'Russo has provided the in-depth coverage that reporters working during the heyday of the mob would have liked to have done . . . an informative, tireless read. It is for followers of mob lore or the beginner who wants to jump with both feet into a subject that has often been only superficially reported.'
—*Chicago Tribune*

'A fascinating tale.'
—*New York Post*

'An impressive in-depth history of Chicago's elusive crime syndicate . . . Russo humanizes the shadowy gangsters without denying their violent proclivities . . . this is the book to beat in examining this midcentury criminal empire.'
—*Publishers Weekly*

'This is the most in-depth, dispassionate study of organized crime and big business to date. Russo located most of the skeletons in this masterful probe.'
—Jack Clarke, Special Investigator for Chicago Mayors Kennelly through Daley, and Illinois Governors Stevenson through Kerner

'A serious and entertaining read.'
—*Baltimore Magazine*

'Nothing is left out.'
—*Chicago Sun-Times*

'Absolutely captivating! For a "wiseguy" like me it was like going back to the neighborhood for an education. I couldn't put it down.'
—Henry Hill, the inspiration for the film *Goodfellas* and the bestselling book *Wiseguys*

'*The Outfit* is an outstanding work of investigative reporting about a crucial juncture in American parapolitics. The index alone is worth the price of admission. Congratulations, then, to Gus Russo for digging so deep and writing so well about a very mysterious place in time, and the murderous characters who gave it so much glamour.'
—Jim Hougan, former Washington editor of *Harper's* and award-winning investigative author of *Spooks: The Haunting of America – The Private Use of Secret Agents* and *Secret Agenda: Watergate, Deep Throat, and the CIA*

The Outfit

The Role of Chicago's Underworld
in the Shaping of Modern America

Gus Russo

BLOOMSBURY

NEW YORK · BERLIN · LONDON

Published by Bloomsbury, New York and London

The Library of Congress has cataloged the hardcover edition as follows:

Russo, Gus, 1949–
The Outfit : the role of Chicago's underworld in the shaping of modern
America / Gus Russo.
p. cm.
Includes bibliographical references and index.
ISBN 1-58234-176-1
1. Outfit (Gang) -- History. 2. Mafia -- Illinois -- Chicago -- History. 3.
Chicago (Ill.) -- History. 4. Chicago (Ill.) -- Politics and government.
I. Title
HV6452.I32 O877 2002
364.1'06'0977311 -- dc21
2001056637

Paperback ISBN 1-58234-279-2

This paperback edition published 2003

10 9 8

Typeset by Hewer Text Ltd, Edinburgh
Printed and bound in the United States of America by
R.R. Donnelley & Sons Company, Harrisonburg, Virginia

For Anthony and Sadie Russo, my parents.

And for

Augustino & Rosina Russo and Anthony & Rose Cascio,
my grandparents,

with love and gratitude.

Contents

Introduction

In the New Cabaret Artistes, an illegal strip joint in Liverpool, a buxom stripper named Janice gyrated to the rhythms of twenty-year-old John Lennon and his even younger mates, Paul McCartney and George Harrison. In Cuba, youthful new prime minister Fidel Castro nationalized the formerly American-owned oil refineries. Meanwhile, the first ten U.S.-supported volunteers arrived at a secret Panama Canal Zone facility to begin training to retake their Cuban homeland back from Castro. The results of these and other events would be well documented in history books yet to be written. But the momentous conference under way in the mansion at 915 Franklin Avenue would, by mutual decree of the participants, never be chronicled.

It was June 1960, and in far-removed corners of the world unseen events were unfolding that would define a revolutionary era to follow. In fact, multiple revolutions – cultural, political, and sociological – were in their embryonic stages. This was the interregnum – the transition between the misnamed "happy days" of the Eisenhower years, and the terrifying brinksmanship of the Cold War sixties.

The palatial estates on Franklin, in the tony Chicago suburb of River Forest, were the setting on this otherwise unexceptional Thursday evening. Lawns were being tended by caretakers; Mercedes sedans were having their wax jobs refined. Young couples ambled off to the movies, perhaps to see *Spartacus,* or *Psycho.* The typical residents, stockbrokers, lawyers, and the like, were going about their lives.

In a much different manner, an atypical neighborhood denizen, a son of Sicilian immigrants named Antonino Leonardo Accardo, was also going about business as usual; with his lifelong friend Murray Humphreys and two other associates, he would, after a sumptuous lasagna dinner, decide who would become the next president of the United States.

For decades, these Thursday-night meetings were convened at the manse owned by "Joe" Accardo, as he was known to friends. Decisions made at these soirées ran the gamut: from who to "whack" for an indiscretion; to which national labor union to take over this week; to whether they should answer the White House's call to murder Castro; to the creation of a gambling paradise in the Nevada desert; or, as in this case, to go along with Joe Kennedy's request to guarantee his son Jack's "appointment" to the U.S. presidency.

The participants prided themselves on the relatively obscure manner in which they were able conduct their business. "We start appearing on the front page and it's all over," one was heard to say. The phrase became a mantra of sorts. Of course this enterprise *was* known, especially to law enforcement agents, but was so smoothly run that proof of the organizational links were unobtainable – at least for the first fifty years or so.

The colleagues in question were, in fact, the heirs apparent to the empire of bootlegging kingpin Scarface Al Capone. Capone's downfall in 1931 provided an important lesson for the Accardo-Humphreys generation: exaggerated violence and a high media profile were the kiss of death and were to be avoided at all costs. Hundreds of millions were at stake, an amount not worth gambling for the luxury of being seen with movie stars. That was for amateurs.

Be assured, this was not "The Mafia" of the East Coast gangsters, laden with elaborate ritual and internecine rivalry; nor was it "La Cosa Nostra" as described by Joe Valachi when he sang to the feds. This band of brothers had shed the more objectionable traits of "Big Al's" 1925–31 "Syndicate." The new regime's capos shared as much commonality with Capone as modern man does with Cro-Magnon cave dwellers. Perhaps as a nod to their enlightened, modernized dominion, a new name quickly emerged for the Chicago crime organization: The Outfit.

Prologue: Origins

"Booze"

"What hath God wrought?" Although the query posed by Samuel Morse related to the unforeseeable consequences of his "Morse code" telegraphic breakthrough, it could just as easily have been directed at the topic of the religious pilgrimage to America. For it was a God-fearing Pilgrim sect called the Puritans who inadvertently set the wheels in motion for a vast criminal reign that would rule the New World two centuries hence.

Espousing a dogmatic, Bible-ruling theocracy, these seventeenth-century settlers to colonial America set the stage for a hedonistic backlash that reverberates to this day. Their humanity-denying canon in fact helped contribute the most unsightly fabric to the patchwork of the soon-to-be-named United States of America. The "law of unintended consequences" was never more aptly applied.

The late-nineteenth-century immigration wave deposited an assemblage of new citizens on America's shores, many from places far less "enlightened" than the England of Oliver Cromwell. These recent émigrés quickly sussed out that their forerunners were enduring a lifestyle of denial and joyless deprivation. Arriving from Ireland, Sicily, or Wales, the newcomers were more than happy to prosper by supplying a few creature comforts. From gambling to girls, they were the providers, while the corrupt authorities looked the other way.

By the early twentieth-century the shadow economy was already savoring a bull market when an ill-conceived constitutional amendment to ban beer and alcohol created a quick and easy route to extravagant wealth. This disastrous federal legislation, which had been percolating for over a century, was the last stand for the Puritan dream of a theocracy. But the insanity of a national ban on beer and alcohol had a perverse effect: instead of installing God's will in government, it bestowed on Chicago's gangs a foothold on America's infrastructure. And the gangsters in Chicago who would call themselves the Outfit have cherished their gift ever since.

Prohibition: From a Bad Idea to a National Nightmare

Although Puritanical codes forbade drunkenness, they did not exclude mild drinking, especially in the form of beer. In fact, the *Mayflower*'s ship's log notes that the reason for the landing at Plymouth Rock was the need to restock their dwindling beer supplies, making America's first permanent colony nothing more than a "beer run."

Beer was one thing, but hard liquor was something else again, for alcohol was seen to lead inevitably to rowdiness and lewd behavior. Introduced in London around 1720, cheap gin had additionally created an epidemic of addicts. In "the colonies," temperance societies sprang up in a futile attempt to keep the plague at bay in the New World.

The rising tide of hard liquor in America was, however, inexorable. Nowhere was this plague expressed more vividly than among the tribes of the Native American "Indians," who happily exchanged fur pelts for liquor. The effects left entire tribes decimated. By the 1820s, there were thousands of temperance societies, spearheaded from the pulpit by still more thousands of Protestant clergy. But no group raised the temperance banner higher than the nation's distaff side. It was, after all, the women who had to deal with the effects liquor had on their saloon-frequenting husbands. Thus, in 1874, seizing the forefront of the antibooze movement, these crusading women formed the national Women's Christian Temperance Union (WCTU).

This first antibooze wave is best remembered for the fanaticism of its most fervored adherents, especially one Kansas native (and WCTU member) named Carry Nation. The rejected daughter of a woman herself committed to an insane asylum, Nation suffered two failed marriages, one to a hard drinker, before becoming a frenzied evangelist in the "Women's War" against alcohol consumption. (She fantasized that her name was a sign from God that she had a calling to "Carry a Nation.") A large, powerfully built woman who decided that her God-given physical attributes were her best weapons in the Women's War, Nation went from attacking the *idea* of saloons to literally attacking the saloons themselves. Graduating from sledgehammers to thrown billiard balls to hatchets, Nation and her tiny band of followers went on a rampage of saloon destruction throughout the Midwest. She called it hatchetizing.

Although Nation's efforts were both public and private failures (like her mother, she died in a mental institution), she kept the prohibition idea in the public consciousness until more capable advocates seized the baton.

New World Disorder

After the American West was "tamed," the new country was swarmed by a massive wave of European immigrants seeking a better life. Dominated in numbers by the Irish, Italians, and Germans, more than twenty-five million new Americans arrived between 1885 and 1924 alone. In a virtual eyeblink, America was awash in immigrants, and with them, potent German beers, Irish whiskeys, and Italian wines, all served in thousands of saloons owned by the Euro-Americans.

Suddenly, a culture that was founded and defined by white, Anglo-Saxon Protestants (WASPs) was being threatened by hedonistic hordes. It was too much for the overwhelmed WASPs, who refused to stand by and watch their theocratic paradise crumble. The booze business was the only enterprise not dominated by WASPs, and just as it had since the first prehistoric tribes appeared, xenophobia reared its head.

The battle to prohibit booze was thus transformed into a nascent form of ethnic cleansing, a WASP attempt to tighten the yoke on the newer ethnic arrivals. Adding to the mix was the anti-German hysteria in place during World War I. The paranoia manifested itself in the withdrawal of German-language courses from school curricula and the removal of German books from libraries. Whereas the religious argument made for interesting parlor chat, prejudice, jingoism, and racism provided potent fuels for the prohibitionists.

The prohibitionist movement finally coalesced in the person of Wayne Wheeler. A brilliant debater from Ohio's Oberlin College, Wheeler was recruited as the political lobbyist for the most businesslike antibooze organization yet, the Anti-Saloon League. Wheeler set the standard for all future lobbyists. Upon relocating to the nation's capital in 1913, Wheeler aimed his powers of propaganda and rhetoric at a bold target: the total banning of alcohol consumption in America. His tireless efforts on Capitol Hill softened up the opposition until Wheeler was able to brilliantly parlay anti-German fanaticism into legislation. The word *prohibition* was transmogrified into a code word for "patriotism."

Incredible as it now seems, Wheeler was able, with absolutely no evidence, to persuade legislators that German-American breweries were in league with America's wartime enemy, the German government. He also decried the waste of raw materials used in the brewing process, materials that could be better utilized to support the war effort. This led to the wholesale ban of grain sales and the closure of hard-liquor distilleries.

For prohibition to become the law of the land, Wheeler needed to effect one of the most difficult tasks in American politics: the passage of a constitutional amendment. In the nation's first 150 years, only seventeen amendments had been enacted. Wheeler's strategy thus included massive support for "dry" congressional candidates. Soon, robber barons and amoral industrialists fell in line behind the prohibition movement. New converts included the Rockefellers and Du Ponts, who helped bankroll Wheeler's crusade. Auto tycoon, and temperance fanatic, Henry Ford was persuaded that his employees' purchase of booze effectively diverted their meager income from the purchase of his cars.

By 1917, with his strategies aligned, Wheeler made his final push towards codified alcohol prohibition. Using his Congressional clout, Wheeler rewrote a proposed constitutional amendment on prohibition that had been languishing in subcommittees since 1913. Wheeler's Eighteenth Amendment read: "No person shall manufacture, sell, barter, transport, import, export, deliver, furnish or possess any intoxicating liquor except as authorized in this act." The exemptions granted were for industrial, sacramental, and medicinal uses only. After securing a relatively swift two-thirds majority in both houses, the bill wound its way through the nation's statehouses in quest of the needed approval by three-quarters, or thirty-six, of the states.

Finally, on January 16, 1919, after a century of proselytizing, the Eighteenth Amendment was enacted, and Americans were given until midnight, January 17, 1920, to close the saloons. When Wheeler and his "drys" concluded that more legislation would be required to enforce national prohibition, Wheeler persuaded Minnesota Republican congressman Andrew J. Volstead to introduce another bill, again ghost-written by Wheeler. Congressman Volstead was merely the facilitator of the proposal, which placed the Internal Revenue Service in charge of investigating and charging those in violation of the new amendment. Although the Volstead Act was passed in October 1919, it was summarily vetoed by President Woodrow Wilson, who saw his veto quickly overridden. In time, many would come to refer to the Eighteenth Amendment and the Volstead Act collectively as "Volstead." Wheeler's Herculean effort is still considered one of the greatest lobbying successes in history.

The Fly in the Ointment

The suffocating restrictions of Volstead seemed all-inclusive, but they were not. Although selling booze was by and large illegal, *drinking* alcohol was just fine. Added to the fact that the Eighteenth Amendment had absolutely no effect on America's unquenchable thirst, it was only a matter of time before the largest underground economy in history was launched. It was known as bootlegging.

Since the earliest days of the New World's western expansion, when cowboys had illegally smuggled alcohol in their knee-high boots to their Native American victims, "bootlegging" had been an integral part of the American fabric. With the advent of twentieth-century prohibition, the lure of the underground booze business became almost irresistible: astronomical profits combined with virtually no risk made a powerful fusion. It cost $5 to produce one barrel of beer that retailed for $55 minimum. The profit in hard liquor was higher still. George Remus, the powerful lawyer-turned-bootlegger from Ohio, earned $40 million in three years, a staggering amount for the time.

Increasing the temptation to bootleg was that in 1923 the federal government employed merely fifteen hundred prohibition agents nation-wide. Making matters worse, the agents were grossly underpaid (earning less than garbage collectors) and were thus easily corrupted by the big-spending bootleggers. In some instances the agents moonlighted as chauf-feurs for their supposed targets. On the rare occasions when a "collar" was made, the feds imposed the relatively microscopic fine of $1,000.

Underpaid prohibition agents and thirsty soldiers returning from World War I made certain that drinking would remain America's favorite pastime. The *federales* had nowhere to turn for support, since corrupted officials were ensconced at every level of government, up to and including the White House. President Harding, rendered vulnerable as a result of an affair with a twenty-year-old who had given birth to his love child, was under the control of his pro-booze advisers. His attorney general, Harry Daugherty, was later found to have been on the payroll of one of the nation's most powerful bootleggers, George Remus. Remus had been paying Daugherty the astronomical sum of $350,000 per year to allow the booze to flow.

No locale was better positioned to take advantage of bootlegging's riches than the city on Lake Michigan's west bank. And nowhere was this obvious rags-to-riches path more adroitly perceived than in America's "second city." Named for the Ojibwa Indian word for the foul-smelling, river-clogging "wild onion" (*checagou*), it had already elevated political corruption to an art form. Chicago, the future home of The Outfit, embraced prohibition with open arms.

"That Toddlin' Town"

Geography and geology play pivotal roles in the character of any city. Chicago's placement on the map dictated that eastern urbanity come face-to-face with the take-the-law-into-your-own-hands mentality of the recently opened Wild West. After its incorporation in 1837, Chicago became the gateway to this new frontier and as such was guaranteed a steady stream of tourist business. Literally hundreds of wagons, over-flowing with anxious homesteaders, transited Chicago every day.[1]

Chicago soon amassed a glut of discretionary money, its coffers bulging with profits from manufacturing, commodities auctions, and huge stock-yards that "rendered" seventeen million head of Western cattle a year. The party was on, and with the swiftness of a barroom pickpocket, Chicago became transformed into "That Toddlin' Town." Hotels and saloons were jammed with a mostly male clientele who had set out from the East in advance of the womenfolk. And these adventurers saw Chicago as their last chance for a little TLC before their trek into the harsh Western frontier. What transpired next was inevitable: Where there are unsupervised males there are saloons; where there are saloons, there are gambling and girls. The gamblers' haunts acquired their own colorful nicknames, such as Hair-Trigger Block, Thieves Corner, and Gambler's Row.

---

1. Chicago's first boom peaked in the 1830s, with more than 150 buildings going up that summer alone. With fourteen miles of riverfront docking space, Chicago was the new nation's largest inland port, and bullish traders were anxious to exploit nature's gift. But a nationwide bank panic in 1837 and a subsequent depression sent the city's newfound prosperity into a tailspin. In 1847, William Ogden came to the rescue when he built a huge factory to manufacture the revolutionary McCormick grain reaper. Coincident were the completion of the Lake Michigan–Illinois River Canal and the Chicago Union Railroad. While the canal gave the nation's breadbasket farmers access to Eastern markets, the railroad completed the connection to the West. On the Chicago Union's heels there followed five more rail lines laying tracks through the city. By 1855 ten more railroads completed the transition of the infant city into a commercial crossroads. The railroads combined with its natural route (the Illinois River) to the southern port of New Orleans, put the Second City in hyperdrive. As Lloyd Lewis wrote, "Chicago had become Chicago."

Not far behind the saloon owners came the con men and swindlers. On some occasions, the con men *were* the saloon owners. One such character was Mickey Finn, who operated two establishments on Whiskey Row. Finn's now infamous concoction, The Mickey Finn Special, was a drink tainted with a secret powder that rendered the drinker unconscious. While touring the twilight zone, the unfortunate reveler had his pockets emptied by the unscrupulous Finn. As they had throughout time, the criminal element found refuge in a district that seemed to be earmarked just for them. And it was one of the most bizarre vice districts imaginable.

The Underworld

If the good citizens of Chicago desired a law-abiding community in which to plant roots, geology conspired with geography to stack the cards in defiant opposition. For although Chicago *seemed* to be the right place to erect a city, nature had other ideas. The city, it turned out, was built on a smelly swamp/marsh, which was a sort of primordial soup for the gangster empires of the future. By the late 1850s, torrents of mud threatened to engulf the town, which had no paved streets. Cracks in the wooden slabs that functioned as thoroughfares oozed the muck around the wheels of carriages and the shins of well-dressed ladies. Mud Town and Slab Town were added to the list of unflattering nicknames for Chicago.

The city fathers concocted an ingenious, if optimistic, solution to the muddy onslaught: jack up the entire city ten feet while fortifying the surface with stone. Given that the buildings themselves were constructed from relatively light wood, the idea was deemed feasible. Thus, for ten years Chicago existed on stilts, creating a cavernous "underworld," as it came to be known. Soon, the underworld gave shelter to a repellent assemblage of humanity loosely commanded by Chicago's first criminal-empire czar, Roger Plant.

An immigrant boxer from England, Plant built a two-story paean to perversity called Under the Willows. The first floor consisted of round-the-clock boozing and gambling; the second tier was the domain of more than two hundred prostitutes, whose window shades were lettered on the outside with the slogan Why Not?

As unsavory as the Willows was, it paled in comparison to the nether region for which it served as a main point of entry. For just below Plant's "Barracks" was a labyrinthine maze of tunnels, rooms, and underground streets that drew, according to Jay Robert Nash, "hundreds of pickpockets, jackrollers, highwaymen, and killers for hire, the most fearsome collection of hoodlums anywhere in the U.S. at the time."

But by far the most loathsome aspects of the underworld were its crimes against women. In this dungeonlike world, young girls were often forced into "the life," otherwise known as prostitution. In standard operating procedure, "ropers" scoured the country for fourteen- and fifteen-year-old girls who could be lured to Chicago with promises of a big payday. Upon arrival, these girls were raped and otherwise terrorized into submission, kept pliant with opium, and assigned to whichever whorehouse bought them (for a couple hundred bucks plus a percentage of their earnings). For the next few years, while their youthfulness was still in demand, the girls paid their "owner" 60 to 90 percent of their ten-dollar trick fee. When their skin became ravaged by disease, they were tossed out on the streets only to succumb to drug overdoses. It was called white slavery, and it could be argued that it was every bit as brutal as the black variety.[2]

The wanton criminality flourished in large part because Chicago maintained a police department in name only. In 1850, with an exploding population of eighty thousand, there existed only nine "city watch marshals" – as no police department had yet been established. Five years later – and too little too late – a minimalist Chicago Police Department was organized. In five more years, Chicago mayor Long John Wentworth actually decreased the force to a mere sixty cops.

Word traveled fast throughout the nation's criminal network. Soon Chicago sustained an influx of criminals from New Orleans, Mississippi, New York, and virtually every burg with a train depot or a healthy horse. At this turbulent juncture, the first true crime lord, Michael Cassius McDonald, appeared. A resident of "Hair-Trigger Block," McDonald was a noted gambler, and among underworld successes the first to appreciate the importance of the political fix. After coalescing the city's riffraff into "McDonald's Democrats," he engineered the election of Mayor Carter Harrison in 1879. As his reward, McDonald gained the exclusive bookmaking franchise for all Chicago and Indiana. His gambling parlor, The Store, was known as the unofficial City Hall. McDonald, who

---

2. Describing the underworld, Herbert Asbury wrote of "rooms for assignation, procuresses, dens where young girls were raped by half a dozen men and sold to the bordellos, cubicles which were rented to streetwalkers and male degenerates, and hidden rooms used as hideaways by every species of crook."

was known to hate policemen, was once approached by two cops for a two-dollar donation. "We're burying a policeman," one of them said, to which Mike responded, "Here's ten dollars. Bury five of them."

McDonald's organization coined the term *syndicate* to denote his crime consortium. The moniker would be appropriated much more infamously by a Chicago gang of the twentieth-century.

In 1871 denizens of the underworld acquired still another source of revenue: looting. On the night of October 8, after a severe, record-shattering drought during which a scant one inch of rain fell in four months, a cow in the barn on Mrs. Catherine O'Leary's Southwest Side farm knocked over a lantern. Fueled by ferocious gusts that have earned the city still another moniker, The Windy City, the barn fire escalated into the Great Chicago Fire. When it finally ended thirty-six brutal hours later, eighteen thousand mostly wooden buildings that had once concealed the underworld were incinerated. The city sustained more than five hundred deaths and was saddled with more than ninety-eight thousand newly homeless citizens. Fully half the city was consumed. Eyewitnesses described the horrific aftermath: like a pack of rats emerging from the underworld, the con men, scalawags, hoodlums, and whores descended on the ruins, looting anything that had not turned to cinders. Local clergy intoned that God's wrath, not nature's, was punishing this wicked metropolis. The Sodom and Gomorrah analogy was heard more than once in sanctimonious sermons. In time the local assessment became a national one.

On the positive side, the fire afforded Chicago a unique opportunity to rebuild the entire city utilizing the most recent strides in engineering and design architecture. In a mere three years the city was transformed into a distinctly modern city and one of the most potent engines for commerce in the world. Soon many of the world's first skyscrapers dominated the Windy City skyline.

Again, word got out just how appealing the Second City had become. With immigration unchecked and unregulated, the population swelled to over two million by 1900. One half million Poles arrived along with more than one hundred thousand Italians, and still more Germans, Swedes, Jews, etc., all gravitating to their ethnic enclaves.

Although the Chicago of the Gay Nineties achieved many noteworthy civic successes (especially its financial institutions, universities, and museums), it was also a nutrient-rich petri dish for the diseases of crime and corruption. The anemic police department numbered only eleven hundred (vs. a 2.1 million population). More than a dozen vice districts sprang up, with appropriate names such as The Black Hole, Bad Lands, Satan's Mile, Dead Man's Alley, and Hell's Half Acre. Crime gangs flourished throughout the city. A 1927 study counted 1,313 gangs, which boasted over twenty-five thousand members.

At the lowest street level, crime was often inseparable from the gambling element. Unlike other cities, Chicago was content to allow its illegal policy (numbers) rackets to be controlled by the blacks of the South Side. More than five hundred "policy stations," run almost exclusively by brothers Edward and George Jones, thrived on the South Side alone.

In the Italian enclaves, criminals embraced a different means to riches: gang terrorism. Given Italy's turbulent history, it is small wonder many of its citizens distrust authority and seek riches and security in fiercely antiestablishment gangs. For much of the millennium Italy was overrun with foreign occupation. The list of oppressive foreign rulers is daunting: Spanish Bourbons, Greeks, Carthaginians, Arabs, Normans, and French, to name a few. When the invaders were finally cast out in the nineteenth century, the southern regions of Italy did not escape oppression – this time from the northern Romans and Neapolitans. This is to say nothing of Sicilians, who were held in disdain by all Italians and thus trusted no one. In sum, a certain type of crime – the sort that flouts authority – was widely considered an honorable way to get ahead.

The Italian Immigrant Experience

Upon arrival, the Italian-Sicilian masses were met with intolerable prejudice and discrimination, which only served to enforce their fears. Considered "less than white" by fairer-skinned northern Europeans, the Italian experience most closely resembled the racism experienced by African-Americans. The respected *Washington Post* newspaper was among those justifying the prejudice: "The Germans, the Irish, and others . . . migrate to this country, adopt its customs, acquire its language, master its institutions, and identify themselves with its destiny. The Italians never. They remain isolated from the rest of any community in which they happen to dwell. They seldom learn to speak our tongue, they have no respect for our laws or our form of government, they are always foreigners."

From their arrival in the 1890s through at least 1915, Italians were regularly lynched in states from Florida to Colorado. Indeed, the worst mass lynching in U.S. history involved the brutal murders of eleven innocent Italian men in New Orleans on March 14, 1891. In the hysteria that followed, one of the victims' young sons was taken to safety by a Cajun woman, who fled with the boy up the river to Chicago. That boy, Joseph Bulger (Imburgio), went on to graduate law school at age twenty, then became one of the most influential behind-the-scenes legal advisers, or consigliere, for Chicago's coming empire of crime.

Persecution was the ugliest obstacle confronting the Italian immigrants, but not the only one. With an illiteracy rate (57.3 percent) that was nearly triple that of other new arrivals, Italian-Sicilian immigrants were forced to accept jobs no other immigrants wanted: ragpicker, chimney sweep, garbage salvager, ditchdigger – anything to get started. In the South, where recently freed slaves were less than enthusiastic about their tasks, Italians were thrilled to find *any* work. Richard Gambino wrote: "Italian labor seemed like a God-sent solution to replace both nigger and mule. The Sicilians worked for low wages and, in contrast to the blacks' resentment, seemed overjoyed to be able to make the little money paid them.'

Against the odds, the Italian immigrants succeeded in gaining a foothold in the New World. And despite the perception of a crime-prone Italian subculture, the facts reveal just the opposite. Consider the issue of prostitution. Whereas poor girls from most every race and nationality were represented in the nation's bordellos, Italian girls were curiously immune to the temptation – their strong family ties made such a choice unthinkable. After the New Orleans lynchings, a follow-up investigation by the Wickersham Commission discovered that "Italians were charged with only four of the 543 homicides committed in New Orleans from 1925 to 1929." The perception of "lawless" Italians, the study concluded, "seems hardly justifiable."

There were, of course, Italian gangs – just as there were gangs of every ethnicity – and the Italian gangs arguably worked harder than their immigrant counterparts. Although they technically lived in America, the Italian gangs existed in a country of their own imaginations, filled with apprehension, fierce independence, and old-world mystique. Young Italian gang leaders were known to stare into mirrors in efforts to perfect "the look," the menacing, unblinking stare that sent shivers through its unlucky recipient. In Chicago, in their Near West Side haunt called The Patch, Italian gangs utilized a terror method that had flourished for centuries in the Old Country. *La Mano Nera,* or The Black Hand, was undoubtedly the quickest, most direct method for a tough punk to make a buck. Although commonly believed to be a crime society, the Black Hand was actually just *a method* of criminality. It involved nothing more sophisticated than the delivery of a death threat, or Black Hand note, to a prospering Italian immigrant. The note was often inscribed on paper that also bore the imprint of a hand in black ink. The threat would be rescinded in exchange for a payoff. Simple extortion.

The Black Handers made their real mark on history by introducing the bomb as a terrorist weapon. More than three hundred Black Hand bombings and four hundred Black Hand murders went down between 1890 and 1920. When prohibition was enacted, the Black Handers, who by now numbered more than sixty gangs and even more individuals, were given a much more acceptable path out of their barrios and eventually into the lives of all American citizens – whether they knew it or not.

Not-So-Strange Bedfellows

Predictably, the denizens of this shadow economy required shielding from officials charged with enforcing the criminal code. For widescale criminal endeavors to succeed, the tacit approval of City Hall is a prerequisite. And Chicago's unique charter made it the ideal arena in which lawbreakers could flourish.

As if more fuel were needed to inflame Chicago's lawless character, its peculiar system of government known as the ward system played a major role in making it a fertile crescent for corruption. Chicago is divided into fifty wards and three thousand voting precincts, the most coveted being the rich downtown First Ward. The essential features of the ward are the posts of elected alderman and appointed committeeman. The alderman serves the traditional role of legislator, voting on ordinances, budgets, etc. The position of committeeman, however, presents a powerfully seductive invitation to corruption.

In the ward, the real power rested with the committeeman. "The reason was patronage," wrote David Fremon. It was an elegantly simple design: the committeemen were granted by law the power to dispense jobs in return for political support. Most important, these appointments included judges and sheriffs. Kickbacks and favors lavished on the committeemen made the nonsalaried position a plum post for unethical pols. Once elected, the momentum of the incumbent, to say nothing of the gangsters', increased exponentially. Subsequent reelections were pro forma in this perpetual-motion corruption machine. Fremon pointed out that the parties relied on "an army of precinct workers whose civil service – exempt jobs depended on how well they performed on election day." Michael Killian described how the Democratic machine, installed after World War II, operated: "[The Democrats] put together a perpetual motion machine in Chicago that dispensed favors in return for votes, and so long as the voters knew where the favors were coming from, nothing changed . . . The Democratic Party in Chicago is simply a means for earning a living."

For the gangsters, this translated as "we'll get you elected, and we don't even want jobs. Just look the other way when we do our thing." And that's just what the pols did. The hoods used muscle and money to turn out the votes for their handpicked candidates, many of whom operated gang-controlled saloons. Chicago would become infamous for "vote slugging" and "graveyard votes." It was the Windy City that coined the expression "Vote early and vote often." The city was essentially for ransom.

Among the earliest architects of political corruption in the Second City was First Ward committeeman Michael "Hinky Dink" Kenna, also known as "The Little Fellow." Working in partnership with alderman John "Bathhouse" Coughlin, Kenna set the standard and constructed the template for all the official chicanery that would follow.

The sons of Irish immigrants, Kenna and Coughlin rose to power as the twentieth-century dawned, with Chicago's population now swelling to more than two million. Their partnership was fixed when Kenna, the owner of the city's most popular saloon and an influential Democrat, pulled out all the stops in fixing the vote in favor of Coughlin's election. In a short time, with both pols in office, the duo devised a foolproof, if inelegant, scheme that would guarantee them great wealth.

Through black committeemen such as William Dawson, protection payoffs for the "policy" game were made directly to City Hall. However, Kenna-Coughlin predictably took aim at the city's Levee district for their main financial fix.

Like Baltimore's "Block" or New York's "Eighth Avenue," the Levee district of Chicago's First Ward was the epicenter of vice and vulgarity – but on a gargantuan scale. By the 1920s, there were more than one hundred bookie and gambling joints in the Levee area alone, with eight hundred more scattered throughout the city. Houses of prostitution spread like wildfire. These brothels took on monikers rich in connotation: The House of All Nations, The Bucket of Blood, and the low-end Bed Bug Row, where action was available for a mere two dollars.

Since Kenna-Coughlin's control of the First Ward (and its jobs) was total, no one – not cops or inspectors – would make a move that went counter to Kenna-Coughlin, who were now bringing in sixty thousand dollars a year each above their annual official salaries. However, it was the dynamic duo's chosen "collectors" who would go on to become the patron saints of the Outfit, the men who would extend organized crime's tentacles beyond anything as parochial as the vision of Bathhouse and the Little Fellow. They were known in the Italian ghetto as Big Jim and The Fox.

The Outfit's Forefathers

Giacomo Colosimo was born in Calabria, Italy, around 1880. Some seventeen years later he and his parents emigrated, eventually arriving in Chicago. Americanizing his name to Jim, the youngster followed the lead of the countless Italians who had arrived before him and started at the bottom – literally. Jim Colosimo first earned money in America as a ditchdigger. But this type of servitude did not suit Jim, who soon discovered that easy money came to a young man with his peculiar talent for pickpocketing. From there the now muscular "Big Jim" graduated to Black Handing, moving quickly up the crime evolutionary ladder to the far more lucrative position of *ruffiano:* a pimp.

Initially, Jim's new vocation flopped. After a confrontation with Chicago's finest, Colosimo laid low, returning – albeit briefly – to a life of honest work. Working for two dollars per day as a "white wing" (the shoveler who followed horse-drawn wagons) would seem to offer upward mobility to only the most enterprising laborer. Such was Big Jim. He quickly rose through the ranks to foreman and went on to organize his own social club. Soon he was elected to the leadership of the Street Laborers Union and the City Streets Repairers Union. Kenna-Coughlin were not unaware of Colosimo as a rising star.

Kenna-Coughlin, constantly on the lookout for votes outside the Irish strongholds, saw Colosimo as their ticket to support in the burgeoning Italian ghettos. In short time, Kenna-Coughlin made the momentous decision to adopt the first Italian-American into corruption, City-Hall style. It was a critical juncture in the history of the Outfit, assuming mythic status in future underworld folklore.

Big Jim's success in delivering the vote prompted Kenna-Coughlin to place him in the "protected" post of Democratic precinct captain. In effect, this made Big Jim immune to police harassment. More important, he was reacquainted with the world of the *lupanare,* or whorehouses, from where he collected Kenna-Coughlin's payoffs. The Kenna-Coughlin-Colosimo enterprise became referred to as The Trust, and for a time it hummed along effortlessly. For Big Jim, the role of graft collector for Kenna-Coughlin was indeed life-defining, since in that capacity he made the acquaintance of the Levee's premier madam, Victoria Moresco.

After a whirlwind two-week courtship, Big Jim and Victoria, who was twice his age, made it legal. Soon, another dimension was added to their marital relationship: a business partnership. By 1912, they owned more than two hundred brothels. This translated to $600,000 per year in "under the table" income for the Colosimos. When the First Ward was redistricted in a show crackdown in preparation for Chicago's first World's Fair, Kenna-Coughlin lost their power base and soon drifted off the scene. Not so Colosimo. The Trust was now so powerful, it no longer needed to court the corrupt pols; the pols had to court *them*.

As his empire expanded, Big Jim pioneered a style that went on to become de rigueur for the stereotypical twentieth-century pimp, sporting diamond rings on each finger, diamond cuff links, diamond studs, diamond-encrusted belt and suspenders, a diamond horseshoe brooch, all accenting a garish snow-white linen suit checked with (what else?) diamonds.

Colosimo's ostentatious style made him an obvious candidate for Black Hand extortion – the same thuggery he had himself once espoused. Although Big Jim had personally murdered three Black Handers who had previously threatened him, one particular threat seemed beyond his capacity to ameliorate. On this occasion, he was being extorted for the unthinkable sum of $50,000. When Colosimo decided he needed outside help to cope with the situation, his wife, Victoria, suggested her cousin from New York. In placing the call, Big Jim would paradoxically save his life in the short term and guarantee his own extermination eleven years later. More important for history, the man Colosimo brought in for damage control placed Chicago gangsterism one giant step closer to the creation of the Outfit.

In Brooklyn, New York, Johnny "the Fox" Torrio answered the call of his cousin Victoria's husband, Big Jim Colosimo. Born in Italy in 1882, Torrio was the leader of the Lower East Side's notorious James Street Gang. By the age of twenty-two, he owned a pool hall, a saloon, and a brothel, in addition to his gang of burglars, hijackers, and extortionists.

One of Torrio's most important traits was his willingness to forge alliances with rivals. In New York, Torrio brokered an important coalition between his James Street Gang and the powerful Five Points

Gang, strong-armed by a professional killer and Black Hander named Frankie Yale (Uale). Like Torrio, Yale would also play a pivotal role in the twists and turns of the Chicago crime world.

Torrio possessed still another skill that would prove indispensable in his future Windy City home: an appreciation of the importance of controlling the political system. While still in his early twenties, Torrio led his gang in a total war on the electoral process. In 1905, with Torrio's help, the Five Points Gang ensured the election of their mayoral candidate by systematically stealing ballot boxes and mugging (or "slugging" as it was known in Chicago) their opponent's supporters.

Although Torrio was the undisputed brains of the gang, he never personally dirtied his hands in the commission of a crime. As the brilliant capo, he was too important to be placed in jeopardy. Years later, near the end of his life, he bragged – probably honestly – that he had never fired a gun in his life.

This would not be the first time that Torrio had traveled to Chicago to extricate Colosimo from the clutches of the Black Handers, but this time his ticket to the Second City would be one-way. On this occasion, Torrio, as per his style, attempted to negotiate with the Black Handers who now threatened Big Jim. Failing in this, Torrio agreed to meet the extortionists and deliver the money. On meeting the trio of Black Handers, Torrio brought guns instead of gold. Two of his gunmen emptied their clips into the extortionists, and Johnny instantly ascended to the role of Big Jim's right-hand man.

In short time, Torrio found himself running Colosimo's empire. But Torrio clearly viewed his stewardship of Colosimo's businesses as merely a stepping-stone. He had big dreams that orbited around the central concept of a limitless crime empire. Colosimo gave Torrio the go-ahead to build his own organization, and the new crime baron set up headquarters in the Four Deuces, a four-story office building named for its address, 2222 South Wabash. Above the first-floor saloon, Torrio installed gambling dens and, on the top floor, a brothel. Chicago historian Herbert Asbury described Torrio's typical day at the office in his keystone book, *Gem of the Prairie:* "There he bought and sold women, conferred with the managers of his brothels and gambling dens . . . arranged for the corruption of police and city officials and sent his gun squads out to slaughter rival gangsters who might be interfering with his schemes."

Flush with success, Torrio rapidly expanded his vice trade into the compliant Chicago suburbs. His personal empire now numbered over a thousand gambling joints, brothels, and saloons. One suburban club, the Arrowhead, employed two hundred girls and netted $9,000 per month. Torrio was grossing over $4 million per year. And prohibition's windfall had yet to arrive.

During the graft-ridden mayoral term of William "Big Bill" Thompson, Kenna-Coughlin-Colosimo-Torrio were given free reign to plunder the city.[3] In Chicago, the term *underworld* was now but a humorous oxymoron, since there was no longer a need, or attempt, to conceal the wanton criminality.

The Second City Meets the Eighteenth Amendment

When Volstead passed, Chicagoans reacted swiftly: On December 30, two weeks before prohibition became law, infamous Second City gangster Dion O'Banion single-handedly hijacked a truckload of whiskey in anticipation of the exorbitant prices it would fetch on the last "wet" New Year's Eve. "In twenty minutes we had buyers for the whole load," Dion later boasted. "We sold the truck separately to a brewery in Peoria." On January 16, 1920, six hours before the bill took effect, a West Side gangster crated off $100,000 worth of medicinal liquor from freight cars parked in the Chicago railyards. On the other side of town a liquor warehouse was looted. Still others utilized printing presses and forged phony withdrawal slips for presentation at government-bonded warehouses.

In short time, some fifteen thousand doctors and fifty-seven thousand druggists applied for "medicinal" liquor licenses. In prohibition's first year, sacramental wine sales increased by eight hundred thousand gallons. This in addition to the illegal trade, which eclipsed the officially sanctioned variety. Windy City "speakeasies" popped up on every corner. Breweries operated in plain sight, with at least twenty-nine in Chicago alone. Countless more were established in suburbs such as Joliet, Cicero, Waukegan, and Niles. As Dion O'Banion said at the time, "There's thirty million dollars" worth of beer sold in Chicago every month and a million dollars a month is spread among police, politicians, and federal agents to keep it flowing. Nobody in his right mind will turn his back on a share of a million dollars a month.' Roger Touhy, a former car dealer who seized bootlegging's brass ring, wrote, "There wasn't any stigma to selling beer.

---

3. When Thompson died in 1944, over $2 million in gold, cash, and stock certificates was found in his safe-deposit boxes.

It was a great public service." Touhy continued, "Clergymen, bankers, mayors, U.S. senators, newspaper publishers, blue-nose reformers, and the guy on the street all drank our beer."

Meanwhile, Colosimo was falling in love with a lissome young woman named Dale Winter. From the first moment Big Jim eyed her singing in his bistro, Colosimo's Café, located at 2126 South Wabash, he was smitten with the girl less than half his age. Colosimo's primary objective now was, to the astonishment of his friends, quiet domestic bliss.

Johnny Torrio, by contrast, had visions of the streets of Chicago paved with gold. He, like Touhy and most other businessmen, grasped the obvious. At last there was a clear road map to riches for the immigrant entrepreneur. When Torrio approached Big Jim with his master plan, Torrio must have been stunned by the response: a vehement no.

In a sad irony, it was now Torrio's sponsor (and relative) who stood in his way. The Fox made what must have been an agonizing decision: his "uncle" had to be eliminated.

On May 11, 1920, three weeks after marrying Dale, and a scant four months after Volstead became law, Big Jim Colosimo was murdered in the lobby of his own restaurant. Official sources let it be known that their prime suspect was Torrio's New York associate Frankie Yale. Although police questioned thirty suspects, including Torrio, no one was ever charged in the crime. One witness, a porter, who had initially described an assailant who fit Yale's profile, refused to ID him in a lineup. Although never charged, Torrio was widely believed by police to have paid Yale, or *someone*, $10,000 for the rubout of Big Jim.[4]

As Big Jim's second-in-command, Torrio took charge of the Colosimo empire at a time when the Chicago crime world was in chaos. Rough-and-tumble gang warfare was out of control, with opposing sides clearly

---

4. No better symbol is needed to illustrate the collusion between City Hall and the gangsters than Big Jim's funeral, and absolutely no effort was made to conceal it. At the lavish affair, Kenna and Coughlin knelt by the coffin. One thousand members of the First Ward Democratic Club and five thousand constituents also accompanied Big Jim to his final resting place in Oakwood Cemetery. Honorary pallbearers included an assistant state's attorney, three judges, nine aldermen, and a state representative, all marching side by side to the cemetery with Johnny Torrio and his goon squad. Torrio, after paying all the funeral expenses, expressed grief and wept, "Big Jim and I were like brothers." Many of his gang let their beards grow until after the funeral, as per Italian custom.

divided along racial and ethnic lines: Irish vs. Italians, Greeks vs. Poles, Jews vs. gentiles, and blacks vs. whites. In a frantic effort to establish turf in the newborn high-stakes business of bootlegging, countless gangs flexed their collective muscle. The period was characterized by continual intergang terrorism featuring bombings, truck hijackings, and kidnappings. In a sixteen-month period, 157 Chicago businesses were bombed. Taking their cue from the Black Handers, the bootleggers, led by bomb masters such as Jim Sweeney and Joe Sangerman and their experts, Soup Bartlett and George Sangerman, detonated more than eight hundred bombs between 1900 and 1930, dynamite and black-powder bombs being the weapons of choice. (Before the prohibition wars, the explosives were used in labor union struggles.)

Immediately upon assuming leadership, Torrio, as he had in New York, brokered a gangland agreement that resulted in a mutually beneficial crime consortium: essentially, a truce. Convening the leaders of all the Chicago crime fiefdoms, Torrio built his case on irrefutable logic: thanks to Volstead, there was no longer a need to fight over the now massive treasure or to dabble in petty crime. There was enough money to go around. At Torrio's suggestion, the gangs carved up the city into discrete and sovereign territories.

The essentials of the arrangement held that the Torrio "Syndicate," as it was now called, took the downtown Loop and part of the West Side; the South went to Danny Stanton's gang; the Northwest to William "Klondike" O'Donnell's contingent; smaller districts to the Frankie Lake–Terry Druggan gang and others. Only the South Side O'Donnells, Spike and Walter (no relation to the Northwest O'Donnells) refused to participate, a big mistake since all five brothers were quickly executed by Torrio's gunmen. A U.S. district attorney now referred to Torrio as unsurpassed in the annals of American crime; he is probably the nearest thing to a real mastermind that this country has yet produced.

Torrio soon branched out into the suburbs. Within weeks of Big Jim's murder, Torrio's army of whores and roulette-wheel spinners were overrunning dozens of surrounding communities. And of course the booze flowed freely as Johnny's bootlegging dreams became reality. Torrio's source of strength, his ability to broker cartels and alliances, was in fact the reason his own bootlegging empire would become so formidable. Displaying brilliant foresight, Torrio had engineered a long-standing alliance with two key Chicago powerhouses: the Genna family and the Unione Siciliana.

The Genna family, who had arrived in Chicago's Little Italy from *big* Italy in 1910, virtually owned the enclave. Known as wild men, and Black Handers, the boys established themselves as a collective to be reckoned with. After Volstead they immediately applied for one of the few exempted licenses for the production of industrial alcohol. "The Terrible Gennas" – brothers Angelo, Pete, Sam, Mike, Tony, and Jim – siphoned off most of their licensed industrial alcohol, colored it with various toxins known to cause psychosis, and called it bourbon, Scotch, rye . . . whatever. Glycerin was added to make the concoction smooth enough to be swallowed.[5]

The brazen and volatile Gennas paid more than four hundred police to escort their booze-carrying truck convoys. Their distilleries operated within blocks of police stations, with workers on twenty-four-hour shifts. In fact, so many men in blue made appearances at their warehouse, locals jokingly nicknamed it The Police Station. In no time at all, the Gennas were grossing $300,000 a month, only 5 percent of which went to overhead, that is, official graft.

The Gennas paid Sicilian families $15 per day (ten times what they would have earned at hard labor) to distill fifty gallons of corn-sugar booze. The arrangement, and the compliance of the largely illiterate Sicilian families, was made possible because the Gennas, old-world, blood-oath Sicilians, had the support of "The Unione."

The Unione Siciliana di Mutuo Soccorso negli Stati Uniti was founded in New York in the 1880s and eventually incorporated thirty-two branches across the country. As a fraternal organization, the Unione played a vital role in the lives of the new arrivals, providing jobs, housing, low-cost insurance, and burial benefits. Sicilian families paid weekly dues that quickly established a huge treasury fund, perhaps the largest of any such union. The Unione also taught English and generally helped immigrants adjust to the American way of life. When there were legal problems, the Unione functioned as a mediator between Sicilian immigrants and American authorities. The Unione had its own influential national publication with a large circulation. It settled disputes, some of

---

5. The "fake" hooch was in fact deadly. When Groucho Marx joked in *A Night at the Opera* that he went to a party that was so wild he was "blind for a week," the remark was rooted in fact; alcohol like the Gennas' was also known to cause blindness. Ironically, this was just the sort of brew that should have been prohibited but was in fact created by the Volstead Act.

which involved Black Hand extortion, between members who distrusted
the American system (police were usually answered with a broken-
English "Me don't know" when asking an Italian to testify). The Chicago
branch, chartered in 1895, counted twenty-five thousand Sicilian members (vs. five hundred thousand Italians in Cook County), and it wielded
great power in the community.

Inevitably, all elements of Sicilian society were represented in the
Unione. Perhaps because it was savvy to the ways of the New World,
the gangster component, like the Gennas, often muscled its way into
leadership positions in the Unione, but this in no way reflected the wishes
of the illiterate, gullible rank-and-file members. This faction was also the
custodian of the darker old-world customs, "blood brotherhood" tradi-
tions, and the law of *omerta,* or silence.

Johnny Torrio, although not Sicilian, numbered among his good
friends one Mike Merlo, the Unione president. Merlo gave the Torrio
Syndicate his blessing, and by inference its partnership with the Gennas.
With his huge gambling and vice empire, Torrio could purchase all the
hooch the Gennas and their cottage industry could produce – and then
some. A key part of the arrangement held that Torrio would purchase the
raw "cooking" materials, with the Gennas supplying the the labor force.

The Torrio-Genna-Unione triumvirate now possessed unmatched
power. Throughout the years, the Syndicate would stop at nothing to
maintain its control over the Unione leadership. The Torrio-Genna
compact was seemingly all-powerful.

In addition to distilleries and breweries in Chicago, Canada supplied
prime brands that were smuggled across Lake Michigan. Still more
flowed northward from the Caribbean. From his headquarters in the
Four Deuces, Torrio oversaw an enterprise that was, thanks to Volstead,
now pulling down over $10 million a year from combined booze and vice
in greater Cook County.

With thousands of speakeasies, gambling joints, and brothels, Torrio
needed to beef up his security operation, especially since countless independent operators had not endorsed the peace pact. Just as Colosimo
had reached out to New York years before, Torrio brought his cousin, a
bouncer in a Brooklyn brothel, to his aid. Torrio would eventually teach his
charge the power of the payoff. "Bribe everyone" was Torrio's mantra.

The boy from Brooklyn, who had years before worked in Torrio's
gang, was a powerful and fiercely loyal muscleman for his cousin. Soon
after his arrival in the Second City, he would be implicated in the decade's

most infamous murder. A witness to Jim Colosimo's demise, his secretary Frank Camilla, described the fleeing assailant as a heavyset man with scars on the left side of his face, a portrayal that effectively narrowed the field to one: Torrio's newest imported muscleman. After his own notorious reign in Chicago, this enforcer's coterie, the Outfit, would achieve a level of success that had eluded even him, Alphonse Capone.

The Capone Years and the Chicago Beer Wars

You get more with a smile and a gun than you get with just a smile.
                                        –Al Capone

He was, like Johnny Torrio, a product of the New York to Chicago, First City to Second City, gangster pipeline. Born in 1899, Alphonse Capone was the last link in the criminal evolutionary chain that gave rise to the Outfit.

As a teenager in New York, Al joined Johnny Torrio's James Street Gang and tended bar for Torrio criminal associate Frankie Yale at the Harvard Inn. Al Capone was big *and* driven, but with an uncontrollable temper that got him expelled from the sixth grade for punching a teacher. He also possessed the Look, taking it to the level of an art form. While he was still in his teens, a barroom brawl with another tough guy named Frank Galluccio left him with three deep knife scars on the lower left side of his face and a new nickname, Scarface.

By inducting Capone into his Five Points Gang, Yale turned Capone from just another thug into a full-fledged gangster. As such, Al graduated to the big leagues, where a player had to be able to perform the ultimate sanction without hesitation. At about the same time he committed his first murder for Yale in 1918, a nineteen-year-old Capone lost his heart to Mae Coughlin, an Irish lass two years his senior. Nine months hence, and as yet unmarried, Mae gave birth to Albert Francis "Sonny" Capone on December 4, 1918. On December 30, Al married Mae. By this time Al and Johnny Torrio had grown so close that Torrio was named Sonny's godfather.

After a brief stint in Baltimore, where he made a momentary attempt at the straight life, Capone returned to New York in 1920 to attend his father's funeral. The homecoming was momentous, since Al fell back in with Johnny Torrio. Capone never returned to Baltimore, or the straight life. In short time, he beat an Italian-hating Irishman named Arthur Finnegan to death. Finnegan's boss, the terrifyingly dangerous William Lovett, then made it known that Al was a dead man.

For Capone, the call from Johnny Torrio couldn't have been more timely. Now, just as Colosimo needed Torrio, so too Torrio needed Capone, and Capone had to go on the lam to avoid being eviscerated by Lovett. In Torrio's Chicago, Capone would go from a $15-a-week mop boy (and occasional whore-beater), to one of the most powerful and wealthy men in the world in a mere six years.

Upon arrival, Capone was given the job of "capper" at Torrio's Four Deuces. In that capacity, Al, who now used the surname Brown, had the lowly task of standing out in the frigid Chicago night coaxing prospective clients inside. "Got some nice-looking girls inside," the scar-faced barker would entice. Capone would flash a sense of humor when he handed out his newly struck business card, which read:

AL BROWN
Second Hand Furniture Dealer
2222 South Wabash Avenue

When asked to elaborate as to what sort of furniture he sold, Capone would quip, "Any old thing a man might want to lay on." After Torrio waxed enthusiastically about their potential empire of booze, Al had his brothers Ralph and Frank join him from Brooklyn. His first cousins, brothers Charlie and Rocco Fischetti, also boarded the New York to Chicago underworld railroad. For a brief time, the quartet lived in the same apartment building on South Wabash Avenue.

In 1923, the newly elected mayor, William Dever, made a serious attempt at clearing the bootleggers out of downtown Chicago. When Dever's police chief proved immune to bribery, Torrio and Capone were forced to abandon the Four Deuces and find a more hospitable locale. They chose the near west suburb of Cicero, a bleak, depressing town of fifty thousand submissive Bohemians, most of whom found work at the huge Western Electric factory. For Torrio-Capone, the choice was a stroke of genius. The Czech-born, beer-drinking Ciceronians resented prohibition almost as much as they resented people of color. Gangsters arriving was one thing, but God forbid a clean-living "Negro" family wanted in.

Setting up their headquarters at the Hawthorne Inn, the boys systematically took over a town that never stood a chance. The local Republican contingent knew a gift horse when they saw one and quickly struck a deal with their new neighbors.

The Syndicate's challenge was to guarantee the reelection of Cicero mayor Joseph Klenha. At the time, the local Democrats were making noise about deposing Klenha as a requisite to – if one could believe it – a reform movement. Since a growing number of Cicero's citizens appeared anxious about the recent gangster immigration, action was needed before reform caught on. Thus on election night more than one dozen touring cars, crammed with Capone's thugs, hit the streets, ensuring that the vote went the right way. There was nothing subtle about their electioneering technique: voters had gun barrels pointed at them while instructed to pull the Democratic lever; still others were shot, knifed, mugged, and slugged into submission. One of Cicero's finest, Officer Anton Bican, attempted to intervene and woke up in a hospital. Local officials, knowing they were outmanned and outgunned, sent out an SOS. Some seventy police were dispatched from Chicago, but while they engaged the Syndicate in street battles, the "democratic process" ran its course. During one of the police skirmishes, Al's brother Frank was killed. It was a tough price for Capone to pay, but Klenha and the Syndicate prevailed.

Before the city had a chance to mop up the bloodstains, one hundred saloons and one hundred and fifty casinos had sprung up in Capone's Cicero. By the next spring, however, the honorable Mr. Klenha gave an interview to a local paper in which he warned that the boat was about to be rocked. He soon regretted the interview. Klenha stated that while he was appreciative of the Syndicate's "support" in his election, he intended to run his office independently of the gangster element.

Upon reading the report, Capone jumped into his touring car and made a beeline to the mayor's office. This time Capone personally meted out the punishment, beating Klenha unconscious on City Hall steps while nearby cops wisely looked the other way. On another occasion, Capone sent his enforcers directly into a town council meeting, where they proceeded to drag out a councilman who had the temerity to propose legislation inimical to the Syndicate's interests. Capone later explained that since he had bought Cicero (and Klenha) lock, stock, and barrel, disobedience could not be tolerated. Capone's forces even dominated the Cicero police station. *Tribune* journalist Walter Trohan realized this when, arriving at the police station for a scheduled meeting with Capone, Trohan was frisked by *Capone's* boys.

Capone was now Cicero's de facto mayor, and he flaunted his power for all it was worth. When his former employer from Baltimore came through Cicero, Capone decreed that there would be a parade in his honor. Of course no one in Cicero had ever heard of Baltimore's Peter Aiello, but Capone wanted a crowd, and he got one. Literally thousands lined the streets to cheer the bewildered stranger.

The Syndicate was now grossing $105 million a year, including the combined income from booze, gambling, vice, and to a diminishing degree (about $10 million) from extortion. Capone began dressing in grand style, typified by brightly colored $5,000 suits and custom-made fedoras. His pals nicknamed him Snorky, slang for "elegant."

Snorky Capone also indulged his passion for music, and in doing so he unwittingly became a major architect of the American musical landscape. Al had always insisted that his speakeasies employ live musicians. In his own home he maintained an expensive grand piano. Now, flush with discretionary cash, the gangster without a racist bone in his body made a momentous decision: he would bring to Chicago the best jazz musicians in the country. The overwhelming majority of these were of African descent and were playing for spare change in the dives of New Orleans, forbidden from playing in the white clubs.

Whereas New Orleans invented jazz, Chicago legitimized it by introducing many soon-to-be-legendary black musicians into the white-attended clubs – and this seminal occurrence was largely due to the efforts of Al Capone.[6]

But the good times were not to last, for the Syndicate's weakest link, the North Side Irish gang, was under the leadership of a madman who decided to confront the Italians. Mayor Dever's crackdown, which resulted in the confiscation of many alcohol stockpiles, had emboldened many gangs; some, like the North Siders, returned to the old days of stealing from one another. Poachings and hijackings began to escalate.

---

6. After opening the Cotton Club in Cicero, Capone initiated the exodus of black musicians from the Big Easy (and elsewhere) to the Second City. Players such as Louis Armstrong, Jelly Roll Morton, King Oliver, Duke Ellington, Milt Hinton, Lionel Hampton, Fats Waller, and Nat King Cole were now making the kind of money they deserved. Capone developed genuine friendships with these players, treating them like family. Great jazz bassist Milt Hinton has spoken of how the Big Guy paid his hospital bill when a nearly severed finger threatened to nip his brilliant career in the bud. One night, pianist Fats Waller was "kidnapped" from the Sherman Hotel by armed gangsters, only to be delivered to Al Capone as a birthday gift. Capone treated Waller like a king, and when the three-day party finally waned, the extraordinary pianist found that Capone had lined his pockets with thousands of dollars.

But only one gang leader had the temerity to steal from Capone. His cretinous decision set off a chain of events that ruined everything for everybody; it would also precipitate the collapse of Capone's reign.

Deanie – the Instigator

The disintegration of Torrio's truce with the North Siders came as no real surprise, given the ethnic rancor that was always just beneath the surface. Even so, the admittedly fragile agreement might have lasted until the Eighteenth Amendment's repeal a decade later if not for the ambitions of the Italian-loathing North Side baron, Dion "Deanie" O'Banion. Possessed of a venomous tongue, the reflexively hateful Irishman referred to Italians as "greaseballs" and "spic pimps."

A living contradiction, Deanie O'Banion was a childhood choirboy at Holy Name Cathedral by day, a gang terrorist by night; he was a vicious racist murderer who was always home by five, where he stayed with his loving wife, Viola, for the rest of the evening. A gifted floral arranger, he owned a flower shop; as "the mob's florist," Deanie might spend his lunch break blowing a competitor's brains out. A casual killer, O'Banion was said to have killed more than sixty people. When he branched out still further into bootlegging, he often made his beer deliveries in his florist truck.

Just as Cicero had its Capone, North Side politicians cowered at O'Banion's terror tactics. While Torrio-Capone dictated Cicero's election results, O'Banion matched them bullet for bullet in his district's Forty-second Ward. The irascible Irishman was witnessed "electioneering" with his thugs at polling places, in direct view of election judges and clerks. "I'm interested in seeing that the Republicans get a fair shake this time," Deanie wailed. He then made a show of checking that his revolver was loaded. Democrats were physically stopped from voting. In one election, his Republicans squeezed by with a scant 98 percent of the vote.

But O'Banion differed from Capone and Torrio in that he was most assuredly certifiably crazy. After his partner, Sam "Nails" Morton died in a horse-riding accident on May 13, 1923, O'Banion's only moderating influence was gone. O'Banion began to make highly questionable decisions. Even to other gangsters, O'Banion's behavior became frightening, since it often made no logical sense. First, O'Banion had his enforcer, Louis "Three-Gun Louis" Alterie execute the poor horse that had thrown Morton. On one occasion, O'Banion was nabbed for a safecracking because, after the hit, he and his escaping crew could not resist the temptation to ascend a stagelike Dumpster and belt out a popular song of the day. In his most infamous booze heist, the Sibley Warehouse robbery, he bought the pilfered hooch from the burglars with a fake certified bank check, marked with bank seals. What made the purchase so bizarre was that O'Banion had hired the same forger that the burglars had hired to make the warehouse withdrawal slips they had utilized to acquire the load.[7]

As his behavior deteriorated, it became apparent that Deanie was the victim of some then unknown mental disorder, a condition that now steeled him to confront the Syndicate powerhouse. During prohibition, O'Banion of course maintained his own breweries, but he decided it was easier to hijack Torrio-Genna shipments. "Let Torrio make the stuff and I'll steal what I want of it" was O'Banion's famous battle cry. In addition to stealing the Gennas' inferior hooch, he thought nothing of pilfering thousands of gallons of Capone's best alcohol. In one heist he felt compelled to leave a humorous calling card, replacing Capone's booze with water. Incredibly, the Capone organization often turned the other cheek. They could afford to. But the Genna brothers had never looked the other way in their lives. They spoiled for a fight.

Deanie's hatred for the Sicilian Gennas was legendary. His innate abhorrence of Sicilians in general was further inflamed by the knowledge that the Gennas, with their rotgut booze, were able to drastically undercut O'Banion's going price for hooch. Torrio, as per his style, attempted to mediate the rivalry, but O'Banion refused to cut a deal. Despite his own predilection for patronizing whorehouses, O'Banion was said to abhor Torrio's vice trade, and the murdering florist drew the line at dealing with an immoral whoremaster. Torrio finally washed his hands of the entire affair, knowing full well that the volatile Gennas would whack O'Banion at their first opportunity. But that could only happen if Torrio and the all-powerful Unione leadership sanctioned such a move. It would be O'Banion himself who would guarantee such a consensus.

After numerous skirmishes with the Gennas, O'Banion was poised to

---

7. The quixotic O'Banion once reminisced about one of his adventures, explaining how a safecracking attempt was interrupted by a policeman: "I was just about to shoot that yokel cop when I remembered that [my partner] the Ox had a pint bottle of nitroglycerin in his pocket. One shot in that room would have blown the whole south end of the Loop to Kingdom Come." Competitors like Capone wondered who could talk sense with such a man.

create his gangster masterpiece: an imaginative double cross of Torrio himself. In the spring of 1924, Deanie informed Torrio that he was getting out of the booze business. He then offered to sell Torrio his interest in the Seiben Brewery, which was coowned by him and Torrio, for $500,000. Torrio jumped at the offer, further agreeing to attend O'Banion's final beer loadout on May 19.

One has to wonder about Torrio's mental state, accepting such an obvious Trojan horse from a man with O'Banion's reputation. Nonetheless, in the early-morning hours on the appointed date, with their paid-off cops standing guard, Torrio and O'Banion observed the beer trucks filling their tanks at the Seiben warehouse. The operation was suddenly halted when squads of Chicago police converged on the scene, arresting everyone in sight. As they were taken to federal prohibition authorities to be charged with Volstead violations, O'Banion was seen whistling, singing, and generally looking like the cat that had eaten the canary.

When Torrio was booked, he gave his favorite alias, Frank Langley, to the police, knowing that if they discovered his true identity, there was no way to avoid doing hard time. The cheery O'Banion, on the other hand, knew that since this was his first prohibition arrest, he would only receive a puny fine. Laughing uncontrollably, O'Banion sent out for breakfast for all thirty-one detainees.

In fact, the crazy Irishman had been tipped off about the imminent raid and thereby set about planning his crowning masterpiece and ultimate practical joke. While Torrio's lawyers set about stalling his trial for six months, Torrio and Capone now joined the Gennas in demanding O'Banion's head. But Mike Merlo, the prestigious president of the Unione, wanted peace. When he died from cancer on November 8, the Syndicate wasted no time, quickly maneuvering Angelo Genna into the Unione presidency. They also set about writing the final scene in the life of the Irish pest.

Torrio customarily sent to New York for Frankie Yale. On November 10, 1924, fresh from muscling the Democrats in a North Side election, O'Banion was working overtime filling floral orders for the huge Merlo funeral. At eleven-thirty in the morning, two of Torrio's most ruthless hitmen, Albert Anselmi and John Scalise, accompanied Yale into O'Banion's Flower Shop. Believing the strangers were there to purchase flowers for Merlo, O'Banion extended his hand, effectively preventing him from grabbing his pistol when they shot him six times, point-blank.

Typically, there were no arrests, but soon after O'Banion was hit, Scalise and Anselmi were seen sporting $3,000 rings. Like a Second City leitmotiv witnesses refused to come forward. ("Me? I didn't see anything.") Another recurring theme was the indifference of the police, who were happy to let the gangsters kill off each other. Chief of Police Morgan Collins said of O'Banion's demise, "Chicago's archcriminal is dead. I don't doubt that O'Banion was responsible for at least twenty-five murders in this city."

Deanie's corpse was placed in a $7,500 bronze coffin, the best made, appointed with solid silver posts and encased in a solid copper box. Like Colosimo and Merlo, the Irish gangster was afforded a huge funeral; some ten thousand marchers followed the hearse to Mt. Carmel Cemetery. More than two dozen cars were enlisted to haul the flowers alone, including a tribute from Torrio and one in roses "From Al," both of which were summarily placed in the trash heap outside. At the tense wake, which both Capone and Torrio attended, mourners checked their guns at the door. Torrio was given the silent treatment by O'Banion's crew. Perhaps out of respect for O'Banion's family, his crew refrained from icing Capone and Torrio on the spot, but the battle was now joined.

The Chicago Beer Wars

If you smell gunpowder, you're in Cicero.

Torrio and Capone braced their troops, numbering some eight hundred gunmen, for the inevitable bloodletting that was to come. With their leader dead, the North Siders were now led by second-in-command George "Bugs" Moran, who stepped up their attacks on the Torrio-Capone gang. The Beer Wars had evolved into an ethnic war, chiefly the Irish versus the Sicilians. The Irish were emboldened in their anti-Syndicate efforts by their acquisition of some newly invented Thompson submachine guns, or tommy guns, which unleashed a barrage of eight hundred rounds per minute. Not surprisingly, the gangsters had machine guns before the cops, who found them too expensive and inaccurate. Although the weapons retailed for $175, the cash-rich gangsters were happy to buy them for $2,000 on the black market, where they quickly earned an appropriate moniker: the Chicago typewriter.

There were now four or more gang-related murders per month in the Chicago area. One journalist noted, "Two thirds of the deaths in Chicago are due to the beer-running trade." On January 24, 1925, Johnny Torrio himself was seriously wounded by North Side chieftain Hymie Weiss. Torrio was hit multiple times, with gunshots to the chest, stomach, and arm. It appeared that the attackers were trying to emulate O'Banion's wounds, including the coup de grâce to the head, which Yale had administered to Deanie. But the shooter ran out of bullets, then had to flee as witnesses approached. Still, Torrio suffered so many hits that the attackers must have believed they had accomplished their mission.

When he heard of the attack, Al Capone raced to the hospital, anxiously asking, "Did they get Johnny?" Capone moved into the facility, occupying the adjacent room and ordering thirty bodyguards to stand watch. "While I'm there, nobody will bother him," Capone sobbed. Near death for two weeks, Torrio rallied to a remarkable recovery; however, after his convalescence, he still had to serve time for the Seiben Brewery raid. Torrio first attempted a futile, $50,000 bribe to the DA, but was sentenced to nine months in the Lake County Jail. While "away at college," Torrio's forced reflection time chastened the weary boss, who had once dreamed of a vast crime cartel. From his confinement, Torrio summoned Capone and, upon his arrival, told him, "Al, it's all yours." And so, at forty-four years of age, Johnny "the Fox" Torrio took his $30 million and headed back east to Brooklyn.

The Commission

If Capone believed that Johnny actually intended to retire, then he was just another of the wily Fox's victims. Torrio guessed that Capone was a train wreck just waiting to happen and decided to bail out and hitch his wagon to an idea that dwarfed even the Torrio-Capone Syndicate: an affiliation with New York gangsters Meyer Lansky, Ben Siegel, and Lucky Luciano. Torrio was the first to realize that the entire substructure of the country was up for grabs, and if a national syndicate could be formed, all concerned would grow rich beyond their dreams while they ruled from the shadows. Soon after arriving in New York, the revered Torrio called a summit and presented his vision of "open cities" in which the combined forces of New York and Capone's heirs in Chicago could flourish. In doing so, Torrio prophetically outlined the rest of America's twentieth century.

What happened at the gangster conclave would have gone unreported were it not for a highly placed snitch who later reported what he had seen to the Brooklyn district attorney in a deal to beat a murder rap. Abe

"Kid Twist" Reles was the top gunner in Lepke Buchalter's Murder, Incorporated. During his career, Kid Twist was arrested forty-one times, but he was always able to dodge a murder conviction. From Twist, and a number of other sources, it has been learned that the meeting took place in a four-star Park Avenue hotel. Those in attendance with the then twenty-eight-year-old enforcer included Lucky Luciano, Lepke Buchalter, Longy Zwillman, Joey Adonis, Frank Costello, and Meyer Lansky.

"Why don't you guys work up one big outfit?" Torrio asked the New York contingent. He was initially met with skepticism, especially over which boss would take a backseat in such an operation. However, the Fox had all the answers: "Each guy keeps what he's got now. We work as equal partners, but we make one big combination . . . It's my feeling that a mixture of the legitimate and the other stuff is our strongest card." The hoods finally grasped the concept and signed on to the plan. Costello said, "I've always liked Chicago as a market, but of course one guy doesn't have the organization to work all the towns. A thing like we're talking about is exactly what we need." Joey Adonis agreed, adding, "It'll cut a hell of a lot of fat from the bundle, and when the pols see they're up against a united front, they'll settle for what they can get."

The *New York Times* was leaked the story by sources in "official circles." It ran a front-page investigative piece on October 26, 1935, in which it named the participants in the momentous powwow. The article concluded: "Torrio is the power behind the scenes. The gang under his tutelage has seized control of the rackets." When Reles/Twist gave details of the meeting to authorities in 1941, he broke a gang rule so sacred that his very existence was put in jeopardy. Thus on November 12, 1941, his body was found after having fallen (or been pushed) from his sixth-floor room in New York's Half Moon Hotel.

The national Commission, as it was often called, would meet from time to time over the coming decades and facilitate the takeover of Hollywood, the founding of Las Vegas, and a national network of bookmaking and other sundry chicanery. Although both the New York and Chicago gangs would profit from the new cartel, the bosses from the Windy City would enjoy a far longer reign, while the New Yorkers routinely decimated their own ranks with internecine infighting, instigated in part by their adherance to old-world "Mafia" rules and rivalries. Chicago's bold decision to abandon ancient ceremony allowed its bosses to outlive and outsucceed their Eastern counterparts. As for Johnny Torrio, he would eventually retire to Brooklyn, where he died on April 1957 at seventy-five, extreme old age for a gangster.[8]

Al Capone was now a twenty-six-year-old tycoon, albeit one embroiled in a nasty gang war. His operation devoured $300,000 a week in overhead, which consisted largely of meeting the thousand-man payroll and official graft disbursements. The Capone Syndicate set up new headquarters in Chicago's Metropole Hotel, where it appropriated between fifty and sixty rooms on two floors. The gang had its own private elevator, service bar, and wine vault, bringing its total hotel tab to $1,500 per day.

The Unione Siciliana Wars

Both warring gangs knew that victory was assured to the faction that held sway over the Unione, which in turn lorded over the massive Sicilian home distillery network. Not surprisingly, the fight for control over the Unione involved gallons of spilt blood. On May 26, 1925, Unione president Angelo Genna and his brother Mike were killed. Some believe Capone himself was behind the Genna hits, as he may have heard they were about to make a power play against him. Soon Tony Genna was killed by Joseph "the Cavalier" Nerone, who had links to Capone, and who was himself soon whacked by a Capone enemy. In the rabid feeding frenzy, Sam and Pete Genna fled to Italy, which proved wise, since within weeks, Angelo's successor, twenty-six-year-old Sam "Samoots" Amatuna met the business end of an assassin's rifle.

Chicago was now the capital of unsolved murders. Murder counts routinely topped those in New York, a city with twice the population. In a five-year period, there were 136 gang killings, with only one conviction. It remains an amazing fact that – federal prohibition laws excluded – no top member of Capone's Syndicate was ever convicted of any local crime in Chicago.

---

8. Johnny "the Fox" Torrio suffered a fatal heart attack while in his barber's chair in Brooklyn. He and his wife, Anna, had led such a hermetic existence for the previous two decades that only a smattering of neighbors showed up at his wake, a far cry from the mammoth send-offs given fellow Chicago kingpins Jim Colosimo and Deanie O'Banion. So inconsequential was his passing that newspapers did not learn of it for three weeks. Just five weeks earlier (February 26, 1957), Torrio's former nemesis Bugs Moran died in Leavenworth prison, where he had recently been imprisoned for bank robbery. The heist came just days after his 1956 prison release, after a ten-year stay, on a similar charge.

With the Gennas gone, filling the Unione power vacuum became everyone's obsession. Joey Aiello, a prosperous Italian bakery owner who coveted the top Unione post, formed an alliance with the North Siders in a plan to kill Capone and take over the Syndicate. Aiello extended a blanket offer to the nations' gangsters: any man who killed Capone could collect a $50,000 bounty. Aiello once offered a cook $35,000 to poison Al, but the frightened would-be assassin confessed to Capone, who then had his men riddle Aiello's bakery with two hundred machine-gun rounds. In short time, there were more than a dozen attempts on Capone. On one occasion, Aiello brought in two out-of-town murderers, who promptly made their return trip in body bags. On September 20, 1926, North Siders Bugs Moran, Hymie Weiss, and Vincent Drucci fired more than a thousand rounds into the Hawthorne Inn restaurant where their prey was eating. But no matter what they tried, the North Siders could not hit their mark. Capone retaliated by having his boys kill as many North Side triggermen as they could hunt down.

The war of attrition with the North Siders was only one facet of Capone's world in 1926. Capone faced additional vicissitudes to the south, where the O'Donnell gang had begun encroaching on Capone's territory, undercutting the Syndicate's booze prices and stealing its customers. When the O'Donnells began moving in on Cicero, they pushed the wrong button. On the night of April 27, after Capone was tipped off that the South Siders were heading to a bar in Cicero, he dispatched a thirty-man, five-car motorcade that included Capone himself. Capone obviously venerated Machiavelli's theory of massive retaliation.

When the stalkers located the O'Donnell car parking curbside by the Pony Inn, onlookers were once again treated to the recurring spectacle of a drive-by drama. As a bonus, they witnessed a rarity: Capone himself was one of the gunmen. In what would prove to be one of the Syndicate's biggest miscalculations, to say nothing of its worst display of marksmanship, they murdered the wrong guy. The unfortunate soul was a twenty-five-year-old assistant state's attorney named Bill McSwiggin, who, for reasons never determined, was out drinking with the O'Donnells. Some have opined that McSwiggin's link to the O'Donnells represented a kind of Irish solidarity; others claimed that McSwiggin was on the take, for although he had a tough reputation, with seven death penalties obtained in eight months, he had never sought capital punishment for a gangster.

Despite six grand juries impaneled to study the McSwiggin killing (at a cost of $200,000), no indictments were obtained. But the death of the young prosecutor both inflamed and united Chicago's citizenry. With Capone hiding in Michigan for the next four months, police sought reprisal, ransacking Capone's speakeasies, gambling joints, and whorehouses, some beyond repair. His most lucrative suburban brothel was burned to the ground.

When Capone returned in July, he reported to the police, who had sought him for questioning. As to the charge that he had killed McSwiggin, Al said, "Of course I didn't kill him. Why should I? I liked the kid. Only the day before he was up at my place, and when he went home, I gave him a bottle of Scotch for his old man." Fully aware that the rising antigang sentiment would not be mollified so easily, Capone embarked on an ambitious public relations campaign aimed at convincing the public that he was a victim of circumstances. As a prelude to the kinder, gentler next phase of his regime, Capone decided to broker an intergang peace conference.

On October 4, 1926, Capone sent out invitations to all the gangs announcing another Torrio-style peace summit. His invitation to Judge John H. Lyle to act as arbiter was met with indignant refusal, while North Sider Hymie Weiss RSVP'd that if he attended, it would be with grenades exploding and shotguns blasting. Weiss was obsessed with avenging Deanie. "I want the heads of [O'Banion's killers] Anselmi and Scalise," Weiss demanded of Capone. Al was willing to go to great lengths to end the gang wars, but there was no way he could deliver the heads of his own Syndicate members. Capone later told a cop friend that Weiss was a madman. "When a dog's got rabies, nobody's safe," Al said. "The dumb thing's just got to be killed." One week later, Weiss, leaving a court hearing to seat a jury for a murder indictment against him, was murdered in front of the late Deanie O'Banion's flower shop by gunmen firing from the second story of a rooming house.

With the Weiss matter settled, the October 20 conference at the Hotel Sherman – located directly across the street from the chief of police headquarters – proceeded as scheduled. All the surviving major gang leaders showed up. One of the North Siders opened the proceedings by imploring, "Let's give each other a break. We're a bunch of saps, killing each other this way." Al Capone later described his presentation: "I told them we're making a shooting gallery out of a great business, and nobody's profiting." He also made reference to his newly awakened paternalism. "I wanted to stop all that because I couldn't stand hearing my little kid ask why I didn't stay home," Al said. "I had been living at the Hawthorne Inn for fourteen months. He's been sick for three years . . .

and I have to take care of him and his mother. If it wasn't for him, I'd have said, 'To hell with you fellows. We'll shoot it out.' " Years later, Capone would expound on this theme to Babe Meigs, publisher of the *Chicago Evening American:* "I can't tell you what it does to my twelve-year-old son when the other schoolchildren, cruel as they are, keep showing him newspaper stories that call me a killer or worse."

The conference produced results, albeit temporary ones. Among the adopted treaty's provisions: a "general amnesty" mandated that retributions cease; signees would solve disputes with arbitration, not gunfire; discrete territories were agreed to with no poaching of customers. The conference ended in a glow of good fellowship and a standing ovation.[9]

Despite Capone's best efforts, Chicago's era of tranquillity would be short-lived. The Hotel Sherman peace treaty held fast for only ten weeks. On January 6, 1927, the North Siders killed Capone's buddy and the owner of the Hawthorne Inn's restaurant, Theodore Anton. Although Capone sobbed openly for his friend, he adhered to the Hotel Sherman agreement and sought no retribution. Days later, Joe Saltis of the West Side ordered the killing of a runner for Ralph Sheldon, with whom Saltis had agreed to share the district. Capone, a friend of Sheldon's, could restrain his primal urges no longer. He ordered the execution of two of Saltis' hit men, and soon thereafter Saltis himself retired to Wisconsin.

*   *   *

9. Capone's image transformation was inspired in part by the counsel of *Chicago Evening American* editor Harry Read, who was happy to trade advice for inside stories from the Big Guy. Speaking to Capone on one occasion, Read advised, "Al, you're a prominent figure now. Why act like a hoodlum? Quit hiding. Be nice to people." (Read would eventually be fired from the *American* when the *Tribune* published a photo of him catching rays with the Big Guy at Capone's Palm Island, Florida, estate.) Apparently, Read's words struck a chord with Capone, who soon began venturing out in public, the most accessible gangster the world had ever seen. He began holding regular press conferences to win back the public. He even announced to a throng of disbelieving journalists for whom he had dished up a spaghetti dinner at his home, "I am out of the booze business." Incredibly, Al Capone became the toast of Chicago – at least among the city's downtrodden blue-collar segments. He was cheered at prizefights, racetracks, and at Cubs games with five-minute standing ovations; he gave writers and perfect strangers tips on fixed fights and horse races.

While Capone busied himself with gang wars and conferences, his empire continued to expand. As the millions poured in, Capone did not neglect the task of keeping the upperworld powers in check. It turned out that the conquest of Cicero was just the prelude to the main event. Now fully cognizant of the power of political liaisons, and experienced in the ways of "electing" a mayor, Capone tried his hand at the real plum: Chicago's City Hall.

Choosing former mayor Big Bill Thompson as the recipient of his largesse, Capone put the laissez-faire pol back in office virtually single-handedly. The transplanted son of wealthy Bostonians, Thompson had been displaced in 1923 by reform candidate William Dever after many of Thompson's appointees were convicted in a payola scheme. It was widely known that the short-on-intellect Thompson was really just a front for power-broker businessmen Fred Lundin and William Lorimer. What was most important for Capone's interests was that Thompson, an unabashed defier of Volstead, had years before given wide berth to Johnny Torrio's operation.

Capone spent $250,000 on Thompson's campaign. The requisite thugs, numbering about a thousand, hit the streets to the sound of broken arms and legs of Thompson opponents. During the primary, Capone's sluggers heaved so many grenades into polling places where his opponent was favored that the contest was nicknamed the Pineapple Primary. After his election, Mayor Bill Thompson disappeared on an extended fishing trip, while the real power, Capone and his Syndicate, set up shop in the Second City.

Now firing on all cylinders, Capone also attempted to ingratiate himself with his most avowed enemy – the newly formed Chicago Crime Commission (CCC), a private organization representing business leaders and citizens who shared the vision of a gang-free Chicago. Al brought seventy-six-year-old Frank J. Loesch, president of the CCC, to one of his headquarters, the Lexington Hotel. Seated below portraits of George Washington, Abraham Lincoln, and Mayor William Thompson, Loesch asked Capone to keep his thugs away from polling booths in an upcoming election. "All right," Al said. "I'll have the cops send over the squad cars the night before the election and jug all the hoodlums and keep 'em in the cooler until the polls close." True to his word, seventy cop cars worked all night, rounding up the hoods. "It turned out to be the squarest and most successful election in forty years," Loesch later said.

Meanwhile, the struggle for control over the Unione Siciliana was unrelenting. The North Siders, led by Bugs Moran, wanted Unione copresident Joe Aiello to preside over the powerful organization and were seconded by New York chapter president Frankie Yale. Capone, however, installed Tony Lombardo as president of the Unione, and Yale was promptly murdered. When Capone moved to murder Aiello, his gang went to the jail where Aiello was being held (on suspicion of trying to kill Capone). In a stunning display of audacity, a train of taxis carrying Capone's assassins showed up at the police station to hit Aiello while he was in custody. After entering Aiello's cell, Capone's boys decided to merely put the fear of God into Aiello and drive off. Upon his release, Aiello fled town and went into hiding for a year in New York.

Meanwhile, Capone's man Tony Lombardo changed the tarnished Unione's name to the Italo-American National Union. When Lombardo was killed on September 7, 1928, Capone had four of the Aiello brothers killed in return. One can scarcely imagine why anyone would now want the virtual death sentence that was the Unione presidency, but Capone somehow found more candidates. And so Lombardo's successor turned out to be one Pasqualino Lolordo, who was killed on January 8, 1929. Temporarily, Aiello achieved his goal and assumed the top post.

The Massacre

Those silly Irish bastards. They have more guts than sense. If only we'd hooked up, I could have been president.
                    —Al Capone, on the St. Valentine's Day massacre

The war for the Unione – and for that matter Chicago itself – reached its climax in the only manner that was ever really viable: a massacre. It occurred on February 14, 1929, St. Valentine's Day. Since Bugs Moran had been stealing Capone's booze, it was decided that he could be lured into a trap by setting up a buy of "stolen" Capone hooch. After disguising a black rental car as a police patrol wagon by mounting a fake siren on its top, four shooters dressed as cops met seven members of the North Side gang in a garage at 2122 North Clark Street at 11 A.M. to make the transfer.

In the garage, the "cops" pointed their "Chicago typewriters" at the heart of the Moran gang. Some seventy rounds were fired with machine guns, and once the victims were motionless, some of them received point-blank shotgun blasts to their faces. Each victim received dozens of wounds, methodically spread throughout each body. The carnage was so brutal that some corpses were said to have been nearly severed at the waist. When the firing ended a full minute later, a river of blood coursed across the dark, oily basement floor. Six were dead at the scene. Incredibly, the seventh, Frank Gusenberg, lingered for a couple hours, before giving investigators the gangster's response as his last words: "Nobody shot me. I ain't no copper." The shooters were never identified.[10] Although Moran was not there, his operation was mortally wounded. Both he and Aiello went into hiding, with the departing Moran telling police, "Only the Capone gang kills like that."

Although it was quickly learned that Capone was in Miami (meeting with the Dade County solicitor) at the time of the shootings, there was little doubt that he had ordered the slaughter of his sworn enemies. There was simply no one else so vicious and with so much to gain by hitting the North Siders. Capone, of course, proclaimed his innocence, at one point mocking Moran's own theory when he chided, "The only man who kills like that is Bugs Moran."

With the war essentially won, Capone named Joe Guintas to head the Unione. This appointee survived in that post the extremely long span of three months, only to be killed by Capone's gang. It seems that two of the suspected Valentine's Day triggermen, John Scalise and Albert Anselmi, were conspiring with Guintas to take Unione back from Al. On May 7, 1929, Capone and his boys met the three conniving traitors at a prearranged dinner party at a roadhouse in Hammond, Indiana. After a nightlong repast, Capone turned on the three quislings. When their bodies were found the next morning in an abandoned car parked by an Indiana highway, they were unrecognizable, having been beaten unmercifully with baseball bats and then riddled with bullets. The coroner assigned to the case said that in his thirty years of experience, he had never seen human bodies so mutilated.

---

10. Ten months after the massacre, evidence gathered at another murder gave a strong indication as to the identity of one of the shooters. At the time, the science of ballistics was in its infancy, but it had already been learned that gun barrels leave unique scratches, or rifling marks, on exiting bullets. Rifling marks on the bullets recovered from the scene of the December 1929 murder of a St. Joseph, Michigan, policeman matched identically the marks on bullets from not only the St. Valentine's Day massacre, but also the assassination of Frankie Yale. More important, the bullets from the policeman's slaying were matched to a weapon that was traced to gang hit man Fred "Killer" Burke. Burke was captured and sentenced to a life sentence in the police murder, never standing trial for the St. Valentine's Day shooting.

All told, adding in the preemptive strikes and various retaliations, eighteen gang leaders died in the War for the Unione. Of course, no one was ever so much as arrested. After the Indiana sanctions, Capone headed for Atlantic City to attend the first national meeting of all the major crime lords, aka the Commission.

The conference ran from May 13 to 16, 1929, and was held in Atlantic City's Hotel President. Thirty gang leaders participated; the roll call read like a Mafia Social Register. Included among the lawless luminaries were Albert Anastasia, Dutch Schultz, Louis Lepke, Frank Costello, Lucky Luciano, Longy Zwillman, Moe Dalitz, Ben "Bugsy" Siegel, and Al Capone. Of particular note was the presence of the notorious Kansas City machine politician Tom Pendergast, the sponsor of Harry Truman, future president of the United States. The legendary Johnny Torrio, working behind the scenes in New York with Lansky et al., surfaced for this convocation. The racketeers were able to avoid arrest because the Atlantic City rackets boss, Enoch "Nucky" Johnson, had paid off the local police. Befitting their exalted stature, the boys luxuriated at posh hotels such as the Ritz and the Breakers. The dons made themselves conspicuous, not only by their garish "mob chic" attire, which was not exactly designed for a day at the beach, but also by their choice of venue. It seems that the boys felt the traditional hotel meeting rooms to be insecure, so while they slept at the President, they adopted a bizarre MO for conducting their discussions: Conversations of great national significance were held in that boardwalk staple, the two-man pushcart. The leaders met two at a time, then changed partners: a Mafia version of musical chairs. Often, at the end of their rides, they would stroll the beach in full attire and complete their negotiations. During breaks, the mobsters ambled the world-famous boardwalk, perhaps sampling the Turkish Taffee. If they were trying to blend in, there is little doubt they failed.

In short time, it became clear that the first order of business was in fact Al Capone himself. Capone got his first inkling of this agenda when his mentor, Johnny Torrio, made a personal appeal to Capone to end the violence. Even the mobsters were cognizant that the "G" (government) would only be pushed so far before it cracked down. But there was also a thinly veiled subtext to the proceedings: the other gang lords were jealous of Capone's prosperity. And Lucky Luciano had been at odds with Capone since their gang days in New York, when Lucky had sided with the man who had inflicted the scars on Al's face. It was Luciano who had instructed Al not to seek revenge, lest he dig his own grave. When Capone discerned the depth of the antagonism at the conference, he lashed out, hurling obscenity-laced accusations in all directions one minute and withdrawing into silence the next. Consequently, Capone was shunned by many of his mobster competitors. It is now believed that Al's mood swings were the result of a syphilitic condition that would not be diagnosed until years later – a disease that ultimately claimed his life.

The conventioneers were so proud of themselves that they waged a PR campaign and leaked details of the proceedings to craving journalists. In the end, a fourteen-point peace plan was adopted. In addition to swearing off violence, the plan's key planks were aimed squarely at the Capone Syndicate, which was to be dismantled immediately, with all of his gambling joints being surrendered to the Commission, now headed by Torrio. As expected, Capone adamantly refused to be forced into this humiliation by the Atlantic City decree. Compounding Capone's woes, Joey Aiello was named to head the Unione Siciliana (Capone would eventually have him iced on October 30, 1930).

Despite the looming difficulties, Capone, now thirty years old, was worth an estimated $40 million, with his Syndicate pulling down $6 million per week. But all the money in the world could not buy peace of mind for someone on the Commission's hit list. Feeling the heat from all sides, Capone spent much of 1929 traveling with his bodyguard Frankie Rio. Since Capone had long desired to retire to the family life, he used the opportunity to decide on a retirement locale. After being turned back as "undesirable" by authorities in, among other places, Los Angeles and the Bahamas, he eventually bought property in Miami.

While on an extended vacation in Florida in the winter of 1928, Capone was quick to acquire well-placed friends, among them Parker Henderson, Jr., the son of the former mayor of Miami, and John Lummus, the current mayor. Henderson picked up Al's disbursements from Chicago – some $31,000 sent to "Albert Costa," while Lummus, also a leading Realtor, sold Capone a home on Palm Island on the Intracoastal waterway for $40,000 ($350,000 by current standards). For political purposes, Lummus told his constituents that he was maneuvering Capone out of town. To cover their tracks, Capone and Lummus instructed Henderson to take title to the property. Capone kept a low profile when in Miami, save for his temperamental, but futile, appearances on tennis courts and golfing greens, where he was seen hurling rackets and clubs in hacker's frustration.

But no matter where he traveled, Capone was never far from a

Commission stronghold. It did not take extraordinary brainpower for Capone to realize that he could not fight all the hoods now aligned against him. To survive, he had to lie low. But even his new Florida estate could not supply the security needed to forestall the professional killers who were nipping at his heels. Johnny Torrio advised, "The safest place in the world is inside a jail. Let's ask Boo-Boo."

Max "Boo-Boo" Hoff was the boss of Philadelphia much as Al was in Chicago. In a prearranged "collar," Hoff tipped two Philadelphia cops, whom Capone saw socially when they visited Florida, that Capone would be transiting their town carrying a concealed weapon. Capone further tipped them $20,000 when they arrested him. He was sentenced to a year in jail. While incarcerated he told a Philadelphia public safety director that he was tired of the gang life. "I've been in this racket long enough," Capone said. He spoke of his longing for peace of mind. "Every minute I was in danger of death . . . I'm tired of the gang murders and the gang shootings . . . During the last two years I've been trying to get out. But once in the racket you're always in it, it seems. The parasites trail you, begging you for favors and for money, and you can never get away from them, no matter where you go."

Capone was placed in the Eastern Penitentiary, where he was provided for like the king that he was: a cell with thick carpets, a phone with which to make limitless long-distance phone calls at the state's expense, a matching cabinet radio and chest of drawers. When asked by the warden if he desired that a stock ticker be installed, he responded, in typical Syndicate style, "No thanks. I never gamble."

In March 1930, Capone decided he wanted out of lockup, and so he left. What happened next will never be completely comprehended. In 1930, Capone adopted a Christ-like persona, performing every charitable work imaginable short of raising the dead. This period crystallized the inherent contradiction of the gangster as Robin Hood. Whether it was a coldly calculated, Madison Avenue–worthy attempt to sway public opinion back in his direction after the public relations disaster of the Valentine's Day massacre, or a genuine conviction of the heart, will never be known. Historians note that a possible incentive was an appeasement of the Unione membership, who were disgusted with the gangster involvement in their leadership putsches. Al may also have sensed his upcoming legal denouement, and thus the need to sway the potential jury pool. In any event, the largesse dispensed by Capone in what turned out to be the waning days of his reign is nothing if not staggering, with everything from handing out money to the needy to creating soup kitchens that fed some ten thousand per day.[11]

The sudden display of altruism was to no avail. On the home front, as well as in Washington, serious challenges were being mounted against Capone's dominion. The newly elected "reform" mayor, Anton Cermak, launched a war on gangsters in general, and Capone in particular. Cermak even allied with the "respectable" bootlegger Roger Touhy in an effort to isolate the Capone gang. (As will be seen, Cermak was not a reformer at all, and his alliance with Touhy stemmed from his desire to grab his own share of illicit jack.) There were numerous arrests, gun battles, and shot-up gangsters, as Capone's end appeared imminent.

In the nation's capital, momentum against Capone had been growing since 1926, when Vice President Charles Dawes had initiated a federal assault on the crime boss. President Calvin Coolidge's second-in-command hailed from Illinois and, along with his brother Rufus, owned a family bank in Chicago's Loop. In addition, Rufus was the president of the World's Fair Corporation, which was formed to coordinate the Fair's 1933 arrival in Chicago. Known as "A Century of Progress," the Fair was viewed as critical to Chicago's future growth and reputation. Over the next few years, Dawes lobbied Coolidge and his successor, Herbert Hoover, in his quest to dethrone Capone. Both presidents joined the fray by exploiting a 1927 Supreme Court ruling (*U.S. v. Sullivan*) – that illegal income was taxable. In March 1929, one month after the St.

---

11. With county clerks on his retainer, Capone was kept informed of any meaningful event that took place in the lives of Italians and Sicilians. Thus cards, gift baskets, and flowers were sent to families mourning a recent death, or celebrating a birth, marriage, or high school graduation; every hospitalized Italian or Sicilian who came to Al's attention received a personal note attached to a floral arrangement; Capone spent Sunday mornings in the Italian districts personally handing out money to the needy. He attended christenings and wakes of perfect strangers; baskets of food were sent weekly to the infirm and the needy, and this being the Depression, the roster was bulging; Capone's soup kitchens became the stuff of legend. After using his muscle to convince local food producers to "do your bit, or else," he hired good cooks for his spotless facilities and fed some ten thousand per day. When winter came, the destitute were served chili, beef stew, rye bread, and coffee or hot chocolate. Lastly, Capone gave slum children Grade A milk for the first time in their lives, ordering his sluggers to force the Chicago City Council to adopt a date stamp on milk cartons. After his death, upperworld capitalists had the law repealed.

Valentine's Day massacre, *Chicago Daily News* publisher Frank Knox led
a citizens' delegation to ask new president Herbert Hoover for help.
Knox, accompanied by Chicago Crime Commission director Frank
Loesch, informed the president that only federal help could save their
city. Like the Dawes brothers, Knox knew that bank investors were
becoming leary of depositing their money in Gangland, USA. At the time,
there were some sixty-three gang murders per year in Chicago.

Although Coolidge and Hoover may have been well-intentioned, the
Chicagoans' "crusade" was in large part a self-serving exercise in hypocrisy. The effort was funded in part by the Secret Six, a group of "crime-
fighting" Chicago businessmen who put up hundreds of thousands of
dollars (including $75,000 to IRS chief Elmer Irey). In fact, this cartel was
just another xenophobic lynch mob that had no qualms about establishing its fortunes on the backs of the musclemen provided by Capone's
Syndicate. Their civic activism was a barely concealed attempt to improve
their own business fortunes by getting the gangs off the streets in time for
the upcoming World's Fair. Worst of all, they backed Frank Loesch, an
unabashed racist, who had earlier struck an election accommodation with
Capone, and who now headed the Chicago Crime Commission (CCC).

With Loesch at its helm, the Chicago Crime Commission was in high
gear. It launched a brilliant PR campaign against the gangsters when it
established the Public Enemy list. Of course, Capone was the CCC's first
Public Enemy Number One. But Loesch was also battling inner demons.
Addressing students at Princeton University in 1930, Loesch disclosed
his true agenda when he wailed, "It's the foreigners and the first
generation of Americans who are loaded on us . . . The real Americans
are not gangsters." He went on to explain that "the Jews [are] furnishing
the brains and the Italians the brawn." Of course, Loesch failed to
inform his audience that he himself was a first-generation American of
German parentage. But no one debated Loesch's motives, since the
Public Enemy list had struck a chord with the American public. Meanwhile, in Washington, Hoover's inquiry was taking off. It was the
beginning of the end for Capone.

The special prosecutor sent from Washington, Dwight H. Green,
received his marching orders from U.S. Attorney George Johnson: "Your
job is to send the Chicago gangsters to prison. You can call on revenue
agents, special agents, or agents of the Special Intelligence Division of the
Treasury Department. You can have the staff you need as quickly as you
can show the need for it. Go to it." Green hired Agent Arthur Madden to

direct the field operation, while Frank Wilson looked into Capone's spending habits. The team pieced together their evidence from physical artifacts and the paper trail, not from corrupted officials. Simultaneously, IRS chief Elmer Irey focused on Capone's 1928 purchase ($31,000 cash down) of his $40,000 Palm Island estate. Using the pseudonym Michael Lepito, one agent, Pat O'Rourke, actually infiltrated Capone's Lexington Hotel headquarters. That led the team to Capone's bookkeeper, eventually found hiding in Miami.

As per custom, Capone dispatched legal emissaries to the nation's capital to put in the fix. The guardians of the public trust were more than happy to take the money, but delivered nothing in return. One of Capone's lawyers, his tail between his legs, reported back to the boss, "I spent forty thousand dollars in just one office, spreading it around." He told how he had placed a bundle holding $30,000 in a deserted Senate office and watched from his hiding spot as a U.S. senator made off with it. "Later I learned that we had not bought a goddamn thing," the legal eagle lamented. Capone also went after Irey himself and must have been stunned when Irey refused the enormous bribe put forward. Irey told the Capone bagman, "So far as I am concerned, Al Capone is just a big fat man in a mustard-colored suit." Reportedly, the bribe attempt only fueled Irey's zeal to destroy Capone.

At least one member of the team developed a grudging respect for The Big Guy. George Johnson recognized Capone's obvious talents and spoke of them with his son, George, Jr. "My father said many times that Al Capone could have been a brilliant businessman," remembered the younger Johnson. "[He] meant that he had the organizational ability, cunning, intellect, and street smarts it took to succeed."

After three years, Johnson, Irey, and Green had enough evidence. First they collared Capone's second-in-command, Frank Nitti, who had spent at least $624,888 in three years alone. He was sentenced to eighteen months and a $10,000 fine. Al's brother Ralph was sentenced to three years at Leavenworth and a $10,000 fine on tax evasion.

In pretrial proceedings, Capone cut a deal with Attorney Johnson that threw out the five thousand prohibition violations that would have cost Capone an astounding twenty-five thousand years to life in jail. Capone smiled throughout the pretrial proceedings, never imagining he would lose. After all, he had gotten away with murder for a dozen years. Nonetheless, Capone purchased extra insurance by bribing the entire list of prospective jurors, which his boys had characteristically acquired.

Finally, the big show, the trial of Scarface Al Capone, took place over four days in October 1931. Judge James Wilkerson, who earlier had thrown out Capone's plea deal with Johnson, now displayed the wisdom of Solomon: He switched the jury-pool list at the last minute and secured an untainted jury. A now somber Capone watched as a parade of witnesses attested to his lavish lifestyle. Although it represented a small fraction of Capone's total funds, the government was able to show that between 1924 and 1929 Capone had netted at least $1,038,660.84, for which he should have paid $215,080 in income tax. Capone's high-priced legal team appeared impotent, seeming to have spent no time trying to develop an explanation for Al's warehouse of expensive possessions. On October 17, 1931, after deliberating for eight hours, the jury returned their verdict of guilty, ending Al Capone's six-year reign. At his sentencing a week later, Capone was sent to federal prison (Atlanta, then Alcatraz) for eleven years, in addition to a $50,000 fine and a $30,000 fee in court costs. No other tax delinquent, before or since, has received such punishment.

Practically before Capone's handcuffs could be affixed, the word began to spread that he had been set up, as some pointed to his inept defense. The bottom line held that, since Al's removal would be better for all concerned, an unholy alliance had been formed between his criminal heirs and the taxman. Teeth were put into the rumors in 1936 when Mrs. Gus Winkler told the FBI that her husband had worked to clear Capone of the tax charges before his conviction. Gus Winkler had confidently advised Paul Ricca that Capone's case could be fixed for a mere $100,000 back tax payment. However, before Winkler's gambit could gain momentum, Frank Nitti and Louis Campagna showed up at the couple's apartment. According to Winkler, the duo ordered her husband to back off. "They wanted Capone in jail," she remembered. At the time of Al's trial, Paul Ricca allegedly said to an associate, "Al was bad for business and it was better that he left the scene." Insiders whispered that Capone's own men had tipped the feds to the crucial financial records that sealed his fate. Although these theories have not been proved, they are widely accepted by many Chicagoans in a position to know.

While temporarily incarcerated at the Cook County Jail, Capone stayed true to form. His boys managed to bribe his jailers, allowing their boss a life of privilege known to few on the outside: The constant stream of guests imbibed whiskey that Capone was supplied by the gallons; his mistress paid conjugal visits, as did a pimp named Bon-Bon, who happily supplied his girls to the boss. Eventually there was a crackdown when the prison warden was caught driving Capone's sixteen-cylinder Cadillac. After a slew of delaying – but futile – legal tactics, Capone was eventually sent away to Atlanta in May 1932. While in prison, he was diagnosed with third-stage syphilis. When his illness became severe, he was granted an early release in 1939, with the disease finally claiming him in 1947.

Immediately after Capone went away, payments commenced to Al's wife, Mae. Gang couriers arrived at his home with moneys tithed by the gang to guarantee Mae's and her young child Sonny's welfare. Mrs. Capone is said to have received $25,000 per year until the day she died many years later. The "pension fund" was among many of the new traditions to be instituted by Capone's heirs. From its inception until the gang's downfall many years later, a monthly stipend was delivered to the families of all the gang's leaders who were incarcerated or dead. It was one of many corporate-like regulations adopted by Capone's heirs – the Outfit.

Part One

The Outfit

1.

Young Turks in Charge

While imprisoned in Philadelphia in 1930, Big Al Capone underwent the kind of self-reflection that is an inescapable by-product of incarceration. For Capone, it resulted in a grand scheme he bequeathed to his successors. Later, in Chicago, in anticipation of his 1931 tax conviction, Capone held one last Syndicate meeting before what he assumed would be a brief incarceration. Summoning his most loyal and indispensable soldiers to his side, Snorky presented his vision: a national crime corporation that would be run not by an all-powerful boss, but by a board of directors, a corporation of thieves partnering with the Torrio-Lansky Commission, whose goal was to make a swift transition into more legitimate white-collar scheming. Until now, this world had been dominated by the upperworld robber barons and Wall Street swindlers, whom the nation held to an infinitely lower standard of justice than the rest of the population. By encouraging his heirs to follow that path, Al Capone was orchestrating his legacy.

The new regime heeded the mistakes of the old, adopting a modus operandi that would serve them effectively well into the future. Capone's heirs apparent grasped the obvious: Al's downfall was largely due to his refusal to hide his money or to provide an explanation of what he did for a living. Capone's personal style only increased his vulnerability. Combined with his penchant for violent retaliation and a high profile – fancy clothes, flashy cars, and movie-star hangers-on – Capone was his own worst enemy. His heirs would contrast Capone's style with one of their own: anonymity. No effort would be spared to avoid press coverage of the new bosses.

Al Capone took every opportunity to point out the judicial double standard in rationalizing his crime wave. Although unschooled, Capone learned on the streets what respected academics such as Ferdinand Lundberg acquired in research libraries. In his seminal 1968 book, *The Rich and the Super-Rich,* Lundberg described how the fortunes (and social standings) of Carnegie, Whitney, Rockefeller, McCormick, and others were built on a foundation of white-collar thuggery, or as Capone called it, "legitimate rackets." Robber baron Cornelius Vanderbilt hardly recoiled at the accusation, asking, "You don't suppose you can run a railroad in accordance with the statutes, do you?"

Among the crimes Lundberg attributed to the country club set were "embezzlement; big fraud; restraint of trade; misrepresentation in advertising and in the sale of securities; infringement of patents, trademarks, and copyrights; industrial espionage; illegal labor practices; violations of war regulations; violation of trust; secret rebates and kickbacks; commercial and political bribery; wash sales; misleading balance sheets; false claims; dilution of products; prohibited forms of monopoly; income tax falsification; adulteration of food and drugs; padding of expense accounts; use of substandard materials; rigging markets; price-fixing; mislabeling; false weights and measurements; internal corporate manipulation, etc."

The victims of white-collar crimes numbered in the millions, many of whose lives were destroyed in stock market swindles and labor abuses. At the time of his 1931 pretrial proceedings, Capone gave an interview to *Liberty* magazine, in which he recalled:

Why, down in Florida, the year I lived there, a shady newspaper publisher's friend was running a bank. He had unloaded a lot of worthless securities upon unsuspecting people . . . One day his bank went flooey. The crooked publisher and the banker were urging bankrupt depositors who were being paid thirty cents on the dollar to put their money in another friend's bank. Many did so; and just about sixty days later, that bank collapsed like a house of cards too. Do you think those bankers went to jail? No, sir. They're among Florida's most representative citizens. They're just as bad as the crooked politicians. I ought to know about them. I've been feeding and clothing them long enough. I never knew until I got into this racket how many crooks there were dressed in expensive suits and talking with affected accents.

Another robber baron who may have fueled Capone's rationale was Boston-based banker/political patriarch Joseph P. Kennedy. According to numerous reports, Al Capone had known Kennedy since they cut a bootlegging arrangement in 1926. By the time Capone was imprisoned, Kennedy was widely known to have been one of the most offensive robber barons of the era.[1]

Fueled by such rationalizations, Capone's heirs set about engineering their version of the American Dream. Such an enterprise required distinct divisions of labor and brainpower, and in his preprison powwow, Capone installed an executive team with the requisite talents. Virgil Peterson, who headed the Chicago Crime Commission for three decades, later remembered that a friend of his was offered a $25,000-a-year job to direct a "new corporation." Further investigation revealed that the "corporation" was in fact the Capone Syndicate. Peterson's friend passed up the offer, but the Syndicate continued their head-hunting, and Capone's eventual appointment of a CEO-type successor incorporated a deceit characterized by a stealthy brilliance.

In naming forty-two-year-old Frank Nitti (né Nitto) to the top post, Capone employed a strategy that has been largely ignored in discussions

---

1. In the midtwenties, banker-investor Joe Kennedy purchased the Film Booking Office as well as controlling interest in RKO Productions. When he branched into Pathé Films, he plundered its stock, giving insiders such as himself stock worth $80 per share, while common stockholders were reimbursed to the tune of a mere $1.50. Many lost their life savings, while Kennedy walked away with a cool $5 million. The swindled stockholders tried to file suit but to no avail.

At the same time, Kennedy worked for Guy Currier's Boston investment firm, and when Currier was away, Kennedy scrutinized his private files to gain insider information. Currier's family now says that Currier felt double-crossed by Kennedy, whom he believed to be corrupt.

In 1929, Kennedy attempted a hostile takeover of the California-based Pantages theater chain. When owner Alexander Pantages balked, Joe Kennedy paid a seventeen-year-old girl $10,000 to accuse Pantages of rape. Pantages was charged and sentenced to fifty years in prison (later reversed), and Joe Kennedy got the theater chain at a greatly undervalued price. Four years later, when the girl wanted to admit her role in the frame-up, she suddenly died, apparently of cyanide poisoning. On her deathbed, the twenty-one-year-old admitted her conspiracy with Kennedy, who had promised to make her a film star (see Ronald Kessler, *Sins of the Father*, pp. 51–59).

It has been well documented that Kennedy used insider information to 'sell short' before the 1929 stock market crash, making millions off the misery of his fellow citizens.

of Chicago crime: the boss is quite often a lightning rod, intentionally positioned to deflect attention from the real power, i.e., the lower-profile board of directors. Nitti's appointment was also predictable given his Sicilian birth and seniority over the other members of the Outfit, as they now called themselves, most of whom were barely thirty when Capone was collared.

Nitti was never the tommy-gun-wielding "enforcer" that has been depicted. He earned his sobriquet The Enforcer because his role mandated enforcement of the internal rules adopted by the board of directors. This responsibility did not entail gunfire, only arbitration. Born Francesco Raffele Nitto in Augori, Sicily, in 1889, Nitti was in fact a smallish, introspective gangster, but like Capone's other successors, he appreciated the effect of the occasional show of power. Within two months of Nitti's installation as "CEO," bombs went off in forty warehouses and offices in and around Chicago. No one was hurt, and little actual stock was destroyed. The attacks were a forceful announcement to Chicago's citizens that the Outfit was now in charge.

Virtually every mass media portrayal of Frank Nitti has bordered on the fallacious. Most recently, in the 1987 film *The Untouchables,* Nitti was depicted as the villainous archenemy of the equally misrepresented "heroic" prohibition agent Eliott Ness. In the film's dramatic climax, the intrepid Ness pushes Nitti off a rooftop to his death. In fact, nothing like that ever occurred. Nitti's death had absolutely nothing to do with Ness, who ironically was a womanizing, antibooze enforcer who ultimately drank himself to death.[2]

Nitti's parents brought him to America when he was three years old, settling in Brooklyn, the New York borough that had given rise to so many Chicago bosses. It is not known if he associated with Capone, Torrio, et al., during this period, although it is highly likely, given where he would soon end up. After learning the barber trade, Nitti entered the New York to Chicago gangster pipeline around 1920. In the Windy City,

---

2. The role of Ness went to Kevin Costner, who appeared to be making a career of historical misrepresentations when, in the 1991 film *JFK,* he portrayed the bullying New Orleans district attorney Jim Garrison as Jimmy Stewart reincarnated. Costner continued the theme in 2000, when he starred in and produced the dramatic recreation of the Cuban missile crisis *Thirteen Days.* In that role he played presidential adviser Kenny O'Donnell, who had no known input in the crisis; virtually all of "O'Donnell's" actions and words in the film are invented.

Nitti quickly made his name as one of Chicago's premier "fence" operators. With his extensive network of shady buyers for stolen goods, Nitti was perfectly positioned in 1920 to make the transition to bootlegging with Torrio's Syndicate. Nitti made his bones with Torrio-Capone as a successful smuggler of top-shelf whiskey from Canada to Chicago and, in 1930, was convicted of lesser tax charges than his boss, Capone, who was jailed one year later. With his loyal wife, Anna, spearheading his early-parole petition, the prison received character references from, among others, a mortuary owner who was a longtime friend of the gangster's – one can only wonder how much business the Syndicate had sent his way. Nitti himself promised the parole board that, if paroled, he would immediately move to Kansas City and accept a position in the dairy business. He would of course do neither. Granted parole soon after the Big Guy "went away," Nitti instead returned to Chicago and accepted the leadership post bequeathed to him by Capone.

With Nitti in place to draw the flak, the board of directors – the Outfit – was free to forge the consummate gangster "think tank," devising schemes that allowed their enterprise to flourish for decades. More important, their stewardship effectively granted their descendants a seamless merge with the upperworld, old-money tribe. Beyond doubt, the most significant member of this board was the twenty-five-year-old referred to by his associates as Joe.

Joe

Accardo has more brains for breakfast than Al Capone ever had all day.
    –George Murray, *Chicago American* columnist

Antonino Leonardo Accardo was born in Chicago on April 28, 1906, the son of a Sicilian immigrant shoemaker. The youngest of five siblings – with three brothers and a sister – he grew into a five-foot-nine-inch, two-hundred-pound barrel of muscle. As a teenager raised in Little Sicily on Chicago's Northwest Side, he got his parents' assent to join the workforce instead of enrolling in high school. Little is known about Accardo's youth. The young Antonino held various jobs, among them grocery clerk/delivery boy and truck driver. Those were his day jobs. By night, the teenaged Accardo made a rapid ascent up the ladder of crime, starting as a pickpocket, graduating to house burglar and then car thief. Although he was hit with numerous arrests, the youngster never spent a night in jail – and as an adult he never would. Years later, FBI agents would describe his language as laced with profanity, while grudgingly admitting that he was never a braggart or a liar. After the excesses of his youth, Accardo would become renowned for his fairness.

When Volstead passed, Accardo's parents, like many of their Sicilian neighbors, joined the cottage industry of alcohol home cooking. Their son, along with his punk chums, gravitated to Claude Maddox's Circus Café, located on North Avenue. Maddox was on the periphery of the Torrio bootlegging Syndicate, tithing the requisite percentage to the gang from Cicero. Young Antonino's pals at the Circus included Vincenzo Gibaldi, aka the infamous "Machine Gun" Jack McGurn, Capone's chief hit man. With such liaisons, Accardo was brought under the Torrio umbrella, where he functioned as an enforcer, compelling the Syndicate's "franchised" bar owners and loan-shark debtors to pay up. He wielded his baseball bat so forcefully – at human heads, not baseballs – that he soon acquired the moniker Joe Batters. His closest friends addressed him as Joe so regularly that his given diminutive, Tony, was all but forgotten – even years later by his own wife.

At the height of the Chicago beer wars, with Capone forced to swell the ranks of his personal army, young Accardo first came to Capone's attention. According to some accounts, Joe was brought to Capone by one of the Big Guy's bosses, "Tough" Tony Capezio. Still others believe McGurn suggested the young muscle. In any event, the seminal first meeting between Capone and Joe, as deduced by the FBI, occurred in early 1926, when the twenty-year-old youngster was ushered into one of Capone's headquarters – the Four Deuces, the Lexington, or the Metropole Hotel. His enlistment procedure was quite simple by Italian mob standards: There was no elaborate East Coast Mafia ritualism, melodrama, and symbolism. Most likely, there was a quick oath of loyalty to Capone and the Syndicate, with the young capo-to-be swearing to uphold the most intrinsic Sicilian beliefs: respect for wives and families, and contempt for "stoolies."

Joe Accardo thus became a fixture in the lobbies of Capone's headquarters, where the young tough often sat guarding the entrance, "Chicago typewriter" in his lap. Completely loyal to the Syndicate, Joe made his bones with Capone-Torrio by eliminating traitors to the regime. When the North Siders' convoy of assassins fired on Capone on April 26, 1926, it was Joe who pulled his boss down and shielded him with his twenty-year-old body. Capone was rightfully impressed and elevated Accardo to the role of his personal driver and chief bodyguard.

(It will be seen that the role of driver for the boss often presaged a future leadership post.)

Accardo's star rose quickly, and it is widely assumed that he was a key player in the notorious St. Valentine's Day massacre in 1929. Former Chicago FBI agent and Accardo biographer Bill Roemer held that Accardo was actually one of the gunmen, along with John Scalise, Albert Anselmi, and Jack McGurn. Accardo also matched the description of the man using the name James Morton who rented the getaway car, which had been disguised as a police car. Four months later, when two of the assassins (Anselmi and Scalise) were murdered in Indiana by Capone after plotting a mutiny, they were beaten to a pulp with a baseball bat. Agent Roemer is among those who believe Accardo wielded the stick. Subsequently, Capone was heard to say about Joe, "This guy is a real Joe Batters."

After the madness of that spring, Joe accompanied Capone as his personal bodyguard when the boss and a dozen other Syndicate members attended the 1929 Atlantic City mob convention. During a break, Accardo went to a tattoo parlor and had a bird emblazoned on the back of his right hand. The creature appeared to flap its wings when Joe opened and closed his fist. Unimpressed, Capone chastised his young soldier, "Kid, that will cost you as much money and trouble as it would to wear a badge with the word *thief* on it." Despite the thoughtless act, Joe remained close with the Big Guy. Later that year, Joe was arrested for vagrancy in Florida while golfing with Capone and Jack McGurn. When Capone's archenemy, temporary president of the Unione Siciliana Joey Aiello, was murdered in October 1930, Joe was considered the prime suspect.

In 1934, three years after the Outfit assumed control, twenty-eight-year-old Joe Accardo wed Clarice Porter, twenty-two, a beautiful blond chorus girl and the daughter of Polish immigrants. As best as can be ascertained, Joe was a faithful husband, as well as a doting father to their two sons and two daughters. In a short time, Accardo became a capo, a young boss with his own crew of ten. Among his chief responsibilities was overseeing the Outfit's gambling operations. Attempting to put a veneer on his image, Joe insisted that his associates refer to him as JB, a moniker more befitting the country club set. But try as he might, the name Joe stuck.

Years earlier, as a teenaged runner for the Torrio-Capone organization, Joe had often worked side by side with with a young man nine years his senior named Felice De Lucia, better known as Paul Ricca. They became each other's lifelong best friends. Their fellowship would span decades; their shared stewardship of the Capone regime's residue would become the stuff of local legend.

Paul

Felice De Lucia was born in 1897 in Naples, Italy, making him thirty-four years old when Al Capone was convicted of tax evasion. In Italy, Felice committed his first murder at age eighteen, when his sister Amelia was disgraced by the family of a boy she was dating. In a fit of rage, Felice murdered the suitor, Emilio Perillo. After serving two years, Felice tracked down and murdered the witness who had fingered him. On the run, De Lucia stole the identity of fellow Neapolitan Paul Maglio and made his way to New York and the New York to Chicago gangster pipeline. In the Windy City, De Lucia assumed the name Paul Ricca and took work as a waiter, a job that would earn him the appellation Paul 'the Waiter' Ricca.

Ricca worked to establish a far different persona from the violent one he had earned in Italy. In Chicago, his reputation was that of a soft-spoken, well-mannered businessman. In his late twenties, Ricca took work as a manager of Little Italy's World Playhouse, a side enterprise of the Torrio-Capone combine. His superior intellect was not unnoticed by the Big Fellow, and Ricca's star rose quickly. When Ricca married in 1927, his new best friend, Al Capone, stood up for him as best man. Soon, Capone appointed young Paul as his personal emissary in dealings with syndicates from other cities. When Johnny Torrio established the Commission with Lucky Luciano and Meyer Lansky in New York, Ricca was honored with the critical role of liaison to the gang from the Big Apple. The coming decades would see yearly powwows convened in mob-favored restaurants, with the gangs intent on maintaining and coordinating the alliance. At such times, Paul Ricca played either the host in Chicago or the traveling emissary to New York.

At the infamous 1929 Atlantic City mob confab, New York mob boss Meyer Lansky advised a young Paul Ricca on how to get rich in the rackets: "Play the waiting game," said Lansky. "Keep your name out of the newspapers and build your own organization." Ricca and his Outfit colleagues took the admonition to heart. With Nitti as the interim front man, it was only a matter of time before the real brain trust took over. As Paul patiently waited his turn at the helm, his nickname, the Waiter, became a double entendre.

Simultaneous with the enlistment of Joe and Paul in the midtwenties, Capone installed another key member of his team. Capone met the young man when the new recruit was twenty-seven years old. The newest Syndicate soldier combined great style and charm with one of the fiercest intellects in the annals of organized crime. His closest friends knew him as Curly.

Curly

He was a man of many aliases. John Brunswick, G. Logan, Mr. Lincoln, Dave Ostrand, Cy Pope, and John Hall are among more than two dozen listed by the FBI. The press referred to him as The Camel, or The Hump, but it was the nicknames bestowed on him by people who actually knew him that spoke volumes: Mr. Einstein, The Brainy Hood, and Mr. Moneybags. If he had chosen the straight life, Llewelyn Morris Humphreys could have been an adviser to presidents or the CEO of a Fortune 500 firm. A master of syllogism, Humphreys' gift for didactic reasoning left everyone in awe. Tall and nattily attired, he moved as easily among Hollywood studio heads and nationally known politicians as he did among the gang that frequented the Four Deuces.

Although he had no compunction about meting out the ultimate punishment to an enemy, he did it rarely, and only as a last resort. To the rest of his acquaintances Humphreys was a charming, soft-spoken, and rakish dandy. He was often described as the nicest member of the Outfit. The only known Welsh gangster, Humphreys was so courteous and trustworthy that when told of his passing, his FBI case officer reportedly had to stifle a tear. Arguably the most fascinating hoodlum who ever lived, he was so obsessive about his low profile that he remains for many "The Unknown Gangster."

Humphreys was born in Chicago on or about April 20, 1899, to Welsh immigrants. Since no birth certificate has ever surfaced, the exact date remains in question. As best can be determined, Humphreys had one brother and three sisters, he being the third born. As a youngster, his mane of dark, curly hair earned him the nickname by which his close friends would know him from then on: Curly. Precious little is known of his early years, as he always demurred at discussing them. Even in congressional testimony decades later, Curly Humphreys refused to open up about his formative period. What little has emerged suggests that, as a boy, Curly sold newspapers, but soon gravitated to petty theft and street gang fights. As a thirteen-year-old, he came under the influence, perhaps by court order, of a Chicago judge named Jack Murray, who saw in Curly a rare brilliance.

According to various accounts, Murray attempted to school the bright young rebel in the ways of the political world, an attempt that would backfire, as young Curly heard only what he wanted: there was a double standard for the great turn-of-the-century robber barons and the rest of the world. Curly appears to have taken this as a clarion call to join the life of the amoral criminal in a world without reason. In honor of the well-intentioned judge, and to thank him for the political education, Curly changed his name to Murray Humphreys. He also became a talented jewel thief.

Little is known of Curly's life over the next few years. FBI records indicate that as a sixteen-year-old, he was nabbed for petty larceny, for which he served sixty days at the House of Correction. Humphreys, who even by this tender age had mastered his use of "persuasion and payoff," had had the charge reduced from felony burglary, which would have mandated a much longer prison term. George Murray, a journalist and acquaintance of Humphreys', recalled that Humphreys first obtained a private meeting with the prosecutor. The precocious young man was in rare form as he argued: "You try to get me indicted for burglary and I will weep in front of the grand jury. They probably won't indict me because I am only sixteen. But even if you get me to court the do-gooders will say that because of my extreme youth I ought not to be sent to prison. However, if you reduce the charge to one of petty larceny, I will plead guilty. I will get a light sentence. You will get a conviction that looks good on your record. Everybody will be happy. What's more, you will receive a suitable gift before the case goes to court."

The prosecutor was persuaded, and the next day an expensive, diamond-studded wristwatch was placed anonymously on his desk – and Curly's modus operandi was now carved in stone. As the Big Guy would later say, "Anybody can use a gun. The Hump uses his head. He can shoot if he has to, but he likes to negotiate with cash when he can. I like that in a man."

Curly's style became so famous in Chicago that to this day hoods and nonhoods alike happily quote aphorisms they attribute to the disarming Welshman. Among the most quoted:

- "Love thy crooked neighbor as you love thy crooked self" – inscribed on a plaque hung above his fireplace.

- "Go out of your way to make a friend instead of an enemy."
- "No good citizen will ever testify to anything if he is absolutely convinced that to do so will result in his quick and certain death."
- "The difference between guilt and innocence in any court is who gets to the judge first with the most."
- "If you ever have to cock a gun in a man's face, kill him. If you walk away without killing him after doing that, he'll kill you the next day."
- "Vote early and vote often."

Years later, Curly would hang another wall plaque with an inscription many believe represents his finest intellectual achievement. In 1951, acting on Curly Humphreys' advice, Outfit bosses befuddled a Senate panel with a plea legislators had never heard before: citing their Fifth Amendment privilege, they refused to answer the investigators' questions. Although the refusal had been voiced in criminal court, Congress had not previously experienced this tactic, and believing the exemption could not be enforced in their venue, they cited the bosses for contempt. Much to their consternation, the committee was informed by the courts that Curly's precedent-setting ploy was in fact legal. Soon, a plaque was seen hanging in Curly's Oklahoma house: "I refuse to answer on the grounds it might incriminate me."

In 1921, while on the lam for a jewel heist, Curly fled to his brother's home in Little Axe, Oklahoma. The slick-talking Humphreys took work as a door-to-door Victrola salesman. On one of his rounds he met, and charmed, a beautiful half-Cherokee college student named Mary Clementine Brendle. Clemi, as she was known, would become an indispensable component in the financial workings of the Outfit. Said to have possessed total recall, Clemi would eventually commit to memory the names of one hundred union presidents – unions Curly would be controlling.

After a brief courtship, the couple married and returned to Chicago, where the heat had cooled on the new bridegroom. Now in his early twenties, Curly found work as a short-order cook at Messinger's Restaurant on Halsted Street. There he met another brilliant (and perhaps the only college-educated) gangster, Fred Evans. Evans had studied accounting, engineering, and architecture, earning his degree at age nineteen. At the time he met Humphreys, Evans was earning his walk-around money buying and selling jewelry and distressed merchandise that he acquired at government auctions, taking advantage of a pre-Black Tuesday financial depression that prompted insurance companies to hold auctions in an attempt to recoup their losses.

Inevitably, the two prodigies were drawn to each other like magnets. Curly opined that if the two joined forces, they could "fence" pilfered merchandise, which included repainted stolen cars (acquired by Curly's gang), alongside Evans' goods at the warehouse Evans rented. As with everyone else who met Curly, Evans was charmed, and a partnership was born. Not surprisingly, their enterprise quickly escalated into the big-money operation of bootlegging. However, with no breweries of their own, the young men took the direct approach – they hijacked the other bootleggers' trucks. Humphreys proved to be not only a talented booze thief, but an effective kidnapper as well. Often, bootleggers were kidnapped until their partners paid up in either booze or money. Among the gangs, kidnappings were a nuisance that came with the territory. All was going along swimmingly until Curly made the first, and possibly last, stupid mistake in his life: He hijacked a shipment owned by Capone.

After fleeing in terror from the gun-toting Humphreys, Capone's driver scurried back to the Four Deuces and reported what had happened. In short order, Capone had the young upstart hauled before his tribunal of one. Instead of relegating the curly-headed thief to the heap of corpses of previous transgressors, however, Capone was inveigled by the defendant. Just as he had before the juvenile division prosecutor, Curly somehow (details are unknown) talked himself out of being sanctioned, and before he was through, he was not only acquitted, he was offered a job. Curly never forgot Capone's act of forgiveness and became one of his most loyal charges. Later, Curly would name his pet dog Snorky in homage to Capone.

After a brief stint as a beer-truck driver for the Syndicate, Humphreys was given a role more suitable to his intellect: the protection racket. Curly quickly became adept at the ways of extortion and graft. Curly's preference for the payoff resulted in his masterminding of the 1931 Capone jury pool bribery. Through his contacts in the judicial system, he obtained the list of jurors, who, had they not been switched at the last minute, were totally corrupted and poised to acquit Capone. When Capone eventually went to jail, Curly, Joe, and Paul paid regular visits to the man who had brought them all together.

Al Capone once said, "Nobody hustles like the Hump." This truism rendered Curly's role in the Outfit a no-brainer: He assumed control of union takeovers, political liaisons, and protection rackets. He also would develop into a brilliant legal tactician, inventing novel defense strategies for his oft-indicted associates. Curly's future successes were predicted by the Chicago Crime Commission, which named Humphreys the new Public Enemy Number One after Capone "went away." With only a brief prison term in his future, Curly proceeded to establish himself as one of the Outfit's most powerful chieftains for decades to come.

Johnny

One of Curly's most important Outfit associates was a largely absentee member named Johnny Rosselli. Like Curly, Rosselli was another affable Outfitter, and the country's original gangster-patriot, referred to as The All-American Mafioso by his biographers. Another gangster with a penchant for thousand-dollar silk suits, Rosselli loved his high style almost as much as he loved his adopted country. In addition to being the Outfit's traveling emissary to locales such as Hollywood and Las Vegas, Rosselli partnered with the intelligence community and the Kennedy White House in their efforts to remove Cuban dictator Fidel Castro. And Rosselli was likely the only one involved who refused to accept payment for his services. When he died, a high-ranking CIA executive who had worked with him wept openly, much as Curly's death moved his FBI case officer.

Rosselli was born Filippo Sacco in Esperia, Italy, in 1905. Six years later, his family brought him to New York, on their way to permanent residence in East Boston. As a youngster, Sacco, like his other future Outfit mates, was drawn to the world of street gangs, seduced by the allure of easy money. Like so many before him, young Sacco spent countless hours at the mirror practicing *malocchio* (the evil eye), or the Look. Years later, Rosselli counseled a friend, "The secret is not to look in their eyes. You pick a spot on their forehead and zero in. That way you don't blink, you don't move. It intimidates the hell out of them." Judging from the career he went on to have, one can assume Sacco, like Capone, mastered the Look.

Dropping out of school, Sacco took work as a driver of a horse-drawn milk wagon, the better to provide cover for his chief enterprise, narcotics trafficking, specifically morphine. Milky, as he was called, was collared twice in 1922, the result of a sting operation involving a pliant drug informant. After spending six months behind bars, Sacco was released, and the informant was soon found murdered. Authorities put two and two together and decreed Filippo Sacco suspect number one. Seventeen-year-old Sacco took his cue and fled to New York City, where he assumed the name John Stewart. After a few months distinguishing himself in the local gang scene, Sacco/Stewart was quickly farmed out to the big leagues via the New York to Chicago gangster pipeline. Eighteen-year-old Sacco became Joe Accardo's predecessor as Al Capone's driver and bodyguard.

Capone and Sacco/Stewart became so close that some believed them to have been cousins. One night, Al convinced Sacco to adopt a more appropriate Italian surname. Back at home, the young gangster leafed through an encyclopedia until he chanced upon an entry concerning a fifteenth-century painter who had added Last Supper frescoes to the walls of the Sistine Chapel: Cosimo Rosselli. From then on, Filippo Sacco *was* Johnny Rosselli. Even his family seemed to forget his birth name when speaking of him.

During his time with Capone, Rosselli, like Paul, Curly, and Joe, grew to appreciate the importance of appearance. But unlike Capone, who was drawn to garish, often flamboyant attire, Johnny mimicked the suave, understated sophistication of Paul Ricca and his peers. In time, Rosselli began acquiring his own fitting nicknames, among them Mr. Smooth.

Just as the Syndicate was about to take off under Capone's rule, unforeseen troubles cut short Rosselli's stay in Chicago. Rosselli may have been tough on the outside, but no amount of staring into the mirror could strengthen his inherited weak lungs (his grandfather died of tuberculosis, his father of influenza). After a typically harsh Illinois winter, Rosselli was diagnosed with incipient tuberculosis. After consultation with Capone, Johnny was dispatched to the West Coast to be the eyes and ears of the Syndicate, on the lookout for opportunities should the infant Hollywood "dream factory" catch hold. Capone was smart: During the Depression, the only people who appeared to flourish were gangsters and entertainers (in the year after the 1929 stock crash, Warner Brothers Pictures was valued at $160 million).

Arriving in Los Angeles, Rosselli quickly attached himself to the bootlegging operation of Anthony Cornero Stralla, aka Tony "the Hat" Cornero. The stylish Cornero, a perfect match for the dapper Rosselli, made his living transporting alcohol on ships from Canada and Mexico. He became so successful that he soon earned the moniker King of the Western Rumrunners. At the time, Cornero was engaged in bloody sea battles with rival rumrunners that conjured up images of pirate exploits. As a trusted associate, Rosselli's star, and income, rose with Cornero's. Tony the Hat eventually came to feel police pressure and fled to Canada, where he turned his interest to gambling. By 1930, he would relocate in Nevada, where Rosselli and Humphreys were spreading Capone's money around to any member of the state legislature who would vote for the Wide Open Gambling Bill.

With Cornero in absentia, Rosselli gravitated to Jack Dragna's crime organization. Considered Al Capone's alter ego, Dragna, né Anthony Rizzoti, was the City of Angels' own bootlegging/extortion/gambling kingpin. The local press named him "the Al Capone of Los Angeles." Dragna's operation flourished largely due to his friendship with Mayor Frank Shaw, the most corrupt chief executive in Los Angeles history. The Rosselli-Dragna liaison was mutually beneficial. Rosselli needed a sponsor to gain acceptance in his new home; Dragna valued not only Johnny's street smarts, but his ties to the powerful Chicago Syndicate, which Dragna hoped would amplify his own purchase in the national crime hierarchy. In a police raid on the office of Dragna's lieutenant Girolomo "Mo Mo" Adamo, evidence was found of the growing cooperation between Dragna's gang and Rosselli's Outfit: Adamo's phone book contained the addresses and private unlisted phone numbers of Curly Humphreys and Joe Accardo.

Throughout the twenties, Rosselli maintained close contact with Capone. In September 1927, Capone threw a weeklong party to honor his friend boxer Jack Dempsey, prior to Dempsey's ballyhooed title fight against champion Gene Tunney. (Capone offered to fix the fight; Dempsey, however, declined. He should have accepted – Tunney won.) The fight was the largest spectacle ever to hit Chicago, with over 150,000 fight fans arriving from all over the country to view the fisticuffs at Soldier Field.

Arriving by train from Los Angeles was Johnny Rosselli. After the fight, he accompanied Capone's cousin Charlie Fischetti back to the Metropole Hotel, where Capone's bacchanal was in full swing. For sheer extravagance, Capone's bash ran a close second to the proceedings at the stadium: Pianist Fats Waller played, Al Jolson sang, and the top-shelf alcohol and women were in great abundance – all paid for by Capone. "There must have been a thousand people in that place," Rosselli later said in Senate testimony. Polly Adler, the famous New York madam, attended the bash and later recalled in her memoir, *A House Is Not a Home,* "Capone was certainly a grand host – Lucullus and those old Roman boys could have taken lessons from him."

Johnny attempted to return the hospitality when Capone journeyed to L.A. later that year. When Capone was booted from the posh Biltmore

Hotel, Johnny tried to intercede with the local police, offering his home to Capone and his entourage. The authorities refused the deal and put Capone et al. on the next train east.

In due time, Rosselli would gravitate to the burgeoning movie business, a move that would have profound repercussions for the Outfit. In that milieu, Rosselli made the acquaintance of the robber baron already known to Al Capone and Curly Humphreys, Joseph P. Kennedy. Like Capone and his gang, Joe Kennedy was anxious to discover what the new people's opiate would be, now that booze was widely available. The get-rich-quick crowd desired another tightly controlled product that was in big demand – what Curly Humphreys described to his wife as "the new booze." It seemed that Capone, via Rosselli and Humphreys, wasn't the only bootlegger who grasped that the new booze was the Hollywood dream factory. As he later testified, Johnny Rosselli often played cards and golf with the Kennedy patriarch, who was now a prime mover in Tinseltown. All told, Kennedy's 1920s contacts with the Outfit were but a prequel to a partnership arrived at four decades in the future.

While Mr. Smooth took full advantage of the hedonism of the movie capital, back in Chicago his sartorial polar opposite, "Greasy Thumb," was going about the mundane but essential task of attending to the Outfit's bookkeeping.

Jake

In the Outfit's ruling system, a spot on the second rung was reserved for Russian-born Jake Guzik. At forty-four years old, he was twelve years Al's senior when they both went to prison for tax evasion in 1931. As a child (one of twelve siblings), Guzik witnessed his parents' arrests on white-slavery charges. Jake and his five brothers eventually became pimps themselves after starting out as errand runners for the prostitutes owned by their parents. Guzik was well-known for his lack of personal hygiene; his former driver, George Meyer, remembered the plump pimp: "Everything he ate for a week you could see on his vest. And the B.O.!"

Guzik was not only Capone's bookkeeper at the Syndicate's Four Deuces headquarters, he was his closest friend and confidant. They became so simpatico that friends began calling Guzik "the Little Fellow," a reference to Al's sobriquet "the Big Fellow." In 1924, when a bloodied Jake showed up at the Four Deuces, mugged by a thug named Joe Howard, Capone went into a rage. In what was becoming an increasingly rare show of hands-on revenge, Capone tracked down Howard in a

Wabash Avenue saloon, placed a pistol an inch from Howard's head, and squeezed the trigger, killing him instantly. Capone's display of loyalty to someone as repellent as Guzik was not unnoticed or unappreciated by other gangsters unaccustomed to receiving such support from on high.

During the Torrio-Capone regime, Guzik had operated in a room leased by Torrio for "A. Brown, M. D." The office, just one block from the Four Deuces headquarters, was illegally raided by Mayor Dever's men in 1924. Although the material seized could not be entered as evidence – the raiders had neglected to obtain a search warrant – the bounty gave an insight into the Torrio-Capone operations, as well as Guzik's role in it. Included in the seizure were numerous ledgers kept by Guzik, which detailed the inner workings of the regime. Among the docket headings were alcohol suppliers; Canadian and Caribbean route information; a list of commercial wholesale alcohol buyers (hotels, restaurants, etc.) and illegal speakeasies; officials (politicians, police, etc.) on the payoff schedule; a list of breweries owned by the Syndicate; and a list of brothels and gambling dens owned by the Syndicate.

The press nicknamed Guzik "Greasy Thumb" for reasons that are still debated. One explanation holds that the financial whiz earned the name as a sloppy waiter who often let his thumb dip into the soup. The more probable version postulates that the name reflects Guzik's role as "the palm greaser" who disbursed countless stacks of greenbacks to corrupted cops and politicians. These payments were made from Guzik's regular table at St. Hubert's Old English Grill and Chop House (which he owned behind front-man owner Tommy Kelly). Whatever the source for the nickname, there is no evidence that anyone outside the working press referred to Guzik as Greasy Thumb.

Capone shared his bounty with Guzik, who reportedly earned millions, for which the government could show no paid taxes. So trusted was Guzik by Capone that he was given the honor of chairing Al's 1926 peace conference. Guzik was convicted on tax charges one year before Capone and would serve five years, before returning to the Outfit as its financial and legal consigliere.

This then was the Outfit's starting lineup: Joe Accardo, Curly Humphreys, Paul Ricca, Johnny Rosselli, and Jake Guzik. Their efforts were buttressed by a supporting cast of hundreds. No effort was spared to insulate the leadership from the violent enforcement inflicted by the expendable ones. Among the troops who ran the gauntlet were Rocco and Charlie Fischetti (beer distribution); Joe Fusco (liquor); Frank Pope and Anthony Volpe (gambling); Peter Penovich, Jr. (floating casinos); Duke Cooney (brothels); Hyman Levin (collections); Jack McGurn, Louis Campagna, and Frank Milano (gunmen-enforcers); James Belcastro and Joseph Genaro (bomb squad); Sam "Golf Bag" Hunt (enforcer; found with Jack McGurn at the scene of a murder with a bag of golf clubs mixed in with a still-warm machine gun).

The Outfit adopted, whether arrived at casually or as result of formal discussion, a strict set of personal guidelines for the new regime: The board would hold daily meetings; at least six days out of the week, they put in twelve-hour workdays; Outfit leaders would dress the part, just as corporate directors of the upperworld; wives and families were to be respected at all times and kept insulated from the business of the Outfit; boozing and drug usage were not tolerated. The antinarcotics stance was a remnant of Capone's own beliefs. "Only two kinds of hustlers I can't stand: a pickpocket and a hophead," Al had told his gang. Capone's abhorrence of drugs was said to have resulted in his ordering the murders of users within the gang. Years later, Paul Ricca learned the meaning of Capone's fears firsthand when his son became a drug addict. The edict against using was mild in comparison to that against dealing. During the reign of the Outfit, drug trafficking was strictly prohibited, and those who succumbed to the temptation of easy money in the narcotics trade were removed with great dispatch. When one member, Chris Cardi, was arrested for drug dealing, he was made an example when the bosses let him serve out his sentence, only to have him killed immediately upon his release.

The gang's bylaws also had a practical rationale. One alcoholic union thug named George McLane, who was to be conscripted against his will into the Outfit, recalled his meeting with Capone's successor, Frank Nitti. "He told me to stop drinking and get on the wagon," McLane said. "Nitti said that there was an unwritten law in the Outfit. They are not allowed to drink, because they might shoot their mouth off. If they shoot their mouth off, they will be found in an alley." But what thoroughly shocked McLane was that "they didn't even chase broads during business hours." Lastly, the Outfit continued Capone's nondiscriminatory work ethic: No one was excluded from the Outfit due to race, religion, or nationality. But the leadership and key decisions were still reserved for Italians only.

The work of the Outfit was thus transfigured from amorphous hooliganism to the "business" of crime, and one its most important agendas, the control of the city's workforce, was delegated to Curly Humphreys.

2.

Curly's Racket:
The Union Takeovers

Honest to God, we've been in the wrong racket all along.
                                                    —Al Capone to Curly Humphreys, 1930

One of the first enterprises embarked on by Al Capone's heirs was in fact initiated during the Big Guy's reign. Local lore holds that soon after his recruitment into the Syndicate, Curly Humphreys explained to Capone how the dreadful state of labor-employer relations could work to the gang's benefit. Humphreys had once again absorbed the essence of recent American history, churned it around in his cranium for a while, and produced a synthesis that would benefit both him and his gang. It was classic Humphreys, displaying the great foresight that saw him dominate the early years of the Outfit's reign.

In 1886, when the American Federation of Labor (AFL) was formed, workers began enjoying a period of great success. With improving wages and workplace conditions, laborers finally had a voice to be reckoned with: the union. For four decades, laborers enjoyed the benefits of unionization, until a post-World War I recession ended the party. Throughout the Roaring Twenties, unemployment quietly rose, as wages began dropping. In addition, the corporate world began to employ the same Communist-scare tactics that the anti-ethnic groups had used in proselytizing the virtues of alcohol prohibition. Given the nation's postwar patriotic fever, Americans were coaxed to equate "workers" and "unions" with Marxist philosophies. Those who remained loyal to the unions were marginalized as Bolsheviks. With labor relations rapidly deteriorating, the workers' unions seemed impotent against the onslaught of antiunion sentiment.

Union membership thus dropped from a prewar high of four million to two million by the late twenties. Employers now felt emboldened to enforce strikebreaking, blacklisting, and vigilantism in their antilabor fervor. The corporate world appeared to be trying to undo labor's four decades of success.

Employers lost their advantage when businesses began failing by the thousands. Given the precarious atmosphere, businessmen wanting to remain solvent now desperately sought concessions from the workforce. But with workers already in near revolt and the battle lines long-since drawn, the two sides were locked in a chaotic economic free fall. Both employers and employees needed someone who would understand their plight and advance their interests. And Curly Humphreys saw his next great scam: He would offer to represent both sides, while in reality playing them off against each other as the Outfit robbed them both blind. The added beauty of the plan was that it exemplified a maxim that Humphreys had long since adopted as his personal credo: It is far easier to muscle in on established businesses than to build them from scratch.

Even before Humphreys was recruited by Capone's Syndicate, the young Einstein of Crime had deduced the potential gains to be had in the operation later called labor racketeering. In 1922, at the tender age of twenty-three, an independent Curly had made a futile attempt to convince the milk drivers' union to ally with the janitors' union, giving them more than double the bargaining power with tenement owners. Humphreys was more successful in convincing elevator operators to allow him to extort high-rise dwellers. Curly put a simple proposal to the residents of the upper floors: "No pay, you walk up and down twenty floors every day." To be sure, Curly Humphreys did not invent labor racketeering, but he was the only Chicago gangster capable of bringing out its full potential. The beauty of Humphreys' synthesis was that he knew where the real profit was located.

The essential elements of a labor racket consisted of terrorizing small businesses into needing protection (euphemistically called a *trade association*), for which they paid a percentage of their gross income. Simultaneously, as perfected by Humphreys, the racketeer represented the workers (*a union* in name only) in their grievances against their employers and their trade associations. It was perhaps the most laughably obvious conflict-of-interest arrangement that has ever existed.

In the Chicago of the 1920s more than two hundred such rackets existed, with names that covered every conceivable business with any income worth extorting: the Concrete Road, Concrete Block, Sewer and Water Pipe Makers and Layers Union; The Jewish Chicken Killers; The

Kosher Meat Peddlers' Association; The Master Photo Finishers; The Newspaper Wagon Drivers and Chauffeurs; The Vulcanizers Union; The Undertakers; The Excavating Contractors; The Master Bakers of the Northwest Side; The Distilled Water Dealers; The Street Sweepers Association; and so on.

Al Capone agreed with Curly's assessment and began planning phase two of his regime, with Curly Humphreys to have a prominent role. Once Capone gave Curly the go-ahead, the takeovers commenced. Humphreys was prescient enough to know just where to turn for an insider's education into the labor situation: George "Red" Barker. Barker was a bookkeeper by trade, and an avid reader and scholar. But his intimate knowledge of the labor situation inspired his recruitment by Humphreys and Capone. Through his connections with bankers and financiers, Barker obtained union balance sheets and details of the size of their individual treasuries. With Barker's advice, Humphreys and Capone decided which unions and associations were ripe for takeover. Barker's first victory for Capone was in taking over the seat of Local 704's president, James "Lefty" Lynch, on the Teamsters Joint Council.

Local 704 represented the Coal Teamsters, responsible for much of the fuel deliveries to the lucrative Loop area of downtown. The takeover of such a union would allow Capone's boys to extort all the hotels and businesses when the bitter cold Chicago winter hit. Lynch had unwisely decided not to step down voluntarily and consequently had both of his legs shot out from under him by Capone's enforcers. At the next council meeting, his chair was assumed by Barker, with no objections from the other petrified council members. In short time, Barker raided 704's treasury and transferred virtually the entire bounty into Capone's bank account. When winter hit, the extortions began, with Capone actually passing on some of the largesse to coal-truck drivers, who received handsome wage increases.

Barker also orchestrated the takeover of the Ushers' Union. At the time, Chicago utilized thousands of ushers at movie theaters, burlesque houses, ball games, prizefights – virtually any indoor or outdoor event. Typically, Barker not only forced promoters to use his union, he had the businessmen bribe him to underpay his workers. In typical racket style, both sides were played.

Having proved his value, Barker became Curly Humphreys' right-hand union adviser. Barker's relationship with Humphreys was not a one-way street, however, as Barker learned the art of "persuasion" at the foot of the didactic master; whenever possible, Curly coaxed and cajoled his targets, explaining how he alone could deliver both the worker and the employer from the throes of underpayment and/or overpayment, depending on whom he was cajoling. When his charm failed, Curly resorted to threats and kidnappings, quickly earning a reputation as Chicago's premier kidnapper. The abductees were rarely harmed, and although ransom was demanded, the focus of the slugging was the takeover of the organizations.

Curly got his start in big-time labor racketeering when he fixed his crosshairs on a prey that proved surprisingly easy to bag: the Midwest Garage Owners Association (MGOA). At the time the Syndicate began focusing on labor racketeering, David "Cockeyed Mulligan" Albin owned the MGOA, a modestly profitable operation. Curly Humphreys saw a quick and easy way for garage owners, and the Syndicate, to increase their cash flow exponentially. But first Humphreys had to take over the MGOA. That was quickly accomplished when Curly and his partner, George "Red" Barker, paid a visit to Albin.

As was his style, Humphreys attempted to cajole Albin into bringing in the Syndicate as his partner, adding that Albin would be wise to stop attending association meetings; Curly would be MGOA's new mouthpiece. Albin declined Humphrey and Barker's overture, and the gang was forced to ratchet up the stakes. One night, Syndicate enforcer Danny Stanton came to Albin with *his* partners, Smith & Wesson, leaving Albin to agonize over a bullet wound through his foot. Like Lefty Lynch of Local 704, Albin was never again seen at an MGOA meeting, his chair now occupied by Curly Humphreys.

Humphreys had reckoned that if automobile vandalism rose drastically, it would be far easier to convince car owners to garage their vehicles. Therefore, next, a willing group of thugs were enlisted to do the dirty work. For that, Humphreys and Barker turned to the 42 Gang, a group of young toughs from the Maxwell Street area who specialized in just such malevolence. The gang, which consisted of dozens of young boys who revered Ali Baba and the Forty Thieves, adopted their name when they realized they had two more members than Baba's claque. (One future Outfit boss, Salvatore "Mooney" Giancana, would rise from this gang after a stint as Joe Accardo's wheelman.)

As per Curly's plan, the gang spread throughout Chicago, often led by Humphreys himself, wielding ice picks to puncture hundreds of car tires. Soon, a newspaper ad appeared, taken out by Humphreys' MGOA, offering the union's secure garages to the troubled car-owning populace. When the MGOA's business doubled overnight, the Outfit collected not only their monthly association dues, but an additional kickback for each car stored. For their efforts, the 42 Gang would collect 10 percent of the take.

Invariably, some disabled cars were left unrepaired for a time, but Curly had that covered as well. After a few palms greased at City Hall, the MGOA became Chicago's official car-towing contractor, hauling off the now ticketed vandalized vehicles. Policeman issuing the tags received a five-dollar kickback.

Although Humphreys proceeded to maneuver his way into scores of unions and associations, he was far from fulfilled in his racketeering ambitions. The young schemer quickly realized that there was no real money in associations with such arcane names as the Golf Club Organizers, or the Safe Movers. The real plums were intimately tied to the Windy City's position as America's service industry capital, and to the beverage that was in even more demand than booze. Thus the Outfit, under the expert counsel of Curly Humphreys, set their sights on the cleaning industry and the milk business.

The Laundry Wars

Chicago's hotel industry, to say nothing of its countless brothels, required hundreds of thousands of sheets and towels to be cleaned every day. This, combined with the personal needs of millions of residents and tourists, meant that the revenues of the cleaning business actually rivaled those of bootlegging. At even a few cents per item, simple mathematics demonstrated that the laundry trade was the place to be. With the Outfit's huge two-faced "protection" fees added on, the profits could be astronomical.

In anticipation of a future career as a laundry kingpin, Curly Humphreys took his first step by acquiring his own laundry businesses. In the case of the Boulevard Cleaners, owner Paddy Berrell was paid an early-retirement buyout of $35,000 to let Curly take over. It is anyone's guess how Humphreys came to own the long-established Drexel Cleaners, but the acquisitions were brilliant strokes that, like all of Curly's ventures, served multiple purposes: They gave Curly a "front" job to legitimize his income; and they gave the Syndicate somewhere to practice creative accounting, making moneys disappear and reappear as needed. The in-store book work was handled by Curly's first wife, Clemi, while Jake

Guzik held up his end at the Syndicate headquarters. Humphreys' second wife, Jeanne Stacy, laughs when recalling a Curly pun that she firmly believes was its first usage: "He used to joke about the money he was hiding at his laundry. He called it 'laundering money.'"

But most important, Humphreys' ownership of laundries like Drexel and Boulevard gave him a foothold in the industry he would soon engage in a massive hostile takeover. Curly considered it going to school. As a strong believer in adult education, Humphreys knew that to successfully take over the laundry business, he had to first learn the business from the inside. In addition, as a bona fide boss in Capone's organization and a legitimate member of the dry-cleaning business, Humphreys now possessed a double-barreled arsenal he could use to cajole both the employers' trade associations and the workers' unions.

By the time Capone and Humphreys targeted the laundry industry, Walter Crowley was already running the scam for the upperworld. As manager of the Master Cleaners and Dyers Association, Crowley oversaw the terrorizing of hundreds of small neighborhood tailor shops, forcing them to submit to his protection association. The tailor shops were not desired for their minimal "tailoring" profits – sewn buttons and so on – but for their role as drop-off points for soiled linens and clothing. These items had to be jobbed out to huge central cleaning facilities, where the profits were infinitely larger. Recalcitrant shops were burglarized and bombed, or acid was thrown on the clothes they had consigned. With many of the little shops in line, Master Cleaners made its first tactical mistake by launching assaults on the holdout shops that had combined to form their own protective association, the Central Cleaning Company. Crowley hired thugs who took brass knuckles to the faces of Central's drivers; delivery trucks were overturned; clean garments were smeared with oil, and when that failed to work, they were sprinkled with acid. The immediate beneficiaries of all the terrorizing were the hired sluggers, the best of whom could earn a tidy $1,000 a week.

In desperation, Central's president, Ben Kornick, turned to the North Side gang, led by George "Bugs" Moran, for protection. The North Siders were paid $1,800 per week to have their enforcers ride shotgun on Central's delivery trucks. Kornick's strategy succeeded, and Crowley's Master Cleaners backed down, only to redirect their arsenal at Morris Becker's operation. It was the beginning of the end for Crowley, and the entrée that Humphreys, quietly running Drexel Cleaners, had long awaited.

Between 1910 and 1928, Morris Becker had built the ten largest cleaning and dyeing facilities in Chicago. Crowley's dream of acquiring total control of the cleaning business necessitated Becker's compliance. As had been the case with Kornick's Central Cleaning, Becker's employees were slugged and robbed, and his facilities bombed. For the coup de grâce, Becker's unionized workers were ordered to strike. Soon, the inevitable occurred when Crowley met with Becker and assured him that his troubles would end immediately after Becker joined Master Cleaners and anteed up a $5,000 "initiation fee." "We had to go to Walter Crowley," Becker later recalled to the local news media, "and stand on the carpet and receive our punishment for being born in America and thinking we had some rights as American citizens in a free country." Not long after showing Crowley the door, Becker was visited by Sam Rubin, Crowley's strong-arm.

"I'll tell you something, Becker. You have to raise prices," Rubin dictated. Crowley's forces wanted Becker to force a 50 percent price rise, most of which would be siphoned off to Master Cleaners. Becker replied, "The Constitution guarantees me the right to life, liberty, and the pursuit of happiness – and to set my own prices."

"The hell with the Constitution," said Rubin. "As far as you are concerned, I am a damned sight bigger than the Constitution." Again, the demand for $5,000 was leveled. Again, Becker refused. Becker's actions over the next few days displayed his naïveté: He sought relief from Chicago's corrupted legal system. Becker and his son delivered volumes of specific and corroborated evidence to the state's attorney's office. Soon the grand jury brought indictments against fifteen members of the Master Cleaners and Dyers Association. If Becker felt optimistic, he had no knowledge of the similarities of upperworld and underworld crime: The white collars could put in the fix with the best of them.

Master Cleaners wisely retained the services of a litigator famous for legal bombast and melodrama, Clarence Darrow. Perhaps the most famous American trial lawyer of all time, Darrow gained fame for his rhetoric-heavy defense of the downtrodden and underprivileged, as well as his staunch support of the union movement. As a social reformer, he made history in his 1925 defense of John Scopes' right to teach evolution. But in his zeal to give voice to the voiceless, Darrow also defended murderers. In 1924, Darrow perorated against anti-Semitism while defending the undeniably guilty murderers Nathan Leopold, Jr. and Richard Loeb. In his lifelong support of the union movement,

Darrow gained the acquittal of Big Bill Haywood, a union leader charged with murder. That Master Cleaners was a corrupt, strong-arm union did not discourage the seventy-one-year-old Darrow from leading their defense.

As Chicagoans tell it, the fix was in "from top to bottom" for the Master Cleaners' trial. After an anemic presentation by the prosecutor, and despite a mountain of incriminating evidence, the jury took all of fifteen minutes to acquit Crowley and his colleagues. Morris Becker quickly found the nearest phone booth and asked the operator for the number of the Metropole Hotel. As Becker later recounted, "The police, the state's attorney, the United States attorney would, or could, do nothing. So, we called a man who could protect us – Al Capone. He did it well."

Actually, the task was delegated to Curly Humphreys and was just the opening he needed to initiate one of the Outfit's most lucrative takeovers ever. The very day after the court's verdict, Morris Becker and five other cleaners met at the Metropole with Capone, Humphreys, Guzik, and two of Capone's lawyers. An arrangement was reached to form a new corporation, Sanitary Cleaning Shops, Inc. On the board of the new venture, along with five other business owners, was Al Capone. For his participation, Capone was paid $25,000 plus a large percentage of the profits, while Curly received $10,000 per year to act as "arbiter" in labor conflicts. Big Al Capone began telling people, "I'm in the cleaning business."

INDEPENDENT CLEANERS BOAST GANGSTERS WILL PROTECT WHERE POLICE FAIL ran a local headline. The mere inclusion of Capone's name on Sanitary's incorporation papers was all that was needed to end Crowley's vision of a Master Cleaners dynasty. As Morris Becker later said, "I have no need of the police, of the courts, or the law. I have no need of the Employers Association of Chicago. With Al Capone as my partner, I have the best protection in the world." When interviewed many years after his retirement, Becker still insisted that the alliance with Capone was the right thing to do, and that Capone was an honest partner who lived up to his end of the bargain. "If I had it to do over again, I would never ask for a more honest partner in any business."

With Master Cleaners on the run, Humphreys went for the jugular. Sam Rubin and his fellow Master Cleaners thugs began receiving late-night phone calls in which they were warned that their wives would be dipped in acid unless Master Cleaners brought in Curly Humphreys to run the shop. After a few broken arms and blown-up porches, Humphreys was invited into Master Cleaners. He had finally bagged the golden goose, along with its $300,000 treasury nest egg. The grand plan was completed when Humphreys grabbed Local 46 of the Laundry, Cleaners, and Dye House Workers International Union.

In all, some 157 businesses were bombed during the sixteen-month laundry war. It should be noted, however, that when Curly employed the bomb, he made certain that it went off at 5 or 6 A.M., to minimalize the chance of casualties. Predictably, when the ashes had settled, Capone's Syndicate stood victorious. Although Curly and the Syndicate were now the dominant forces in local laundering, one obstacle remained to total control: Al Weinshank. As a labor racketeer, Weinshank had recently allied with Bugs Moran's North Siders, who in turn had partnered with Ben Kornick's Central Cleaning Company. As a criminal version of the Civil War, this contest pitted Weinshank and the North against Humphreys and the South, climaxing with Chicago's own version of Antietam. In fact, the manner in which this final thorn was removed from Humphrey's side may have been an overlooked component to one of the nation's most infamous crimes.

When the bootlegging war with the North Siders reached its bloody St. Valentine's Day climax in 1929, Curly Humphreys may have played a silent but critical role in its planning. Ostensibly, bootlegging rival Bugs Moran had been targeted by Al Capone, but the death of Weinshank had at least as much effect on the laundry wars as it did on the bootlegging wars. The real target may have been Weinshank, who was killed in the Valentine's Day bloodbath, not Moran, who was not even present. And the planner may have been Humphreys, not Capone. "The St. Valentine's Day massacre never really made sense," asserted Chicago researcher Mike Graham. Graham reasoned that Capone would not have assented to such a suicidal attack, i.e., Capone's Syndicate could never have weathered the inevitable civic backlash. Graham and others believe that the agenda for the killings is still open to speculation. For some, the Humphreys-Weinshank rivalry is at least as plausible a theory as any other, since Humphreys was the chief beneficiary of the Weinshank murder. Curiously, on Valentine's Day, 1936, seven years after the massacre, one of its supposed triggermen, Jack McGurn, was gunned down after trying to muscle back into the Outfit. On his body was a sardonic Valentine's greeting that smacked of Curly Humphrey's sense of humor:

You've lost your job
You've lost your dough
Your jewels and handsome houses
But things could be worse, you know
You haven't lost your trousers

It is not widely known, but McGurn was a scratch golfer who might have turned pro if he had lived. Once, when playing the Western Open in Illinois, the Chicago police "goon squad" was dispatched to the links to harass McGurn, who was in danger of actually winning the event. "You fuckin' dago," the cops yelled as McGurn (born Vincenzo Gibaldi) putted on the last four holes.[1] Their tactics worked, and Jack "the Duffer" McGurn went in the tank at the end of the round.

Got Milk?

By 1931, Curly Humphreys felt confident enough about his racketeering skills to revisit the milk industry, which he had approached without success in 1922. Since his induction into the Syndicate in the midtwenties, Humphreys had been trying to convince Capone to get into the dairy business. Curly saw it as a direct way for the underworld to enter the upperworld: The boys could at last combine wealth with the respectability that accompanied legitimate, upperworld, white-collar scams.

Curly was his usual convincing self, and according to Chicago journalist and Humphreys' friend George Murray, Capone began extolling the virtues of milk to his fellows: "Do you guys know there's a bigger markup in fresh milk than there is in alcohol? Honest to God, we've been in the wrong racket all along." During one prolonged soliloquy, he sounded like an evangelist who had just seen the light: "You gotta have a product that everybody needs every day. We don't have it in booze. Except for the lushes, most people only buy a couple of fifths of gin or Scotch when they're having a party. The workingman laps up a half a dozen bottles of beer on Saturday night and that's it for the week. But with milk! Every family every day wants it on their table. The big people on Lake Shore Drive want thick cream in their coffee. The big families of the yards have to buy a couple of gallons of fresh milk every day for the kids."

---

1. Gibaldi, a talented athlete in many sports, was given the name Jack McGurn by his boxing manager. Irish brawlers, à la Jack Dempsey, were perceived as more marketable at the time.

Although by 1931, Capone was facing serious court battles with the government, he also knew that convicted tax cheats only served a few months prison time, on average. He may have seen his imminent incarceration as a much needed rest, from which he would reemerge as an upperworld milk baron. Curly was given the OK to infiltrate the milk business.

Humphreys' experience told him that the quickest way to take over an ongoing upperworld racket was to first gain control of the relevant workers' unions. His style mandated that force be used only as a last resort: The velvet glove of the payoff was always offered before the hammer of kidnapping. His assault on Local 753 of the Milk Wagon Drivers' Union began in the late spring of 1931. This powerful union was sitting on a treasury of almost one million dollars. At the time, Robert G. "Old Doc" Fitchie was the local's president, and Steve Sumner was its business manager. History showed that part of Humphreys' modus operandi was the use of a trusted partner, such as Fred Evans or Red Barker, in his operations. For the milk operation, he once again teamed with his garage-scam confrere, Red Barker, and a third conspirator, named Frankie Diamond, whose brother was married to Capone's sister, Mafalda.

On a spring night in 1931, not long after Capone's tax indictment, Humphreys and Diamond paid a visit to Steve Sumner. According to later testimony by Sumner, Humphreys took the floor and in his typically charming tones asked Sumner for a favor. "Since 1926," Curly began, "Capone has been trying to diversify his investments in legitimate business while consolidating his brewing and distilling empire. He is opening a retail dairy business."

While Curly initially stated that he was only approaching Sumner as a peace gesture, asking that Sumner refrain from giving Al's new operation any union troubles, it wasn't long before Curly got around to the real purpose of his visit: He wanted Local 753 to stake Al's new business. When Sumner refused; an unhappy Humphreys lowered the boom: "Your union has a million dollars in the treasury. I will hand you a hundred thousand dollars cash. All you have to do is walk away. Leave town. I'll take over from here."

Sumner replied, "That's out of the question," and the meeting broke up. Steve Sumner was no fool. He immediately began fortifying both his office and his home in anticipation of the Humphreys bomb squad: bulletproof glass was installed on his car; his headquarters was shielded with sheet-metal plates; bodyguards were employed.

But Curly Humphreys was no fool either. In December 1931, while Sumner was circling the wagons and Capone was starting his jail term, Curly and Red Barker kidnapped the union's president, Old Doc Fitchie. In short time the ransom note appeared, demanding $50,000 for Fitchie's safe release. Sumner immediately caved. "I handed Murray Humphreys fifty thousand dollars cash in December," Sumner later testified. Fitchie was released unharmed, and two months later Humphreys chartered a new corporation named Meadowmoor Dairies, with an initial capitalization of $50,000. Meadowmoor then had the effrontery to sue fifty-one other unionized dairies to prevent them from forcing Meadowmoor into becoming a union shop. This would allow Meadowmoor a "vendor's license," allowing Curly et al. to pay lower wages and hire underage delivery boys, much as newspapers are allowed to employ newsboys. Once Meadowmoor was established, with one C. W. Schaub fronting as president, secretary, and corporate director, the business prospered.

And though his recent travails were with Humphreys and the underworld, Steve Sumner would later inform an investigating tribunal something it would probably rather not have heard about its own culpability. He testified about the true essence of organized crime in Chicago, and by extension the entire United States: the upperworld. "The racketeering started here in Chicago years ago," Sumner advised. "It was first brought in by big business. The men whom we generally look to as being above the average were the very men who were the lowest. They brought them [the underworld gangsters] in." Or, as one veteran Chicago investigator concluded, "The Irish, the Germans, the Poles – they got here first and had already made the move up to judicial corruption and white-collar crime. The Italians were just the last ones here, so they'll be the last ones out."

Much as Capone's soup kitchens created goodwill among the city's less fortunate, so too did Meadowmoor have a lasting positive impact on the way milk was bought and sold in the Windy City. Through the Outfit's representatives in the city council, new rules were adopted that for the first time established a definition of Grade A milk, forbidding lesser grades to be sold within the city limits. Further, the Outfit's pols gained passage of the city's first dated-milk ordinance, which established the first guidelines that allowed mothers to protect their children's health by screening the milk they ingested. Throughout the parliamentary debate over these bills, the upperworld politicians fought hard against the measures, which they feared would cripple the established dairies. But the Outfit fought harder and prevailed. Meadowmoor prospered for decades and still exists under the banner of the Richard Martin Milk Company, the name having been changed in 1961, and the present owners are not controlled by the underworld.

Unmentioned in most gang histories are the benefits that accrued from an association with Curly and the Outfit, not the least of which was protection. Dr. Jay Tischendorf remembers a story told by his grandfather, who drove a horse-drawn milk wagon in the years after Curly Humphreys had taken over the Milk Wagon Drivers' Union. "My grandfather was robbed at gunpoint by two men who took all that day's receipts," Tischendorf says. "My grandfather was distraught. He apologized to his boss, who told him to not worry. The boss said they were not going to the police. Instead they were going to the union." In one week's time, the two scoundrels' bodies were found floating in Lake Michigan.

Regretfully, not all the Outfit's racketeering takeovers were as bloodless as the laundry and milk operations. When Humphreys set his sights on Ben Rosenberg's dry cleaning business, Rosenberg resisted Humphreys' cajoling. Typically, the pressure escalated to Plan B, when Curly dispatched Philip Mangano and Louis Clementi, who spilled acid on clothes in four of Rosenberg's trucks. When that failed, they beat Rosenberg mercilessly. Then Ben Rosenberg did the unthinkable: Instead of rolling over, he went to the police. When a grand jury returned indictments against Mangano and Clementi, Rosenberg turned up dead, murdered before the case could come to trial.

Humphreys remained largely unscathed throughout the many years of his labor racketeering. On the few occasions when Humphreys was detained for questioning, he was able to either talk his way out of arrest or pay off the cops before they had time to announce their appearance. On one occasion, a witness to one police confrontation with Humphreys witnessed the payoff king whip out his wallet as soon as he encountered the officers. Proceeding to count out ten $100 bills, Curly asked, "Can't we settle this right here among friends?" Usually they could.

Humphreys' union struggles were only one of the responsibilities he assumed when Big Al "went away." Given his natural talents, Curly became, most likely by default, the Outfit's liaison to their political and law enforcement allies. In a tradition going back as far as Chicago's nineteenth-century bosses, compliant, graft-addled cops and politicians were an integral part of organized crime's success in Chicago. Humphreys' sharp-witted second wife recently described her husband's modus operandi: "He was buying cops like bananas – by the bunch." Humphreys' hold over Chicago's finest became so total that veteran policemen were routinely dismissed for harassing Outfit members. The gang's Einstein had similar success in the city and state legislatures, where Outfit-controlled pols routinely blocked anticrime bills. When one Illinois governor threatened to pass get-tough laws, the Outfit sent an emissary directly to the governor's mansion with their proposal. "Drop the crime bills, chief, and we'll pass the two main planks of your program for you," offered the gang's representative. When the chief executive refused to cave in, the Outfit made good on its threat, killing a key bill to establish a state Fair Employment Commission, and a bill calling for a badly needed new state constitutional convention.

Starting with Capone's reign the gangsters looked to one politician in particular to advance their interests. His name was Roland V. 'Libby' Libonati. With Capone's and the Outfit's support, Libonati was propelled upward to the state legislature, where he served for twenty-two years, and from there to Washington (1957), where he became "the mob's congressman," installed on the powerful House Judiciary Committee. After all, it was said, the "white collars" had their representatives, why shouldn't the Outfit?

Libby developed a colorful persona, and a verbal style that earned him the moniker Mr. Malaprop. Libonati waged a one-man war on the English language with phrases that are remembered in the Windy City to this day: "No one should speak asunder of the governor"; "I am trying not to make any honest mistakes"; "The moss is on the pumpkin"; "Chicago is the aviation crosswords of the world"; "I resent the insinuendoes"; "Chicago will march on to new platitudes of learning"; ". . . for the enlightenment, edification, and hallucination of the alderman from the Fiftieth Ward . . ."; and the unforgettable "walking pedestrians and tantrum bicycles."

Libonati, whose attorney brother Eliador also frequently represented Capone, flaunted his role with the Outfit, appearing often in public with the Big Guy himself, even being photographed sitting with Capone and "Machine Gun" Jack McGurn at a Chicago Cubs baseball game. "I was very proud when he [Capone] asked me at the ball game to speak to his son," Libby later recalled. "Mr Capone showed me great respect as a person of Italian extraction who represented one of the pioneer families in Illinois . . . I treated him with like respect as I would any American. If people treat me nice, I treat them nice." In 1930, when the Chicago police's goon squad wanted to round up some of the boys for routine questioning regarding Capone's whereabouts, they knew right where to go: Libby's campaign headquarters, where he was celebrating his election to the state legislature. There, according to police reports, they bagged some twenty gangsters "hanging out." On that occasion, Curly was among those taken in for questioning. Libonati was himself once arrested while in the company of Curly, Paul Ricca, Frankie Rio, and Ralph Pierce. When Frank Nitti was imprisoned in 1931, Libby was a regular visitor. That same year he represented Joe Accardo when Accardo was arrested for a hit. In that instance, counselor Libonati came to the rescue, seeing to it that the indictment was nol-prossed. He did likewise for Paul Ricca years later. Three decades later, Libby's top aide, Tony Tisci, would become the son-in-law of future boss Sam Giancana.

For more than four decades Libby and Curly would work together to stall the efforts of the G, especially future attorney general Bobby Kennedy, to prosecute the Outfit.

Under Curly's stewardship, and with his wife, Clemi, keeping the books, labor racketeering was perfected, turning a modestly profitable con into a multimillion-dollar operation, with the Outfit controlling as much as 70 percent of the city's unions. In 1928, the boys were seeing an estimated $10 million a year in profit from Curly's rackets; by 1931, estimates escalated to over $50 million – small by bootlegging standards, but with unlimited potential, since unlike Volstead, labor was never going to be repealed.

While the unions were coming under Humphreys' control, Joe, Paul, and Johnny were quietly laying plans for future conquests with a national scope. However, before the Outfit could put its bold new schemes into motion, a number of temporary hurdles needed to be overcome.

3.

Playing Politics

While the G was building its tax case against Al Capone, local officials were being embarrassed into action against the gangsters. One year before Capone's 1931 conviction, federal officers had stumbled onto a bombshell. While searching for Frank Nitti at a known Syndicate hangout, the agents discovered a list prepared by local police chief John Ryan. The one-page memo targeted forty-one gangsters for prosecution. Informed individuals asserted that Curly Humphreys had bribed an official to obtain the secret memorandum. The list found by the officers showed X's next to eight of the names, who were Capone's hierarchy (including Humphreys, Accardo, Hunt, and Campagna). It was learned that after Ryan had dictated it, the list had been retyped for official distribution. When the Nitti list was compared to the four copies in possession of police officials, those key names no longer appeared. Supposedly, Curly had delivered the note to Capone, who had himself penciled in the X marks and somehow managed to get the Syndicate-edited list into official circulation.

The local police were forced to escalate their inquiries into Nitti and the others. After Nitti was released from a brief tax-evasion term in 1932, he found that the heat on him had not dissipated. With the upcoming Democratic National Convention and the 1933 World's Fair both being hosted in Chicago, local officials desired to give at least the appearance of civility. This quest manifested itself in the person of the newly elected mayor, Anton "Ten Percent Tony" Cermak. During the mayoral campaign, Capone's Syndicate had naïvely thrown its considerable weight behind Cermak, believing Tony's racketeering background would render him sympathetic to the gang's needs. In fact, Cermak was playing a dangerous game, planning to backstab the hoods once they had helped get him elected.

"The mob doesn't know how I really feel about them," Cermak told Judge John Lyle days before the election. "I think I can get some support from the mob during the campaign. I'll take it. But after the election I'll boot them out of town." After his 1931 ascension to the mayoralty Cermak thus joined the long list of Chicago's faux "reform" mayors. On his first day in office, Cermak double-crossed the gangsters. Loudly promising to "assign some tough coppers" to chase out the hoods, Cermak concealed his real intent: to eliminate the *Italian* gangsters, who were prone to settling their differences in full public view. But more important, Cermak wanted to anoint a set of less embarrassing law-breakers whom he could control from within City Hall. It was a pattern he had established early in his career. The newly installed mayor vowed to show the world that the upperworld ran Chicago, not the underworld.

Anton Cermak was born in 1875 in Kladno, Bohemia. After his family's immigration to America, Tony, as he was called, worked his way out of poverty, eventually becoming an Illinois state legislator. To facilitate his chief goal in life (becoming rich), Cermak began building political organizations. While in the statehouse, Cermak assumed leadership of the United Societies, a lobby of saloonkeepers, distillers, and brewers. A Chicago historian described the arrangement: "As leader of an organization which assumed the misleading name of United Societies, Cermak aroused and organized the underworld to enforce its demand for a wide-open town. For a quarter of a century, any politician, whatever his party, who dared to support any measure that would curb the license of those antisocial hordes, was immediately confronted by Cermak, snarling and waving the club of the underworld vote."

Simultaneously, Ten Percent Cermak maintained sideline real estate and business insurance operations. Using insider information he acquired in the legislature, Cermak's real estate business quietly purchased land that the state soon coveted for parkland. Meanwhile, Cermak's insurance company obtained lucrative contracts from businessmen seeking favors in the statehouse. By the time he was elected mayor, the interest-conflicted Tony Cermak, the son of a poor Chicago policeman, was worth over $7 million. But the king of insider information had even greater ambitions: His sources had told him that Volstead was going to be repealed and the time was right to seize control of the soon-to-be-legal booze and gambling rackets.

Mayor Cermak understood that Al Capone would never relinquish control of his Syndicate's speakeasies and gambling joints. Even though

Capone himself was on a fast track to prison in 1931, Cermak concluded that the same fierce independence had been inherited by the new Outfit. Thus Cermak struck a fateful alliance with a successful independent bootlegger and gambling czar named Roger Touhy.

At the time of Cermak's election, thirty-three-year-old Roger Touhy ran a thriving slot machine and hooch operation out of the suburb of Des Plaines, fifteen miles northwest of Chicago. By 1932, Touhy and his brothers had overrun the Chicago Teamsters organization, which preferred the evil of the Touhys over the evil of Capone. Until his alliance with Cermak and the subsequent battles with the Outfit, Touhy was most notable not only for being the last major Irish bootlegger since the fall of O'Banion, but also for his continued refusal to cave in to the Syndicate. The ingenious Touhy once averted a threatened raise in police bribery fees by purchasing a fleet of Esso gasoline delivery trucks with which to secretly make his booze deliveries.

Capone had first tried to cajole Touhy into a partnership, but to no avail. Soon, Capone began a campaign of terror, kidnapping and assaulting Touhy's men. The Teamsters bequeathed the Touhy brothers $75,000 to wage war with the Capones. In responding to Capone's thuggery, Touhy made a monumental miscalculation: He confronted Capone in a show of bravado, threatening Capone in his own headquarters. Showing up one night at the Four Deuces, Touhy played his hand, telling Capone, "Stay out of my business. I tell you that for every man of mine kidnapped, I'll kill two of yours." With that Touhy turned and left. Capone may have been briefly amused by Touhy's act of lunacy, but in time Touhy would learn that Capone had a thin skin. He never forgot Touhy's insolence.

One of Capone's many efforts to ensnare Touhy came in 1930, while the Big Guy was in the Philadelphia lockup. By telephone, Capone instructed Humphreys to pay a call on Roger "the Terrible" Touhy. Previously, Curly had kidnapped Touhy's partner, Matt Kolb, prompting a $50,000 payout by Touhy. Now, accompanied by his driver, James "Red" Fawcett, Humphreys dropped in on Touhy at his Schiller Park headquarters. In Touhy's office, Curly made his best effort to convince Touhy of the mutual benefits of an alliance, suggesting Touhy come to Cicero to form a partnership with Nitti and the Outfit. At one point in the discussion, Touhy was called out of the room to take a phone call from a Capone soldier who owed Touhy a favor. "Don't go to Cicero, they're going to kill you," the informant warned.

On his return to the office, Touhy declared that Nitti should come to him if he wanted to talk. Curly feigned bravado saying, "You know, Touhy, we can take care of you anytime we want to." Touhy grabbed an ornamental shotgun off the wall, causing Curly to tremble visibly, much to Fawcett's surprise. Humiliated, Curly offered Touhy his limousine if he spared his life. Touhy declined the offer, but allowed Curly and Fawcett to crawl back to Cicero. Like Capone, the chagrined Humphreys never forgot his encounter with Touhy and kept a watchful eye for the chance to avenge it. Not long after Cermak's election, the opportunity would present itself.

Touhy's operation stood out as one of the few that had successfully resisted assimilation into the Capone organization, while Mayor Cermak's putsch manifested itself in a precipitous rise in the number of Capone-linked mobsters killed by cops, ambushed by Cermak's "special squad." It was not unnoticed by the Outfit that Touhy's vast enterprise remained curiously untouched. It was soon learned that Touhy was a longtime friend of Cermak's, for whom he supplied barrels of beer when Cermak hosted the Cook County Board of Commissioners' annual picnic. One of Cermak's most trusted insiders told the Illinois parole board in 1959 that he had witnessed the formation of a Touhy-Cermak alliance. Meeting in Cermak's office, the mayor offered to help Touhy wage a full-scale war on the Outfit. To insure that Touhy would have sufficient manpower, Cermak offered to put his five-hundred-man police force at Touhy's disposal. "You can have the entire police department," Cermak said.

What had to be more infuriating for the Capone gang was the apparent defection of one of their own to Team Cermak. Teddy Newberry was a gambling-club owner and ward boss from the North Side who had sided with Capone's Syndicate after the Beer Wars against the O'Banion crew. Such was Big Al's gratitude that he had lavished on Newberry a diamond-encrusted belt buckle. Newberry became so trusted by the Outfit that he had assisted Curly Humphreys in a protection scam as recently as early 1932. Sometime that year, Cermak apparently made Newberry a better offer, and the triumvirate of Cermak-Touhy-Newberry began plotting a serious assault on Nitti and the Outfit. The assault had a personal impact on Curly Humphreys when his trusted labor adviser George "Red" Barker was gunned down by Touhy's killers. When word reached the Outfit that Touhy and Newberry were Cermak's approved gangsters, Curly and the Outfit set about plotting their revenge. All the while, events in Washington would force the gang to diversify its interests; the cash cow of booze was soon to disappear.

Repeal

The violence associated with Capone's regime was the last straw in the fast-growing movement to repeal Volstead. The Great Depression and the gangster era exposed the prohibitionists' hollow promise that banning alcohol would lead to a prosperous nation. Too late, the nation realized that, in addition to rampant alcoholism, the ill-considered legislation had created powerful gangs. Once again taking the lead, America's women, shepherded by Pauline Sabin's Women's Organization for Prohibition Repeal, pushed for repeal. It was a fitting development, given that women had been largely responsible for the birth of the prohibition movement. With pro-repeal sentiment taking off, the "dry unions" were now greatly outnumbered. Newspaper polls estimated the repealers at 80 percent of the populace.

By 1931, New York governor and presidential aspirant Franklin Roosevelt had joined the campaign against prohibition, asserting that $300 million could be raised in alcohol taxes to fight the depression that had gripped the country since the October 29, 1929, stock market crash. Furthermore, booze at least provided some comfort during the Depression. For the gangsters, Roosevelt's potential election, and the possibility of an end to bootlegging, foreboded a massive drop-off in revenue.

On February 20, 1933, Congress passed the Twenty-first Amendment, nullifying the Eighteenth. Ten months later, the needed three-fourths of states had ratified the measure. On December 5, 1933, the bootleggers were officially out of business, at least the booze business. The labor rackets were in full swing, under the guidance of Curly Humphreys, while Joe Accardo concentrated on gambling. But the profits from these activities would pale in comparison to the riches that awaited the boys in a few short years. In the meantime, the Outfit experienced firsthand what Big Al had often told them: "Nobody's on the legit."

The Outfit's Political Education

The Outfit-Touhy counterplots took some time to coalesce, and so by June 1932, a stalemate was in place as the Chicago elite held its breath while welcoming the Democratic national delegation. And although both Curly and Joe advised the Outfit to keep violence to a minimum, there were nonetheless more than thirty gangland murders that year.

The 1932 Democratic nomination was tightly contested by two New York governors: Franklin Delano Roosevelt (the incumbent) and former four-time governor Al Smith. The Outfit had a front-row seat to the internecine backdoor warfare that chose the candidate. The boys would put this education in politicking to good use in many future presidential contests.

Accompanying the nation's party hacks to Chicago were members of the Torrio-Luciano Commission. In his authorized biography, *The Last Testament of Lucky Luciano,* New York gang chief Charles "Lucky" Luciano recalled how he arrived in town with other mob luminaries, including Meyer Lansky, Longy Zwillman, Moe Dalitz, Phil Kastel, and Frank Costello. The group also included Kansas City machine boss Tom Pendergast, who was sponsoring the ascendancy of future president Harry S Truman. The mobsters were ensconced in six-room suites at the posh Drake Hotel overlooking Lake Michigan. Whereas the delegates were hosted by the local Democratic elite (headed by Mayor Anton Cermak), the gangsters were squired by Ricca, Accardo, Guzik, and the rest of the Outfit. "They supplied all the booze we needed for free," Lucky remembered. Luciano said that the scene at the convention was similar to that at the Drake: "Liquor was for sale openly to any delegates at stands run by the heirs of Al Capone. In the hospitality suites run by the Outfit, liquor was free to all comers, and it was poured steadily and unstintingly all hours of the day and night. The bar was never closed and the buffet tables were constantly replenished."

The nomination proved a dogfight, with a bitter Al Smith leading a vigorous "Stop Roosevelt" faction that succeeded in denying FDR the needed support for the first three ballot votes. Then, as they would in many future presidential contests, the upperworld turned to the under-world for assistance. The candidates' aides and their sought-after dele-gates swarmed to the Chicago Stockyards and proceeded to maneuver the powerful ganglords. As Luciano recalled, "We waited until the very last second, and we had Roosevelt and Smith guys comin' out our ears. They all knew we controlled most of the city's delegates."

While the mobsters procrastinated, Frank Costello held a meeting with Roosevelt's advisers. Costello's faction required a concession of their own: As governor, Roosevelt had recently unleashed Judge Samuel Sea-bury on a civic corruption investigation, and the New York "mob delegation" wanted the dogs called off. As Luciano recalled, "When Frank got the word that Roosevelt would live up to his promise to kill the Seabury investigation – I mean like tapering off so he could save face – it was in the bag for him." The gangsters instructed their delegates to support Roosevelt.

Luciano was saddled with the task of breaking the news to Al Smith. According to Luciano, Smith, who had long coveted the White House, broke down in tears on hearing the news. When told the details of the deal, Smith warned, "Frank, Roosevelt'll break his word to you. This is the biggest mistake you ever made in your entire life by trustin' him. He'll kill you." Ignoring the warning, the mob threw their considerable weight behind Roosevelt, who won on the fourth ballot. In the subsequent general election, Roosevelt handily defeated the incumbent Herbert Hoover. Joe Accardo's wheelman at the time, the young Salvatore "Mooney" Giancana, allegedly told his brother years later that the Outfit financially supported the Roosevelt effort in Chicago, support that would greatly escalate in Roosevelt's subsequent reelections. "Shit, he got to the White House thanks to Syndicate money," Giancana supposedly told his brother (in Chuck Giancana's *Double Cross*). Luciano was a bit more restrained in his summary, adding, "I don't say we elected Roosevelt, but we gave him a pretty good push." Although unproven, Lucky's and Mooney's allegations, if true, would help make sense of Outfit-related controversies a decade later.

Regretfully for the New York mob, the trap predicted by Smith proved accurate: After his inauguration the following year, Roosevelt turned Judge Seabury loose on his investigation. In *The Last Testament of Lucky Luciano,* Lucky talked of the hard-learned lesson:

> Roosevelt had been a prick all along, but I gotta give him credit for one thing – he was really smooth . . . I always knew that politicians was crooked; that you could buy 'em anytime you wanted and you couldn't trust 'em around the corner. But I didn't think it was the same with a guy who was gonna be President. I never knew that muscle could buy its way into the White House. I never knew that a guy who was gonna be President would stick a knife in your back when you wasn't looking. I never knew his word was no better than lots of racket guys'. But I guess nobody should become President of the United States on the back of a gangster.

Despite Roosevelt's alleged betrayal, the Outfit would continue to dabble in presidential politics. Only Luciano's close Outfit chum, Curly Humphreys, remained the voice of reason in these dealings. Three decades later, he alone would caution against the Outfit's coddling of bootlegger/robber baron Joe Kennedy and his son Jack. Curly had not forgotten the Roosevelt double cross.

Although the Democratic convention came and went without incident, Mayor Anton Cermak remained obsessed with ridding the city of the Italian gang element before the spring 1933 opening of the World's Fair. Local banker Rufus Dawes, brother of former U.S. vice president Charles Dawes, was directing the Chicago-hosted Fair, slated for a May 27, 1933, grand opening. Given the Great Depression setting, the Fair's name, "A Century of Progress," seemed a contradiction. But the title was meant to illustrate the great strides made by the Windy City since its incorporation one hundred years earlier and had been in the planning stage a year before the stock market's 1929 Black Tuesday.

Dawes and Cermak allegedly had nightmare visions of millions of Fair patrons witnessing the sideshow to which Chicagoans had become accustomed: gangland drive-by shootings. Such a spectacle could hardly be expected to lure investment capital – the real purpose of the Fair – into the city. Of course, Cermak's actual agenda remained the same: to establish his own criminal organization. Thus the anti-Syndicate crackdown continued.

The Cermak-Outfit war finally entered its climactic phase on December 19, 1932, five months before the Fair's opening. As the Outfit later learned from its spies, Teddy Newberry met with Cermak "special squad" detective sergeant Harry Lang, paying him the then astronomical sum of $15,000 to dispose of Nitti once and for all. Joined by Patrolmen Harry Miller and Chris Callahan, Lang drove to Nitti's fifth-floor office at 221 North LaSalle Street, an address provided them by Cermak. The officers encountered six men, including the typically unarmed Frank Nitti. In later testimony, Callahan described what happened next: "We took the six men from the little anteroom into a larger office. We searched them. Nitti had no gun. While I held Nitti by the wrists, Detective Sergeant Lang walked up to Nitti from behind and shot him three times." He had been hit twice in the back and once in the neck. While falling, a shocked Nitti gasped to Lang, "What's this for?" Callahan recalled that Lang then returned alone to the anteroom and shot himself in the hand, the better to claim that he had shot Nitti in self-defense.

With Nitti's injuries seemingly fatal, a police physician arrived and tended to Lang's trivial hand wound while the bleeding Nitti lay unconscious. Later, at Jefferson Park Hospital, the gangster regained consciousness long enough to tell his treating surgeon (his son-in-law), Dr. Gaetano Rango, "I didn't shoot Lang. I didn't have a gun." He then slipped back into unconsciousness. While Nitti appeared to be at death's door, Lang and Miller were lauded by the City Council, given bonus pay and meritorious service awards. But back at Jefferson Park Hospital, unbeknownst to the self-congratulatory officials, Nitti was making a miraculous recovery.

When word of Nitti's condition reached City Hall, Cermak, Lang, Newberry, and Miller were gripped with fear. They knew the Outfit's retribution would be swift and bloody. Cermak changed addresses, doubled his personal security, and placed guards at the homes of his daughters. According to newsman Jack Lait, the Outfit placed a bomb under Cermak's car when it was parked in the Loop, but the device malfunctioned. On December 21, Cermak, Lang, and Miller suddenly left town for an extended stay in Florida. The official explanation for the trip was Cermak's need to recuperate from a bout of dysentery. Many, however, believed that the timing of his illness was far too convenient to be coincidental. Before his departure, a clearly shaken Cermak told a reporter that the Outfit had threatened his life, and so he had bought a bulletproof vest. His parting charge to his troops was "Wage bitter war on the gangsters until they are driven from our city." Two weeks later, Teddy Newberry's body was found in a ditch in suburban Indiana. He was still wearing the diamond-studded belt buckle given him by Al Capone years earlier.

Word of Newberry's passing terrified the trio of tourists visiting the Sunshine State. Five weeks later, on February 13, 1933, Mayor Cermak attempted to mend fences with now President-elect Roosevelt, who was visiting Florida, and whom Cermak had not supported at the previous summer's Democratic National Convention. It has been also said that Cermak hoped to persuade Roosevelt to attend opening day of the upcoming World's Fair. What happened next eerily presaged the assassination of President John F. Kennedy thirty years later: A lone nut fires three shots at a political leader on a Southern-state tour, with rumors spreading of organized crime involvement.

After greeting Roosevelt at a public appearance in Miami's Bayfront Park, Cermak, who had uncharacteristically neglected to don his protective vest, was shot by a former Italian army sharpshooter named Giuseppe Zangara. When his Chicago secretary rushed to his hospital bedside, Cermak managed to say, "So you arrived all right. I thought maybe they'd shot up the office in Chicago too." The fifty-year-old Cermak lingered for three weeks before succumbing to gangrene and pneumonia, and Zangara was summarily tried and executed.

The accepted version of the murder has it that Zangara was a complete psychopath who, despite being a sharpshooter, missed his real target, Roosevelt, a man whom he paradoxically said he admired. But in Chicago, another theory held sway: Cermak's killing was intentional, a fallout from the Outfit-Cermak power struggle. Municipal Judge John Lyle, Chicago's fiercest and most knowledgeable antimob jurist of the era, opined, "Zangara was a Mafia killer, sent from Sicily to do a job and sworn to silence." The expounded theory posits that Zangara, whose occupation was betting on dogs and horse races, owed the mob huge gambling debts and was ordered to kill Cermak or be tortured to death. It was also alleged that he had been promised that his mother would be cared for should he be caught in the act. Lastly, renowned criminal attorney and criminologist August Bequai learned in his research for his book *Organized Crime* that Zangara gave an interview shortly before his execution in which he admitted that he had been ordered by the Outfit to kill Cermak. Although, when recently queried, Bequai could not recall the source of his contention, it was likely none other than the most famous syndicated columnist of the time, Walter Winchell. Using all his powers of persuasion to finesse his way past Zangara's prison guard, Winchell obtained the only interview with the killer. According to what Winchell told his editors, Zangara was ordered to kill Cermak, and that had he missed, the fallback plan was to assassinate the troublemaking mayor on the opening day of the World's Fair. Winchell's editors declined to print the story since Winchell had no way to prove its veracity. However, sixty years later, thousands of Secret Service records obtained by investigative journalist John William Tuohy virtually proved the mob-hit allegation.

It turns out that the thirty-three-year-old Zangara had immigrated to America ten years before the Cermak murder. Settling in New Jersey, Zangara became a bootlegger, which resulted in his 1929 arrest for operating a massive thousand-gallon still. After spending seven months in Atlanta Federal Prison, he relocated to Florida, where he became addicted to gambling at both the horse and dog tracks. Zangara's addiction was worsened because most of his bets failed to deliver. According to government records, Zangara became "juiced up" and was forced to work off his vigorish by becoming a drug mule: He couriered narcotics from a south-Florida processing plant to members of the New York Commission. However, for reasons unclear, Zangara went afoul of his controllers. Documents hint that he was possibly caught cheating them out of their profits. In any event, Zangara was earmarked for elimination. However, before the hit was enacted, Paul Ricca picked up the telephone.

The Waiter called Dave Yaras, a feared Outfit enforcer and labor liaison to Florida, who was moonlighting with Zangara's New York dope pipeline. Ricca informed Yaras that the Cermak situation in Chicago had become unbearable, and that the Outfit had decreed that Cermak should be whacked, most suitably when out of town. And he was on his way to Florida. Did Yaras have any ideas? Yaras offered up the doomed Zangara. With Ricca's consent, Zangara was made an offer he couldn't refuse: either be killed horribly on the spot or kill Cermak and take his chances by pleading insanity in a state with liberal laws regarding mentally unstable criminals. Zangara chose the latter.

Unbeknownst to Zangara, he had more to fear than the Florida legal system. Sources told the Secret Service that Ricca dispatched two of his best killers, Three Fingers Jake White and Frankie Rio, to kill Zangara in the post-assassination confusion. On the morning of February 13, tipped by the gangsters, Zangara first proceeded to the Bostick Hotel, where Cermak was going to privately call on the owners, Horace and May Bostick, who were longtime friends. However, by the time Zangara arrived, Cermak had departed. The owners of the hotel nonetheless remembered seeing him on the premises stalking the Chicago mayor. "Zangara's object in coming here," May Bostick told the Secret Service, "was to kill Cermak."

At 9:25 that night, Tony Cermak was seated on the park's bandstand as Roosevelt's car approached, and while Zangara waited in the crowd of fifteen thousand, Roosevelt's vehicle stopped mere feet from Zangara. With Roosevelt lifted onto the trunk, Zangara had a clear shot at the president's back – but did not take it. Instead, he waited for the president to spot Cermak: "Tony! Come on down here." Cermak walked down and spoke with the president for about three minutes, then returned to the stage area. With Cermak at one end of the stage, and Roosevelt's car on the other side, some thirty feet away, Zangara fired three shots *in Cermak's direction*. William Sinnot, a New York policeman injured in the attack, said, "He was no more shooting at Mr. Roosevelt than I was." Mark Wilcox, a Florida congressman who witnessed the shooting, stated emphatically, "He was shooting at Cermak. There is no doubt about that. The killer waited until Mr. Roosevelt sat down and then fired." For his part, Roosevelt agreed with the other eyewitnesses that he was not the target. For the rest of his life he reiterated the opinion that Zangara was "a Chicago gangster" hired to take out Cermak.

Upon hearing news of the attack, the Chicago police department moved to have the Miami authorities round up eighteen Outfit associates known to be in Miami. However, Chicago state's attorney Tom Courtney, known to be in the pocket of the Outfit, countermanded the department's request before they could send it. Meanwhile, the imprisoned Zangara, who futilely pled insanity, took the prison's warden, Leo Chapman, into his confidence. Chapman told the Secret Service that Zangara was anything but insane, and that he was in fact linked to "some sort of criminal syndicate." Zangara's last words before receiving twenty-three hundred volts in the electric chair were "Go ahead and push the button. *Viva Italia! Viva Comorra!*" *Comorra* is an Italian word synonymous with *Mafia*.

Back in Chicago, firehouses sounded their alarms in celebration upon hearing of Cermak's death: The late mayor had hounded the firefighters with unannounced midnight raids to catch men who might be dozing on the job. In short time, Sergeant Lang was fired from the police force and tried for assault with intent to murder Nitti. After hearing damning testimony from both of Lang's partners, the jury returned a guilty verdict. Lang, however, had other ideas. "I will blow the lid off Chicago politics and wreck the Democratic Party if I have to serve one day in jail," he threatened to a throng of reporters. Within hours he was granted a new trial, and when bail was posted at $15,000, so many worried politicians chipped in that the court was awash in $45,000 cash. Lang was said to have chuckled when he heard. He must have laughed harder when his new trial was postponed into oblivion and never occurred. Interestingly, after his firing from the force, Lang left the Cermak sphere and sided with another crook, Maxie Eisen, a racketeer and former associate of none other than Big Al Capone.

After the trial, Nitti took a much needed vacation at the Florida home of Capone's cousin, Charlie Fischetti. Chicago crime experts believe that Nitti never fully recovered from his injuries, suffering lasting neurological injuries that rendered him incapable of taking charge of the Outfit. Some months later, acting as the "caretaker" chief of the Outfit, Nitti returned to Chicago and met with his board at what the locals referred to as Little City Hall, on the third floor of the Capri Restaurant on North Clark Street, directly across from official City Hall. According to a union boss who was taken to the Capri, the Outfit maintained a supersecret room on the third floor where they held daily meetings. "This dining room was so private," the labor organizer said, "that you couldn't get in there unless the elevator operator recognized you." In attendance were Curly, Joe, Paul, Sam Hunt, and the Fischettis. Nitti advised his crew of decisions made at a meeting at Charlie Fischetti's Biscayne home that summer, a convocation also attended by the Lansky brothers from New Jersey, and Jack Dragna, Rosselli's Los Angeles partner. At the Capri, Nitti ticked off an agenda largely dictated by Chicago's position as the country's hotel and service industry mecca:

- Invest in beer and liquor businesses, then control restaurant and bartenders' unions to increase the sales of their own brands.
- Expand into hotel and food operations, building on the groundwork already laid by Curly Humphreys.
- Get into the entertainment business, especially nightclubs and musicians' unions.
- Take over the race wire and bookmaking businesses.

Nitti advised his gang, "The bartenders" union is our biggest lever. After we get national control we will have every bartender in the country pushing our brands of beer and liquor.' But Nitti was wrong. Although the control of the bartenders' unions would be lucrative, it would pale in comparison to other schemes soon to be devised.

While waiting to assault the Touhy half of the Cermak-Touhy alliance, Humphreys, Nitti, and the Outfit spent the spring cashing in on the "Century of Progress." Even before the gates were opened on the first day of the Fair, the Outfit reaped huge profits. With land having to be cleared on Northerly Island, just off Lake Shore Drive, and massive construction projects necessary, the organizers were at the mercy of the trucking and construction trade unions, which in turn were controlled by the Outfit. Curly and his boys saw nothing wrong with taking a 10 percent cut "off the top" on all work performed at the Fair. After all, the upperworld had been collecting its 20 percent graft for decades. That fee was the price fixed to guarantee work permits for lucrative jobs. Private contractors automatically added the fee to their job estimates, a tribute paid "to take care of the boys downtown," as one such businessman put it. The Outfit, led by Curly Humphreys, paid a visit to the Fair's builders and convinced them of the wisdom of tacking on the added 10 percent for the Outfit. Held on the Lake Michigan shoreline between Twelfth and Thirty-ninth Streets, the 1933 World's Fair ran for two years, attracting more than thirty-nine million visitors. Its main theme was the number of recent scientific breakthroughs in use of lighting (the Fair's lights were turned on when rays from the star Arcturus were focused on photoelectric cells at disparate astronomical observatories, transformed into electricity, then transmitted to Chicago).[1]

Not all the fair's exhibits were high-minded. The earthy, hedonistic pleasures were in evidence, if not advertised by civic promoters: Exotic "fan dancer" Sally Rand showed her wares at the Streets of Paris emporium; wine and women flowed at the Ann Rutledge Tavern. With so much money to be made at the Fair, the members of the Outfit were not about to look the other way after construction was completed. They were, in fact, among the chief beneficiaries of the tourist largesse. While Chicago's newest corrupt mayor, Edward Kelly, squired dignitaries around the grounds, Al Capone's heirs controlled many of the Fair's critical functions, including parking, hot dog, hamburger, soda, hatcheck, towel, and soap concessions. What services they did not operate outright, they nonetheless profited from by collecting "protection" money. Curly Humphreys owned the most popular ride at the Fair and, with Fred Evans, controlled the popcorn concession. While Curly was on the lam later that year in Mexico, he hired a manager who picked up the weekly profits from each booth. Al Capone's brother Ralph virtually cornered the market on bottled water and sodas, while Paul Ricca ran the San Carlo Italian Village, where the Outfit socialized after hours. The roulette wheels were spinning and the dice rolled under the supervision of Outfitter James Mondi. Outfit boss and Capone cousin Charlie Fischetti said at the time, "If a wheel turns on the fairgrounds, we get a cut of the grease on the axle."

When the fairgrounds emptied at night, the adult attendees partook of the Outfit's other amenities scattered throughout the rest of the city: brothels, casinos, massage parlors, and saloons. Prohibition came to an

---

1. The Chicago Crime Commission's director, Virgil Peterson, described the Fair: "[It] epitomized a new age – an age of steel, electricity, chromium, aluminum, and modernistic architecture. Most of the buildings were completely without windows. Day and night they were illuminated by electricity. At night, colored illumination added to the beauty of the exteriors of the futuristic buildings. The Travel and Transportation Building was a block and a half long. Inside were locomotives, multiple-motored transport planes, and a cross section of an ocean liner."

end during the first year of the Fair, an event that only escalated the partying at the Outfit's clubs, which operated twenty-four hours a day. With these and other gang enterprises enjoying robust business, the transition to post-Volstead was reasonably smooth.

Curly's Revenge

With Cermak removed from the scene and the "Century of Progress" filling the Outfit's coffers, Curly Humphreys was free to redress the personal attack by Roger Touhy, not to mention the murder of his friend Red Barker and the shooting of Frank Nitti. Humphreys' vengeance had the added bonus of simultaneously removing a major Outfit adversary. The plot was brilliant in concept and actually played out over several decades before reaching its denouement. At the time, an English friend of Curly's, John "Jake the Barber" Factor, was living in Chicago, on the run from the law in Great Britain. Factor, brother of future cosmetics baron Max Factor,[2] had been charged with participating in an $8-million stock swindle involving South African diamond-mine securities ($160 million by today's count). It seemed that Jake had struck a partnership with the king of New York bootleggers, Arnold Rothstein, to stake him $50,000 to set up the swindle. Among Factor's victims were widows, clergymen, elderly investors, and most significant, members of the British royal family and the chief of Scotland Yard. When the scam was discovered, Factor fled to Monte Carlo, where he quickly created another crime syndicate that successfully broke the casino bank by rigging the tables. Before authorities caught on, Factor had fled once again. In 1931, when the British government located Factor in Al Capone's Chicago, they commenced extradition proceedings.

Factor was by now a multimillionaire, thanks to the profits from the British and Monte Carlo swindles, and enlisted a strong legal team to stall the federal government for over two years, but by 1933, they had run out of maneuvers. When Curly Humphreys learned that the statute of limitations on the extradition would soon run out, he envisioned his

---

2. Max Factor single-handedly reinvented Hollywood's look with his development of Pan-Cake makeup. Prior to this, stars were painted with vaudeville-style greasepaint. Factor was also the originator of the pouty-lip look and is widely considered the father of the cosmetics industry. When his products went commercial, they dominated stores for decades. Factor, who was immortalized in the Johnny Mercer song "Hooray for Hollywood," died in 1938.

elegant, if elaborate, revenge against Touhy. Only a mind like Curly's could see the connection.

Factor had been summoned to appear in federal court on April 18, 1933, for what was certain to be his one-way ticket back to England. By amazing coincidence, Jake the Barber's nineteen-year-old son, Jerome, chose this moment in history to become a kidnapping victim, coincidentally giving Jake an incontestable excuse for having the proceedings postponed yet again. With a $200,000 ransom on Jerome's head, Chicago police, apparently unaware of Factor's friendship with Curly, raided the headquarters of the the best kidnappers in Chicago, the Outfit. There they encountered Curly Humphreys, Joe Accardo, and Sam "Golf Bag" Hunt. The gangsters were incredulous, telling the cops that they were in fact strategizing on how to get the young boy freed. Jake himself admitted that he went to Curly for help. After all, Curly was not only Chicago's best kidnapper, but also one of its best negotiators.

Eight days later, Jake and a carload of Outfitters rescued Jerome on the city's West Side, but they failed to catch the kidnappers. "We spotted them in their car," the Barber recounted, "but some policemen came along and the criminals sped away." Neither Jerome, who was allegedly blindfolded the entire time, nor Jake could identify the scoundrels. With Jake's legal confrontation in D.C. temporarily postponed, phase one of Curly's plan was complete.

On May 29, frustrated Supreme Court officials reset the date for Factor's hearing. It was a last-ditch motion, since the statute was due to expire in early July. But by a propitious turn of events, this time Jake Factor himself turned up kidnapped.

On June 30, 1933, Jake Factor disappeared after leaving an Outfit-controlled saloon in the northwest suburbs. Twelve days later he surfaced, walking the streets of suburban La Grange, appearing bleary-eyed and bearded. He told a policeman he had paid $70,000 in ransom to his kidnappers, whom he could not identify. But the totality of Factor's physical appearance invited skepticism. As later described by the detaining patrolman, Bernard Gerard: "Well, his tie was in place . . . and he was wearing a light linen suit, which was clean. His sleeves were wrinkled. His pants were somewhat wrinkled. His shoes were quite clean, no marks or dirt on them; no marks of dirt on his hands. He also had a white handkerchief, which was very clean – wrinkled, but no marks of dirt on it. His nails and hands were perfectly clean, cleaner than mine, and I have just cleaned them . . . The cuffs of his shirt were pressed and clean. His collar was straight [and] in place."

But the discrepancies didn't matter to a state's attorney's office controlled by Curly and the Outfit. Touhy was soon named the chief and only suspect in the case. Many years later, mob-fighting federal judge John P. Barnes described the arrangement between the Outfit and a compliant state's attorney's office: "The [Capone] Syndicate could not operate without the approval of the [state's attorney's] office . . . The relationship between the State's Attorney's office, under [Tom] Courtney and [Dan] Gilbert, and the Capone Syndicate, was such that during the entire period that Courtney was in office [1932–44], no Syndicate man was ever convicted of a major crime in Cook County."

In rapid succession, Courtney's goons arrested Roger Touhy and persuaded the Washington authorities to cancel Factor's extradition proceedings, now that he was a material witness in a capital case. Touhy was tried twice in the Factor case, the first jury unable to reach a decision. Although Factor identified Touhy, his admission was suspect given that he had earlier testified that he had been blindfolded the entire time. Two weeks later, the second trial produced a surprise witness, Isaac Costner, or Tennessee Ike, who, when asked under oath to state his occupation, replied, "Thief." Ike stated that he was with Touhy during the kidnapping but he was against the idea. Touhy was found guilty this time around and sentenced to ninety-nine years in prison. Meanwhile, Jake the Barber was allowed to stay in the country as "a friend of the court." Twenty years later, Ike filed a deposition in which he admitted that he was put up to the false testimony by U.S. assistant attorney general Joseph B. Keenan, who promised to cut Ike a break on a thirty-year sentence for mail robbery if he agreed to testify against Touhy. When Keenan reneged, Ike filed the damning deposition.

But it was too little too late for Roger "the Terrible" Touhy, who languished in prison until 1959, when the abomination was finally reversed. When Judge Barnes finally reviewed the case, he concluded that "the kidnapping never took place." The parole board agreed. Unfortunately for Touhy, he released his autobiography, *The Stolen Years*, simultaneously with his release from prison, wherein he referred to Curly Humphreys as a pimp.[3] Compounding his error, Touhy an-

---

3. Joe Accardo saw to it, however, that Teamster truckers would refuse to ship the book, and that Chicago bookstores were frightened off from carrying the memoir.

nounced that he intended to sue Factor, State's Attorney Tom Courtney, Ricca, Humphreys, and Accardo for $300 million for wrongful imprisonment. One wonders what Touhy could have been thinking; it was obvious to many that he was signing his own death warrant. By this time, the Outfit, in collusion with its New York Commission partners, was on the eve of bilking the Teamsters Pension Fund out of hundreds of millions of dollars to finance casino construction in Las Vegas. Touhy's suit held the ominous potential for exposing this massive conspiracy. Thus it came as no surprise when, on December 16, three weeks after his emancipation, Roger Touhy was murdered with five shotgun blasts, while Jake Factor dined at the Outfit's Singapore Restaurant. The *Daily News* reported two days later that "police have been informed that the tough-talking Touhy had given Humphreys . . . this ultimatum: 'Cut me in or you'll be in trouble. I'll talk!' On his deathbed, the former gangster whispered, 'I've been expecting it. The bastards never forget.'"

Jake the Barber continued his association with the Outfit for many years. After finally serving six years in prison for mail fraud involving the fraudulent sale of other people's whiskey receipts, Factor moved on to Las Vegas in the 1950s. At that time, the Outfit had expanded its empire into Sin City, and Curly Humphreys sponsored Jake for a position as manager of one of Vegas' (and the Outfit's) first premier hotel-casinos, the Stardust. In 1960, just months after Roger Touhy's release from prison and subsequent murder, Factor sold Curly Humphreys four hundred shares of First National Life Insurance stock at $20 a share, then bought them back after a few months for $125 per share. Curly netted a tidy $42,000 profit.

In the 1950s, Factor began drawing on the great fortune he had amassed during his early British stock swindle, to embark on a successful PR campaign aimed at creating the persona of Jake the Philanthropist. His frequent six-figure donations to various charities earned him numerous humanitarian awards. Some have asserted that another reason for Touhy's murder was that a free Touhy could easily destroy the Barber's hard-won reincarnation as the beneficent John Factor.

In 1960, the Immigration and Naturalization Service (INS) was considering deporting Factor back to England to face the massive mail-fraud charges brought against him decades earlier. Also in 1960, Jake Factor contributed $22,000 to the presidential campaign of Joseph Kennedy's son Jack, becoming JFK's single largest campaign contributor. In 1962, the INS moved to deport Factor, but was thwarted when Attorney General Bobby Kennedy brought Factor to Washington to speak with him and review the INS case. Factor later told the press that Bobby Kennedy slyly brought up that he needed donations to help secure the release of 1,113 Cuban Brigade soldiers captured by Castro's forces after the disastrous April 1961 Bay of Pigs invasion. Reports had been circulating for months that Bobby Kennedy was placing threatening calls to business leaders with tax or other pending legal matters, practically extorting the funds from them. In conversations monitored by the FBI, the Outfit was clearly impressed by Kennedy's mastering of the "velvet hammer" extortion approach. On one occasion, the agents reported that Giancana aide Chuckie English "pointed out that the attorney general raising money for the Cuba invaders makes Chicago's Syndicate look like amateurs." After a number of meetings with the Barber in December 1962, Bobby Kennedy recommended to his brother that Factor be pardoned. Factor told reporters that he had contributed $25,000 to Kennedy's "Tractors for Cuba" fund.[4] President Kennedy granted Jake's parole on Christmas Eve, 1962, the same night the prisoners landed in Miami, and just one week after the INS had announced its decision to deport Factor.

But soon after, the inexperienced attorney general began to have misgivings about what he had done. Jack Clarke, who worked in the investigative police unit of Chicago's Mayor Daley, recently recalled what happened next. "Bobby Kennedy called me and asked if there would be any problem if Jake Factor were pardoned. When I explained the details of Factor's Outfit background – Capone, Humphreys, the Sands, et cetera – Bobby went, 'Holy shit!' He then explained that he had already approved the pardon." Clarke adds that Bobby's dealings with the Factor case were not atypical. "RFK didn't know what he was doing in the Justice Department. He had no idea of the subtleties, the histories of these people."

It is impossible to know if Bobby Kennedy grasped the historic and complex relationship between the upperworld barons, such as his own father, and the hoods with whom the barons consorted. If he did, he may have thought twice before launching his full-scale assault on the underworld.

---

4. It was reported that Factor's payoff to RFK was an Outfit practical joke: The money came from the skim the gang was taking from Las Vegas casinos, about which more will be seen.

Eventually settling in Los Angeles, the much traveled Factor took particular interest in the welfare of underprivileged black youth in the Los
Angeles district known as Watts. In the 1960s, after bestowing a million-
dollar endowment (allegedly through the Joseph P. Kennedy Foundation)
on a Watts youth center, a *Los Angeles Times* reporter brought up his
ties with the Outfit. Factor broke into tears, asking, "How much does a man
have to do to bury his past?" The reporter could easily have countered,
"Perhaps an apology to Roger Touhy's family, for starters."

Factor died of natural causes in 1984 in Beverly Hills. His *Los Angeles
Times* obituary headline read JOHN FACTOR, NOTED PHILANTHROPIST,
DIES AFTER LONG ILLNESS.

On June 27, 1933, "the Man" finally caught up with Curly Humphreys
and his labor racketeering. Apparently the Milk Wagon Drivers' Union
business manager, Steve Sumner, was not intimidated by the Humphreys
muscle. Although Sumner could not prove who actually snagged his
partner, Doc Fitchie, he was certain who collected the $50,000 ransom:
Curly Humphreys. Without a witness to the actual kidnapping, the court
found itself in a quandary and was forced to indict Humphreys on the
only charge that seemed to stick in 1930s Chicago: federal tax charges.
Thus Humphreys earned the distinction of becoming the only man known
to have been charged with not paying taxes on a ransom he received for a
kidnapping of which he was never accused.

Instead of answering the charge, Humphreys took the opportunity to
pursue one of his favorite hobbies: traveling. After hiring a manager to
look after his affairs at the "Century of Progress," Curly fled the Windy
City, "lamming it," as he put it, for sixteen months. This period gave the
first hints of trouble in the Humphreys' marriage. According to conversations overheard by FBI bugs planted years later, Humphreys spoke
of how he was accompanied by "a little blonde I used to have" on his
escape. Among other locales visited by Curly and his mistress was
Mexico, where Humphreys pursued his passions for fishing, reading,
and photography. In future years, Curly expanded into documentary
filmmaking.[5] The Chicago Crime Commission quickly named Curly its

---

5. Humphreys shot one such epic on location at Alcatraz, sarcastically dubbing the
sound track with the popular song "Hail, Hail, the Gang's All Here." (His heirs still
proudly display examples of Curly's photographic prowess, including 8mm footage
from Hawaii, Europe, Africa, Havana, and Asia.)

new Public Enemy Number One. In its previous list of twenty-eight hoods, the Commission had failed to even name Humphreys, who now leapfrogged the competition to gain the top spot.

Returning to Chicago some fifteen months later, Humphreys pled guilty to the tax charge, adding that he alone was responsible for the financial misunderstanding. His performance as a "stand-up guy" succeeded in securing the release of others who had participated in the scheme. Curly paid his taxes (with interest and penalties) and calmly headed off to Leavenworth Federal Prison on October 31, 1934. Some knowledgeable observers perceived Humphreys' acquiescence as reminiscent of Capone's tactical vacation spent in the Philadelphia lockup. That conclusion was bolstered by the grand schemes to be undertaken by Humphreys upon his release from prison fifteen months later. On his departure for jail, Humphreys informed the press: "While I'm down there, I intend to study English and maybe a little geometry." For Curly, the term *college* was not a just a cute euphemism.

The Big House was not such a cavalier subject, however, for the gang's original architect, Al Capone. Initially placed in the overcrowded Atlanta federal penitentiary, Al displayed gallows humor mixed with some sense of optimism. "Uncle Sam got me busted on a bookkeeping rap," Al told a fellow prisoner. "Ain't that the best!" He added hopefully, "If I could just go for a walk. If I could just look at buildings again and smell that Lake Michigan, I'd give a million." Any optimism Capone might have harbored was quickly tempered by the awful truth of his current situation. Soon after arriving in Atlanta, the Big Guy received a triple whammy: he was diagnosed with central-nervous-system syphilis, gonorrhea, and a perforated septum due to chronic cocaine abuse. He was only thirty-three years old.

As Al's health went downhill, so did his temperament. He became prone to mood swings and long-winded boasting about his accomplishments. He was constantly harassed by some of the nation's most violent miscreants, who were more than a little jealous of Capone's previous life. "Where're the broads and booze now, fat boy?" they taunted. The Big Guy was resented by low-life inmates, who dismissed his soup kitchen endeavors, instead perceiving him as an ostentatious rich bloat. He was practically a white-collar criminal locked up with child rapists. For the most part, the threats led to nothing and evaporated. Capone spent his days in the shoe repair shop and settled in as best he could. Just as Capone seemed to be coming to terms with his plight, his world was rocked by news that presaged Capone's total descent into hell. In the fall of 1934, Capone was informed that he was being transferred to the penal system's newly completed monument to sadism: The Rock, aka Alcatraz. This bleak institution, situated on a small island in San Francisco Bay, was already being whispered about in the mess halls of America's prisons.

Although inmates are prone to exaggeration, there was no way they could inflate the truth of this torture chamber. One prisoner transferred to Alcatraz said, "The buildup makes Alcatraz pretty bad, but the reality is worse." The prison sat above an abandoned military garrison on a 120-foot promontory. Prisoners were housed in single-occupancy, five-by-nine-foot cells, not allowed to communicate with one another, or the guards for that matter. With the exception of cafeteria time, the prisoners were kept in silent confinement. Men were routinely driven over the edge by the boredom alone. Rule infractions landed a prisoner in D Block, or solitary confinement, in which the cells were completely devoid of light, and the prisoners received only bread and water through a slit in the door. This sadistic chamber broke down some men in six minutes, others in a couple days, yet some were kept in for as long as six months, exiting into the light of day clinically insane. One unhinged inmate, assigned to chopping wood on the dock, suddenly began chopping the fingers off his left hand. After removing them all, he begged a guard to amputate his chopping hand.

When Capone got the news of his transfer, he was fully aware of what it meant, as were his prison tormentors. "You're going to the Rock, Al, have a nice long ride to Alcatraz," someone teased. Capone exploded in all directions. His cellmate, Red Rudensky, later wrote about the event: "All the fire and hate and strength and torment erupt[ed] suddenly." Capone let loose a profanity-laced tirade at the guards, attacking them with all his might. "You'll never take me out of here!" he shouted before flinging himself at a guard, who signaled for help. When it arrived, the Big Guy was thrown into a wall, slumping to the floor unconscious.

Capone had good reason to be frantic over the news. His tenure on the Rock, coupled with his insidious illness, was nothing short of a prolonged nightmare. Initially, Capone's work assignment was on the bucket brigade, mopping the bathhouse floor, where he earned the nickname The Wop with the Mop. After a year of begging, Capone persuaded the warden to allow him twenty minutes a day to form a band with other prisoners. Al had his family send him top of the line banjos, mandolins, and music charts and he succeeded in teaching himself some rudimentary songs. On drums was "Machine Gun" Kelly, while sax chores were handled by kidnapper Harmon Whaley. The ensemble was disbanded after a violent row erupted during a rehearsal.

After the disbanding, things went quickly downhill for Capone. As in Atlanta, there were factions who hated Capone simply because he was Capone. He was a racketeer businessman imprisoned with two-bit thugs. One Alcatraz clique known as the Texas Cowboys made it their mission to kill the Big Guy. After one of the gang stabbed Capone repeatedly with a scissors from the barber shop, Capone was rushed to the hospital. The offender was given an incredible six months in solitary. Meanwhile Capone's sexual paresis had spread to his brain, and he became increasingly delusional and disoriented. Physically, he lost his impressive girth, his hairline, and his Italian-olive complexion. After one frightening bout of delirium in 1938, Capone was placed in a mental ward, but it was clearly too late. When Capone got into a disgusting feces-throwing battle with a patient in an adjacent cage, officials knew it was only a matter of time before he would be remanded to his wife's custody.

In 1935, with Curly, as well as Jake Guzik, now imprisoned, Frank Nitti, Paul Ricca, and Joe Accardo were left to oversee the Outfit's business. Although Nitti had seniority, it was Ricca, as liaison to the Commission, and Accardo who took charge behind the scenes. Ricca seized the moment and nourished private relationships with Meyer Lansky and Lucky Luciano. Although Nitti was allowed to sit on his leather throne at the Bismark Hotel, the Ricca-Accardo-Humphreys triumvirate created a power fusion that far exceeded Nitti's own designs. While Ricca's work was mostly ambassadorial, Accardo's talents, which differed from Humphreys', drew him to a racket much more suited to his tough-guy exterior: gambling.

4.

Joe's Racket: Running the Games (The New Booze)

Bootlegging was always seen by the gangsters as a temporary cash cow. When the Eighteenth Amendment's repeal became imminent, the Outfit kept a watchful eye for new sources of treasure, such as the union invasions that were scripted by Curly Humphreys. Or perhaps the new windfall would come from the groundwork being laid by Johnny Rosselli in the embryonic Hollywood "dream factory." But while Curly and Johnny concocted grand schemes, looking for the "new booze" as Curly called it, someone had to tend to the relatively mundane task of keeping the ship of crime afloat. The job required a decisive executive who understood the importance of instilling fear in rivals, but who nonetheless appreciated that violence had to be kept to an absolute minimum. Much as the smooth-talking Humphreys was the only choice for the role of union mastermind, streetwise Joe Accardo topped the short list of Outfitters equipped to oversee the universal staple of gang rackets: gambling.

Joe's World

At the time Joe Accardo took control of the Outfit's "games," Chicago gambling was a multiheaded hydra that included card and dice games, slot machines, and sports betting, especially on horse racing. (See the Appendix for a detailed history of gambling in Chicago.) In a few years, Accardo would expand his gambling empire to include the forerunner of the now legal lottery, "numbers," also known as policy, and the jukebox racket. The Outfit made certain each game was rigged in its favor; the gamblers knew it but played on regardless. Although they assumed many forms, the Outfit's gambling endeavors were not as closely scrutinized as their union machinations. By the time Accardo took the reins, there was little need for early-morning bombings that were guaranteed to invite newsprint.

Thus details are scarce regarding Joe's day-to-day exploits during this period. However, much is known about the gambling world he lorded over. Joe's responsibilities consisted of having his crew police the pool-rooms, barrooms, and secret gambling parlors, keeping the proprietors in line, making sure they paid a cut to the Outfit. A compulsive gambler himself, Joe was known to attend many of the floating games, where surprisingly he often lost. Joe also became a devout billiards enthusiast, albeit with mixed results. On one occasion, Accardo was hustled by a pool shark who had rigged a table to be slightly off-kilter. After adjusting his own stroke accordingly, he challenged the Outfit boss, who accepted and was soundly beaten. When the subversion was detected, one of the Outfit's enforcers offered to whack the foolish pool shark. "Nah. Leave him alone," decreed Accardo. "He cheated me fair and square." Although there existed numerous permutations of the games, the key variations were as follows:

1. Card Games

Throughout much of the history of card gambling, the games of choice fell into two categories: percentage games, such as poker, where the players challenge one another equally, with the house keeping a fixed percentage of every winning pot; or banking games, such as blackjack, faro, and baccarat, where the player is pitted against the house directly. Both percentage and banking games can be further subdivided into contests largely determined by chance, or those by skill.

By far the most popular card game for both the professional gambler and the house is the game of chance known as blackjack, the object of which is to draw cards whose face value is as close to twenty-one as possible without exceeding it. The gambler likes it because the action is fast, with a lucky streak bringing in a few minutes what it might take a poker player all night to amass. The house prefers blackjack because it allows a multitude of ways to gain a cheater's advantage: Cards can be marked in numerous ways; shills can drive up the stakes against the "mark" (victim); the dealer would be hired by the gang for his skills of prestidigitation, which permitted him to to palm or insert cards into the deal at will; a well-positioned mirror kept the dealer informed of what the mark was holding. The mathematics of the game, even without cheating, affords the house an average 10 percent advantage over the player. In other words, the house will always win in the end.

An example of a skill game is poker, wherein the players make continuous mathematical calculations attempting to improve their hands and discern the hands held by their adversaries. Unlike many card games that can be played purely for social enjoyment, poker is virtually non-existent outside the realm of gambling. Poker is the most intense card game, with gamesmanship ("poker faces" and "bluffs") a key component of success. Due to its antisocial, adversarial nature, poker attracts rugged individualists, willing to do anything to defeat their opponents, including waiting them out: The poker champion must possess great patience, given that a marathon game can last for days. All the above factors add up to make poker the passionate interest of a relatively small minority. (Studies conducted in Las Vegas casinos showed that poker accounted for only 1.7 percent of total gambling revenues.)

2. Dice Games and Roulette

Dominating the many variations of dice games is craps, in which two dice are thrown in hopes of rolling a 7 or 11. The house wins on rolls of 2, 3, or 12, with the remaining numbers being rollovers, or "points."[1] When played honestly, the lightning-fast craps game can be among the fairest, with the house holding only a 5 percent advantage. The trouble was that the Outfit, and other hoods, rarely played it straight. Craps is among the easiest games to manipulate, or "gimmick": Dice can be "loaded" (weighted), with the fixed die inserted into the game by a shill adept at palming; tables and dice can be manufactured with magnets installed to force the winning house numbers 2, 3, or 12.

Roulette is another game of chance favored by some weekend gamblers. With thirty-eight slots on a spinning wheel ready to catch one ball, the game has two slots (0 and 00) reserved for the house, thus giving the player 36–1 odds of winning on a single-number bet. But the house pays out only 34–1, giving it a guaranteed profit. In addition, like craps, roulette is easily gimmicked with magnetic circuits or mechanical pins that pop up to block a slot while the wheel is spinning. Although estimates vary, it is safe to say that illegal profits from dice and roulette games netted crime gangs in the hundreds of millions per year nationally.

---

1. The game had its origins in eighteenth-century Europe, where it was known as hazard. It was introduced to America in New Orleans, where it became popular with African-Americans, who are widely credited with creating its playing rules. Much like jazz music, craps quickly expanded beyond the borders of the Big Easy, migrating up the Mississippi River to the Windy City.

3. Coin-Operated Devices

Conveniently for the Outfit, slot machines (also known as one-armed bandits) and pinball machines were mass-produced in the Chicago environs, arguably the capital of those games. The slot machine was invented in California by Charles Fey at the turn of the century with the introduction of the Liberty Bell device. It was improved in 1906 by Stephen Mills of Chicago. From that time on, all ten slot-machine manufacturers set up shop in the Windy City, where by 1931 they fell under the control of the Outfit. Not merely content to control the devices' distribution, the Outfit created more revenue by manufacturing the machines. For this enterprise, they employed the services of former boxer and Outfit wheelman Joey Aiuppa. Aiuppa set up shop in Cicero, where he ran Taylor and Company, ostensibly a furniture manufacturing shop. In reality, the only furniture they produced were slot machines. When Taylor's bookwork was later confiscated, it was determined that the Outfit was pulling down an extra $300,000 per year from selling their one-armed "furniture."

The slot machine was a brilliant distillation of all the requisite gambling elements into a cheap mechanical beast: it took the money in, set the game in motion, and made the payouts. The typical arrangement had the Outfit splitting the profits fifty-fifty with the bar hosting the device. Added to its allure was that an initial investment of $100 for the purchase of the machine was typically paid off in its first ten days of operation. A Senate investigation estimated that a gangster who placed two hundred slot machines realized at least $5,000 per week after splitting the take with the storefront owner. The slot was attractive not only to the hoods, but also to the gambling masses, since it allowed Depression-era players, who could ill afford the high stakes of horse racing, to take their chances one nickel at a time.

The fundamentals of the slots are elegantly simple: When a coin is inserted and a lever pulled, three cylinders of twenty characters each (displaying pictures of bars, bells, cherries, lemons, oranges, and plums) begin spinning. When the reels stop, a player wins if all three cylinders show matching icons. Although the player has a reasonable chance to win, the payout odds change constantly, from a 1–1 prize to the exceedingly rare jackpot. Of course the machine's criminal owners make certain the payout is dwarfed by the amount wagered. The machine is also preadjusted so that its profits are guaranteed: typically from 25 to 50 percent of all moneys inserted. Even so, the one-armed bandits, like craps, were a huge success with both the player and the Outfit, which grossed untold millions of tax-free dollars.

Crime gangs like the Outfit subverted the antigambling laws by asserting that the machines were "for amusement purposes only." However, the machines could easily be rigged to dispense tokens, chewing gum, or free plays to a winner, but then with a secret pull of a lever by the proprietor, pay out cash. Payouts could also be made on the sly, with patrons stealthily exchanging their worthless chips and trinkets for cash.

Nationally, estimates put the gross take from slots at over $100 million annually, with 20 percent of that earmarked for official corruption. With so much at stake, only the most trusted Outfit associates were given the slot machine racket. Of course, Joe Accardo was the overall boss, but directly under him was Eddie "Big Head" Vogel, who had started running slots during the waning days of Al Capone's regime. Under Accardo and Vogel, the Outfit spread one-armed bandits to many other states. Often these extra-Illinois ventures solidified the Outfit's association with other crime gangs, especially those of New York, led by Lucky Luciano, Ben Siegel, and Meyer Lansky.[2] By the 1940s, an estimated 140,000 slot machines were in operation nationwide, grossing an astonishing $540 million per year, with only half the machines legal, taxpaying "amusement" gadgets.

4. Pinball

With the slot games coming under scrutiny by officials, some bar owners installed another game – this one a descendant of the Victorian parlor game bagatelle – known as pinball. In this variation, a ball is released into a glass-covered table, while the player uses hand-operated flippers, and more than a little body English, in an attempt to force the ball to knock over as many "pins" as possible. Although initially conceived as an amusement game, the hoods appropriated the game for gambling purposes, with machines that paid off in cash instead of free games and sundries. The machines cost approximately twice as much as slots to manufacture, and the table's large size (fifty by twenty inches) made them harder to ship and less easy to fit into bars. Thus, pinball was a distant runner-up in popularity to the slots. Games of lesser importance included 26, faro, keno, the punchboard, and chuck-a-luck. No matter how trifling the profit, the Outfit missed no opportunity to run a game.

---

2. The intergang agreement is believed to have been reached when the New York bosses met with Outfit leaders in a Chicago restaurant in 1934.

5. Dog and Pony Shows

Equal in importance to "parlor game" gambling rackets for Joe Accardo was the game known as the sport of kings. Horse racing itself did not provide direct income – the Outfit did not aspire to own horses – but the ancillary world of "making book" on the race results provided staggering amounts of easy-to-skim hard cash.

Even before the Outfit assumed the reins, their father figure, Al Capone, had already made inroads into the race game, first with dogs, then later with horses. (For details, see the gambling appendix.) Once entrenched in the sport, the gang learned that racetracks provided them important benefits that eclipsed those derived from race fixing.

Although the races themselves brought great profits to the Outfit – according to his own paperwork, Paul Ricca's cut was $80,000 per year from two tracks alone – the real allure of the racetracks for the Outfit has never been grasped by the public. According to Jim Ciatola, who worked for Unione Siciliana consigliere Joseph Bulger (Imburgio), "The tracks provided truckloads of cash, which made them an ideal setup for money laundering." Previous to the track ploy, members of the Outfit made so much cash during the bootlegging days that, fearing tax problems, they often buried it in their backyards or in other parts of their homes. "Very often they put the money in five-gallon cans in which they drilled air holes," says Ciatola. "What the Outfitters failed to realize was that after a few years the money got moldy and developed a stench. They were worried that if they took it to the bank or tried to spend it, the bank tellers or the IRS would get suspicious. In addition, the Treasury had just changed the size of U.S. currency, so old bills were conspicuous. So they used the tracks to exchange the bills. Sometimes they paid the winners with old bills, but most of them were sent to the Federal Reserve. It was hilarious. The G was laundering money for the Outfit and didn't know it."

One Outfitter with a huge cash overflow was Paul Ricca. Knowledge-able sources assert that the Waiter hid half a million dollars in a hidden space under his roof. In fact, the gang stashed so much bootlegging money that it is a virtual certainty that there are still undiscovered stashes throughout Chicagoland.

6. Bookmaking

The racetracks became a money mill in every sense of the word. Not only were the fixed races generating profits and the tellers laundering money as fast as they could count it, but the racetracks provided the scaffolding for the real profit machine known as bookmaking. The bookmaker's key function is to allow gamblers to place offtrack bets on sporting events (predominantly horse racing), then illegal in every state except Nevada. (Decades later, when state-run offtrack betting was legalized, bookmakers expanded their domain to cover other sporting events such as football, basketball, and boxing.) Although the upperworld barons saw to the enactment of legislation such as the 1894 Percy-Gray Law in New York, which outlawed offtrack bookmaking, the bookies continued to flourish. The Internal Revenue Service estimated that by 1940 there were fifteen thousand individual bookmakers nationwide. Joe Accardo and his associates even dabbled, albeit briefly, with the idea of "going legit" with their bookmaking enterprise. At the Outfit's urging, Mayor Ed Kelly sponsored a state bill to legalize racing handbooks in Illinois. Not only would the Outfit benefit from legislation that legitimized one of the "games" they already controlled, but Kelly could multiply his income as a result of the graft that would accompany the licensing procedure. During the period of debate in the state legislature (1935–36), two representatives strongly opposing the bill were shot to death. Although the bill passed, Governor Henry Horner vetoed it. It didn't matter. With the Kelly-Outfit arrangement, there were soon more than one thousand bookie joints in the Windy City.

Once again the European immigrants were ahead of the curve: They knew that offtrack betting was widely accepted, and legal, in Europe, where it was the principal form of horse-race wagering. "Off-course" betting was legalized in France in 1930, largely as a method of discouraging bookmaking. The combined offtrack bets in England and France accounted for 85 percent of all bets placed. It was only a matter of time before the American upperworld prevailed and seized the action.[3]

At least one key bookmaking takeover was assigned to Joe Accardo during this period. One can imagine Frank Nitti, Paul Ricca, Curly Humphreys (before going off to "college"), and Joe Accardo at one of their daily morning meetings deciding to acquire the bookmaking opera-

---

3. New York's Off-Track Betting Corporation opened its doors for business in 1970 at Grand Central Terminal. Within five years it would command 147 locations and become the largest "retail establishment" in New York, grossing $758,673,000 per year.

tion of the Russell brothers.[4] In the thirties, Harry "the Muscle" Russell and his brother David ran the most profitable 'lay-off' operation in the Loop from their headquarters at 186 North Clark Street. In bookie parlance, a lay-off joint is a place that takes bets based on odds and the results it receives over the telegraphic wire service provided by a larger organization. At these locations, bettors pick three numbers they hope will correspond to three winning horses assigned the same numbers. Author Joseph Albini described the lay-off in his book *The American Mafia*: "By knowing the results of the first two races [from the wire service], the operators can foretell how many potential winners they have . . . If they find that they have a large number [of bets] with the first two winning digits, they can then 'lay off' a portion of these bets with other gamblers. The 'lay-off' here refers to the process whereby the operator bets with a larger gambling concern a portion of the customers'' bets having the first two digits. By doing this, should the last digit create a large number of winning tickets, the operator can collect from the lay-off source and hence balance his own losses.'

Of course the lay-off was only employed on the rare occasion when large numbers of bettors held the same two winning numbers. Nonetheless, the wire information was crucial to keeping bookies from having what could have been a catastrophic day. Key among other reasons for the bookies' dependence on the wire reports were that bettors might have race results relayed by telephone without the bookie knowing the contest had been concluded (such "postbetting" could destroy a bookie); or conversely, a crooked bookmaker with information right off the wire could accept losing bets for a race he knew was already decided. For these and many other reasons that will be seen, the wire service was indispensable to the race betting business. The wire operation, controlled by an upperworld collusion with Western Union, was able to extort huge sums from all bookies for their precious information. The profits far surpassed even what the Outfit took in from the bookies. It would therefore become targeted for takeover by the Outfit, but the process would not go into high gear for a few years to come. In the meantime, Joe and the Outfit were happy to run their stable of bookies and muscle in on Harry the Muscle.

---

4. During this period, the boys met at a revolving list of Italian restaurants and saloons, so as to remain untroubled by the authorities. According to one insider, the gang had no fears of being overheard while conducting business: "When they came in, everybody else cleared out."

Joe Accardo was fast mellowing in his role, having learned the art of the velvet glove from Curly. Just a few short years earlier, a bat-wielding Joe Batters would have dispensed with the Russell brothers in a markedly sanguine manner. Now, the nattily attired *boss* Accardo simply arranged a business merger. It was a partnership that flourished, expanding into other states, for over a decade.

7. The Sharks

Backstopping the gang's gambling revenue was the affiliated scam known as loan "sharking," a bastardization of Shakespeare's "Shylock," the Jewish moneylending antagonist of *The Merchant of Venice*. With so many of their customers losing at their almost-impossible-to-win games, the Outfit became a full-service provider, offering high-interest loans to those who could not meet obligations made to bookies. The scam consisted of the Outfit's channeling a portion of their huge profits to loan sharks at, say, 2 percent interest. The sharks, known in the Chicago vernacular as juice men, then loaned the money out to the "juiced-up" loser at double or triple that interest *per week*. This compound interest is known as the sharks' vigorish, or vig. It is easy to see how a debt can rise exponentially in short time: A $100 loan becomes $120 at the end of week one, $144 a week later, $172.80 the third week, and $207.36 the fourth week, etc. Often, a minimal-paying client ends up paying back the original loan numerous times over – much like the now legal version of loan-sharking known as credit cards.

Given that their victims were believed to be other lowlifes, the sharks were virtually unmolested by police. And since no one was being arrested, loan-sharking benefited from low overhead, as graft was unnecessary. With millions loaned out at any one time, loan-sharking was second only to gambling in profits for the Outfit.

With the combined revenues from sharking, bookmaking, and the innumerable versions of gambling, the Outfit's coffers were bursting. And the booming business was supervised for the Outfit by Joe Accardo, who personally tapped Outfit chieftain Louis Campagna to run two gambling joints, the Austin Club and the El Patio, in Cicero. Years later, Campagna testified that he "bought into" the operation for $1,500, but netted over $75,000 per year. Accardo's other key crewmen helping to hold it all together were Frankie Pope (bookies), Pete Penovich (games of chance), and Hymie "Loud Mouth" Levine (collection).

By 1934, Joe Accardo was overseeing an empire that numbered more than seventy-five hundred gambling establishments in Chicago alone. In 1941, the *Chicago Tribune* unearthed some of the Outfit's books and reported that by then "the boys" were grossing $320,000 per month; estimates of the portion of the take that was funneled to Ed Kelly and his bribe-infested City Hall have run as high as 50 percent. The headquarters for the graft exchange was the Lawndale Scrap Iron & Metal Company on South Kedzie Avenue. In what must have appeared a surreal scene, politicians and gangsters met at prearranged times inside the Lawndale office. In one line were the gangsters with cash in hand; in the other, the pols waited with open palms outstretched. From behind his desk, a former investigator for the state's attorney's office coordinated the corrupt circus, periodically announcing, "You're next."

With Joe Accardo's games running smoothly, the gang continued to keep its antennae scanning for the next source of treasure. The next target chosen was the logical extension of local union work already under the aegis of Curly Humphreys. According to Curly's daughter Llewella, the scam had its genesis some years earlier when she'd overheard her parents in conversation. "It all started with my mother," Llewella recalled. "She was a fan, crazy about movie stars. So she mentioned to my father, 'Why don't we go into this business so that I can meet everybody?'"

The subsequent extorting of the entire motion picture industry gave the Outfit a foothold in Hollywood that it never entirely relinquished. Although a high-profile bust-up of the racket in 1941 gave the impression that the scam was over, in truth the convictions were too little, too late. The gangsters from the Windy City had so thoroughly infiltrated key unions and production houses that their influence remained intact for decades to come. In its embryonic stage, the assault on Hollywood followed Curly's proven formula that combined political payoffs and labor racketeering. Years before Humphreys went to jail in 1934, he laid the groundwork for the "Hollywood Extortion Case" when he met his next pawn, Thomas Maloy.

Part Two

Going National

5.

The Local Takeovers

"**N**o politician ever turned his back on a bundle of currency," Tommy Maloy once said to his union subordinates. Emulating knowledgeable hoods like Curly Humphreys, Maloy followed up his words with action. As the boss of Local 110, the Motion Picture Operators' Union, the feisty Irishman resembled Humphreys in one other way: When the payoff failed, Maloy upped the ante until he got what he needed. Although he succeeded for a time, Maloy learned the hard way that he was a mere stepping-stone in a great Outfit scam that saw them plant permanent roots in the City of Angels. In a three-stage operation that included Outfit takeovers of two key unions and Johnny Rosselli's maneuvers in Los Angeles, the gang from Cicero undertook the first of many endeavors that propelled them permanently onto the national scene.

Thomas E. Maloy was born in Chicago in 1893 and spent his youth gaining a reputation as a tougher-than-usual gang member. Eventually he came to the attention of local union strong-arm Maurice "Mossy" Enright, known as the boss of the building trade unions as well as the garbage workers. For a time, Enright had been a slugger for North Side gangster Deanie O'Banion, before evolving into a fearsome union organizer who did not shy away from bombing a recalcitrant business owner's building. Maloy became Enright's chauffeur, squiring Mossy around in his long, terrorist-filled sedan known as the Gray Ghost. The young Maloy also became Mossy's protégé, absorbing his teacher's insights until one day in 1925, when Enright earned the distinction of becoming Chicago's first drive-by shooting victim.

Maloy proceeded to take work as a projectionist in a small Chicago movie house, while simultaneously running a craps game under the theater's stage. After performing muscle work for the theater operators' union boss, Jack Miller, Maloy was bequeathed the top spot when Miller resigned. Maloy retained his position through intimidation backed up by blackjacks and dynamite. Supposedly, at Maloy's first official union meeting, the membership erupted in a near riot, threatening strikes against the theaters and violence against its own leadership. Maloy wasted no time asserting his position by spraying the union hall's ceiling with bursts of machine gun fire. The members lost their nerve and became submissive to Chicago's newest "alpha dog." With his theater as a base of operations and with Enright as inspiration, Maloy quickly began slugging his own way up, becoming a never-convicted suspect in nine murders, including that of one unbowed theater owner murdered in Maloy's office.

Tommy Maloy's chief scam, and the one that brought him to the attention of Curly Humphreys, was the systematic extortion of local movie theaters, especially the lucrative Balaban & Katz chain of houses. Barney Balaban, who later moved west to run Paramount Pictures with his brother, and Stan Katz, future VP of MGM, started with one theater in 1908 and by 1930 had built up Chicago's most prosperous movie chain, numbering dozens of houses. The B&K empire was obviously dependent on its film operators, and by extension, Tommy Maloy's Motion Picture Operators' Union. In a manner that would have brought a smile to the face of his mentor Mossy Enright, Maloy extracted huge sums from B&K (among others) for the promise of union tranquillity. At the time, union rules mandated that there be two workers in the projection booth, one for picture and one, the fader, to synchronize the phonograph machine to the then silent movies. It was known that one man could perform both tasks, so Maloy told B&K he could arrange for one-man projection suites in their theaters for a "contribution" to his favorite charity: Tommy Maloy. In addition, Maloy was able to squeeze small wage increases from his marks, thus keeping his membership placated. Like so many other labor racketeers, Maloy made a show of throwing crumbs to his membership while simultaneously robbing them blind.

While Maloy enjoyed his $125 per week B&K kickbacks (in addition to his $25,000-a-year union salary), his workers made their own contributions to the Maloy Fund: "Special assessments" were added to union dues whenever Maloy needed a Caribbean cruise, or a $22,000 European vacation with his mistress; unwitting members rewarded their leader with gifts of a $4,000 bathroom and a $5,000 bar, so he could ostensibly conduct business at home. Investigators later conservatively estimated that Maloy plundered half a million dollars from his union treasury.

It was a virtual impossibility that Maloy's golden goose would evade the Outfit's radar. In fact, the gang had been interested in the entertainment business since the days when Al Capone had first booked his favorite jazz bands into his speakeasies. At that time, Capone had developed a relationship, likely a silent partnership, with Dr. Jules Stein in his infant booking agency with the inflated name the Music Corporation of America (MCA). Native Chicagoan Stein got his start as a booker of bands and sometime bootlegger. Like Capone, Stein battled with Roger Touhy, who tried to muscle Stein out of the booze business. It is widely believed that Stein allied with the Syndicate to gain protection from Touhy. As one Chicago investigator told writer Dan Moldea, "Touhy was nothing next to Capone and his boys, and that's where Stein's connections were." Stein was soon using Capone's musclemen to force theaters to book his acts. One such thug, Willie Bioff, would figure prominently in one of the Outfit's boldest takeovers. Among Stein's earliest clients was a young actor named Ronald Reagan, who frequented the Club Belvedere in Iowa, which was owned by the Outfit.

An interesting sidebar to the saga of Capone hitman Jack McGurn reflects the increasing camaraderie between gangsters and the Hollywood glitterati during the Syndicate era. Recently, Bing Crosby biographer J. Roger Osterholm wrote of the crooner's periodic rounds of golf played with partner Jack McGurn: "Crosby just loved golf; he didn't care who he played with," said Osterholm. "I stress that it was just very innocent; it was just to play golf." Osterholm adds that Crosby ditched McGurn when he learned of his line of work. But the biographer vastly understated the true nature of the Crosby-McGurn liaison.

Recently released FBI documents and interviews with knowledgeable Chicagoans add a far more sinister dimension to Crosby's odd golf pairing. The FBI's documentary record shows that Crosby was the unlucky recipient of numerous Black Hand-type extortion threats, some of which are included in his FBI file. According to the Bureau, Crosby paid out many thousands of dollars over the years to the extortionists. At some point, Crosby had enough, according to one witness who circulated on the Outfit's periphery. That witness, a woman whom we will call Ruth Jones, was McGurn's golfing partner. One day, Jones asked McGurn how he came to play golf with Crosby, and McGurn told her the origins of their friendship.

"Crosby was doing a gig at the Chicago Theater on Wabash," says Jones, "when he was met backstage by two freelance Black Handers." The extortionists gave Crosby two days to pay up, or else. The savvy Crosby knew where to seek relief: his manager, the legendary Dr. Jules Stein, founder of MCA. As a man familiar with the workings of the Capone Syndicate, Stein knew just where to turn for help with Crosby's Black Hand problem. His name was Jack McGurn.

On the appointed day, McGurn arrived at the theater, where he was introduced to Crosby in advance of the extortionists' arrival. The two thugs arrived at what they thought was Crosby's dressing room, only to be met by the legendary enforcer McGurn. "They knew very well who Jack was and what they were in for," recalls Ruth Jones. "Jack beat the shit out of them and then threw them out into the back alley, which borders the dressing room."[1] Bing Crosby was both beholden and enthralled. He engaged McGurn in a lengthy conversation, at times asking what favor the singer could do for the gangster. McGurn refused all the overtures, but when the conversation turned to their mutual love of golf, McGurn's resolve weakened: "Well, there is one thing you might do – meet me for a round of golf." Crosby happily obliged, and the two were soon hitting the links at Chicago's Evergreen Country Club. The friendship blossomed, with McGurn playing rounds with Crosby on McGurn's visits to Los Angeles to do business with Johnny Rosselli and other Outfitters. Stein later moved to Hollywood, where MCA would live up to its vaunted moniker, becoming the most powerful agency in town. It should also be recalled that prior to Hollywood's christening as the movie capital, the Windy City had that distinction. Like Stein, many other local

---

1. McGurn was certainly versed in the ways of muscling entertainers. In 1927, he was given a 25 per cent interest in the North Side Club the Green Mile for settling the club's dispute with comedian Joe E. Lewis. After the popular Lewis, who had been the club's star attraction for a year, jumped ship for a better offer at a rival club, McGurn was brought in to talk some sense into Lewis. Before opening at his new venue, the Rendezvous, Lewis was informed by McGurn, "You'll never live to open." Lewis did in fact open, but one week later he was met by three thugs, two of whom crushed his skull with pistol butts, while the third hacked away mercilessly at Lewis' face with a large knife. Incredibly, he recovered, but the resultant brain damage left him unable to talk for months, and the knife wounds left him disfigured. During his convalescence, Lewis received a $10,000 gift from Al Capone. The story was dramatized in the 1957 Frank Sinatra film *The Joker Is Wild*.

movie folk relocated west, forming the backbone of the motion picture industry as it is known today.[2] In the 1920s, one fifth of all films shot were produced in Chicago, and since these productions needed cooperation from Syndicate-controlled trade unions, Capone (via Curly) became well acquainted with the workings of the movie machine. Ironically, the studios paid the Syndicate's unions off for the privilege of immortalizing many of Chicago's own hoods in gangster films starring actors such as Jimmy Cagney and Edward G. Robinson.

The Outfit's encroachment into the theatrical world was, in hindsight at least, a predictable expansion of its empire. Al Capone reportedly ordered the takeover of Maloy's union from his "vacation" home on the island of Alcatraz. Others believe the decision was reached in an Outfit meeting with Joe Accardo, Frank Nitti, Curly Humphreys, Paul Ricca, and attorney Joe Bulger in attendance. Of course, the scenarios are not mutually exclusive. In any event, the gang bided their time, waiting for the perfect opening. They did not have long to wait, since Tommy Maloy's road to riches was becoming bumpy, and like so many before him, he sought out the help of Al Capone's heirs.

For years, a number of theater owners had refused to pay Maloy to waive the union's two-operators-per-booth requirement. By 1930, with the nation's financial depression adding to their woes, the owners had had enough and began complaining to local politicians, prompting a Cook County state's attorney to open an investigation into Maloy's activities. In desperation, Maloy turned to the Outfit's payoff guru, Curly Humphreys. Together the two men trundled off to the state capital in Springfield and began spreading around bags of cash. Consequently, legislation was introduced mandating the use of two operators "for the safety of the public." This was long after moviemakers began syncing the sound on the filmstrip, making the fader operators even more redundant. At the same time, one of Maloy's rivals for the union leadership turned up murdered. Some believe the description of the dapper young shooter with the mane of curly, dark hair precisely described Curly Humphreys. However, as with other gangland murders, nothing ever came of it.

---

2. Carl Laemmle, founder of Universal, started in Chicago, likewise Adolph Zukor; Barney Balaban, president of Paramount; Sam Katz, VP of MGM; and Leo Spitz, president of RKO. Actors from Chicago included Wallace Beery, Tom Mix, and Gloria Swanson.

The Hollywood Kid

With the Outfit's hooks now firmly embedded in Maloy's union, events unfolding in Los Angeles were about to play into its grand scheme. By the early thirties, the gang's West Coast ambassador, Johnny Rosselli, had also began to focus on the world of entertainment, very likely at the directive of his Chicago superiors. Rosselli's bootlegging partner, Tony Cornero, had moved on to Nevada, where he opened a gambling casino, cashing in on the newly passed Wide Open Gambling bill. The legislation was helped along by Johnny and Curly, who had made special graft-delivery trips to the state capital. Now Rosselli glommed onto the movie studio bosses, who were themselves enamored of gambling and gangsters.

Propitiously, Rosselli had recently become the Outfit's Los Angeles gambling czar, thanks to deals made back in his gang's Chicago headquarters, and agreements reached with their Commission counterparts in New York. By the time Capone "went away," he had struck a partnership with upperworld race-wire king Moses Annenberg: Capone's boys were paid $100,000 to muscle out Annenberg's Chicago competitors in the nascent wire business. Although the Outfit was not content to merely stay a partner in the lucrative wire service, at least it had a toehold. Out in the City of Angels, Johnny Rosselli became the point man for Annenberg's expanding empire, forcing bookies to subscribe to the service. With L.A. mayor Frank Shaw thoroughly bribed, the operation flourished. Given the studio bosses' predilection for the ponies and their infatuation with hoods, the suave Johnny Rosselli was a natural fit. Long before the Outfit's studio takeover scheme congealed, Hollywood had entered into a fawning relationship with gangsters: Ben Siegel of the New York gang was already a known conqueror of starlets; Frank Costello was chummy with Columbia's Harry Cohn and the William Morris Agency's George Wood; box office sensation (and gambling addict) George Raft was a virtual member of Owney Madden's gang out of New York (and later Arkansas).

Johnny Rosselli became the movie honchos' bookmaker and personal adviser, placing bets and socializing with the likes of Joe Schenck (United Artists), Harry Cohn (Columbia), and Joe Kennedy (RKO and Film Booking Office). As bookie to the studio heads, Johnny would glean information vital to the Outfit's movieland aspirations. By either threatening to expose hidden skeletons or to call their vigorish, Rosselli was able to acquire silent partnerships for the Outfit in many Hollywood careers. It is believed that in this way the hoods "sponsored" actors such as George Raft, Chico Marx, Jimmy Durante, Jean Harlow, Cary Grant, Clark Gable, and Marilyn Monroe. Rosselli's near fraternal bond with Harry Cohn gave him, and by proxy the Outfit, an education in the ways of the motion picture business. Cohn typified the thug as businessman. A former small-time crook from New York, "White Fang" Cohn was a ruthless executive who openly spoke of his reverence for Benito Mussolini, as well as his disdain for workers' unions. Although Depression-era Hollywood suffered huge drop-offs in profits, studio heads like Harry Cohn continued to live extravagant lifestyles, but the skilled workforce was forced to make concessions. By early 1933, studio employees watched in disbelief as their high-living employers slashed wages by a staggering 50 percent. On July 24, 1933, the International Alliance of Theatrical Stage Employees (IATSE) struck. The strike by IATSE, then the largest union in the entertainment field, and affiliated with 99 percent of the nation's theaters, could not be ignored by the studios and their collective, the Association of Motion Picture Producers (AMPP). When the AMPP resolved to break the strike, the choice for the role of strike-breaker was easy: Cohn's new tough-guy buddy from the Chicago Outfit, Johnny Rosselli.

Since many of Hollywood's glitterati were transplants from the Windy City, they were well acquainted with just how thorough the Outfit could be. "They asked if I could help," Rosselli later testified. "I said the only way to help is to fight fire with fire." And he did. Hiring a crew of local toughs, Rosselli kept the gates open for scab strikebreakers desperate for work. In one bitter, ugly week it was over, with the IATSE practically destroyed after its members deserted ship en masse when the union caved in to Rosselli. On the winner's side, the dapper Johnny Rosselli was elevated to the status of hero by the movie moguls, and he was soon seen at their palatial estates, enjoying tennis, swimming, and cavorting with an unending stream of beautiful starlets. Back in Chicago, Curly Humphreys began referring to Johnny as "the Hollywood kid," while his Hollywood friends nicknamed the affable mobster Gentleman Johnny. But it was not all play for Rosselli, who used his newfound propinquity to soak up intelligence on the inner workings of Hollywood. Little did Joe Schenck, Harry Cohn, and their producers' union realize that in schooling their bookmaking chum from Chicago, they were setting up the Outfit with a permanent, and lucrative, presence in the film industry. When he was put on the permanent AMPP payroll, Johnny Rosselli knew he had arrived.

Before long he invited his Chicago mates to barrel through the opening he had created.

In Chicago that same year, 1933, the final component of the master plan fell into place when a falling-down-drunk labor boss picked the wrong place to shoot off his mouth. The racketeer with the alcohol problem was George E. Browne, business manager for Local 2, the 450-member stagehands union, having assumed the post by pummeling the head of his predecessor with a lead pipe. Browne moonlighted by selling "protection" to the chicken dealers in Chicago's Fulton Street Market. Although Browne was believed to have been drunk every night of his life, this particular bender actually had a reason: Browne was celebrating the culmination of a highly lucrative scam.

Word of a good racket traveled fast in Chicago, and like the Outfit, George Browne had become aware of Tom Maloy's blackmailing gig with the Balaban & Katz theater chain. When Browne likewise decided to hop on the B&K gravy train, he had no idea he would end up as merely the middleman for the firm of Nitti, Accardo, Humphreys, et al.

Critical to the success of George Browne was his partnership with a brothel owner and all-around thug named Willie Morris Bioff. He would also prove to be the Achilles' heel of the entire operation, a player whose imprudence caught the Outfit by surprise too late in the game. The Russian-born Bioff was by all accounts an evolutionary malfunction. By the age of ten he was plying girls with candy, not for his own pleasure, but so that he might palm them off on older boys for ten cents apiece. When a girl attempted to rebel, he tortured her before beating her up. "Next time you talk this way," he scolded, "it's a dime's worth of acid in the face." Before he was twenty, the revolting Bioff was a full-fledged pimp on his way to owning his own brothel. For his "legitimate" day job, the pudgy Bioff became a $35-dollar-a-week union slugger responsible for enforcing dues payments. After serving time for pandering, Bioff took up the slightly less unsavory occupation of extortion: He sold protection to kosher chicken sellers in the same Fulton Street Market as George Browne.

When Bioff met George Browne, probably at Fulton's chicken stalls, Bioff grasped the financial implications of Browne's position. "No matter what anybody tells you, people do not have to eat," Bioff lectured Browne (as later recounted by Browne). "The only thing they really got to do is get laid or see a show whenever they can dig up the scratch." Since Bioff had the sex angle under control, he saw Browne as his ticket to untold riches.

Browne was likewise enamored of the repulsive beater of women and hired Bioff as chief slugger for his stagehands union. It was a marriage made in mob heaven: a goon who sold protection to kosher chicken dealers linked with one who protected the gentile chicken retailers.

Browne and Bioff's first extortions involved kickbacks paid them by strip-club owners who feared competition. The owners knew that if Browne and Bioff were kept comfortable, they would instruct their stagehand members not to work for any start-up clubs, effectively keeping them from operating. Browne and Bioff made the rounds, telling the established club owners that the movie house down the block was about to move into the far more lucrative strip-show trade. Suitably frightened, the owners always anted up.

Browne and Bioff believed they were doing fine until they learned about Tom Maloy's fleecing of B&K. Despite the Depression's having slowed business at the B&K chain, George Browne headed straight for Barney Balaban's hospital room, where he was awaiting treatment, to shake him down. Under the guise of a concerned union leader who had to sadly report that his workers were in desperate need of a 25 percent raise, George Browne made his appeal to Balaban. Balaban saw through Browne's transparent show of sympathy and cut right to the chase. Browne later testified to Balaban's response: "He said he was paying Tommy Maloy one hundred and fifty dollars a week. He said he would like to take care of me like that." After leaving to think it over, Browne called Balaban with his decision: He wanted $20,000 up front to cover retroactive pay cuts back to 1930. "Twenty thousand on the barrelhead or stink bombs at the busiest hours in every B&K house in town," Browne warned.

Balaban capitulated, on the stipulation that Browne come up with a way for Balaban to disguise the payoff from his stockholders. That proved easy, since Bioff had instituted a soup kitchen for unemployed stagehands. Balaban made his check out to the soup kitchen as a donation. The soup kitchen itself was meant to be anything but altruistic. The food was obtained for free, Capone-style, and was separated into two categories: cheap soup and bread for the unemployed and a free "deluxe menu" for politicians, cops, and judges – the real intended recipients of the largesse. "I never saw a whore who wasn't hungry, and I never saw a politician who wasn't a whore," Bioff said. "So we'll let them eat for nix." Writer George Murray described the deluxe menu thus: "It consisted of roast chicken with chestnut dressing, roast duck glazed with orange juice basting, roast prime of beef, broiled double lamb chops or pork chops, or tender porterhouse steaks. [It] occasionally had such delicacies as braised calf shank, oxtail stew, beef and kidney pie."

Balaban signed a $20,000 check over to The Stage Hands Union Soup Kitchen, $19,000 of which was split by Browne and Bioff, with the remaining $1,000 covering Balaban's attorney's fee. The money was supposed to go to the workers as a retroactive reimbursement of the 1929 pay cut. That was the ruse, in any event. As Bioff later testified, "The restoration of the pay cut was forgotten. We were not interested in that then or at any other time. We didn't care whether wages were reduced or raised. We were only interested in getting the dough, and we didn't care how we got it." Bioff and Browne did offer one display of altruism: The soup kitchen received two cases of canned soup, costing Browne and Bioff $2.50 each.

Browne and Bioff did their best to conceal their childlike glee from Balaban when he handed over the bribe. But once out of earshot, the duo celebrated as if they had just hit the trifecta at Sportsman's Park. "As soon as we were alone, Willie and me laughed and did a little fandango dance step in our office," Browne later testified. "Then we decided we ought to go to the Club 100 to have a few drinks and talk to the girls. We both knew the guy who ran the club, Nicky Dean."

The decision to party at the Club 100 was momentous. The former Yacht Club on East Superior Street was now run for the Outfit by Al Capone's cousin Nick Circella, also known as Nicky Dean. His brother, August, ran burlesque houses, thus the Circellas were well acquainted with the stagehands union and Browne and Bioff. "Pride goeth before the fall," warns the old maxim, and it was never proven more accurate than in the events and repercussions of that night at the Club 100. George Browne had a reputation as a loudmouthed drunk, often making the rounds of the speakeasies, where he brandished his pistol and pretended to be a gangster. The real gangsters saw him as a buffoon, a harmless court jester. However, on this night, Browne, the village idiot, and his chum Willie the pimp, would actually impress the professional hoods when they let on about their newest scam. Although tonight they were in ecstasy over their brilliant B&K maneuver, they would most certainly come to wish they had never concocted it.

After a couple of hours in the club's first floor playing the dice game 26, the inebriated pair took a couple of the club girls upstairs to play craps. By now the liquor had typically loosened George Browne's tongue as he sought to impress his new lady friend with the story of his financial windfall. Word quickly got back to Circella, and before the revelry ended,

Circella had managed to spend an hour alone with Browne, who happily bragged about the clout of his stagehands union.

The next day, Circella met with the Outfit for lunch at the Capri Restaurant, where he informed Nitti and Ricca what he had learned. A call was placed to Browne, who was still sleeping off the previous night's bender. A frightened Browne listened as Outfitter Frankie Rio ordered Browne to meet him at a Chicago intersection. Rio drove Browne around the city while the tearful union boss pleaded for his life. Unbeknownst to Browne, the Outfit's intent was nonviolent; they merely intended to put the fear of God in him. They succeeded. Two days later, Browne and Bioff were directed to the the Riverside home of Rio's bodyguard (and Frank Nitti's next-door neighbor), Harry Hochstein. Although they were led to believe that they were going to a social soirée with abundant female participation, upon arrival Browne and Bioff quickly realized that this was in fact an Outfit business meeting. In attendance were Nitti, Ricca, Charlie Fischetti, and an out-of-towner, Louis "Lepke" Buchalter. Browne and Bioff knew Lepke by reputation: He was the most notorious killer in the New York crime gang of Lucky Luciano. Although Curly Humphreys was not known to be in attendance, it is a virtual certainty that his union expertise played a large role in the Outfit's evolving strategies. Some believe that Curly was a participant, but that when details of the meeting emerged in later testimony, he was intentionally spared by witnesses due to his irreplaceable role in the Outfit.

Pieced together from subsequent testimony, key details of the Riverside meeting are known. After a sumptuous buffet, waiters served up Italian espresso and spumoni ice cream as Nitti called the meeting to order. He stated at the outset that he was aware Browne coveted the IATSE presidency, and that he had in fact narrowly lost his election bid at last year's convention. The next convention was to to be held one year hence in 1934 in Louisville, which brought Nitti to the point. "You gonna run for president again?" Nitti asked Browne. When Browne responded that he hoped to do just that, Nitti hypothesized, "Suppose this time we saw to it that you had enough votes to win. Hands down. No contest. Would you like that?" Of course Browne liked it. At that point Nitti made George Browne a classic "offer he couldn't refuse." "In this world if I scratch your back, I expect you to scratch mine. If you can win by yourself, you don't need us," Nitti teased. "But if you want our help, we'll expect you to cooperate. Is that fair enough?"

"That's fair enough," answered the Outfit's newest inductee, Browne.

Nitti nodded to Buchalter, signaling that he report back to Lucky Luciano, who would in turn deliver the New York stagehands union's delegation.

If the Outfit's "secret" agenda was not synthesized at the time of the Riverside meeting, it would soon be. In March 1934, three months before the IATSE convention, Johnny Rosselli returned east to update the Outfit on his Hollywood experience. It was decided to convene at Big Al's estate in Palm Island. In attendance were Nitti; Ralph Capone, who had been back and forth to Hollywood working with Johnny; Paul Ricca; Nicky (Dean) Circella; Charlie Fischetti; and Curly's assistant, Ralph Pierce. One mystery surrounding this critical planning session was the extent of Curly Humphreys' revered counsel. Although local scribes wrote that Curly spent his entire "lam" in Mexico, from where his liaison with the Outfit would have been problematic, it turns out that he was much closer to the action. According to numerous FBI sources noted in the huge Humphreys file, Curly and his unidentified blonde traveling companion spent many months in Bloomington, Indiana, a mere 234 miles southwest of Chicago. However, Jake Guzik likely had little involvement in this confab, as he was still serving out his tax conviction sentence. Browne and Bioff were not invited.

When the meeting was called to order, Johnny regaled his superiors for over an hour, explaining in detail the inner workings of the movie industry. Essentially, Rosselli explained, the Hollywood trade unions, such as IATSE, had been broken. The major studios, Johnny continued, were churning out a feature film a week, and fully 40 percent of their overhead was in the craft services. The monopolistic style of the major studios rendered them vulnerable to a strong union, should one emerge. Having already subsumed Maloy's Operators' Union and Browne's stagehands union, and poised to take over the weakened IATSE at the national convention, the Outfit was well positioned to "go Hollywood." Even Nitti had done some homework, arriving at the meeting armed with newspaper clippings from the Chicago financial pages. His research informed him that, despite a Depression-era drop-off, the movie business was the fourth-largest industry in the United States. Nitti had also determined that many of the major Hollywood studios were subsidiaries of the theater chains. Barney Balaban's brother John, for instance, ran Paramount studios. The Loew's theater chain was a holding company for Metro-Goldwyn-Mayer, while the president of Twentieth Century-Fox was the brother of Loew's president. Since the gangsters now had direct control over the exhibitors' employees, the theater owners, many with headquarters in New York, became the studios' Achilles' heel and were therefore chosen as the Outfit's first front of attack.

"So the guys in New York are already softened up for us," Nitti said. "They are just waiting for us to walk in the door and ask for money." He recalled how Al Capone had often expressed his desire to move in on Hollywood. It was well-known that many stars and producers were either juiced up or had other skeletons in their closets. If nothing else, they were vulnerable to blackmail. Nitti then concluded colorfully, "The goose is in the oven waiting to be cooked."

Nick Circella was designated Browne's nonstop watchdog, while Johnny Rosselli was directed to look over the shoulder of Bioff, who would soon be dispatched to Los Angeles. Before the meeting adjourned, the Outfit had voted to institute a methodical plan to infiltrate the business of movies, with Nitti closing the meeting by saying, "I think we can expect a permanent yield of a million dollars a year."

6.

"Hollywood, Here We Come" (The New Booze II)

In August 1933, the entertainment industry's biweekly newsletter *Variety* reported on the widely circulating rumor that "the Chicago crowd," was fixed to launch an assault on the 1934 IATSE convention. Although the trade paper was making reference to George Browne's predicted second try at the union presidency, the prognostication was more accurate than could be known at the time. In fact, the most significant "Chicago crowd," the Outfit, was about to hijack the convention, with George Browne as its front man.

On June 34, 1934, the IATSE delegates convened their biennial assemblage in Louisville, Kentucky, at the ominously named Brown Hotel on Broadway. In an unusual move, IATSE barred the local press from the closed-door proceedings. John Herchenroeder, editor of Louisville's *Courier-Journal*, recalled for crime reporter Hank Messick years later, "We sent a reporter over to the hotel, but he couldn't get in, so we ignored the convention." It soon became clear why prying eyes were not allowed to witness the furtive gathering. In attendance alongside union delegates were mobsters from all the major crime families: Meyer Lansky, Ben Siegel, Lucky Luciano, and Lepke Buchalter from New York; Longy Zwillman from New Jersey; Big Al Polizzi from Cleveland; Johnny Dougherty from St. Louis; and of course the hosts, Chicago's Outfit. With Buchalter as the gangsters' "floor manager," gunmen patrolled the aisles, sat on the dais, and lined the room's perimeter. Many observers had the impression that there were more gunmen than delegates in the hotel's auditorium. Not surprisingly, IATSE delegates were quickly persuaded to anoint Browne as their new president. So frightened was the membership that no one else dared ask to be nominated. George Browne ran unopposed. (After the convention, the Outfit billed IATSE for the gangsters' hotel rooms and traveling expenses.)

The new IATSE president took the stage, feigning astonishment at his fortune. His performance set a new standard for maudlin behavior as he cried profusely, seemingly unable to muster the strength to give a speech. All he could do was repeat over and over, "Thank you, boys. Thank you." He was likely addressing his gangster benefactors.

After the convention, Browne, Bioff, and Circella were sent to New York, where they informed the Producers' Association of their intent to revitalize IATSE. After the meeting, Bioff was taken by Circella to the Medical Arts Sanitarium, where Johnny Rosselli was undergoing treatment for his chronic tuberculosis. It was time for Bioff to meet his Los Angeles overseer. "Johnny Rosselli here is our man," Circella intoned. "He handles the West Coast for us. If there is anything that goes on on the West Coast with any producing company, we will know. There is nothing you or George can do that we won't know."

Browne and Bioff spent the remainder of 1934 in Chicago bringing holdout unions into line with their power play. In later testimony, Bioff explicitly detailed his modus operandi (expropriated from Tommy Maloy) when he recalled his approach to theater owner Jack Miller: 'I told Miller the exhibitors would have to pay two operators in each booth. Miller said: "My God! That will close up all my shows." I said: "If that will kill grandma, then grandma must die." Miller said that two men in each booth would cost about $500,000 a year. So I said, well, why don't you make a deal? And we finally agreed on $60,000 . . . You see, if they wouldn't pay, we'd give them lots of trouble. We'd put them out of business – and I mean out.'

Another movie house owner, Nathaniel Barger, recalled to an IRS investigator how he was coerced into paying Bioff approximately $50,000 over three years: 'After my theater had been opened for approximately two months, Bioff walked into the office and said, "Well, partner, how is business and how do we stand?" There seemed nothing I could do – either close up the theater and go out of the business I had been in all my life or bow to Mr. Bioff. So, later, I started paying Mr. Bioff half my profits. When there were losses in the theater, he did not share any loss, nor did he put in any money at any time.'

Bioff later recalled, "Barger raved and said it wasn't fair, but I told him that was the way it had to be if he wanted to stay in business. He went along." When Barger was forced to divest himself of a burlesque house to offset his loss in profit, Bioff helped himself to half of the sales price. One harassed theater owner lamented, "We are being unmercifully persecuted by a notorious method of racketeering by a gang of inhuman scoundrels. Our theaters are being stench-bombed, tear-gas-bombed. Three have been burned. They are broken into at night and motion picture machines, seats, carpets, draperies, are destroyed." The Outfit made it clear that their newest business plan was not to be denied. One by one, theater owners in Illinois and surrounding states caved in to the gangs' will.

In the near term, the Outfit was forced to proceed without the daily counsel of its Einstein: In October, Curly Humphreys surrendered himself to the authorities and began serving a prison term in Leavenworth. He had been indicted for tax evasion on a kidnapping ransom payoff he'd received, but had never been indicted on the kidnapping itself. According to Curly's daughter, her father uttered an upbeat farewell as he packed for the big house: "While I'm down there, I intend to study English and maybe a little geometry." However, many believe that he actually focused on business math, for when he was released fifteen months later, he helped design the Outfit's strategy for ambitious business takeovers on a national level. Many government officials, as well as Humphreys experts in the fourth estate, are certain that the Brainy Hood was in constant contact with his crew during his stay in "college." Royston Webb, a Welsh scholar who conducted a five-year doctoral study of Humphreys, noted recently, "There is no doubt that Humphreys, much as Capone had done years before, orchestrated the key decisions of the Hollywood takeover from behind bars. It was also to his great fortune that he was unavailable for the initial face-to-face meetings with Bioff and Browne. It gave him deniability in the future." It also rendered Paul Ricca, Johnny Rosselli, and the others vulnerable, should the caper be unraveled by authorities.

After giving Curly a rousing send-off, the Outfit mulled over where to install Nick Circella in the union hierarchy. At the time, Nitti was worried that Maloy would succumb to IRS pressure, and the Outfit's titular head was not anxious to go back to the slammer. In a convenient turn of events, the solution to the Maloy problem simultaneously answered the question of Circella's future. On Christmas Eve, 1934, the Outfit met and pronounced a death sentence on Maloy. At noon on February 4, 1935, as Maloy drove on Lake Shore Drive, along the now deserted "Century of Progress" grounds, the union boss received two fatal shotgun blasts from two gunmen in another vehicle. Chicago FBI agent Bill Roemer strongly asserted that the hit men were Joe Accardo and a young up-and-comer named Gus Alex.

One of Maloy's pallbearers was none other than George Browne, who, after the service, headed straight to the offices of Maloy's Local 110. Not long after his coup, Browne named Nick Circella to Maloy's vacant post. As with so many other figures of Chicago infamy, Tommy Maloy was given one of the largest funerals in the city's history, marked by a three-hundred-car procession. In July, another obstacle was unceremoniously removed from the Outfit's road to the promised land. Three Gun Louis Alterie, the stubborn holdout president of the Theater Janitors' Union, and the executioner of the horse that had thrown Dean O'Banion's partner years earlier, was shot to death. Still another unsolved Chicago gangland rubout.

Another Battlefront

With the Browne and Bioff situation now operating under its own inertia, the emboldened Outfit decided to spread its wings. As noted, one of the gang's initial goals was the infiltration of the bartenders' unions. Even with his union mastermind Curly Humphreys in jail, Nitti felt sufficiently confident for the assault and decided the time was right to make the move. The hoods' chosen point of attack, George B. McLane, was the business agent for Local 278, the Chicago Bartenders and Beverage Dispensers Union. Although the local comprised only fifty-three hundred members, it was affiliated with fifteen other similar guilds with a combined thirty thousand members. The Outfit planned to take them all.

McLane's nightmare began, he later testified, in the spring of 1935, when an Outfit union slugger in Curly's crew named Danny Stanton telephoned him at his union headquarters. McLane recalled, "I knew Stanton was a slugger for Red Barker and Murray Humphreys. He said he wanted five hundred dollars to go to the Kentucky Derby. He said he would send over two men for it. I told him I had no right to give out union funds." Stanton ignored McLane's rebuttal, saying, "I'll have two men over in a half hour to to pick up the money." When the thugs showed up, McLane turned them away, which prompted an angry Stanton to call again. "You son of a bitch," Stanton yelled. "We will get the money and take the union over." Within days, McLane was summoned to Nitti's office at the LaSalle Hotel. Nitti demanded that McLane install an Outfit member in his union's hierarchy. The courageous (or foolish) McLane refused Nitti's demand. Nitti exploded. "We have taken over other unions," he blustered. "You will put him in or get shot in the head." Within days, McLane was brought to Nitti again, this time at the Outfit's private third-floor dining room at the Capri Restaurant. Once inside, McLane was confronted by a star chamber that included Nitti, Ricca, Campagna, and partners of the imprisoned Curly, Fred Evans and Sam "Golf Bag" Hunt. Again Nitti threatened, "How would your old lady look in black?" This time McLane softened, saying he'd see what he could do.

When months went by with no action, McLane was back at the Capri before an Outfit that was losing its patience. McLane explained to Nitti that he had asked his board if they would accept an assistant named by Nitti, and they had turned down the suggestion. Nitti demanded to know the names of the opposing board members. This time he told McLane, "This is your last chance. Put our man in or wind up in an alley."

"I went back to the union and told them about the threats to me and to them – what it meant," McLane later testified. "They had no alternative. They agreed to putting a man on." In short time they were introduced to one Louis Romano. "His salary will be seventy-five dollars a week out of the union treasury," Nitti ordered McLane. "You'll have to make provisions to raise it later. Romano will see that all the Outfit places join the union." The Outfit clearly had its sights fixed on the thirty thousand members of the affiliated unions. For the next five years, the gang, via Romano, called the shots in the bartenders' union, while collecting $20,000 per month in dues. According to McLane, Romano admitted that he was whisking the money off "to the boys in Cicero." McLane said that over the years, Johnny Patton, "the boy mayor of Burnham" and Outfit racetrack maven, attended the Outfit's board meetings. Patton gave reports about which brands of booze were being sold at the gang's dog tracks. "Patton said the bartenders were not pushing the right stuff," McLane said. The brands manufactured by the Outfit, especially Fort Dearborn whiskey, were "the right stuff."[1] "Tell those bartenders that if they don't push our stuff, they will get their legs broken." The Outfit and McLane maintained the status quo of the bartenders' union until Curly was released from prison to oversee its expansion. Until then, the gang profited (approximately $3–5 million per year) from their liquor sales and the monthly dues extracted from the union's five thousand members.

Meanwhile, the movie scam began to get serious. Browne and Bioff were soon ordered to New York, where they were brought further into the loop

---

1. Other Outfit brands at the time included Great Lakes draft beer, Badger and Cream Top bottled beer, Gold Seal liquors, and anything made by their breweries: Manhattan Brewery and the Capitol Wine and Liquor Company.

of the New York–Chicago national crime consortium. As it was learned in subsequent testimony, the duo, accompanied by Paul Ricca and Nick Circella, was directed to Tommy Lucchese's Casino de Paree restaurant in Manhattan, where they were joined by gang leaders from other major cities. Among the attendees were Rosselli's partner Jack Dragna from Los Angeles and New York associates Lucky Luciano and Frank Costello. After the meeting, Ricca instructed Bioff that he would soon be working both coasts, ferrying between Manhattan and Hollywood. "Feel free to call on Charlie Lucky or on Frank Costello if you find any difficulties here in our work," instructed Ricca. "If you need anything, be free to call on them, because they are our people." Torrio's dream of a national crime consortium had come to fruition.

Soon Browne, accompanied by Bioff and Circella, flexed his muscles. On July 15, Browne called an IATSE strike in New York against the Loew's and RKO theater chains. It was his way of introducing himself to the moguls of the movie business. By noon, General Leslie Thompson, chairman of RKO, became the first victim of the grand scheme. After a period of tense negotiating, Thompson handed over $50,000 for strike insurance, adding another $37,000 the next morning. "A good morning's work," Bioff said, laughing.

Next, the trio paid a visit to Nick Schenck, president of Loew's. Willie Bioff and the Schenck brothers shared similar backgrounds, being Russian-born Jews who knew the value of mixing a criminal and honorable ethos simultaneously. Joe Schenck, Nick's brother and L.A.-based partner, was another known to walk through life with one foot in the upperworld and one in the underworld. On one hand, his generous donations to Roosevelt gave him carte blanche with the White House, especially with Jim Farley, FDR's New Deal director. In addition, Schenck's cozy relationship with the California state legislature, again thanks to donations, saw him well treated on the local level. "Whatever Joe Schenck wanted, I got for him," said the de facto boss of the state legislature, Arthur Samish. On the other hand, Schenck was well known to be in bed with the famous gangsters of the era. As has already been noted, Schenck had been a close friend of Johnny Rosselli's for years. But Johnny was just one of Schenck's many hoodlum acquaintances. "He came to know every element of the gangster world, from the lowest ranks on up to the top echelons," recalled Schenck's screenwriter friend Anita Loos.

Johnny Rosselli, meanwhile, continued to ingratiate himself with

Hollywood's movers and shakers, performing favors for them that only a man with his résumé could undertake. In 1935, Johnny was given a delicate task by Will Hays, who now ran the AMPP. It had long since become customary for thugs to attempt to shake down Hollywood's glitterati through blackmail. Now a case had arisen where some freelance extortionists had put their hands on a pornographic film, one of several made by a starving nineteen-year-old actress who was now one of MGM's hottest upcoming stars. Her name was Joan Crawford. Although the blackmailers demanded $100,000 to turn over the negative, the studio would go no higher than $25,000. Rosselli was asked to be the "negotiator." Now the freelance hoods were in way over their heads. Rosselli met with them and calmly explained who he was and whom he really worked for, the Outfit. Unless the print was handed over, Rosselli told them, their corpses would make those of the St. Valentine's Day massacre victims seem unscathed. Sooner than they could say "Chicago typewriter," the amateurs handed over the print, never to be heard from again. And Johnny Rosselli pocketed the $25,000.

In New York, Joe Schenck's brother Nick was now also about to cut a deal with the devil. The producers readily agreed to pay the gangsters $150,000 for a seven-year no-strike contract, two thirds of which went to the Outfit. But it was anything but simple extortion. Not only would producers profit from a no-strike, low-wage deal, but it gave them a buttress against the National Labor Relations Act (the Wagner Act), passed just weeks earlier on July 5, 1935. The act was a pro-worker bill that codified their rights to collective bargaining. Just as the movie industry was beginning to come out of its Depression-era financial doldrums, the Wagner Act threatened to derail its progress. Schenck and his peers also feared the recent establishment of the Congress of Industrial Organizations, or CIO, by John Lewis and Sidney Hillman. Worried that new labor organizations would demand profit-sharing, producers were ready for a savior in the form of the Outfit. Thus the deal also held that Browne would reduce worker wage-increase demands by two thirds.

But Schenck and friends feared that somebody might get wise if the deal was arrived at too quickly, so the Outfit offered the skittish producers an ingenious way out: In typical Hollywood fashion, it decided to "put on a show." Browne would call a phony strike, forcing the moguls to "capitulate" and grant IATSE total control over the studio's workforce. The producers would grant IATSE the first "closed shop" agreement in the history of the entertainment business. In return, the Outfit-backed Browne and Bioff would suppress any worker calls for wage increases.

The sham walkout was triggered in late November 1935, when a non-IATSE Paramount film crew arrived in New York to film aerial footage for the movie *Thirteen Hours by Air*. On Saturday night, November 30, with date-night crowds filling movie theaters, a seemingly irate Browne ordered his IATSE projectionists to walk out of more than five hundred Paramount theaters from Chicago to New York. According to later testimony by Bioff, the double-dealing allies then staged an "emergency" closed-door meeting at the Union League Club in New York to settle the strike. Since the deal had been cut in advance, one can only wonder what went on behind the closed doors – perhaps a discussion of the most recent New York Giants game. When the partners emerged from their confab, it was announced that IATSE would be granted a closed shop, 100 percent labor jurisdiction on the studios' lots. This of course presupposed that the producers had legal rights to make such a pronouncement; they did not. In later testimony involving the estate of Frank Nitti, the studio executives sheepishly admitted that their labor-racketeering partnership with the Outfit had saved the studios approximately $15 million.

Variety and the rest of the national press were completely hoodwinked by the charade. No one suspected that greedy producers had formed an unholy alliance with embezzling union leaders willing to sell out their own membership in exchange for bribes. Of course, the Outfit's back-stabbing of the workers was only a temporary stepping-stone to the its real goal: double-crossing the conniving producers once the gangsters were granted complete control of the studio shops.

December 1935 was a festive month for the Outfit, starting with the release from prison of its accounting wizard, Jake Guzik. According to Outfit tradition, a lavish "coming out" party was thrown whenever one of its members was sprung from the big house, and the venerated Guzik undoubtedly received the full treatment at one of the gang's favorite restaurants. Within days, the Outfit's leadership, including Rosselli from Los Angeles, headed to the Sunshine State where their itinerary included both business and pleasure. The business involved the annual IATSE executive board meeting at the Fleetwood Hotel in Miami. With the Outfit brain trust by his side, Browne introduced the IATSE executives to their new bosses, adding that Bioff would now head the Hollywood local. After leaving the grim IATSE officials to contemplate their new lot, the Outfitters repaired to Big Al's Palm Island estate, where Ralph Capone hosted his Chicago pals. George Browne, the legendary quaffer, was stunned by the Outfit's work ethic, even here in Florida sitting by Al Capone's pool. He later remarked to Bioff, "These guys don't know how to relax. They just work all the time, day and night, and never take time to spend their money." The frustrated Browne implored Nitti, "Jeez, Frank, we just got here. I haven't had a dozen bottles of beer today. Nobody has been in the pool. Nobody went over to look at Miami Beach. Can't I get a little bit of this sun?" Nitti was stunned by Browne's backward priorities. Nitti sternly informed Bioff that Rosselli would be his overseer, and that he must also find a way to put Rosselli on the union payroll. He then said, "OK. Go ahead. Have a night on the town." But it would soon be back to work, with assaults to be mounted on movie business fronts in New York and Hollywood.

The new year, 1936, brought more good news for the Outfit. On January 8, its legal and political shaman Curly Humphreys was released from Leavenworth, mandating yet another coming-out gala. Almost before recovering from his welcome-home party, Humphreys got back to work, quickly taking over the Individual Towel Company, which had a $45,000 annual contract with the Chicago Board of Education, and becoming an executive with an entity known as the Mid West Oil Corporation. With his brother, who went by the name Jack Wright, Humphreys seized control of a number of local movie houses, where the duo were known as the Wright Brothers.

With Curly and Jake back in the game, the gang was now fully armed for its assault on the entertainment industry. Simultaneously, Willie Bioff and his wife, the former Laurie Nelson, relocated to Hollywood, where their cruise ship was met on arrival by Rosselli and Browne. In short time the scheming trio tended to the key first item on their agenda: informing the local IATSE rank and file that the Outfit was now in charge. Bioff muscled the holdout unions into joining IATSE. Having been granted the franchise by the studio bosses, Bioff presented the twelve thousand studio technicians with both the carrot and the stick: sign on with IATSE and get a 10 percent raise; otherwise, get no work at all. Writer George Dunne, who closely studied Bioff's time in Hollywood, described one pivotal meeting at the union's headquarters: "Bioff walked into a meeting of the union officers on Santa Monica Boulevard with these two hit men from Chicago, one on either side. Each one had a violin case under his arm, just like they do in the movies. Bioff stood up and said, 'We're taking over the union – the international is,' and they dismissed the local officers right there."

With Bioff as its front, the Outfit set up its West Coast headquarters in the penthouse of Hollywood's twelve-story Taft Building, previously notable as a locus for movie star dentists. Although comfortably ensconced, Bioff continued to receive his marching orders from Chicago, including one directive that resulted in Browne and Bioff obtaining still more personal income for their efforts. In this instance, Nitti instructed the duo to hire one Izzy Zevlin to manage their books. "Izzy has forgotten more about accounting than those Internal Revenue Service guys ever knew," Nitti boasted. Upon meeting Bioff and Browne, Zevlin enlightened the thugs as to how they could reap vast sums that Nitti and the gang would not have to learn about. With Zevlin maintaining two sets of books, one supposedly hidden from the Outfit, Bioff and Brown wasted no time in levying a new 2 percent surcharge on the IATSE members' paychecks – for the strike insurance fund, they claimed. Of course, Bioff and Browne were being paid by the producers *not* to call a strike, but there was little chance the workers would learn of that sub-rosa compact. Bioff assumed the Outfit had little chance of discovering the secret surcharge connived by Zevlin. This "assessment" income was noted in the second set of books, kept in a vault, supposedly below the Outfit's radar.

It is not known how Nitti learned of the rip-off – perhaps Zevlin was merely his agent provocateur – but when he did, he exploded. In Chicago, Nitti confronted Browne. "Nitti got so mad he backed me into the bathroom," Browne later testified. "I thought he was going to push me out the window." To Browne's feeble protestations, Nitti yelled, "There's a lot of guys in the Outfit that have to be taken care of." Then, like a scolding parent, Nitti announced their punishment: "From now on, whatever money we get won't be split fifty-fifty. You keep one third for you and Willie, and I'll take two thirds for my people." According to court testimony, the surcharge scam eventually netted the conspirators over $6.5 million, two thirds of which was sent back to Chicago. The surcharge was merely a hint of things to come. With all the pieces now in place, the time had at last arrived for the "Chicago crowd" to apply the coup de grâce.

In April 1936, the studio heads were thunderstruck upon learning that their wicked alliance had backfired: The moguls themselves were but mere pawns in the Outfit's game. On April 16, Willie Bioff, George Browne, and Nick Circella showed up at Nick Schenck's New York office, and Browne let the other shoe drop. "I want you to know that I am the boss," Browne intoned, "and that I want two million dollars out of the motion picture industry." Schenck turned pale. He later testified that he thought Browne had lost his mind and was talking nonsense. "At first I couldn't talk," remembered Schenck. He recalled Bioff's saying, "You know what will happen. We gave you a taste of it in Chicago. We will close down every theater in the country. You couldn't take that. It will cost you many millions of dollars over and over again. Think it over." George Browne then chimed in and assured Schenck that Bioff and he were serious and gave Schenck a few hours to ponder his fate. During the break, Nick Schenck met with Sidney R. Kent, the chief of Loew's sister company, Twentieth Century-Fox. Kent begged the entrapped Schenck, "Talk them out of it. They'll wreck the industry." But Kent was probably unaware of Schenck's previous deal with the Outfit that now tied the industry's hands.

When the gangsters returned that afternoon, Schenck told them there was no way he could raise the $2 million. Willie Bioff cut him off, countering, "All right. I'll take one million." Schenck again tried to spar with Bioff, who ended all discussion when he stood up to leave, saying, "One million. That's my final offer." Sidney Kent's objections aside, the studio heads really had no choice; they had happily allowed the Outfit to take over and reinvigorate IATSE, and now they had to pay the price. It was now impossible to operate the studios without IATSE. The next day, the gang returned and Bioff dictated the payment schedule: $50,000 per year from each of the four major studios (Fox, Warner Bros., MGM, and Paramount), and $25,000 from the smaller firms (RKO and Columbia, for example). Making matters worse, Willie the pimp was in a hurry: "Oh, yes, and I want one hundred thousand up front."

Within three days, the beleaguered Kent and Schenck raised the cash and delivered it to Bioff and Browne at their suite at the Waldorf-Astoria. Although the two gangsters nervously harbored the thought that the movie executives might turn up with the feds, their fears were quickly dispelled. As per Bioff's instructions, both producers carried plain brown-paper bundles, each containing $50,000 in hundred-dollar bills. Adding to their indignity, the studio heads were forced to cool their heels while the gang meticulously counted the one thousand individual C-notes. "There were twin beds right there in the hotel suite," Schenck later told a jury. "I put my money on the right-hand side of the bed. Bioff took half the money and started counting it. He put the other half on the other bed and told Browne to count it." As Willie Bioff later said, "I had Hollywood dancing to my tune."

With Fox and Loew's in line, Bioff headed back to Los Angeles to inform the other studio chiefs of their fate, while Browne took care of business in Chicago. Willie Bioff knew no other game than hardball, and one by one, the studios surrendered to the gang. When studios balked at the extortion, there were threats. Louis B. Mayer, of MGM, later testified that he capitulated only when Bioff threatened to kill him before dawn. In some cases, such as the deeply in debt Warner Bros., Bioff had to settle for less than he demanded. Major Albert Warner cut a deal for $10,000 in advance plus regular installment payments. Financially strapped Paramount produced $27,000. Books were juggled routinely to keep the arrangement from the prying eyes of stockholders. Albert Warner's brother Harry noted one $12,000 payment as "Christmas presents for critics."

Only Columbia studios was protected from Bioff's strong-arm ways. Recall that Columbia's head, Harry Cohn, was Johnny Rosselli's best friend in Los Angeles. When Bioff put pressure on Cohn's studio with a wildcat strike, Cohn immediately picked up the phone and called his buddy, Gentleman Johnny, who raced over to Bioff's office, despite being told by the secretary that he was out. Finding Willie behind his desk as expected, Rosselli raged, while Bioff pleaded that he had Frank Nitti's blessing. For Johnny, that did not matter where a close friendship was involved. Besides, Nitti was only a figurehead. The real power was with Accardo, Ricca, and Humphreys. They would understand the difference between business and personal loyalties. "To hell with you and Nitti," Rosselli screamed. Bioff refused to bend and Rosselli stormed out. But later that night, Rosselli turned up at Bioff's home with the "Al Capone of Los Angeles," Jack Dragna, and read Willie the riot act. Bioff called Cohn to announce the strike was canceled. "The strike is off," Bioff said. "You can thank Johnny – nobody but Johnny could have done this for you" It was Cohn's last problem with IATSE.

In the first year alone, the Outfit amassed over $1.5 million from the studio extortions and the 2 percent union members' surcharges. They amplified their profit by anointing the bookmaker for each studio lot. Chicago transplants such as Izzy Adelman handled thousands of bets a month for the studio employees. With all the action in Hollywood, the gang accrued inestimable moneys. "To top it all off, they were getting to screw the best broads in America," one Outfit associate fondly recalled. Then the original "Slick Willie" engineered a new variation of the extortion scam to take some heat off the studio heads: He had himself appointed "purchasing agent" for all raw film stock acquired from Du Pont Chemicals. His 7 percent commission, for which he did no work, netted Bioff a combined $230,000 in 1937 and 1938. He kept the studios reasonably placated by living up to his end of the bargain: over the next four years, IATSE members in various cities saw their wages decline 15 to 40 percent. When the rival Federation of Motion Picture Craftsmen struck in 1937, Bioff imported some notorious Chicago sluggers to break the strike by breaking some heads. Although the strikers had hired tough longshoremen for protection from Bioff and Rosselli (and by implication the studio bosses), they were far outmuscled by the out-of-towners. The workers watched in terror as thugs armed with Chicago typewriters arrived in Lincoln Zephyr town cars at the Pico Street gate of Twentieth Century-Fox. They met little resistance. The efficiency of the mogul-mobster relationship left even Sidney Kent impressed. "We have had less interruption of employment, less hard feeling, less recrimination," he declared in 1938, "and have built more goodwill than any industry I know of in the country." Harry Warner chimed in, admitting that it was just plain "good business" to have a relationship with Bioff.

Joe Schenck knew exactly what Warner meant by "good business." As Bioff would later testify, the Schenck brothers were in the middle of their own scam when they entered into one with him: They were diverting theater receipts in a profitable scheme that was robbing their stockholders blind. Over six years, as a favor to his new partners, Bioff made at least a dozen courier trips from New York to Hollywood, wherein he delivered bundles of the purloined cash from Nick Schenck to his brother Joe at his house. One such delivery alone amounted to $62,500. Often sitting by his pool while taking the lucre, Joe would ask Willie, "Did Nick take care of your traveling expenses?" When Bioff replied in the negative, Joe handed him $500 from the bundle, "to cover the two cross-country trips you made." The Shencks attempted to convince Willie that the money was intended to line the pockets of bribed state legislators, not theirs. But Willie knew better. "These businessmen are nothing but two-bit whores with clean shirts and a shine," Willie philosophized.[2]

And the Schenck brothers were not the only studio heads who saw the silver lining to be gained by entering into a relationship with gangsters.

---

2. According to Mooney Giancana, the Outfit also used its Hollywood partner Joe Schenck to funnel a half million dollars to Roosevelt's 1936 reelection campaign.

George Skouras of the eighteen-theater chain of Fox movie houses in New York paid Bioff $25,000 to handle his competition, the Frisch-Rintzler circuit. At the time, the banks were chiding Skouras for mismanaging his theaters to the tune of $60,000 more than it cost Frisch to operate the same number of theaters. Since Skouras had no desire to cut his perks and extravagances, he asked Willie to make certain that his competitors' operating costs became intolerable. Bioff later recalled that the answer was simple: "As a result of that conversation, I called up the heads of the Frisch-Rintzler circuit and increased their [union pay] scale sixty thousand dollars per year." Even more disquieting was that the courier for the Bioff bribe was Sol Rosenblatt, former general counsel to the Democratic National Committee, and an administrator in Roosevelt's National Recovery Act program. For his services, Rosenblatt took a 25 percent commission. As writer Stephen Fox concluded, "Bioff did not have to 'corrupt' Hollywood any more than he had needed to corrupt the stagehands union. In both instances he merely folded smoothly into the environment."

Back in Chicago, George Browne quickly moved to consolidate his union's power. The dissolution of the L.A. local the previous winter was followed in the coming months by the forced nullification of union branches around the country. On July 10, 1936, Browne and his "board" declared marshal law: The union, they pronounced, was in "a state of emergency." Local meetings and elections were banned, and the Outfit began exporting its Chicago craftsmen to Hollywood, where they were placed in key IATSE posts. According to one Outfit insider, "Ricca, Accardo, and Humphreys made one thing clear – their people should be placed in the infrastructure of IATSE, not just in the vulnerable roles of leadership." This brilliant strategy would ensure the gang's presence in the film business for decades, even if Bioff took a fall.

Going Hollywood

With the Outfit allowing Bioff to keep fully a third of the take, he began to compete with the Hollywood set in ostentatious lifestyles. After fifteen years of subjecting his family to life in hotel rooms, Willie the pimp went domestic: In 1937 he purchased an eighty-acre farm and built a spacious home in the L.A. suburb of Woodland Hills. Bioff christened his new home Rancho Laurie after his wife. Instead of hookers, his neighbors were now Hollywood celebrities such as Barbara Stanwyck, Robert Taylor, Tyrone Power, and Clark Gable; he filled his home with Louis XV furniture; he collected rare oriental vases; he built a wood-paneled library that was stocked with rare volumes, although he himself was never known to read beyond the comic-book level; he planted alfalfa and $600 olive trees. "My wife is nuts about flowers and so am I," Willie told the press. "We grow all our own fruit and vegetables. I'm building a playhouse so I can have a place to entertain my pals." Bioff later recalled how he furnished his lavish new digs: He muscled $5,000 worth of furniture from RKO executive Leo Spitz. "So I went to Leo and I said, 'Leo, I gotta have some drapes and other things for my new home and I thought maybe you could get them for me wholesale through RKO's purchasing department.' Of course I didn't intend to pay for them."

Not all of Rancho Laurie's amenities reflected domestic bliss. In the home where the Bioffs raised seven children there also dwelled a phalanx of bodyguards; not well concealed on the home's adobe exterior were adornments not normally seen on suburban homes: gun turrets. Willie Bioff took to dressing in "Al Capone chic," featuring garish, brightly colored tailored suits. When the press teased Willie for wearing $150 suits and $15 shirts, he had a standard retort: "It's the union that's rich, not Willie Bioff."

Bioff audaciously ordered studio heads around as if they worked for him. Once, when a studio gate security guard denied Bioff's car entry to the lot, Bioff ordered Louis B. Mayer, then the highest-paid executive officer on earth, to drop what he was doing and come out to give the guard a tongue-lashing. Warner Bros.' president, Harry Warner, so feared the erstwhile panderer that he hired a personal bodyguard. In 1939, Mr. and Mrs. Bioff took a cruise to Brazil; as described by historian Alson Smith, Bioff's cabin suite overflowed with "flowers and farewell gifts from the movie men whom he was persecuting; most of whom were fervently praying he would drown."

Willie Bioff was now the cock of the walk, and he never let anyone forget it. His temerity even extended, albeit briefly, to his relations with the Outfit. One nervy perpetration nearly cost him his life. Bioff's close shave was precipitated by a Commission decision to absorb a vaudeville performers' union called the Artists and Actors Association of America within IATSE. Since the crime bosses of New York and Chicago controlled so many nightclubs where the vaudevillians worked, the alliance would obviously assist with bookings and pay negotiations. But Willie Bioff opposed the move, coveting this one union, and its treasury, for himself. As if unfamiliar with the Outfit's talent for retribution, Willie refused to facilitate the gang's directive. Bioff later testified that a few days after his foolhardy show of independence, he received a call from Paul "the Waiter" Ricca. "You're in trouble, but good," Ricca bellowed. The Outfit boss then ordered "Willie the Maverick" to catch the next plane to Chicago. On his arrival in the Windy City, Bioff went directly to Nitti's office at the Bismarck Hotel, where he was met by Ricca. "He said he came early to warn me," Bioff later said. Willie was about to become the defendant in a kangaroo court presided over by all the Outfit members. Local journalist George Murray described the scene:

> Then came Nitti, Charles Gioe, Louis Campagna, and the others. All were grim-faced. There was no laughter or greeting. Nitti waited until all were seated, then he spoke. "Bioff, you been trying to muscle in. You think you're going to run things for yourself. You're trying to put yourself in front of George Browne. You're trying to take personal charge of this vaudeville actors" union and its treasury and its dues. You're just headed for a hearse . . . From now on, Charlie Gioe will run this actors' union. Now let's hear no more about it.

Bioff came to his senses and groveled back to California with his tail between his legs.

With its coffers bulging, the Outfit's Chicago-based members also began enjoying the spoils of victory, like Bioff in California. After 10 percent of the profits were allocated to the Outfit's mutual fund, a sort of corporate treasury, the hoods indulged themselves. The Capone style was much in evidence, if not in the way the Outfit bosses conducted business, than at least in the manner in which they spent their earnings. Much as Capone had relaxed at his brother's Mercer, Wisconsin, farm, and at his own digs in Florida, so did his heirs. Paul Ricca, who filed his tax returns as a marble importer and owner of the World Playhouse Movie Theater, acquired an eleven-hundred-acre farm in Kendall County, Illinois, for $75,000. At about the same time, Paul had suffered multiple fractures (back, pelvis, leg, and foot) when a Loop building elevator in which he was riding fell three floors. For a time, Sunday-night Outfit meetings were held at his farm while he recuperated. Ricca's wife, the former Nancy Gigiante, kept the pasta flowing as the men made their plans. Likewise, Louis Campagna and his wife, Charlotte, purchased an eight-hundred-acre farm, the L.C. Ranch, in Fowler, Indiana, and a second eighty-eight-acre spread in Berrien Springs, Michigan. At the L.C. Ranch, Campagna devoted most of the acreage to cultivating crops such as wheat, corn, and soybeans; the remaining land was set aside for his two hundred head of cattle. In the years to come, Curly Humphreys, as well as Capone's cousin Charlie Fischetti, also followed the Big Guy's lead and bought vacation homes in Florida.

Unlike Accardo and others, Humphreys believed the Outfit should refrain from purchasing ostentatious digs in Illinois. When in Chicago, Curly lived in a succession of upscale hotels, the Bernard, the St. Clair, and later the Morrison. By this time, the Humphreys family included their toddler daughter, Llewella, born in 1935.[3] The new arrival prompted Curly to purchase a nondescript Chicago house, although he continued to lease hotel rooms for the many nights he would be away from home. In the yard of the family's 7710 Bennett Avenue home, Curly built his daughter an intentionally crooked garden playhouse, a reference to Curly's way of life.

As the years wore on, Humphreys spent an increasing amount of time in Norman, Oklahoma, the place of his half-Cherokee wife's upbringing, taking the opportunity to build by his own hand a modest home on his three-square-mile parcel of land. The house contained a secret entrance to a basement that was believed to be used for gang business and money storage. Curly's sense of humor was much in evidence at the Norman house: His in-ground pool had silver dollars affixed to the bottom so he could watch in delight as guests dove in to try to retrieve them. Curly insulated his Oklahoma relations, who referred to him as Uncle Lew, from his line of work, and he and Clemi often spoke in Italian when discussing Outfit business in their presence. Humphreys bonded with the Native American inhabitants in the area, paying them extravagantly for house chores and groundskeeping. His gardener, a Native American known as Skybuck, educated Curly to the tragic plight of his fellows, initiating Curly's lifelong devotion to their cause. Curly's nephew Jimmy O'Neill recalled, "Every holiday, Uncle Lew would go downtown, fill the station wagon with turkeys and other food, and give it to the under-privileged Indian children." To this day, old-timers fondly recall Curly Humphreys' handing out silver dollars to complete strangers who appeared destitute. So total was the break from his life in the Windy City that Curly the Welshman took to dressing in cowboy attire when in town.

---

3. Family friends hold that Llewella was actually an adopted child, the progeny of an illicit affair between an Outfit boss and Clemi's sister, Isola.

Some Outfit bosses, such as Humphreys and Accardo, traveled extensively. Humphreys' widow maintains a photo scrapbook stuffed with pictures of family vacations to China, Egypt, France, Cuba, and Hawaii. The Accardos enjoyed European getaways and trips to Nova Scotia and the Caribbean, where Joe became an accomplished deep-sea fisherman. While Curly Humphreys and Joe Accardo preferred international travel, others took sumptuous vacations to venues like the "gangsters' spa" in Hot Springs, Arkansas, owned by New York bootlegger Owney "the English Godfather" Madden. Often, the gangsters took the opportunity to visit their new fiefdom in southern California. On one such getaway, Louis Campagna was awestruck when he saw his first lawn sprinkler system on the front yard of a Beverly Hills estate. Inspired, the gangster purchased five hundred such sprinkler heads for his newly acquired Chicago mansion.

The Comely Courier

Nick Circella and George Browne were more businesslike with their shares, forming a side partnership to create the lavishly appointed Colony Club, a bistro that fostered a number of relationships that had serious consequences for the entire national Commission. One such liaison involved one of the many call girls working the Colony. Virginia "Sugar" Hill was a voluptuous redheaded prostitute who had moved to Chicago from the impoverished steel town of Lipscomb, Virginia, as a teen in 1933. Born Onie Virginia Hill, the youngster joined thousands of others who gravitated to the promised bonanza known as the "Century of Progress" under construction in the Windy City. As fate would have it, before her job at the Colony, Hill had found work as a waitress at the Outfit's San Carlo Italian Village on the fairgrounds, where it was rumored that every gang member had made a play for her.

Hill was brought into the Outfit's confidence by Jake Guzik's chief lieutenant and money launderer, Joe "Joey Ep" Epstein. As the man responsible for the collection of the gang's moneys from racetracks, handbooks, studio shakedowns, and other sundry ventures, Epstein was always casting about for nonsuspicious methods of transporting the money back to the gang, laundering it, and finally, depositing it in the Outfit's numerous offshore and Swiss bank accounts. One of his tried-and-true methods was the enlistment of classy-looking women who would not invite suspicion from the authorities. At this time, according to a friend, Epstein was employing the services of three women from the

Near North Side. Epstein decided to groom Hill for the job and furnished her with the finest upperworld wardrobe and coiffures. In time, Hill distinguished herself from her peers and became Epstein's top courier. Hill began traveling from city to city under dozens of aliases, collecting the gang's lucre, and often cleaning it at the tracks herself. With Epstein calling the shots, Hill took thousands of gang dollars to the tracks, where she was directed to bet on races where the winner had been predetermined. Hill then brought the "new money" back to Chicago, and from there to Switzerland.

In her insatiable quest for fame and celebrity, Hill had dalliances with countless gang bosses in every major city, including one, still known only to a handful of insiders, with Moe Dalitz, of Detroit's Purple Gang. (This liaison would play a pivotal role in one of gangland's most infamous rubouts, that of Bugsy Siegel.) Epstein and the Outfit soon decided to offer Hill an even more dangerous assignment: She was asked to spy on prominent bosses throughout the country, such as New York's Joe Adonis (Doto), with whom the Outfit had entered into partnerships. When in Chicago, Hill became the Outfit's token female member, the first (and only known) woman invited to sit at the backroom table of Accardo, Humphreys, and the rest. And for her critical role in the Outfit's smooth running, Hill was well compensated. Not only did she receive a healthy commission for moneys delivered, but she was also tipped to numerous fixed races (known by the hoods as boat races), allowing her to bet heavily and win big. No one knows exactly how much Hill was worth at her peak, but she owned or leased posh homes in many big cities such as New York, where she encouraged the rumor that she was, according to the *New York Journal-American,* a "twenty-three-year-old Georgia oil heiress."

In New York, Hill became grist for the society and gossip columnists, who regularly reported on her legendary parties. In 1941, the *Journal-American* called her a "much photographed Manhattan glamor girl." The paper also gave her the distinction of being the woman with the most fur coats in the country. (The wags were unaware that Hill supplemented her income by selling "hot" furs to her society girlfriends. Hill had seen how many gamblers were pawning off their wives' furs to her real Chicago love, gambling boss Ira Colitz. Hill convinced Colitz to convert his North Clark Street Clover Bar backroom into a walk-in cooler to store furs that Hill in turn sold to her uptown pals; Hill also occasionally trafficked in hot diamonds acquired in the same manner.) In time, Hill would cast her spell on more top hoods in every sector of the nation, making a fateful assignation with Ben Siegel, about which much more will be seen.

In addition to his Colony Club investment, George Browne diversified into the profession of benefit-concert promoter. With Chicago's Grand Opera House as his main venue, Browne promoted a series of concerts featuring a virtual who's who of the legitimate stage: Sophie Tucker, Amos 'n' Andy, Helen Morgan, Fanny Brice, Gypsy Rose Lee, and the Ritz Brothers, to name a few. Of course, 100 percent of the costly $20 tickets sold "benefited" only George Browne's personal bank account.

The Outfit elite making the trek to Hollywood found themselves warmly received by the fawning studio heads and, after some encouragement, began to buy into the studios as silent partners. With insider information from the moguls' bookie, Johnny Rosselli, the gangsters knew more about the studio chiefs' financial condition than even their own families. One word from Johnny about an executive with vigorish problems was all that was needed for the gang to offer their lending services. While some hoods became consultants on gangster flicks, Johnny Rosselli and New Jersey boss Abner "Longy" Zwillman became full-fledged producers, together responsible for more than half a dozen box-office hits. Not surprisingly, their crime-genre films were praised by critics for their realism.

Even the hoodlums' kids found something to appreciate about their parents' association with Hollywood. Children of Outfit members have described private, "closed set" tours of the Hollywood studios, conducted not by teenaged tour guides, but by the movie moguls themselves, much to the dislike of their contract players. On all their trips West, the gangsters were "comped" by IATSE, with all travel expenses charged to the union. Louis Campagna had a preference for his union-supplied seaside digs in the expensive Malibu enclave. The gang's new friendships in Tinseltown occasionally provided more practical benefits. On at least one occasion, Joe Accardo hid out with Hollywood producer Howard J. Beck while he was being investigated in Chicago by the Civil Service Commission. Other Outfit hoods on the lam, among them Butch Blasi and Sam DeStefano, were dispatched to Hollywood, where they were given cushy union jobs and temporary new identities until the heat cooled in the Second City.

Behind the scenes, Curly, Joe, and Paul called the shots. Occasionally this meant looking out for the interests of their Commission partners back

East. In one instance, using trusted aide Ralph Pierce as intermediary, Curly Humphreys directed Johnny Rosselli to keep an eye on Longy Zwillman's girlfriend. The stunning young actress, born Harlean Carpentier in Chicago, had become a box-office sensation under the name Jean Harlow. The platinum blond Harlow, nicknamed Baby, was also the stepdaughter of Chicago mobster Marino Bello, who earned dirty money by pimping her to many studio executives.[4] Zwillman thus was reassured to learn that Johnny Rosselli would escort Harlow in Longy's absence.

With the exception of new homes purchased out of state and in upscale Chicago suburbs, and Nick Circella's new investments in his nightclub enterprises, the Outfit kept a low profile on their home turf of Chicago. Thriving associates who found it difficult to keep their names out of the newspapers were harshly punished. Joe Accardo and Curly Humphreys, not wishing to repeat Big Al's mistakes, were in total disdain of any publicity. But for all their planning, the gang's six-year-old scheme in Hollywood was about to unravel. The endgame would bring about prison terms for some Outfit bosses, who then refined their enterprise still again, giving them a future virtually unmolested by their upperworld adversaries.

---

4. When she married Paul Bern, assistant to brilliant MGM producer Irving Thalberg, Bello wasn't pleased. Two months later Bern was shot to death. Longy Zwillman had previously made a deal with Bern to bring him into the New York mob "so long as Longy can fuck the Baby."

7.

Waking Up
in the Dream Factory

Although a number of factors played into the eventual demise of the Outfit's Hollywood spree, one largely avoidable oversight was crucial: The Outfit neglected to teach Willie Bioff how to launder money. Long experienced in the ways of rendering truckloads of bootleg cash untraceable, the gang's failure to pass their expertise on to Willie the pimp would come back to haunt them. As previously noted, the Outfit used many methods to launder their money, especially favoring the natural subterfuge provided by cash flow at their racetracks. But in Hollywood, Willie Bioff had no clue how to avoid walking into a bank with a $100,000 cash deposit in his pocket. Ironically, of all the illegal chicanery orchestrated by Bioff, it was his benign desire to build a home that led to the collapse of his Hollywood reign. It would also temporarily derail key bosses in Chicago.

"A chain is only as strong as its weakest link" goes the aphorism, and it was the most compelling lesson learned by the Outfit in their IASTE finagling. The weak link in the Hollywood scam, to no one's surprise, turned out to be Willie Bioff. Like so many before him, Bioff believed that by demanding payoffs in cold cash he would effectively protect himself from a paper trail of his covert criminal transactions. In the short term he was correct, but he had not learned the lesson of the bootleggers: Spending vast amounts of cash is an invitation to official scrutiny. By the time Bioff realized his mistake, he had to scramble. Thus, when he desired to place a down payment on his Rancho Laurie purchase in 1937, Bioff was by then aware that even a rookie bank officer's eyebrows might raise at the sight of a thousand $100 bills dropped on his desk. In what would prove to be a fatal move, Willie Bioff turned to Joe Schenck to launder his funds and bail him out of his predicament.

Since Bioff had facilitated the Schenck brothers' money laundering on numerous occasions, he expected, and received, a quid pro quo. Instead of depositing his cash in the bank, Bioff consigned it to Joe Schenck, who in return made out a company check to Willie for the same amount, $100,000. With his money now in a nonsuspicious form, Willie marched down to the bank and deposited a Twentieth Century-Fox business check, which he could claim, if asked, was a commission payment for his film-stock agenting deal. The transfer went unnoticed for the better part of 1937. However, when one of Willie Bioff's growing number of enraged adversaries was pushed to the brink, the exchange was brought to light, triggering a series of events that ended with the collapse of the entire enterprise.

A number of disparate forces had opposed Bioff's handling of IATSE, but had been stymied in their attempts to oppose the powerful Bioff-Browne-Rosselli-Outfit alliance. Bioff's enemies were too numerous and motivated, however, to give up the fight, and their diligence was soon to be rewarded. One such foe, a coalition known as the IA Progressives, engaged in pitched battle with Bioff's IATSE muscle. Courageously led by Irv Hentschel and Jeff Kibre, the IA Progressives fought to "get the mob out of the union." Forming their own scab union-within-a-union, Kibre and Hentschel persuaded growing numbers of workers to defy Bioff's orders.

The same year he constructed his paean to domesticity in the valley, Bioff began making noise about muscling in on the Screen Actors Guild (SAG). After SAG meetings, guild members would emerge to find their car tires slashed. Other members were mugged and threatened, but despite the assault, the SAG contingent refused to capitulate. Instead, they conducted their own investigation of Willie Bioff. Under the leadership of its president, actor Robert Montgomery, SAG financed an inquiry that uncovered the $100,000 payment Schenck and Fox had made to Bioff. With the examinations by the IA Progressives and SAG making headlines, the California state legislature began its own review. Under oath, Bioff stated that the transaction was merely a loan, obtained so that he could purchase land. The Assembly's investigation allowed them to append Bioff's résumé to include "former panderer from Chicago." The IA Progressives seized the opportunity to distribute leaflets boldly illustrated with Bioff's Chicago mug shot. Despite the setback, Bioff was not about to take the insults lying down. Using Curly Humphreys' tried-and-true MO, Willie was able to nip the Assembly problem in the bud by paying Assembly Speaker William Jones and his investigator William Neblitt

$5,000 to kill the investigation. The move would grant Bioff only a temporary reprieve: 1938 was a bad year to be on the wrong side of the law in California, as the political climate was undergoing one of its periodic reform movements. In Los Angeles, the public was calling for gangster-corrupted mayor Frank Shaw's recall, eventually succeeding in September 1938. Nitti and the Outfit sensed the obvious and sent word to Bioff that he should step down from his IATSE post, at least publicly. Bioff complied with the order, but continued to draw a salary and shadow his boss, George Browne.

Whereas Nitti and the gang began to express concern, George Browne exuded confidence. At the 1938 IATSE convention, Browne came to his friend Willie's defense. His oration to his delegates also included jingoistic verbiage that would conveniently be adopted by firebrand pols for the next four decades: He labeled the Progressives "Communists" and "parlor pinks." With Browne's Red-baiting diatribe ringing the rafters of the auditorium below him, Willie the pimp took two of his goons to Irv Hentschel's hotel room, where they beat the daylights out of him. It was Willie's last stand; the battle for the union had just begun.

Bartenders' Union Redux

The year 1938 not only provided drama on the IATSE front, but also for the continuing Outfit battle for control of Chicago's bartenders' unions. Having successfully placed Louis Romano on the board of the five-thousand-member Local 278 three years earlier, the gangsters embarked on an expansion that appeared to backfire, but actually helped embroider the growing legend of the Outfit's legal sage, Curly Humphreys.

The union's business agent, George McLane, later recalled how one day in 1938, Louis Romano, accompanied by Curly Humphreys and his partner from the bootlegging days, Fred Evans, arrived at his office. Robert Satchie, president of Local 278, had died of natural causes, prompting Curly Humphreys' decision that Romano should be elevated to the presidency of the Chicago bartenders' union. "As they sat down, Romano told me, 'I'm taking over,'" McLane recalled. "My desk drawer was open a few inches and they noticed my pistol. Humphreys and Romano pulled pistols and ordered me away from the desk."

"We're taking over," Romano repeated. "You will receive your pay." McLane took the demand to his board, which initially refused to grant Romano and the Outfit the top spot. When McLane reported back to the Capri, Curly Humphreys gave him the Look and coldly said, "Tell us who opposes it. We will take care of it." McLane asked his counsel what he should do. "Turn it over to them" was the reply. If McLane hadn't made up his mind by then, he would when he reached inside his coat pocket. "They slipped me a bullet," McLane testified. A bullet placed in a man's jacket was the standard Outfit warning of imminent death to its recipient. McLane went on a forced three-month vacation. When he returned, Curly and Romano had formed a "joint council," having muscled fifteen other unions to fall under their umbrella. The Outfit's dues-paying bartender serfs had now grown from five thousand to thirty thousand.

While the Humphreys-McLane tango continued, events were quietly occurring elsewhere that marked the end of an era. In April 1939, Johnny Torrio conceded defeat to the IRS after having been charged with evading $86,000 in taxes for the years 1933 to 1935. The feds had even gotten to the near-demented Al Capone in prison and persuaded him to testify against his mentor. However, his ramblings turned out to be incoherent and useless. Although Torrio initially pleaded not guilty, he changed his plea, it is assumed, so that the prosecutors would not pry open a door that would lead them into the heart of the all-important Commission. After serving twenty-three months in Leavenworth, Torrio was paroled on April 14, 1941. He had done his time like a man of honor and had earned the right to retire as a living legend among those who knew what he had accomplished in a life dedicated to forging profitable alliances. The man whose vision had created first the truce between the James Street Gang and the Five Points Gang, then organized the original Chicago Syndicate, and finally the national Commission, was fifty-nine years old when he decided to take his millions and enjoy the good life.

The same year that Torrio was sent up on tax charges, his protégé, Al Capone, was liberated. On November 7, 1939, with his health in steep decline, Capone was released to his wife's custody. He would spend the next few years in seclusion at his Palm Island estate.

Meanwhile, McLane continued to haggle with Nitti and the gang about Romano. Now the Outfit wanted the union to nominate Romano for the national bartenders' union presidency at the upcoming convention, the ploy used so successfully with George Browne and IATSE. McLane recalled one occasion when Curly Humphreys visited him at the union office, and the master of the velvet-glove approach was in rare form. "Why don't you have some sense? You have been in the labor game all your life, but you don't have a quarter." Curly promised that the Outfit would make McLane as rich as Bioff and Browne. But McLane was unyielding. "I can't go to sleep at night," McLane said. "I ain't going to push people around for you or anybody else." Humphreys was taken aback, saying, "That's the trouble. We call it business and you call it pushing people around."

McLane later testified that at some of these meetings he met Bioff, Browne, and Circella. Clearly, the movie scam was to be used as a template for the gang's national control of all forms of pleasure. Eventually a compromise was reached wherein the Outfit agreed to prop up McLane himself instead of Romano for the national leadership of the bartenders' union. When Nitti first suggested the new strategy, McLane tried to school the mobster. "I told Nitti that, as it would be known that I was an Outfit yes-man, I would wind up in the penitentiary, or in an alley." But Nitti would hear none of it. "They told me they had run other organizations and had taken other organizations through the same channels," McLane said, "and all they said they wanted was two years of it and they would see that I was elected." McLane capitulated to Nitti's demand, and just as Browne had been forced on IATSE, McLane would be installed at the top of the national bartenders' union.

When the convention occurred, the Outfit miscalculated somehow and McLane was defeated. By this time, George McLane had had enough. He went to Chicago's master of chancery, Isadore Brown, telling the city official of the death threats he had received from the boys from Cicero. This led to the impanelment of a Cook Country grand jury in 1940. When the state's attorney announced publicly on June 5, 1940, the subject of the grand jury's inquiry, the gangsters had to move fast. In the days of Capone's Syndicate, the situation would have demanded that the gang dust off their Chicago typewriters. But Curly saw things differently: If the grand jury sent up indictments, a trial might provide him a laboratory in which to field-test some legal maneuvers he had been studying. If he had done his homework properly, the trial could be the best thing that ever happened to the Outfit. Thus, instead of using force to stop McLane from repeating his story before the grand jury, Curly told his colleagues to keep their distance. Curly's move was meant to inform his associates that they could use brains over brawn. Furthermore, there would be no intimidation of the judge or jury. His grand strategy predicated that McLane be allowed to talk to the grand jury, and that the resultant trial go forward. And talk McLane did, with his testimony culminating in the indictments

of Nitti, Humphreys, Ricca, Romano, Evans, and a slugger named Tom
Panton. Ricca and Campagna promptly went on the lam, probably to
Hollywood. Local 278's council was dissolved and the union placed into
receivership until untainted directors could be placed in charge. Why the
Outfit would so break with tradition by allowing a trial to proceed
seemingly without interference would soon be made abundantly clear.
The stage was now set for Humphreys' brilliant manipulation of the legal
code.

Although other attorneys were reported as defense counsels of record
when the case came before the criminal court, it was actually Curly
Humphreys who masterminded the legal strategy that left even his
adversaries in awe. Just before the November 29, 1940, trial, George
McLane reported that his union was now healthy, persuading the court to
terminate the receivership. At this point, McLane's attorney, A. C. Lewis,
should have suspected something. On the first day of the trial, McLane
informed Lewis that he was fired. In his place was a former judge named
Alfar Eberhardt, a close friend of Curly Humphreys'. After this introductory shock, Humphreys made his grand entrance. Curly's biographer
John Morgan described the scene: "The Welshman strolled into Criminal
Court, with his lawyer Roland Libonati in tow, smiling courteously at the
assembly, placing his vicuña coat on the back of his chair and gracing the
judge with a smile." Knowing what was about to transpire, Humphreys
must have had a difficult time stifling his glee.

Following the requisite introductory remarks, the state prosecutor
swore in his crucial star witness, George McLane. After McLane gave
his name and address, the bombshell exploded, ignited by a seemingly
innocent interrogatory:

Prosecutor: "What is your wife's given name?"

McLane: "I must refuse to answer on the grounds that it might tend to
incriminate me."

Prosecutor: "Do you know the defendant Murray Humphreys?"

McLane: "I must refuse to answer on the grounds that it might tend to
incriminate me."

And so it continued, with Curly Humphreys "beaming at the witness,"
as reported by the *Chicago Tribune*. With the state's only witness to the
threats suddenly gone mute via the Fifth Amendment, the case against all
of the defendants was dropped. But more important, with the charges
heard in open court, the defendants could not be tried again on the same
complaint. Humphreys let the world know he had studied the "double

jeopardy" clause of the Constitution. Ricca and Campagna could return to the Windy City and show off their tans with knowing smiles. They proceeded to successfully infiltrate the bartenders' union. After the receivership was rescinded, James Crowley, the man who won the union presidency at the 1941 convention, quickly appointed Outfit members to key union posts.

Two decades later, the FBI learned what had happened behind the scenes at the McLane trial; thanks to a hidden microphone in one of the Outfit's headquarters, the G-men heard Curly brag repeatedly about his 1940 legal triumph. According to one of the agents, after the trial was announced, Humphreys warned McLane that if he uttered a word in court, "his wife, Christine, would be abducted and kept alive as her husband was daily sent one of her hands, then her feet, then her arms." Humphreys added, "I not only had McLane, I had the prosecutor, and I even had a juror for good measure. I was taking no chances." Humphreys then instructed McLane in another legal maneuver he had been studying: the Fifth Amendment's protection against self-incrimination. Of course, McLane had done nothing wrong, but the court could not know that. It is one of the first times that the underworld sought refuge behind the Fifth Amendment.[1]

Thanks to Humphreys' masterstroke, Ricca and Campagna had dodged one legal bullet. But even Curly could not entirely defuse the situation that confronted his pals as a result of their West Coast operations. However, his intercession would greatly reduce the damage to his partners in crime.

The Taxman Cometh

While George Browne and Willie Bioff frantically treaded water in their fight against the IA Progressives, three more adversaries were creating tidal waves for the beleaguered hoods. In fact, things were happening so fast that accounts vary as to which came first. One opponent was the ubiquitous taxman. Elmer Irey, the IRS chief who had relished using the tax code against Big Al Capone, suddenly became interested in *l'affaire* Bioff. Irey had been looking into Hollywood tax dodgers since the 1920s, when many movie stars were regularly evading taxes. One tax consultant named Marjorie Berger represented seventy celebrity clients, simulta-

---

1. It is believed that the first gangland use of the Fifth Amendment shield was devised by attorneys for legendary New York bootleg kingpin Arnold Rothstein.

neously teaching them how to pad their expense accounts. In that investigation, twenty-two stars pleaded guilty, and Berger went to jail for three years, eventually paying $2 million in back taxes.[2] In the end, the IRS did not adjudicate its tax case against Bioff, but it did get Schenck, and Schenck's trial would throw a bright spotlight on Bioff's more serious infractions. Meanwhile the trades began reporting in earnest on the IATSE boss' travails. Moreover, a California grand jury had begun delving into Bioff's $5,000 payoff of the General Assembly.

Another ominous event was the recent involvement of a member of the fourth estate, a journalist with a terrier's tenacity. In Connecticut, syndicated columnist Westbrook Pegler followed *Variety*'s coverage of the unfolding SAG and California Assembly investigations. One version holds that it was Pegler who tipped off SAG's investigators as to Bioff's true background. According to that telling, Pegler was introduced to Bioff at a Hollywood party. Having worked the crime beat in Chicago for years, Pegler immediately recognized the notorious whore-beater and leaked the information to the authorities. In the best gumshoe style, Pegler journeyed back to Chicago, and with the assistance of police lieutenant Make Mills, began poring over dusty old police records. They hit paydirt, for which Pegler later earned a Pulitzer Prize, when they located a 1922 "open" conviction of Bioff for beating a whore. The bottom line: Bioff owed the state of Illinois six months in the slammer. In November 1939, Bioff received by telegraph a warrant for the 1922 conviction. A battery of high-priced lawyers delayed but could not prevent Bioff's incarceration. While the stalling tactics ensued, Elmer Irey's IRS indicted Willie for underestimating his 1937 tax bill by $69,000. George Browne responded by inviting right-wing Senator Martin Dies to Hollywood to ferret out Communists, and while perorating at the 1940 IATSE convention, Browne stepped up his attacks on the alleged Communists in the IA Progressives. In *Hollywood's Other Blacklist,* a study of Hollywood's union struggles, authors Mike Nielsen and Gene Mailes described Browne's presentation: "In Browne's remarks the line was blurred between communism and fascism . . . Browne maintained that communism 'not only exists within the country, but within the ranks of our

---

2. Among those pinched in related inquiries were Tom Mix ($100,000), Marion Davies ($1 million, which publisher W. Randolph Hearst paid off), and Charlie Chaplin ($1 million). Chaplin eventually left the country to avoid paying the balance of his penalty.

organization as well' . . . Browne mixed the motives of the communists with those of the producers, as if the two groups had somehow conspired to overthrow IATSE. Why the communists would want to help Louis B. Mayer or Joe Schenck was never clearly explained."

The IATSE chief then praised his secretary, Willie Bioff, evoking images of a saintly and tireless advocate of the downtrodden rank and file. "William Bioff is the victim of a merciless series of scurrilous attacks," Browne decried. "It was not hard to see that instead of the legislature being investigated, the IATSE was being investigated, and it became apparent that this was another fishing expedition to embarrass my personal representative, William Bioff." The speech remains the only time on record that Willie the pimp was referred to as "William." The nation's talking heads joined the fray, with many castigating Pegler as a front for the Communists. Even Eleanor Roosevelt, the wife of the president, sided with George Browne when she wrote critically of Pegler in her daily newspaper column (years earlier, President Roosevelt had invited Browne to relocate his IATSE headquarters to Washington).

While Browne was spewing his rhetoric at the IATSE convention, an eventful proceeding was quietly taking place in New York, as Joseph Schenck was indicted for fraud. On April 15, 1940, Bioff entered Bridewell Prison on the pandering charge, from which he was released five months later. While in jail, the Outfit sent Charles "Cherry Nose" Gioe (pronounced *joy*) to check on Willie, who was near the breaking point. Bioff informed Gioe that he was going to quit the Outfit. The next day, Gioe's immediate superior, Louis "Little New York" Campagna, appeared at Willie's jail cell. It came out in later testimony that Louis Campagna educated Willie Bioff to one of the Outfit's bylaws: "Anybody who resigns from us resigns feet first." Willie Bioff then headed back to Hollywood, oblivious to the ramifications of the Schenck indictment, and continued his IATSE racketeering as if nothing had changed.

In April 1940, the same month Willie Bioff entered prison on the pandering charge, Johnny Rosselli married actress June Lang (born Winifred Vlasek), one of the many starlets he had been escorting on the Hollywood party circuit. Within two years, after fights over Johnny's jealousy and weeklong disappearances, the marriage ended. (After his 1943 divorce from Lang, Johnny never remarried.)

In New York, young federal prosecutor Boris Kostelanetz (younger brother of famed New York Philharmonic conductor Andre Kostelanetz), using the $100,000 transaction as leverage, cut a deal with Joe Schenck: In return for a reduced sentence, the movie mogul agreed to rat out Bioff, Browne, and Circella. At the same time, Elmer Irey indicted Bioff on tax charges, for allegedly underpaying his 1937 tax bill by $69,000. A still feisty Bioff posted bond on this charge, declaring "big business" was out to get him. The tax charge would soon be dropped, in favor of a much more damning complaint, the first hint of which surfaced during the Schenck fraud trial.

Joseph Schenck knew the tax charges could be just the tip of the iceberg: If the jurists sussed out the full extent of his labor racketeering, gambling, illicit cash transfers, and collusion with the Outfit, the mogul might never see the light of a Beverly Hills day again. He decided to cooperate with his prosecutors, but disclosed only enough to guarantee a reduced sentence. In essence, Schenck would admit his payoffs to IATSE, via Bioff, Browne, and Circella, and pray that they would leave it at that (in terms of Schenck, they did). When Johnny Rosselli was called before a New York grand jury, he knew from the tenor of the inquisition that someone was going to have to take a fall. Hopefully, with sufficient damage control and a little luck, the bleeding could be stopped before proving fatal to the gang leaders back in the Windy City. After emerging from the inquest, Rosselli telephoned Willie Bioff in California. "Everybody you have done business with has squawked," scolded the gangster. Within days, on May 23, 1941, Bioff and Browne were indicted on tax and racketeering charges, while Circella was sought as a material witness. (After some tense intramural squabbling, Elmer Irey's IRS was persuaded to drop the tax charges, since they would most likely run concurrently with a racketeering sentence.)

So far as the Outfit was concerned, the trio were small potatoes, and highly expendable. What was most important was that the grand scheme, the virtual shadow government known as the Commission formed with the New Yorkers, survive. The stakes were too high. Immediately after the indictments were announced, Rosselli raced out to Rancho Laurie to engage in some witness tampering. To save his own skin, Gentleman Johnny came armed with Bioff's script. A submissive Bioff agreed to testify that, although Rosselli was a good friend of George Browne, Bioff had met Rosselli only once, in 1936. With Rosselli's role seemingly obfuscated, the likable gangster took his leave. Willie probably knew that this session was merely a prelude to the day when the knock on his door came from the big boys back East. In

Chicago and New York, the Commission met to decide how best to limit the damage, but there was really only one choice for the role of Bioff's handler: Sidney Korshak.

Damage Control by the Liaison Extraordinaire

With the erratic Bioff now dangling in the wind, the Outfit and the Torrio-Lansky New Yorkers needed a legal expert who would guarantee that Bioff and Browne would not take down the entire enterprise with them. That role would be assumed by a man who would go on to rank among the most shadowy and influential power brokers of the twentieth century. A 1930 graduate of Chicago's DePaul University Law School, Sidney R. Korshak was a well-spoken, dapper young criminal attorney who was rumored to have earned beer money during his college years as a driver for Al Capone. An aging New York boss recently said, on condition of anonymity, that he knew for a fact that Big Al Capone had paid Korshak's law school tuition, hoping Korshak would later care for Capone's legal needs. Upon passing the bar, Korshak indeed began defending young thugs, quickly moving up to represent Outfit bosses who were being harassed with vagrancy arrests.

Korshak had numerous associations that gave him purchase with Chicago's hoodlum crowd. Chief among Korshak's connections was his friendship with the state's attorney's office, run by Tom Courtney and his investigator from the police labor detail, Dan Gilbert. With such important consorts, Korshak not only controlled the city's Outfit-unionized workforce, but was able to negotiate practically all gang criminal citations down to misdemeanors. Before long, Korshak had no need of the courts at all, since his clients had their cases resolved with a phone call. As one of his fellow lawyers said, "Sid Korshak is a lawyer who tries few cases – but he has one of the most important law practices in town." Rising swiftly in the local business world, the personable Korshak maintained a fitting lifestyle: He lived in a $10,000-a-year suite in the Seneca Hotel, owned by Frank Nitti's investment adviser, Louis Greenberg.

By 1939, Korshak had formed a law partnership with Harry Ash, together setting up their office in the same building that housed the Outfit-ruled First Ward Democratic Headquarters; Curly Humphreys and Jake Guzik practically lived there, orchestrating their local political corruption. During those years, as Korshak settled strikes at Outfit-controlled racetracks, he became close friends with a native of horse country and future vice president to Harry Truman, Alben Barkley of Kentucky.[3]

Experts believe that it was either Guzik or his bodyguard, Gus Alex, who recommended Korshak for the role of West Coast fixer for the Outfit. Since 1935, Korshak had been making frequent trips to visit his fiancée, an actress who was a friend of Longy Zwillman's girl, Jean Harlow. As overheard by FBI bugs planted years later, Curly Humphreys approved Korshak's recruitment. The Bureau also learned that Korshak communicated with Humphreys in code, referring to his superior as Mr. Lincoln. Given his talent and suave sophistication, Korshak was the perfect front for the gang's California expansion.

Sidney Korshak would never practice law in California; his task was more subtle, more shadowy. He was the fixer for both the Outfit and the Commission, his role being that of dealmaker or dealbreaker, depending on what Mr. Lincoln or Mr. Lansky ordered.[4] With the studios at the mercy of the mob-controlled craft unions and talent agencies, dealing with Korshak became the first order of business for any studio that wished to stay solvent. Korshak's indispensable mediating skills set a trend in Hollywood that exists to this day. As many a producer can attest, in modern Hollywood, the entertainment business is now virtually run by attorneys. One Hollywood insider recently joked, "In Hollywood, they cast a lawyer like they cast an actor." And they probably cast the lawyer first.

Over the decades, Korshak maintained close relationships with former Capone associate Jules Stein and Stein's partner at MCA, Lew Wasserman. These friendships were vital to assuring the Outfit's continued weight in movieland over the decades. Like Jake the Barber (who was a Korshak client), the Schencks, the Annenbergs, and innumerable others before, Sidney Korshak mastered the art of walking through life with one foot in the upperworld and one in the underworld. Other Korshak connections to the entertainment world were of obvious attraction to

3. When he was a congressman from the Bluegrass State in the 1920s, Barkley had fought hard against the political influence of the upperworld's Kentucky Jockey Club, which by virtue of its agenda to monopolize horse betting was also a natural enemy of Korshak and the Outfit's.

4. When Torrio had devised the national Commission in New York, he had had Lansky bring Korshak aboard to oversee the New Yorkers' Western business interests.

hoods anxious to make a mark in that industry. As with Stein, Korshak was a lifelong friend of CBS president Bill Paley, who, like Korshak, had risen out of Chicago's Twenty-fourth Ward.

Korshak's wife, Bernice, a model and Ice Capades skater, obtained a glimpse of Sidney's clout early on. After returning from the honeymoon, Mrs. Korshak read from a list of coded messages that awaited her new husband.

"George Washington called, everything is status quo. Thomas Jefferson called, urgent, please call ASAP. Abraham Lincoln must speak with you, important. Theodore Roosevelt called three times, must connect with you before Monday."

"Your friends sure have a strange sense of humor. Who are they?" asked Bernice.

"Exactly who they said they were," was Sidney's terse response. "Any other questions?" According to producer Bob Evans, who was told the anecdote by Bernice, "Fifty years later, Bernice has never asked another question."

In Los Angeles, Joe Accardo's longtime associate and gambling expert Charles "Cherry Nose" Gioe who, like Korshak, lived at the Seneca, had first introduced Sidney Korshak to Willie Bioff. "Sidney is our man," Gioe had instructed, "and I want you to do what he tells you. He is not just another lawyer. He knows our gang and figures our best interest. Pay attention to him, and remember, any message you get from him is a message from us." Three days after Bioff's indictment, Korshak renewed his acquaintance with the man who formerly pummeled prostitutes in Chicago's Levee.

"You will admit to being Schenck's bagman and do your time like a man," Korshak explained to Bioff when they convened at L.A.'s Ambassador Hotel two days after the indictment. Bioff knew that defying Korshak meant defying the Outfit. He accepted his fate and prepared for the trip back to New York to plead guilty. Korshak obtained $15,000 from his Chicago bosses, a gift to Bioff to defray his attorney fees. It is assumed that similar arrangements were made with George Browne, who also turned himself in.

The third defendant, Nick Circella, the most obvious link to the Chicago bosses, disappeared after his indictment the following September. His flight invites the reasonable inference that he was ordered to go on the lam by the Outfit, since his interrogation would leave a key gangster open to being "turned" by the government. It was a chance, however remote, that the gang was unwilling to take. Circella went into hiding with his girlfriend Estelle Carey, a thirty-four-year-old, beautiful, blond hostess at Circella's Colony Club. Carey, a former 26 game dice girl,[5] had moved up to the lucrative position of hostess when she hooked up with Circella. As a hostess, Estelle's primary responsibility was to steer potential high rollers from the legal 26 game to the illegal, big-money craps tables on the second floor. The role also called for the occasional bedding of a client in a third-floor suite, if that's what it took to keep him happy. Circella, who was known to share Estelle with his Outfit associates, often crowed about her talents. "I once saw her steer an oilman from Tulsa to the tables," Circella boasted. "He lost ten grand in an hour. She kept him happy all the time, and after that, whenever he came to Chicago, he wanted Estelle." Now on the run with Nick Circella, Estelle Carey dyed her hair black, abandoning the high life of Chicago's nightclub district for the suburbs.

The summer of 1941 saw a battery of legal maneuvers that stalled Bioff and Browne's trial opening as long as possible. On October 6, 1941, the trial finally commenced, opening with pleas that were unheard of in gang circles: Both defendants defied Korshak's directive and pled not guilty, assuring that witnesses would be heard who could tip the prosecutors to the real scope of the operation. In Chicago, the bosses seethed, worrying that the capricious Bioff might trump his mistake and take the stand. To the gang's increased consternation, he did. Now all they could do was hold their collective breath and hope for the best. Bioff's testimony showed that he had decided he could fight the charges without giving up the Outfit. His one-note defense was inventive, if nothing else: "They bribed me. I didn't extort them." Bioff claimed weakly that the producers sought him out to guarantee labor peace.

Although Bioff himself spared the Outfit, the gang's fears were eventually realized when the trial heard from another witness. As a result of Schenck's limited cooperation, prosecutors Boris Kostelanetz and Matthias Correa had deposed a number of other movie moguls. Lightbulbs went off in the prosecutors' heads when they inadvertently picked up a bombshell from the lips of Warner Bros.' head, Harry Warner. The beleaguered executive

---

5. In 26, an attractive girl holds a cup of ten dice at a three-foot-square board. For a quarter, a customer gets a roll; if he gets 26, he wins a drink (legal). Many clubs had a backroom version where bettors played for money (illegal). According to Chicago Code 191, Section 1, "All gambling is illegal."

recalled that on one occasion when Willie Bioff had upped his cash demands, he had let slip the true scope of the racket. "The boys in Chicago insist on more money," Bioff had blurted. That was all the prosecutorial team needed to hear. They were now certain that Bioff's Chicago background was more than happenstance, since it went straight to the heart of the regime of Al Capone's heirs, the Outfit. Although it was too late in these proceedings to vet the new revelation, the prosecutors were salivating over the potential for future investigations. After three weeks of testimony, and after only two hours of deliberation, the jury returned a guilty verdict. Soon Bioff received his ten-year sentence, while Browne got an eight-year term. On December 1, one week prior to America's declaration of war against Germany and Japan, and within weeks of the Bioff and Browne verdicts, Circella was apprehended while having breakfast at Shorty's Place on Cicero Avenue, miles from his normal haunts on the Near North Side. To the great dismay of the prosecutors (and the relief of the Outfit), Circella played his role true to form: He clammed up. On March 8, 1942, Circella pled guilty and quietly went away to prison.

For the prosecutors, the work had just begun. Putting away the heirs to Al Capone was potentially a career-making case, and the team gave it the requisite attention. The were emboldened by the June 1934 passage of the Federal Anti-Racketeering Act (the Copeland Act), which gave law enforcement new weapons to train on gangsters. With Schenck serving a lenient three-year sentence (which was reduced to one year and a day), and Browne and Bioff facing hard time, the prosecutors strategized over how to build their case against the Outfit. Initially, they focused on the double-book-keeping Izzy Zevlin, hoping he might provide the link to the Outfit. He would be indicted later that year, but without providing the fatal blow to the Outfit. Meanwhile, the other Outfit bosses lay low, hoping the heat would die down. Some even sought to embellish their biographies with patriotic gestures. Curly Humphreys utilized his Hollywood connections to organize a wartime bond rally at Chicago's Soldier Field. Pressed into service were such luminaries as Bob Hope, George Raft, Jimmy Durante, and a young up-and-comer named Frank Sinatra. Johnny Rosselli, in his effort to wave the flag, went so far as to enlist in the army. The thirty-seven-year-old sufferer of chronic tuberculosis was a recruitment long shot at best. However, after an initial rejection, the persistent Rosselli was inducted on December 4, 1942. Although his patriotism was never in question, his biographers labeled his move for what it was, an "all-American alibi."

Throughout 1942, the intrepid federal prosecutors in New York prodded Bioff, Browne, and Circella with little success. Circella toyed with the idea of cooperating with investigators. "He never agreed to spell everything out for us, but there was a measure of cooperation," Kostelanetz told writer Ed Becker decades later. But with the dawning of 1943, a horrific piece of savagery turned the tide in the government's favor.

At 3:09 in the afternoon on February 2, 1943, Chicago firemen were called to an apartment at 512 Addison Street on the North Side near Lake Michigan, where neighbors had smelled smoke. Racing up the stairs to the third-floor apartment, the firemen found the still-smoldering corpse of a redheaded young woman on the dining-room floor. Her remains were in a horrid state: She had been stabbed with an ice pick, beaten, and set afire after being doused with a flammable liquid. The flash fire had burned the flesh off her legs up to her knees. The apartment's condition bespoke of a fierce struggle. The woman's blood and hair covered the walls and floors in the kitchen and dining room. In the kitchen, investigators found the bloody objects used to assault the woman before she was set ablaze: a blackjack, an ice pick, a knife, an electric iron, and a broken whiskey bottle. The police concluded that the crime had occurred just hours before their arrival. The victim, it was learned, had been on the phone with her cousin when she had had to answer the door. "I'm expecting someone" were her last words as she hung up. Although two fur coats were missing, the victim's much more valuable jewelry was untouched. Police wondered if the coats were taken to give the appearance of a robbery. Also, the bottle of flammable liquid found in the ashes had not belonged to the deceased or her roommate, and burglars are not typically known to carry combustibles with them to a heist.

Virtually no one suspected organized crime involvement in the tragedy, since killing a wife, girlfriend, or any woman for that matter violated the gangsters' unique moral dogma. In addition, since the Outfit had taken over, innocent bystanders were insulated from the fray even more so than in Capone's day. What gave the investigators pause was that both the victim's given surname, Smith, and her blond hair had been changed several times, and that most recently she had been known as Estelle Carey, the talented nightclub hostess and lover of Nick Circella.

Investigators learned that Carey had dyed her hair still again (this time red) and gone into hiding after Circella's indictment, taking up with a roommate named Maxine Buturff. Although police initially suspected a mob hit, they never determined why Carey would feel threatened by gangsters whose code prohibited the terrorizing of women. Like most other Chicago murders of the era, Carey's would go unsolved, allowing speculation to fill the void. One theory holds that Carey had been two-timing Circella and had divulged his hideout to authorities; another view maintains that both Circella and Carey had skimmed from the Outfit's Hollywood extortion operation and thus courted punishment; another hypothesis postulates that the Outfit killed Carey to dissuade the defendants from entertaining the notion of testifying against the bosses; lastly, there remains the possibility that the crime was just a ghastly coincidence, having nothing to do with the Outfit or the Hollywood trial. This last possibility certainly jibes with the Outfit's aversion to involving women in its affairs. It is widely believed in Chicago that Carey was seeing Outfit enforcer Marshall Caifano on the side, and that she was using her cachet with him to manipulate, and infuriate, countless creditors. But tending to verify the gang's culpability was that coincident with Carey's murder, George Browne's wife received an anonymous phone call warning her and her husband not to cooperate with the investigation, lest her lifeless body turn up in somebody's trunk.

Whatever its motive, the murder of Carey, combined with the death threats, produced powerful but opposite effects on Circella and Bioff. If Nick Circella had seriously entertained the thought of singing to the G, he quickly thought better of it after the slaughter on Addison Street. "As soon as [Carey] was killed, that was the end of it," prosecutor Kostelanetz recalled. "[Circella] turned off, boom, just like an electric light." Unlike Circella, Willie Bioff, fearing for his beloved Laurie and their children, reacted with rage, saying, "While we do time for them, they are murdering our families." Bioff proceeded directly to the prosecutor's office asking, "What do you want to know?" For his part, George Browne took the middle ground, cooperating only minimally with the investigators.

Now a friendly prosecution witness, the reckless Bioff attempted to enhance his appeal to the government by adding patriotism to his rationale for giving testimony, telling prosecutors, "I am a loyal American. I just want to get out so I can do my part against the Axis." Bioff was not the only culprit attempting to play the patriotism card. Called before a grand jury that summer, Johnny Rosselli left his army barracks at Fort McPherson, Georgia, and journeyed to New York, where he took up residence at the Waldorf-Astoria. When he appeared before the jurors, the "all-American mafioso" showed up in full army dress. But his posturing was futile. Not even an appeal to America's opposition to

the evil Third Reich could derail the government's high-speed investigative train. Within days, on March 18, 1943, conspiracy and extortion
indictments were returned against Rosselli, Nitti, Campagna, Ricca (De
Lucia), and Gioe, as well as Phil D'Andrea, Frankie Diamond (Maritote),
and a New Jersey union boss named Louis Kaufman, who had helped
engineer Browne's takeover of the Kentucky IATSE convention.

Rosselli was still in New York when the ax fell and thus became the
first defendant picked up by the police. Instead of accompanying his
Eighty-first Battalion to Normandy, a uniformed Private Rosselli was
arraigned and hauled off to jail. The same night the indictments were
returned, the news was widely reported on Chicago radio. A hastily
arranged Outfit meeting convened that night at Nitti's Riverside home. At
this caucus, out of necessity, the torch was passed from Frank Nitti to Joe
Accardo and Curly Humphreys. Paul Ricca would also have been
included, except that he was virtually assured a stiff prison term. In
short time, Paul Ricca lit into the fifty-eight-year-old Nitti. "Frank, you
brought Browne and Bioff to us," Ricca yelled. "You masterminded this
whole thing and it went sour." Ricca then pronounced sentence: Nitti
should take the fall honorably, just as Big Al had done.

"But it's a conspiracy charge," countered Nitti. "We all have to hang
together." Nitti had had such a rough time in his previous incarceration
that he was determined not to go away again without a fight. Tempers
flared as the combatants rose to scream at one another. "Frank, you're
asking for it," threatened a panting Ricca. One boss' threatening another
brought the room to an uneasy silence. In a daring breach of traditional
etiquette, Nitti walked to the door, opened it, and indicated that his
former friends had to leave. Walking out into the fittingly chilly March
night, the Outfit executive board members knew that, in one way or
another, they had seen the last of their old compadre Frank Nitti.

The following day brought a freezing rain to Chicagoland. As the
2 P.M. train crawled down the tracks of the Illinois Central Railroad, its
crew was startled to see a clearly drunk man stumbling toward them on
the tracks. He was holding a whiskey bottle in one hand and a .32-caliber
pistol in the other. The train ground to a halt after the well-dressed,
smallish man made threatening gestures in its direction. In fact, he just
wanted the workers to keep their distance. With the railroad men
watching in horror, the despondent man aimed his gun at his head
and fired two shots, but he was so drunk that he missed, putting the
bullets instead through the crown of his fedora. On his third attempt,

Frank Nitti's gun found its mark, blowing his brains out in full view of the onlookers. His death remains to this day the only suicide of a high-ranking gang leader. Gang historians surmise that the Outfit gave Nitti the choice of going to prison or facing the business end of a Chicago typewriter. Nitti chose neither.

Seemingly unfazed, the Outfit bosses moved on to new business, the most pressing of which was the need to post bail of $500,000. The money was raised in much the same way that the gang had produced much of its alcohol during prohibition: the Unione Siciliana was recruited into the effort. Soon, thousands of small checks began arriving at the Outfit's headquarters, sent by the tightly knit community of Italian immigrant families, formerly the gang's alky cookers. Contributing to the effort was a mixed assortment of crooked bookies and legitimate small-business men, all of whom felt they owed something to "the boys." The FBI later identified some eighteen individuals who appeared at the Chicago offices of the American Casualty Company, the enlisted bail-bond company, toting tens of thousands of dollars each. They arrived bearing personal checks, money orders, cashier's checks, and boxfuls of cash. One married couple, Jack and Betty Sussman, arrived with $50,000 in cash. The organizer of the fund drive was the mysterious "supreme president" of the Italian-American Union (formerly the Unione Siciliana), and the former twenty-one-year-old mayor of suburban Melrose Park, attorney Joseph I. Bulger (Imburgio).[6] Bulger, now in his early fifties, was born in New Orleans, from where he was rescued by a Cajun woman after his father was lynched by the local xenophobes. The woman brought the youngster to Chicago, where he prospered, eventually graduating at age twenty from the John Marshall School of Law. After becoming one of the youngest presidents of the Unione Siciliana, Bulger assumed the role of consigliere for the Outfit, and lawyer of record for the gang's bosses, having personally handled a lawsuit for Ricca involving a fire at his Berrien Springs farm years earlier. Some believe Bulger was the hidden "ultimate leader" of the Outfit, working from his 139 North Clark Street office to link the organization back to the old country, which in turn siphoned off a percentage of the ill-gotten profits from the Windy City. This belief, though widespread in Chicago's Italian ghettos, is virtually impossible to prove.

---

6. Bulger also held the position of chief of the West Side Park District until his death decades later.

After a summer of predictable stalling maneuvers, the trial of the original "Chicago Seven" commenced on October 5, 1943. One by one, studio heads testified about the extent of the shakedown. In contrast to the reluctant witness George Browne, Willie Bioff gave unrestrained, detailed testimony that left the courtroom stunned. Of course, by the time of his testimony, Bioff had secured a deal with the prosecutors for a shortened jail term, protection, and a new identity upon his release. All he had to do was finger the Outfit leaders, and Bioff more than held up his end of the bargain. The former pimp readily admitted that his prior testimony in the 1941 trial, denying the extortion, was a total fabrication: "I lied, and lied, and lied." In fact, Bioff said, "We had about twenty percent of Hollywood when we got in trouble." The Outfit would have taken over 50 percent, Bioff added, if they hadn't "loused up." Summing up his tawdry life, Bioff said, "I am just a low, uncouth person. I'm a low-type sort of man. People of my caliber don't do nice things." This particular colloquy concluded with Bioff's introspective no-brainer: "Oh, yes, I am a very despicable man."

But the extortion admission was just one of Bioff's bombshells. He also recounted how studio heads such as the Schencks were stealing from their stockholders; how Nick Schenck had paid a federal investigator $200,000 not to investigate him; and in a statement that sent ripples of fear through the members of the Outfit's New York-based Commission partners, Bioff named Sidney Korshak as "our man in Hollywood." However, Willie "the Canary" stopped just short of naming Curly Humphreys or Joe Accardo, whom he had never met face-to-face. Keeping these key figures insulated from Bioff and Browne was a key strategy that allowed the Outfit to continue to function despite the monumental setback.

The defendants' legal team decided against putting their clients on the stand. Instead they chose to cross-examine the studio heads and Bioff in a futile attempt to to prove that the extortion was in fact bribery by venal businessmen who desired to control labor. Of course there was some truth to that defense. When a federal court investigated the estate of Frank Nitti six years later, the presiding judge noted, "The monies were extracted [from the studio heads] with full knowledge on their part as to Browne's and Bioff's activities and assurances; and no effort was made to secure the assistance of law enforcement authorities." But Kostelanetz's prosecution team was also correct about the Outfit's master plan, and the Outfit was charged in this trial, not the studio heads. In the end, the jury heard vastly more testimony about the gang's connivances than it did about the movie industry's own expedience.

On New Year's Eve, 1943, after a seventy-three-day trial, the jury delivered their guilty verdict, which carried a maximum ten-year sentence, at the discretion of the judge. In two weeks' time, the litigants returned to debate the imposition of punishment. Prosecutor Kostelanetz gave a blistering synopsis of the gang's criminal past and alleged violent associations, even arguing that the judge might see fit to extend the requisite ten-year sentence "by one or two years, as Your Honor may feel appropriate." One of the Outfit's attorneys, A. Bradley Eben, in asking for a light sentence, called attention to the obvious when he reasoned, "There is not one chance in a thousand that they will be pardoned when they first become eligible for it." Another member of the legal team added, "Your Honor may know that they will probably serve nearly every day of the sentence that Your Honor imposes." After hearing the opposing pleas, the judge pronounced punishment: Ricca, Campagna, Rosselli, D'Andrea, Maritote, and Gioe were sentenced to ten years in prison plus $10,000 fines. Louis Kaufman, the New Jersey union strong-arm, was given seven years. After three months of futile appeal motions, during which the convicts languished in New York City's dreaded Tombs prison, the gang packed its toothbrushes for what their pursuers assumed would be a decade "in college." Although Nick Circella had been sent to Leavenworth federal prison in Kansas, a day's drive from the gang's Chicago headquarters, the new convictees were remanded to the notoriously strict, 60 percent overpopulated, and hideously unsanitary Atlanta federal facility, 720 miles from the Windy City.

In Atlanta, Warden Joseph Sanford made a preemptive gesture, aimed at informing the gang bosses that they should not expect special treatment while under his watch. When Phil D'Andrea feigned illness, Sanford personally entered his cell and beat the fifty-two-year-old father of three unmercifully. When word got back to the rest, they lay low, with Rosselli even earning a job as prison library clerk, where he pursued an interest in the Bible. Rosselli also maintained his liaisons with Hollywood. During his prison stay, he received hundreds of letters from friends such as talent agent Danny Winkler and actress Beatrice Ann Frank. But for the forty-five-year-old Paul Ricca, the man who by rights should have assumed Nitti's leadership post, the ignominy was unbearable. He had paid off too many pols in his life to suffer such an outrage. But Ricca and the Outfit soon learned a valuable lesson: It was one thing to own high-placed politicians and judges, but pressure exerted by energetic scribes such as Westbrook Pegler could render all the bribes in the world moot. This epiphany caused a knee-jerk reaction in the humiliated Ricca, who instructed his lawyer that he wanted the crusading Pegler killed. Ricca was quickly disabused of this notion, however, and was counseled to go back to being "the Waiter." The Chicago contingent settled in as best they could, but Paul Ricca never believed for a moment that he could not pull off the impossible and get sprung on the first day he was eligible for parole in three years. Were he a betting man, he could have gotten great odds, since virtually no one else believed it possible.

In Chicago, enough of the brain trust survived to keep the enterprise not only afloat, but prosperous. With the Welshman Curly Humphreys as consigliere, the baton of leadership passed from the deceased Frank Nitti, leapfrogging over the imprisoned Paul Ricca, directly into the hands of Joe Accardo. Reenergized by the input from a recently sprung, tough-as-nails wheelman named Mooney Giancana, the Accardo regime would go on to achieve prosperity unmatched in America's criminal history.

8.

The Outfit:
Back from the Brink

J oe Accardo's reign commenced without missing a beat. Despite the temporary loss of such key players as Ricca, Campagna, and Rosselli, the tenacious Outfit licked its wounds and moved forward at full speed. At this time, the gang was meeting regularly in a backroom of the Morrison Hotel, Capone's old haunt, on Madison Street in the heart of the Loop, using the phone in the hotel barbershop to receive cryptic messages. During one of their confabs, they were approached by a recently released ex-con from the slum area known as the Patch. This wiry, ill-mannered roughneck had owed the G some time for illegal alcohol manufacturing. Although his personal style conflicted with the corporate-like sophistication of Accardo, Ricca, and Humphreys, what he had to say blinded the dapper bosses to the man's total lack of refinement. While "in school," the hood had learned of a lucrative scam, called policy, that he believed might be of interest to the Outfit. The man who was championing it, and who would go on to dramatically affect the Outfit's future, was known in his environs as Mooney.

Mooney's Story

The pitchman was born, according to the Bureau of Vital Statistics, Gilormo Giangona on May 24, 1908, in Chicago. However, baptismal records disclose that he entered the world as Momo Salvatore Giancana on June 15 of that year. In any event, his name somehow transmogrified into Salvatore "Sam" Giancana. Sam's parents, Antonino and Antonia, or Lena, had arrived in America from Sicily in 1905, at the ages of twenty-four and nineteen respectively. As a youth, Sam frequented the streets of the Chicago ghetto known as the Patch, which the Italian immigrant community had transformed into a replica of the Old Country: Street vendors, such as Antonino, sold fruit in the open-air marketplace, while wine and song flowed in countless clusters of friendly gatherings. Outsiders came to refer to the Patch as the Spaghetti Belt.

When Sam was but two years old, he was met with unspeakable tragedy: the tragic death of his young mother at age twenty-four due to internal hemorrhaging. Thus as a child, the callow Sam was largely unmonitored and free to succumb to the temptations of the street. It was said that boys from his enclave either became hoods or saints, and those like Sam who took to the streets were the hoods. Life for street kids in the Patch consisted of daily turf battles with the numerous ethnic groups that occupied the various districts encircling the Spaghetti Belt, predominantly the Irish, French, Jews, Greeks, and Bohemians. When not defending their territory, the youngsters stole whatever was not nailed down, delivering their plunder to the vendors in the Patch street bazaar. The other chief preoccupation was more primal: The boys used abandoned buildings for "gang shags," or gang rapes, perpetrated against the neighborhood's young female population. This distasteful rite of passage went largely unpunished, save for the rampant and often deadly cases of venereal disease that plagued the Patch's young male population.

When they were old enough to drive, the boys adopted street racing as a favorite pastime and show of machismo. By now, many had sided up with gangs that took measure of their virility in intergang drag racing. Coursing dangerously through crowded streets at all hours, the boys honed their skills at moves such as "whipping," the taking of turns at high speeds, often on two wheels. Young Sam became known as one of the best wheelmen in the Patch, commandeering souped-up muscle cars that would remain a trademark throughout his life. Sam's wild, unrestrained talent as a wheelman (among other things) earned him the nickname that would stick with him for the rest of his life: Mooney, or crazy. The danger implicit in such high-velocity antics often led to tragedy, and in at least one case, irony. In October 1926, a pedestrian named Mary ran after her four-year-old son, Charley, who had scampered into a Patch street just as a member of Mooney's gang screeched toward him in his Cadillac. Shielding her child, the terrified woman took the full brunt of the impact, which killed her but spared the child. The woman was Mary Giancana, Mooney's stepmother, and Charley was his stepbrother.

The gang that recruited Mooney's talents was the most notorious in the Patch. As noted previously, the 42 Gang harbored terrorists deemed indispensable to the union organizers and politicians, as well as drivers for the bootleggers. The gang had been organized around 1925 by Joey

"Babe Ruth" Colaro, a suave, smooth-talking delinquent who specialized in tire snatching, auto theft, and police bribes. Colaro was one of the prescient gang leaders who determined that the local police force was largely composed of ravenous immigrants like himself, anxious to have their palms greased. One 42 member later recalled, "When we were making so much, we thought the police were scums, shysters. They could be bought for so little; they were money hungry."

By the time Mooney worked the streets with the 42s, Volstead had been enacted, opening up a wider variety of criminal choices for young hoodlums. While many of their parents made ends meet as alky cookers, the boys performed liquor runs for the bootleggers or assisted them in election "slugging." These jobs were considered noble since the bootleggers were respected by most immigrants as businessmen, heroes who provided a service and gave lucrative jobs to the otherwise unemployed. Mooney quickly rose to a leadership role in the same 42 Gang that provided the muscle in the infamous 1927 Pineapple Primary and assisted Curly Humphreys and Red Barker in their tire-slashing putsch against the Midwest Garage Owners Association.

Mooney Giancana did not emerge unscathed from his illicit adolescence. The hyperactive gang member was arrested numerous times for auto theft, burglary, and attempted burglary. In 1926, the eighteen-year-old was indicted for murder, only to have the charges dropped for lack of evidence. His constant need of bail money, combined with the fines that often accompanied his convictions, kept his father in permanent impoverishment.

By the midthirties, Mooney Giancana had married and fathered two daughters. During this period Mooney and his driving prowess came to the attention of a genuine Patch big shot, Outfit boss Paul Ricca. The revered Waiter honored young Sam with the offer to become his personal driver. Although this association would open doors for Mooney in the future, Giancana had to survive in the present, and squiring the dapper mob boss did not get him any closer to the end of the rainbow in the short term. With a growing family to feed, Giancana continued to cast about for more lucrative opportunities, while still chauffeuring Ricca. He believed he had found his pot of gold when he met another Patch entrepreneur named Guido "Joe Greco" Gentile. Although Volstead had been repealed, operators such as Gentile were keenly aware that there was still a fortune to be made in illegal alcohol. During the thirteen-year era of prohibition, spoiled alcohol wholesalers had grown accustomed to buying cheap, untaxed spirits and thus continued to purchase moonshine whenever it became available. Gentile would become one of the suppliers.

After locating a suitable facility, a farm in suburban Grand Prairie, Gentile enlisted his crew from the Patch gangs. Mooney Giancana was one who answered the call, giving his name to Gentile as "Albert Mancuso." Once set up, Gentile's still churned out thousands of gallons of illegal alcohol per day for more than sixteen months before the IRS uncovered the operation. After the farm was successfully raided on January 17, 1939, Gentile's crew, including Mooney, were charged with nine counts of alcohol law violations. By this time, Sam's father was nearly insolvent, and thus it fell to the hood's father-in-law to put up the $5,000 bail. The following spring, however, Mooney was dealt a four-year prison sentence, to be served, after an initial two months at the federal penitentiary in Leavenworth, in the Terre Haute, Indiana, lockup. And like so many other convicts, Mooney Giancana used his time in school to study criminality at the feet of more experienced fellow classmates. One from whom he learned the most was an African-American policy kingpin, Eddie Jones, assigned to Mooney's cellblock. As youngsters, Jones and his two brothers had prospered in one of the few rackets that had not been preempted by the Outfit: numbers.

Numbers

The game goes by numerous names: bolita, lottery, numbers, polizza, and policy. But they are essentially all variants of one of the cheapest and simplest forms of gambling that exists. Taking a chance on a drawing of numbers has been a staple, both legal and illicit, of American culture, the concept extending at least as far back as the seventeenth century, when King James I utilized the lottery to finance the growth of the colony of Virginia. Historian Henry Chafetz has written: "The American colonies were floated on lotteries." The proof of his statement is everywhere, given that state-controlled lotteries financed institutions such as the British Museum; universities such as Harvard, Yale, and Brown; Boston's Faneuil Hall; and the development of the Cumberland Pass. The games were ongoing until the 1890s, when, due to widespread corruption, they were discontinued. However, the game only went underground. And like bootlegging and horse wagering, it did not need to go very deep below the surface.

The underground variant first took hold in the poor African-American communities in the South, then, much like jazz music, migrated to the

North, where it took root in the European immigrant population. The African-Americans used to refer to the Italian gangs who came to control the game as "spigoosh." In addition to being cheap (typically a 1940s bettor wagered five cents on a three-digit number combination), the outlawed version was wonderfully convenient and accessible. In most Chicago immigrant neighborhoods, young boys earned money as runners, picking up the gambler's bets at his home or place of business. From there, the runners deposited their booty to one of Chicago's two thousand collectors, known as drops, and from there it went to the gang that controlled the action. The most common numbers wager consisted of placing a nickel bet on a number from 000 to 999, with the winning combination being drawn from a can, or "wheel." Each ethnic cluster maintained its own version of numbers: the Italian barrios called it *polizza*, Italian for "lottery ticket." Every Friday night, the *polizza* winning number was supposedly drawn from a wheel in Italy by a blind boy. The winning number was then cabled to America, where it was distributed via sundry handouts and publications.

Although there were differing methods of determining the winner (such as using the last three digits in the day's closing stock market volume or U.S. Treasury balance), the wheel variety was the most popular. The wheel, or can, consisted of a large, crank-turned tin can about half the size of an oil drum. The wheels were produced by a Chicago factory specifically for the numbers operators, who secreted the machines in remote locales where the drawings were made.

The wheel operations acquired colorful, if meaningless, names and vernacular. There were the Erie-Buffalo, the Rome-Silver, the Calcutta–Green Dragon, the Whirlaway, and the Beans–Ham Gravy wheels. A player did not have a three-number choice, he had a "gig"; a winning number was not chosen, it had "come out." Although the odds against winning were 1,000 to 1, the group controlling the action typically paid off at 600 to 1, at best. With the games often rigged, the house was estimated to keep eight of every ten dollars wagered, the rare winner seeing a payoff of about $25 for each nickel bet. Players in the black communities were further abused when they were hoodwinked into buying useless "dream books," which assigned a number to a specific dream subject that a person may have just experienced. Black preachers were often ordered by the policy operators to give certain numbers to the faithful from the pulpit. The numbers were rarely correct, but the seeming imprimatur of the church built excitement for the game.

For years, Capone's Syndicate had little interest in the operation, which they dismissed as "nigger pool." With the vast riches derived from bootlegging, the nickel-per-bet policy game hardly seemed worth the time. On one occasion, when a Syndicate underling tried to muscle in on a black policy ring, Capone had the rogue offender run out of town. The Big Guy himself apologized to the threatened policy directors, saying, "That's your racket, boys. I don't want no part of it." This indifference had given the Joneses free reign build their empire. Capone's philosophy remained intact until Mooney Giancana convinced the Outfit to reconsider.

After his release from Terre Haute in December 1942, Giancana took a legit job as a salesman in his brother-in-law's envelope company. During the height of the World War II troop mobilization, Mooney was ordered to report to the draft board, where he lived up to his moniker and then some. In a high-volume tirade, Mooney recounted to his examiner the criminal exploits of his 42 Gang in minute detail. When he was asked what he did for a living, Giancana gave a now infamous response: "I steal." In bestowing the street thug a 4-H exemption, the draft board labeled him psychopathic. (During the same troop buildup, Jake Guzik received his notice. He informed the board that his fifteen-year record of friction with the law should render him ineligible for the draft. He further noted that if they insisted on drafting him, the board would have to come and get him.)

In short time, Mooney Giancana became restive in the straight life. After his third daughter was born, he began to consider ways to break into big-time gangsterism. Recalling the friendships he had formed in Terre Haute, Mooney Giancana decided it was time to seek out Eddie Jones. Soon, Giancana located the policy king, and together they struck a partnership, wherein Jones staked Giancana to the tune of $100,000 to oversee still another of the Jones' rackets: jukebox distribution.

The coin-operated jukebox, a key improvement over the noncoin variety, was devised in Chicago in 1934 by David Rockola. Before his breakthrough, Rockola was employed as a slot machine inspector for the Syndicate-infiltrated O. D. Jennings slot machine manufacturing company. It was later found that Jennings had shipped thousands of his slot machines to New York Commission member Frank Costello, who had in turn flooded Southern states such as Louisiana with Jennings' contraption. Rockola was charged in 1929 in a huge slot machine scandal, wherein he freely admitted his involvement with gangsters, corrupt politicians, and police. Although acknowledging that he had made numerous payoffs, Rockola escaped prison by cutting a deal in which he would implicate his boss, James "High Pockets" O'Brien. Now, in 1934, Rockola's new device provided gangs an easy way to skim money: Since no one could prove how many nickels were inserted, the owner of the machine could siphon off any amount of pretax lucre he desired.

Much as they ignored the numbers game during the bootlegging era, powerful gangs like the Outfit mistakenly gave little priority to the jukebox racket, using it primarily to launder money with bar owners. The opportunistic Jones brothers once again filled the breach. They had realized that Depression-era Chicagoans would gravitate to the machines. "During the Depression, people who made three dollars a week bought a nickel beer and put a nickel in the jukebox, or seven plays for a quarter, and that was their weekend," remembered Rockola's assistant, Frank Shultz. "A person who made fifty dollars a week went out to hear a band." David Rockola and the Joneses held the same philosophy: Pinball machines might go out of style, but not music.

In 1934, Rockola opened the Rock-Ola Manufacturing Company, employing thirty-two hundred workers, and covering four city blocks on Chicago's North Kedzie Avenue. Not only did his machines take coins and play more selections, but they were priced at $198, $52 cheaper than his competitors' versions. As will be seen, the Outfit became the largest purchaser of "jukes" in furtherance of its rackets. Under Mooney's guidance, the jukebox racket provided a pleasant surprise for the Outfit, reaping huge profits for decades to come.

In 1945, with his income rising steadily, Mooney purchased a spacious home in the Chicago suburb of Oak Park for $32,000. Although an exponential improvement over life in the Patch, it was not enough. Giancana had seen firsthand the extravagant lifestyle of his partners for three years now, and he grew to covet the lucrative holdings they had generated so painstakingly. Despite Eddie Jones' display of altruism toward Mooney, this greedy new partner had no qualms about betraying his benefactor. Although details are lost, it is believed that before Giancana made his move, he sought to impress the Outfit with his plan, thereby to create entrée with the big boys. Obtaining an audience with Accardo, Humphreys, and Guzik at the Morrison was no small feat, especially for one so noncorporate as Mooney Giancana. Fortunately for Giancana, one of those whom he had befriended in Terre Haute was William "Billy" Skidmore, a gambler who was both close to Johnny

Torrio and a former bagman for Jake Guzik. Combined with his former driver's role years earlier for the now imprisoned Paul Ricca, Giancana's link to Skidmore most likely paved the way for his access to the Morrison's backroom. In the winter of 1945, Mooney made his sales pitch about the wonders of policy.

The Jones brothers' Maine-Idaho-Ohio policy wheel, as Mooney had learned, generated over $1 million a year profit, much of which the ambitious brothers funneled into legitimate real estate investments, including department stores and four hotels. In addition to their mansions in Chicago with Lincolns in the driveways, the Joneses owned villas in Europe and Mexico. Most appealingly, from his vantage point on the inside of the Jones' enterprise, Giancana knew that they were no match for the muscle of the Outfit. The "black belt" areas of the South and West Sides, Mooney concluded, were ripe for a takeover.

After extolling the virtues of a racket that the Outfit had given little attention, it is believed that Giancana made the Morrison confreres an offer: If he could find a way to take over the Joneses' policy operation and provide the Outfit its cut, he would be invited into the inner sanctum of the heirs to Al Capone. The bosses possibly wondered if this uncouth thug was indeed a diamond in the rough. Perhaps former contacts, such as the prison psychiatrists at Terre Haute who had tested his IQ at a lowly 71 verbal and 93 nonverbal, had terribly misread a man with the kind of street smarts that defy measurement. He had clearly done his homework regarding policy. When the vote was taken, the decision was made to sanction Mooney's coup attempt against the Joneses' operation.

It was soon reported that Mooney Giancana was now performing his driving services for Joe Accardo, much as he had years earlier for Paul Ricca. In February 1945, Mooney and Joe were arrested together for questioning in a kidnap case. During this period, Giancana's family began seeing new visitors to their equally new Oak Park home. In her autobiography, *Mafia Princess*, Mooney's daughter Antoinette wrote of the changes in her father's lifestyle: "It was really from 1945 on that I became aware of the frequent comings and goings of Sam's 'business associates,' men whose names engendered fear in Chicago's underworld for decades . . . Mother never knew how many men Sam was bringing home, but two or three times a week there were guests, and they would arrive promptly for dinner."

Among the individuals Antoinette came to recognize was Curly Humphreys. A key topic of "business" was almost certainly the Outfit's planned theft of the Joneses' operation. However, for reasons unknown, the takeover did not commence for over a year. Finally, in May 1946, after months of meticulous planning, Mooney made his move. After closing his Ben Franklin department store for the night, Eddie Jones and his wife, Lydia, instructed their limo driver to also drop off the store's cashier at her home on their way to the suburbs. Unbeknownst to the limo's occupants, they were being tailed by two cars. After dropping off the cashier, the Joneses' driver was prevented from driving off by two shotgun-toting men from the tailing cars, their faces hidden behind kerchiefs. With Lydia screaming hysterically, Eddie was knocked unconscious by a blow from a rifle butt and dragged into one of the kidnappers' cars. As they screeched away, the abductors left the police, who had just arrived, with the impression that these drivers displayed talents similar to those of the notorious 42 Gang wheelmen.

For six days Jones languished in captivity while the word in the Patch was that the kidnappers were demanding anywhere from $100,000 to $250,000 for his release. The story made front-page news in Chicago and its environs. Suddenly, on the sixth day of his ordeal, the policy boss was released, but with no details divulged to the press, and no one charged. But knowledgeable Chicagoans had their suspicions. Giancana's FBI file reflects what the word was on the streets of the Windy City: "The Chicago Police believe, but can't prove, that Giancana was the brain in the $100,000 kidnapping of Jones, Negro policy king." When officials tapped their sources, the truth emerged: Mooney Giancana had taken Eddie Jones to an undisclosed location, and while captive, Jones was told to surrender his most lucrative policy wheels to Giancana or face the shotgun. In addition, he was advised that it would be wise of him to relocate to his Mexican villa, where Mooney would send him a cut of the action. Within days of his release, Jones took his family to Union Station, where they boarded a train to Mexico by way of Texas. They never lived in Chicago again.

Giancana's performance understandably impressed the Outfit's brain trust, and his stature within the gang was elevated as he became its boss of all numbers and jukebox rackets. Thanks to Giancana's ingenuity, the Outfit had more than made up for the loss of the Hollywood extortion gambit. By 1949, the Outfit's Standard Golden Gate policy alone grossed over $5 million per year. Incredibly, it was estimated that there were some thirty such wheels in Chicago. The Chicago Crime Commission estimated that by 1954, Chicago's policy racket netted some $150 million. And as per custom, Jake Guzik kept officialdom at bay by dispensing the gang's largesse. Each month, Greasy Thumb delivered bribes to Ward Committeeman William Dawson at his office at 180 West Washington Street. Dawson, an appointee of the equally corrupt Mayor Ed Kelly, went on to become the era's most powerful African-American politician, later serving eighteen years in the House, eventually becoming vice chairman of the Democratic National Committee.

Thanks to Dawson, the Outfit was able to spread its empire of gambling and loan-sharking into Chicago's African-American community. Like bootlegging, numbers running ingratiated the gangsters with the downtrodden among the immigrant population. Profits were funneled, Capone-like, into charitable causes such as food and lodging for the unemployed and homeless. In his book *Street Corner Society,* William F. White described the impact of racketeering on the immigrant community: "In all their activities, legal or illegal, the racketeers perform the important function of providing employment for a large number of men. Most of the employees have no background of experience and skill to prepare them for jobs in private industry . . . The rackets provided them with jobs which were difficult to find by other means."

Although the gang's numbers success was the most obvious of Giancana's triumphs, the jukebox racket churned on in the background, bringing in vast profits, while burnishing Mooney's rising star.

Jukin' with the Outfit

It was long an industry policy not to sell machines to bar owners, selling them instead to regional distributors, who in turn distributed them to operators who represented a number of storefronts in specific subregions. This modus operandi played right into the hands of crime gangs like the Outfit. Once Giancana was given the green light by Accardo and Humphreys, he brought in his own underlings, such as Charles "Chuckie" English and Bill McGuire, who together set up Lormar Distributing Company, named after a contraction of their wives' names, Lorraine and Mary. Jake Guzik was tapped to head a jukebox distribution company called Century Music in partnership with former Capone gang lieutenant Dennis Cooney. Guzik's son-in-law, Frank Garnett, ran Automatic Musical Instrument Company (AMI), whose machines were distributed in the East by the Runyon Sales company, owned by the notorious gangster Abner "Longy" Zwillman. Zwillman also co-owned New York's Riverside Music Company with Mike Lascari, who fronted for Lucky Luciano and Meyer Lansky. In 1949, AMI was taken over by Mooney Giancana himself. The Outfit next installed Fred "Jukebox Smitty" Smith as head of the jukebox division of the International Brotherhood of Electrical Workers Local 134; Jukebox Smitty's protégé, Mike Dale, became owner of the Commercial Phonograph Survey, which charged fees for jukebox permits. With all facets of the business in line, other nonaligned distributors withered away. Ted Sipiora, owner of Singers' One-Stop Record Service, testified that his business dropped off by 90 percent, or $800,000.

As with almost every criminal endeavor undertaken by the Outfit, the jukebox operation succeeded in large measure because the underworld easily found upperworld partners to help grease the skids. Chief among their above-the-law accomplices were jukebox manufacturers, such as the Wurlitzer Corporation. When Wurlitzer's vice president, Milton J. Hammergren, testified before Congress, his admissions to then counsel Robert Kennedy ran the gamut from shockingly candid to downright arrogant:

Kennedy: "How were you able to achieve distribution where you had difficulty in the past?"

Hammergren: "Well, let's take Chicago. I had a very intimate friend named Goldberg . . . Al Goldberg was a very aggressive and well-connected, so to speak, individual."

Kennedy: "What do you mean 'well-connected'? He had connections with the underworld element in the United States?"

Hammergren: "Yes, I would say so . . . In New York we weren't so successful . . . We proceeded to reorganize and set up a more aggressive distributorship . . . We put in Eddie Smith, Meyer Lansky, Bill Bye, and I had a piece of it myself."

Kennedy: "Were company officials upset about the use of force?"

Hammergren: "Company officials, of which I was one; yes, we didn't like it, but we still had to sell jukeboxes."

Kennedy: "If somebody, just in the course of trying to get your boxes distributed, if somebody was killed, that was taken as part of the trade?"

Hammergren: "That is one of the liabilities of the business."

Kennedy: "And the people that you found, as a general rule – the only people who could get this kind of distribution achieved – were these people with underworld connections, as a practical matter?"

Hammergren: "Yes, that is true."

Hammergren went on to admit that he had sold some 550 jukes to Jake Guzik's Century Music Company. He also conceded that he had made "arrangements" with the Outfit's St. Louis associate Buster Wortman, and in Miami with a strong-arm named Angelo Meli. Kennedy asked Hammergren if he was aware that at one time Meli was Public Enemy Number One. "Yes, I knew about it," Hammergren replied. In a 1946 grand jury investigation in Detroit, a local union secretary, Eugene James, said about Hammergren: "I know what he does here, and what he does everywhere else . . . He has always used the mob wherever he goes."

The jukes and their racket spread like wildfire across the country. In New York, Meyer Lansky, via his association with Alvin Goldberg in the Emby Distributing Company, became a major distributor for the Wurlitzer Corporation; Goldberg also teamed with Joe Accardo and Jake Guzik's son-in-law to distribute Wurlitzers in Chicago via their Chicago Simplex Distributing Company. Sam Taran took the Florida franchise; Carlos Marcello worked the scam in New Orleans; William Bufalino lorded over Michigan. Many of the jukebox machines shipped to these locales originated in Windy City factories owned or secretly controlled by the Outfit.

From June 15 to June 21, 1947, the Wurlitzer Company staged the jukebox version of the mob's infamous 1957 Apalachin summit. Wurlitzer's distributors' confab took place at Crosslake, Minnesota, and was attended by numerous "connected" individuals who were assigned to share cabins like teenagers at summer camp. Among those known to attend were Lansky's juke partners Alvin Goldberg and Willie Bye. In another cabin were Guzik's son-in-law Frank Garnett and Sam Taran. Other attendees included Henry Friedman of the mobbed-up Mercury Records Corporation and a partner of Chicago bookies Frank Harmon and Max Hoffman. One cabin was assigned to someone named Siegel, with no further clarification that his first name was Ben. The Chicago Crime Commission concluded: "The underworld was well-represented at the meeting. Several of the most important Wurlitzer distributorships were in the hands of notorious racketeers."

As with its other takeovers, the Outfit's brain trust devised numerous ways to squeeze peripheral profits from the jukebox racket. In one variation, the hoods began to cross-promote singers of its own choosing. The gang could literally turn no-talents into national sensations by manipulating the key benchmark of popularity: At the time, jukeboxes were the fastest way to promote a singer's career, and the Outfit decided whose records were placed in the boxes, which position they occupied on the machine's index, and the machine's play counters. Distributors were ordered to place certain records in the coveted number one position on the box. One aspiring twenty-four-year-old vocalist, Tommy Leonetti, was personally handled by the notorious Felix "Milwaukee Phil" Alderisio, a dreaded enforcer-for-hire. A program director for a Chicago TV station reported that "the mob actually owns 150 percent of Tommy Leonetti, and Leonetti, who is actually working on an allowance, is a very, very sorry boy." Chicago distributor Ted Sipiora recalled how he was paid a visit by a gang underling who demanded Sipiora promote a recording by Leonetti. Sipiora said the hood, John Ambrosia, doubled as Leonetti's agent and had allegedly once managed Dean Martin and Jerry Lewis. Ambrosia initially stopped in to deliver fifty copies of a Leonetti single. He later returned to express his displeasure with the sales of the record. "We told him it wasn't good enough to get on the boxes," Sipiora said. Ambrosia then began tossing a bullet in the air, saying, "These things can be dangerous. They penetrate flesh."

To this day, Chicagoans are quick to recount the tale of how one of their own became the beneficiary of the Outfit's jukebox domination to become a nationwide singing sensation. Recent conversations with both the singer's relatives and associates of Unione Siciliana president Joe Bulger demonstrate how the gang's support could boost a nascent show-biz career. In the 1930s, Bulger was the trustee and president of suburban Melrose Park, a community largely composed of blue-collar Italian laborers and craftsmen. In 1934, Bulger appointed one Mike Laraia, a distant relative through marriage, to be comptroller of Melrose Park, a powerful position that dispensed public works contracts throughout the town's labor force.

When not working civil projects, many of the town's artisans serviced the homes in neighboring upscale enclaves such as River Forest. According to local lore, when River Forest's most powerful resident, Joe Accardo, undertook the extensive renovations on his palace, Mike Laraia dispatched Melrose Park's best carpenters, plumbers, etc. Years later, when Laraia's talented teenaged daughter cut her first record, Bulger told Accardo to put his considerable weight behind the high-schooler, who had not an inkling of the favor about to be bequeathed her.

"It's time we did something for one of our own," Bulger told Accardo. Thus when Laraia's daughter released her first record, it received prime placement in the tens of thousands of the jukes under the gang's control, an incalculable advantage for a new talent. According to one Laraia cousin, "Everybody got behind the record. She's a phenomenal singer, and she deserved it."

Mike Laraia convinced his girl to change her name before going national to something more easily pronounced by non-Italians. Heeding her father's advice, Carol Laraia became Carol Lawrence, the soon-to-be Broadway sensation of the musical *West Side Story,* and countless other Broadway, recording, and television triumphs. She would marry Robert Goulet, the matinee idol star of Jack Kennedy's favorite musical, *Camelot.*

In addition to the power they wielded at the jukebox, the Outfit's relationship with Jules Stein's MCA placed it in the powerful position of starmaker for Stein's favored musical acts. Once the chosen artist's records were inserted, a phony measure of popularity was concocted: Soon after jukeboxes became a national fixture, Stein, perhaps with the gang's involvement, invented the Top Ten List, which later became the Top Forty. The gang solidified its hold on the recording industry by rigging the jukes' play count. The Outfit thus anointed Top Ten hits and created instant celebrities. They had mastered the art of "spin" in more ways than one.

Lastly, a related enterprise involved the production of counterfeit records. Some of the inferior bootlegs were made at Lormar, others at Apex Music, run by the Outfit's slot king, Eddie "Dutch" Vogel. As with the boxes themselves, the gang's bogus discs were marketed well beyond the borders of Illinois. In his book *Brothers in Blood,* Pulitzer Prize-winner David Leon Chandler recounted how the mob in Louisiana, which worked in tandem with the Outfit, used counterfeits to return a political favor.[1] In the 1940s, then governor of Louisiana Jimmie Davis helped push through legislation that allowed local boss Carlos Marcello to open gambling casinos in New Orleans. At about the same time, Davis, a longtime country-western singer, recorded the umpteenth version of his classic composition "You Are My Sunshine." Despite the public's ennui

---

1. FBI wiretaps obtained years later verified the links between New Orleans boss Carlos Marcello and the Chicago Outfit. The taps disclose how they worked on numerous crime operations in consort, and how Outfit bosses cherished their fall hunting trips to Marcello's Churchill Farms estate and Grand Isle hunting camp, both in Louisiana.

with the overrecorded chestnut, the recording by "The Singing Governor" inexplicably turned up everywhere, especially in countless mob-controlled jukeboxes across the nation. Twenty years later, when New York authorities dredged some hundred thousand of the mob's counterfeit records from the East River, they discovered that most of them were Davis' recording of "You Are My Sunshine." The cache represented a rare failed attempt by the mob to promote a recording. The FBI concluded that Davis "had done a favor for the 'Cosa Nostra,' and in return, the mob-owned jukebox companies of America had bought the Davis recordings and placed them in tens of thousands of jukeboxes."

Within ten years there were more than seven thousand jukes in Chicago alone, grossing $36 million annually. Nationwide, the Outfit controlled many of the half million machines, which generated a tidy $300-million cash flow. Rarely mentioned, though, were the enormous ancillary industries that descended from the Outfit-controlled coin-operated jukebox operation. Consider that in 1939 the Mills Novelty Company of Chicago invented the "visual jukebox," in which, for twenty-five cents a play, a patron could view "soundies," or filmed performances of a requested song. After World War II, the French improved the design and marketed their version, known as the Scopitone. The American rights to Scopitone were purchased in 1963 by a Chicago firm with rumored Outfit connections, Tel-A-Sign, which succeeded in placing tens of thousands of its machines around the country in the midsixties.

The predecessor to the music video explosion of the end of the twentieth century might have taken hold permanently had it not been for the owners' flawed strategy of promoting middle-of-the-road talents (Debbie Reynolds, Bobby Vee, Vikki Carr, Donna Theodore, etc.), while downplaying the rock-and-roll juggernaut. Also, in the early sixties, Robert Kennedy's mob-hunting Justice Department began looking into Tel-A-Sign's links to organized crime. By 1966, as RFK's quest seemed about to bear fruit, details of the inquiry were leaked to the *Wall Street Journal*. MOVIE JUKEBOX PROBE: GRAND JURY LOOKS INTO EVERYBODY LINKED WITH SCOPITONE: TEL-A-SIGN ASSAILS INQUIRY ran the April 26, 1966, headline. Combined with dwindling interest in their star roster, and the proliferation of television sets in public places, Kennedy's probe caused a panic that fueled a sell-off by stockholders and distributors. By 1969, Scopitone was out of business, its machines auctioned off for pennies on the dollar, with many finding their way into the nation's peep-show industry.

In sum, the Outfit's championing of David Rockola's coin-operated jukebox helped pave the way for both the Top Forty and the music video industry. It is widely assumed that many of the gang's descendants went on to become fully legitimized participants in both of these Wall Street megaliths. Like the lottery's, the music industry's lineage is firmly entrenched in the legacy of Mooney Giancana and the Outfit. But the gang had many more worlds to conquer, most of which involved beating the upperworld to other treasures, such as off-track betting, motion picture production, and casino gambling in the Nevada desert.

9.

Wire Wars

In 1942, while Boris Kostelanetz was still trying to compel Bioff, Browne, and Circella to cooperate, an unrelated but equally substantial Outfit endeavor was finally beginning to bear fruit in Los Angeles. In July of that year, the Outfit's West Coast representative, Johnny Rosselli, was playing hardball with an Outfit adversary named Russell Brophy. Rosselli, Jack Dragna, and Ben Siegel of New York had recently set up the Commission's wire operation, the Trans-America News Service, in L.A. They tried to pressure Russell Brophy of the dominant Continental Press into a partnership. He refused. A week later two thugs showed up at his ninth-floor office. "We tore that fucking office apart," one of the hoods later admitted to a reporter. "In fact, we busted Brophy's head open pretty good because he got out of line a little bit. But actually, the instructions were to knock him in pretty good anyway."

The gang's strong-arm tactics worked in L.A., but for the next four years in Chicago, Brophy's father-in-law, as well as Continental owner James Ragen, continued to oppose Outfit muscle in that key city. In 1946, when Mooney Giancana and his rackets were being absorbed into the Outfit, and Paul Ricca et al. were cooling their heels in prison, James Ragen was paid a visit by Curly Humphreys and Jake Guzik, who had come to inform him that the Outfit had lost its patience. The confrontation brought to a climax decades of warring over the lucrative race-wire business. The acts of brinkmanship by Joe, Curly, Johnny, and the rest were in direct proportion to the importance of the race-wire business.

The History of the Race Wire

The onset of horse-race betting in nineteenth-century Europe instigated a rivalry between illegal offtrack bet-takers (bookies) and the upperworld racing establishment. After a period in which racing was banished, the tracks resurfaced both abroad and in the United State, with powerful new weapons aimed at driving the bookies out of business: antibookmaking legislation and the pari-mutuel machine.

Convinced of the allure of race betting, the equine-owning elite first utilized their influence to have bookmaking outlawed. Once the game was centralized on-site at the tracks, the owners, much like their underworld counterparts, sought to rig the system in their favor. They were facilitated in this effort by the recent invention of the pari-mutuel system. Invented in the 1870s in France by Pierre Oller, the Paris Mutuels is a ciphering apparatus that constantly recalculates the relative amounts bet on each horse, continually changing the odds, so that the bettors are betting against each other, not the track. Before the odds are reset, however, the pari-mutuel machine subtracts both the owners' take and the state's tax cut off the top, guaranteeing their profit (the upperworld's precursor of the underworld's Las Vegas skim). The state-regulated machines also offer a powerful incentive to the bettor, given that there is less chance that the state will fix a race, since their profit is in place regardless of the outcome. (In America, the machines are sold by the American Totalizator Company.)

Just when it seemed that the upperworld had the bookies on the ropes, another invention leveled the playing field once again. This breakthrough was known as the race wire. It allowed the offtrack handbook operators to obtain the same instant results as the state-sanctioned pari-mutuel machines, while preserving the convenience and accessibility of the numbers runners for the bettor. In addition, the allure of forming a personal relationship with a bookie was more attractive than feeding a machine. It was such an instant and powerful profit-maker that gangs like the Outfit never abandoned their goal of controlling it.

Invented in 1900 by John Payne, a Western Union worker in Cincinnati, Ohio, the race wire utilized fixed telegraph wires to transmit, in coded form, the names of riders, track conditions, scratches, and, most important, results. In many cases an on-site spotter would signal the information, by telephone or semaphore, to a cohort who had leased long-distance lines from either Western Union or AT&T. From there the valuable intelligence was sent to whichever bookies paid for it. As previously noted, the information garnered from the wire was priceless to all concerned (see chapter 4). The instant transmittal of track information was so crucial that no nonsubscribing handbook operator could compete with those that did. Not surprisingly, Chicago was the largest handbook center in America, with so many cops on the take that an underworld joke soon emerged: It was harder to rob a handbook than a bank, since more cops frequented their bookie parlors than their financial institutions.

Soon after Payne announced his breakthrough, Jacob "Mont" Tennes, who had inherited Mike McDonald's gambling empire, purchased the Chicago franchise from Payne for $9,000 per month. Windy City handbook operators in turn paid 50 percent of their profits to Tennes' wire service. With thousands of bookies subscribing to the service, and Tennes' in-pocket politician, alderman Johnny Rogers, keeping the official wolves at bay, the Chicago franchise was soon generating $25,000 a month in profits. Tennes solidified his position by personally bribing officials such as Mayor Fred Busse and Chief of Police George Shippey. In the next mayoral contest, Tennes secured Carter Harrison's mayoral election.

But Tennes' greed took hold, giving him dreams of having the national rights to the race-wire nest egg all to himself. In 1910, after bombing John Payne into retirement, Tennes organized the General News Bureau. With this development, Tennes became the acknowledged offtrack gambling czar in the United States and Canada. Tennes was so attuned to the gambling world that he learned before the infamous 1919 World Series that New York gambler Arnold Rothstein had paid eight Chicago players to throw the contest to the Cincinnati Reds.[1]

The Annenberg Years

In 1927, after the gang battles that forced Johnny Torrio to leave Chicago, Tennes announced that he was getting out of a business he could no longer protect in a city under siege. In a watershed event, a newspaper circulation manager and tip-sheet operator named Moses Annenberg bought 48 percent from the retiring Tennes. After enlisting Capone's sluggers to oust the other major General News shareholder, Jack Lynch, Annenberg set about creating a legend all his own.

Born in Prussia in 1878, Annenberg in 1885 came to Chicago, where his father owned a small grocery store in the Patch. "Moe" earned his first

---

1. Tennes tried to warn Sox owner Charles Comiskey, who couldn't do anything, since, if it was true, the revelation would destroy his franchise, which was built by underpaying his players by 50 per cent. Although Rothstein fixed the players' 1921 trial, they were banned for life by the just installed first commissioner of baseball, Judge Kenesaw Mountain Landis.

paycheck as a messenger for Western Union, a position that would offer valuable insights for his future ventures. During the early part of the century, young Moe was hired by William Randolph Hearst to be his "general" in the newspaper circulation wars. Pre–World War I Chicago had eight metropolitan newspapers, and circulation not only meant sales, it meant fighting pitched battles to ensure the papers were delivered at all. In the no-holds-barred contest, newsstands were smashed, delivery trucks bombed, carriers beaten, and papers stolen and thrown into Lake Michigan. Interestingly, Moe sided with Hearst's *American,* while his brother Max Annenberg commanded the troops of Colonel Robert McCormick's *Chicago Tribune,* where he assumed the post of circulation director. Since Hearst was the new kid on the block, his men had to fight especially hard to gain a toehold. Moe Annenberg himself was not above the fray, often joining barroom brawls in the service of his appreciative employer.

The Annenbergs' need of circulation-war soldiers first introduced them to the efficiencies offered by the gangsters. In the powerful and heated Annenberg sibling rivalry, the brothers emulated Mont Tennes and utilized the talents of well-connected sluggers to gain the upper hand. In the 1920s, Max turned to the Torrio-Capone Syndicate, while Moe enlisted North Siders such as Bugs Moran and Deanie O'Banion, and future union thugs such as Mossy Enright, who went on to nurture the professional life of motion-picture-union strong-arm Tommy Maloy. In fact, it was the circulation wars that initially divided up the city along the geographical battle lines that would soon prevail in the Beer Wars of 1925. In one instance, Max Annenberg asked for Capone's help in preventing a strike by the paper's drivers' union. Capone later said, "Them circulation fights was murder. They knifed each other like hell . . . And who do you think settled all them strikes and fights? Me, I'm the guy that settled all their strikes and all their circulation raids." When Capone delivered for the *Tribune,* Colonel McCormick himself met with Al to thank him. "You know you're famous, like Babe Ruth," said the Colonel. "We can't help printing things about you, but I will see that the *Tribune* gives you a square deal."

For years, Moe Annenberg maintained a sideline operation to his newspaper endeavors, since the corner newsstand operators he controlled doubled as bet-takers. As Jake Guzik told syndicated writer Lester Velie, "Almost every newsboy, bartender, and cigar-stand keeper has become a bookie." Patrons armed with scratch sheets or the *Racing Form* typically bought their morning paper, then made their wager. When the afternoon-paper delivery truck arrived with the latest edition, the driver, often a gang member, picked up the bets and delivered them to the circulation manager, who split the profits between the winners and Annenberg, who himself rarely placed a bet. Annenberg soon began publishing his own racing newspaper, the *Daily Racing Form,* purchased in 1922 for $400,000. With his profits, Annenberg purchased the *Wisconsin News* and his crown jewel, the *Philadelphia Inquirer.* Hearst also brought him to New York to publish Hearst's *New York Daily Mirror,* competitor of the *New York Daily News,* which employed Max Annenberg as circulation director. While in New York, Annenberg employed the slugging services of Lucky Luciano, much as he had done in Chicago. Luciano later said, "I used to think of the *Mirror* as my paper. I always thought of Annenberg as my kind of guy."

In 1926 Annenberg quit Hearst, the hard-copy magnate having come to appreciate the value of selling electronic, high-speed race information, either to gamblers or bookies or both. One year later he purchased 48 percent of the retiring Tennes' General News Bureau. Having settled his differences with Capone, Annenberg enlisted the services of Al's Syndicate, in this case to relay results from inside the track to a nearby telegrapher. It was widely reported that Moe Annenberg attended the May 1929 mob convention in Atlantic City, where he was approached on the boardwalk by Al Capone, who tried to form a partnership. Instead, Annenberg established the Nationwide News Service, in collusion with the New York gangsters, choosing again to use Capone's forces merely as hired hands. After Capone was sent to prison, Annenberg's alliance with the new Outfit was strengthened. Over the next few years, Annenberg depended on the Outfit's muscle to harass his competition; in return for their services, the gang's bookies received the wire service free of charge. For years, the Outfit was beholden to Annenberg's wire service, coveting the lucrative operation for themselves, and lying in wait for the opportunity to grab it.

On January 2, 1935, Annenberg paid $750,000 to buy out a Nationwide minority owner who had previously rebuffed such offers. On the same day, according to an affidavit found after his death, Annenberg's operations manager and longtime buddy James Ragen couriered $100,000 in $100 bills to Frank Nitti for the gang's help in convincing the shareholder to sell. It has never been determined exactly what methods were employed, but it remains a strong possibility that the master negotiator Curly Humphreys counseled the gang from his "college dorm" at Leavenworth. Despite their symbiotic relationship with Annenberg, the Outfit never abandoned their aspiration of controlling the race wire outright. And while the underworld jockeyed for position, their corporate partners were granted a free ride directly to the bank.

The Upperworld's Stake in the Wire Service

Much as the upperworld attempted to control horse-race betting by combining restrictive legislation with its pari-mutuel system, it simultaneously profited from the nascent illegal wire operation. When John Payne devised the race-wire encoding system, of necessity he leased the long-distance wires of Western Union Telegraph Company for $2 million per year to transmit the vital data. In the first decade of the twentieth century, under pressure from reformers, Western Union gave up its lucrative, albeit indirect, arrangement with the nation's gangster bookies. The fledgling telephone company AT&T was more than happy to fill the void. The breadth of the operation eventually encompassed some sixteen thousand miles of leased wire to three hundred handbook areas around the country. In 1935, the Nationwide service alone paid AT&T $500,000, becoming its fifth-largest client.

Federal investigators had little luck in breaking up the Tennes-AT&T collusion, or the Trust as the operation was called. Tennes could now afford to retain the best legal counsel with which to keep the courts at bay. Thus when Tennes and AT&T were brought before an investigative tribunal in 1916, they were represented by Clarence Darrow. The probe, which resulted from pressure brought by a newspaper probe, was stalled into oblivion by Darrow's legal machinations. Judge Kenesaw Mountain Landis, the first commissioner of baseball, excoriated Tennes and AT&T, calling them a corrupter of youth, whose profits were "covered with dirt and slime because young men are being made criminals." But all the fire and brimstone was to no avail, since Judge Landis was no match for the upperworld gangsters of AT&T and the legal bombast of Clarence Darrow. Alson Smith, in his book *Syndicate City,* described the proceedings: "The investigation finally came to nothing when the Illinois Bell Telephone Company refused to cooperate on the grounds that interstate transmission of sporting news was not a crime and that local gambling was not within the jurisdiction of the Federal court."

However, by the midthirties, after three decades of sharing its bookie-derived profits with its shareholders, AT&T felt sufficient pressure from the FCC to abandon the race wire. By this time, Western Union was in such dire financial straits that it was more than willing to jump back into the game. With its transmission lines in great disrepair since their construction six decades earlier, and with the advent of air mail, Western Union was in a financial free fall, and desperate for a cash influx. But another factor appeared to sound the death knell for the company. According to a 1939 FCC report, "the financial condition of Western Union is definitely unfavorable . . . Probably the most important factor contributing to these conditions is the development of competing forms of communication." In other words, the telephone.

Alexander Graham Bell's invention had by now so proliferated that fewer Americans than ever were reliant on the telegraph for fast communication. To make matters worse, in 1937 the Department of Justice had filed charges against Western Union, alleging violations of the Sherman Anti-Trust Act. Stockholders feared the utility was about to come under increased federal supervision as a result of its monopolistic practices. A Senate report on the telegraph industry in 1939 summed up the situation, pointing out that Western Union profits in 1938 were down $38,529,000, or 31.1 percent, since 1926. Thus, when the race-wire gangsters came calling, Western Union gratefully accepted the deal. Years later, a congressional committee chaired by Senator Ernest McFarland uncovered an internal Western Union memorandum from the company's vice president urging his board "to pursue expeditious handling" of the race-wire business, noting that the corporation could expect to earn over $30,000 per month in much needed profits.

Like AT&T before it, Western Union could not be bothered to cooperate with government investigators. In one of its few swipes at corporate white-collar crime, the Senate's 1951 Kefauver Committee described the company's hubris:

> The backbone of the wire service which provides gambling information to bookmakers is the leased lines of the Western Union Telegraph Company. This company, in many parts of the country, has not been fully cooperative with law-enforcement officials who have been trying to suppress organized criminal rackets which make use of telegraph facilities. By permitting its facilities to be used by bookmakers, Western Union has given aid and comfort to those engaged in violation of gambling laws. In some cases, Western Union officials and employees actually participated in bookmaking conspiracies by accepting bets and transmitting them to bookmakers.

Appearing before McFarland's committee, the heads of both AT&T and Western Union played dumb, attempting to convince the probers that they had no inkling of who leased their lines or for what purpose. An exchange between the committee and Western Union's Assistant Vice President Walter Semingsen was typical and revealing. McFarland's interrogation of Semingsen is worth reprinting at length, so revelatory it is about the upperworld's attitude toward, and involvement in, the propagation of organized crime. The ludicrous back-and-forth comprises dozens of pages of testimony, with exchanges that presaged both the self-serving responses of the jukebox manufacturers, and the end-of-century strained testimony by tobacco-company executives professing that nicotine is not addictive. At one point in the hearings, Senators Tobey and McFarland expressed disbelief when the company VP claimed to have no interest in what was being transmitted over the company's wires:

Semingsen: "We have no way of knowing about illegal use of these facilities until the law-enforcement authorities so inform us."

Tobey: "What do you think goes on? . . . The point is that these [wire] messages are their means of doing business and carry information on which the bets are based. Is that not correct?"

Semingsen: "I do not know."

Tobey: "What do you think they are used for?"

Semingsen: "I have never been in any of the establishments, and I could not tell you personally."

Senator McFarland then ticked off the names of dozens of "racing information" parlors in different states that leased the wires, asking, one by one, what Semingsen believed they did with the information. To each query Semingsen's responses were similar: "I have not the slightest idea," "I have no way of knowing," "I have not the slightest idea how they make use of the information." Tobey then began to lose his temper.

Tobey: "Do you know what the trouble is in this country? Nobody accepts responsibility . . . We know that these lines are being used for disseminating race track information. We know it is so; you know it is so. A child six years old knows that."

Semingsen: "I disagree with you. We do not know it is so."

Tobey: "Do you mean to stand there and say, under oath, that in your judgment you do not know that these leases are being used for disseminating race track information? . . . When you carry the information into the state where bookmaking is illegal, you become an accessory after the fact, do you not?"

Semingsen: "You are assuming that all these persons to whom we are leasing facilities are bookmakers."

Tobey: "No; I do not assume that at all. I assume some of them are, and so do you . . . The moral law – the law of society – does not interest you a bit, as long as you get the revenue; is that right? . . . Western Union is a necessary cog when the Western Union is used to accept money from the bettor and transmit it to the bettee, through their offices, by accepting the money and paying out at the other end on the facts circumscribed in the telegram; is that right?"

Semingsen: "That is correct."

Tobey: "I should think – and I say this without prejudice – that certainly makes Western Union a party to the illegal transaction of business, because in some states those things are illegal."

Semingsen: ". . . I do not know what the laws are."

In the end, not one director or employee of Western Union or AT&T was ever charged with collusion in the bookmaking racket. The huge profits they reaped from illegal betting were somehow deemed beyond the law, whereas countless underworld bookies in the Outfit and other crime consortiums regularly faced the prospect of hard time.

In contrast to the free ride given to the white-collar criminals, Moe Annenberg felt the full weight of the government's muscle. In 1935, the combative, omnipresent Elmer Irey focused his attention on Annenberg's operation. Instead of investigating "the backbone of the wire service," Western Union, its stockholders, or board of directors (such as Vincent Astor, Percy Rockefeller, Paul Warburg, William Truesdale, Donald Geddes, William Vanderbilt, W. A. Harriman, and Jay Cooke), Irey's IRS chose to persecute the most recent immigrants, such as Annenberg, to have become millionaires. After all, Western Union's founder, Ezra Cornell, had long ago legitimized his company when he endowed Cornell University. For Annenberg and the gangsters, this lack of prestige-purchasing turned out to be a key oversight.

After studying Annenberg's books for a full five years, Irey's men garnered enough evidence to indict Moe for $5.5 million in tax evasion. Also named was Annenberg's son Walter, who had initially pleaded with Moe not to get into the wire business, but had eventually helped run the company. However, when Moe agreed to take the fall and pay an $8-million fine (the largest personal tax fine to date), he negotiated his boy's removal from the charge. Due to the diagnosis of a terminal brain tumor,

Annenberg was released from prison after having served two years of a three-year sentence. He died at home on June 11, 1942. Since few large corporations could survive five years of such scrutiny, the question was begged, why did Irey target Annenberg in the first place? The answer appears to be twofold. First, Annenberg attained his wealth too quickly, and with the cooperation of Capone and the Outfit, infuriating old-money types, who promulgated the charade that they themselves would never engage in illegal activities. The nouveau riche have always been snubbed. After years of frustration in trying to prove that the wire operators knew about the hoods at the other end of their transmissions, the feds fell back on the dogs of the IRS.

In his decision, the presiding judge in Annenberg's case delivered closing remarks that weakly attempted to explain why he could not vacate a jail sentence altogether. To do so, the judge said, would be to say to all businessmen, "you may organize your affairs in a network of corporations and avoid the payment of your just taxes, and when called to account by the Government for what you really owe, nothing worse will happen to you than to be compelled to pay what you would have paid long ago." That sort of privilege, after all, was reserved for Western Union, AT&T, the Morgans, Rockefellers, Du Ponts, and assorted other robber barons.

Second, Annenberg had drawn the ire of the notoriously thin-skinned President Franklin Roosevelt. For months Annenberg had used the bully pulpit of his influential *Philadelphia Inquirer* to editorialize against what he perceived to be the shortcomings of FDR's New Deal. Annenberg was not alone in concluding that, while FDR deserved praise for his success in jump-starting a flagging economy, many New Deal entitlement policies were destroying initiative and encouraging strikers to demand more concessions from the business world. Furthermore, Annenberg supported the Republican slate in Pennsylvania and rubbed FDR's nose in it when the Republicans triumphed. PENNSYLVANIA HAS REPUDIATED THE NEW DEAL screamed the *Inquirer*'s headline.

In a paranoid style that would have impressed Richard Nixon three decades later, Roosevelt tasked his treasury secretary and attorney general with investigating the tax status of his enemies in the press. After attempting to instigate legislation that would label policy dissenters as criminals (Moe promptly called the move Hitler-like), Roosevelt's senior aides stepped up their attack. Soon, Roosevelt met with Attorney General Homer Cummings to discuss tax delinquents, singling out Annenberg and demanding, "I want him in jail." When Treasury Secretary Henry Morgenthau met Roosevelt for lunch, he asked the president if he could do anything for him. "Yes," a seething Roosevelt replied. "I want Moe Annenberg for dinner." To which Morgenthau replied, "You're going to have him for breakfast – fried."

Eventually, Roosevelt prevailed, thanks to Irey's IRS. In discussing presidential abuse of the tax code, David Burnham, author of *A Law Unto Itself: Power, Politics and the IRS*, wrote, "President Franklin Delano Roosevelt may have been the champion abuser." Under pressure from the feds, Nationwide was forced to cancel its contract with AT&T, which was itself attempting to escape prosecution from the previously noted FCC probe. In its desire to escape the FCC's clutches, AT&T got out of the race-wire business altogether. Moe's son Walter quickly struck up a deal with the struggling Western Union.

Democrats themselves quietly admitted that Annenberg's prosecution was nothing short of a White House-directed vendetta. They knew that had Moe's anti-New Deal editorials appeared in the *Lubbock Avalanche,* Roosevelt could have ignored them. But his adversary could not be granted a forum as visible as the *Inquirer.* As discovered by Annenberg's biographer Christopher Ogden, even the IRS accountant who dissected Annenberg's books knew the case was a sham. The accountant, William Hopewell, wrote to Walter Annenberg in 1981, "The tremendous injustice done to him has been on my mind – on and off – for years. I am sure your father was not guilty as charged." Moe Annenberg concluded the obvious in an *Inquirer* editorial: He had been indicted because "it was important to the Democratic Party that I be destroyed prior to the 1940 elections."

After his indictment on August 11, 1939, Moe Annenberg walked away from the Nationwide wire business in exchange for the government's sparing of his son Walter. A mere five days after Nationwide ceased operations, Continental Press was established, allegedly after the new owner, Mickey McBride, paid Annenberg for his infrastructure. In short time, McBride sold Continental to James Ragen, who finessed the legalities of the wire business by selling his race information to distributors, not directly to illegal bookies. "Selling information is legal, [and] what the distributors did with it is none of my concern," Ragen said, sounding remarkably like his upperworld counterparts at Western Union. When Congress investigated Continental in 1951, it was likewise not fooled by Ragen's insouciance. It determined that Continental received wildly varying weekly fees from its distributors (from $500 to $10,000 per week), depending on how much "business" they did with the information. One congressional probe, the McFarland Committee, concluded: "The facts support the thesis that Continental today has a near monopoly in the transmission of racing news which ultimately reaches the bookmakers in the country. Continental does choose its distributors, assigns them exclusive territories, and charges them on the basis of size and amount of business done in such territory."

A second federal inquiry added: "[Continental's distributors] are nearly all dummies, set up to insulate the Continental Press Service against the charge that it deals directly with persons engaged in illegal operations."

This then was the atmosphere when, in 1946, the Outfit got serious about its desire to control the underworld sector of the wire business. For years, Ragen, owner of Continental Press, had rebuffed Outfit attempts to work their way into his operation. Ragen later testified that he had once been approached by Frank Nitti, who told him, "If you come along with us, we will kill [owner] Annenberg in twenty-four hours." Ragen refused, and Annenberg mollified the gang by paying them $1 million a year in protection fees. For years under Annenberg, Nationwide had coexisted in a delicate standoff with the Outfit, but now Nationwide's descendant, Ragen's Continental, began to view the Outfit as its enemy.

Eventually, Accardo and the Outfit, tired of waiting to take over Continental, formed their own service, Trans-America, with their Commission partners in New York. The new venture, referred to in Chicago as the Dago Wire Service, peddled wire information pirated from Ragen's Continental Press. The Outfit also ordered their thousands of bookies to buy the pirated information from Trans-America. One noncompliant bookie, Harry "Red" Richmond, was gunned down in front of his own home. Gamblers loyal to Continental were ordered to get out of town. One who ignored the order, an ex-con named Frank Covilli, was shot to death in early 1946. The furious James Ragen understandably decided to revoke the Outfit's no-fee status, prompting a bitter war of words with the gang's accountant, Jake Guzik. Ragen requested a meeting to defuse the growing tension. Joe Accardo agreed and dispatched his master negotiator, Curly Humphreys. Accompanying Humphreys to the pow-wow in Jake Guzik's Room 1837 in the Chicagoan Hotel were Guzik and the mobbed-up state senator Dan Serritella, who was also Guzik's partner in a scratch-sheet operation.

Curly's initial suggestion, that Ragen sell his Chicago franchise, the Midwest Wire, to the Outfit, was rejected by Ragen. As his last offer, Humphreys gave Ragen the option of giving the Outfit 40 percent of his profits. As Ragen later described: "I said to Humphreys, 'Why should you want to be a party in breaking up something that is supplying your books with news, and which if there was an alliance of any kind or deal, and Edgar Hoover found out about it, he would chop up the business?' [Humphreys] went on to try and sell me that Hoover need not know anything about this. We argued for an hour."

With Ragen's continued refusal to fold, heated words were exchanged as the summit broke up.

Joe Accardo then declared war, ordering his army of bookmakers to stop using Ragen's service. A now desperate Ragen turned to the politicians he had been paying off so handsomely for years. To his great dismay, Ragen was informed that the pols had a higher allegiance, and it was not to justice, but to the Outfit. It should have come as no surprise to the embattled wire king that Al Capone's heirs practically owned City Hall, the mayor's office included. Ragen wrote that he then realized that the Outfit "is as strong as the United States Army."

Ragen next sought relief from the Cook County state's attorney, William Touhy. One year later, county officials released details of their meeting. In a transcript comprising ten thousand words, over ninety-eight pages, it was finally learned what had transpired at the showdown with Humphreys and his associates. According to a congressional probe that later obtained the statement, Ragen said his life had been threatened, and he fully expected the threat to be carried out. "If he were killed," the congressional report summarized, "he said the probable killers would be Accardo, Guzik, and Humphreys . . . it is corroborated in part by the testimony of Dan Serritella, Jake Guzik's partner in [the Outfit's] scratch sheet." Ragen apparently did not believe that Touhy would do much more than the impotent City Hall officials. Ragen's next move pushed the Outfit's patience over the limit: he went to J. Edgar Hoover's FBI.

Until James Ragen sauntered into the Chicago Field Office of the FBI, J. Edgar Hoover, whose jurisdiction forbade local crime investigations, had avoided delving into the murky world of organized crime. Convinced until this time that there was little hard evidence of interstate gangsterism, Hoover was content to chase bank robbers and "Commies." Hoover was obsessed with success, and he knew that pursuing the shadowy connections of far-flung hoods could prove disastrous to the Bureau's vaunted reputation: "We always get our man." Now comes James Ragen, who described to the agents the national scope of his illegal race wire. Although Ragen himself admitted he had paid over $600,000 to pols over three years (nicknamed "the widows and orphans fund"), the agents were more interested in another aspect of his tale, namely Ragen's charge that Al Capone's heirs had also muscled into the game. It was now impossible for Hoover to ignore the obvious. It is not clear if the Bureau offered Ragen immunity for his cooperation, but it appears it did, since Hoover decreed the formation of a special investigation with a code name that gave away their focus: CAPGA. The name stood for "Capone Gang."

Soon, Accardo, Humphreys, Guzik, and their buddies were being followed by agents from the G. More important, the agents succeeded in gaining access to the gang's Morrison Hotel headquarters. There they tapped into the phone in the hotel's barbershop that served as the hoods' key link to the outside. This last affront pushed the hoods past the breaking point; they had had enough and needed to act fast. Meanwhile, the local police concluded that the threat against Ragen was serious and gave him twenty-four-hour protection. Ragen, however, soon hired his own bodyguards, but they were unable to prevent the inevitable. On April 29, 1946, Ragen found himself pursued in a fifteen-mile, sixty-mile-per-hour car chase, which he was able to deflect only by heading straight for a suburban police station. It was to be a temporary reprieve.

On June 24, 1946, Ragen's fatal prediction came true. On that day, under heavy police protection, Ragen was driving down State Street on the South Side during rush hour. With his protectors in a follow-up car, Ragen saw a hoary, tarpaulin-covered delivery truck pull alongside his vehicle. When the truck got close, the tarp was raised and the shotgunners underneath began firing from behind orange crates. Ragen's trailing guards fired at the fleeing truck in vain. When the abandoned vehicle was later located, it was found to have been fortified with quarter-inch steel plates over its rear section.

Turning to their boss, the bodyguards found Ragen with serious wounds to his right arm and shoulder. Rushed into emergency surgery at Michael Reese Hospital, his blood was transfused ten times. Over the next few weeks, Ragen appeared to be recovering when, to everyone's surprise, his kidneys, which had not been injured in the attack, began to fail. On August 8, Ragen again underwent emergency surgery. However, four days later he died. His autopsy revealed that his blood contained traces of the lethal chemical mercury. It was widely believed that Joe Accardo had gotten to someone on the hospital staff, bribing the employee to dose Ragen with the poison. Sergeant William Drury, a twenty-four-year veteran Chicago detective, spent months running down leads in the case, putting particular heat on Jake Guzik. The gang's accountant, and chief palm-greaser, responded by putting his own spin on the case. "If I were to talk," Guzik told all within earshot, "some of Chicago's best citizens would go jumping out of windows." When Drury hauled Guzik in for a lie-detector test, Drury's boss, Outfit-friendly Police Commissioner John Prendergast, shook his head and said, "*They* won't like it." Thus it came as no real surprise when, for his efforts, Sergeant Drury was fired from the force for harassing Outfit members.

It was as clear as ever that Chicago's infrastructure was corrupt from top to bottom. Ragen had done as much as he could to encourage authorities to clamp down on the Outfit, and he was killed in broad daylight for it – again without a suspect arrested. A *Chicago News* editorial asked its readers, "How do you like it, Chicagoans?" The scathing diatribe was noteworthy for its denunciation of the system as much as the gangs themselves: "[The Ragen murder] paints a sordid and depressing picture of what happens to a community when politicians consort with thieves and criminals; when a political machine allies itself with racketeers, when the racketeers, in fact, become the real power behind local government."

Although indictments were returned against Outfit hitmen William Block, Lenny Patrick, and the gang's Miami liaison Dave Yaras, the charges were dropped when the star witness backed out of the case. Soon, it was announced that Mickey McBride's twenty-three-year-old son, Eddie, would run Continental. One month later, the Outfit closed down its Trans-America operation, fooling no one. During a 1951 Senate probe, McBride senior was asked: "Weren't you afraid that your boy would be bumped off?" After he responded in the negative, this question was put to young Eddie: "You are a complete figurehead and dummy, is that right?" To which the young man candidly replied, "I guess you could put it that way if you wanted to." The committee's report concluded the obvious: "The Continental Press national horsetrack service is controlled by the Capone mob in Chicago." The gang from Cicero, after a two-decade struggle, had finally attained its goal, and the rich rewards that followed.

A congressional investigation estimated that the combined take from all the nation's bookies ran into the billions of dollars, and many experts believed the race wire to be the savior of organized crime after the repeal of prohibition. Len O'Connor, a Chicago newsman and political analyst, wrote that "the instantaneous transmission of information vital to illicit bookmaking was the nerve system of organized gambling, the foundation stone of syndicate crime." In his 1975 book, *Clout,* O'Connor described the Outfit's role in the national wire network: "The Chicago race wire was the nation's bookmakers' only available source of instantaneous information concerning *all* the betting opportunities currently existing at *all* the tracks, and, indeed, the cash flow of the bookie joints was significantly greater than that of the tracks."

Dying along with James Ragen was Hoover's short-lived interest in organized crime. With his key witness gone, Hoover lacked the enthusiasm to pursue the case. To make matters worse, orders came down from the executive branch to cease and desist, according to Hoover's number two, Cartha DeLoach. "Then, quite suddenly, the attorney general, Tom Clark, told us to discontinue our operations," DeLoach later wrote. It will be seen that Clark was understandably viewed in Chicago as Outfit-friendly. The CAPGA unit was thus disbanded until eleven years later, when events forced Hoover back into the investigation of organized crime. The decision to close the CAPGA case was a costly one, for it gave the Outfit a virtual free ride to expand its empire into domains as far removed as the Nevada desert and the White House. And they never relinquished their hooks into Hollywood, or their liaison, Sid Korshak.

Moe Annenberg's son Walter went on to exponentially increase the value of the tattered business he'd inherited, founding such publications as *TV Guide* and *Seventeen.* In 1969, Walter was appointed U.S. ambassador to Great Britain by Richard Nixon. And in a manner that even eclipsed the rebirth of Jake Factor, Walter devoted the second half of his life to philanthropy, establishing a foundation valued at over $3 billion. In 1991 alone, he gave away $1 billion; likewise in 1993. In his father's honor, Walter endowed the prestigious M. L. Annenberg Schools of Communication at the University of Pennsylvania and the University of Southern California.

Part Three

Scandals and Investigations

10.

Playing Politics II:
The Truman Connection

By 1945, barely one year into their ten-year term, Paul Ricca and his incarcerated cohorts had reached the end of their patience. Enduring the privations of their Atlanta prison hellhole was bad enough, but doing so while their fellows on the outside lavished in the wire and numbers profits was unbearable. Rubbing salt into their wounds were the early releases, in December 1944, granted to stoolies Willie Bioff and George Browne, both of whom immediately went into hiding. The situation was especially intolerable for the forty-seven-year-old Ricca, who, had he not been pinched for the Hollywood scam, would now be the boss of the Outfit. Thus Ricca made his decision: He and his fellows wanted a quick transfer to Leavenworth, a prelude to an unthinkable early parole.

Ricca initially attempted to obtain the transfer in the traditional way by having his attorney, Edward Monaco, who had brokered Ricca's Indiana farm purchase, write a letter asking for it. When prison warden Joseph Sanford wrote to the Bureau of Prisons opposing the request, he noted his fears that "money is being paid to obtain the transfer of these men to Leavenworth." Sanford added that he wanted the Atlanta prisoners sequestered from Nick Circella, who was already at Leavenworth, and kept distanced from their Chicago allies. The Atlanta Parole Board agreed with Sanford and let its federal superiors know it. When he was told of Sanford's stance and the Atlanta board's agreement, Ricca was shocked, so unaccustomed was he to having his demands refused. He decided to go over their heads, resorting to a strategy that had always succeeded: He called Chicago. When Ricca got word back to Accardo and the Outfit, the seemingly impossible task predictably fell to the gang's political mastermind, Curly Humphreys. This would be verified fifteen years later, when the FBI overheard Accardo describing how the events had played out. Curly knew that such an undertaking would require every bit of political leverage he had acquired over the years, and then some. Fortunately for Ricca and the rest, Humphreys had spent the recent past forging alliances with pols whose influence extended even into the Oval Office. After considering the problem, Humphreys hit upon the solution: He would tap a sixty-eight-year-old Missouri attorney named Paul Dillon, a litigator he had employed in 1939 when he'd needed to obtain indictment dismissals for two Outfit thugs named John Nick and Clyde Weston, strong-arms used in the IATSE takeover. Humphreys' kinship with the Missouri-based Dillon was a natural result of his role as the Outfit's political liaison to that state. And in the shadowy world of underworld-upperworld collusions, this linkage gave Curly Humphreys leverage over the most powerful politician in the United States.

Truman's Shadow World

When Curly Humphreys hit upon Paul Dillon as the solution to Ricca's problems, he did so with the knowledge that Dillon was the St. Louis, Missouri, version of Chicago's Sid Korshak, with one notable exception: Dillon's gangster associates in Kansas City, Missouri, had sponsored the ascendancy of the thirty-third president of the United States, Harry S Truman. Humphreys knew that by playing the Kansas City card he was subtly threatening to open a Pandora's box that Washington would be forced to address. For those like Curly Humphreys who knew the level of corruption in the upperworld, the rules of the game had to be bent. The Missourians were a Capone-like gangster named John Lazia, a Kansas City Democratic boss named Tom Pendergast, and an eager politician named Harry Truman. This triumvirate gave rise to *President* Truman and his appointees; their subservience to the Chicago Outfit virtually guaranteed that mountains would be moved for Paul Ricca.

Kansas City was known far and wide as Cow Town, since much of the cattle slaughtered in the Chicago stockyards originated from sales in Kansas City's Livestock Exchange, a 205-acre parcel known as the Kaw, where ten thousand Western cows were sold daily. And the cattle connection to Chicago was merely the beginning. If Chicago was the most corrupt city in the country, Kansas City was a close second, with its municipal police department run by a former Capone gangster. Imported as prohibition muscle from Chicago by the Kansas City machine, ex-con Johnny Lazia quickly rose in the ranks from bootlegger to gambling czar. During Volstead, Lazia kept in regular contact with the Capone Syndicate, which counted Kansas City as one of its bootlegging distribution hubs. On one visit to Chicago, Lazia was officially anointed by Capone as the boss of Kansas City. Lazia mimicked his Chicago superior and alter ego in many ways. Using brute muscle, Lazia controlled not only local politicians, but also the city's police force. At one point, Lazia forced the Kansas City Police Department to hire sixty ex-cons as cops. A former Kansas City FBI man recently recalled, "If you called the police station, Lazia was more than likely to answer the phone."

By 1934, 10 percent of the city's police force had a criminal record. In 1934, a reporter for the *New York Herald-Tribune* wrote, "If you want excitement with roulette, cards, dice, the races . . . ask a patrolman on the Kansas City streets. He'll guide you." One thief recalled, "This town was fast, had good booze joints, plenty of targets, and some of the laziest cops in the country." During Lazia's tenure, which lasted until he was murdered in 1934, Kansas City possessed a host of social ills that rivaled those of its Windy City big sister: unsolved kidnappings and murders, rigged elections, and labor sluggings. In 1939, federal judge Albert L. Reeves said, "Kansas City is a seething cauldron of crime, licensed and protected."

Lazia was allowed to flourish for decades due to his partnership with Democratic boss Tom Pendergast. In a city with a mayor's office that was legislated to be weakened, ward boss Pendergast thrived. Much as Jake Guzik sat on his throne in Chicago dispensing the Outfit's largesse to a line of supplicants, so did Pendergast rule from his dingy Main Street office in Kansas City. All morning long (the office only stayed open until noon), Pendergast handed out political favors and city contracts to his subjects. "All right, who's next?" Pendergast would grumble from his swivel chair and rolltop desk.

Tom Pendergast's machine mirrored Big Al's Syndicate in other ways. When his favored pols faced election day, Pendergast's organization brought in Chicago-like vote sluggers. In the 1936 general election, Pendergast oversaw the posting of more than eighty thousand "ghost" votes. Like Capone with the Sportsman's Park sideline, Pendergast brought horse racing to Kansas City at his Riverside Park Jockey Club. As Kansas City grew increasingly amoral under Lazia-Pendergast, the predictable vices such as gambling and prostitution took hold, all dancing to the tune of the world-class jazz musicians who gravitated to Kansas City as they did to Chicago. Rising stars included Lester Young, Coleman Hawkins, and arguably the world's greatest jazz sax player, Charlie Parker, who was born in Kansas City in 1920. "Most of the jazz spots were run by politicians and hoodlums, and the town was wide open for drinking, gambling, and pretty much every form of vice," pianist Mary Lou Williams remembered.

As his stature grew, Pendergast formed an alliance with the Chicago–New York Commission. When he traveled to New York, Pendergast was seen in the company of Lucky Luciano and Frank Costello. He showed up at the infamous 1929 Atlantic City gangster convention and was on hand with the Outfit in Chicago when they and their New York brethren decided to support the presidential candidacy of Franklin Roosevelt. The Kansas City contingent also delivered the vote for FDR. According to IRS investigations, Pendergast delivered 20,687 votes in his First Ward, although the sector only maintained 19,923 registered voters. A local reporter found that one voter had registered forty times, using different names, but the same birth date. When the Lazia-Pendergast alliance was held responsible for a botched hijacking of a federal prisoner in 1933, in which four federal agents were killed, the machine rocketed to the top of the federal authorities' priority list.

What is most critical in any discussion of corruption in Kansas City is an understanding of the relationship between the Outfit and the Pendergast machine, a relationship that figured into Curly Humphreys' overall strategy. From the days of Al Capone, the Pendergast-Lazia machine fell under the ultimate control of the Chicago Syndicate, and later, the Outfit. Bill Roemer, an FBI agent in Chicago who would later use hidden microphones to eavesdrop on the Outfit's most private conversations, summed up what he learned of the Chicago–Kansas City gangster linkage: "The Kansas City mob is a subsidiary of the Chicago mob. Every family of La Cosa Nostra west of Chicago belongs to Chicago . . . the Outfit takes a hunk of their income and oversees their activity." As his personal representative in Missouri, Curly Humphreys utilized the talents of St. Louis' Egan Gang muscleman Thomas Whalen. Humphreys also formed Outfit partnerships with St. Louis handbook operator Tony Giardano and racketeer Frank "Buster" Wortman. Authorities noted frequent trips by these men to Chicago, especially Wortman, who became a close personal friend of Humphreys'.

When Johnny Lazia went on trial for tax evasion in 1934, he threatened to "blow the lid" on corruption in Kansas City. Instead, he was murdered on July 10, 1934, gunned down at 3 A.M. as he arrived with his bodyguard at his home. Among the secrets Lazia took to his grave was the connection of Boss Pendergast to the official infrastructure of Kansas

City. One of the keys to the survival of the Lazia-Pendergast machine was its sponsorship of county judges who gave them both credibility and a wide berth for their shenanigans. Tom Pendergast and Johnny Lazia, the men who sanctioned election-day beatings, kidnappings, and murders, chose as their main "front" an army pal of Pendergast's nephew Mike Pendergast. The beneficiary of the machine's power hailed from Independence, Missouri, a small town just a few miles to Kansas City's northeast. His name was Harry S Truman.

Like the city that fostered his career, Harry Truman was a split personality. A well-liked World War I hero, Truman was, on the one hand, a gregarious, hardworking public servant who was never proved to have been anything but scrupulously honest. These personal attributes, however, confound psychohistorians who attempt to reconcile them with his blind allegiance to friends and sponsors who were among the most corrupt of the era. As his entrée to political corruption in 1922, Harry Truman was first given, by Tom Pendergast, the plum role as the machine's county judge, a position that included many executive responsibilities, such as setting budgets and allocating county contracts. Pendergast's fixing of the election was so blatant that Truman won by the astonishing count of 137,000 to 9,000. Although Truman's tenure as judge was highlighted by his hardworking dedication to saving taxpayers' money, it also included the occasional nod to his patron. In return for Pendergast's continued support, Truman made what some have called illegal justice-of-the-peace appointments and gave road construction contracts to Pendergast's shady friends. Truman biographer Richard Lawrence Miller wrote that Truman "not only knew of the machine's illegalities but participated in some of them." Truman himself noted that he had looked the other way while his patron plundered the city's treasury. Between 1930 and 1934, Truman maintained a handwritten journal in which he candidly described how he returned Pendergast's support. The documents, now residing in the Truman Library, are referred to as the Pickwick Papers, since Truman made the jottings on Pickwick Hotel stationery. "I had to let a former saloon keeper and murderer, a friend of the Big Boss [Pendergast], steal about $10,000 . . . from the general revenues of the County to satisfy my ideal associate," wrote Truman.

Kansas City old-timers assert that Truman did much more than look the other way. Roger Morris, a prize-winning author and former senior staff member of both Presidents Richard Nixon's and Lyndon Johnson's

National Security Councils, recently related a family story of growing up in Boss Pendergast's Kansas City. As a young boy in the late forties, Morris was watching television with his grandmother as President Truman appeared on the screen. "Grandma, it's the president," said young Morris. "Oh, that's just Harry. I could tell you all about him." Morris eventually learned his grandmother's story: In the 1920s, the woman had run one of the most successful brothels in Kansas City. Staying in operation obviously entailed payoffs to the Pendergast machine. The man who had picked up the weekly bribe was none other than Harry Truman, Pendergast's bagman.

After the heat came down on Pendergast-Lazia in the wake of the 1933 massacre that claimed four federal agents, Pendergast decided he needed to boost his influence if he was to survive. He thus decided to elevate his judge, Harry Truman, to the position of U.S. senator. During the ensuing 1934 primaries, in which Pendergast funded Truman for senator, ghost voting was rampant, as was political terrorism; at the height of the electoral frenzy, four political activists were shot dead. When he was asked about vote irregularities in Kansas City in 1934, Truman gave a cynically crafted response: He had nothing to do with Kansas City politics; he voted in Independence.

As senator, Truman consistently turned away those seeking federal relief employment if they bypassed proper channels, i.e., the Pendergast machine, which controlled the local branch of the Works Progress Administration (WPA). To one supplicant Truman curtly replied: "If you will send us endorsements from the Kansas City Democratic Organization, I shall be glad to do what I can for you." When U.S. Attorney Maurice Milligan announced that he was going to investigate the Pendergast machine's role in the massive 1936 election fraud, Truman immediately returned to Kansas City and met with Big Boss Pendergast. Soon Truman announced he was going to use his senatorial privilege to block the attorney's renomination by the full Senate. Only after pressure was exerted by President Roosevelt himself did Truman cease his obstructionism. An infuriated U.S. district judge, Albert Reeves, who was a prime mover in the election investigation, described Senator Truman as "a man who had been nominated by ghost votes, who had been elected with ghost votes, and, if the truth were known, [had] a ghost writer."

Not only was the underworld aware of Truman's shady sponsors, but President Roosevelt himself expressed dismay at the collusion. "I told Harry Truman the other day that he better get away from that crowd out there," Roosevelt told the U.S. attorney from Kansas, Maurice Milligan, in 1939. However, when Pendergast was finally reined in that same year by Milligan and the carnivorous IRS chief Elmer Irey and sentenced to a fifteen-month term, Senator Truman personally called the prison director to ensure Pendergast's fair treatment. "I want you to know he's a friend of mine," implored Senator Truman. "I'm not asking for any favors for him, do you understand, but I wanted him treated no differently from anybody else." As Truman himself later explained: "I never desert a sinking ship. He was my friend when I needed him, and I will be his." Elmer Irey responded by calling Truman "a creature of Boss Pendergast." Pendergast was paroled after one year and died five months later.

Seemingly free of the Big Boss' legacy, Truman went about the business of the Senate. After Pendergast went away, his empire was taken over by another Chicago-connected gangster, Charles Binaggio, who strengthened alliances with the Outfit and its wire service, the Trans-America. With such powerful allies, Binaggio became, like Pendergast, a fearsome Missouri power broker, with several politicians in his pocket. One of his representatives, state senator Edward J. "Jelly Roll" Hogan, often attended secret Democratic caucuses with the imposing Binaggio sitting at his side.

When Binaggio sought to purchase the gubernatorial election of Forrest Smith, he borrowed $200,000 from the Outfit. Binaggio was believed responsible for the fraud and murders that accompanied the defeat of Truman's nemesis Roger Slaughter. With Binaggio using the services of Outfit gunmen such as Tony Gizzo, Mooney Giancana began referring to Truman as "our boy." Curly Humphreys' daughter, Llewella, then an eight-year-old, recalled that on one of her family's vacations, her father gave them the grand tour, impressing the youngster with his Capitol Hill connections. "He even knew Harry Truman, and at one time when Mother and I were in Washington, Harry Truman showed us around," Llewella recalled in 1984. "He became president of the United States shortly thereafter."

Truman: A President the Gangs Could Control

As the 1944 Democratic National Convention loomed conveniently in Chicago, the nation's pols began positioning themselves to control the all-important vice-presidential nomination: Insiders knew that the failing Roosevelt did not have long to live and that the VP nomination actually amounted to the de facto presidential pick. Since virtually no one supported the current vice president, Henry Wallace, who was deemed too liberal and detached for the job, the jockeying began for pretenders to the throne. The issue was fairly settled, although without Wallace's knowledge, on June 27, when Democratic National Committee chairman Robert Hannegan told Roosevelt that Wallace had to go. President Roosevelt agreed and soon found himself lobbied not only by upperworld personages, but also by representatives of the underworld. This was still the era of the smoke-filled-room dealmakers, decades before the 1972 primaries wrested some of the nominating power back to the general public. The underworld wanted Pendergast's boy Harry Truman in the number two slot, against even Truman's own wishes. According to Truman expert Marquis Childs, Truman was "scared to death" of the nomination, fearful his association with the Big Boss would be dragged out into the light. Truman called the Chicago convention "that miserable time." But Truman's own desires mattered little. The underworld wanted a president it could manipulate in a crunch, such as the Ricca parole affair. And one of the key components of the underworld's Truman putsch was their long association with Roosevelt's top adviser, labor leader Sidney Hillman.

Sidney Hillman: Labor Statesman with a Secret Life

Forget everything else. The key to Ricca's parole was the White House. And we held the keys to the White House – we had the Pendergast machine, and we had Sidney.

               –A retired Outfit associate

"Labor's Statesman" Sidney Hillman straddled the moral chasm as deftly as any duplicitous personage in history. A 1907 Russian immigrant to Jim Colosimo's Chicago, and from there to New York in 1914, Hillman and his wife quickly rose from the garment-worker rank and file to leaders of that industry's workers' unions. An icon of the labor movement, Sidney Hillman was president and cofounder of the Congress of Industrial Organizations (CIO). At the time of the 1944 convention, Hillman was Roosevelt's key labor adviser and a prime influence on FDR's choice for a running mate. Lionized as a champion of workers' rights, Hillman was undeniably responsible for improving the plight of America's workforce, teaming up with Roosevelt to forge such New Deal legislation as the Fair Standards Act. At one point, Hillman was considered the second most powerful man in America. However, Hillman's secret relationship with the underworld gave the nation's gangsters a powerful voice in delivering the VP slot to Tom Pendergast's protégé.

Rising up from the bitter struggles of the New York labor movement, Sidney Hillman used the muscle of the Outfit's Commission partners to fortify his Amalgamated Clothing Workers (ACW) in its violent rise to the top of the New York labor scene. A man described as cocksure, self-absorbed, and relentlessly hateful, Hillman made deals with the devil to force holdout garment manufacturers to recognize his fledgling ACW. In one instance, manufacturer Guido Fererri was murdered days after having a bitter argument with Hillman's Amalgamated. The prime suspect was labor slugger and kingpin of the Commission's "Murder, Inc." Lepke Buchalter, the same Lepke who had participated in the Commission's formative meetings and had also traveled to Chicago as the New Yorkers' representative in the Hollywood studio extortion scheme. When Lepke was questioned for the Fererri murder, he called Hillman, who quickly arrived with his attorney, future New York mayor Fiorello La Guardia. Lepke was never charged. In 1941, when Lepke was serving a forty-four-year sentence in Leavenworth for narcotics and racketeering violations, New York DA William O'Dwyer tried to extradite him for the Fererri murder, for which he could have received the electric chair. However, Hillman's great friend Franklin Roosevelt continually procrastinated in signing the extradition papers. Meanwhile, Pulitzer Prize-winning journalist Westbrook Pegler reported in the *New York World-Telegram* (syndicated in 121 papers) that Lepke had worked for the ACW when Hillman had ordered the murder of an independent trucker named Joseph Rosen.

Eventually, Lepke was returned to New York, where he was executed for the Rosen hit in 1944, becoming the only gang boss (to this day) to receive that ultimate official sanction. While on death row, Lepke detailed the revelations Hillman had hoped would never come. Buried in the Bureau of Narcotic's Murder, Inc. files at the New York Archives is a mountain of testimony detailing the relationship between Hillman and Lepke, much of it from the mouth of the imprisoned Lepke. From 1932 to 1937, Hillman paid Lepke $350 per week, with $50 going to the Commission's Lucky Luciano. For his pay, Lepke terrorized laborers and manufacturers into kowtowing before Hillman's ACW. Hillman gave Lepke huge bonuses of $25,000 when he successfully broke a strike, and another $25,000 for fixing a murder rap. As for the Fererri murder, Lepke told authorities it was ordered by Hillman. Both the FBI and the Bureau of Narcotics corroborated the Lepke testimony. Harry Anslinger, the thirty-year veteran crime fighter and head of the Bureau of Narcotics concluded, "The facts fitted together too precisely for error." However, no one was about to go after the second most powerful man in America.

Truman on the 1944 Ticket

On Monday, July 17, 1944, killer Lepke's sometime employer Sidney Hillman called FDR's train from his suite at Chicago's Stevens Hotel. Along with Robert Hannegan, Hillman argued for Truman's recruitment. FDR agreed. The next day, Hillman began massaging the reluctant Truman at a breakfast meeting at the Ambassador East Hotel. Hillman informed Truman that labor could not back Truman's choice of the White House's War Mobilization Director Jimmy Byrnes as Roosevelt's partner. Hillman told Truman, "If it can't be Wallace, we have a second choice, but it isn't Byrnes."

"Who then?" asked Truman.

"I'm looking at him," answered Hillman.

Hillman's influence-peddling was backstopped by Outfit-corrupted Chicago mayor Ed Kelly, who also worked behind the scenes in the anti-Wallace clique at the convention. Meeting with FDR, Kelly and the rest made their case for Truman with the sickly president. But it was Sidney Hillman whose opinion mattered most. Arthur Krock of the *New York Times* reported that when Robert Hannegan asked Roosevelt about potential veep nominees, Roosevelt replied, "Clear it with Sidney."

The last person to fall into line was Truman himself. After two days of waiting for the recalcitrant Truman to agree, Roosevelt lost his patience, slamming down the phone on Hannegan when the party sachem reported that Truman was still balking. Roosevelt then employed a strategy later utilized by President Lyndon Johnson, who in 1963 pressured Chief Justice Earl Warren to head up the investigation of the assassination of President John F. Kennedy. On that tragic occasion, Warren demurred from the appointment, citing among other things his heavy workload at the Supreme Court and the "separation of powers" precept of the Constitution. Johnson then made an appeal that Warren could not refuse, telling Warren that only his imprimatur could prevent a Cold War conflagration. "Why, if Khrushchev moved on us, he could kill thirty-nine million in an hour," Johnson exhorted. "I'm asking you something and you're saying no to everybody when you could be speaking for thirty-nine million people." After Warren wiped the tears from his eyes, he said, "I just can't say no." Roosevelt was no less insidious, telling Hannegan to relay a message to Truman. "You tell him if he wants to break up the

Democratic Party in the middle of a war, that's his responsibility." To which Truman replied, "Well, if that is the situation, I'll have to say yes, but why the hell didn't he tell me in the first place?"[1]

Mooney Giancana was among many inside and outside the Outfit who believed that Truman's links to Kansas City bosses and to FDR's key New Deal adviser Sidney Hillman had guaranteed his placement on the 1944 ticket. The hidden agendas behind Truman's selection, referred to as the Second Missouri Compromise, did not go unnoticed by the upperworld either. A dismayed Interior Secretary Harold Ickes was moved to write: "I react strongly against the method of his nomination and the seeming dominating position that the corrupt city bosses now have in the Democratic National organization.[2] Eleanor Roosevelt wrote to the disappointed Henry Wallace, "It looks to me as though the bosses had functioned pretty smoothly." The *Chicago Tribune* was the most vitriolic when it editorialized: "[We] are faced with the grinning skeleton of Truman the bankrupt, Truman the pliant tool of Boss Pendergast in looting Kansas City's country government, Truman the yes-man and apologist in the Senate for political gangsters."

As president, Truman appeared on the surface to have severed his ties to the Pendergast machine. A closer inspection of the record, however, gives a different reading. In 1946, Truman declared war on Congressman Roger Slaughter, a Republican contrarian who consistently opposed Truman's legislative initiatives. To counteract Slaughter, Truman sought help from his old Kansas City backers, but by this time, Tom Pendergast was deceased. President Truman therefore placed a call to Tom's nephew and successor as boss, Jim Pendergast, himself a frequent weekend guest of Truman's at the White House. As a result of Jim's interference in the next primary, Slaughter was defeated. The *Kansas City Star* uncovered evidence that the Pendergast-Truman machine had rigged the nomination

---

1. Robert Hannegan, castigated by the Missouri press for secretly attempting to steal the state governorship from the 1940 Republican victor, was nonetheless named to head the DNC and the IRS district in Missouri by Senator Truman and was later appointed postmaster general by President Truman.

2. Ickes knew from whence he spoke: He was a former Chicago newsman who was the most influential supporter of 1920s reform mayor William Dever, one of the few Chicago mayors who actually tried to confront Syndicate-influenced political corruption.

process. During a subsequent inquiry, a female election watcher was shot to death on her front porch and the fraudulent ballots were destroyed in a City Hall safe that was blown up by dynamite.

When Congress hinted at an investigation of the Kansas City election fixing, Attorney General Tom Clark, about whom much more will be seen, assured the legislature that he had conducted a thorough investigation and that no facts supported the fraud allegations (although it later surfaced that Clark had not even read a 355-page FBI report on the election before he had cut off the probe.) However, a Kansas City grand jury concluded otherwise and indicted seventy-one vote sluggers, and the *Kansas City Star* conducted its own investigation and also found massive vote fraud, including many voters who had showed up at the polls only to learn they had already voted. Thus despite Clark's pronouncements, Congress proceeded with its inquiry, and when Tom Clark came under fire from the committee chairman, he responded by saying that if he had conducted a full investigation "no one would be ruined except the Democratic Party." The candid response prompted the chairman to retort, "And you are one of them. This was a family affair."

Maurice M. Milligan, the U.S. attorney who had prosecuted Pendergast, wrote that "Harry S Truman's career, without the help of Boss Pendergast, would have ended far short of the White House." Milligan summed up the career of Truman thus: 'When the Senator became Vice-President in 1944, the political stock of the renascent Pendergast machine boomed, but it was nothing compared with the golden opportunities that came on Mr. Truman's succession to the Presidency. New offices, vacancies and resignations which were within the gift of the President, all kinds of Federal patronage found grateful acceptance in the ranks of good machine men, all friends of the President.'

And Pendergast's nemesis, Maurice Milligan, was promptly relieved of duty by the new president, who appointed a new U.S. attorney to the region. The dismissal came not before Truman's friends concocted a nefarious scheme to manipulate Milligan to their own ends. When Truman's Senate reelection bid had come up in 1940, it was widely assumed he would be beaten by the "good government" candidate, Missouri governor Stark. Truman's people believed that their only hope was to persuade a third candidate, a sure-loser type, that he could actually win, convince him to run, thus splitting the good-government vote with Stark. Realizing that Milligan, a dull bureaucrat and lousy public speaker, was considering a run for the Senate, one of Truman's closest friends, Tom Evans, paid a visit to Milligan's brother to put in the fix. Evans convinced the naïve Milligans that his intention was pure and that he firmly believed Milligan could be victorious. And to show his conviction, he handed Milligan a $500 campaign contribution. Truman wrote to his wife that if both Stark and Milligan ran, "that would be too good." As planned, Milligan and Stark nullified each other while Truman snuck through with only a plurality of the vote. Truman historian Robert H. Ferrell wrote: "Truman could not have been renominated without the entrance of Milligan."

By any measure, Truman's presidency was as mixed as his personal ethos. To his admirers, he defeated the Japanese and Germans in World War II, established the state of Israel, and organized NATO. To his detractors, Truman was morally culpable not just for his Missouri compromises, but for the decision to drop an atomic bomb on the population of Nagasaki, after he had already done so on Hiroshima; his formation of NATO was a prime reason Soviet-U.S. relations chilled, leading to the costly and dangerous Cold War; he unnecessarily committed U.S. troops to Korea, fifty thousand of whom returned in body bags. Of Truman's enigmatic moral code, Richard Lawrence Miller wrote, "Truman loved politics, but he held democracy in contempt . . . [He] would always act insensitively about terrors committed by his political allies in Jackson County . . . He had no patience for anyone, great or small, who felt honesty and public service more important than aid to the Pendergast organization . . . Was Truman really indifferent, or could he just not bear to think about his role and responsibility?"

The Transfer

By the time Truman walked away from a presidential reelection bid in 1952, he was dogged by scandalous accusations, not the least of which concerned his possible role in events surrounding Curly Humphreys and the Outfit's imprisoned Hollywood extortionists. But while Truman was in office, Chicago's Outfit was little concerned with debating his historical legacy. For the gangsters, all that mattered was that his past rendered him impotent in the face of pressure from America's empire of crime.

Fully knowledgeable of Truman's vulnerabilities, Curly Humphreys placed a call to Pendergast's legal mouthpiece in St. Louis, attorney Paul Dillon. For years, Dillon was the lawyer of record for Pendergast's muscleman Johnny Lazia. In 1934 and 1940, Dillon managed (at Pendergast's request) the St. Louis campaign offices for Harry Truman's two fraud-filled senatorial elections, with the '34 contest earning the title "The Bloody Election." With his friend Harry Truman now president, Dillon had an open door at the White House, one of the rare few able to call on a president unannounced. As an added bonus, Dillon counted among his best friends T. Webber Wilson, chairman of the federal parole board.

Curly next enlisted Edward "Putty Nose" Brady to deliver to Dillon a list of the men he wanted transferred. Years later, when Congress launched a major probe into the transfer, they were denied access to the FBI files that disclosed the Bureau's plumbing of the Brady connection. When Brady died in 1945, his widow, Helen, was allegedly the recipient of a $20,000 bequest, courtesy of the Outfit, according to a Cicero-based Outfit associate, Willie Heeney, who claimed to have delivered the gift.

Agreeing to take up the Outfit's case, Dillon traveled east and began peddling his influence. Upon his arrival in Washington, Dillon first visited the assistant director of the Bureau of Prisons, Frank Loveland, to whom he introduced himself as a close friend of the president's. Loveland allowed Dillon to make his plea, but ultimately denied the attorney's request. Aware that his Outfit client Paul Ricca would not accept failure, Dillon proceeded up the chain, and on August 8, 1945, the Atlanta inmates, except for Rosselli, were transferred to Leavenworth, over the objections of prison officials. One year later, Johnny Rosselli was transferred to Terre Haute, Indiana. It may never be known exactly whom Dillon leaned on, but buried in documents discovered years later among the Bureau of Prison files is a memo noting that "[Attorney General] Tom Clark would like the subjects transferred to Leavenworth." According to FBI sources, the gang left nothing to chance in its push to obtain the transfers. Years later "a reliable confidential informant" in Chicago reported that Johnny Rosselli had enlisted a well-known D.C. lobbyist, gambler, and ex-con named Samuel Roy Beard in the cause. The informant reported that "through his connections [Beard] was able to arrange the transfer of Rosselli and his associates." The Bureau never determined exactly how Beard figured into the parole strategy.

While in Washington, Paul Dillon nurtured his friendship with the parole board chairman, T. Webber Wilson, with whom Dillon shared many social dinners. In two years, this friendship, in combination with Dillon's other political purchase, would play a pivotal role in the fortunes of the Outfit.

Meanwhile in New York, Johnny Torrio's Commission suffered a major setback: In February 1946, founding member Charles "Lucky" Luciano was deported to Italy. He had been languishing in New York State's infamous Dannemora Prison for ten years on white-slavery charges. Luciano's thirty-to-fifty-year sentence was reduced when he used his underworld connections in both the New York harbor and in Sicily to aid in the World War II Allied effort. Within months, Luciano relocated to Havana, Cuba, from where, according to Curly's second wife, Jeanne, he made clandestine trips into the United States. "We used to meet him at the Plantation Yacht Club [Plantation Key]," Jeanne recalled. "The boys always threw big 'coming out' bashes for Lucky at the club."

Lucky's removal only served to exacerbate New York's intramural Mafia squabbles, a proclivity that has haunted them ever since. By contrast, Chicago's Outfit was more unified and focused than ever, even considering the recent extortion convictions. The power this unity afforded them was soon to be put on display for the rest of the country.

11.

The Parole Scandal

What I need is a lawyer with enough juice to get Ray Charles a driver's license.

–Lenny Bruce, political satirist

The transfer to Leavenworth lessened Ricca's dissatisfaction, but far from eliminated it. Now, at least, the gang boss might be able to turn visiting day into a covert council with his Chicago confreres, Joe Accardo and Curly Humphreys. Of course, felons were not allowed visits from anyone other than family and attorneys, but the Outfit was not about to allow a bureaucratic rule prevent their corporation from holding business meetings. The key facilitator in these powwows at Leavenworth was once again attorney Joseph Bulger, the "supreme president" of the Unione Siciliana.

With Ricca, Campagna, Gioe, D'Andrea, Maritote (Diamond), and Circella now confined together, all that was missing for an Outfit quorum were Accardo and Humphreys. However, taking turns impersonating attorney Bulger, Joe Accardo and Curly Humphreys accompanied Eugene Bernstein, the gang's tax attorney from the Twenty-fourth Ward, to the high-security lockup to confer with their associates. Bernstein, a former ten-year IRS agent, later said that he had never met Accardo or Humphreys before; he had merely been instructed to deliver them to Leavenworth. "Bulger said he will send someone who is acquainted to help me," Bernstein later testified. Ricca would later admit to federal investigators that his friends had signed in on visitors' day by forging the name Joseph Bulger.

By Bernstein's own admission, these trips numbered over six, but it is believed that that was an huge understatement. For over a year, the secret Outfit meetings proceeded, with one piece of new business always at the top of their agenda: obtaining an early parole for their "stand-up" partners.

Ricca's demand was virtually inconceivable for countless reasons: They had criminal records and incorrigible reputations as the heirs to Capone; the outstanding mail-fraud indictments involving the IATSE dues were still untried in New York; they owed $600,000 in back taxes and penalties. Despite the obstacles, the Outfit was convinced that its strong ties to Truman's shadow world would save the day. Putting its nose to the grindstone, the empire of crime confronted the obstacles one by one.

The Mail-Fraud Problem

The gang's brain trust, led by Humphreys, typically decided to attack the problems systematically. First, they took on the impending mail-fraud troubles. Recall that the gang was initially charged, but never tried, for bilking some forty-six thousand IATSE members out of $1 million in dues, most of which had gone into the Outfit's coffers. By the spring of 1946, after months of planning, the powerful prisoners were ready to approach the man they would delegate to accomplish phase one, a high-powered, Dallas-based attorney named Maury Hughes, considered the best trial lawyer in the South. However, Hughes was employed to use his connections to *prevent* a trial and to obtain a dismissal of the pending mail-fraud indictments. Hughes had a long association with the Windy City, having defended a number of its more colorful citizens.[1] The FBI developed information that led them to conclude that Hughes was also acquainted with Harry Ash, Sid Korshak's First Ward law partner and Charles Gioe's parole adviser.

But it wasn't Hughes' Chicago links that were of interest to the gangsters. More important, Hughes was a boyhood friend of fellow Texan, and present attorney general, Tom Clark, Hughes having attended school with Tom's younger brother Bill. According to his son, Maury, Jr., Hughes was also a friend of President Truman's and, as a high-ranking Democratic national committeeman, attended the 1944 Chicago convention, working with Sidney Hillman and the rest to guarantee Truman's addition to the ticket. With his friend Clark controlling the parole board, and his friend Truman controlling Clark, Hughes was the perfect man for the job.

In the spring of 1946, a man described by Hughes to be of clear Italian descent, with "a swarthy complexion and olive skin," appeared at Hughes'

---

1. Among his Chicago clients was Mike Potson, the former manager of (Big Jim) Colosimo's Cafe. At the time, Potson was a known Outfit gambling boss with IRS problems.

Dallas law office. Sporting a gangster-chic pinkie ring with a large diamond, the man introduced himself as "Mike Ryan." The six-foot-tall, fiftyish man said he lived in Chicago, where he was in the trucking business, but had other interests in California, such as a string of horses he owned.

"I have a friend in the penitentiary that has a case pending in New York," Ryan said. "His name is Paul De Lucia."

Hughes later told investigators that, despite his familiarity with Chicago, he had never heard of De Lucia/Ricca, or the other defendants. Ryan told him that Ricca had wanted to be a priest as a youth, but had made a wrong turn. "All right, tell me something about the case," responded Hughes.

Ryan described the mail-fraud charge that threatened to scuttle Ricca's parole chances. The gang's first parole opportunity was over a year away, but they wanted enough time to cover all the contingencies. Hughes agreed to think it over and advise Ryan of his decision. About ten days later, Ryan and two associates met with Hughes in Chicago's posh Stevens Hotel. Ryan offered Hughes a $1,000 retainer against an extravagant $15,000 fee, plus expenses, if he was successful in having the fraud charges dropped. Hughes' experience told him that this could be the easiest $15,000 he would ever earn, since courts rarely wasted the time or money for a trial in which a sentence would likely run concurrently with a previous conviction, as they both stemmed from the same general crime. All Hughes would have to do was let the authorities know who his friends were (Truman, Clark, etc.) and demand habeas corpus: either go to trial now or drop the fraud charges. Hughes' prediction was canny. Although (possibly) unbeknownst to the Dallas attorney, prosecutor Boris Kostelanetz's own opinion was that the fraud charges should be dropped, since there was little chance the prisoners would be released before 1953. Joe Bulger, who was in the courtroom the day the appeals were heard, reported that Judge Knox said, "I am not going to put any time on this mail-fraud case. You have a conviction in one case, and if that sticks, we are not going to waste any time on these cases." Hughes' involvement seemed, according to Congress, to represent nothing more than "an insurance policy."

Whether having known or merely intuited the authorities' recorded views, Hughes accepted Ryan's offer and proceeded to contact the defendants' previous lawyers as well as government authorities such as Kostelanetz in New York, and Attorney General Tom Clark's assistant Peyton Ford in Washington. Over the next year, Hughes journeyed to New York, Washington, and Chicago lobbying for his new clients. (Back in Chicago, on October 9, 1946, the legendary Michael "Hinky Dink" Kenna died. Assorted gamblers and First Ward machine bosses paid their respects. Representing the Outfit, Jake Guzik attended the funeral.)

During the hotly contested 1946 off-year elections, *Chicago Tribune* reporter Jim Doherty was among the first to learn of the next phase of the Outfit's parole strategy. "We began hearing that there was considerable agitation in the Italian wards of Chicago, that efforts were being made to push Republican Italians over into the Democratic fold," wrote Doherty. Hitting the streets of the Italian ghettos, Doherty was told, "The word is out, we all got to go Democratic this time." One of Doherty's editors got to the bottom of the vote push when an Italian friend disclosed, "We have got the word. We have to go Democratic this time so four guys can get out on parole." Doherty subsequently located Italian Republican ward leaders who were later punished by their party for succumbing to the peer pressure and actually delivering the vote to the Democrats. "The facts were and the record showed that those Italian Republicans did vote Democratic," Doherty testified. "Those Italian Republican leaders delivered ten thousand or fifteen thousand votes to the Democratic organization." According to Mooney Giancana, the Italians were putting on a show; they merely wanted to prove to Truman what they could do for him when his election came up in 1948.

With the parole gambit moving apace, the Outfit did not ignore the day-to-day business of organized crime. In December 1946, Joe Accardo headed an Outfit delegation to a national Commission meeting in Havana, organized by Meyer Lansky, who had been invested in Cuban casinos since the midthirties, and the deported Lucky Luciano, who had snuck into Cuba. More than two dozen regional bosses and their families arrived on December 21, finding themselves ensconced on the top four floors of the luxurious Hotel Nacional.[2] As with any upperworld convention, meeting rooms and banquet facilities were all booked in advance, while the criminal conventioneers conducted their business in a manner not unlike that of their upperworld counterparts. On the first night of the conference, December 22, the attendees threw a lavish bash in which they paid tribute to Luciano by handing him envelopes stuffed with

---

2. In addition to Accardo, Lansky, and Luciano, others in attendance included Vito Genovese, Joseph Bonanno, Albert Anastasia, Joe Adonis, Carlos Marcello, Santo Trafficante, Moe Dalitz, Doc Stacher, and Longy Zwillman.

cash. When Luciano totaled the $200,000 Christmas gift, he announced he would use it to invest in the Naçional's casino.

Over the Christmas holidays, the bosses met to deal with the key items on the conference agenda: the infighting of New York's five "families"; the wisdom of engaging in the narcotics trade (Luciano and Costello were against it); and the "Ben Siegel situation." Siegel had been spending the Commission's money as if it were water in the Nevada desert, constructing the first of the glitzy Las Vegas hotel-casinos, the Flamingo. His original budget had been $1.5 million, but Siegel had managed to squander over $6 million, with rumors rampant that he was skimming from his Commission partners.

On Christmas Eve, the confreres were treated to a party honoring Frank Sinatra, who had arrived from Chicago with Accardo and the Fischetti brothers. In his memoirs, Luciano asserted that years earlier he had put up $60,000 to jump-start Sinatra's fledgling career. Congressional investigators believed that Sinatra couriered a briefcase stuffed with over a million dollars to Luciano at the Havana conference, as the return on Lucky's investment. In later years, Sinatra would visit Luciano in exile in Italy. Syndicated columnist Walter Winchell wrote, "When Italian police raided Lucky's lavish apartment in Rome, they found a sterling silver cigaret case, inscribed: 'To My Dear Friend, Charlie Luciano,' over one of the most sought-after American autographs, that of a young star, a known gangster lover." Although Winchell did not name him, the facts soon emerged that the signature read, "Frank Sinatra."[3]

---

3. Tales abound of Sinatra's associations with hoodlums, going back to his days running the streets of Hoboken, New Jersey. In fairness, at the time of Sinatra's emergence as a singer, there was no practical way of avoiding making some accommodation with gangsters, who controlled much of the entertainment industry. But Sinatra clearly went overboard with his affinity for the hoods. Senate investigator Norman Polski wrote: "Mickey Cohen, Frank Sinatra, and a Jimmy Tarantino were believed to have operated the *Hollywood Nite Life Magazine*, and were closely associated in the fight racket with [the Outfit's] Barney Ross . . . In the latter part of 1949, Sinatra was supposed to have provided a $75,000 bankroll to back a fight that was held on the West Coast. It is believed he worked in close contact with [Los Angeles mobster] Mickey Cohen and Blinkie Palermo, manager of [boxer] Ike Williams."

Sinatra's 1,275-page FBI file is loaded with the crooner's connections to the mob, the strongest of which appears to be with Chicago's Fischetti brothers, with whom Sinatra became extremely close in the midforties. Sinatra's first wife, Nancy, was a cousin of a top hood in New Jersey boss Willie Moretti's gang.

When the conference ended, the bosses returned to their respective dominions. For Joe Accardo, that meant back to work on the disposal of the mail-fraud charges and the complex parole issue. His bags were hardly unpacked when the Outfit heard the news from Florida: At his Palm Island estate, Big Al Capone, the gang's forty-eight-year-old patriarchal figure, had suffered a massive stroke on his January 18, 1947, birthday and died one week later. The event was likely related to his raging case of syphilis, which had rendered him both weak and demented. After being released to his family on November 16, 1939, Capone underwent a program of experimental syphilis remedies at Baltimore's Union Memorial Hospital.[4] While the treatments actually succeeded in slowing the progression of the disease, they could not stop the inevitable. After four months, Al Capone retired, finally, to his villa in Florida, where he spent his final years with his beloved wife and son in near seclusion.

Shortly after his death, Capone's body was secretly loaded into a laundry truck and driven to a local funeral parlor, where it was then embalmed and placed in a hearse. Ten days after Al Capone's passing, the $2,000 coffin bearing his disease-ravaged corpse arrived by hearse from Miami, with Capone's family arriving by train. At around 2 P.M. Scarface was interred in the Mount Olivet Cemetery on Chicago's Far South Side. From behind a police-guarded periphery, a couple hundred gawkers braved the frigid eleven-degree winter air to observe the amazingly small (by Chicago standards) gangster funeral. The top bosses who did attend arrived in rental cars, hoping to avoid identification by police. The intimate gathering was the result of a decree by boss Joe Accardo: "We gotta draw the line someplace. If we let 'em, everybody in Chicago will crowd into the cemetery. Al had no enemies."

The curious throng watched as only Al's most trusted friends and relatives drove up to burial plot fifty-eight near the south end of the cemetery. The Campagna family and Al's brother Ralph attended, as well as Capone's in-laws and other relatives from New York. But those who were of most interest to the press and public were the pinkie-ringed, well-dressed men alighting from the follow-up cars, a who's who of Chicago crime paying their respects to Al's mother, Theresa Capone; his widow, Mae; and son, Sonny. Some Outfitters considered "too hot" at the time were barred from

---

4. In one protocol Capone was repeatedly injected with a form of malaria, the theory being that by inducing high fevers, the syphilis bug might die from heat. He later became one of the earliest recipients of the powerful new antibiotic penicillin.

the proceedings by Accardo; they were instead allowed to pay their respects indoors at the Rago Brothers Chapel, the site of the private wake held earlier. Wake attendees later spoke of the hoods' reliving old times, bringing smiles to one another's faces. Curly Humphreys especially was noted as having lightened the mood with war stories that kept the likes of Guzik chuckling. Now graveside, the mischievous mourners were more true to form with a distraught Charlie Fischetti barking at a press photographer who attempted to take a picture of Al's distraught mother, "I'll kill the son of a bitch that takes a picture." Al's younger brother, Matt, also threatened the press. The grief-stricken older brother, Ralph "Bottles" Capone, was more restrained as he pleaded, "Why don't you leave us alone?"

Under the funereal canopy, Monsignor William J. Gorman conducted the brief reading as Al's mother sobbed profusely, comforted by Joe Accardo. Before reciting the traditional prayers of the Catholic Church, Gorman offered his own thoughts on the occasion: "The Roman Catholic Church never condones evil, nor the evil in any man's life. But this ceremony is sanctioned by our archbishop in recognition of Alphonse Capone's repentance, and the fact that he died with the sacraments of the Church."

In a few years, due to their disdain for curiosity seekers, the Capone family had Al's remains secretly transferred to a family plot in Mount Carmel Cemetery on Wolf Road in the western suburb of Hillside. His spare, flat grave marker notes merely his name, birth and death dates, and a quotation: "My Jesus, Mercy."[5]

On May 6, 1947, the fraud charges were finally dropped in New York. According to sources developed by reporter Jim Doherty, the order for the dismissal came from Washington, from Attorney General Tom Clark, the same Tom Clark who one year earlier had ordered the FBI's CAPGA (Capone Gang) probe disbanded; and the same Tom Clark who scuttled an FBI investigation into the Kansas City vote fraud that defeated Truman's sworn enemy Congressman Roger Slaughter and resulted in the murder of a female election official. After the court proceedings, Hughes met with Ryan to collect the balance of his fee. Ryan walked Hughes to the Manhattan's Corn National Bank, where, as promised, he transferred a $14,000 cashier's check to Hughes. After saying their good-byes, Ryan and Hughes

---

5. Apropos of Capone's life, the multitude of flower arrangements were carted off to hospitals and orphanages in Chicago's poorest sectors, while the Outfit went back to the office to again consider the business of paroling Al's most trusted protégés.

went their separate ways. Hughes said he never saw the mysterious Ryan again. When pushed by congressional investigators, Hughes admitted that he had possessed Ryan's phone number, but had lost it when a pickpocket had lifted his address book at a Chicago Cubs game.

The Tax Payments

Undoubtedly the easiest preparole penalty to satisfy was the issue of Ricca's and Campagna's back taxes and penalties, totaling over $600,000. Although the dollar figure was irrelevant to a crime cartel pulling in millions per month, Humphreys believed the punishment excessive and decided to have it lowered; he may have also relished the opportunity to show off the long reach of his growing personal influence. Almost immediately, the penalty was lowered to a paltry $126,000, while the Outfit's law enforcement adversaries threw up their collective hands in frustration and bewilderment. It has never been explained just how Curly accomplished this feat of legerdemain.

Humphreys then accompanied attorney Bernstein to Leavenworth to report the good news to Ricca, who, according to Bernstein's later testimony, repeated the gang's mantra: "Go see Bulger." After consultation with the enigmatic Joe Bulger, Bernstein waited for the other shoe to drop. Meanwhile, Bulger, the "supreme president" of the twenty-five thousand-member Unione Siciliana, put the word out once more: "The boys need some money." Apparently, Ricca and Campagna had demurred from tapping their personal fortunes to settle the matter. Without hesitation, the same loyal Sicilians answered the call as they had four years earlier when they'd contributed to the gang's bail fund. Out of the blue, men began arriving at Bernstein's office, bringing sheaves of banknotes, saying, "This is for Paul" or "This is for Louis." The FBI estimated that some forty-two separate drop-offs were made. It was as though, according to Bernstein, money fell from the sky. Bernstein later told a rapt, if dumbstruck, congressional committee, "This sounds like fantasy, I agree with you. It sounds fantastic." To the end, Bernstein contended that he never identified the men who contributed to the fund. When Louis "Little New York" Campagna learned of the windfall, he feigned astonishment, exclaiming, "It's an act of God!" Later, when grilled by congressional investigators, Campagna was asked by a sarcastic Congressman Clare Hoffman, "Do you believe in Santa Claus?" To which a bemused Campagna answered, "Yes. I mean, if you were me, wouldn't you?"

The fraud charges and the tax penalties dispensed with, the stage was set for the coup de grâce. Crime historians agree that the obtaining of an early parole for Capone's heirs is one of the greatest examples of the influence of organized crime in U.S. history.

The Impossible Parole

In 1947, some eleven thousand requests were made for early paroles, with roughly 50 percent granted. When word reached Chicago that Al Capone's protégés were under consideration, virtually no one believed it would be possible. No one, that is, except the Outfit. At the gang's direction, the letters of reference began arriving at the parole board's office. Dozens of influential Chicagoans, including one bishop and four other clerics, spoke up in testament to the redeeming qualities of their friends, Ricca et al. Steve Healy, the owner of the landmark Stevens Hotel and one of Chicago's premier public-works contractors, also worked for the gang's release. Calling from California, Sidney Korshak suggested to his Chicago law partner Harry Ash that he act as Charley Gioe's parole supervisor, the revelation of which would later cost Ash his irony-laden patronage job as the Illinois superintendent of crime prevention. Korshak had stayed in regular contact with Gioe, visiting him many times in Leavenworth. Meanwhile, the Chicago press reported that rumors were circulating about an alleged Jake Guzik trip to New York. The allegations, never investigated, stated that Guzik had New York boss Frank Costello offer Postmaster General, and former Democratic National Committee chairman, Robert Hannegan $350,000 if he could secure the paroles.

At the same time, Louis Campagna's wife, Charlotte, was instructed to call Paul Dillon to enlist his services once more. Dillon later said he accepted the offer to make up for what Bioff and Browne had done; they were the ringleaders, he said, and he had personal experience with Browne, whom he knew to be a liar. "[Browne] was as unreliable a man as I ever dealt with," Dillon later testified. "When I found that his testimony was the main testimony that convicted these men, I said I wouldn't believe in their conviction under any conditions."

Although Dillon claimed to have met with Wilson only as a favor for Mrs. Campagna, he in fact admitted cashing a $10,000 check from the Campagnas at the conclusion of his minimal work on their behalf. Also added to the legal team was Ricca's attorney from the original extortion trial, A. Bradley Eben. It is possible that Eben was brought in on the chance that his connections might hold some sway on the eventual outcome: His mother, Mary Agnes Eben, worked in the White House as assistant secretary to President Harry Truman.

Dillon, who routinely traveled to the nation's capital every other week, immediately went to Washington to call on his friend parole board chairman T. Webber Wilson, where he greeted Wilson's secretary saying, "Wilson will know me. I'm a friend of the president." Dillon was informed that Wilson was out of town and that the board would not be considering the gang's parole until it came due in early August. Dillon then filled out the requisite paperwork, formally requesting the paroles for his clients. Per custom, the original judge in the case (John Bright) and the prosecutor (Boris Kostelanetz) were sent Bureau of Prison Form 892, asking their opinions on the the impending decision. Kostelanetz wrote back in strong opposition: "The convicted defendants are notorious as successors to the underworld power of Al Capone. They are vicious criminals who would stop at nothing to achieve their ends. The investigation and prosecution were attended by murder, gunplay, threatening of witnesses, perjury, etc." As Kostelanetz later told Congress, "I opposed parole in each case, except the case of Gioe." He explained that the court was never able to demonstrate that Gioe profited from the extortion scam. Judge Bright concurred: "I beg to advise you that I would oppose a parole." Bright then enumerated the laundry list of crimes in which the men were involved. "I know of no better way to suppress these kinds of activities than severe punishment . . . When I sentenced [Ricca] and his coconspirators to prison I felt very strongly that the full sentences should be inflicted."

Despite the perceived obstacles, the gangsters were confident. In Chicago, Mooney Giancana, privy to Truman's vulnerable past, told his brother that Ricca and the rest would be out "real soon." In his own hyperbolic manner, Giancana described how Truman's shadow world in Kansas City would be used to leverage the eventual early release of the Hollywood-extortion prisoners:

It's just like Chicago out there. They had a mick mayor, Pendergast, on the take big time . . . loved to bet on the ponies. And they got the Italians [Lazia] for muscle and to make money with the rackets. So, fact is, Truman owes everything he's got to us. Pendergast made him a judge and then, with Italian muscle behind him, got him into the Senate. When the 'forty-four election came up . . . Kelly here in Chicago got him on the ticket with Roosevelt. Shit, Chicago got Roosevelt and Truman nominated and elected. We were good to Roosevelt; he was good to us. He died and Truman's been our man in the White House ever since. It's been smooth sailing with him there.

On August 5, Dillon again showed up at the office and met with Wilson and another of the board's three members, Fred S. Rogers. (Both Rogers and the third member, Boleslau J. Monkiewicz were appointed by Maury Hughes' longtime friend Attorney General Tom Clark.)

On August 11, 1947, after the parole board had conducted what Congress later called "perfunctory" investigations into the defendants' histories, the paroles were approved by Wilson and Rogers, over the objections of Kostelanetz, Bright, and a host of Chicago newsmen. In Leavenworth, Ricca and pals began packing their bags, and two days later, when Monkiewicz came to Washington, he added the final imprimatur. Rogers later said that Wilson had convinced him that "the Al Capone Gang [the Outfit] was not functioning in Chicago." According to Rogers, Dillon persuaded the board that Bioff and Browne "testified themselves out of the penitentiary and testified these men in." Incredibly, the board never learned of the defendants' phone-book-thick rap sheets. Jim Doherty, an investigative reporter for the *Chicago Tribune,* interviewed the parole board about their action and came away from the interview perplexed: "They [the board members] were very vague and mysterious. They seemed to have had no idea of who these men were. They never heard of the Capone gang. The Capone gang to them was something that might have come out of a fairy tale or might have been something in ancient history, but they didn't know, or at least they wanted me to believe they didn't know, the menace of the Capone gang to the city of Chicago."

Syndicated columnist Drew Pearson had his own theory about the parole board's baffling pronouncement. Parole Board Chairman Wilson "was crooked," Pearson informed the FBI. According to Pearson, Wilson had compromised his position on at least two occasions when "money changed hands in connection with the granting of paroles." Soon after their controversial ruling on the Outfit's paroles, Wilson and Rogers resigned their posts.

On the first day Ricca and friends became eligible for parole, only one week after Dillon's meeting in Washington, they exited the confines of Leavenworth. Unquestionably a massive "coming out" party was thrown at one of the Outfit's restaurants. Throughout Chicagoland, Outfit associates celebrated their bosses' triumph. Perhaps the grandest coming-out party was thrown by Paul Ricca five months later, on the occasion of his daughter Maria De Lucia's wedding to Alex Ponzio, the owner of an electric supply company. Maria had postponed her marriage until her father was released from prison.[6]

After the ceremony, some five hundred guests feasted at the Blackstone Hotel, where, according to the bridegroom, the tab came to between $27,000 and $30,000, an astronomical sum in 1948. Jules Stein's Music Corporation of America (MCA) supplied the Buddy Moreno big band at a cost of $1,000. Before the day ended, the Ponzios were the recipients of the traditional Italian envelope presentations from the guests, and given the stature of the father of the bride, no one was about to present a thin wrapper. According to Alex Ponzio, the couple received an amazing $35,000 in cash, in addition to a $20,000 trust gift from Paul Ricca to his daughter.

The Uproar

The good cheer, however, was not universal. One month after the paroles, and after reading Jim Doherty's work in the *Trib,* Illinois congressman Fred E. Busbey, a member of the Committee on Expenditures, fired off a letter to Attorney General Tom Clark, demanding an investigation. Clark complied with the request and tasked Hoover's FBI to investigate. While waiting for the FBI's report, Busbey and Michigan congressman Clare Hoffman, the committee chair, initiated their own congressional probe. Between September 1947 and June 1948, the committee interviewed 56 witnesses under oath, while the FBI spoke with some 275. Although the committee was never able to prove a bribe had been paid for the gang's release, they were highly suspicious of the administration's actions.

Fueling the committee's suspicions was the total lack of cooperation of Clark's Justice Department and Truman's White House, since both refused to turn over the FBI's interviews to the committee.[7] Congressman

---

6. A federal investigator described the extravaganza for a congressional committee thus: "This wedding breakfast and reception, which has been facetiously referred to as De Lucia's "coming out" party, was held on January 24, 1948 . . . and has been unexcelled for gaiety, splendor, and lavishness by few if any of the parties staged by the first families of Chicago."

7. In his closing statement, Hoffman wrote, 'There is no evidence in the record that the Federal Bureau of Investigation, which, because of an executive order and because of the instructions of the Department of Justice, refused to make available to the committee information presumably in its possession, in any way assisted the committee or its investigators . . . The Department of Justice . . . gave the committee no assistance whatsoever.'

Busbey wrote: "To this day, members of this committee have been unable to get even a hint of [the FBI's] results, nor what was learned from interviewing 275 or more witnesses." On two occasions in October 1947, Hoffman wrote to President Truman, beseeching him to issue an executive order commanding Clark to release the FBI material to the committee. Truman never responded, but merely instructed Deputy Attorney General Philip Perlman to deny the request based on the principle of separation of powers. In its final report, Hoffman's committee concluded: "The syndicate has given the most striking demonstration of political clout in the history of the republic."

Just how politically sensitive the findings of the withheld FBI report were can be seen in the recently released portions of the document, in which the Bureau ended with the following summary and caution:

> It is noted that Humphreys' involvement in the above situation is consistent with his functions to act as the mastermind of the strategy utilized by Chicago area hoodlums when confronted with prosecution of any type. Extreme caution should be exercised in the use of this information. It should not be included in the body of a report even though paraphrased. It should not be used . . . unless specific clearance is obtained from the Bureau and from Chicago. This is an extremely delicate and sensitive source which the Chicago office is making every effort to protect.

In 1948, under extreme pressure from Hoffman's powerful committee, the reconstituted parole board revoked the paroles, but the Outfit's lawyers posted bail and succeeded in introducing a barrage of delaying tactics that stalled the case into oblivion.

Throughout the committee's investigation, legislators repeatedly hinted that "big money" had been paid to secure the gang's release. In Chicago, street hoods claimed to know for certain that this money went not just to attorneys, but "into the White House and the attorney general's office." And more than money may have been used in the bribery. According to Mooney Giancana, Curly Humphreys relayed a Ricca offer to the attorney general. "Ricca even promised Clark a seat on the fuckin' Supreme Court if he helped get him out," Giancana said. According to his brother Chuck, Mooney told how the allegedly extorted Hollywood studios made a $5-million personal gift to Truman for the granting of the paroles, with Tom Clark guaranteed the Supreme Court post for his role. The Outfit also promised Truman its support in the 1948 elections. As far as Truman went, "We own him," said Giancana. "We own the White House." In that contest, Truman's friends in Chicago reportedly returned the parole favor. "Boy, does Truman owe Chicago," Giancana said. "Thirty thousand votes . . . that's all he won by. Jesus, we had to beg, borrow, and steal to swing the son of a bitch . . . No way the man doesn't know who got him elected." After the razor-thin 1948 election, the Outfit felt they had increased their "marker" on the Oval Office.

Mooney was corroborated in part when a hidden FBI bug picked up Curly Humphreys bragging in 1964, "The trick was to get to Tom Clark. He had the power to see that the New York indictment was vacated. But he had a lot of problems with that. What a cry would go up if the 'Capone guys' were dismissed. Finally a deal was made: If he had the thick skin to do it, he'd get the next appointment to the Supreme Court." Clark played along, and when the next Supreme Court opening came two years later, on October 3, 1949, Clark indeed received Truman's nomination to the nation's highest court. The *Chicago Tribune* immediately responded to Clark's appointment, noting "Clark's utter unfitness for any position of public responsibility and especially for a position on the Supreme Court." The paper called for Clark's impeachment when it editorialized, "We have been sure of Clark's unfitness ever since he played his considerable role in releasing the Capone gangsters after they served only the bare minimum of their terms." A few years later, Congress' massive Kefauver hearings on organized crime would call the episode "an awesome display of the syndicate power and ability to wield political influence." The FBI's hidden mikes overheard Humphreys' more prosaic summary: 'Attorney General Tom Clark was always one hundred percent for doing favors.'

Though the early parole and the appointment of Clark were two of the major scandals of the Truman presidency, no one ever pursued the linkage of the Outfit and Truman beyond the hamstrung congressional probe. Therefore, it was never learned how the Outfit was able to guarantee that Truman would go along with Clark's court appointment. And it will likely never be proved that Truman himself personally prevailed upon his appointees to spring Ricca and his pals. It is worth noting that President Truman had a record of granting highly questionable pardons, many of them to members of the Pendergast machine, not to mention the 1945 pass he granted Nick Schenck. Most of Pendergast's paroled thugs had been convicted of participating in the

Kansas City voting fraud that not coincidentally helped place Truman in the Senate.[8]

In Truman"s defense, Mafia expert Hank Messick wrote, "Truman was just too busy with the United Nations, the cold war, and the state of the economy to pay much attention to internal corruption." Truman himself was conflicted concerning his path to the Oval Office. He told his wife, "The terrible things done by the high ups in Kansas City will be a lead weight on me from now on." About one of his political fixes for Pendergast, the distraught Truman wrote, "Was I right, or did I compound a felony? I don't know." Perhaps the most trenchant summary was written by historian and Truman expert Richard Lawrence Miller: "The fanatic, unthinking, and eternal devotion Truman demanded from everyone ever associated with the Pendergast machine has no justification in normal American political practice or in the history of Kansas City politics." In later years, as Miller wrote, Truman engaged in internal dialectics "to ease his own guilty conscience about his role as an honest front protecting the power of thieves and murderers."

The bust-up of the Hollywood extortion scam caused many to conclude that the Outfit had ceased its hegemony in the movie capital. That assumption could not have been more erroneous. With their associates now permeating every facet of the movie industry's craft and teamster unions, and with labor negotiator Sid Korshak still in place manipulating the unions and studios like chess pieces, the gangsters' presence in Hollywood was as strong as ever, if less blatant. "We're not about to turn our back on so much money and power," said Mooney Giancana. "Besides, those guys [Cohn, Mayer, Warner] are more than business contacts . . . they're our friends now. Rosselli's got them in his pocket." Giancana's assessment was dead-on. After his release from prison, Johnny Rosselli was sponsored right back into the motion picture business by, of all people, Joe Schenck, who had also been imprisoned during the Hollywood shakedown and had supposedly been extorted by Rosselli's Chicago bosses. Working as a producer at Eagle Lion Studios, Rosselli cranked out hit gangster films

---

8. Truman also shocked many when he pardoned "Ice Pick" Danny Motto, a New York labor thug convicted of murder and racketeering. The Justice Department had scheduled Motto's deportation, but Truman intervened at the last moment.

that were noted for their realism.[9] In short time, he moved into the legendary Garden of Allah bungalow apartments, home to stars such as Humphrey Bogart and Edward G. Robinson. As if making up for lost time, Johnny went on a starlet-dating binge, romancing the likes of Lana Turner, Betty Hutton, Donna Reed, and Virginia Hill, girlfriend of the recently whacked Ben Siegel. On the side, Rosselli continued loan-sharking to the stars, with millions of Outfit lucre loaned out to juiced-up actors with gambling problems. The technique remained a tried-and-true method for the hoods to get off-the-books shares of stars' careers.

It was even obvious to the children of the Outfit members that the gang's stature in Tinseltown had not diminished one whit. As she later recalled, then fourteen-year-old Antoinette Giancana, Mooney's youngest daughter, was given a personal tour of MGM's facilities by top producer Boris Pasternak in 1949. Pasternak saw to it that she was introduced to such stars as Jimmy Stewart and Spencer Tracy. Llewella Humphreys, Curly's only child, spoke of a studio head who escorted her and her mother, Clemi, onto Joan Crawford's closed set. Suddenly, the feisty Crawford, whose past had been secreted by Rosselli, acted the diva: "Get those two out of here," she fumed. "I will not have it on my set. It's closed." Whereupon the studio honcho shot back, "Either they stay or you go, and you are through in the movies." Llewella's photo scrapbook holds photographs of the youngster with Jimmy Stewart, Tony Bennett, and Fay Wray. Lest there be any confusion about the Outfit's continued influence in Hollywood: When teenaged Llewella needed an escort to her high school prom, she asked her daddy if he could arrange for Frank Sinatra to be her date. One call from Curly and the bobby-sox idol was on the next plane to Chicago.

Not all of the favors given to Outfit members were the result of intimidation, real or implied. Many successful upperworld habitués genuinely liked most of the Chicago bosses, many of whom preserved Capone's tradition of Good Samaritan beneficence, freely sharing their ill-gotten wealth with the downtrodden. One only has to stay in Chicago for a day to find octogenarians with tales of gangster-style humanitarian-

---

9. Among the Rosselli-produced pics were *T-Men, Canon City,* and *He Walked by Night.* Years before his incarceration, Rosselli allegedly worked with his boss at Eagle Lion, Brynie Foy, in producing the B movie *Roger Touhy, Gangster,* which was released by Twentieth Century-Fox in 1944; the film's legal adviser was none other than Sidney Korshak.

ism. It is generally agreed that Curly Humphreys was the "nicest hood" ever to make the Public Enemy List. Not only was Humphreys beloved in Oklahoma by the Native Americans whose cause he championed decades before it became chic, but he was known in Chicago as a man who quietly helped anyone in need. FBI reports note that Humphreys was the one gangster who looked after just-released convicts who needed jobs, and who made certain the Outfit gave pensions to widows and disabled associates. A telling example of Humphreys' silent altruism occurred in 1950, according to a number of retired Chicago police officials. Informed by a friend on the force that a relative of Attorney General Tom Clark's had gotten into a legal jam with the park police, Curly contacted park police chief Ot Lewis and persuaded him to deep-six the written complaint. Humphreys then met with the complainant, paying him off to drop the charge. When asked if this was Humphreys' way of returning Clark's parole board favor, a park police retiree said, "No. It was just typical Humphreys – just doing the right thing to help a guy."[10]

As the nation entered the Fabulous Fifties, so did many of the Outfit bosses enter theirs. Fittingly, the underworld barons began to aspire to less demanding lifestyles, wishing to spend more time with their families and hobbies. Some contemplated a life away from the stresses of the "business world," hoping to enjoy the fruits of their labor in comfortable retirement. One by one, however, they would learn that getting out was exponentially more difficult than getting in; by now, too many associates and their families were dependent on their founders' continuing leadership.

Joe Accardo was so enamored of the easy life that he made one ostentatious purchase that caused a good degree of friction between him and his cohorts. For years, the Accardo family had lived in a modest ranch house at 1431 Ashland Avenue, in the Chicago suburb of River Forest, where Joe was known as a beer distributor. In 1951, Accardo decided he deserved a home fit for a king, which in many ways he was. Curly Humphreys, the avowed apartment dweller, was among those who warned against such an extravagance. "The smart money don't go to the suburbs," Curly said. "You and your family will stick out like a sore thumb and the feds will always know exactly where you are." Jake Guzik, now in his

---

10. Although the author knows the names and specifics of the case, it would serve no purpose to divulge them, especially since both the complainant and the alleged perpetrator are still alive.

sixties and semiretired, agreed with Curly and stayed at the Chicagoan Hotel when in town. Guzik bought his dream house on San Marino Island, off the Miami coast, far from the prying eyes of Chicago police and the feds.

Ignoring Curly's counsel, Joe purchased a red-roofed, twenty-two-room mansion at 915 Franklin Avenue (also in River Forest), just two blocks from his pal Paul Ricca. At the price Accardo paid, $125,000, the home, which came to be known as the Palace, was a steal. It had been built by a millionaire manufacturer in 1930 for $500,000; four decades after Joe's purchase, it would sell for almost $2 million. Curly's wife remembered that "Curly was mad as hell at Joe after he bought the Palace. He didn't speak to him for weeks."

Accardo's stone palace was a local showplace, far and away the most opulent home in a neighborhood of impressive dwellings. Its amenities included high-vaulted rooms, an indoor pool with a garden on its roof for Joe's queen, Clarice, a gun and trophy room, a pipe organ, a walk-in safe, wood spiral staircases, carriage and guest houses on the backyard half-acre. The property was encircled by a seven-foot-high, wrought-iron fence and two electrically controlled gates. But even this much opulence was not enough for Accardo. After moving into his new digs, Joe installed a $10,000 black onyx bathtub and an indoor, two-lane bowling alley. He had the plumbing refitted with gold fixtures and added a massive barbecue pit to the backyard. Even Mooney Giancana's sixteen-year-old daughter, Antoinette, was taken aback by the garish spread. "It was almost obscene the way he flaunted his wealth," she later wrote. "He reminded me of some medieval Sicilian godfather dispensing baronial favors from his stately, wood-paneled library filled with valuable and classical gems that I bet he never bothered to open, let alone read."

The Palace's backyard would become the scene of legendary Fourth of July cookouts, attended by all the Outfit leaders, foot soldiers, and their families. Typically, these patriotic frolics were surveilled from the other side of the iron fence by a gaggle of curious press and Chicago detectives. Joe liked to entertain his guests by toying with the prying officials. One year, a detective yelled from the periphery, "Hey, Joe, you gonna have fireworks?" Feigning shock, Accardo answered back, "Certainly not, Officer, that would be illegal."

Sharing the new home with Joe were his wife, Clarice, and their four children: Anthony (born 1936), Marie (1939), Linda Lee (1941), and Joseph (1946). Both of the Accardo boys were adoptees. Clarice, like her husband, was an opinionated leader, assuming the responsibilities commensurate with her role as the Outfit's first lady. Afternoons at the Palace often found Clarice hosting teas with the spouses of other gang bosses. From her wives' club, Clarice regularly gleaned information useful to her husband and the orderly running of his business. "Joe's wife told him what the gang's wives said," recalled one Outfit member. On one occasion, Clarice informed Joe that Scotty Stevenson, a foot soldier married to a Capone relative, was neglecting his family. Stevenson was summoned to Accardo, who pulled the subordinate aside. "I'm paying your wife from now on," Joe decreed. "You will get paid by her. If I can't trust you to take care of your family, how can I trust you to take care of my business? This shit keeps up and you ain't going to be around."[11]

Accardo, who was never known to cheat on Clarice, was especially terse with members who flaunted their infidelities in public. Although discreet liaisons with mistresses were tolerated, men who brought pain or dishonor to their family were dealt with harshly – often beaten, or ousted from the gang altogether. The transgressions were not only frowned upon for moral reasons; as Joe was well aware, the antiphilandering edicts also served a pragmatic function. Consequently, Accardo was heard to scold more than one adulterer, "You're embarrassing *us*."

Marital woes were not confined merely to the lower-level members of the gang. In 1951, the Outfit's chief strategist began a seven-year affair with a dice girl who would eventually become the next Mrs. Murray Humphreys. With Curly's wife, Clemi, and daughter, Llewella, living full-time on their Oklahoma property, Curly had been spending increasingly longer periods alone in his Chicago apartment, where he had free rein to indulge his weakness for young blondes.

During this period, Curly frequented numerous Windy City bistros, among them a Near North restaurant called Ye Olde Cellar Club, where Jeanne Stacy was among the most attractive of the dice-rolling 26 game girls. Stacy was born Betty Jeanne Neibert in St. Charles, Missouri, in 1928. By the time she was seventeen, she had the looks of actress Tippi Hedren and the independent spirit and razor-sharp wit of Mae West. Seeking adventure, the teenaged Neibert, now using the name Stacy, headed for Chicago, where she quickly hooked up with a third-tier Outfit bookie twenty-five years her senior named Irving Vine, whom she married after a short courtship. "It was a marriage of convenience,"

---

11. Accardo's intercession may indeed have saved the Stevensons' relationship. Many years later, Mrs. Stevenson buried her husband after fifty years of marriage.

Jeanne explains today. "I was a minor when we got together, and I needed a place to live. We shared the rent, and for the last three years we weren't even a couple." The marriage to Vine, an underling of slot and jukebox king Eddie Vogel, lasted six years, and Stacy soon fell in with Humphreys.

When Humphreys first eyed Jeanne Stacy in the Rush Street restaurant, he merely admired the youngster from afar. "I was a teenager when I came to his attention," Jeanne recalls, "so he didn't make any moves. He waited till he was ready, till the time was right." The "right time" turned out to be a scene worthy of the film *Married to the Mob*. At the time, Curly's driver, Hy Gottfried, had been carrying on his own affair with another pretty blonde who lived in Stacy's building. Gottfried devised moneymaking schemes for the Outfit, often with unreliable cohorts. Curly was once heard to remark, "I spend half my time straightening out this guy [Gottfried] with the boss." Gottfried's tenuous purchase with Accardo made his adultery all the more perilous. "Hy's wife eventually found out about his girlfriend and hit him over the head with a bottle of beer," Stacy says. "He blamed me. He thought I had told his wife." Fully aware of Joe Accardo's decree about keeping infidelities secret from the wives, Gottfried was furious that Stacy might have jeopardized his standing with the boss (to say nothing of the harm it caused his marriage). "He wanted to mug me, break my arms or something," Stacy remembers. "One day, while he's driving Murray, he comes by my place to do a drive-by. When Murray saw it was me, the dice girl, he called it off. He told Hy, 'You can't hit a sweet little thing like that.'" Humphreys' attraction to the young dice girl was coupled with Stacy's obvious preference for older men: Curly was a full twenty-nine years older than the liberated Jeanne Stacy. Soon, Stacy and Humphreys, whom she always refers to as Murray, began seeing each other on the side. Few women can say that they met their future husbands at a drive-by where she was scheduled to be his victim.

The combined stress of his illicit affair and his pressure-filled role as the Outfit's mastermind took its toll on Curly. According to his FBI file, Humphreys suffered the first of a series of heart attacks in 1950. Upon his admittance to the hospital, the fifty-one-year-old gangster guru gained notoriety among the facility's staff. As recounted in Humphreys' FBI report: "When he was questioned about whether he had hospitalization insurance by the admitting officer, he pulled out a roll of $100 bills and waved them around, demanding, 'Is this hospitalization enough?' This story made the rounds of the hospital, so that very soon everyone who worked there was aware of the identity of Humphreys."

12.

"Senator Cow Fever" Hits Chicago

Although its members' personal lives were in transition, the Outfit's business affairs proceeded uninterrupted. Bookmaking and jukebox operations continued to fill the gang's treasury, and the Accardo regime even had a bootlegging resurgence, shipping booze to dry states such as Kansas and Curly's adopted home of Oklahoma. But by far the most dramatic example of the gang's expansionism was the move it made on bookmaking in southern Florida in the late 1940s.

Since the days of Al Capone's Palm Island estate purchase, the Outfit had maintained a presence in the Sunshine State. Under the watchful eye of their racetrack boss, Johnny Patton, the gangsters controlled four of Florida's premier dog tracks. With the local bookmakers subscribing to the Outfit's Continental Wire Service, it was no secret to the Chicago gang which Miami bookies were the most successful. Towering over the competition was a Miami bookmaking consortium called the S & G syndicate (for "Stop and Go"), which supplied its services to hundreds of resort hotels. Observers placed S & G's annual gross at an astounding $40 million, with the five partners taking home $2 million in profits. At this point, the Chicago bosses were only realizing approximately $100,000 in profit from each of their Florida dog track operations. It was only a matter of time before Joe Accardo charged his troops with the takeover of S & G.

The prime soldiers entrusted with the S & G coup were Johnny Patton and Harry "the Muscle" Russell. Like Patton, Russell was a Chicago native who, years earlier, had himself been muscled into a bookmaking partnership with Accardo (see chapter 8). Fronting for Patton was a former bookkeeper, William H. Johnston, from the owners' barns at the gang's Sportsman's Park track in Illinois. In another elegant Outfit plan, the gang chose to enlist the Florida governor's office to force the S & G partners to their knees. All they had to do was guarantee that their candidate prevailed in the 1948 gubernatorial contest. The man picked for the job, Fuller Warren, was a friend of Russell's and a frequent visitor at the gang's Miami Beach Kennel Club. Using Johnston as a conduit, the Outfit pumped $100,000 into Warren's campaign, helping to ensure his eventual victory. All told, Johnston convinced friends to contribute $404,000 to the campaign, fully half of the budget. Within days of his 1949 inauguration, Warren appointed another Russell friend, William O. "Bing" Crosby, as his special investigator. Crosby was so close to "the boys" that he visited their Miami Beach Kennel Club four times per week. Given a list by Russell of the addresses of the S & G bookmaking facilities, Crosby directed Miami sheriff Kelly (who had been spotted by the FBI in conferences with Accardo, Humphreys, and Guzik) to begin raiding the dozens of establishments. Adding the coup de grâce, Joe Accardo simultaneously cut off the wire service from the besieged S & G. When the bookmaking consortium tried to siphon the critical information from other Florida operations, Accardo scuttled the wire service to the entire state. S & G was now forced to suspend operations; when it reopened two weeks later, it had a new partner, Harry Russell.

For the sake of appearances, S & G noted in its books that Russell had merely bought into the partnership for $20,000. However, a congressional investigation located records showing that at the same time Russell entered into the conspiracy, S & G paid Joe Accardo, who now leased a ranch-style home on Collins Avenue in Miami Beach, the coincidental sum of exactly $20,000 to purchase his yacht, the *Clari-Jo*. There was another curious coincidence: as soon as S & G reopened with its new partners, Warren and Crosby abruptly halted their raids on the consortium, and William Johnston and his friends received a major share of Florida's contracts for road-building materials. A 1949 Florida grand jury concluded the following about S & G's bookmaking transactions: "There appeared to be little effort to curb them, although they were being carried out right under the eyes of the police."

Although the vast profits accrued from the race wire were well-known, few in authority seemed interested, and even fewer desired to do anything about it. Most politicians were keenly aware of the upperworld and underworld alliance that had buttressed this fragile house of cards. For his part, FBI director J. Edgar Hoover had accurately deduced that the collusion went so deep and was so vaporous that securing convictions would prove futile. And Hoover prided himself on always "getting his man." Therefore, the boss remained focused on bank robbers and Communists. One pol naïvely believed he could walk the fine line between investigating gambling crime and sparing his fellow legislators (not to mention his president, Harry Truman). He also relished the bright national spotlight that would naturally fall on him, hopefully boosting his own White House aspirations. Although Estes Kefauver's investigation would prove a short-term irritant to the Outfit, it would be years before its revelations produced any real effect on the fortunes of the Empire of Crime.

The Kefauver Hearings

In 1950, while the Outfit was sinking its teeth into the Florida book-making bonanza, forty-seven-year-old Estes Kefauver was the freshman U.S. senator from Tennessee. His physical and moral stature, seen as grave but honorable, gained him the accolade "Lincolnesque." Kefauver came from a religious Southern Baptist family, the grandson of a Madisonville preacher. In 1939, after years as a practicing attorney, Kefauver was sent to Congress on a reform platform. During that contest, his political opponent in Tennessee, machine boss Ed Crump, called him a pet coon. The gibe only inspired Estes Kefauver to don a coonskin cap on the campaign trail. It became a favorite trademark.

Not long after his ascendancy to the Senate in 1949, Kefauver became intrigued with organized crime, a topic thus far assiduously avoided in any legislature. The new senator decided that when the time was right, he would introduce a bill aimed at penetrating the murky world of interstate gambling crime. He would not have long to wait. An organization of big-city mayors called the American Municipal Association held a 1949 conference on syndicated crime in Cleveland. One year later, Attorney General J. Howard McGrath held a national conference on organized crime in D.C., attended by district attorneys, mayors, and police. After Truman addressed the gathering's opening session, the press coverage increased, leading to a public outcry. The nation began to believe itself a helpless victim of an evil conspiracy, and it demanded action. In January 1950, after calling the race wire "Public Enemy No. One," Kefauver finally introduced Senate Resolution 202, which called for a Senate investigation into interstate gambling. Many observers perceived the motion as an attempt to bolster his national visibility. One of Kefauver's best friends from Knoxville, Jack Doughty, called the proposal "the most opportunistic thing Kef ever did." But the first-term senator was savvy enough to know that the inherent drama in such a proceeding could propel him into the national consciousness faster than any other of his freshman-class peers. For his part, Kefauver noted that his interest in organized crime had honest roots, dating back to days as a congressman assigned to examine judicial corruption. In that probe, Kefauver had worked closely with committee investigator Boris Kostelanetz, who later prosecuted the Outfit in the Hollywood extortion case.

The Senate membership was less than excited about Kefauver's bill, delaying the impanelment of the committee until events forced its hand. Senator Pat McCarran of Nevada, chairman of the Judiciary Committee, stalled on the bill out of fear that any investigation might threaten the nest egg created by the upperworld and underworld in his Las Vegas gambling mecca. Senate Majority Leader Scott Lucas of Illinois also feared the consequences of a full-blown investigation in his thoroughly corrupt state, the home of the Outfit. The debate was resolved on April 6, 1950, when two Missouri gangsters with Outfit connections, Charles Binaggio and Charles Gargotta, were killed in Kansas City's First Ward Democratic Headquarters, the seat of power that had launched President Truman's career. After the killings, Congress could no longer disregard Kefauver's request for the nation's first major investigation of organized crime. Republicans such as Forrest C. Donnell of Truman's home state of Missouri now backed the initiative, hoping the probe would uncover the truth about Truman's shadow world. With the Senate torn between the public's call for action and its own members' political skeletons, the entire subject was touchy, a point proven by the floor vote, which tied at 35–35, with Vice President Alben Barkley breaking the stalemate. The new committee, comprised of Democrat Kefauver, two other Democrats, and two Republicans, was given a $150,000 budget and was named the Senate Special Committee to Investigate Organized Crime in Interstate Gambling. Although the Republicans hoped that Kefauver's interest in gambling would enlarge into a full-fledged probe of Democratic corruption, Kefauver would steadfastly attempt to tiptoe around that political land mine. At every turn, however, Kefauver would come face-to-face with the very upperworld chicanery he hoped to avoid.

Harry Truman likewise knew that the urban-focused investigation was likely to hurt him and his urban-based Democratic Party much more than the farm-belt Republicans. When Kefauver announced that the hearings in Kansas City would commence on September 28, prior to the 1950 off-year elections, Truman called him disloyal and began mocking him as

"Senator Cow Fever." Even after the hearings ended, Truman continued to vent. "When the time came for a report to the United States Senate, the 'great crime investigator' took his report, copyrighted it, and sold it as a book over his own name," Truman bellowed. "Talk about ethics – well, he has none."

The bulk of the committee's background research was delegated to Rudolph Halley, a thirty-seven-year-old attorney from New York with previous experience as a congressional investigator. Halley's public persona was that of an expressionless, monotone-voiced litigator, and a legendary workaholic. The monumental task of memorizing thousands of government reports forced Halley to endure eighteen-to-twenty-hour workdays preparing for the investigation. When hearings started, Halley was known to pull forty-eight-hour cramming sessions prior to questioning a witness. With no time left to educate the senators, it fell to Halley to conduct most of the grilling.

As Kefauver began to take his own crash course in organized crime, Virgil Peterson of the Chicago Crime Commission became his guru, guiding the senator's research and agenda. When Peterson eventually gave formal testimony, it lasted two days and filled eighty-nine tightly spaced pages of transcription. Kefauver also sought out the expertise of Harry Anslinger of the Bureau of Narcotics and Boris Kostelanetz, the federal attorney who had kindled Kefauver's interest during the earlier House probe. In time, Kefauver bought into the idea of a mysterious Mafia, which he called "a secret international government-within-a-government."

And while Kefauver continued to memorize the hoodlum hierarchy, his president and vice president made a May 1950 trip to Chicago to address the National Democratic Party Conference, a three-day event held at Chicago Stadium. On the way to President Truman's late-night address to the conventioneers, the president and vice president were feted with a torchlight parade by some of the luminaries Kefauver was reading about. The key organizers of the parade were two notorious committeemen from the infamous "bloody Twenty-fourth Ward," Peter Fosco and Arthur X. Elrod. Fosco was an admitted close friend of Paul Ricca's who would eventually lose his ward post when it was revealed that one of his underlings had played Joe Bulger's courier for the moneys raised in the Hollywood extortion case paroles. He was also a dominant figure in the Building Laborers' Union, where he manipulated the city's labor force with the likes of Curly Humphreys and Sid Korshak. Arthur Elrod, who acted as chauffeur for Sid Korshak's friend Vice President Barkley in the motorcade, had gained notoriety for, among other things, turning out absurd Democratic electoral pluralities in the precinct where he was captain. In 1944, his Twenty-fourth Ward used Outfit muscle to turn out the widest margin of victory of any ward in the entire country for the Roosevelt-Truman ticket: 29,533 for FDR to 2,204 for Dewey. In 1948, when Truman ran for president, Elrod's precinct gave Truman a 300–1 victory. When Truman appeared at a party in Chicago after the election, Elrod presented him with the precinct tally sheet displaying the ludicrous totals. Truman jokingly asked Elrod, "Who was the one?" To which Elrod replied, "I don't know, I'm still looking for him."

When the first official "Kefauver Committee" hearings commenced in Miami, Outfit bosses made themselves scarce, hoping to avoid subpoenas. Joe took his family to Mexico, accompanied by Charles Fischetti, while Curly holed up in Oklahoma. A subpoena sent to Harry "the Muscle" Russell, the gang's Florida representative, likewise received no response. Reporters covering the committee jokingly wrote about the bouts of "Kefauveritis" spreading across the land. Pressing ahead in Miami, the committee settled for whoever was available, a decision that brought it face-to-face with the hoods' upperworld partners. Although Kefauver's goal was to expose "Mafia"-type gambling, he was now forced to address official corruption. In south Florida, investigators learned that the sheriff of Dade County (Miami), Smiling Jimmy Sullivan, had been accepting bribes for years from the wire operators. Although Sullivan's annual salary averaged $9,500, his assets purchased in five years were valued at more than $65,000. When Sullivan's subsequent indictment was dismissed on a technicality, Governor Fuller Warren, whom Johnny Patton and the Outfit had done so much to elect, reinstated him as sheriff. The *Miami Daily News* called Warren's act "lousy, stinking – and obvious."

After Miami, the committee's executive staff spent the summer of 1950 taking depositions in Washington, New York, and Missouri, home of President Truman. In Missouri, the committee walked on eggshells attempting to avoid the Truman-Pendergast controversy, choosing instead to focus on the Kansas City wire operation, which was tame in comparison to the machine corruption that had sponsored the president's career. A possible subconscious tone may have been set by the fact that Rudolph Halley, the committee's chief investigator, had been friends with

Truman since 1941, when he had served as the then senator's chief investigator on the Truman Committee, which had looked into the awarding of defense contracts. When the Kefauver Committee wound up its Missouri foray, it was roundly lambasted for its timidity by the local press.

While his advance investigative staff went to school in Chicago, Kefauver and his fellow senators brought Paul Ricca, Louis Campagna, and Charles Gioe to Washington to hear some preliminary testimony. Since these men were in regular contact with their parole officers, they were easier to subpoena than Accardo, Humphreys, and the others. The questions revolved around whom they associated with, what they did for a living, and what property they owned. The trio successfully parried with their inquisitors and revealed little or nothing of their gambling activities, except to say that they had legally won most of their savings at the track. Their responses set a new standard for vagueness, leaving the officials visibly frustrated.

September 19, 1950, should be memorialized in legal annals as the day the Outfit set jurisprudence on its ear, establishing a key precedent for all who would follow them into a congressional grilling. The setting was the Senate Office Building, where the Kefauver Committee gathered at 2:45 P.M. to take the long-sought subpoenaed testimony of Harry "the Muscle" Russell.

Soon after Russell's requisite swearing in, dumbfounded senators and their counsels received a taste of what Chicagoans had been experiencing for years: the brilliance of Curly Humphreys. It is commonly accepted that Humphreys, acting as the gang's legal adviser, instructed his pupils to hide behind the shield of the Fifth Amendment, much as he had done eleven years earlier in the bartenders' union trial. Although the tactic was now used routinely in criminal courts, it had never been tested in Congress.

Unaccompanied by a lawyer, Russell braced for the first pertinent question. It came from chief counsel Halley, who wanted to know why Russell had not responded to the committee's subpoena when it was in Florida. "I refuse to answer that question on the ground that the answer may incriminate me," came Russell's historic response.

"That is no excuse," shot back an off-guard (and misinformed) Halley. "I advise you that you have no privilege that protects you from answering a question that might tend to incriminate you except under federal law."

When it became clear that Russell believed otherwise, the committee recessed, allowing the legal minds to reconnoiter. Kefauver recommended Russell bring a lawyer with him when he resumed his testimony in three days. When the testimony resumed on the twenty-second, Russell again arrived without an attorney, but with a firm resolve to cling to his rights. When Russell again claimed his rights, Kefauver intoned, "The chair rules that you have no right to decline to answer that question." Russell answered that he believed the good senator was mistaken, prompting Kefauver to ask, "Who informed you of that?" The bookmaker claimed that he had studied the Constitution himself, although few believed him. Over and over, the committee ordered Russell to respond, at one point calling him selfish.

"What is selfish about wanting to protect your own rights?" Russell queried. At that point, Senator Alexander Wiley of Wisconsin fulminated, "You can lose your citizenship." And before ending the proceeding, Kefauver threatened to charge Russell with contempt of Congress, but the witness still refused to fold. If the probers believed they had had their worst day, they were mistaken. The testimony by Russell was but a dismal preview of things to come.

Protecting Sidney

Before Kefauver visited Chicago in October 1950, he made it known that one of his prime targets would be Sidney Korshak. In July, shortly after announcing his committee's September trip to the Second City, Kefauver obtained Korshak's tax records for 1947–49 from the secretary of the treasury. Committee investigators already on site in Chicago subpoenaed Korshak's financial records for 1945–48. Korshak promptly complied with the request. The full-court press continued as former Chicago detective William Drury, who had dogged the Outfit in the 1946 James Ragen killing at the cost of his own job, was enlisted by a Miami newsman to monitor Korshak's movements, the reports of which were shared with Kefauver's investigators. The Drury surveillance operation ended abruptly on September 25, 1950, when Drury was shot to death in his garage. He had not only been focusing on Korshak, but had been scheduled to deliver explosive new evidence in the Ragen murder, a case that he had continued to investigate. When the Kefauver Committee touched down in Chicago, the prospects for a Korshak inquisition intensified.

Although Kefauver had steadfastly repeated that he was not going to investigate political corruption, the Outfit saw troubling warning signs that prompted them into damage-control mode. Most distressing was the committee's interest in Korshak, and its staff's exposure of Chicago police captain and chief investigator for the state's attorney, Dan "Tubbo" Gilbert. The corrupt cop had amassed an astounding $300,000 nest egg, much of it by betting with Outfit-controlled bookies, and unbeknownst to the committee, running his own handbook on the side. When his executive-session testimony was leaked to the press, the local papers dubbed Gilbert "The World's Richest Cop." (In fact, Gilbert had made his real profit by investing his winnings in the stock market with brother-in-law Dan Rice, an investment banker.) Under intense questioning, Gilbert, who was running for Cook County sheriff at the time, admitted that he had in fact earned big winnings by gambling on baseball, football, prizefights, and even elections. He also admitted that he had placed his bets with the Outfit-connected bookie John McDonald.

The committee's flabbergasted chief counsel asked Gilbert if his activity was legal. Gilbert answered haltingly, "Well, no, it is not legal, no." After hearing from Gilbert, the committee interrogated his superior, Police Commissioner John C. Prendergast, the same man who had objected to Sergeant Drury's "persecution" of Outfit members after the Ragen shooting. When Counsel Halley asked Prendergast rhetorically if any of Al Capone's heirs still operated in Chicago, the commissioner answered with a straight face, "I have no personal knowledge. I have nothing in my reports to indicate they are." Prendergast's false display of naïveté did nothing to repair Gilbert's tarnished reputation. In the November election, Gilbert was defeated in his bid for sheriff by more than 370,000 votes, beaten by a last-minute Republican entry. In another mini-victory for the committee, police captain Thomas Harrison was exposed for accepting $32,000 in graft from gambling racketeer John J. Lynch. By the end of the month, Harrison was permanently relieved of duty. (Sharing the local newsprint this headline-filled month was news on October 20 of the death of the man who was arguably Chicago's most corrupt mayor, Edward J. Kelly, who had run the city for fourteen years after the assassination of Anton Cermak in 1933. Kelly had openly allowed the Outfit to flourish after the capture of Capone. After Kelly's passing, it was learned that he owned homes in Illinois, Wisconsin, and Palm Springs, California, with a combined value of over $686,799. It was believed to represent just a fraction of his fortune, which was never located.)

Like the rest of Chicago, Joe Accardo read the Gilbert disclosures, but viewed them with a different subtext, one appreciated only by the underworld: For years, Gilbert had worked as chief investigator for the Outfit-corrupted state's attorney, Tom Courtney. During their reign, thousands of felony charges lodged against Outfit bosses and crews were reduced to misdemeanors.[1] But more important, Gilbert was in charge of the police labor detail, a position of critical importance to the efficient running of the city. The bottom line was that the city's business community depended on Courtney and Gilbert working closely with the Outfit as Curly Humphreys took over one union after another. Frank Loesch, when president of the Chicago Crime Commission, said, "Few labor crimes have been solved in Chicago because of the close association between labor gangsters and law enforcing agencies." The entire scheme was facilitated by Courtney-Gilbert's alliance with none other than the gang's young labor lawyer, Sidney Roy Korshak. An associate of Gilbert's recently said, "Gilbert worked both sides – labor and business – and he took to Sidney. Sidney learned at his knee." With Korshak representing the Humphreys-controlled unions, Gilbert became a powerful voice in Chicago's power structure. One Gilbert acquaintance recently recalled, "Dan Gilbert was the only guy in town who could stop a strike with a phone call." A call to Sidney Korshak, to be exact.

Given Korshak's key position at the junction of so many Outfit and Commission national endeavors, Joe Accardo decided to protect Korshak from a public grilling when the Kefauver Committee arrived in the Windy City to conduct formal hearings. Just like other Washington insiders, the Outfit was aware of Estes Kefauver's vulnerabilities. When the Tennessean arrived in Chicago, the gang was poised to exploit these weaknesses for self-preservation.

Kefauver's Little Problem

Prior to his marriage to the former Nancy Pigott in 1935, Estes Kefauver had a reputation as a stereotypical Southern ladies' man, a landed-gentry Lochinvar. After his marriage, Kefauver cleaned up his act – at least in Tennessee. Charles Fontenay, who covered Kefauver for the *Nashville Tennessean*, wrote, "A lot of people knew of his propensity for women, but

---

1. When investigators pressed Gilbert about the paucity of gangster arrests, Gilbert replied that he had arrested Roger Touhy for the Jake Factor kidnapping. At this time, of course, Touhy was still wrongfully imprisoned, and the Humphreys-Courtney concocted sham had not yet been exposed.

he was clean as a whistle in Tennessee." However, in Washington, and wherever else his travels took him, Kefauver was known as a legendary drinker and womanizer. William "Fishbait" Miller, the longtime House "doorkeeper," who supervised some 357 House employees, called him the "worst womanizer in the Senate." On Kefauver's premature death of a heart attack, Miller wrote, "He must have worn himself out chasing pretty legs." The senator himself provided the fuel for the talk. When on tour in Europe, Kefauver caused a scandal after escorting a famous call girl to a society ball. On another occasion, he trysted with a woman in Paris who was not told of his wife in Tennessee. Afterward, Kefauver recommended his courtesan to a friend who was about to tour France.

On future campaign junkets, Kefauver would become infamous for dispatching his aides to procure women for him. *New York Times* columnist Russell Baker recalled one night with the candidate on the tour bus when Kefauver was feeling particularly randy. On arrival in a small town "in the middle of the night," Baker overheard Kefauver telling one of his minions, "I gotta fuck!" Capitol Hill lobbyist Bobby Baker, who would become the first American to have a scandal named after him, wrote that Kefauver regularly put himself "up for sale." According to Baker, "[Kefauver] didn't particularly care whether he was paid in coin or in women." The Outfit, well aware of Kefauver's proclivities, utilized this knowledge to protect Sidney Korshak, and the secrets he held about the Outfit's vast empire.

Showdown in Chicago

Finally, in October 1950, months after his investigative team had arrived, Kefauver and his senior staff descended on Chicago. Kefauver took a room in the Palmer House, while the rest of the staff and investigators stayed at the hotel that was also home to Curly Humphreys (as well as the Outfit's former meeting place), the Morrison. Perhaps not coincidentally, the committee's chief counsel, Rudolph Halley, complained that the staff's phones were tapped. But the staff never learned of the Outfit's planned setup of the chairman. In 1976, reporters Sy Hersh and Jeff Gerth began to unravel the inside story of Kefauver and Korshak in a four-part profile of the well-connected lawyer in the *New York Times*. A close friend and business associate of Korshak's told the writers how Korshak and the Outfit had blackmailed the ever-randy Kefauver. The informant told the reporters that he had seen compromising photos of the senator taken in a suite at the luxurious Drake Hotel. Recent interviews have shed more light on the incident.

According to the new telling, Kefauver was enticed to the Drake (on whose board sat Outfit-connected Anthony Ponterelli), where two young women from the Outfit's Chez Paree nightclub entertained him. "The Outfit had a guy at the Drake, a vice cop who moonlighted as the hotel's head of security," a friend of the Korshak family recently divulged.[2] "Korshak got the girls; the security guard set up an infrared camera and delivered the prints to Korshak." The source added that a private meeting was arranged between Kefauver and Korshak. In the brief encounter, Korshak, who had been pre-interviewed on October 26 by Committee investigator George Robinson,[3] flung the incriminating photos on Kefauver's desk. "Now, how far do you want to go with this?" Korshak asked. Kefauver never called Korshak to testify before the committee, despite his being the first of eight hundred witnesses subpoenaed.

On the committee's October junket to Chicago, the only Outfit boss questioned under oath was Johnny Rosselli, who turned on the charm, admitting he was a small-time bootlegger in the twenties, but insisting that he had cleaned up his life. He spoke of his strikebreaking work for the Hollywood moguls, and how he was now a legitimate film producer. As Ricca had done one month earlier, Rosselli admitted to meeting many gangsters, including Capone, but said he had no business with them. A frustrated Kefauver told Rosselli, "You look like a man who would like to be helpful, but I don't think you are telling us as much about it as you could tell us." To which Rosselli replied, "I wish I could."

Before the Christmas break, the committee heard testimony from the Outfit's racetrack chieftain, Johnny Patton. Like Russell, Patton had been dodging the committee's subpoena in Florida, only to finally be tracked down in Chicago. Counsel Halley inquired as to why Patton had refused to come to the door when his wife had been informed that the Senate

---

2. The security guard's name is known to the author, but attempts to locate him have been unsuccessful.

3. When speaking with Robinson, Korshak calmly stated that he believed his targeting by Kefauver was due in large part to a recent exposé of Korshak by Lester Velie in *Collier's* magazine. Korshak explained that Velie had not only exaggerated the facts, but often invented them. But according to Sidney, there was a reason for the Velie attack: Velie had held a twenty-year grudge against Korshak since their college days at the University of Wisconsin, where Korshak, a boxing champion, had punched Velie (whose real name was Levy) in the nose.

investigator Downey Rice was waiting to serve him. "I told my wife to pay no attention to him," Patton answered. "I thought it was Jack Rice, our publicity man, always calling me up for a touch. That is why I ducked that."

"Mr. Patton, that is the best one I have heard yet," said Halley.

"Well, it is a good one," agreed Patton.

After an hour of denials of any criminal associations, Kefauver called an end to the circus, saying, "All right, Mr. Patton. We will see you again sometime." To which Patton responded, "I hope not."

Returning to Washington, the committee called no other Outfit notables until Al Capone's brothers, John and Ralph, were brought to Washington on December 20, for another round of perfunctory testimony.

Curly's Marionettes Take the Fifth

During the Christmas holidays, the committee's subpoena finally caught up with Joe Accardo. In January 1951, the man who, unbeknownst to the senators, was the secret boss of the Chicago Outfit testified in Washington. Accompanied by his lawyer, George F. Callaghan, the middle-aged Accardo quietly gave the same response to almost all the questions posed to him: "I refuse to answer." He let Callaghan explain that the Fifth Amendment's shield against self-incrimination was the basis for Accardo's lack of cooperation. In all, Accardo took the Fifth 140 times, only answering a handful of benign inquiries. Callaghan had to explain to dismayed senators that his client had every right to refuse to answer. Senator Charles Tobey of New Hampshire, a righteous member whom Kefauver called "the committee's lightning rod," and whom legendary New York UPI reporter Harold Conrad called "about as well-equipped to be investigating gangsters as Shirley Temple," was particularly frayed by the encounter and interrupted the interrogation to address Kefauver: "I [have] sat here with feelings of rising disgust, and listened to a man come before this committee, and through his answers or refusal to answer, insult this committee and its counsel; and I think it is a new low in the conduct of witnesses before this committee, and we have had some tough ones . . . And so, with a feeling of disgust in my heart toward the witness" attitude and that of his counsel, I move you, sir, that he be cited for contempt.'

Tobey, who regularly toted a Bible into the hearings, inveighed so forcefully at times that he often launched into God-fearing diatribes against the witnesses and, on one occasion, brought himself to tears. Railing against one corrupt police official, Tobey intoned, "Why don't you resign and get out and put somebody in there that can handle it – somebody who has some guts . . . It is revealing and disgusting that a man like you can continue in office! I simply cannot sit here and listen to this type of what I call political vermin!"

Before dismissing Accardo, Tobey led the senators in a unanimous vote for a contempt citation. As will be seen, the charge would wind its way through the courts before its precedent-setting resolution. The Outfit's bold legal maneuver would trigger a landslide of similar encounters, not only in this investigation, but in many congressional tribunals that would follow. Two weeks after Accardo's presentation, Joey Aiuppa, the fast-rising Outfit slot-machine manufacturer from Cicero, reprised the performance, refusing to answer all questions. Aiuppa quickly tired of giving the same response; eventually, he sat mute.

"Let the record show that the witness just sits there mute, chewing gum, saying nothing," a frustrated Halley said before excusing the gangster. Like his boss, Aiuppa was also cited for contempt.

Later that month, the committee arrived in New Orleans, where television station WNOE acquired permission to televise the hearings, pre-empting its entire commercial schedule. The gambit was such a success that subsequent hearings were televised in New York, St. Louis, Los Angeles, and San Francisco. Also attempting to cash in on the drama was a company called Movietone News, which produced hour-long edits of the New York testimony and leased them to theaters across the nation. Kefauver, who initially coveted the attention afforded by the telecasts, eventually found the cameras' presence to be a drawback, as the committee members began to play to the audience, careful not to become too bogged down in detail that might bore the viewer. Chairman Kefauver tried to cancel the arrangement, but it was too late, commitments having been made to broadcasters. The viewing public was captivated by the event, with some 20–30 million viewers (twice the audience for the 1950 World Series) tuning in regularly. "It is the best thing we have had since television came in," said one New York viewer. Kefauver biographer Charles L. Fontenay described the reaction of the home audience: "Housework was neglected and movie theaters and stores were nearly deserted as the number of home television sets turned on rose from the normal less than 2 percent to more than 25 percent in the morning and from the normal less than 12 percent to more than 30 percent in the afternoon."

As expected, the broadcasts made Kefauver a household name over-night, distinguishing him as the first politician to create a national image using the new medium. During those initial New Orleans broadcasts, the committee attempted to probe the gambling empire of local boss Carlos Marcello, a syndicate chief known to be in regular contact with the Outfit. Once again the committee was hit with a tidal wave of responses that began with "I refuse to answer." In all, Marcello demurred 152 times. When the committee returned to Washington, they heard from one malaprop-prone gang member who lightened the proceedings when he garbled his Fifth Amendment plea by saying his answers might "discriminate against me."

"Murray went nuts when he heard how the 'spaghetti benders' almost screwed up what he had worked so hard on," recalls Humphreys' then mistress, later wife, Jeanne Stacy. "He had to type it out on index cards so they got it right. Then he worried if they could even read." Humphreys had little time to chafe over the performance of his inferiors, as the committee finally succeeded in serving a subpoena on him in the spring of 1951. It seemed fitting that his testimony would come near the end of the hearings, a worthy climax that did not disappoint those in attendance in the Capitol in Washington.

Curly and the Stooges

On the morning of May 28, 1951, the Kefauver Committee sat on its raised dais, but it was Curly Humphreys, in rare form, who held court. Although Humphreys' initial intention was to not answer any questions at all, he soon found he could not pass up the opportunity to match wits with his interrogators. Resorting to the Fifth only on occasion, the master negotiator, who appeared without counsel, preferred to verbally joust with his inquisitors.

After instructing the committee to send photographers out of the room, which they did, Curly politely requested that he be allowed to make an opening statement. For the first five minutes, the committee tried to change the subject, but Curly would hear none of it. "I would still like to get my statement into the record at this time . . . I have requested to make my statement when I first came into the room." Then he advised, "It will save you time." Like so many people before, the committee relented under Curly's articulate purposefulness. Finally granted his demand, Humphreys politely responded, "Thank you." He then quoted the Fifth Amendment to his questioners, again ending with "Thank you." Curly then had a longer written statement placed in the record, elaborating on his privilege under the Constitution. At that point, one of the committee counsels unwisely challenged Humphreys on his understanding of the amendment.

"You understand that if we ask you questions, the answers of which will not tend to incriminate you, that you have to answer, and that the only questions you can refuse to answer are the ones which will tend to incriminate you?"

Curly cut him off. "Would you mind telling me your name, sir?"

Kefauver interjected, "This is Mr. Richard Moser, chief counsel for the committee."

"Oh, I am sorry. I just like to know who I am talking to." Humphreys then added, "Well, I don't understand it that way." Curly next turned self-effacing, saying, "Well, I'm not a lawyer here, and I would like to help this committee if I possibly could, but I don't feel like I am amongst friends, just to be plainspoken."

Senator Charles Tobey of New Hampshire naïvely believed he could cajole Humphreys by resorting to the "good cop" tactic: "Don't you think, as a good citizen, that you ought to tell us all you know about the sordid characters of the underworld?" Curly deflected him with, "Do you doubt whether I am a good citizen or not?" After teasing the senators by answering their questions about his childhood, Curly started pleading the Fifth when asked about his business dealings. At this point Kefauver interjected, "You do understand in regard to all of these that you are directed to answer by the committee, and you still decline for the reasons you stated?"

Humphreys: "Yes, Mr. Chairman. Thank you very much."

In one of many droll exchanges, Humphreys refused to tell Senator Tobey whether he'd flown in from Chicago with Rocco Fischetti. Humphreys would only admit that he had arrived on the ten-o'clock Capitol Airlines flight from Chicago. A surprised Tobey said, "I was on that flight too."

Humphreys: "You were? Well, we had a distinguished guest on it then, didn't we?"

Tobey: "I can say that goes both ways. However, if I had seen you there, maybe we could have settled this all before we got in town."

Humphreys: "Well, if I had seen you, Senator, I think I would have tried to get off."

In another verbal joust, Humphreys denied having anything to do with

the 1931 Fitchie kidnapping, explaining that the Milk Wagon Drivers'
Union boss had framed him in a fit of vengeance. "His revenge was
caused by my being in the milk business," Humphreys said, "and that was
one way of getting me out of the milk business." The probers were
dubious, however, that the genteel man who now appeared before them
was ever in the milk business. Tobey attempted to trip Humphreys up,
asking, "Which side of a cow do you sit on to milk?" To which an
unfazed Humphreys quipped back, "Well, I don't know if I have ever
gotten that low yet."

When Senator Lester Hunt of Wyoming started asking about Curly's
wife and daughter, Humphreys let him know he would have none of it:

Humphreys: "I don't see where that has anything to do with this
hearing."

Hunt: "All you have to do is to say you refuse to answer."

Humphreys: "Let's start right now. I refuse."

Hunt: "Do you want to tell me what year your daughter is in high
school?"

Humphreys: "I will refuse to answer that, so long as you have
suggested that."

Hunt: "What is your daughter's first name?"

Humphreys: "I don't see where my daughter has anything to do with
this hearing."

Hunt: "It is not for you to pass on the type of questions I ask at all. If
you don't care to answer, just say so."

Humphreys: "Would you like to have people asking questions about
your family?"[4]

Hunt: "You are not questioning the senator; the senator is questioning
you. You are the one who is the witness."

Humphreys: "I realize that, but I still resent the line of questioning,
Senator."

Hunt: "You are going to be cited for contempt; I can tell you that."

Humphreys: "I am sorry to hear that, sir."

---

4. Humphreys was particularly sensitive about this issue, since his daughter, Llewella, suffered from mental instability and had spent three years in a sanitarium in
Kansas, setting Humphreys back some $36,000. Years later, the FBI's hidden
microphone picked up Humphreys talking about the Kefauver incident: "When
you get into something, like when he starts out, you know, about my daughter –
"Is your daughter nuts?" – I could have up and powdered the guy."

But the Welshman was not really worried, so certain was he of his interpretation of the Constitution. The set-to concluded with Curly's asking Hunt, "Then you are under the impression that I am a criminal, is that it?" At this point, a frustrated Hunt threw Humphreys' legal masterpiece back in his face: "I would refuse to answer the question because it might incriminate me. I have no further questions." When Kefauver moved to stop the questioning, Humphreys made another demand. He wanted the committee to send a copy of its interim report to whichever court was to hear his contempt citation. This request reminded Kefauver of a similar request by Rocco Fischetti just moments before. It then dawned on Chairman Kefauver that Curly had been coaching the other witnesses. Curly readily admitted his tutelage of the gang. Unable to resist a bit of swagger, he added, "And you know, the longer you fellows work, the more we understand what our rights are." Having totally disoriented the august body, Curly took his leave, but not before reminding them to forward their report to the courts. With that, Humphreys stood up and smiled courteously, saying, "Thank you very much."

While Curly Humphreys' testimony provided comic relief during the public hearings, the secret executive sessions were enlivened by the appearance of the Outfit's feisty courier-spy, Virginia Hill. Just hours before her public testimony on March 15, 1951, the committee wisely chose to pre-interview the scorpion-tongued vixen behind closed doors during their New York road trip. According to Kefauver aide Ernie Mittler, Senator Tobey refused to drop the topic of Hill's enormous surfeit of money. Like most other witnesses, Hill had been appropriately vague about her business with the Outfit, but when she had had enough of Tobey's line of questioning, she knew exactly how to stop it dead in its tracks.

"But why would [Joe Epstein] give you all that money?" Tobey asked for the umpteenth time.

"You really want to know?" Hill teased.

"Yes," Tobey said. "I want to know why."

"Then I'll tell you why. Because I'm the best cocksucker in town."[5]

---

5. The author spoke with one of Hill's many Chicago lovers who recalled, "I once told her that she played a prick like Harry James played a trumpet. She laughed and said, 'That's funny. Spread the word.'" She was quite proud of her abilities."

As UPI correspondent Harold Conrad described the scene: "Tobey all but swallowed his Bible." After the private tête-à-tête, Hill exited the chamber and headed for the open hearing room, where she was met by a horde of flash-camera-toting reporters shoving microphones in her face. The ever *un*quotable Hill yelled, "Get your fucking cameras out of my face, you cheap fucking bastards! Get out of my fucking way! Don't I have fucking police protection? I hope the fucking atomic bomb falls on every one of you!"

After a couple of hours of evasive public testimony by Hill, Kefauver announced that he had sealed Hill's earlier private session, and that, in addition, no questions about what she had said could be asked of the committee. Soon after her dismissal, Hill caught a plane and went into globe-hopping exile, evading the clutches of Elmer Irey's IRS, which had named her for massive tax evasion. During her fifteen-year odyssey, Hill continued to receive a cash pension from Epstein and the Outfit, which was said to total over $250,000.

The Legacy of the Kefauver Committee

After hearing eight hundred witnesses in fifteen cities, traveling more than fifty-two thousand miles and transcribing more than 11,500 pages of testimony, at a combined cost of $315,000, the Kefauver Committee hearings came to an end. And with eleven months of grueling investigation behind him, Kefauver stepped down, anxious to spend time with his children, who had layered their television with fingerprints attempting to "touch Daddy." At the time, the chairman said, "I can't go on. I have got to get some time to get home." Senator Herbert O'Conor assumed the chairmanship, his chief assignment being the drafting of proposed legislation. Rudolph Halley had the onerous task of writing the committee's final report, a monumental chore that ultimately resulted in his hospitalization for exhaustion.

For all his efforts to ensnare "the Mafia" and avoid upperworld corruption, Kefauver learned more about the latter than he desired. Kefauver knew that the Hollywood parole scandal, which he called an "abomination," said more about the Truman administration than it did about the Mafia, but he shuddered at the thought of learning the truth of the matter. Kefauver likewise had to face that Florida's Governor Warren and Sheriff Sullivan were happy to let the Outfit flourish in their state. In Illinois, Police Commissioner Prendergast, and Captains Gilbert and Harrison were "mobbed up," not to mention sundry state's attorneys and legislators. Upperworld crime appeared to eclipse the underworld variety. And Kefauver's field investigators turned up the proof regularly:

- In Saratoga Springs, New York, Detective Walter Ahearn pretended not to be aware of the profligate bookmaking facilities in that gangster haven. "I never tried to find out certain things," Ahearn testified. Kefauver later learned that Ahearn earned extra cash by moonlighting as the bookie's vigorish courier, hauling the gilt from their handbooks and plush casinos to the bank. Saratoga's police chief, Paddy Rox, also testified that he had no knowledge of illegal gambling in his district. In New York City, it was learned that former mayor William O'Dwyer had received a $10,000 bribe from a firemen's union, had paid a visit to the apartment of Commission boss Frank Costello, and had refused to prosecute hitman-boss Albert Anastasia.
- In Miami, Lieutenant Phil Short was asked why he had not investigated the S & G bookies. He answered, "I've been an officer for better than twenty years, and I know what hot potatoes were." Also in Florida, Tampa sheriff Hugh Culbreath candidly admitted to running a handbook operation out of his office.
- In Philadelphia, the local gang's bagman admitted to paying out $152,000 *per month* in "ice" (graft) to the city's police department.
- As he had in Truman's Missouri, Kefauver also sidestepped the touchy subject of Louisiana corruption, which was intimately linked to the committee's stated interest, gambling. Kefauver investigator Claude Follmer filed a report that spelled out how in the 1930s the mob had "made arrangements" with the governor's office to allow New York's Frank Costello to set up syndicated gambling in the Bayou State. Follmer's report added that a U.S. congressman and a U.S. senator were also the recipients of Costello payoffs. Two years after the hearings, Aaron Kohn, head of the New Orleans Metropolitan Crime Commission, released a damning report on Big Easy mayor deLesseps "Chep" Morrison. According to Kohn, Morrison's initial 1946 campaign was financed largely by Carlos Marcello. In return, Marcello was allowed the city's bookmaking franchise, which necessitated the use of the Outfit/Commission/Western Union race wire. At the same time, New Orleans sheriff John Grosch stashed $150,000 in an attic strongbox according to his divorced wife's testimony. The money, said Grosch's ex, had been delivered to

the home by well-known known local underworld figures. Jefferson Parish sheriff Frank "King" Clancy was found to have allowed gambling to flourish in the open. (When Clancy tried to change his ways after the hearings, a local newspaperman wrote: "Clancy is making a spectacle of himself by enforcing the law.")

- Calling for Mayor Morrison's resignation, Kohn gave voice to the topic too sensitive for the politically ambitious Kefauver: "Finding corruption in New Orleans was like making a virgin gold find when the nuggets were lying on the top of the ground." But Kefauver was keenly aware of Morrison's role as a powerful Southern Democrat, and as a likely delegate to the party's upcoming national convention, where presidential aspirant Estes Kefauver would need all the friends he could get.

Upperworld criminals in politics and big business were fully aware that they had dodged a bullet. As an added bonus, the Kefauver Committee's hearings riveted the public's attention to the underworld, and away from the upperworld. *Mafia* was now a household word.[6]

The legacy of the Kefauver Committee is decidedly mixed. On one hand, none of the committee's nineteen legislative recommendations were enacted, in part stalled by the powerful chairman of the Judiciary Committee, Nevada senator Pat McCarran, widely perceived as an upperworld ally of gangs just now descending on Las Vegas. It was no secret that McCarran feared any legislation that might impact his home state's cash cow, legalized gambling. In addition, the country's infant television industry made urgent pleas to members of the committee, imploring them to drop most of their contempt citations. Many of the witnesses had objected to being forced to testify on national television, and it was feared that the gangsters might win massive civil judgments against the fledgling corporations if their cases were heard in the highest court.

---

6. In his seminal 1968 book on the power elite, *The Rich and the Super Rich,* Ferdinand Lundberg reached sober conclusions on the Kefauver episode: "Senator Estes Kefauver found representatives of the vulpine Chicago Mafia ensconced in the Illinois legislature, which has been rocked by one scandal of the standard variety after the other off and on for seventy-five or more years. What he didn't bring out was that the Mafians were clearly superior types to many non-Mafians."

On the other hand, the public reaction to the inquest initiated the formation of more than seventy local anticrime commissions. If nothing else, Kefauver gave the nation its first glimpse into the shadow economy of the underworld, and just a hint of its alter ego in the upperworld. The committee conservatively estimated that the annual illegal gambling take was $15–$20 billion. When Kefauver learned of those figures he asked: "This fifteen billion dollars is about two billion dollars more than the appropriation for our military establishment the last year, is it not?" It would take another decade before the interest generated by Kefauver's probe translated into meaningful legislation, such as the Wire Act of 1960, which abolished the race wire once and for all, and the outlawing of interstate shipment of slot machines. But by then, of course, the Outfit had moved on to other lucrative opportunities.

In a 1951 interview for *Collier's* magazine, Rudolph Halley openly admitted the committee's failures with regard to penetrating the Outfit: "We knew that Chicago was the crime capital of America, the home of a nationwide crime organization. Yet we never translated our findings into live testimony as we did in other cities . . . We linked [the Outfit] to Florida through income-tax records, and we exposed the Guzik-Accardo invasion of the numbers rackets. But we never smashed behind that awfully thick wall that shields the Capone mob. We just skirted the edges."

Halley lamented that he might have been more successful "if there had been two years" time instead of just eleven months, and if there had been a staff of two hundred investigators instead of just a dozen.'

For a time, Kefauver, a new folk hero, was the front-runner for the 1952 Democratic presidential nomination. With his coonskin cap on frequent display, he entered sixteen primaries, fourteen of which he won. But backroom party hacks, worried about his private indiscretions and his "disloyalty" to fellow party members caught up in his probe, held more power than the primary voters. Not only were many of his party embarrassed by his revelations, some, such as Chicago's Senator Scott Lucas, the majority leader and Truman spokesman, saw their careers destroyed. Lucas, who lost his seat to Everett M. Dirksen, openly blamed Kefauver for his defeat, due to his committee's revelations regarding police corruption in Chicago. Florida's Governor Fuller Warren, implicated by Kefauver's bookmaking probe in the Sunshine State, worked tirelessly against Kefauver in the Florida primary.

When the Republicans assembled in Chicago, two weeks before the

Democrats, they made official corruption their major issue. The 1952 Democratic National Convention, also held in the Outfit's Chicago, became the scene of bitter behind-the-scenes party bloodletting.[7] When Truman arrived at the convention, he lobbied hard to wrest the nomination from Kefauver and deliver it to Illinois' governor, Adlai Stevenson, who, like Truman before him, had absolutely no desire for the candidacy. The president sent one of his aides to order candidate Averell Harriman to withdraw and toss his votes to Stevenson, which the subservient Harriman did. "Had I not come to Chicago when I did," Truman later wrote, "the squirrel-headed coonskin cap man . . . who has no sense of honor would have been the nominee."

"Nobody's on the Legit." –Al Capone

For all his publicized concern about gambling, it became known after the hearings that Kefauver himself not only attended the races at tracks like Laurel, Pimlico, and Hot Springs, but also wagered on their outcome. In a private meeting during the hearings with Commission partner Meyer Lansky, the New York boss asked the chairman, "What's so bad about gambling? You like it yourself. I know you've gambled a lot." Kefauver replied, "That's right, but I don't want you people to control it." Nobody's fool, Lansky penetrated Kefauver's righteous veneer and so informed his biographer years later: "I was convinced that he meant 'you Jews and Italians,' and that infuriated me."

There were more troubling dimensions to the Kefauver story. Although the Tennessee crusader was constantly broke, perhaps due to gambling, the local press learned that he had deposited $25,000 into his Chattanooga bank account on January 3, 1951 – at the height of the committee's hearings. The source of the windfall was never learned. Locals also found the timing of Kefauver's committee resignation to be suspect; just weeks before the chairman's departure, a Knoxville numbers boss and Kefauver campaign contributor named Herbert Brody was arrested. Although it was revealed that Brody had contributed $100 to Kefauver's 1948 campaign, insiders whispered that he had actually chipped in $5,000.

In his autobiography, Bobby Baker, the infamous Washington influence peddler, described how he had delivered a briefcase stuffed with $25,000 in cash to a Kefauver aide in 1960. The money had originated

---

7. Ironically, Kefauver selected as his Chicago organizer attorney A. Bradley Eben, who had been the Outfit's lead lawyer in the Hollywood extortion trial.

with a Texas group hoping to acquire an NFL franchise, but who were opposed by Washington Redskins team owner George Marshall. After the money changed hands, Kefauver's committee conveniently found that Marshall had been operating an illegal monopoly with his Washington Redskins Television Network, which televised their games throughout the South. That same year, the Dallas Cowboy franchise was awarded to a group headed by Texas oilman Clint Murchison, Jr.

After his death in 1963 at age sixty, it was learned that Kefauver had owned stock valued at $300,000 in drug companies that he had been charged with regulating in the Senate. His chief counsel and close friend from Tennessee, attorney Bernard Fensterwald, Jr., said at the time, "My God! What if a hostile newspaper had gotten ahold of that?"

In the year after the Kefauver Committee disbanded, the forty-six "contempt of Congress" citations it had issued were heard in court, with only three being upheld. In overturning one such charge, Judge Martin of the Sixth Circuit U.S. Court of Appeals ruled that Humphreys and the Outfit had in fact outwitted the combined wisdom of the Senate's gaggle of attorneys. "The committee threatened prosecution for contempt if [the witness] refused to answer, for perjury if he lied, and for gambling activities if he told the truth," the court concluded. Judge Martin added that "to place a person not even on trial for a specified crime in such a predicament is not only not a manifestation of fair play, but it is in direct violation of the Fifth Amendment to our national Constitution." And despite Halley's constant promises that his questions could not implicate witnesses in a federal crime, the court believed otherwise. In the case of Joey Aiuppa's citation, Judge Martin wrote in his opinion:

> The motive of the committee and its examiners in calling Aiuppa as a witness was largely to connect him, by his own admission, with the operations of nefarious organizations engaged in criminal activities on a national scale . . . It is evident that most of the information sought to be elicited from Aiuppa concerning his activities was already in the hands of the committee . . . The courts of the United States could not emulate the committee's example and maintain even a semblance of fair and dispassionate conduct of trials in criminal cases.

In the years since the Kefauver hearings, the public has been treated to the sight of countless gangsters, as well as unfairly persecuted leftists, repeating for various congressional tribunals the mantra introduced by Curly Humphreys and the Outfit. After his legal triumph, Curly took a much deserved vacation at Owney Madden's gangster spa in Hot Springs, Arkansas. There soon appeared over the fireplace in Curly's Oklahoma home a new wooden plaque he had carved while on vacation. The inscription read, "I Refuse to Answer on the Grounds That it Might Incriminate Me." It was his self-bestowed award for his invaluable gift to future congressional witnesses.

The Outfit's long history of financial success owed much to its awareness that every scam it conceived had a built-in, finite life span. Nonetheless, if the gang was fortunate, an operation might be milked for years before the G would crack down or the upperworld would appropriate it for itself. Thus when Western Union, under pressure after the Kefauver investigation, began clipping its wires to suspicious distributors such as the Outfit's Continental Press, Accardo and his minions took it in stride. After all, by this time, Chicago's empire of crime was awash in profits, and the nation's newest immigrants were nothing if not the definition of survivors. In addition, closing down Continental would be only a temporary halt in the gang's bet-taking franchise, as the resourceful rogues would eventually oversee a massive sports betting operation that included everything *but* racing; with the growth of gamblers' interests in professional sports teams such as baseball, football, and basketball (not to mention boxing and college sports), there would be few tears shed over the loss of the ponies. In a few years, after being forced to relinquish their handbook invention over to the upperworld, who labeled their version "offtrack betting," the Outfit's bookmaking network merely adapted to the new situation.

While Accardo and his buddies enjoyed the good life, starry-eyed, Outfit-connected Chicagoans continued to bring new ideas to the table, hoping to mimic the success of Mooney Giancana, who had "made his bones" with the bosses when he'd brought them the numbers and the jukebox rackets, which continued to bring treasure to the confederation. One of the more inventive, if distasteful, scams concocted during this period involved duping the city's entire population for almost two years, while the hoods netted a quick couple million. When the deception was revealed, Windy City citizens were sickened, literally. In January 1952, federal inspectors revealed that since 1950, millions of unknowing Chicagoans, as well as tourists, had been ingesting horse and mule meat when they thought they were eating hamburger.

Filly Mignon

Months earlier, Governor Adlai Stevenson had begun hearing rumors that the Outfit had been selling millions of servings of "horseburgers" in the Chicago area, arguably the meatpacking capital of the world. An initial investigation by the state's superintendent of foods and dairies, Charles Wray, was fruitless, with Wray declaring that he was unable to prove the allegations. A subsequent inquiry by the federal government's director of the Office of Price Stabilization (OPS), Michael Howlett, reached a much different conclusion: For the last two years, Illinoisans who had ordered Black Angus were instead ingesting Black Beauty.

The allure of the new racket was obvious: Horsemeat could be purchased wholesale for ten cents a pound, whereas ground beef was fetching four times that price. Gang-controlled processing plants were producing a blend of 40 percent horseflesh and 60 percent ground beef. The malicious mixture was then doctored with "dynamite," a chemical that gave the meat a red tint and also disguised any rotten portions. Finally, the concoction was sold to restaurants for eighty cents per pound. If the hoods' consciences needed assuaging, they could rationalize that Europeans, and especially those from southern Italy, had eaten horsemeat continually for ages.[8] "It's all in your mind," admitted one UPI reporter covering the story. "Horsemeat is as clean as beef or pork." Although the surfacing of the operation led to allegations that the horsemeat was spoiled, these contentions were not corroborated by any statistical surge in intestinal maladies. Apparently, no one even detected a difference in taste.

During the swindle, millions of pounds of the meaty concoction were served to the public. One of the equine suppliers later admitted to selling one hundred thousand pounds of horseflesh per week to the plotters. Another supplier sold fifty-five thousand pounds in thirteen days, and one small wholesaler was found to have bankrolled $250,000 in four months. And since the "blended" product sold at a cheaper price, otherwise honest meatpackers had adopted the practice in order to compete with their less scrupulous competitors. Eventually, more than twenty-five large wholesalers had joined the racket, and many of the city's best restaurants, such as the swank Blackhawk on Randolph Street, had fallen prey to the fraud. The local wags had a field day, utilizing an assortment of peptic puns as

---

8. During the 2001 European mad-cow-disease scare, French restaurants openly sold meals featuring horsemeat as a substitute for beef.

they invented new names for the fare on local menus: "chili con filly," "colt cuts," and "porterhorse steaks," all followed by a "pony of brandy."

The initial arrests naturally involved the underworld masterminds. In Louis Campagna's Berwyn suburb, Meyer Ditlove, who managed a horse-slaughtering plant, was arrested for bribing a state food inspector to not inspect his meat shipments; in Lake Zurich, authorities nabbed Joe Siciliano, the owner of the Lake County Packing Company, who expressed shock over his arrest, exclaiming, "Gee, you'd think I ground up Man o' War!" But as the investigation proceeded, it became apparent that the horseburger episode was just one more proof of Al Capone's contention that "nobody's on the legit." The gangsters had once again exploited a culture that was, with a few exceptions, corrupt from top to bottom. The feds eventually learned why state food inspector Charles Wray had failed to unravel the deception: He had been paid $3,500 by Joe Siciliano to look the other way while the gang "loaded" the ground-beef stocks. Wray was fired and indicted, and more than a dozen other state inspectors were likewise relieved of duty, with some admitting to having taken $450 per month to allow the horsemeat to flow. Both Chicago's chief food inspector and its health commissioner, who had held the post for almost thirty years, were forced to resign. The commissioner was soon indicted, but the charge was eventually dismissed.

Surveying the growing list of civil servants and politicians of both parties caught up in the scandal, *The Nation*'s Carey McWilliams wrote that it was "silly" to blame the scandal on the underworld alone. After the revelation that some 4.5 million pounds of horsemeat had been eaten in Chicago in twenty-four months, a number of the city's most famous restaurants were forced to close, some permanently. Grocery stores reported that sales of hamburger dropped 50 percent, and a flurry of ads began appearing in the local media in an effort to reassure consumers. One business owner, Chris Carson, gave away more than one hundred thousand hamburgers "with all the trimmings" to help restore customer confidence in his product.

The public's reaction to Kefauver's "Mafia" and the loss of the horseburger racket appear to have marked a turning point in the Outfit's business plan. Combined with the 1950 passage of the Johnson Act, which outlawed slot machines in every state but Nevada, the charged atmosphere convinced the Outfit bosses to reconnoiter. After years of bootlegging, bookmaking, and labor racketeering, the hoods decided they had amassed a bankroll sufficient to fulfill the ultimate immigrant dream:

investing in legitimate upperworld businesses. Throughout the early fifties, the gang acquired countless Chicago-area companies. In addition to massive real estate tracts, car dealerships, food processing and distribution plants, restaurants and liquor stores, the gang purchased eight local hotels, according to the *Chicago Daily News*. An article from the period in the *Chicago Tribune* noted, "The millions rolling in from the rackets touched [Joe] Accardo with gold. He acquired stocks, bonds, hotels, restaurants, auto agencies, liquor firms, appliance companies, and a sprawling stone house in River Forest, where even the plumbing was gold-plated." Writing in *The Nation* in 1952, Carey McWilliams concluded: "The gambling racket is dead. The mob is now infiltrating into big business – all business – and all the political power it can muster will be used to put official 'muscle' into operation against legitimate merchants and manufacturers."

But the gambling racket was far from dead; only the illicit variety was temporarily drying up. As chance would have it, a new, and legal, gambling venture was now available to any individual or consortium with deep enough pockets to meet the prohibitive start-up costs. It became apparent to the newest Second City entrepreneurs that the legitimate commercial venture with the greatest profit potential was the embryonic casino industry, sanctioned only in Nevada and in the nation's offshore playground, Cuba. The concept was a no-brainer from the start. Since casino gambling was legally structured to give "the house" the advantage at the tables, owners had no need to fix games to make a profit. (The house's built-in advantage ranged from 1 percent for blackjack to 5.2 percent for roulette to a staggering 20 percent for keno. The numbers seem small until they are multiplied by the billions wagered yearly.) It soon became a gangster truism that the only gamblers who win are the ones who own the tables. In addition, with the vast amounts of clean cash wafting through the count room, the gangs would have an ideal setup in which to launder income from less savory enterprises; not to mention what could be stolen, or "skimmed," from the uncounted stacks of cash.

The upperworld typically waxed euphemistic when describing its participation in one of the oldest of vices. For the sake of appearances, gambling was now to be called gaming, and in the 1950s the Outfit, as content with the hollow distinction as anyone, jumped headfirst into the gaming industry.

Part Four

Vegas
(The New Booze III)

13.

Cohibas and Carpet Joints

The glitzy, high-stakes world of casino gambling was anything but alien to the bosses of organized crime at midcentury. The Outfit had dipped a tentative toe into those waters during the previous two decades, but the New York and Florida gangs had been the first to take the concept seriously. Although the casino enterprise was one of the few gambling ventures in which the Chicagoans were behind the curve, they would soon make up for lost time. The Outfit's decision, in the wake of Kefauver, to go increasingly legit, was not a total transformation, however; they had not lost their habit of making truckloads of money quickly. And the illegal opportunities afforded by legal casino gambling provided the perfect link in the hoods' evolutionary chain.

The boss who had run the gauntlet years earlier for all the gangsters who would follow was Curly Humphreys' East Coast alter ego, the genius of the New York Commission, Meyer Lansky. After rising to the top of the New York bootlegging trade, the greatest Jewish gangster in history focused his immense talents on casino gambling. And he chose as his laboratory the tropical paradise of Cuba with its amenable president, Fulgencio Batista y Zaldívar.

A Sunny Place for Shady People

Meyer Lansky first came to Havana in the 1930s, having already earned a reputation as the owner of the best "carpet joints" in America. These gambling parlors were the first to deliver the card, wheel, and dice games from the backrooms and sawdust floors of saloons into their own dedicated, upscale nightclubs. Lansky was thus among the forefathers of the plush gaming industry, establishing clubs up and down the East Coast. Naturally, for these illegal clubs to operate in the open, the compliance of local officials was required, and Lansky, like every other gangster boss, took advantage of the inherent greed of the upperworld. With officials properly satiated, Lansky oversaw carpet joints that succeeded wildly, due in large part to their reputation for fair gaming and intolerance for cheats. These Lansky traits brought him to the attention of Cuba's new military leader, Fulgencio Batista, a U.S.-sponsored strong-arm with visions of creating a combination of Paris and Monte Carlo in the Caribbean.

Batista's dream of a Cuban music and gambling paradise was hindered by his homeland's notorious reputation as an unregulated haven for cardsharks and swindlers. In this free-for-all atmosphere, where come-on games with names like "razzle-dazzle" and "cubolo" flourished, casual tourists were being robbed, and serious gamblers had no reason to play in the first place. To make matters worse, the races at regime's premier, beautiful racetrack, Oriental Park, were rightfully perceived as being fixed daily. Again, the serious bettors and horse owners stayed away. When Batista sought to remedy the scandalous state of affairs, he wisely sought the expertise of a Polish-born, Brooklyn-bred thirty-five-year-old expert with a reputation for running the most honest gambling concessions in the United States. Born Mair Suchowljansky, he was now known as Meyer Lansky, the New York head of the Commission.

Unlike the Outfit, Lansky and pals had been transshipping their boot-legged alcohol through Caribbean ports for over a decade and were well acquainted with the allure of the tropics. At the time of Batista's takeover, Cuba's two main gambling parlors consisted of a small, plush venue inside Oriental Park, and the classic Grand Casino Nacional nightclub, with its Greek architecture, fountains, and statues in the nearby town of Marianao. With Lansky agreeing to kick back 30 percent of the take to Batista, a successful partnership that would last for three decades was formed. Lansky more than lived up to his end of the deal, bringing his own trusted pit crews from his Florida carpet rooms, and single-handedly building a new reputation for Cuban casinos that eventually succeeded in attracting the hemisphere's high rollers. The partnership flourished until 1944, when the new Cuban president ousted both Batista and Lansky. They both relocated to southern Florida, where they stayed close friends and neighbors, waiting until the day when the United States would reinstall Batista at the helm of his corrupt dictatorship.

During this period, the extent of the Outfit's interest in Cuba is impossible to determine. With scant FBI (or later CIA) penetration in the offshore haven, the degree of American investments on the island has

A painting by Edward Mendel depicting the creation of Chicago's literal "underworld" in 1857.

[the OUTFIT]

[rogues GALLERY]

Capone's mayor, Big Bill Thompson, being serenaded with a song about himself.

Jim Colosimo

George "Bugs" Moran

Frank "The Enforcer" Nitti (1932)

Al Capone, waiting to be interrogated at the Chicago Police Department headquarters (c 1928).

Johnny "The Fox" Torrio, recovering from wounds suffered during the 1925 Chicago beer wars.

Capone and his child Sonny chatting with Chicago Cubs player Gabby Hartnett. To Sonny's right is "the mob's congressman," Roland Libonati (1931).

The St. Valentine's Day Massacre, February 14, 1929.

[antonino leonardo ACCARDO]
"JOE BATTERS"

Accardo's record is as follows:

31, 1923, disorderly conduct – fined $200 and costs

ary 3, 1924, disorderly conduct – discharged.

ary 19, 1924, disorderly conduct – fined $10 and co

7, 1924, disorderly conduct – fined $25 and costs.

er 13,   rly conduct – discharged.

ary 6,   conduct – discharged.

March 3,   duct – discharged.

June 6,   ct – discharged.

October   onduct – dischar

January   conduct and carry
discharg

February,   h "Machine Gun" Ja
                     Indicted in the
                  on March 13, 1931 up

              sorderly conduct – discharge

             disorderly conduct – discharg

            rrested with Charles Gioe on charge o

May 10,   four
gangster   Mike
vice ove

May 3, 1   y 24,

May 17,

August 1   ek an
investiga

Arrested   Cain
with murd   cella
Dean was   sente
tentiary with other members of the Capone mob.

Bettmann/CORBIS

Chuck Schauer

Chuck Schauer

Chuck Schauer

Bettmann/CORBIS

Infant Curly (r.) with sister.

Don Llewellyn

[llewelyn morris HUMPHREYS]
"CURLY"

Jeanne Humphreys

Ernest Brendle

Don Llewellyn

Don Llewellyn

Ernest Brendle

Proof — Chicago — Miami 1939

Curly, Clemi, and Luella (c 1941).

Rosselli (c.) leaving the U.S. District Court in New York after being told he could not wear his army uniform to the Hollywood extortion trial.

Bettmann/CORBIS

Young Filippo.

David R. Nissen

Early mug shot.

[filippo SACCO]
"JOHNNY ROSSELLI"

The Look.

David R. Nissen

Bettmann/CORBIS

Johnny with his new bride, June Lang, on honeymoon at the Grand Canyon (April 9, 1948).

Attorney Frank Desimore with client Rosselli in Los Angeles (Sept. 1948).

Los Angeles Daily News Photographic Archive, Dept. of Special Collections, Charles E. Young Research Library, UCLA.

New York, 1965.

Chicago, 1965.

[salvatore GIANCANA]
"MOONEY"

Wheelman Mooney (l.), with cousin Anthony DeMarco (c 1935).

[felice DeLUCIA]
"PAUL RICCA"

"The Waiter"

National Archives

Ricca with Louis "Little New York" Campagna waiting to be interrogated about their early paroles in the Hollywood extortion case (August 25, 1947).

Bettmann/CORBIS

Jake "Greasy Thumb" Guzik

Library of Congress NYWTS

Gus "Slim" Alex

Kefauver Committee photo files, Library of Congress

Federal Bureau of Investigation

Roland V. "Libby" Libonati, the mob's congressman.

John "Jake the Barber" Factor, on the day he was released from his "kidnappers" (July 7, 1933).

National Archives

Meyer Lansky (1949)

Meyer Lansky's partner, Vincent "Jimmy Blue Eyes" Alo.

A typical Chicago "handbook" joint.

Police raid a slot machine distributor.

Benjamin Siegel (l.) with actor and gangster wannabe George Raft.

Siegel slain

Benjamin "Don't Call Me Bugsy" Siegel.

A bank receipt from one of Joe Epstein's payments to Virginia Hill and Barney Ross.

Kefauver Committee evidence file

Virginia Hill, the Outfit's courier, in a 1947 Hollywood glamour shot.

Hill testifying before the Kefauver Committee (March 15, 1951).

Luella Humphreys (l.) leads a dance line of Hollywood bigwigs. Note actors Jimmy Stewart (third from left) and George Burns (fourth from left).

Ernest Brendle

Don Llewellyn

Luella with her high school prom date Frank Sinatra.

Don Llewellyn

Luella with her lover, actor Rosanno Brazzi, in Italy (early fifties).

Willie "The Pimp" Bioff "before," in Los Angeles (1939).

Sally Rosenthal

Attorney Boris Kostelanetz, still going strong in 2000.

Bioff "after." His remains scattered around his Phoenix neighborhood on November 4, 1955.

Los Angeles Daily News Photographic Archive, Dept. of Special Collections, Charles E. Young Research Library, UCLA

Bettmann/CORBIS

Senator Harry S Truman (l.) with his sponsor Tom "Boss" Pendergast (second from left) at the 1936 Democratic National Convention in Philadelphia.

Senator Estes Kefauver (r.) discussing coonskin caps with television's "Davy Crockett," actor Fess Parker (c.).

Curly and Jeanne on the town—

Jeanne Humphreys' well-worn passport. Note dozens of stamps from Switzerland, where she and Curly couriered funds to Virginia Hill.

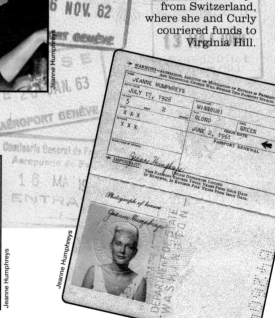

—and on tour in the Middle East.

Senator John F. Kennedy, campaigning in Chicago, with Mayor Richard Daley seated to his left (November 4, 1960).

Counsel Robert F. Kennedy and Senator John Kennedy give rapt attention to a witness before the McLellan Committee.

Teamster boss Jimmy Hoffa (l.) and Allen Dorfman (r.) leave the federal courthouse in Chattanooga, Tennessee, during a recess in their jury tampering trial. Hoffa's son-in-law, Robert Crancer, also pictured (February 18, 1964).

The Cal-Neva Casino (1950).

Nevada Historical Society

Entrance to the Cal-Neva Lodge.

[under SURVEILLANCE]

Commission courier
Sylvain Ferdmann leaving
Philadelphia airport with
Las Vegas skim, bound
for Zurich.

Ida Devine (r.), Virginia Hill's successor,
at Union Station in Chicago, delivering
$115,000 in skim from Las Vegas.

Curly caught on
hidden camera
outside his Key
Biscayne home.

Curly, in his "feeble
man" getup used
to elicit sympathy
from jurors.

Don Llewellyn

Johnny Rosselli on his way to the
Senate Select Committee on Intelligence
hearings (June 24, 1975).

Bettmann/CORBIS

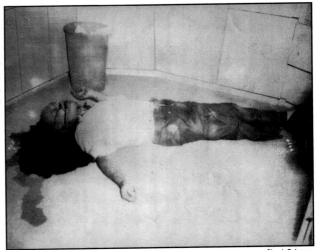

The body of Mooney
Giancana, where it
was found in his
basement on June
18, 1975.

Chuck Schauer

The weapon used to kill
Giancana, a .22 automatic
with homemade silencer,
found alongside the road
on the way to aide Butch
Blasi's home.

Chuck Schauer

Don Llewellyn

Curly's last trip—being escorted back to Chicago from Oklahoma (June, 1965).

One of the last photos of Johnny Rosselli.

David R. Nissen

Don Llewellyn

Curly signs his release papers just a few hours before his death on November 23, 1965.

The notoriously camera-shy Sidney Korshak, caught off-guard outside his Beverly Hills home in 1994 by former *Hollywood Reporter* scribe Dave Robb. "I'm sure he thought I was the hit that he'd been waiting for for fifty years," Robb recalled.

David Robb

always been shrouded in mystery. However, numerous well-placed sources have emerged over the years telling a consistent story of Windy City ties to Cuba. It was widely believed that the Chicago gang had a hidden stake in Havana's Sans Souci, Capri, and Tropicana casinos, owned in part by Santo Trafficante, Jr, the numbers boss of Florida. Trafficante, the only gangster to stay behind after Batista's 1944 fall from power, would install a Mooney Giancana underling named Lewis McWillie as his pit boss at the Trop. McWillie would later perform the same service for Mooney at a casino hotel he secretly purchased in Reno, Nevada, in 1960. Federal narcotics agent Charles Siragusa told investigative reporter Dan Moldea that the Outfit hit man who had been indicted in the 1947 James Ragen murder was the gang's chief liaison to all things Cuban. "Dave Yaras was probably one of the first members of the Chicago underworld to 'discover' Florida after Capone was sent to jail," Siragusa said. "He ran a number of gambling operations on the island [Cuba] and was also the Chicago mob's liaison to the Cuban exile community after the fall of Batista."

Other Outfit members had maintained a presence in the Cuban paradise. As captured in photos in extant family albums, Curly Humphreys had been traveling with his family to Cuba at least since the early 1940s. Likewise, it was oft reported that Joe Accardo enjoyed regular deep-sea-fishing vacations to Cuba and other Caribbean destinations. However, it is unknown if they conducted gang business on these outings. Despite the dearth of offshore intelligence, hints of the Chicago gang's growing interest can be seen most conspicuously in the movements of Johnny Rosselli, always the most visible of the core Outfit members.

After the Kefauver circus, Johnny Rosselli's star began to dim in Tinseltown. When his friend Brian Foy left Eagle Lion Studios, the owners let Rosselli's contract expire, while Johnny's parole adviser was telling him that the best way to avoid suspicion was to hold down regular employment. The loss of the Eagle Lion gig was stressful, but it was the dismissal of Johnny by his longtime pal Harry Cohn of Columbia that convinced "Mr. Smooth" to seek out greener pastures. Cohn stunned Rosselli when he refused to give him a producer's job on the studio lot. "Johnny, how could I give you a job?" Cohn asked. "The stockholders would scalp me." "You're a rotten shit," an angry Rosselli fired back. "Did the stockholders complain when I got ten years of prison because of you?"

There is some compelling evidence that before Rosselli abandoned

Hollywood he managed to redress his snub by Cohn. At the time, the once meteoric career of gangster hanger-on Frank Sinatra was in free fall. With his voice in great disrepair, his marriage to Ava Gardner failing fast, and his MGM film contract recently canceled, "The Voice" was believed by his closest friends to be on the verge of suicide. Meanwhile, Harry Cohn was casting for the World War II film *From Here to Eternity*. Sinatra had read the book and was obsessed with landing the role of Private Angelo Maggio, a scrawny Italian-American soldier with a heart bigger than that of GI Joe. It was believed at the time that the film would be awash in Oscar nominations the following year, and Sinatra envisioned the film's resuscitating his flagging career. The trouble was that Harry Cohn wanted only legitimate seasoned actors to read for the part.

Sinatra managed to sit down with Cohn, and over lunch the producer pulled no punches. "Look, Frank, that's an actor's part, a stage actor's part," Cohn told the crooner. "You're nothing but a fucking hoofer."

Dismayed but not yet resigned to defeat, Sinatra had his white-hot actress wife, Ava Gardner, lobby his case with Cohn's better half. Other friends were conscripted into the cause, but Cohn gave little indication that he was interested in Sinatra. At this point, according to a number of well-placed sources, Sinatra enlisted the aid of the Outfit's Johnny Rosselli. News reports initially surfaced that noted New York Commission boss Frank Costello was telling friends that his longtime pal Frank Sinatra had approached him for help with the Cohn situation. Columnist John J. Miller told writer Kitty Kelley that this was not uncommon. "Sinatra and Frank C. were great pals," Miller remembered. "I know because I used to sit with Frank C. at the Copa and Sinatra would join us all the time. He was always asking favors of the old man, and whenever Sinatra had a problem, he went to Frank C. to solve it." Apparently, this newest accommodation was facilitated by the Outfit's Johnny Rosselli.

Although studio executives have denied that a Rosselli intervention ever took place, Rosselli admitted his role to his niece shortly before his death many years later. Former publicist and Rosselli pal Joe Seide said in 1989 that one of Costello's key men told him how he had flown to L.A. to enlist the Outfit's Rosselli in the cause. According to Seide: "The Maggio role, Sinatra wasn't going to get it. There were no two ways about it . . . Johnny Rosselli was the go-between. Johnny was the one who talked to Harry – he was the one who laid it out. That was serious business. It was in the form of 'Look, you do this for me and maybe we won't do this to you.' . . . It wasn't even a secret in the business."

To no one's surprise, *From Here to Eternity* was nominated in ten categories for the 1953 Academy Awards, winning eight of the coveted statuettes. Among the winners was Frank Sinatra for Best Supporting Actor. And as he had hoped, Sinatra's career took off and the singer never looked back. The pivotal role Rosselli played in Sinatra's turnaround, if in fact it happened, goes a long way toward explaining their lifelong friendship, which began about this time. The episode might also account for Sinatra's dutiful obliging of Humphreys' daughter when she needed a date for her high school dance. It was the least he could do for a gang from Chicago who had changed his life forever.

The alleged Rosselli-Sinatra incident was fictionalized in the 1969 novel *The Godfather* (which the Outfit played a key role in getting made as a movie, as will be seen). In that telling, a down-in-the-dumps Italian singer named Johnny Fontaine had his mob sponsors make a studio head "an offer he couldn't refuse" in order to land their boy a plum film role. In the movie version, the mogul woke up to the sight of his prized race-horse's severed head in his bed.[1]

The Outfit's Emissary Goes Tropical

Rosselli's friends in Hollywood had not deserted him socially, but they drew the line at having professional relationships with the now infamous ex-con. Thus the Outfit's travelling emissary set out to conquer new worlds, simultaneously smoothing the way for his associates in Chicago. The top spot on Johnny's new itinerary was Cuba.

Although his presence on the island is mentioned in only one FBI document, Rosselli's business expansion into Cuba, as recounted by numerous associates and government agents, is undeniable. The timing for Rosselli and the Outfit could not have been better, since in 1952, Batista-Lansky had retaken the island nation and made up for lost time in establishing their Caribbean Monaco. Batista quickly placed Lansky in charge of gambling at the plush Montmartre Club and the more modest

---

1. The entire episode recalls a story told by bandleader Tommy Dorsey to *American Mercury* magazine in 1951. For years the story had circulated that when Sinatra's singing career had first taken off, he was desperate to escape a long-term contract with Dorsey. As the persistent rumor went, Sinatra went to Costello, who sent his goons to visit Dorsey. The thugs allegedly shoved the barrel of a gun in Dorsey's mouth until he signed Frank's release agreement. After years of such rumors, Dorsey himself admitted that he was in fact visited by three enforcers who instructed him to "sign or else."

Monseigneur Club, both in downtown Havana. As Batista's "adviser on gambling reform," Lansky took an above-the-table retainer of $25,000 per year, and untold millions below. His money-counting crew had a saying that would become a mantra in Las Vegas: "Three for us, one for the government, and two for Meyer."

Lansky next installed a casino in the elegant ten-story Nacional Hotel, over objections by expatriate Americans such as Ernest Hemingway, who viewed the placid, noncommercial gardens of the Nacional as their private club. Designed by art deco icon Igor Plevitzky, who also drew the plans for The Breakers in Palm Beach and The Biltmore in Coral Gables, the Nacional was (prior to Lansky-Batista) the last place one would expect to find the gambling ilk. With its manicured lawns on a bluff overlooking Havana Harbor, the Nacional had been the perfect setting for afternoon teas and bridge parties for the leisure class. But the avaricious Lansky-Batista changed all that with the addition of a bar, a showroom, and a casino. The Cuban gold rush was now on, and the Outfit's interests were represented by Los Angeles exile Johnny Rosselli.

In her autobiography, Mooney Giancana's daughter Antoinette remembered her father "constantly hopping a plane" for Havana in the years before her mother's death in 1954. As Antoinette recalled: "Sometimes he was with Accardo, or the Fischettis, or Gus Alex, or Johnny Rosselli. Rosselli managed one of the Cuban hotel casinos, the Sans Souci, with the boss of the Florida crime family, Santo Trafficante."

When Trafficante testified before the House Select Committee on Assassinations in 1978, he admitted having known Rosselli since at least 1945. That same committee referred to government sources who, like Antoinette Giancana, knew that Rosselli "had a management role" in the Sans Souci. In 1990, the former casino floor manager at the Nacional, Refugio Cruz, said in an interview that he saw Rosselli there several times in the midfifties, dining with Lansky. "It was as if royalty was visiting," the Cuban recalled. Likewise, an anonymous source told Rosselli's biographers that he was hired by Rosselli during the same period to oversee publicity for acts appearing in some of Havana's casino showrooms. The FBI believed that Rosselli, like Dave Yaras, had also coordinated hidden investments for the Outfit in Cuban gambling.

The lack of FBI surveillance in Cuba effectively curtails further investigation into the specifics of the Outfit's Cuban casino investments. However, the steady growth of the gang's fascination with gambling in the Nevada desert is well documented.

The Outfit Explores the Green Felt Jungle

When the subject of the Las Vegas casino boom is broached, invariably the first name that comes to mind is that of Meyer Lansky's partner Ben "Don't Call Me Bugsy" Siegel, whom many credit with creating the industry when he built his Flamingo Hotel-Casino in 1946. But in financing Siegel's dream, Lansky's Commission (which included the Outfit) was acting on the groundwork laid two decades earlier by none other than Curly Humphreys, Johnny Rosselli, and the Big Guy himself, Al Capone. And the Outfit's interest in the desert oasis demonstrated once again the gang's uncanny prescience and survival skills, talents that saw them beat the upperworld to still another pot of gold. It is a certainty that, as early as the 1920s, someone in Chicago's empire of crime was versed in the history of the desert Southwest, a history that made the locale ripe for Outfit expansionism. (See gambling appendix.)

Wide-Open Gambling

In the early twentieth century, the combined effect of the nation's Depression and the depletion of the southern gold and silver mines sent Nevada officials scurrying to invent ways to revive the state's flagging economy. While the locals debated remedies, the U.S. Bureau of Reclamation was about to break ground on a project that would propel much of the Southwest into an era of prosperity. For over twelve years, federal officials had argued over what to do about the disastrous periodic flooding of the fourteen-hundred-mile-long Colorado River. Finally a bold plan was approved that would, if successful, not only tame the Colorado, but provide water and hydroelectric power throughout the West: The government moved to construct the world's largest dam thirty miles to the southeast of Las Vegas. Since no city can grow without an adequate water supply, the construction of the massive Hoover Dam, which broke ground in 1931, went a long way toward making the idea of Las Vegas viable. The project had the ancillary benefit of employing more than five thousand workers, many of whom relocated to Nevada from out of state.[2] With so many hardworking, hard-partying laborers spend-

---

2. Most were desperate unemployed Depression victims. In the first three weeks after the project was announced, some twelve thousand employment hopefuls contacted the planners, willing to work in the 130-degree desert seven days a week for $1.15 per day. They would be allowed only two days off per year – Christmas and the Fourth of July.

ing their paychecks in nearby Las Vegas, the predictable vices once again flourished, happily tolerated by officials.

Much as Roosevelt would call for a repeal of Volstead in order to avail the economy of an alcohol-tax windfall, so too did Nevadans start talking of legalizing gambling. One editorial writer for the *Reese River Reveille* summed up what many were thinking: "If we are going to have gambling . . . let's have it in the open and be honest with ourselves. Regulate the thing and use the revenue for some good purpose." This was happening at the same time that the Outfit, preparing for the end of prohibition, was casting about for "the new booze." With their racetrack maven Johnny Patton already operating illegal dog tracks outside Reno, the Chicago bosses, like the Nevada upperworld, concluded that a legalized-gambling mecca would allow them to expand their race operations and construct gambling joints. It now appears that the Outfit dipped into its treasury to persuade any statehouse holdouts of the wisdom of wide-open gambling.

By the time Nevada governor Fred Balzar signed the law legalizing gambling on March 19, 1931, there were already whispers that some state legislators had been the recipients of graft from gambling entrepreneurs. As A. D. Hopkins wrote in a 1999 article in Las Vegas' *Review-Journal:* "It is commonly believed that cash was spread around to lubricate the passage of casino gambling in 1931, but the source of that money has long been the subject of speculation." Of course, if Chicagoans were involved in such a thing, it was a good bet that Curly Humphreys, the Outfit's political payoff mastermind, would have been the coordinator. The FBI's massive file on Humphreys notes his constant travel to grease the skids for Outfit business. In one example, Humphreys traveled to New York State to bribe legislators to repeal the Sullivan Act, which forbade ex-cons from carrying a weapon.[3] Irv Owen, a Norman, Oklahoma, native and retired attorney who had known Humphreys' extended family and friends since 1937, recently made the emphatic statement that he knew exactly how the Wide Open Gambling Bill came to be enacted. "In the 1930s, Humphreys and his protégé Johnny Rosselli [whom Curly always called the Hollywood Kid] bribed the Nevada legislature into legalizing gambling," Owen said. "Las Vegas owes everything to Murray

---

3. Humphreys often visited St Louis, Kansas City, Los Angeles, and Dallas, where he helped expand the gang's numbers racket; in Oklahoma, he was believed to have masterminded the flow of booze into that dry state; he made frequent trips to the nation's capital to visit with the "mob's congressman," Roland Libonati.

Humphreys." Regarding Outfit money passing under the table at Carson City, Owen was recently corroborated by John Detra, the son of one of Las Vegas' earliest gambling-club owners.

John Detra's father, Frank Detra, had moved from New York to Las Vegas in 1927. A year later, according to his son John, thirty-one-year-old Frank Detra and his family began receiving visits from none other than Chicago's Al Capone, then twenty-eight years of age. Although John has no knowledge of how the two met, it was clear to him that they were close friends. (It is possible that the friendship goes back to New York, since both men were there at the same time and were of the same age.) The younger Detra still retains a gold pocket watch Capone gave his father, the back of which bears the inscription "Franco Amici Alphonse," which translates as "Frank and Alphonse are friends." Detra and Capone were obviously planning a business partnership, says John.

After a brief stint as a dealer in downtown's Boulder Club, Detra was staked by a still unidentified Eastern entity to build his own club five miles outside the city line, on a section of old Highway 91 (the future Las Vegas Boulevard) that would later be named The Strip. His club, The Pair-O-Dice, would make history as the Strip's first upscale carpet joint. In the vicinity at the time, there was only The Red Rooster sawdust roadhouse. Although Detra's club was a speakeasy of sorts (a password was needed to enter), it boasted all the refinements of Vegas lounges that would hold sway three decades later. Open only at night, the Pair-O-Dice featured delicious Italian cuisine, jazz and dance bands, fine wine, and, of course, table games. To keep the operation afloat, the requisite bribes were in force. "The old man went to town every month with envelopes, several of them, and came back without the envelopes," John says.

When the 1930 debate over gambling legalization was joined, young John began accompanying his father as he made deliveries of cash-stuffed briefcases and envelopes to influential Nevadans across the state. Frank Detra admitted to his son that the money was being spent to ensure the passage of the Wide Open Gambling Bill. John believes the money had to have come from the Capone gang, since Capone was the only major player close to his father. John was aware that some monies were being paid to state legislators, but his father's role may have been even more critical to the pro-gambling strategy: Frank Detra's contacts superseded the local power brokers. "They were all federal people, top-drawer people who influenced the state people," John remembers. On one trip to Reno, John was asked to make the delivery himself. "Dad gave me a little briefcase and said, 'See that house over there? Go ring the bell,'" John recently remembered. "I went over and rang the doorbell, and a man came to the door and said, 'Oh, thank you,' took the suitcase and closed the door."

After gambling was legalized in 1931, Frank Detra openly operated the Pair-O-Dice until 1941, when he sold the business to Guy McAfee, who incorporated the club's structure into his Last Frontier Club. Detra, who died in 1984, went on to operate clubs in Reno and Ely.

Outfit associates not only moved quickly to open the first legal upscale nightclubs like the Pair-O-Dice, but also established Nevada's first casino-hotel. After gambling legalization, Las Vegas city commissioners issued only seven gambling licenses for downtown clubs, most of which had maintained illegal gambling operations for years. Among the license recipients were the Boulder Club, where Frank Detra had briefly worked as a dealer, and the Las Vegas Club.[4] Club owners with Outfit affiliations were among the first to cash in on the Las Vegas gambling rush. On May 2, 1931, Johnny Rosselli's bootlegging partner from Los Angeles, Tony "The Hat" Cornero, opened Las Vegas' first legal hotel-casino, The Meadows, just east of the city. Unlike the small, sawdust-coated downtown casinos on Fremont Street, Cornero's place was a Lansky-like "carpet joint," but combined with well-appointed hotel accommodations. The May 3 *Las Vegas Age* newspaper described the Meadows: "Potent in its charm, mysterious in its fascination, the Meadows, America's most luxurious casino, will open its doors tonight and formally embark upon a career which all liberal-minded persons in the West will watch closely."

Although visionary, The Meadows was a huge gamble for the Depression era. In southern Nevada especially, there were not yet enough well-to-do patrons to sustain the business. In just a couple years, The Meadows closed, only to reopen as a high-class bordello. Cornero would resurface in the 1950s to open another Vegas hotel-casino, the Stardust, which was quickly appropriated by the Outfit.

The Outfit's fingerprints can be seen in other parts of the state in the immediate aftermath of legalization. In downtown Reno, a large crew of laborers began tearing out the walls of adjacent buildings on Center Street even before the bill was signed. The gambling parlor that would occupy the space in a matter of days was John Drew and Bill Graham's Bank Club.

---

4. The others were the Northern, the Rainbow, the Big Four, the Railroad Club, and the Exchange Club.

According to Chicago FBI agent Bill Roemer, Joe Accardo had given Drew his start at Joe's Owl Club in Calumet City, Illinois, before dispatching Drew to Reno to manage the Bank Club. Bryn Armstrong, former chair of the Nevada State Parole Board, revealed in a recent interview that none other than Johnny Rosselli, a good friend of Graham's, represented "hidden financial interests" (read "the Outfit") in the Bank Club. Graham was likely critical for the legalization push in the first place, since, according to Rosselli's autobiographers, "he knew every politician in the state and could obtain licenses and government concessions when other men could not."

Despite their best efforts and visionary concepts, Outfit liaisons such as Detra, Cornero, and Drew were ultimately the victims of bad timing. The nation's depressed economy kept the number of available affluent high rollers to a minimum. Economic conditions around Las Vegas were even worse, since after the Hoover Dam was completed in 1935, the area saw the exodus of the five-thousand-man workforce and their families. The situation thus remained in stasis as Vegas once again became synonymous with low-rent dude ranches, cowboy casinos (with gamblers' horses harnessed out front), and sawdust-floored gambling roadhouses. Out-of-towners were dispossessed of a bit more cash by state legislators, who passed no-fault quickie-divorce codes. But roadhouse gambling and quickie divorces were not panaceas for a flat state economy. However, redemption would come soon after World War II in the form of a handsome New York hoodlum who had been peddling the Outfit's Trans-America wire service to the downtown gambling joints. The movie-star-handsome thug came up with the best scam idea of his life: He decided that the time was right for Las Vegas (and the Commission) to revisit the hotel-casino notion pioneered by Tony Cornero in 1931 with The Meadows. With the Chicago–New York Commission's financial backing, Ben Siegel gave new life to Nevada while ironically sacrificing his own. In doing so, the fortunes of Nevada, and particularly Las Vegas, would forever improve.

The Bugsy One

He is best remembered as Meyer Lansky's childhood pal and crime partner. Together with Meyer, Brooklyn-born Benjamin Siegel graduated from terrorizing pushcart vendors for chump change to organizing the infamous murder-for-hire racket known as Murder, Inc. By the age of twenty-one, Siegel was said to have perpetrated every crime in the book, including white slavery, bootlegging, hijacking, robbery, rape, extortion, narcotics running, and numerous contract murders. Ben Siegel's hooligan thoroughness was equally matched by his borderline pathological outbursts, which earned him the nickname Bugsy, a moniker no one dared use in his presence. Until the end of his life, Siegel was known to pistol-whip those who committed the transgression, regardless of whether the faux pas occurred in private or by a crowded Las Vegas poolside. Lansky once said of his childhood friend, "When we were in a fight, Benny would never hesitate. He was even quicker to take action than those hot-blooded Sicilians, the first to start punching and shooting. Nobody reacted faster than Benny."

By 1936, the thirty-year-old Siegel himself became a marked man in New York, much as had Al Capone, after committing an ill-considered high-profile gang rubout (that of Tony Frabrazzo). Instead of boarding the New York to Chicago underground railroad like Capone, Siegel was ordered to Los Angeles by his superiors, Lucky Luciano and Meyer Lansky. It was a fitting venue for the movie-star-handsome Siegel, whose legendary vanity was right at home in a city that had turned self-love into an art form. Soon after his arrival, Siegel hooked up with another transplanted Brooklyn pal who had already scored in Hollywood, actor George Raft. Siegel also made the acquaintance of the town's social lioness, Countess Dorothy Dendice Taylor di Frasso, who became one of Siegel's countless lovers. With the well-placed Raft and di Frasso as his connections, a starstruck Siegel soon met celebrities like Clark Gable, Jean Harlow, Gary Cooper, and many others. Through Johnny Rosselli, Siegel met studio barons like Harry Cohn and Louis Mayer, and labor thug Willie Bioff. And although Siegel had relocated to Hollywood with his wife and daughters, he bedded more starlets than most single lotharios.

Siegel quickly established himself financially, since Luciano had greased the skids by ordering Los Angeles boss, and Rosselli associate, Jack Dragna to partner in his lucrative gambling and labor racketeering operations with the outcast Siegel. "Benny is coming west for the good and health of all of us," Luciano had told Dragna. Expanding his empire, Siegel formed a partnership with another Rosselli cohort, Tony Cornero, and began fronting for the Outfit's Trans-America wire service, scattering agents throughout the Southwest. Siegel guaranteed his new empire's success by bribing countless state politicians and law enforcement officials, all the way up to the state attorney general's office.

Bugsy Siegel's selection as the Outfit's wire representative in the Southwest was understandable: He had known the gang's patriarch, Big Al Capone, since both their formative days in the Williamsburg section of Brooklyn, where they had worked in consort as strikebreaking thugs for garment-industry upperworlders. When Capone had come under intense heat from rival Arthur Finnegan in 1920, he had gone into hiding with one of Siegel's aunts before subsequently making for Chicago. In later years, Al entertained Siegel at his Palm Island estate in Florida.

Siegel took to the superficiality of Tinseltown as though he had been born there. His vainglory now in overdrive, Siegel began dressing in custom-made designer clothes, every item of which was monogrammed; he took acting lessons; he combed his hair every five minutes; and he applied face creams and eye shades nightly. Once, when George Raft sent him a toupee as a joke for a birthday present, Bugsy drove over to Raft's house in a rage and screamed at the actor, "I oughta shoot you, you motherfucker!"

Inevitably, Bugsy's voracious sexual appetite drew him to his female alter ego, the Outfit's money courier/spy/nymphomaniac, Virginia Hill. Opinions vary as to how the pair met, but since they floated through the same New York/Chicago/Los Angeles hoodlum cliques, their meeting was inevitable. According to Joe Adonis (Doto), New York gambling boss and Commission partner of Lansky's and Luciano's, he set Hill up with Bugsy. As he told UPI correspondent Harold Conrad in 1946, "Great broad, but she was out in front all the time, giving orders and fighting me for the dinner checks. That can de-ball you when you got a broad always grabbing the checks. So I hedged her off to Benny."

As unstable as Bugsy's, Hill's fiery temper matched that of her paramour slug for slug. The tempestuous pair became known for their furious rows, after which the regularly bruised Hill would often attempt suicide by overdosing. To their friends, Bugsy and Virginia explained that the painful fisticuffs were more than ameliorated by their conjugal bliss, which was said to feature explosive sex. In later years, this woman of a thousand liaisons never hesitated to say, "Benny was the best sex I ever had." During rare moments of solitude, Virginia called Siegel "Baby Blue Eyes," while Siegel gave her the pet name Flamingo, referencing her red hair and long legs. Although Hill assisted Siegel in setting up a Mexican narcotics pipeline, she never relinquished her allegiance to the Outfit, and especially her Chicago handler, Joe Epstein. Through Epstein-Hill, Ac-

cardo and Humphreys were kept well informed of Siegel's management of
their affairs.

The Vegas Idea

In 1941, just after the race wire was legalized in Nevada, Siegel sent his
aide and lifelong Brooklyn friend Moey Sedway to Las Vegas with a
charge to install the Outfit's Trans-America wire service in the downtown
Vegas haunts of the serious gamblers – casinos such as the Golden
Nugget, Horseshoe, Golden Gate, and Monte Carlo. The task was
virtually effortless, since the "Glitter Gulch" casino owners saw bookie
wagering as a draw and hoped that in between races the bettors would
sample the other games of chance on-site.

The money was huge. In no time, Siegel was receiving a $25,000-per-
month cut from the Las Vegas wire alone, which he called the Golden
Nugget News Service. Sedway became a civic-minded philanthropist,
who, for a time, considered running for public office – that is, until Bugsy
set him straight. In a typical fit of rage, Siegel screamed at Moey, "We
don't run for office. We own the politicians."

Soon, Siegel let Sedway in on another secret, when, on a 115-degree
summer day in 1945, he drove Moey out of Las Vegas on Highway 91.
About five miles out, they pulled to a stop in the middle of nowhere, and
Bugsy pointed to a couple of dilapidated buildings, leaving Moey
befuddled.

"For God's sake, Ben. What is it?" Moey asked

"Thirty acres, Moe," said Siegel. "Thirty acres for a few nickels and
dimes."

After Sedway had questioned his buddy's sanity, Siegel described his
master plan: "Moe, we're going to buy this hunk of land. And we're going
to build the goddamnest biggest hotel and casino you ever saw. I can see it
now. 'Ben Siegel's Flamingo" – that's what I'm going to call it. I'm going
to have a garden and a big pool and a first-class hotel. We're going to
make Reno look like a whistle-stop.'

In truth, Siegel's vision, like so much else in his life, had been stolen, this
time from one of Johnny Rosselli's best friends, Billy Wilkerson. As the
publisher of *The Hollywood Reporter* and the owner of successful L.A.
nightclubs on the Sunset Strip, Wilkerson had hoped to create a new
"strip" on the Las Vegas outskirts. After Wilkerson made the initial land
purchase, his financing fell through. Enter Bugsy Siegel. Wilkerson's
gangster friend not only agreed that the time was right to revisit the

idea of Tony Cornero's ahead-of-its-time Meadows, but Siegel knew that he could avoid haggling with city commissioners for a casino license if he built his dream outside the Las Vegas city limits. Siegel estimated that his pleasure palace would need $1.5 million in financing. In no time, Siegel, as majority stockholder, formed a partnership with Wilkerson and a handpicked group of other investors, such as Meyer Lansky, who chipped in an initial $25,000, adding $75,000 more later. Years later, the FBI would learn that there was also a hidden partner in the Flamingo project. As Chicago FBI agent Bill Roemer recounted, "We learned how Hump [Curly Humphreys] went there in 1946 to assist Bugsy Siegel in establishing the first hotel-casino on what is now known as the Strip . . . Hump worked with Siegel, Meyer Lansky, and others of the New York mob putting the Flamingo together . . . Chicago gained an early foothold in Vegas through Humphreys" work.' Two decades later, the FBI would listen via hidden microphones as Curly recounted this period to a protégé named Gus Alex. "I was there when Bugsy Siegel was there," Humphreys said. "[Contractor Del Webb] was the big boss there at the time, 'cause he used to sit with Bugsy Siegel when Bugsy was building that joint, you know? And I sat there with him. He used to come over and meet Bugsy every morning."

By 1948, Virgil Peterson of the Chicago Crime Commission had determined the exact amount of the Outfit's investment in Siegel's operation. In a letter to the Nevada Gaming Commission, Peterson notified the Nevadans that, via the Fischetti brothers, Chicago had transmitted over $300,000 to Bugsy. If the figure is accurate, it would make the Outfit the most substantial shareholder in the Flamingo, since the largest investor of record, Siegel, had endowed only $195,000.

Bugsy's Fall

At about the same time that ground was broken on the new casino (December 1945), Bugsy received bad news that presaged his coming downslide into tragedy: His long-suffering wife, Esta, had finally filed for divorce in Reno. The adulterous Siegel was remorseful in his decision not to fight Esta, and he readily agreed to pay her a settlement of $600 per week for life, a staggering amount at the time. Back at the job site, the inexperienced Siegel was being robbed blind by his subcontractors, who marked up their raw-material costs or stole material off the site at night only to resell the same products to Siegel the next day. During the construction, Siegel's chief builder, the popular Del Webb of Phoenix, picked up a key insight into his employer's psyche. In conversation with Webb, Siegel let on that he had personally killed twelve men. "He must have noted my face, or something," Webb later recalled, "because he laughed and said that I had nothing to worry about. 'There's no chance that you'll get killed,' he said. 'We only kill each other.'"

Siegel's flair for extravagance contributed to the project's spiraling cost overruns. His insistence on using only the best imported marbles and woods was made all the more unrealistic given postwar supply shortages. With costs skyrocketing, Siegel obtained emergency moneys from his Hollywood friends such as George Raft, but he needed more than they could produce, so Bugsy went East to secure additional investment from his gang friends. With Lansky's approval, and Siegel's passionate guarantees of success, the New York Commission staked Siegel an extra $5 million.

As the Flamingo absorbed money like a black hole throughout 1946, rumors began to waft eastward that Siegel was skimming the gangs' investment. Although one of the goals of the Flamingo enterprise was to skim money off the top of losers' trove before the owners were assessed for taxes, some Commission and Outfit members began to suspect they were the ones being taken for a ride. Under pressure, Bugsy decided to open the casino even before the hotel was completed. When the big day arrived on December 26, 1946, everything seemed to conspire against Siegel. Bugsy had spared no expense for entertainers such as George Jessel, Rose Marie, George Raft, Jimmy Durante, and Xavier Cugat's Orchestra. In 1996, Rose Marie recalled her stint at Bugsy's place: "The show was spectacular, everything was great, but no locals came. They were used to cowboy boots, not rhinestones. Las Vegas was cowboy hotels; this was Monaco . . . We worked to nine or ten people a night for the rest of the two-week engagement." But despite his best efforts, Siegel was thwarted by Mother Nature and local politics, the combination of which guaranteed the Flamingo's opening would be a disaster. In Los Angeles, a winter storm grounded the two planes Siegel had chartered to ferry celebs to the gala; those who did arrive, such as Clark Gable, Lana Turner, and Joan Crawford, either drove the 350 miles from L.A. or took a train. While in Nevada, most local gamblers, accustomed to the sawdust joints, had no desire to don dinner jackets and buy overpriced drinks merely to play a round of blackjack.

Although most of the serious players were in absentia, those who did show appeared to have entered into a conspiracy against Siegel and the

Flamingo. Some owners of competing downtown casinos tried their luck at the tables, and with the collusion of some of the dealers, beat the house consistently, a virtual impossibility. When Siegel learned of one big cheat, he had to be restrained after screaming, "I'll kill that son of a bitch." (Ironically, one of the only big losers, to the tune of $65,000, was Siegel's pal George Raft.) It thus came as no surprise that the Flamingo lost $100,000 in its first ten days.

Frantic to stop the casino's money hemorrhaging, Siegel closed the operation down in January for six weeks, affording him time to complete hotel construction and repopulate his pit crews. In April, Siegel took Virginia Hill to Mexico, where it is widely believed (but has never been proven) that the two married. When the casino reopened in March, it was a rousing success, so much so that it reported a $250,000 profit by June. However, all was not well in the inner sanctums of his powerful backers. Back East, both the Chicago Outfit and the New York Commission remained convinced that much of their combined $5-million investment had found its way into Siegel's and Hill's Swiss bank accounts. In California and Nevada, smaller investors held similar grudges. In addition, West Coast bookies were also infuriated, because they were now forced to buy both the Outfit's Continental and Siegel's Trans-America.

And Bugsy had still other problems nipping at his heels. A number of powerful gangsters, including Joe Epstein, were furious over Siegel's continued battering of Virginia Hill, the gang's courier and spy whom Epstein and the Outfit had been bankrolling for over a decade. One key adviser to a Commission founder recently stated in no uncertain terms that his boss (whom he asked not be named) had told him that Siegel's treatment of Hill was the straw that broke the camel's back. "Just before Bugsy was killed," says John DeCarlo (pseudonym), "he had beaten the hell out of Virginia, who had carried on a secret affair with my boss. To this day, only a handful of people are aware of the relationship. When Virginia showed him what Bugsy had done, the contract went out."

Although DeCarlo is reluctant to name his boss, one other knowledgeable Angeleno is not. Screenwriter Edward Anhalt (*The Pride and the Passion, Becket, Jeremiah Johnson, Not as a Stranger*, etc.) recently recalled a conversation with the Outfit's West Coast negotiator, Sid Korshak, who also represented Bugsy Siegel. Anhalt had sought out Korshak with the intent of getting background for a possible film on Siegel.

"You know all that bullshit about Ben being killed because he spent too much money?" Korshak asked. "Absolute fiction." Korshak then gave the same rationale as DeCarlo, only he added one more detail. The man who ordered the contract was Hill's first lover, "the guy from Detroit . . . the guy from the Purple Gang." The only man from the Purple Gang with the power to order such a hit was none other than future Las Vegas sachem Moe Dalitz, about whom more will be seen. "He was very offended by it [Siegel's battering of Hill]," said Korshak. "He warned Siegel, and Siegel paid no attention to the warning, and they whacked him."

Unbeknownst to both Anhalt and DeCarlo is a paragraph from the recently released FBI file on Siegel: "Early in June 1947, Siegel had a violent quarrel with Virginia Hill at which time he allegedly beat her so badly that she still had visible bruises several weeks later. Immediately after the beating she took an overdose of narcotics in a suicide threat and was taken unconscious to the hospital. Upon recovery she immediately arranged to leave for an extended trip to Europe."

And there was more. Another of Bugsy's egregious foul-ups was the cavalier manner with which he had been addressing the Outfit's cash cow, the wire service. Bugsy's Chicago employers had been telling him for months to surrender the Trans-America wire service, which they no longer needed since seizing Ragen's Continental. When Joe Accardo personally ordered Siegel to relinquish his outlets, Siegel unwisely balked at the directive, attempting instead to extort his Chicago boss by telling him he could have Trans-America back for $2 million.

Given all the backroom disparaging of Siegel, Bugsy's ears must have been on fire. For the most part, the complaints slid away like water off a duck, but when Siegel learned that the Commission had discussed his fate at the Christmas, 1946, Havana conference, to which he was not invited, he was seized with fear. As recounted by Ed Reid and Ovid Demaris in *The Green Felt Jungle,* Siegel flew to Havana to beg the deported supreme Mafia boss Lucky Luciano for more time. Supposedly, Luciano was intransigent.

"Look here, Ben," Luciano said. "You go back there and start behaving. You give the Chicago boys the wire and no more bullshit. Those boys are fed up. This has gone far enough. You understand?"

"You bastard," Bugsy screamed back, "No one dismisses me. And no son of a bitch tells me what to do. Go to hell and take the rest of those bastards with you. I'll keep the goddamn wire as long as I want."

Quite possibly there was no one reason for the rubout of Ben Siegel. His numerous offenses may have had a cumulative effect that forced his bosses to say "Enough is enough." With so many aligned against Siegel, there was little shock among insiders when the events of June 20, 1947, transpired. On that balmy southern-California evening, Bugsy was sitting with local hood Alan Smiley in the living room of a Beverly Hills mansion (810 Linden Drive) rented by Virginia Hill, where he had arrived from Las Vegas that very morning. While talking with Smiley and reading the *Los Angeles Times,* Siegel was shot four times by a gunman positioned outside the living room window. Hit twice in the face and twice in the chest by slugs from a .30-caliber M-1, the forty-one-year-old Bugsy died quickly, or as Flamingo comic Alan King put it, "Bugsy took a cab." Alan Smiley later told a Chicago friend, "His right eye flew right past my face." It was found by police fifteen feet away on the dining room floor. John DeCarlo said that the blasts to Siegel's face were no coincidence, but poetic justice for his disfigurement of Hill's visage. " 'A face for a face' was what I was told," says DeCarlo.

If Siegel lived long enough to feel the first shot hit him, it surely came as no surprise. The previous day in Vegas, he had been stalked by four underworld goons, who consistently missed him by minutes. Throughout that day, the Flamingo received anonymous long-distance phone calls, with the caller warning Siegel, "Bugsy, you've had it," before hanging up. On that same day, Siegel gave his bodyguard, Fat Irish Green, a briefcase that government investigators believe held as much as $600,000. Siegel informed a stunned Green, "If anything happens to me, you just sit tight and there'll be some guys who'll come and take the money off your hands."

Twenty minutes after the shooting, before police even arrived, the Outfit's Phoenix bookie chief, Gus Greenbaum, along with Moey Sedway and Morris Rosen, walked into the casino at the Flamingo and announced that they had taken over. The next day, Virginia Hill's Chicago paymaster, Joe Epstein, arrived to do the books.

Over the next year, Greenbaum used $1 million in borrowed Outfit money and bank loans to enlarge the hotel's capacity from ninety-seven to more than two hundred rooms. It turned out to be a good investment, since in its first year the Flamingo showed a $4-million profit, skim not included. Although Greenbaum did a brilliant job as the Flamingo's manager, his own alcohol and gambling addictions would ultimately produce tragic results. In the meantime, Greenbaum was proclaimed the first mayor of Paradise Valley – or the Strip.

Typically for gangland rubouts, Siegel's murder, the first ever of a Commission board member, was never solved, but "solutions" to the

Siegel killing were as numerous as his enemies. Some have claimed to *know* that Lansky or Luciano or Accardo or local Las Vegans ordered the hit. Lansky, for his part, strongly denied any sanction of his lifelong friend's murder. Shortly before his own death in 1983, Lansky told writer Uri Dan, "If it was in my power to see Benny alive, he would live as long as Methuselah." One piece of evidence, long buried in the files of the Chicago Crime Commission, seems to tilt the possibilities in favor of the Outfit, which was seething over Bugsy's theft of its lucrative wire. The artifact is a letter originally mailed to Beverly Hills police chief Clinton H. Anderson from Chicago three weeks after Siegel's slaying. The unsigned letter read:

Dear Chief,
Here is the real inside on the Bugsy killing. One week before he was killed, Murray Humphries [*sic*], a Capone gangster, and Ralph O'Hare [*sic*], one of the mob's front men, were at the Beverly Wilshire Hotel under phoney names. The story is that Bugsy owned the Golden Nugget News Service in Las Vegas. He owed the Trans-America Wire Service $25,000. O'Hare was the head of that outfit which the Capone gang owned. It seems there was quite an argument in Humphries room when Bugsy stalled about the 25 G's. Humphries told him to pay O'Hare the dough or he would have a lot of bad luck.

The "Ralph O'Hare" mentioned in the missive was actually Ralph J. O'Hara, the kingpin appointed by the Outfit to run the day-to-day affairs of its wire service. Police Chief Anderson also learned that Bugsy's Baby, Virginia Hill, had been ordered by the Outfit back to Chicago on June 10, ten days before Siegel's murder. From there she traveled to Europe, where some mistakenly believed she begged Lucky Luciano to intercede on her lover's behalf. In fact, according to both the FBI and John DeCarlo, Hill went to Europe to recuperate from her recent savage beating by Siegel and possibly undergo plastic surgery. In the days after the Siegel killing, Chief Anderson gave a series of press statements in which he hypothesized about the ultimate authors of the murder: "There was money – a lot of money – behind this killing. It wasn't just a cheap gambling murder, you know. I do not believe that Siegel was wiped out because of anything which occurred in Las Vegas . . . a Chicago racketeer probably engineered the killing . . . Benjamin Siegel was killed because he demanded hush money from the Chicago mob . . . probably the Fischetti brothers, Charles, Rocco, and Joe."

Not only was the planning of the murder unresolved, so too was the identity of the actual shooter. Recent interviews suggest that the contract for the hit, whatever its origin, was accepted by a California entity. John Carter (pseudonym), a Chicago investigator who prefers to remain anonymous, claims that he was told details of the shooting by Bobby Garcia, the skipper of Tony Cornero's luxury gambling ship, *The Rex*. Cornero had partnered with Siegel in the *Rex* operation, and for years Siegel had refused to cut Jack Dragna, Johnny Rosselli, and the Outfit in on the action, even after Dragna had help set up Siegel when he'd arrived out West. "Bobby Garcia told me the contract went out to an Italian immigrant from San Diego who wanted to get staked in the olive-oil import business," says Carter, who himself had personal relationships with Outfit members dating back to the 1930s. "The shooter had become an American citizen by joining the army during World War II. He used his army carbine to hit Bugsy." Carter claims that he has forgotten the name of the shooter, who he said drove up to Beverly Hills from San Diego in a little pickup truck and waited in the bushes for Bugsy.

In the immediate aftermath of the Bugsy episode, the Chicago–New York Commission began investing in other Sin City casinos, such as the New Frontier (formerly the Last Frontier), then the Thunderbird (owned by Meyer Lansky), and the Desert Inn (Moe Dalitz of Cleveland). By 1952, with newly empowered local crime commissions placing gangsters in many major cities under the microscope, the hoodlum exodus to Nevada increased dramatically. The "Kefauver refugees" from around the country made the trek into the Nevada desert, anxious to shed their past like some desert reptile sheds its skin. Soon, more gang-controlled facilities such as the Sands (opened in 1952 by numerous Commission members, the Outfit, and Frank Sinatra) and the Sahara (Al Winter of Portland) opened for business. In some cases, the hotels were owned, or fronted, by an upperworld consortium, while the hoods managed the all-important casinos. "The hotels and the lounges were just window dressing," said one Outfit member. "All that mattered were the casinos."

During this period, Chicago's interests, as coordinated by Curly Humphreys, were limited to minor investments in a number of the casinos. But with the Outfit pushing to go increasingly legit after Kefauver, Joe Accardo and associates decided it was time to own some Las Vegas properties outright. Accardo therefore packed his bags in early 1953, bent on checking out the desert opportunities for himself.

14.

The Frenzied Fifties

Surveillance records maintained by both federal and local authorities reflect that Joe Accardo set out for Las Vegas by way of Los Angeles on January 15, 1953. Accardo's itinerary included a brief stopover in L.A. to confer with Johnny Rosselli before traveling on to Sin City. Accompanying Accardo was his personal physician, Dr. Eugene Chesrow, whom Joe had maneuvered into the top post at Oak Forest Hospital, and fast-rising underboss Mooney Giancana.[1] The foray also represented something of a school field trip for Giancana, who was being groomed by Accardo to take over the day-to-day running of the Outfit. In addition to the constant harpings of Clarice for Joe to retire, the IRS was making rumblings that it was going to do to Accardo what it had done to Capone twenty-four years earlier. Joe wisely decided to concentrate on his tax case, with Curly as adviser, while Mooney Giancana fronted the organization, much as Nitti had done after Capone's imprisonment. Although key decisions would still be authorized by the old guard of Accardo, Humphreys, and Ricca, for public consumption Mooney was now the boss. With his elevation came the ascendancies of his crew, many of whom were buddies from the old 42 Gang: Sam Battaglia, Felix Alderisio, Marshall Caifano, Jackie Cerone, and Butch Blasi among them.

At the time of the Chicago trio's westward journey, the L.A. Police

---

1. Chesrow's elevation was a typical Outfit move. The Oak Forest Hospital was directly across the street (159th and South Cicero) from a building referred to by the gang as The Wheel. This facility was a gambling joint and a clearinghouse for prostitutes recently arrived from various Midwestern states. The girls would stay at the Wheel for a week while going through a battery of medical checkups before being dispatched to Windy City brothels for their three-month "tour." This rotation, or wheeling, was overseen by none other than the good doctor Chesrow.

Department (LAPD) was focused on discouraging any more out-of-town hoods from setting up shop in the City of Angels, as Accardo (ticketed under the name S. Mann) was soon to discover. With the country's most aggressive intelligence unit on guard at the city's key points of entry, the LAPD gained a reputation for spotting gangsters as they alighted from trains, planes, and buses, mugging them and then tossing them back aboard for a painful return trip home.

After being met at LAX airport by two Outfit members on assignment in L.A., the group proceeded to Perino's Restaurant in Beverly Hills, scrutinized all the while by plainclothes LAPD officers from the "airport squad," who had ID'd them on arrival. Before the group had time to digest their meal, the cops swooped down. Accardo and friends gave the officers their true names after the police had frisked them and discovered the three travelers carried over $12,000 in cash, which may have represented the gang's newest Vegas investment fund. However, before the trio could transport the cash to Nevada, they were sent back to Chicago by the LAPD's front guard, the Organized Crime Intelligence Unit, or OCID.

For the next two years, the Outfit maintained a low profile in Las Vegas, awaiting the perfect opening to make their big move. But the gang was never content to ignore new opportunities while waiting for another to coalesce. According to a long-withheld 224-page report by Virgil Peterson, "The Jukebox Report of 1954," Curly Humphreys devised a scheme wherein the Outfit would "take over ASCAP." The American Society of Composers, Authors, and Publishers (ASCAP) was formed in 1914 by songwriter Victor Herbert as a nonprofit clearing house for coordinating the collection of song-performance royalties as a service to composers. In 1954, ASCAP was pushing to obtain royalty payments from the nation's jukeboxes, many of which were controlled by the Outfit. Humphreys saw this as an opportunity for his gang to complete its vise grip on the entertainment industry: They already controlled the jukes, which were manipulated into creating Top Ten hits for their stable of performers, who in turn were booked by Jules Stein's Outfit-friendly MCA into their clubs in Las Vegas and elsewhere, and finally, the performers' record companies were often run by the Outfit, and when not, the gang simply flooded the market with their own counterfeit versions.

Now Humphreys saw still one more way to squeeze profit from the operation by obtaining either an interest in ASCAP or negotiating a kickback deal, wherein the gang would receive a cut of the composers' royalties for the privilege of allowing their material to be placed in the Outfit's jukes. At the time, ASCAP was realizing approximately $18 million per year in payments. According to Peterson's sources, ASCAP president Stanley Adams and the company attorney, Herman Finklestein, came to Chicago in February 1954 to negotiate with the manager of Jake Guzik's Century Music Company, Daniel Palaggi. At the time, Century was believed to control more than 100,000 of the nation's 575,000 jukeboxes. ASCAP initially proposed that Century contribute one dollar per juke per year into the fund. During the two days of meetings at the Palmer House, Century Music (aka the Outfit) agreed to the payout, but only if ASCAP would kick back 30 percent of the collected royalties to Chicago's Jukebox Operators Association, controlled, of course, by the Outfit. The deal would cost the Outfit $100,000 per year, but the 30 percent cut of ASCAP's $18 million in yearly royalties came to $5.4 million, a $5.3-million profit per year for two days' work at the Palmer. Peterson's report noted, "It is understood that ASCAP is inclined to accept the proposed deal." No further details are known of the duration of the alleged relationship.

During this period, the Outfit also worked to solidify affairs on the home front. One such endeavor entailed throwing their considerable political clout behind a Democratic machine politician's bid for mayor of Chicago. Having backed his career for twenty-odd years, the Outfit brought out the votes in its wards to help ensure the February 1955 election of Richard J. Daley.

Boss Daley

Joe Accardo's gang toiled so diligently on Daley's behalf because they knew him and felt certain he would look the other way while they conducted their business. Their prognostications proved accurate, as Daley neither persecuted nor elevated the Outfit bosses during his long tenure at the mayoral helm. He just seemed to ignore them. Richard "Boss" Daley's laissez-faire attitude toward the Outfit came as no surprise to the Chicago electorate. Savvy locals remembered that the Boss' early patrons were machine pols such as Big Joe McDonough, widely believed to have been in league with the Outfit's predecessor, the Torrio-Capone Syndicate. Daley was also the protégé of Eleventh Ward committeeman Hugh "Babe" Connelly, likewise known to have been the recipient of Outfit payoffs. When Daley assumed Connelly's post in 1947, it was believed that the gang had merely decided it was time for a change. As Alderman Edward Burke told writers Adam Cohen and Elizabeth Taylor, "They were sick of the old man [Connelly]. He was probably taking too big a slice of the gambling and whatever." Just prior to the 1955 mayoral election, the *Chicago Tribune* warned, "If Mr. Daley is elected, the political and social morals of the badlands are going, if not to dominate, then surely to have a powerful influence on its decisions." Despite the warning, Daley won the 1955 contest, due in no small part to a 13,275-to-1,961 plurality in the Outfit-controlled First Ward.

The paper was proven correct when Mayor Daley quickly made three executive decisions clearly favorable to Accardo and Co. First, he replaced the powerfully antimob head of the important, contract-granting Civil Service Commission, Stephen E. Hurley, with William A. Lee, the head of the Humphreys-infiltrated Bakery Drivers' Union. Chicago news analyst Len O'Connor said that the appointment was "patently a political payoff." Second, according to the FBI, when Humphreys ordered the gang's First Ward alderman, John D'Arco, to arrange for the Outfit's man to be appointed that precinct's police captain by Daley, D'Arco and Daley delivered. "D'Arco then contacted Mayor Daley," the report stated, "and advised him that he wanted this captain to command his district . . . The appointment was then announced by [Police] Commissioner [Timothy] O'Connor." Third, in 1956, Daley disbanded the city's intelligence unit known as Scotland Yard. This elite wing of the police department had been compiling thousands of dossiers on Chicago's hoodlums, the result of years of painstaking surveillance. According to the FBI, the unit was disbanded when Daley learned that they had bugged a bookmaker in the gang's Morrison Hotel hangout, where Curly Humphreys had coincidentally lived for a time, and where Daley had had his campaign headquarters. Daley had also been informed that during the campaign, Scotland Yard had bugged Daley's Morrison offices, supposedly under the orders of his incumbent opponent, Mayor Martin Kennelly. After the Yard's offices were padlocked, the Chicago Crime Commission lamented, "The police department is back where it was ten years ago as far as hoodlums are concerned." That year's annual Accardo Fourth of July cookout was thus especially festive, as noted in the July 16, 1956, issue of *Time* magazine: "Chicago hoodlums and their pals celebrated around a champagne fountain at the plush River Forest home of Mobster [Joe] Accardo . . . The Accardo soirée, an annual affair, had a different spirit this year. Where once his guests had slipped their black limousines into a hidden parking lot on the Accardo property, they now made an open show of their attendance, and the Big Boss' gardens rang fresh with ominous joy."

During the early years of Daley's two-decade reign, "Da Mare" used a number of trusted friends as liaisons to the Outfit. As noted again by the FBI, one of these conduits was a childhood friend from the Eleventh Ward named Thomas Munizzo. Daley's FBI file, obtained by Cohen and Taylor, stated: "Munizzo reportedly collected vast sums of money from the hoodlum element for the Daley mayoralty campaign . . . [Munizzo] was considered the contact man . . . between the hoodlums and the mayor's office for favors . . . with respect to gambling or the crime Syndicate." The Bureau further noted that Daley also utilized his former law partner, William Lynch, as a "go-between" for the Outfit and City Hall.

When Daley appeared at the Outfit-controlled First Ward Democratic Headquarters, he actually boasted about his record of giving official jobs and civil contracts to Outfit associates. "I've been criticized for doing this," Daley told the overflowing crowd, "but I'll make no apologies. I'll always stand alongside the man with a criminal record if I think he deserves another chance." Unlike the cocaine-pushing gangs that would succeed the Outfit, the first wave of immigrant hoods were anxious to legitimize their lives, and Daley decided to give them a chance to do it. Predictably, the feeling was mutual. Speaking on behalf of the Outfit, Curly Humphreys was overheard years later on hidden FBI bugs telling Johnny D'Arco, "This mayor has been good to us." To which D'Arco replied, "And we've been good to him. One hand washes the other."

It would be easy to mistake Daley's tolerance of the Outfit for simple corruption. However, the more accurate assessment appears to be that Daley understood better than most that the sooner the hoods were promoted up the social ladder, the sooner they would disappear into the landscape much the same way as the Founding Fathers who institutionalized the enslavement from the African subcontinent, or the westward explorers who orchestrated the demise of more than six million Native Americans, or the aging robber barons who defrauded untold millions of their life savings. Why, Daley may have wondered, should Chicago's greedy frontiersmen be treated any different from their predecessors? Mayor Daley seemed to know innately what Kefauver had failed to grasp, and what Professor David Bell of Columbia University had labeled "the process of ethnic succession": The violence associated with the process was, at least in the case of organized crime, overwhelmingly intramural, and when it spilled over, it seemed to dissipate once the gang obtained what it believed was its rightful share of the American Dream. As Daley once responded to a question about his indulgence of the Outfit, "Well, it's there, and you know you can't get rid of it, so you have to live with it."

The Riviera

With another adherent ensconced in Chicago's mayoral office, the Outfit turned its attention back to the Silver State. As Daley was solidifying his power in 1955, the gang made its first big move in Las Vegas when Joe Accardo and the Outfit secretly financed the $10-million Riviera Hotel, with a group of Miami investors as fronts. The hotel's silent investors also included Meyer Lansky. In an effort to guarantee the casino's success, Accardo decided to turn to an old friend with a proven track record, Gus Greenbaum.

Greenbaum, in failing health, had recently stepped down from the ownership of the Flamingo, taking with him the casino's ledgers, which held the identities of the Flamingo's Gold Club high rollers. After burying the valuable dockets in the Nevada desert, Greenbaum retired in Arizona. In Phoenix, Gus became pals with the state's junior senator, who led a shadow life cavorting with underworld characters. Known on the Las Vegas Strip as a "swinger," Senator Barry Goldwater (né Goldwasser) had been a frequent visitor to Greenbaum's Flamingo. Supposedly, a Greenbaum aide helped ghostwrite one of Goldwater's speeches.

Greenbaum had scant time to settle into his new life before Accardo and Jake Guzik visited him in Phoenix and ordered him out of retirement. Greenbaum initially refused the edict, but a few nights after Accardo and Guzik took their leave, Greenbaum learned that his sister-in-law, Leone, had received a telephone threat. "'They' were going to teach Gus a lesson," she told her husband. In a few days, Leone was found dead smothered in her bed, and Gus Greenbaum packed for Vegas to manage the Riviera.

Most likely ordered by Accardo, Greenbaum drove back out into the desert, where he dug up and dusted off the ledgers containing the priceless list of Flamingo Gold Card members. With the Flamingo list as a foundation, Greenbaum's secretaries were soon busied with mailing out new memberships for the exclusive, well-comped, high rollers' club at the Riviera.

But the Riviera saga was far from over. In an incredible turn of events, Gus Greenbaum committed a cardinal offense when he chose another mutual friend of his and Goldwater's to be the entertainment director for the hotel. Often seen with Goldwater in the senator's private plane was a man with extensive knowledge of the entertainment industry, William "Al" Nelson. As one of Goldwater's first contributors when he ran for Congress (to the tune of $5,000), Nelson and his wife, Laurie, were among the senator's closest friends. Probably unbeknownst to the senator, Nelson had been in hiding from the Outfit for eleven years. Since he had stool-pigeoned the gang's hierarchy in the Hollywood extortion case, former pimp Willie Bioff had assumed his wife Laurie Nelson's maiden name. For unknown reasons, Bioff ended up in Phoenix, where he bought a small farm and hooked up with Goldwater and Greenbaum, who, without informing his Outfit superiors, hired Bioff-Nelson as the Riviera's entertainment director.

Sometime that year, one of the Outfit's most notorious hit men, Marshall Caifano, aka John Marshall, was staying at the Riviera when he spotted and ID'd the accursed Willie Bioff. Caifano promptly reported back to Accardo, who confronted the addiction-addled Greenbaum. With a straight face, Greenbaum explained that he had brought in Bioff for the express purpose of keeping down the entertainers' salaries – something with which Bioff was much experienced. But Accardo would have none of it. In short time, Greenbaum was paid a visit by Caifano, who recited Accardo's decree: "Get rid of that fink or else." When Willie's dismissal was not forthcoming, someone decided it was time for the former whore-beater to pay the price for selling out his fellows. On November 4, 1955, Willie "Al Nelson" Bioff left the front door of his Phoenix home and got behind the wheel of his pickup truck parked in the family driveway. Police later determined that a dynamite bomb had exploded when Willie turned the ignition, sending parts of Willie and his truck all over his Phoenix neighborhood. The incident illustrated something Johnny Rosselli said to a fellow hood: "Us fucking Italians ain't human. We remember things too long, hold these grudges inside of us until they poison our minds."

Bioff's murder stunned Gus Greenbaum, whose personal demons now grew to include heroin addiction. Greenbaum's "horse" problem only exacerbated his health woes, poor gambling abilities, and his growing infatuation with prostitutes. And his decline would only be tolerated for so long by his Chicago taskmasters.

The Stardust

The Riviera would not be the Outfit's only Las Vegas expansion point in 1955. Johnny Rosselli's old bootlegging pal Tony Cornero would (unintentionally) provide the gang another lucrative opportunity in the casino game. In Los Angeles, Cornero had apparently been stewing over the Sin City successes of gangs from Chicago, New York, Cleveland, and elsewhere. After all, the hotel-casino concept had been Cornero's in the first place with the Meadows, and had it not been for the depressed economy of the 1930s, Tony Cornero would now be king of the Vegas Strip. After the Meadows closed, Cornero had returned to Los Angeles, where he made a fortune with his offshore gambling ships, the flagship being the 350-crew *Rex*. When the boom returned to Las Vegas, Cornero took his fortune there and announced that he was finally going to build his dream hotel in the heart of the Strip, the 1,032-room Stardust.

Cornero's concept for the Stardust once again displayed his visionary genius. He rightly concluded that elegant joints like Moe Dalitz's Desert Inn had a finite clientele, whereas a casino designed for the low-roller masses would attract gamblers by the busload. Although the hotel's frontage would boast the Strip's largest (216 feet long) and most garish lighted sign (7,100 feet of neon tubing and more than 11,000 bulbs), the hotel itself would be little more than a warehouse, where guests could stay for a mere five dollars per night. The Stardust's all-you-can-eat buffets and practically free lodging would become a Sin City staple.

A variety of factors caused Cornero's Stardust dream to go bust. Complicating the typical Las Vegas cost overruns was Cornero's own gambling addiction, which quickly depleted his bank account. Just weeks before the scheduled August 1955 opening of the hotel, Cornero learned he was out of money, unable to pay staff or purchase furnishings and gambling instruments. On July 31, Cornero paid a morning visit to Moe Dalitz's Desert Inn, where it is believed Cornero hoped Dalitz would make him an emergency loan. According to one telling, Dalitz met with Cornero for several hours; however, Dalitz ultimately declined to get involved. On his way out of the Desert Inn, Cornero could not fight the temptation to hit the craps tables, where he went quickly into the hole for $10,000. When Dalitz's crew not only refused to extend his marker, but had the audacity to charge him for his drinks (a monumental affront in the pits), Cornero went ballistic. Within minutes, sixty-year-old Tony Cornero was clutching his chest with one hand even as he clutched the dice with the other. He was dead of a heart attack, with less than $800 to show for the estimated $25 million he had made in his lifetime.

The story is then picked up by the Outfit's traveling emissary, Johnny Rosselli, who promptly reported the new vacancy back to his Chicago bosses. According to the files of the LAPD's intelligence unit, which had been tailing Rosselli for years, "Mr. Smooth" had been making the trek to Sin City regularly, cutting deals, and brokering complex intergang partnerships. George Bland, a retired Las Vegas-based FBI man, disclosed that one of the Bureau's illegally placed bugs revealed that one major casino had the skim divided twelve different ways. One partner later called Johnny "the Henry Kissinger of the mob," and Rosselli's business card from the period said it all, and simply: "Johnny Rosselli, Strategist." Rosselli's biographers described his role in Las Vegas as "nebulous, but crucial . . . He maintained open channels to all the different out-of-town factions, as well as to the California-based operators downtown, and served as a conduit to political fixers like Bill Graham in Reno, and Artie Samish, known in California political circles as 'the Governor of the Legislature.'" Rosselli was soon living full-time in Vegas, dividing his time between his suites at Dalitz's Desert Inn and the Outfit's Riviera. In their 1963 book, *The Green Felt Jungle,* authors Reid and Demaris described a typical Rosselli day:

Rosselli spends his leisure hours (that is, all the waking hours of his day) at the Desert Inn Country Club. He has breakfast there in the morning, seated at a table overlooking the eighteenth green. Between golf rounds, meals, steam baths, shaves and trims, Twisting, romancing, and drinking, there is time for private little conferences at his favorite table with people seeking his counsel or friendship. It may be a newsman, a local politician, a casino owner, a prostitute, a famous entertainer, a deputy sheriff, a U.S. Senator, or the Governor of Nevada.

As Johnny remarked to a fellow hood, "I'm now the man in Vegas."

Armed with the news of Cornero's cardiac, Rosselli flew to Chicago, where he met with Accardo, Humphreys, and Guzik at Meo's Restaurant. It was decided that the gang would finish construction and assume the debt of the Stardust in a partnership with Cleveland's contribution to Vegas, Moe Dalitz. However, the Outfit would run the operation. When the time came to name a front for the operation, Chicago brought in an old friend, a gifted con man who owed Humphreys and Accardo a huge favor: Jake "the Barber" Factor. Five years later, Johnny Rosselli described the arrangement to longtime friend, and L.A. mafioso, Jimmy Fratianno: "Jake Factor, an old friend of Capone . . . shit, I used to see him when he came to the Lexington to see Al . . . took over and finished building the place. So I went to Sam [Giancana] and told him we could move into this joint. Listen, Jake owed Chicago a big one. Moe Dalitz wanted in on it and so it's a fifty-fifty deal."

Over the next two years, Factor and the Outfit poured money into the Stardust operation, while Jake continually lobbied the newly formed Gaming Control Board for a casino license, where he was consistently rebuffed. Before the Stardust could open for business, the Outfit had to assign someone who could obtain a casino license and, per custom, simultaneously watch over Jake Factor. Joe Accardo and his new front, Mooney Giancana, once again made the seventeen-hundred-mile journey to Las Vegas to make the appointment. Taking Factor aside, Joe whispered the name John Drew in his ear. As a former Capone crew member, Drew had already obtained, thanks to a few greased palms, a license to operate the Outfit's Bank Club in Reno, where he watched over front man Bill Graham. In subsequent years, Chicago FBI agent Bill Roemer witnessed Drew having a business dinner at the St. Hubert's Grill with his sponsor, Curly Humphreys. Johnny Rosselli later named other Stardust "supervisors" brought in for good measure: "[Sam Giancana] sent Al Sachs and Bobby Stella to help [Drew]. Dalitz's got Yale Cohen to watch his end. But Sam's got a sleeper in there, Phil Ponti, a made guy from Chicago. A real sharp operator."

When the Stardust finally opened for business on July 2, 1958, it proved well worth the effort. After the grand opening, attended by guests of honor then senator and future president Lyndon Baines Johnson and his trusty sidekick Bobby Baker, the money began arriving in Chicago almost faster than it could be counted. "They're skimming the shit out of that joint," Rosselli later told Fratianno. "You have no idea how much cash goes through that counting room every day. You, your family, your uncles and cousins, all your relatives could live the rest of their lives in luxury with just what they pull out of there in a month. Jimmy, I've never seen so much money." Coming from a man who had lived though the phenomenal profits of the bootlegging era, this speaks volumes about the lure of Las Vegas. Carl Thomas, an expert on the skim, estimated that the Stardust was contributing $400,000 per month to the Outfit's coffers. Rosselli would rightfully brag for years, "I got the Stardust for Chicago," and for his role in setting up this windfall for the Outfit, Johnny was also well compensated. "I'm pulling fifteen, twenty grand under the table every month," Rosselli said.

On the Home Front

Back in Chicago, the year 1956 brought with it the regular irksome skirmishes with city officials not on the gang's payroll. At the time, many Chicago police were playing a dangerous game, harassing Outfit members to increase their bargaining power with the hoods; i.e., the gang must pay more to relieve the pressure. According to a close friend, the ailing Jake Guzik was tormented more than most. "Those fucking cops used to run him up and down ten flights of stairs, hoping he'd have a heart attack," the friend said. "They wouldn't stop until he put them on his payroll." On January 13, while the police were attempting to probe gambling at the gang's Owl Club in Calumet City, Humphreys and Guzik were arrested on the Near North Side. The detention was meant as another vexation, and the duo were quickly released. Six days later, both men were again brought downtown, and this time they were charged with disorderly conduct, another harassment that was rarely upheld. When the case was brought before Judge John Pope, the police were chastened instead. "I've seen too many of these cases where the police file DC charges against persons they just want to question," Pope scolded. "You filed false charges and you are trifling with the court." Pope then advised that Curly and Jake had the right to sue the city for false arrest. Of course Curly Humphreys' credo dictated that discretion was the better part of valor, but Guzik promptly enlisted the American Civil Liberties Union, which filed a $50,000 "infringement of civil liberties" suit against the city. But before the case could be decided, five decades of playing cat and mouse with the cops took its toll on the sixty-nine-year-old Guzik.

When heart failure claimed the Outfit's strongest link to Al Capone on February 21, 1956, it happened fittingly at the very spot where Guzik had disbursed official bribery uninterrupted since the 1920s – his table at St. Hubert's Olde English Grill on Federal Street. Also appropriately, with Guzik at the time was the man who had inherited his role as the Outfit's political shaman, Curly Humphreys, who had by now secured the hidden ownership of the St. Hubert's. Humphreys' FBI case officer described what happened next: "Not wanting the body to be found in a mob hangout, Murray Humphreys, who had been with him, had his men carry Guzik's body to his home in the South Shore neighborhood of Chicago's South Side, where the amazed widow was instructed to advise police that he had died there."

The Bureau noted that Humphreys assumed his self-appointed role as the Outfit's benefactor in times of grief or transition. From this point on, according to the FBI, Humphreys sent $200 "every Christmas to Mrs. Guzik, the widow of his former partner in organized crime . . . [he] instructed [Bartenders' Union agent Carl] Hildebrand to mail the cashier's check to Mrs. Guzik without a return address so that she won't know it is from Humphreys."

Bobby's Crusade

By the end of 1956, the nation's lawmakers were swamped with reports that Teamster officials were looting the members' pension fund and forging alliances with the underworld. In December, the Senate Select Committee on Improper Activities in the Labor or Management Field was established to investigate the contentions. Chaired by a devout Baptist Democrat from Arkansas, Senator John J. McClellan, the investigation would eclipse even the Kefauver probe in its scope, lasting over two and one-half years and hearing fifteen hundred witnesses whose recollections (or lack thereof) were laid out over twenty thousand pages of testimony. The WASP chairman made it clear early on that his investigation would be a continuation of the xenophobic battles of the pre-Volstead era. As he viewed in self-righteous disgust the procession of twentieth-century immigrants, most charged with committing crimes that paled in comparison to those of his own forebears, McClellan declared, "We should rid the country of characters who come here from other lands and take advantage of the great freedom and opportunity our country affords, who come here to exploit these advantages with criminal activities. They do not belong in our land, and they ought to be sent somewhere else. In my book, they are human parasites on society, and they violate every law of decency and humanity."

The many inherent ironies of an upperworld investigation of the underworld surfaced almost immediately when the "McClellan Committee" chose as its chief counsel Robert F. Kennedy, the seventh child of Boston millionaire, and former Roosevelt-administration diplomat, Joseph P. Kennedy. Over the years, countless upperworld bosses and ordinary witnesses have attested to Joseph Kennedy's working in consort with the underworld to establish his fortune. Bobby Kennedy quickly commandeered the probe, on which his brother Jack served as a Senate member, with a style alternately described as either forceful or bellicose. When the thirty-one-year-old Kennedy traveled back to Massachusetts for Christmas in 1956, he excitedly announced the full-blown inquiry to his father. Papa Joe, fully cognizant of the extent of the upperworld-underworld alliance that had helped build his dynasty, was not impressed.

According to Bobby's sister Jean Kennedy Smith, the argument that ensued at Hyannis Port that Christmas was bitter, "the worst one we ever witnessed." Kennedy adviser Arthur Schlesinger, Jr. described the row as "unprecedentedly furious." The politically savvy father warned that such an upheaval would turn labor against Jack in his presidential quest. Longtime Kennedy confidant Lem Billings recalled, "The old man saw this as dangerous . . . He thought Bobby was naïve." Bobby, however, saw things differently, believing such a crusade would actually enhance the family's image. Chicago investigator Jack Clarke, who headed Mayor Daley's investigative unit and occasionally counseled Bobby Kennedy, also detected Bobby's personal agenda. "If Bobby really wanted to investigate organized crime, he never had to leave Boston," Clarke recently said. "The McClellan thing was a show. Bobby thought it was just good politics." Clarke's view is supported by Bobby's friend, anticrime journalist Clark Mollenhoff, the Washington editor of the *Des Moines Register*. Mollenhoff, who had been prodding Bobby Kennedy for months to spearhead such an investigation, met with little success until he called Bobby and introduced his brother Jack's presidential aspirations into the debate. "Kefauver did his investigations five years ago and it got him enough clout to beat your brother's butt [at the 1956 Democratic National Convention]." Suddenly, Bobby's interest was piqued. "Well, why don't you come down and we'll talk about it."

Eventually, Bobby began cajoling McClellan about forming the committee, but Joe Kennedy was not yet convinced his son's probe could not be short-circuited. Joe enlisted Bobby's mentor, Supreme Court justice William O. Douglas, to try to talk some sense into the young firebrand. But Douglas' intervention also proved futile, as Douglas later told his wife about Bobby's intransigence, "He feels this is too great an opportunity."

When the committee went out of business, it had established evidence that led to the convictions of ninety-six of its criminal witnesses. And although it steered clear of upperworld liaisons, it occasionally stumbled inadvertently into embarrassing disclosures, such as that several of the targeted unions leased their New York offices from none other than Bobby's father. One of Kennedy's key targets, Teamsters VP Jimmy Hoffa, said years later, "You take any industry and look at the problems they ran into while they were building it up – how they did it, who they associated with, how they cut corners. The best example is Kennedy's old man . . . To hear Kennedy when he was grandstanding in front of the McClellan Committee, you might have thought I was making as much out of the pension fund as the Kennedys made out of selling whiskey."

The Tropicana

While the McClellan Committee did battle with Teamster officials in Washington, the Outfit remained unfettered in its Las Vegas expansion. The success of the Stardust had inspired Rosselli and the Outfit to gear up for still more acquisitions. In a feat of ambassadorial legerdemain that rivaled the latter-day shuttle-diplomacy efforts of President Jimmy Carter, Rosselli brokered a complex partnership in the $50-million Tropicana, designed to be the most luxurious facility on the Strip. The intricate ownership trust of the Tropicana, which opened for business on April 3, 1957, included the Outfit, Frank Costello of New York, Meyer Lansky of Miami, and Carlos Marcello and "Dandy" Phil Kastel of New Orleans. Another curious partner in the deal was Irish tenor Morton Downey, the best friend and business partner of Kennedy family patriarch Joseph P. Kennedy. In 1997, Morton Downey, Jr. said that the Tropicana investment, as well as numerous others made by his father, were conceivably hidden investments of Joe Kennedy's, with Downey acting as the front. "Joe was my dad's dearest friend," Downey, Jr. said. "My father owned ten percent of the Tropicana. I wouldn't be at all surprised if he was fronting it for Joe. That's how they worked. My father often had someone 'beard' for *him* also. I remember when he would jump up screaming at the dinner table when his name surfaced in the newspaper regarding some deal or other. 'They weren't supposed to find out about that!' he'd yell."

To oversee the Outfit's stake in the enterprise, Curly Humphreys sent a trusted associate named Lou Lederer from Chicago to run the casino, which would become the most profitable in Las Vegas. For appearances, the Tropicana operation was fronted by the same man who fronted for the Commission's interest in Miami Beach's Fontainebleau Hotel, Ben Jaffe. Despite this precaution, the hoods' hidden interest in the Tropicana became known when Frank Costello was shot above his right ear by a rival New York gangster on May 2, 1957. Although the wound proved superficial, its unintended ramifications were anything but. While Costello was in the hospital recuperating, detectives found an incriminating handwritten note in his pocket. Written in the hand of Humphreys' guy Lou Lederer, the explosive scrap of paper notated the skim from the Tropicana:

Gross casino wins as of 4/27/57 $651,284
Casino wins less marker 434,695
Slot wins 62,844
Markers 153,745
Mike $150 a week, totaling $600; Jake $100 a week, totaling $400;
L.-$30,000; H.-$9,000

As a result of the serendipitous discovery, Costello was forced to divest his interest in the Tropicana. More important, the local Mormon-controlled banks began denying loans to questionable entrepreneurs, and the Mormon-controlled Gaming Control Board became even more stingy, and discriminatory, with its licensing approvals. Until this time, the gangster owners had financed much of their start-up costs with moneys supplied by the Mormon-owned Bank of Las Vegas. Although they certainly had more than enough disposable income to afford the costs, the hoods' decision to go with a more traditional method served a more important function by not calling the attention of the IRS to their immense hidden nest egg. Luckily for the Outfit, a new, well-endowed bank had just opened in Chicago, and it curiously seemed to prefer gangster clients.

The First National Bank of Accardo

If the Outfit had to face a bump in the road in Vegas, it could not have come at a more fortuitous time than 1957. That year saw the realization of an Outfit Five-Year Plan that gave them "preferred borrower" status for low-interest loans from a new bank, otherwise known as the Central States Pension Fund of the Teamsters Union.

The key players in this unprecedented dispensation were an old Capone associate named Paul "Red" Dorfman, a Teamster up-and-comer from Detroit named James Riddle Hoffa, and the plan's architect, Curly Humphreys.

The FBI called Red Dorfman, titular head of a number of labor unions including the Humphreys-controlled Waste Handlers Union, one of the five or six men closest to Joe Accardo, while a Chicago Teamster described him as "a hood's hood."[2] Another Teamster said about Dorf-

2. For a couple months in the late 1930s, Dorfman's Scrap Iron Union had one temperamental slugger who would achieve infamy after he moved to Dallas in 1947. Known in Chicago as an emotional powder keg, Jacob Rubenstein, aka Jack Ruby, would avenge President Kennedy's November 22, 1963, assassination by whacking his killer, Lee Harvey Oswald, two days later.

man, "He was a small, thin, red-haired guy who'd walk in and throw two bullets on a guy's desk and tell him, 'The next one goes in your fuckin' head.' " In the late forties, Hoffa's ambition to ascend the Teamster power structure was in overdrive. He knew that to achieve his goals he would have to gain the allegiance of the all-powerful Outfit, which by now had a vise grip not only on Chicago's influential local Teamsters, but on the locals of numerous cities west of Chicago, which were also taking orders from Humphreys.

Through a union-busting Michigan steel hauler named Santo Perrone, Hoffa met Humphreys' guy Red Dorfman, who then introduced Hoffa to Accardo, Humphreys, Ricca, and the rest. Hoffa also became close friends with Joseph Glimco (né Guiseppe Glielmi), appointed by Curly in 1944 to run the fifteen powerful Teamster taxicab locals of Chicago. According to the FBI, Red Dorfman suggested to Humphreys that if the Outfit's Teamster locals, which Curly controlled, backed Hoffa's advancement, Hoffa would return the favor by opening up the Teamsters' pension fund vaults to the Outfit and their friends. At the 1952 Teamster convention, where Hoffa was seen schmoozing Joey Glimco and other hoods, the underworld decided to bequeath Hoffa the union's vice presidency, a prelude to his coronation five years later. However, all knew that Hoffa would be the real power behind the "front" president, Dave Beck. According to Rosselli's friend L.A. mobster Jimmy Fratianno, Beck agreed to retire after one five-year term, while Hoffa worked behind the scenes to broaden his own power base, simultaneously proving to his underworld sponsors that he was capable of ruling.

The fine points of the deal dictated that Hoffa would appoint Red's son, Allen, a college phys-ed teacher, to administer the pension fund loans. Technically, a Teamster fund board of trustees, with Allen as a "consultant," had to authorize the loans, but in actual practice, Allen with his intimidating underworld sponsors, called the shots on loan approvals. From that point on, the hard-earned dues of truckers, warehousemen, and taxi drivers from the twenty-two states that comprised the Central Fund would subsidize the Outfit's business ventures in Nevada and elsewhere. And for the next twenty-five years, Outfit-backed Allen Dorfman disbursed the assets of a fund that would be valued at $400 million by the midsixties. By 1961, the fund had lent over $91 million in low-interest (6 percent) loans. In all, some 63 percent of the fund's holdings were made available to borrowers.

For the first few years (until Hoffa assumed the Teamster presidency in

1957), the Outfit kept its "withdrawals" low profile, mostly in the form of business funneled to Allen Dorfman's newly constituted Chicago branch of the Union Casualty insurance company. During those years, father and son Dorfman were estimated to have received over $3 million in commissions. An emergency loan-of-sorts involved the "purchase" of Paul Ricca's Indiana farm by his new friend Jimmy Hoffa's Detroit Teamster locals, this despite labor-union ownership of property being illegal in Long Beach. Hoffa later said that the property was to be converted into a school for Teamster business agents. At the time, Ricca was facing an IRS deadline for payment of tax penalties, so the Teamsters paid Ricca $150,000 for the spread, which was valued at only $85,000. In addition, the Riccas were permitted to live in the house free of charge for over a year.

In 1957, the year of the bank crackdown in Vegas, the Teamsters were preparing to name a new international president to replace incumbent Dave Beck, who was facing federal tax and larceny charges, the result of McClellan Committee revelations. The Outfit's Five-Year Plan, arranged in 1952, would now achieve fruition, with Hoffa's being maneuvered into the Teamster presidency at the upcoming September convention to be held in Miami.

On August 28, 1957, one month before the Teamster convention, the OCID unit of the Los Angeles Police Department watched surreptitiously as the Teamsters Executive Board met with Jimmy Hoffa and three powerful residents of the Windy City at L.A.'s Townhouse Hilton Hotel. An LAPD memo in the files of the Chicago Crime Commission gives further details of what the OCID witnessed:

> According to information given to the LAPD, three men are with Hoffa for the purpose of aiding his cause in becoming President of the Teamsters Union. It is claimed that the men in question are: Murray Humphreys, Marshall Caifano, [and Humphreys aide] Ralph Pierce – all of whom are well-known Chicago hoodlums. It is stated that a member of the Executive Board is being taken before these men singly, and they are advising members of the Executive Board in no uncertain terms that Hoffa is to be the next President of the Teamsters Union.

When the word came down to Dorfman, he dispatched his close friend Johnny Dio (Dioguardi) to New York to organize Teamster "paper locals," which had the sole purpose of assuring Hoffa's control of the

New York Joint Council of the Teamsters. According to one report, Curly Humphreys, who was known to frequent the Sea Isle Hotel in Florida, was on hand one month later at Miami Beach's luxurious Eden Roc Hotel to watch from the shadows as Hoffa accepted the Teamster presidency before seventeen hundred roaring delegates.

In the aftermath of Hoffa's election, Humphreys' personal friendships with Teamster officials only grew stronger. Jeanne Stacy Humphreys remembers that Curly was very close to John T. "Sandy" O'Brien, the international vice president of the Teamsters, whose wife, Marge, just happened to be the secretary of the Teamsters pension fund. According to the FBI, Humphreys and Congressman Libonati used their Teamster connection with the O'Briens to secure yearly Teamster donations for an underprivileged boys' camp in Colona, Wisconsin. Curly Humphreys also maintained a close personal relationship with Hoffa, who often vacationed at the Humphreys' Key Biscayne home. FBI bugs heard Curly tell Joey Glimco, "Hoffa was the best man I ever knew." According to Humphreys, whenever the Outfit told Hoffa to do something, "He just goes boom, boom, boom, he gets it done." Humphreys added, "One thing I always admired about the guy, they tried to fuck him, but he never took a bad attitude about it." On occasion, Humphreys even lent his legal expertise to Hoffa. "I worked on this case for him," Humphreys said, "and paid out a lot of money for him and never got it back." Despite the warming relationship with the new Teamster boss, the hoods would wait a suitable while before making withdrawals from their new bank. But once they commenced, they would be ravenous. In the meantime, key Chicago bosses had to tend to business at home.

On the Homefront II

Under Humphreys' tutelage, the Outfit was enjoying great business successes, but the period was especially trying for Humphreys' personal life. Weary of Curly's skirt chasing, and fully cognizant of the affair with Jeanne Stacy, Clemi Humphreys filed for divorce, after thirty-five years of marriage, in Norman, Oklahoma, on July 6, 1957. Her petition alleged that Curly had 'been guilty of gross neglect and incompatibility has existed . . . for more than three years by reason of which the parties have not lived together.' Within a year, Humphreys married Jeanne Stacy, lavishing on her a beautiful waterfront home in Key Biscayne, Florida. The FBI was never able to confirm the marriage to Stacy, although they combed official records in St. Louis, Chicago, Miami, and even Mexico

City. "That's because we got married in Georgia," Jeanne Humphreys recently said. "The justice of the peace almost fainted when Murray handed him two hundred dollars for a two-minute ceremony."

In Florida, neighbors knew Curly as Mr. Lewis Hart, a retired oilman from Texas. Jeanne Stacy has recalled the numerous Outfit confabs that took place at the Key Biscayne home, where Teamster president Jimmy Hoffa was also a frequent guest.[3]

The home, at 210 Harbor Drive, boasted stunning views across the bay to Miami Beach, where the Humphreys often luxuriated at the mob-friendly Fontainebleau Hotel, also the site of the wedding reception for Mooney Giancana's daughter Bonnie on July 4, 1959. The FBI noted that Humphreys may have made a simultaneous purchase of a country house and adjoining cattle farm at Round Lake, Illinois. According to his new wife, Curly maintained friendly relations with his ex, calling her regularly in Norman. "He had to," Jeanne Humphreys says. "Clemi had done all the gang's bookwork for so many years. Even though they were divorced, they were still in business together."

Humphreys' family distress did not end with his marital upheavals; his daughter, Llewella, provided her own drama. Although details are sketchy, it seems certain that, after high school, Llewella, a gifted pianist, went to Rome to pursue her music studies. In one interview she claimed to have performed three concerts with the Rome Symphony Orchestra,

---

3. Jeanne, a passionate animal lover, populated the new home with sundry wildlife such as mynah birds, parrots, dogs, and a squirrel monkey. 'What made it even more bizarre,' says Jeanne, "was that the mynah birds mocked the dogs and monkeys." The cacophony was a surreal counterpoint to the parade of gangsters who commandeered Jeanne's kitchen for hours on meeting days. On one occasion, Jeanne thanked her Cuban-born housemaid, Modesta, for putting up with the mayhem. "Gracias, mi amiga," Jeanne said. "Mi casa es su casa." Modesta shot back, "Mrs. Hart, no gracias. Su casa es un *loco* casa!"

Besides fishing in the Keys, the "Harts" of Key Biscayne dawdled about in their garden, a hobby that gave rise to a humorous exchange between Curly and Modesta, whose thick accent often made for laughable exchanges. Worried about her boss' health, Modesta once warned him about working too long in the hot garden, adding that if he did not rest, she would tell Mrs. Hart when she returned.

"Do you know what happens to stool pigeons?" Curly asked the housekeeper. Whereupon Modesta went into the kitchen and returned with a stool. "It's where it always is," Modesta scolded.

although this has not been verified. What is certain is that she began an illicit affair with the married Italian actor Rossano Brazzi. Upon returning to America, Llewella, who now called herself Luella Brady (an anglicization of Brazzi), gave birth in California on July 14, 1955, to Curly's only grandchild, George Llewellyn Brady, whom Luella claimed was Brazzi's progeny. Extant photos and love letters from Brazzi appear to confirm the parentage. Brazzi was in California at the time seeking to establish his career in America, and according to Luella, her father used his Hollywood contacts to ensure Brazzi's roles in such films as *Three Coins in the Fountain* (1954), *Summertime* (1955), and *South Pacific* (1958). Curly's new wife suggested in jest that Curly acknowledge George's "Italian genes," thereby qualifying him for membership in the Mafia. Curly, who was anxious to extricate himself from his way of life, found the remark neither wise nor funny.

By January 1958, Luella was experiencing a recurrence of mental instabilities that had plagued her on and off over the years. Curly had her committed to a Kansas City sanitarium, where she would remain for over three years. "Murray spent over thirty-six thousand dollars on her hospital bills," remembers Jeanne Humphreys.

Although Humphreys' heart disease was progressing, he kept up a hectic pace. In addition to having to squire his new young-enough-to-be-his-daughter wife, and caring for his actual daughter and fatherless grandson, Humphreys' legal counseling skills were in constant demand. Even as Humphreys told all within earshot that he was retired from the Outfit – and he may have wanted to be – he had to oversee the Teamster pension fund operations and strategize the Accardo tax situation. The IRS had given Accardo an ultimatum, stating that he could no longer claim vast amounts of "miscellaneous income" as he had since prohibition. According to information gathered by the Chicago Crime Commission, Curly's solution was unveiled at a meeting at the Armory Lounge in Forest Park, headquarters of the new boss, Mooney Giancana.

In attendance with Humphreys were Accardo, Sidney Korshak, Giancana aide Jackie Cerone, Eugene Bernstein (the tax consultant so pivotal in the Hollywood parole deal), and officials from the Fox Head Brewing Company. Humphreys owned twenty-two hundred shares of Fox Head, and he had decided to instruct the company's executives to place Accardo on their payroll to the tune of $65,000 per year. The maneuver only managed to buy time, as the IRS eventually indicted Accardo. During this time, Accardo, in a further effort to decrease the feds' attention on him, put the word out on the streets that Mooney Giancana was now the boss of the Outfit. In time, Joe's decision to make Giancana a Nitti-type flak-catcher would prove to be inspired.

One member of Accardo's legal team, who wishes to remain anonymous, recently recalled how the Outfit conducted a typical brainstorming session at his office. "Joe and Curly would show up late at night with three or four assistants, each of which carried bags of groceries," the attorney remembered. "For two hours they'd cook an Italian meal, which we had to eat before we conducted business. Everything revolved around food." Finally, around midnight, the group would commence work. On the eve of one of Accardo's most important court hearings, the hoods showed up unannounced at the attorney's office for an all-night, last-minute strategy session. After the mandatory cookfest, as they finally started to work, Joe noticed the attorney's secretary was on the verge of tears. Accardo cajoled the woman into an explanation for her sorrow. She told of her recent engagement, and her first meeting with her in-laws, which was to take place the next day. The girl was expected to prepare a meal for her fiancé and his parents, but had no skill in the kitchen. Seeing the gang feasting on an impeccable lasagna had brought her insecurities to the point of breakdown. Accardo told her, "Not to worry." He adjourned the all-important confab, and he and his assistants took off to scour the county for a market open at 1 A.M. – or to open one. When they returned an hour later, they spent the rest of the night preparing a four-course gourmet meal as a wedding gift to the distraught bride-to-be.

"The gang left about five A.M., with no work having been done," recalls the attorney. "We met at the courthouse at nine A.M. and faked it."

The "eat first" ritual reoccurs like a leitmotiv in the business world of the Outfit. Frequently overheard on hidden FBI microphones were good-natured sarcasms about one another's expanding waistlines. On some occasions, gang members discussed which prisons' cuisine was more fattening. Curly was often heard addressing his associates with "Hey, Fat Boy." The importance of food is clearly seen in the bosses' choice of bodyguards, many of whom had to double as cooks. Mooney Giancana was especially fortunate: His driver/bodyguard, Joe Pignatello, was a gourmet chef who eventually opened his own Italian restaurant in Las Vegas (Joe and his restaurant are still there at this writing).

Before Accardo's trial finally commenced in 1960, Humphreys obtained the list of prospective jurors, numbering more than one hundred, and had his boys run background checks on them. Curly found numerous ways to muscle the jury pool. "We have to work on the weakest jury guy and scare the shit out of him," Curly said unknowingly into hidden FBI mikes. When one on the jury list turned out to be a trucker, Humphreys knew exactly how to handle it. As recounted by his FBI case officer, Humphreys "immediately dispatched Frank 'Strongy' Ferraro to . . . call Jimmy Hoffa on the phone, find out whether this trucker was a member of the Teamsters, and if so, what local did he belong to and who could be contacted within the Teamsters to approach this possible juror to understand what a bummer of a case against Accardo this really was."

(Humphreys had things well in hand when the trial finally began in September 1960. However, the court had been tipped by the FBI, which had by this time inherited a bug previously placed in one of the Outfit's meeting places, and the judge reprised what Judge James Wilkerson had done in the Capone tax trial three decades earlier. On the first day of the trial, Judge Julius Hoffman switched juries. When Humphreys found out, he was livid, according to the FBI bugs. Agents listened in as Curly railed about all his hard work, using dozens of "made guys, all down the drain." When Accardo was convicted and sentenced to six years, the case was appealed, allowing Curly to try again, and when the appeal was heard in October 1962, the verdict was reversed, because, according to the FBI, Curly Humphreys had strong relationships with the appellate court judges. That court deemed that Accardo had received prejudicial pretrial publicity.)

Although Joe Accardo was afforded little respect from the federal boys, his prestige in the Windy City was at an all-time high. He had developed close friendships with numerous successful local businessmen, many of whose wives worked with Clarice Accardo on community issues and local charity drives. And though he exercised his power quietly, Accardo's long reach is retold in countless local anecdotes. One such example recalls the time in 1957 when Joe purchased a used car as a surprise high school graduation gift for his daughter Marie. Among Joe's friends at the time was John Marino, the manager of the Hendrickson Pontiac Dealership in Forest Park, the largest Pontiac franchise east of the Mississippi. As a regular customer, Joe was well-liked by the mechanics, who knew him as the dealership's biggest tipper. According to Dr. Jay Tischendorf, whose father, Jerry, was the shop supervisor at Hendrickson's, Joe brought Marie's gift in for a tune-up, accompanied by two "assistants."

"I need this done by three," Accardo said to Tischendorf. "My father almost fainted," recalls the younger Tischendorf. "At the time, there was a strike by the mechanics" union, and no work could be taken in.' Jerry Tischendorf started to say, "I'm sorry, Mr. Accardo, but –" when he was cut off by a smiling Accardo, who repeated, "This is for my daughter, it's important. I'll see you at three." Before Tischendorf could catch his breath, Accardo was gone. "My father assumed that Joe had no idea about the strike," says Jay Tischendorf. While Jerry Tischendorf fretted about what to do, Joe Accardo must have been laughing. "Within half an hour, all the shop's mechanics showed up," Jay was told by his father. Apparently, Accardo had his men get the word out to the union, which was likely controlled by Humphreys, that the strike was suspended for two hours to service Marie's car. Accardo returned at three and picked up his immaculately tuned automobile.

That same year, 1957, Paul Ricca also continued to feel the wrath of the IRS, which prevailed upon immigration authorities to commence deportation proceedings. As if the Accardo case were not enough to deplete Curly's energies, he now had to work the Ricca case, which lasted three years. One of his strategies was to hire a New York detective agency to surveil the jurors in an effort to compromise them. However, this strong-arm approach was vetoed by his fellows, Accardo and Giancana. When Ricca was convicted, the gang realized they should have followed Curly's advice. The FBI noted that, since the conviction, "the hoodlums . . . are more inclined to listen to Humphreys in this regard." Although Ricca would eventually be imprisoned on tax charges in 1959, Curly worked tirelessly on his appeal and was able to quash the deportation order.

As if Curly did not have enough to fret over, his laundry empire, which he had never abandoned, continued to expand. By August 1957, Humphreys had formed partnerships with several companies, including Normal Wet Wash Laundries, Modern Laundry & Dry Cleaning, Empire Laundry, and Lewis Wet Wash Laundries and Dry Cleaning. The FBI reported that all the stress was taking a profound toll on the fifty-eight-year-old gangster, who was believed to have suffered three more heart attacks within the last year. The FBI would eventually overhear conversations that gave evidence that Humphreys' legendary mild manner was beginning to fray. "I'm going to retire and go to Wales where there are only Protestants, so I can get away from the Catholics and Jews," Curly complained. On another occasion, Humphreys told Frankie Ferraro that he was off to Florida for a year and a half, bone weary from doing legal work for his inferiors. "The hell with you guys – I've been doing this for thirty years," Humphreys ranted.

In 1957, the frenetic activity under way in Chicago, Las Vegas, and Washington would be eclipsed by a momentous gathering just ten miles west of Binghamton, New York. The assemblage would herald a new era in the epic of the Outfit, an era marked by the gang's volatile, and often contradictory, relationship with the federal government, or, as they referred to it, the G.

Part Five

The G

15.

The Game's Afoot:
The G Gets Involved

While the Outfit struggled with its own nuisances, namely Bobby Kennedy and the IRS, their travails paled in comparison with those of their sometime associates in New York. For unlike in Chicago, which had unified its underworld in one sixty-second shooting spree on St. Valentine's Day, 1929, New York gangsterism was typified by a continuous series of internecine bloodlettings. For years, the New York turf had been parceled out to five "families," the brainstorm of 1930s boss Salvatore Maranzano, even as Charles "Lucky" Luciano attempted to downplay the "old-world" family paradigms in favor of Torrio's modern vision. As writer John Davis says, "What Luciano accomplished was to Americanize and democratize the old Sicilian Mafia, turning it into a huge, and fearsome, moneymaking machine." Despite Luciano's national influence, the five New York bosses continued to squabble, with their leadership increasingly determined at the point of a gun. The recent attack on Costello, which had tipped authorities to the breadth of the Las Vegas collusions, was but the most recent example of the turbulence.

As the situation drifted perilously close to chaos, an emergency meeting of the Commission was called for November 14, 1957. Since Johnny Torrio had conceived the enterprise two decades earlier, the Commission had met regularly every five years to coordinate the members' mutual or exclusive interests. At the top of this year's agenda was the desire to effect a truce among the current ruling Empire State families – Genovese, Lucchese, Gambino, Profaci, and Bonanno. Among those invited to deliberate the warfare's resolution were the Outfit's Joe Accardo and his heir, Mooney Giancana.

It was decided that the eighty-odd bosses and their factotums from around the country would assemble at the rural estate of Joe Barbara, in the south-central upstate New York town of Apalachin (pronounced

"Apple-*ay*kin"). The fifty-one-year-old, Sicilian-born Barbara, a well-liked local philanthropist, had come to America during prohibition and cut his teeth as a bootlegger, later legitimizing to become the regional Canada Dry soft-drink distributor. New York State Police sergeant Edgar Croswell, however, continued to monitor Barbara, believing his distributorship to be a front for an illegal alcohol racket. On November 13, after learning that Barbara's son had been booking rooms at the local Parkway Motel, Croswell drove out to the estate, where he observed a coral-and-pink Lincoln and a blue Cadillac, both with Ohio plates. Croswell returned the next day with his partner and two agents of the Alcohol and Tobacco Tax Agency, this time spotting more than two dozen cars parked behind Barbara's barn. The next sight was even more odd for this rural setting: Scores of suited men were partaking in a sirloin steak barbecue. The 220 pounds of choice cut, valued at $432, had been specially shipped from Chicago the week before.

Before Croswell could gather his thoughts, the men, who had spotted Croswell, took their steak sandwiches and began vanishing into the surrounding woods, while the good sergeant called in for backup. Croswell quickly set up a roadblock on the only route from Barbara's property. The first car to approach the rampart was a new Chrysler Imperial containing none other than New York boss Vito Genovese, with whose reputation Croswell was well-acquainted. From there, things degenerated into a comic opera, with backup police giving chase to a dispersing herd of middle-aged men racing through the brambles and mud in their silk suits and $200 imported dress shoes. Before the officers realized they were rounding up men who were not actually wanted for anything, they had arrested many of the cookout's participants, most of whom had a knee-jerk reaction to run from men in uniform.

By 1 A.M. powerful bosses such as Santo Trafficante and Joe Bonanno, having been rounded up in cornfields, were being processed, if illegally, at the nearby Vestal police station, charged with absolutely nothing. In custody, the bosses were polite in the extreme, as the frustrated cops grasped for incriminating straws. Croswell later admitted to trying to entrap his detainees: "We gave them a rough time at the station house, but we couldn't even make them commit disorderly conduct down there." For their part, the hoods claimed that they were paying respects to an ailing Barbara. All told, sixty-three men had been caught, only nine of whom had no criminal record (their collective record came to 275 past arrests and 100 convictions). The men carried on them the incredible combined sum of $300,000 in cash. One of the bosses, holding ten grand, gave his occupation as "unemployed." A stark reminder of the upper-world-underworld communion was the collaring of Buffalo, New York's Man of the Year, city councilman John C. Montana.

Although sixty-three of the attendees were processed and quickly released, untold dozens more made their exits without being appre-hended. Among them were Accardo and Giancana. Two days later, Mooney showed up at his Thunderbolt Motel in Rosemont, Illinois, managed by his brother, Chuck. "I tore up a twelve-hundred-dollar suit on some barbed wire," Mooney said of his escape in Apalachin, "and ruined a new pair of shoes." He gave Chuck a humorous description of the hoods' flight through Barbara's woods. "You should've seen some of the guys slippin' and slidin' down on their asses, splittin' out their pants." Mooney's daughter Antoinette recalled a similar recap given to Johnny Rosselli at the family home. "These cops close in and start grabbing everyone in sight. I took off like I was some sort of gazelle out the back door . . . I mean, I ran like I was doing the hundred-yard dash in the Olympics," Mooney recounted. "I made the woods in the back by going out the back door."

The Chicago contingent was incensed that the Commission meeting had taken place in a venue they had warned against. Giancana was especially irritated, venting to Rosselli, "I told that fuckin' jerk in Buffalo [Stefano Magaddino] that we shouldn't have the meeting in the goddamn place – that he should have the meeting here in Chicago, and he'd never have to worry about cops with all the hotels and places we control." Years later, Mooney had still not let up about the confab. Utilizing a telephonic wiretap placed in one of the gang's hideouts, the FBI heard Mooney chew out Magaddino personally for the debacle in New York. "I hope you're satisfied," Mooney fumed. "Sixty-three of our top guys made by the cops." To which the chastened Buffalo mobster replied, "I gotta admit you were right, Sam. It never would have happened in your place." In the next few sentences of the FBI's transcript, Giancana said more about the Outfit's influence, and legit business penetration, in Chicago than a hundred editorials: "This is the safest territory in the world for a big meet. We could've scattered you guys in my motels; we could've had the meet in one of my big restaurants. The cops don't bother us there. We got three towns just outside of Chicago with the police chiefs in our pocket. We got what none of you guys got. We got this territory locked up tight."

The national press had a field day with the Apalachin story, an occurrence that gave a temple-pulsing headache to the director of the nation's premier investigative unit, the FBI. J. Edgar Hoover, the portly paladin who was ever protective of his beloved Bureau's reputation, was now being pressured into action against organized crime. For decades, Hoover had denied that crime was anything but a local problem, that just such an assemblage as Apalachin was inconceivable. Now, for the first time publicly, Hoover was seen as being behind the curve. The G's boss moved quickly to make up for lost time. On November 27, Director Hoover fired off a memo to all the FBI field offices. The missive was headlined "Top Hoodlum Program (THP)," and it ordered the FBI to penetrate the inner sanctums of organized crime, define it, and make cases that would stick. Hoover's number two man, Cartha DeLoach, contends that the THP had actually been formed earlier in the year and that Apalachin only energized it. Other agents, such as Chicago's Bill Roemer disputed this.

In either event, the nation's major cities soon saw an influx of new G-men sent to ensure the success of the THP. By far the most emphasis was placed on New York, which welcomed twenty-five new agents, and Chicago, with ten. For the next two years, the new federal arrivals went to school on organized crime. In Chicago, FBI special agents wisely sought out the counsel of the former members of the city's Scotland Yard investigative unit, recently disbanded by Mayor Daley. Although it would take many months before the Bureau was able to acquire connected sources, and critical inside information, it would eventually do so. That success would represent a major turning point in the fortunes of the Outfit. In the short term, the Outfit's chieftains, increasingly desirous of going legit, kept a low profile throughout most of 1958–59, confining their business expansion to the offshore gambling haven of Cuba. While Meyer Lansky had just opened his deluxe twenty-one-story, 440-room Havana Riviera Hotel Casino (the first large Cuban building to be fully air-conditioned), the Outfit expanded in other directions. With Mooney Giancana as his partner, Joe Accardo invested in Havana-based shrimp boats and processing plants, an endeavor that reaped still more millions in profit. Accardo also teamed with Diamond Joe Esposito to cut in on the lucrative Cuban sugar export business. The Outfit's low-profile domestic activity was believed by some to have had one bloody exception: In Vegas, drastic action was taken to prevent the Outfit's Riviera Hotel-Casino plum from going belly-up.

The disturbing reports from Las Vegas were unabated: Gus Greenbaum's personal descent was escalating. He was deep into the abyss of heroin addiction, spending night after hazy night with prostitutes, but only after losing stacks of money at the craps tables. His dreadful condition, which allowed him only a couple hours of afternoon work, predictably spilled over into his administration of the Outfit's Riviera business. Although Greenbaum had worked his managerial magic for a decade in Las Vegas, now for the first time his ledger sheets were awash in red ink. With the Riviera's casino doing a good volume of business, the Chicago bosses knew it could not be losing money – unless Gus Greenbaum was skimming to support his many addictions. Consequently, Greenbaum received another visit from the dreaded Marshall Caifano.

"Sell out or you're gonna be carried out in a box," Caifano ordered.

After Caifano left, Greenbaum consulted with his senior staff, telling them, "I don't want to leave. This goddamn town is in my blood. I can't leave." The stance was either courageous or foolhardy, given not only Greenbaum's current troubles with the Outfit, but also that he still had not repaid them the $1 million he had borrowed for the Flamingo Hotel improvements after Bugsy's death.

What happened next may have come as the result of a Thanksgiving, 1958, meeting of "the Four Joes," 124 miles south of Phoenix. The site was the Grace Ranch, owned by Detroit gangster Pete "Horse Face" Licavoli. The FBI received reports that Joe Accardo had made the holiday trek to Licavoli's outpost to confer with New York Commission bosses Joe Profaci and Joe Bonanno and his brother-in-law Joe Magliocco, all of whom had attended Apalachin. With Accardo playing host, the Four Joes feasted on barbecued steak and discussed their business in Sicilian. It was rumored that one of the business decisions they reached cost Joe Accardo $1 million – the money he had lent to Gus Greenbaum for the Flamingo, which could now never be repaid.

In the late morning of December 3, less than a week after the Grace Ranch summit, Gus Greenbaum's housekeeper happened upon a grisly scene in the Greenbaum bedroom. Still in silk pajamas, Gus Greenbaum's corpse lay across his bed, his head nearly severed by a vicious swipe from a butcher knife. On a sofa in the den fifty feet away was found the body of Gus' wife, Bess, also the victim of a slashed throat. Although no one was ever charged in the murders, the killings were widely believed to represent a Bugsy redux, i.e., the fastest way to effect a managerial change in Sin City. If in fact the Greenbaum murder was sanctioned by the Four Joes, the killing of Bess was a potent departure from the Outfit's rule that prohibited involvement of innocent family members. There is also the distinct possibility that the hired killer overstepped his authority in an effort to dispose of a witness. Chicago insiders believe that the hit was authorized by the Riviera's Miami investors, since police learned that two suspicious men had arrived from Miami the day of the murders, only to return to Miami that very night. Lending credence to this scenario was a conversation Johnny Rosselli had with Jimmy Fratianno two years after the murders. When Fratianno brought up the Greenbaum killings, Rosselli said, "That was Meyer's contract." Meyer Lansky was of course well-established in Miami and was an investor with his fellow Floridians in Greenbaum's Riviera.

Back in Phoenix, the Greenbaums' funeral was attended by three hundred mourners, among them Senator Barry Goldwater.

All the while in Washington, the McClellan hearings churned on. For the Outfit, the tribunal was little more than a nuisance, with the gang having to dodge a spate of congressional subpoenas. Eventually, some of the bosses appeared, only to plead the Fifth Amendment ad nauseam.[1]

Bobby Kennedy expressed a strong initial interest in hearing from Curly Humphreys on the subject of his alleged anointment of Hoffa. According to files in the Chicago Crime Commission (CCC), Kennedy's investigators were also interested in Humphreys' control over the Chicago Restaurant Association and the Hotel and Restaurant Employees Union. "Books of the Union have been sub-poenaed [by the committee] and restaurant owners and workers are being interviewed throughout the city," a CCC memo noted. Chicagoans were therefore shocked when the Welshman never appeared before the McClellan Committee. The mystery was resolved on February 25, 1959, while Robert Kennedy was grilling Chicago slot king Eddie Vogel. Kennedy was essentially reading "for the record," since Vogel pled the Fifth to all questions posed. While ticking off the names of various gangsters with whom Vogel was associated, Kennedy included: "Rocco Fischetti, Charles Fischetti, who is now dead; Murray 'the Camel' Humphreys, *who is now dead . . .*" (Italics added.) The committee had somehow been led to believe that the very much alive Humphreys had passed on.

---

1. Accardo took the "out" 152 times; Giancana read the oath from his Humphreys-supplied index card 34 times. Rosselli, not deemed by the committee to be in the labor racket, was not called to testify.

At least one connected Chicagoan was wise to the scam. Mayor Daley's intelligence chief, Jack Clarke, laughed recently when the incident was brought up. Clarke had assisted the committee's staff on occasion, as when they tried to locate Outfit leaders. "The committee had hired some local detectives to do their skip-tracing," Clarke remembers. "Humphreys slipped them some C-notes and told them to report back that he had died. Apparently, Bobby bought it."

Making the committee oversight even more unbelievable is that that very year, 1959, Humphreys appeared before an Illinois grand jury investigating organized crime and put on one of his seminal performances. It happened on April 1, 1959, and Curly's performance was likely his idea of an April Fools' Day joke. According to the April 4 edition of the *Chicago American,* Humphreys appeared but a pale shadow of his former self. "Humphreys has lost the dapper, erect appearance of his better days," the paper reported. Wearing a crumpled raincoat, and feebly hobbling with a cane, Curly told onlookers, "My left leg is crippled – arthritis. I've gone to fifty doctors, but they haven't been able to correct it." For good measure, Humphreys sported a patch over his left eye. "It's some sort of nervous disorder," he explained. A local journalist quipped, "Humphreys is over the hump." John Morgan, who wrote a Humphreys biography published in Wales, described what happened next, a scene that presaged the climax to the 1995 film *The Usual Suspects:* "Humphreys was asked a few questions: he croaked the Fifth Amendment a few times. After five minutes, the embarrassed court allowed him to leave. He shuffled into the April air, turned into Rush Street, threw away his walking stick, his raincoat and his homburg and skipped as blithely as ever from bar to bar to meet old friends. But the picture of the broken man was in every newspaper."

Despite this widely reported incident, Kennedy and the committee proceeded as if they still believed the gangster to be dead, and made no effort to contact him.

"The Waiter" Is Unmasked

Whereas Curly Humphreys succeeded in disappearing from the G's radar, Paul Ricca had no such luck. For over ten years, and with no fanfare, federal agents had quietly been building a case against a man they had initially believed to be chiefly a tax cheat. They soon concluded that Ricca was also an illegal alien and a murderer. While Ricca was imprisoned on the Hollywood extortion case conviction in 1945, an anonymous tipster apparently contacted the Chicago branch of the Immigration Service and informed them that Ricca had entered the United States on a false passport, using the name of Paul Maglio, a real citizen of a small Italian village of six thousand named Apricena. The investigation took a decade, but Ricca's pursuers eventually stumbled into an astonishing coincidence: The real Paul Maglio had also emigrated to America, and to of all places, Chicago. In a strange twist, Maglio had been leading a parallel life as a laborer in the shadow of his alter ego, one of the most powerful crime bosses in the country. Adding to the bizarre tale was that Maglio had no idea he had been impersonated by Ricca. Even more, Maglio had been the town clerk of Apricena and knew that only one local family was named Maglio, and that there was only one Paul Maglio – him.

At Ricca's Immigration trial, the surprise witness was none other than the real Paul Maglio, who delivered testimony so airtight that Ricca offered no defense. Although he was ordered deported, Ricca was supremely confidant that the order would never be enforced. Ricca boasted, "I'll blow the lid off politics, from the White House down." Through Curly Humphreys, Ricca demanded that all the pols who had been feasting at the gang's trough be marshalled in his defense. In short time, Ricca's petition to remain at liberty was remanded to the federal district court of Judge Michael L. Igoe, who was one of the many friendly officials who had marched behind the coffin of the Outfit's patriarch Big Jim Colosimo in 1920. Ricca was said to have laughed in Igoe's face after the judge granted him his request.

According to Humphreys' second wife, Jeanne, Curly worked tirelessly to have the deportation order quashed, putting in long hours in legal research and strategizing. The work on the immigration issue proved successful, but the feds merely fell back on their charge of last resort, tax evasion. On this charge, even Curly could not obtain a complete dismissal, and on July 1, 1959, Ricca was sent to Terre Haute to start a ten-year sentence, later reduced to three years, with twenty-seven months ultimately served.[2] The real Paul Maglio, who said he had testified to prove that not all Italians are lawbreakers, became a

---

2. During his imprisonment Ricca was not only visited by his cohorts, but also on numerous occasions by Libonati, who astounded prison officials with his lavish displays of affection, hugging the Waiter repeatedly. According to Jeanne Humphreys, Ricca's release mandated a massive coming-out party, attended by the likes of Libonati and Frank Sinatra.

neighborhood hero, still walking fourteen blocks back and forth to work every day.

Ricca's imprisonment caused him to miss by three days the wedding reception Mooney threw for his daughter Bonnie and her husband, Tony Tisci (Congressman Libonati's secretary) at Miami Beach's Fontainebleau Hotel. The muted affair, by gang standards, was held on the very day most mob watchers were in River Forest gawking over Joe Accardo's Fourth of July barbecue. Giancana purposely kept the marriage low-key, after the fallout from the much more lavish reception he had thrown for another daughter, Antoinette, three months earlier. That affair, which had featured more than seven hundred guests at Chicago's LaSalle Hotel, had drawn local headlines and become fodder for questions put to Mooney two months later when the boss appeared before the McClellan Committee. Mooney, therefore, decided to keep Bonnie's wedding off the press' radar. Poor Bonnie was thus prevented from receiving the same kind of envelope largesse as her sister, who collected over $200,000 at her gala. "I never saw most of the money," Antoinette recently said. "I gave it to my father for safekeeping and never saw it again, except for a few thousand dollars he gave me for a down payment on my house."

Cat and Mouse with the G

Although green to the world of the Outfit, Chicago's newly assigned G-men were under such pressure from Hoover that they worked overtime until learning who the leaders were, and where to find them. With Ricca already in "college" and Accardo lying low, the agents became most interested in Curly Humphreys and Mooney Giancana. FBI men like Ralph Hill, John Roberts, Bill Roemer, Marshall Rutland, John Bassett, and Vince Inserra hit the streets, attempting to tail their targets. In many instances, their efforts played out like a Keystone Kops comedy, in which the hoods used their well-honed skills to toy with the agents. Local G-men remember one humorous incident in which they employed a full-court press on Mooney Giancana, dispatching nine cars to his home one morning, intent on following his every move. Little did they know they were about to match driving skills with the most talented wheelman from the Patch. When Giancana drove off, he took his pursuers on a labyrinthine route, causing them to bark excitedly to one another on their radios, at times nearly colliding with one another. After successfully losing all nine cars, Mooney snuck up on one of them from behind, then stopped alongside the agent's car and chided, "Here I am."

On another occasion, Curly Humphreys saw that on one particularly hectic day the G was following him everywhere he went, from a newsstand, to an attorney's office, to a restaurant, to a hardware store, etc. Eventually tiring of the game, Curly had his driver stop the car, then alighted and walked back to the startled agents parked behind him. "Look, this is silly," Curly said. "Instead of wasting all this gasoline, why don't I just send my driver home and go with you guys. That way you'll know exactly where I am at all times." Humphreys then opened the back door of the federal car, got in, and was chauffeured for the rest of the day by the federal government. Needless to say, the agents took a grudging liking to the disarming Welshman, as did almost everyone else who had personal contact with him. The charm he had first cast as a teen on his court-appointed adjudicator was as potent as ever. On one occasion, agents followed Joe Accardo and Curly Humphreys into a movie theater as they took in a matinee of the 1959 film *Al Capone*. Sitting inconspicuously behind the bosses, the agents eavesdropped as the old chums critiqued the adaptation of their patriarch's career. "No. No, it wasn't like that at all," they said repeatedly, nudging each other.

Unbeknownst to the G-men, their routines were also being scrutinized – by the Outfit. The gang knew one agent, Bill Roemer, coached his son's Little League team and had determined the boy's practice schedule, so they coordinated their most important gatherings around little Roemer's baseball. One gang member recalled walking to a meeting with Accardo and worrying about Roemer's surveillance. "He'll be gone by three," Joe replied confidently.

In his memoir, Bill Roemer makes much of the "Family Pact" he reached with Curly, whom he called Hump. At the time, according to Roemer, his wife, Jeannie, had been receiving threatening phone calls. "Your husband is a dead man," they would whisper before hanging up. In addition, Roemer's two sons were seen followed to school by two mysterious men in a car. Wisely, Roemer sought out Curly to intervene. One morning, Roemer approached Humphreys outside his current residence at 4200 Marine Drive and introduced himself.

"Yes, Mr. Roemer, I know who you are. What can I do for you?" Humphreys asked.

Roemer explained what had been going on, and Curly replied, "Mr. Roemer, I understand your situation. I'll look into it." Roemer suggested ground rules that essentially stated, "You stay away from our families and we'll stay away from yours." Curly agreed to take the matter up with his associates and get back to Roemer. A week later, Humphreys reported, "Bill, this was the work of a misguided individual. I have spoken to him, and you can rest assured your family will have no more problems." With that, the two amicable adversaries shook hands on the Family Pact. However, when Humphreys later learned that the G had given the press the name of Frankie Ferraro's mistress, Humphreys and Roemer's mutual friend and restaurant owner Morrie Norman was asked to set up another meeting.

"I thought we had a deal," Curly said. Roemer professed that he had no idea "families" included mistresses. "Bill," Humphreys said, smiling, "there might come a day when you regret this. You might not always be so righteous." The arrangement was soon amended to include paramours. At least that was Roemer's version.

According to Humphreys' widow, the "threatening" calls and visits were greatly misrepresented by the late Mr. Roemer. "Roemer couldn't keep his zipper zipped," says Jeanne Humphreys. Jeanne maintains that it was common knowledge in the Outfit that Bill Roemer and his compatriots had roaming eyes for some strippers working in a downtown joint called the 606 Club. A passage from Jeanne's contemporaneous journal reads, "Gussie [Alex], Henry Susk, and Dave Gardner were trying out the same strippers as the agents and decided to use the strippers to get the goods on the agents." Jeanne recently summed up the gambit, saying, "It was Gussie's idea to rat Roemer out to his wife to get the G off everybody's back. The Family Pact was nothing more than 'you forget about our mistresses and we'll forget about yours.' No one ever threatened Roemer's wife and kids." Curly told his wife of the pact, explaining, "This way, the G will get to keep their lily-white image, and they'll stay away from our families." When Jeanne asked one of the gang if the agents' families had ever been threatened, her source quipped, "Sure, their home life."

Years later, Roemer wrote of his sincere affection for Humphreys: "I actually did like the guy. The truth is, I did have a grudging respect for Accardo. And I had even more respect for Hump . . . There was a style about the way he conducted himself. His word was his bond." Roemer added that he took no glee in harassing his "friend" Humphreys. He much preferred to chase the swarthier, violent types like Mooney Giancana. "In Chicago there were always plenty more mobsters to choose as targets. But none like Hump."

Roemer was well aware of the professional problems that might ensue from his genuine affection for the Hump. As he wrote in his *Roemer: Man Against the Mob*: "I had clearly developed an affinity for Hump – more so by far than I did for anyone else in the mob. Obviously, I had to lean over backward to ensure that my respect for the man did not outweigh my responsibility to do all in my power to neutralize his connections and minimize his role in the mob."

After many months of tails and informant debriefs, the Bureau's effort began to bear fruit as, one by one, the gang's meeting places were identified. At the time, the Outfit maintained a series of venues for use at specific times. At nine in the morning, like clockwork, the old guard of Accardo and Humphreys met with Mooney and his aides at Celano's Custom Tailor Shop, a large second-story facility located at 620 North Michigan Avenue, in the heart of the city's Magnificent Mile. Although the Bureau never learned of it, the gang assembled for lunch twice a week in the Wedgewood Room of Marshall Field's Department Store, where the city's elite ladies gathered for tea. "It was perfect," remembered one hood. "Nobody ever suspected that these tough guys would meet in a room full of women. When we took over the back of a restaurant in those days, we referred to our section as Amen Corner." On Thursday nights, the "boys" came to Joe's River Forest palace to conduct business over a home-cooked meal, while Mooney Giancana met his charges late night at the Armory Lounge at 7427 West Roosevelt Road in the western suburb of Forest Park.

The Bureau first noticed that Curly and the others were showing up every morning just before 9 A.M. at the North Side intersection of Rush and Ontario Streets. The hoods would enter an office building and disappear into a maze of hallways and lobbies. After some weeks of head-scratching, the agents discovered that the building shared a common hall with another edifice that fronted on Michigan Avenue, which took the gangsters ultimately to the backroom of Celano's; the Ontario entrance was meant as a diversion. Once inside, the gang nodded to Jimmy Celano, who abandoned the backroom while the Outfit conducted its business. Accardo et al. met in the sparsely furnished room, which had a couple easy chairs, a large sofa, a desk, a television, a well-stocked wet bar, and a safe.

As recounted often and with great swagger by agent Bill Roemer, the feds obtained a key to Celano's and executed a recent Hoover directive that ordered a wholesale trashing of their targets' civil rights: Hidden microphones would be planted in the hangouts. The order gave witness to the pressure Hoover felt to break the mob. "I decided I would be the first guy to plant a mike," Roemer wrote. "I had been the first and only guy to win four Notre Dame boxing championships. It wouldn't be my first first." Roemer's bravado notwithstanding, Hoover and his agents were fully cognizant of the unconstitutionality of their "black bag job." In his autobiography, Roemer recounted the situation: "If we got caught, we were not to identify ourselves as FBI agents, and we were to attempt to escape without being identified. We were to carry no badge or credentials, no gun, nothing to connect us with the FBI. But, heaven help us if we were apprehended and it eventually came out that we were employed by the FBI; then the Bureau would denounce us. We were 'rogues,' carrying out an unauthorized operation."

Every Sunday night for two months, the G-men surreptitiously entered Celano's, sawing their way through crawl spaces to create invisible wiring ducts. The operation was fraught with danger as the agents bumbled toward their goal. On one occasion reminiscent of a Three Stooges short, an agent fell through the crawl space, exiting the ceiling of the first-floor restaurant below, which was luckily closed. The agents had to race out to find plaster and paint to repair the damage before the eatery opened the next day. On July 29, 1959, Agent Roemer finally completed the task of planting a pineapple-sized World War II microphone (nicknamed Little Al in honor of Al Capone) behind the backroom radiator, hardwiring it into phone lines.[3] Of course, the noise of the radiator when it kicked in obliterated the conversation in Celano's, just the sort of discovery that led to the invention of a new definition for the Bureau's famous acronym: Famous But Incompetent.

Emboldened by their success at the tailor shop, Hoover's mob busters spent the next several years planting bugs at other gang headquarters: Mooney's Armory Lounge (this mike nicknamed Mo); Curly's apartment

---

3. Roemer and the Bureau apparently never learned of another bug planted at Celano's three years later. At the time, the Illinois Crime Commission, under Charles "Cigars" Siragusa, hired a local detective to plant a microphone at the tailor shop. Unlike the G's mike, this one was not hardwired; instead it was planted with a transmitter and broadcast on an FM frequency to anyone who knew where to set the dial. The broadcasts were monitored for an unknown period by the commission's Ed King and James Kelliher.

(Plumb); Johnny D'Arco's First Ward headquarters (Shade); the dry-heat room at Postl's Health Club, where the gang often met; and one in Accardo's lawyer's offices. In addition to the bugs, phone lines were tapped both in Chicago and at the gang's Las Vegas properties. One of the G's intelligence coups was hearing that the Outfit was skimming over $12 million per year in Sin City. They also learned that the gang had at least forty-nine cops on their dole, in addition to various and sundry politicians of both statewide and nationwide notoriety. And invariably, the G came face-to-face with the shadowy connections between upperworld and underworld leaders. Agent Bill Roemer recalled how he once informed Sidney Korshak that he wanted to interview his wife, Bernice. Korshak said, "I'll tell you where you can reach her. She's having dinner at the Mocambo with Peter Lawford and his wife – you know, Bobby Kennedy's sister." At the time, Bobby Kennedy was the inquisitor general on the McClellan Committee. When Roemer reported the intelligence to his superiors in Washington, he assumed that they would rendezvous with Bea Korshak at the upscale eatery. Johnny Leggett, the THP coordinator at headquarters, responded, "Are you kidding, Roemer? They wouldn't touch that with a ten-foot pole."

In passing, Curly mentioned to Jeanne that the G was getting wise to the gang's activity. "Maybe they've got the tailor shop bugged," Jeanne surmised. "No way," Humphreys responded. However, with Humphreys' seeming endless list of infiltrators in the police department, it wasn't long before he confirmed his wife's suspicion. "He also had a source in the Bureau," insists his second wife, who refuses to divulge the name in deference to the agent, who may still be alive. West Side boss Frank Buccieri told one friend, "We knew the place was bugged, so we gave them a show." According to Buccieri, Humphreys knew that the bugs were illegal and thus inadmissible in court. Said one friend, "Curly got a kick out of teasing the G."

The December 1959 murder of alleged kidnapper Roger Touhy is believed by some to have inspired a classic Humphreys tease of the G. For twenty-six years, law enforcement officials had suspected that the actual planner of the Jake Factor kidnapping, for which Touhy had been imprisoned, was Curly Humphreys. When Touhy was gunned down after threatening to sue Humphreys and Accardo in 1959, authorities were all but convinced of Curly's authorship of the hit. Confounding the G was the knowledge that Curly had fled Chicago for Florida on the day before the December 16 murder, much as Capone had done decades earlier, before the St. Valentine's Day massacre. Thus authorities were excited to overhear Humphreys at Celano's discussing Touhy's killing ten days after it had happened. The rest of the story was developed by Chicago journalist Sandy Smith, who was given access to the tapes of the powwow at Celano's. In the middle of a conversation with Joey Glimco, the Humphreys-appointed head of the taxicab unions, Glimco brought up the recent whacking of Roger Touhy.

"What was it with Touhy?" Glimco asked, bringing the G-men to attention in their hidden listening post.

"Well, Joe, I'll tell you . . .," answered Humphreys. At that moment the steam from the radiator that concealed the hidden mike came on full force. For the next ten minutes, Humphreys' voice was obliterated by the gurgling and clanging of the radiator. When the clamor died down ten minutes later, Humphreys' voice returned in its full resonance: ". . . and that's the way it was, Joe."

The opportunity to finally resolve the Touhy case, and the garbled tape that held the answers, sent paroxysms through the headphoned agents. The tape was rushed to FBI headquarters in Washington where the Bureau spent many fruitless months trying to filter out the static. Jeanne Humphreys is certain that the episode was staged by Curly, who merely turned on the radiator manually just as he got the G's attention.

Although Humphreys seemed to have learned of the Celano's bug, he likely never learned of the other microphones, including the one eventually placed in his own apartment. After a time, the entire Celano's charade became even too ludicrous for Humphreys. He began to amuse the agent monitors, many of whom had come to a grudging liking of the hood, with a new meeting-opening address: "Good morning, ladies and gentlemen, and anyone listening. This is the nine-o'clock meeting of the Chicago underworld."

Although the truth of the Touhy murder was obscured from the feds, the cause of another recent hit, also believed tied to a longtime Chicago mystery, was revealed, at least to Humphreys' wife.

Curly's Partner Gets Whacked

On August 23, 1959, Jeanne Humphreys was reading the newspaper and catching some late-morning sun with Curly on the patio of their new Key Biscayne home when her eyes caught an unsettling story emanating from Chicago.

"Fred Evans was killed yesterday," she said to Curly. "Didn't he used to be your best friend?"

"He's no friend of mine," Humphreys responded brusquely, before turning and walking back into the house.

Jeanne Humphreys knew better. The Curly & Fred Show went back to the 1920s, when they had met as Young Turks in Messinger's Restaurant and had thereafter partnered in a freelance fencing operation. From then on, after Curly's graduation to the Outfit's inner sanctums, they had worked closely together on numerous labor rackets, especially those involving the laundry business. In 1940, Curly and Fred had been indicted together in the $350,000 embezzlement of the Bartenders Union. At the time of his death, an up-against-the-wall execution, Evans was running a number of large operations, including the Industrial Garment Service with another Humphreys underling, Joey Glimco. In addition, Evans owned five other large laundry businesses and two luxury hotels in Los Angeles. His net worth was in the millions. But behind the scenes, Evans' life was in turmoil.

Evans' problems had come at him from different directions, and the question never resolved was, which one caused him to be shot twice in the head and twice in the throat as he exited his 5409 West Lake Street offices at high noon on August 22? And for Jeanne Humphreys, the question was twofold: Why had Curly turned against a lifelong friend, and was the desertion connected to Evans' demise? In time, Curly's minimal commentary combined with Jeanne's hindsight reminiscences gave a degree of explanation for the tragedy.

Over the years, explanations for Evans' murder have focused on two possible causes, both of which involved his recent problems with the G. First, Evans had come under attack by the IRS. For over a decade, Evans had been under close scrutiny by the taxmen, and once a year, as ordered, the dry cleaning kingpin toted his books down to the IRS office, where his numbers were put under a microscope. Despite their best efforts, the feds failed to find one penny out of place, so meticulous was Evans' accounting. But by 1959, after McClellan and Apalachin, the G tried a new tactic: It began leaking details of Evans' business to the press. It seemed that Evans' minutely detailed ledgers also included the names of all the gangsters who received a cut of his operation, people like Curly Humphreys and Joe Accardo. Three weeks before his murder, Evans' office was burglarized, the result of which left his files in shambles and many records missing.

The press wondered if Evans' killing was the underworld's way of stopping him from divulging the gang's secret business workings. But G-man Bill Roemer had another theory. "I had a knack for planting bugs," the agent later wrote, "and I developed a knack for recruiting informants. The first one I really recruited was Fred Evans." Roemer described how he and fellow agent Ralph Hill had interviewed Evans at his office just six weeks before his killing: "He was a willing talker. He told us of Humphreys" youth, mentioned a couple of Hump's associates . . . He also told us that Humphreys had a current financial interest in Superior Laundry and Linen Supply Company . . . Ralph and I went back to the office feeling pretty satisfied with ourselves. We had made arrangements to meet with Evans again in the near future.'

Chicago reporter George Murray, with his extensive sources in the underworld, reported what allegedly happened next: "The governing body of the Syndicate [Outfit] sat in judgment of Fred Evans in a kangaroo court. The records snatched in that office burglary on August 1, 1959, were scrutinized by men who understood every accounting entry. Murray Humphreys, as Evans' sponsor, was asked if he wanted to advance any valid reason why the sentence of death on Fred Evans should not be carried out. Humphreys passed."

Roemer believed his meeting with Evans instigated this star chamber. "The shots to the throat may well have been to ensure he would do no more talking to the FBI," Roemer wrote. For his part, George Murray leaned toward the IRS-leak theory. Although both explanations may have contributed to Evans' fate, recent interviews with Humphreys' then wife strongly suggest that the overarching reason was rooted in one of the heartland's greatest tragic mysteries.

In the year prior to the killing, Jeanne Humphreys witnessed a repeat occurrence that seemed trivial at the time, but would later turn out to be the turning point in the saga of Fred Evans. "Murray and I were walking into a restaurant to meet Joe [Accardo] and his wife," recalls Jeanne, "when all of a sudden, Buster Wortman came running up and begging Murray for an audience with Joe Batters." Frank "Buster" Wortman had long been the Outfit's man in East St. Louis, Illinois, and St. Louis, Missouri, where he coordinated the labor rackets for Humphreys, who was a close friend. The Outfit's relationship with Wortman went back at least as far as the 1940s, when Capone's heirs came to Wortman's aid in his protracted gang war with the rival Shelton gang. After eliminating the Sheltons, Wortman built a moat around his Collinsville, Illinois, ranch home.[4]

"I'll see what I can do," Humphreys answered the frantic Wortman. When the sit-down was not forthcoming, Wortman again traveled up from St. Louis a year later with a senior St. Louis hood named Elmer "Dutch" Dowling and visited Curly at home. "They stopped by on a Sunday morning and it was the same story," remembers Jeanne. "They were desperate to talk to Joe." This time Curly was even more terse. "There's nothing I can do for them," Curly said, as overheard by Jeanne. "They got themselves into this, and now they'll have to suffer the consequences." After Fred Evans' death, and unending pestering by Jeanne, Curly gave a short explanation: "Evans and Dowling broke the rules. Buster was begging for their lives, but Joe could not let the Greenlease thing go unpunished."

When Dowling, Wortman's key lieutenant, was similarly executed three years later in Belleville, Illinois, it all began to fall into place for Jeanne Humphreys. The "Greenlease thing" was the tragic 1953 kidnapping and murder of six-year-old Bobby Greenlease in Kansas City. "Apparently, the Outfit wanted them to sweat it out for a while before hitting them," Jeanne says of the interval between Wortman's first entreaties and the killings. Although Jeanne Humphreys learned little else about the rubouts, she knew enough to ask no more questions. However, with her contributions, reasonable inferences can be drawn about the enduring forty-nine-year-old mystery of Bobby Greenlease.

The Midwest's "Lindbergh Baby"

On September 28, 1953, Bobby Greenlease, the son of the wealthy owner of one of the nation's largest Cadillac dealerships, was abducted from his private Catholic school in midtown Kansas City. His captor was a forty-one-year-old prostitute named Bonnie Brown Heady, who together with her partner, ex-con Carl Austin Hall, had meticulously planned the kidnapping for months. The duo took the child across state lines into Kansas, where Hall brutally beat the child before fatally shooting him in the head, then burying the body in the backyard of Heady's St. Joseph, Missouri, home. Next, the pair sent a ransom note to Bobby's parents,

---

4. After the 1968 assassination of Dr. Martin Luther King Jr., John Ray, the brother of assassin James Earl Ray, told authorities that James had hid out in an East St. Louis gambling joint owned by Wortman.

demanding $600,000 in $10 and $20 bills (far eclipsing the 1932 ransom of $70,000 demanded for the murdered baby of famous aviator Charles Lindbergh).

Robert C. Greenlease, Bobby's seventy-one-year-old father, contacted the president of a local bank, Arthur Eisenhower, the brother of the president of the United States, Dwight D. Eisenhower. Before releasing the funds to Mr. Greenlease, Eisenhower had his staff make note of the serial numbers on each and every bill. After the money was delivered, the kidnappers had the bad luck of taking a St. Louis cab from a fleet owned by Joe Costello, a local gangster in the Wortman sphere. Costello had strong ties to Chicago and was married to a Chicago girl. The cabbie, John Oliver Hager, took the kidnappers to a motel run by John Carr, another Wortman-connected hood. Paying with fistfuls of cash, Hall and Heady hired Hager as their personal chauffeur, and he eventually ferried them to an apartment rental in St. Louis. By now, with the abduction a nationwide sensation, Hager became suspicious of the source of the lucre. After Hager informed Costello about the low-rent pair with bags of money, Costello quickly tipped St. Louis police lieutenant Louis Shoulders, a friend of both Costello's and Wortman's, who years later was placed in a position of power in Wortman's St. Louis Steamfitters Union.

Hall and Heady were arrested on October 6 and quickly admitted their roles, telling police where to find Bobby Greenlease's body. A mere eighty-one days later the pair were sitting side by side in the gas chamber – Heady earned the distinction of becoming the only woman ever to be so executed. All the loose ends appeared to be resolved, except for one: At the time of their arrest, Heady and Hall held only $298,000 – less than half the delivered ransom money; it was never determined what became of the missing loot. (At the time of their arrests, Hall and Heady were adamant that all the money was in their apartment when they were arrested.) Over the years, the serial numbers of the ransom bills were repeatedly printed in Midwestern newspapers, becoming a story every time one surfaced. On May 31, 1959, some of the bills turned up in a Chicago bank, the charge for a $686 money order paid to the Outfit's gambling boss Lenny Patrick. The purchaser of the money order was Fred Evans.

James Deakin, the longtime White House correspondent for the *St. Louis Post-Dispatch,* spent years researching the Greenlease case. After spending weeks with the lead FBI investigator, Phil King, and obtaining more than three thousand pages of the Bureau's Greenlease file, Deakin wrote the book *A Grave for Bobby.* "The book should have been titled

Blood Money," Deakin recently said. "The only real mystery was who took the money; but the FBI was certain it went to Chicago to be 'cleaned.'"

In 1962, the same year Dowling was executed, both Shoulders and Costello died of natural causes. Thus, Lieutenant Shoulders' partner, Officer Elmer Dolan, concluded it was safe to tell the truth of what he knew about the missing ransom money. Dolan confessed that he had witnessed Shoulders and Costello take the money to a three-hundred-pound Chicago Teamster leg-breaker, who precisely fit the description of one Barney Baker, a close associate of both Jimmy Hoffa's and the Chicago Outfit's. Both Dolan and the FBI concluded that Baker was a courier, hired to transport the marked notes to Chicago, where, Dolan was told, the hot money was sold for a mere twenty cents on the dollar. In fact, of the 115 bills recovered, 58 turned up in Chicago, and many of those surfaced at the Outfit-controlled Southmoor Bank & Trust Company.

And Elmer Dolan was not the only confessor. A prostitute named Sandy O'Day, who was hired by killer Hall after the murder, admitted to James Deakin that she went out looking for Wortman to inform him of the booty. When she did not locate Wortman, she sought out a close associate of his, whom she did not name, but possibly Dowling. Also coming forward was Mollie Baker, Barney's divorced wife, who told Bobby Kennedy during the McClellan hearings that Barney had admitted to her that "Joe Costello got the Greenlease money." Lastly, a former prostitute named Pat A. has admitted in recent years that she was Lieutenant Shoulders' girl on the side, and that he confessed to her that he had made off with the Greenlease money.

Putting the pieces together, it can be surmised that, through Shoulders-Costello, it was leaked to Wortman and Dowling that the drifters held the $600,000 treasure, which they may have taken to be an extortion payoff.[5] Wortman likely concluded that only one organization was capable of laundering such a large amount of cash, the Chicago Outfit, with which he had a close association through Humphreys. Seemingly without Humphreys' knowledge, a decision was made to launder the money in the massive Evans-Humphreys dry-cleaning empire, and possibly thereafter apply it to Evans' looming travails with the taxman. There is also the remote possibility that Costello had a more active role in the planning of

---

5. It is also believed by some that John Carr, who died a multimillionaire, may have grabbed some of the loot.

the kidnapping, which went awry when the constantly drunk Hall murdered the child.

All the puzzle pieces will likely not be found, but it is clear that Accardo and Humphreys were not happy with what they learned of Evans' and Dowling's connection to the Greenlease caper. And even a long-trusted ally like Buster Wortman could not save them.

Although there were fewer and fewer high-profile rubouts in the Outfit's sphere, the Evans killing was not to be the last that year. Four months later, on December 16, 1959, the double-dealing Roger Touhy was similarly executed.

The Black Book

In Nevada, the fallout from the discovery of Frank Costello's link to the Vegas skim continued, and in 1959 Nevada authorities attempted to place tighter controls over the burgeoning Las Vegas gambling empire. Shepherded through the legislature by Mormon politician James Gibson, the Gaming Control Act of 1959 called for the creation of a five-member Gaming Control Board, which would grant licenses and, supposedly, keep unsavory characters out of the industry. The performance of the Board would soon demonstrate, however, that its real agenda was to guarantee that the gambling treasure remained in the hands of Nevada's WASPs, and not with swarthy outsiders, especially Italians.

In their groundbreaking study of the history of Nevada's gambling regulation, *The Black Book,* University of Nevada professors Ronald Farrell and Carole Case found that the "social control" exerted by the board was but a thinly veiled attempt to wrest control of the lucrative (albeit essentially immoral) gambling industry from those who had created it. The authors' inspection of the licensing record was especially telling. Among those approved for licensing in the board's first year were:

- Frank Soskin, who had a record of illegal gambling.
- Lincoln Fitzgerald, a functionary of the Michigan gambling syndicate, with a criminal record for tax evasion, gambling, bribery, and conspiracy to run a gambling operation.
- Sanford Waterman, a convicted bookmaker who had worked for Meyer Lansky.
- Morris Lansburgh, who the board was informed was fronting for "notorious hoodlums."
- Ike "Cheesecake" Berger, a convicted bookmaker.

- Charles "Babe" Baron, convicted of carrying a concealed weapon, and twice arrested for murder.

The above Anglos had little trouble convincing the board to overlook their bootlegging, bookmaking, and possibly murderous backgrounds. However, it was a different story for the Italian entrepreneurs who wished to enter Nevada's gaming industry. Joseph D. Pignatello, for instance, was a gourmet chef from Chicago who applied for a permit to purchase a restaurant with four slot machines on-site. Although he had no criminal record or history of gambling, Pignatello was denied the license because he had cooked for, and chauffeured for, Mooney Giancana. The board claimed to worry that the restaurant would be a front for Giancana, although one wonders what interest Giancana would have in a mere four slot machines when he was pulling down millions per month from the skim and his interest in many major casinos. (Pignatello got the last laugh when he eventually purchased Vesuvio's Restaurant on East Desert Inn Road, an eatery that thrives to this day.)

Soon, the board established the infamous Black Book, which listed "unsavory characters" who not only could never be licensed, but were barred for life from setting foot in a Las Vegas casino. Accompanying the list was a statement rich in contradiction. The introductory remarks noted that the list had been devised so that certain individuals "not discredit the gaming industry." Discredit gambling? This is the same pastime that the board's Mormon dogma prohibits and labels immoral. All those listed were so included without any formal notification, hearing, or appeal. And the reasons for their inclusion could be mere hearsay.[6] Of the initial eleven placed in the Black Book, eight were Italian, and most had been implicated or convicted in the same sorts of crimes as the WASPs who *were* licensed: bootlegging and bookmaking. Included in the first eleven were the Outfit's Mooney Giancana and Curly Humphreys. (So strong was the board's opposition to Curly that his name was kept in the book for ten years after his death.)

Over the years, 62 percent of those placed in the Black Book have been Italian, dwarfing the numbers of the runners-up, Anglo-Saxons (15 percent). They were judged by a board that has been 75 percent WASP, with most of those Mormons, and of the forty-seven regulators to date,

---

6. When the questionable procedure was challenged in the Supreme Court, the court ruled in favor of the Gaming Board, explaining that gambling was a privilege, not a right.

only two have been Italian, despite the long history of Italian industry in Nevada that preceded the gaming industry, and which helped build the infrastructure of the state. Farrell and Case wrote, "The mere Italian sound of a man's name generated considerable suspicion." In a candid moment, board chairman Harry Reid once said, "The reasons for their being singled out are not important as far as we're concerned."

Farrell and Case were not looking for the pattern they discovered. Nonetheless, they were forced to conclude the obvious:

> The disproportionate selection of Italians for inclusion in the Black Book raises important legal questions regarding regulatory compliance with the 1989 law stating that entry must not be based on ethnicity . . . [Those listed] have presented little threat to the industry. These observations suggest that the function of the regulatory mechanism are indeed symbolic . . . The Black Book also serves to illustrate patterns of dominance and subordination in Nevada: certain groups make the selections, and other groups are selected.

The board's philosophy reverberated into the executive suites of the Mormon-controlled Bank of Las Vegas, which accelerated its denials of Italian business-loan applications. (Until this time, the Bank of Las Vegas had been instrumental in financing the Sahara, the Fremont, the Sands, the Desert Inn, the Dunes, the Hacienda, the Stardust, and the Riviera.) But despite the xenophobia, the Outfit merely implemented Plan B, a strategy that gave it independence from the local banks.

Toward the end of the year, the Chicago underworld, with new upperworld partners, made its first major loan from the First National Bank of Accardo, aka the Teamsters pension fund. On September 3, 1959, a new Las Vegas partnership recorded a deed of sale in Nevada's Clark County Courthouse for a desert tract consisting of hundreds of acres two miles southwest of the Strip. On the same day, papers were entered in Chicago to obtain a 6 percent interest, $1-million loan from the pension fund, with Jimmy Hoffa and his fourteen trustees signing on as beneficiaries. Surprisingly, the intended investment had nothing to do with casino construction. In a move that demonstrated the underworld's awareness of their upperworld predecessors' transition to legitimacy, the hoods decided to build a hospital.

The resultant hundred-bed Sunrise Hospital was more than a public relations ploy. The venture, a for-profit undertaking with built-in guarantees for the investors, would be but a prelude to an even bigger Sin City investment. The partnership chose as the hospital's president Mervyn Adelson, the transplanted son of a Beverly Hills grocer, and currently the "clean" owner of the Strip's Colonial House club (known locally as a magnet for Sin City hookers). Adelson had teamed up with local Realtor Irwin Molasky to build the much needed hospital, but the partnership came up short before they could realize their dream. The duo thus turned to Moe Dalitz (a boyhood friend of Hoffa's) with his Chicago Teamster connections. "We ran out of money and had to take in some investors," Molasky explained to the *Las Vegas Review-Journal*. The hospital's success was made certain when Jimmy Hoffa decreed that the Teamster and Culinary unions' medical fund would pay for treatment only if the rank and file were treated at Sunrise. Thus, the new hospital saw an influx of thousands of "captive" patients. Irwin Molasky called it "an early form of managed care." The lucrative facility also boasted the Sunrise Hospital Pharmacy, Inc., the Sunrise Hospital Clinical Laboratory, and the Sunrise Hospital X-Ray Lab, the only one in the county. Adelson and Dalitz would later parlay their huge Sunrise profits, with the aid of a $27-million loan from Allen Dorfman's fund, into the construction of the luxurious Rancho La Costa Resort, a favorite meeting spot for Joe Accardo and Dorfman, outside San Diego. Federal officials referred to La Costa as "a playground for the mob." One FBI report alleged that La Costa "is used as a clearinghouse for bookie operations. The phones are used to receive incoming lay-off bets." Adelson's share of the Las Vegas and La Costa profits were in turn utilized in 1966 to bankroll his Hollywood juggernaut, Lorimar Telepictures Productions, which produced television's *Dallas* and *The Waltons* series. Adelson and Molasky would also make the original land bequest that endowed the University of Nevada at Las Vegas.[7]

---

7. Other Lorimar credits include *Eight Is Enough, Knott's Landing, Family Matters, I'll Fly Away, Falcon Crest,* and *Alf,* all for television. On the big screen, Lorimar produced *Billy Budd, Sybil, Being There,* and *An Officer and a Gentleman.*

Merv Adelson was briefly married to TV journalist Barbara Walters. He has become great friends with the high and mighty, such as Israel's former prime minister, Benjamin Netanyahu, who attended Adelson's 1992 marriage to Walters. For years, Lorimar was headed by Leslie Moonves, currently the head of CBS Entertainment. Adelson recently merged Lorimar into Time-Warner and placed his money in East-West Capital Associates, which invests in digital motion picture infrastructure. His son, Andy Adelson, runs Filmtrust, which sells film-production accounting software.

But the hospital provided one other service, and this was to the underworld. Per custom, the Dalitz-Outfit faction overlooked no ancillary devices for squeezing profits from the Sunrise Hospital operation. Ed Becker, the former public relations man for the Outfit's Riviera Hotel, recently disclosed one of the hospital's most appealing hidden advantages. According to Becker, Joe Accardo and associates used the hospital to fill the void left when their courier Virginia Hill fled to Europe. "They would send a man out and he would be met at [Las Vegas"] McCarran Airport,' Becker recently recalled. "He was put in an ambulance, driven to Sunrise Hospital, spend a few days there; [then] back in the ambulance, back to the airport, then back to Chicago. That's where the skim was going." Becker, who went on to have business relationships with a number of underworld luminaries, eventually became a Las Vegas private detective and author. And Sunrise Hospital remains a highly regarded Las Vegas moneymaker. The Sunrise Hospital "mediplex" is the largest hospital west of Chicago, with 688 rooms and 1,200 doctors on staff.

The Sunrise Hospital conglomerate was but a prelude to an even bigger moneymaker, the Paradise Development Company. Employing great foresight, the Sunrise partners began developing the adjacent land tract, with the kind assistance of $5 million in government-guaranteed Federal Housing Authority (FHA) loans. With names like Paradise Homes, Desert Palms, and Paradise Palms, the consortium's homes, in the $22,000–$42,000 range, sold by the hundreds. In fact, during one two-year stretch, the abodes were selling at a rate of one per day. Authors Roger Morris and Sally Denton wrote accurately that the "Paradise Development Company shaped the emerging commercial and residential map of the city." The company's profits would be used to underwrite even more massive withdrawals from the pension fund, the result of which transformed Las Vegas from a gambler's getaway into a vibrant Western city. The U.S. Department of Labor estimated that the pension fund's loans in Las Vegas ultimately totaled $300 million, or one sixth of the fund's total assets, all of which was repaid. Since the underworld began to develop the town in the early fifties, the city's population has exploded from under fifty thousand to 1.5 million today. Clark County sheriff Ralph Lamb succinctly summarized the importance of the underworld on the development of Las Vegas. "Don't forget this town owes something to these people," Lamb said. "Without them there wouldn't be a Las Vegas." And none of it would have happened if Joe Accardo and Curly Humphreys had not put their man in charge of the pension fund.

*   *   *

Perhaps in celebration of his gang's successful hijacking of the pension fund, Joe Accardo took his wife, Clarice, and longtime friends Mr. and Mrs. Anthony DeGrazia on a European holiday. The trip featured a stop in Zurich, where Joe probably made a deposit in his Swiss account. What made the vacation even more newsworthy back in Chicago was that DeGrazia was a lieutenant in the Chicago police department. When the press reported the story, the chagrined police commissioner quickly suspended the thirty-seven-year veteran and later fired him upon his return. However, few worried about the financial health of DeGrazia, with his police pension and the friendship of Joe Accardo.

Before the Outfit could continue to siphon pension fund treasure into the development of Las Vegas, it was distracted by the pull of dramas on the national stage. On the less significant side, some gang members were, like many of the country's Italian immigrants, in a lather over the fall 1959 debut of the ABC television series *The Untouchables,* a less than accurate retelling of Eliot Ness' battles with Al Capone and Frank Nitti. The show was a virtual slander of all things Italian and quickly elicited howls of protest from concerned Italian-American organizations across the country. Angered by the "goombah of the week" theme of the show, the protesters pointed out how the show conveniently ignored all upperworld corruption.

The backlash started even before the show's two-hour pilot aired, after word of producer Desi Arnaz's purchase of Oscar Fraley's book of the same name hit the press. In Hollywood, Arnaz braced for the inevitable. "Having gone to high school and been such good friends with Sonny Capone [Al's son]," Arnaz wrote in his autobiography, "I knew damn well, even though I hadn't seen or heard from Sonny in years, that I was going to get a call from him." Coincidentally, Desi and Sonny had attended St. Patrick's High School in Palm Beach together, and Desi described his basketball teammate Sonny as "my best friend there."

On the very day the story hit the papers, Sonny Capone called Arnaz. "Why you? Why did you have to do it?" Sonny asked.

"Sonny, if I don't do it, somebody else is going to do it, and maybe it's better that I'm going to do it," Arnaz answered. Arnaz wrote that he "couldn't get to first base with Sonny." Soon, Arnaz's Desilu company heard from lawyers for Al's widow, Mae Capone, who filed a multimillion-dollar libel and unfair-use-of-image suit against the studio. Although Capone lost her case against Arnaz, the story was far from over. In

New York, Albert "Tough Tony" Anastasia organized demonstrations outside ABC's corporate offices and saw to it that the longshoremen under his control would leave crates of cigarettes made by the show's sponsor Liggett & Meyers untouched on the docks. Within days, Liggett withdrew its sponsorship of the show. In Chicago, however, the Outfit, especially the volatile Mooney Giancana, was far from satisfied.

According to information received by the Chicago Crime Commission's chief investigator Wayne Johnson, Mae Capone called Mooney Giancana, who ordered Sinatra to pay a visit to Arnaz. When Arnaz refused to fold, Sinatra became enraged. In their history of Desilu, Coyne Sanders and Tom Gilbert wrote about the confrontation:

> Frank Sinatra abruptly moved his production company off the Desilu-Gowar lot to Samuel Goldwyn Studios. "What started as a discussion about Italians on Desilu's TV series, *The Untouchables,* ended up close to fisticuffs," said one observer, who noted that Arnaz inflamed the altercation by calling Sinatra a "television failure." *Variety* reported, "Frank Sinatra and Desi Arnaz almost came to blows at Desi's Indian Wells Hotel when Frank looked him up after midnight to discuss the depicting of Italians as ruthless mobsters on the *Untouchables* programs."

Unsatisfied, Giancana wanted Arnaz whacked. In his biography, *The Last Mafioso,* Los Angeles hood Jimmy "the Weasel" Fratianno described one conversation with Johnny Rosselli:

Johnny: Have you seen that TV show, *The Untouchables*?

Jimmy: A couple of times, but I don't have time to watch that shit.

Johnny: Let me tell you something, Jimmy. Millions of people all over the world see this show every fucking week. It's even popular in Italy. And what they see is a bunch of Italian lunatics running around with machine guns, talking out of the corner of their mouths, slopping up spaghetti like a bunch of fucking pigs. They make Capone and Nitti look like bloodthirsty maniacs. The guys that write that shit don't know the first thing about the way things were in those days. Eliot Ness, my ass. The tax boys got Al, not Ness. And what did he ever have to do with Frank Nitti?

Jimmy: Nobody pays attention to that shit. It's like a comic book, a joke. Who cares?

Johnny: I'll tell you, Jimmy. Sam [Giancana] cares. Joe Batters [Accardo] cares, Paul Ricca cares, and I care. Jimmy, what I'm about to tell you has been decided by our family. The top guys have voted a hit. I've already talked to Bomp [San Diego hood Frank Bompensiero] about it. We're going to clip Desi Arnaz, the producer of this show."

Bompensiero and his boys, however, were not as excited about the Arnaz situation as Giancana and made only one cursory attempt to track the producer. Bomp informed Fratianno that his hit men "got disgusted and went back home, so the [Desi Arnaz] deal is down the drain." They also knew that Giancana was moody and that this tantrum would likely soon pass. The situation was further resolved, according to Wayne Johnson, when Mae Capone vetoed the hit against her son's former best friend. For his part, Arnaz defused the situation by making Sinatra a standing $1-million offer to produce any film of his choice at Arnaz's studio. "That concluded the contract," Fratianno wrote. "Desi Arnaz never knew how close he came to getting clipped."

Of far more import was the charged political climate that was encroaching on the Outfit's world. With the 1960 presidential campaign looming, the war rooms of both major parties were appreciative of the clout now wielded by Al Capone's heirs. Their influence stretched from Miami to New York, through the major Midwestern cities, on to Las Vegas and Hollywood. Their sway over the nation's Teamsters and other labor unions alone made the Chicago gang impossible to ignore. Thus, the Outfit would soon be courted by both Vice President Richard Nixon, the Republican candidate, and Joe Kennedy, the father of the Democratic candidate, Jack Kennedy. It now appears likely that Vice President Nixon simultaneously oversaw a 1960 operation that also needed the Outfit's help, an escapade that, if successful, would have all but guaranteed his electoral success: He wanted new Cuban strong-arm Fidel Castro overthrown and, if possible, murdered. Thus, just as it had done repeatedly since the days of FDR, the upperworld White House enlisted the underworld Outfit.

16.

Courted by Old Joe Kennedy:
The Outfit Arrives

His papa bought him the presidency.

> —Lee Oswald, speaking with his wife,
> Marina, about President Kennedy

It consumed our lives that year.

> —Jeanne Humphreys, speaking of
> Curly's work on Jack Kennedy's behalf

The decade that ushered in a sociological revolution of youth and sexual liberation began fittingly enough: On January 20, 1960, Joe Kennedy's forty-two-year-old son, Jack, declared for the presidency, one year after then thirty-four-year-old Fidel Castro had seized America's Cuban playground; on the sexual front, February 29 saw *Playboy* magazine mogul Hugh Hefner, then just thirty-three years old, open his first Playboy Club in the vortex of the Outfit's power structure at 116 East Walton Street in downtown Chicago. These seemingly disparate, but seminal, occurrences held more commonalties than the youthfulness of their standard-bearers: They could not ignore the power and influence of the middle-aged men who composed Chicago's Outfit.

The Second City bosses wasted little time in sinking their claws into Hefner's new "key club" venture. As with most other Near North businesses, the Playboy Club had to make accommodations with the countless semilegit enterprises within the all-encompassing grasp of the Outfit. The intersections started with Hef's liquor license, which had to be approved by the Outfit-controlled First Ward headquarters, where John D'Arco and Pat Marcy reigned supreme.

Much of the club's cutlery was said to be supplied by businesses owned by Al Capone's brother Ralph, while other furnishings had their origin in the gang's distribution warehouses. In addition to the army of Outfit soldiers who were seen cavorting at the new jazz-inflected boîte, Accardo's boys (via Humphreys' union stranglehold) controlled the numerous concessions – bartenders, waiters, coat checkers, parking valets, jukeboxes – so vital to the new enterprise. Local bands that supplied the requisite cool-jazz backdrop were booked by the Outfit's musicians' union. Coordinating the gang's feeding frenzy was the club's general manager, Tony Roma (of later restaurant fame), who was married to Josephine Costello, daughter of Capone bootlegger Joseph Costello.[1]

Outfit bosses were bestowed exclusive Number One Keys, which allowed them to date the otherwise off-limits "bunnies" and drink on a free tab. Slot king, and Humphreys crony, Eddie Vogel, dated "Bunny Mother" Peg Strak, who later became Roma's executive secretary when Roma was promoted to operations manager of Playboy Clubs International, Inc., which oversaw the empire of sixty-three thousand international key holders. Although Hefner himself has never been tainted by his club's unavoidable contact with the Outfit, it is interesting to note that in 1977, when he fought a copyright infringement lawsuit filed by Universal Studios, Hefner employed the services of Sidney Korshak. For a $50,000 fee, Korshak attempted in vain to settle the case with the studio, which was run by his old friend Lew Wasserman.

On the night of the gala Playboy Club opening, the top Outfit men, Joe Accardo, Mooney Giancana, Curly Humphreys, and Johnny Rosselli, were not in attendance. Now at the peak of their influence, the Chicago bosses had been invited to a power summit in New York City.[2] However, this time their host was not another Commission boss coping with internal strife, but was none other than Ambassador Joe Kennedy.

Details of the meeting first surfaced fifteen years later, when Manhattan lawyer Mario Brod gave a series of interviews to historian Richard

---

1. Chicago historian Ovid Demaris described how Roma operated the club: 'One of Roma's first acts as general manager of the Chicago Playboy Club was to award the garbage collection to Willie "Potatoes" Daddano's West Suburban Scavenger Service . . . Attendant Service Corporation, a [Ross] Prio-[Joseph] DiVarco enterprise, was already parking playboy cars, checking playboy hats, and handing playboy towels in the rest room. Other playboys were drinking [Joe] Fusco beers and liquors, eating [James] Allegretti meat, and smoking [Eddie] Vogel cigarets.'

2. An FBI telex of March 10, 1960, notes Rosselli's flight to New York from L.A. The Bureau guessed that Johnny was there on film production business.

Mahoney. Brod had been a liaison between the Central Intelligence Agency and the New York crime bosses since World War II, when the CIA's precursor, the Office of Strategic Services (OSS), had kicked off the U.S. government's long, mutually beneficial relationship with the underworld. The partnership had its known origins in 1942, when the OSS enlisted Meyer Lansky and the imprisoned Charles "Lucky" Luciano in its effort to deter wartime sabotage in the New York harbor. The government also utilized Luciano's Italian contacts to gain intelligence in anticipation of the invasion of Sicily. For his efforts, detailed in Rodney Campbell's book *The Luciano Project,* Lucky Luciano was allowed to leave prison in exchange for permanent exile in Italy. At the time, Brod was an OSS captain in Italy under future CIA counterintelligence chief James Angleton. In that theater, Angleton and Brod coordinated the information received from Luciano.[3] After the war, Brod maintained his contacts with both the underworld and the U.S. intelligence community from his Park Avenue law office. According to Angleton's biographer, Tom Mangold, "[Brod] helped the CIA, on a regular, salaried, contract basis, with all those awkward jobs in the intelligence business that need an untraceable intermediary." Leonard McCoy, a longtime CIA analyst who became the deputy chief for counterintelligence, described the Angleton-Brod relationship thus: "Angleton used Brod anytime he needed to go around normal channels. Brod was involved with organized labor officials, and certain unsavory characters. Whenever Angleton needed to keep the world from knowing the CIA was involved in an operation, he used Brod."

When Bobby Kennedy announced he was going to subpoena Brod in 1963 to ask about his Teamster friends, Angleton personally called Kennedy and advised him to drop the initiative. Angleton came to Brod's rescue again in 1975, when he convinced a Senate committee to drop Brod from its interview list, lest he suffer retaliation at the hands of mobsters who had no inkling of his cozy history with the U.S. government.

*　　*　　*

3. Confidential government sources reported to Johnny Rosselli's biographers that "Mr. Smooth" also had a history of cooperation with the federal government. According to officials of the International Cooperation Agency, Rosselli assisted the CIA-backed Standard Fruit Company in the 1957 ouster of Guatemala's president, Castillo Armas.

Although Brod had no recollection as to which of his mob friends invited him to Felix Young's Restaurant in Manhattan on February 29, 1960, he had a clear memory of who showed up and what was discussed. Rosselli told Brod that Joe Kennedy, whom Johnny had known since both their early Hollywood days in the 1920s, had asked Rosselli to set up the confab. Brod told Mahoney that the New York and Boston crime bosses, whom Kennedy had also asked Rosselli to invite, failed to show up. Once the attendees were in place, Joe Kennedy quickly got to the point: He wanted a large contribution to Jack's campaign, and more important, the Outfit's labor support for the election push. According to Brod, Curly Humphreys objected, noting that Joe's other son Bobby was on an adrenaline-fueled mob-chasing crusade. Mahoney, who finally wrote of Brod's account in 2000, noted, "The elder Kennedy replied that it was Jack who was running for president, not Bobby, and that this was 'business, not politics.'" After that weak argument, Kennedy left the restaurant and his unimpressed guests. However, Rosselli told the group that it was significant that Joe Kennedy had come to *them*. He asked his associates to at least consider the Kennedy alliance. Little did the bosses know, but Joe Kennedy was used to getting his way, and he would continue to arrange sit-downs with the Outfit in hopes of winning them over.

In 1988, ignorant of Mahoney's unpublished interview with Brod, Irish journalist Anthony Summers spoke with Edna Daulyton, the hostess at Felix Young's Restaurant in 1960. She also remembered the February powwow, telling Summers, "I took the reservations." Daulyton recalled an even larger roster than did Brod, informing Summers, "It was as though every gangster chief in the United States was there. I don't remember all the names now, but Johnny Rosselli was there . . . They were all top people. I was amazed Joe Kennedy would take the risk."[4]

But Joe Kennedy believed that he had to take the risk if his son was to stand any chance of prevailing in the upcoming national contest. On the Republican side, Vice President Richard Nixon had allied with Outfit-

---

4. A third corroboration for the Kennedy luncheon at Young's is a contemporaneous handwritten record, names included. Regretfully, the material is stored in an off-limits portion of a federal archive. The author was made aware of it through an employee with access. Out of consideration for the well-being of both the employee and the record, the location cannot be disclosed. There is currently an effort to force an opening of the collection that holds the material.

connected Teamster boss Jimmy Hoffa.[5] (When Nixon was defeated, his part of the deal could not be delivered, but his debt to the Teamster leader would be more than nullified when Nixon eventually became president.)

Papa Joe knew, however, that an arrangement with the Chicago Outfit would trump any alliances formed by the opposition. Joe had had firsthand knowledge of the power of the Chicago gang since his purchase of the world's largest office building, the Chicago Merchandise Mart, in 1945, a virtual impossibility without making concessions to the gang.[6] As to why Joe Kennedy would "take such a risk" in meeting personally with hoods, a clue is offered by an associate of Joe's son-in-law Steve Smith, who overheard Joe telling Smith that the other candidates "didn't have the balls to go straight to the mob themselves." Joe did. But then again, Joe Kennedy had been dealing with the underworld for years, and among Kennedy's earliest shady acquaintances was the gang from Chicago.

Joe Kennedy and the Outfit

Joe Kennedy was Meyer Lansky with a Harvard degree.
>   −A member of the Chicago Outfit

Few doubt that Old Joe Kennedy had the "balls" to deal directly with gangsters. And historians agree that since the days preceding the 1929 stock market crash, when Kennedy had sold short on his stocks, driving the Depression even deeper while he profited from the nation's misery, Joe Kennedy's empire had come first, with patriotism and ethics distant runners-up. As for Kennedy's ability to make deals with the underworld, the story likely begins during Volstead, when many immigrants seized the brass ring known as bootlegging.

It is all but universally accepted as historical fact that in the 1920s Joe

---

5. Senate investigator Walter Sheridan, and separately, journalist Dan Moldea, have detailed how California congressman Allan Oakley Hunter played the go-between in the Nixon-Hoffa dealing. With assurances from Nixon that he would, if elected, ease Hoffa's legal harassment, Hoffa saw to it that the Teamsters executive board endorsed Nixon. Close Hoffa aide Ed Partin has stated that he witnessed Hoffa deliver $1 million to the Nixon war chest, half of it collected from New Orleans boss Carlos Marcello, and half from New York/New Jersey mobsters. Marcello rightfully feared deportation in a Kennedy administration.

6. Completed in 1930, the 4,023,400-square-foot Mart was the largest office space in the world until the construction of the Pentagon.

Kennedy was up to his eyes in illegal alcohol. Leading underworld bootleggers from Frank Costello to Doc Stacher to Owney Madden to Joe Bonanno to Meyer Lansky to Lucky Luciano have all recalled for their biographers or for news journalists how they had bought booze that had been shipped into the country by Joseph Kennedy.[7] On the receiving side of the booze business, everyone from Joe's Hyannis Port chums to the eastern Long Island townsfolk who survived the Depression by uncrating booze off the bootleggers' boats tells tales of Joe Kennedy's involvement in the illegal trade.

Overlooked by most was the 1996 discovery of a written record that described Kennedy's illegal alcohol trafficking. While researching a television documentary based on Edward Behr's book *Prohibition,* the A&E Network producers uncovered the records of a 1926 Canadian government investigation into Canadian alcohol exported to America during prohibition. At the time the report by the Royal Commission on Customs and Excise was compiled, Canadian authorities were attempting to discern how much export tax they were owed by the American bootleggers. The commission's paperwork, displayed on the show that aired, showed that the one American purchaser's name that appeared time and time again was Joseph Kennedy. The files showed that Kennedy had been buying up liquor from Canada's Hiram Walker facility, which had upped its production by 400 percent to meet the demand of Kennedy and the other U.S. "importers." In the same Hiram Walker address book that contained the name Joseph Kennedy were the names of other American bootleggers, among them Al Capone and his "financial director" Jake Guzik. It was the earliest hint of an intersection between Kennedy and the Chicago underworld.

The inclusion of Kennedy's and Capone's names in the same Canadian government bootlegging file may not be coincidence. Rumors have long been rife in Chicago that one of the many hoods Kennedy had cut sales deals with was none other than Al Capone. The core of the allegations is that Kennedy made arrangements with Capone regarding transshipment of booze across Lake Michigan from Canada – a route controlled by

---

7. According to the late talk-show host Morton Downey Jr., the son of Joe's closest friend and business partner, Irish tenor Morton Downey Sr., Joe Kennedy and Downey (accompanied by Mort Jr.) would often meet at Frank Costello's Waldorf-Astoria headquarters, where the foursome regularly went for haircuts.

Capone's Syndicate. Recently, a fascinating corroboration for those stories has surfaced.

In 1994, John Kohlert, a master piano tuner and retired plant supervisor for Wurlitzer Pianos, gave a videotaped oral history just prior to his death at age ninety-three.[8] In his recitation, Kohlert pointed out that he had obtained two master's degrees, one in acoustical engineering from Johns Hopkins University. But he had got his start as a young piano tuner in the speakeasies owned by the man who paid for his college education, Al Capone. On the tape, Kohlert tells his story of Al Capone merely as an unremarkable aside to the history of his life.

One night in 1926, while tuning the home piano of Capone (who had become like a father figure), young Kohlert was invited to stay for a spaghetti dinner. "We're having a special guest," Big Al informed the young man. At the dinner, Joe Kennedy showed up, and Kohlert watched as Capone and Kennedy struck a deal wherein Capone traded his whiskey (from his Canadian distillery) for a shipment of Kennedy's Seagram's brand. The exchanges were to be made in Lake Michigan, off Mackinac Island.

Years later, when Kohlert was arrested in Britain (on stowaway charges – he had escaped Nazi Germany, but had no passport), he got a message out to the now ambassador to Great Britain, Joseph Kennedy. The note said: "I hope you remember me from that spaghetti dinner in Cicero . . . " The next day, Kennedy came to the prison and saw to Kohlert's release. In 1944, when Joe introduced Haig & Haig whiskey to Chicago, his agent was, according to FBI files, Tom Cassara, a Miami gangster who was shot dead soon after arranging the deal with an operative from the Outfit.

Curly Humphreys also remembered Joe Kennedy from the Volstead era. Years later, Curly Humphreys' daughter, Llewella, recalled her father speaking of his distrust of Kennedy, explaining that one of Curly's hijacked booze trucks was hit by bombs tossed by Kennedy's bootleggers, an apparent double cross by Kennedy, the details of which were not clarified for the family. Jeanne Humphreys also has vague memories of Curly speaking about a booze theft by Joe Kennedy's forces. Kennedy's interest in Al Capone's liquor business was buttressed by *Washington Post* reporter and Joe Kennedy biographer Ronald Kessler, whose sources indicated that Joe promised a Chicago friend that "if he got Al Capone's

---

8. The videotape is in the author's possession.

business, he would give him 25 percent. The man got the business, but Joe then fired him and hounded him so he could not find another job."

Curly Humphreys was also said by his family to have connected with Kennedy when the Irish patriarch moved in on the film business and eventually plundered the stocks of operations such as the Pathé newsreel company. Kennedy was a major player in Tinseltown in the 1920s when he purchased Film Booking Office (FBO) and Radio-Keith-Orpheum (RKO). While his family stayed on the East Coast, Joe lived in Beverly Hills for three and a half years producing seventy-six mostly forgettable films for FBO, and conducting a much publicized affair with actress Gloria Swanson. After his 1931 appointment by President Roosevelt to be the first chairman of the Securities and Exchange Commission, Kennedy intermittently returned to Hollywood, most notably to mediate a dispute in the boardrooms of Paramount Pictures, an uproar referred to as a corporate "civil war." This was during the same period that the Outfit, through Johnny Rosselli, controlled most of the craft unions and received kickbacks, or extortion, from most of the major studios.

Still other Outfit leaders crossed paths with Joe Kennedy. Johnny Rosselli told the Church Committee years later that he, like Curly Humphreys, remembered Joe Kennedy from his robber-baron, bootlegging, stock-plundering days. Rosselli testified that he knew Joe as far back as his 1930s Hollywood era, when the two used to golf and play cards together. According to Dade County (Florida) police files, Rosselli maintained his acquaintance with the elder Kennedy for the rest of Kennedy's life, and that in a 1960 golfing chat, Papa Joe expressed his concern to Rosselli about his sons' problems with women. Rosselli gave a similar recounting to D.C. police detective and mob expert Joe Shimon.

Joe Takes Charge of the Backrooms

Joe Kennedy had coveted the Oval Office for three decades, first for himself and then for his namesake son, Joe, Jr., who was killed in World War II. All those who met his second son, Jack, however, readily saw that he had the requisite charm, charisma, and intellect to succeed where the father had failed. It is now clear that Joe Kennedy concluded that for Jack to gain the Oval Office, the cooperation of all was necessary – and Joe meant *all*. As the patriarch himself said, "There are no accidents in politics." He thus informed Jack, "I will work out the plans to elect you president." Joe Kennedy biographer Richard Whalen summed up the ensuing electoral atmosphere: "Jack's campaign had two separate and distinct sides. On display before the voters was the candidate, surrounded by clean-cut, youthful volunteer workers, the total effect being one of wholesome amateurism. At work on the hidden side of the campaign were the professional politicians whom Joe had quietly recruited. In his hotel suite and other private meeting places, they sat with their hats on and cigars aglow, a hard-eyed, cynical band, brainstorming strategy.'

Early on, Joe set his sights on the massive labor vote. Likely unaware of the deal already cut between Nixon and Hoffa, Joe Kennedy attempted to forge a Kennedy alliance with the very man his son Robert was railing against in the McClellan hearings. The senior Kennedy called old family friend Frank Sinatra, asking him to first arrange a meeting with liberal Teamster leader Harold Gibbons. Gibbons met with Joe at the Kennedy compound in Palm Beach, whereupon Joe assured him that Bobby's anti-Teamster vendetta had been put aside. 'Well, Mr. Gibbons," Kennedy advised, "I don't think there's much of a war going on between the Kennedys and Hoffa. I hardly hear the name Hoffa in our house any-more." Although the Hoffa-baiting Bobby was certainly not on the same page as Papa Joe regarding the Teamster overture, there is evidence that his more accommodating brother Jack was indeed. Jimmy Hoffa's strong-arm Joe Franco was present when John Kennedy phoned Hoffa to offer a truce. Hoffa was entertaining the idea when Kennedy then had the temerity to ask Hoffa for a campaign contribution. According to Franco, this sent Hoffa into a screaming tirade against the brother of his nemesis, Bobby Kennedy. Joe Kennedy, however, would continue to assuage the fears of other Teamster leaders throughout the 1960 election year. He became fast friends with Gibbons, often sharing a table at Miami Beach's Eden Roc Hotel, according to Gibbons' secretary and PR director, Jake McCarthy.

Even before the 1960 primary season commenced, Joe Kennedy began his plan to undo the damage caused by his firebrand son, Bobby. John L. Lewis, head of the United Mine Workers Union, related a story to the *Chicago Tribune*'s Walter Trohan. According to Lewis, Joe Kennedy flew in to see him soon after Jack's announcement, asking for help in the important primary in West Virginia – a state overflowing with mine workers. Lewis told Kennedy to relax – he already had the state won. Lewis was well aware of the agents Joe Kennedy had dispensed through-out the state, dispersing cash to county assessors, judges, party chairmen, etc. The average payoff was said to be $4,000 to $5,000. It was under-stood that much of this was undertaken without Jack Kennedy's knowledge. Lewis recalled, "His agents would say, 'Joe Kennedy is very interested in this state and he would like to help you out.' He never mentioned Jack."

By the time Senator John Fitzgerald "Jack" Kennedy declared his candidacy for the 1960 presidential nomination, his father had determined that the electoral-rich state of Illinois had to be guaranteed. However, many experts feel that, given the strong Irish Catholic labor tradition in that city, support for Jack Kennedy was already a lock. Nonetheless, in his desire to acquire the state's twenty-seven electors, Joe decided he couldn't leave anything to chance, his own knowledge of the inner workings of that city having come from his long history as a businessman who had to keep Chicago's local pols, unions, and hoods happy. As early as 1952, according to numerous accounts, Joe Kennedy had sent Kenny O'Donnell, a Harvard friend of Bobby Kennedy's and an early member of the "Kennedy machine," to Chicago to sow the seeds for young Jack's eventual campaign for the presidency. O'Donnell would become the patriarch's liaison to Chicago mayor Richard Daley. Joe Kennedy and Richard Daley were longtime political cronies, who lunched together often at Joe's Merchandise Mart. So close was their relationship that Daley was seemingly cleared to spend Joe's money as he saw fit. On one occasion, when candidate Kennedy was speaking in Chicago, Daley wanted the event televised nationally, at a cost of $125,000. The mayor instructed an aide: "Go over to Mr. [Joe] Kennedy at the Merchandise Mart, and he'll give you the check." Which is exactly what happened.

In truth, Richard Daley had a selfish motive in getting out (or inventing) Chicago's Democratic vote. Within the last year, Republican Ben Adamowski, the state's attorney who was on the Republican slate, had announced major indictments against members of Daley's infrastructure.[9] Most disconcerting for Daley and the Outfit was the rumor that the

---

9. Adamowski was a strait-laced anticorruption crusader who had broken from the Democratic ranks in protest of Daley's ties to both the underworld and the party machine's patronage gravy train. In 1959, Adamowski unearthed a $500,000-per-year traffic-ticket-fixing scheme in the city's traffic court, with the kickbacks ending up lining the pockets of Daley appointees. At the beginning of 1960, Adamowski had broken the Summerdale Scandal, in which a twenty-year-old burglar admitted that, for two years, twelve Chicago policemen had assisted in his wholesale thievery by acting as lookouts, then using their patrol cars to cart off the goods to be fenced.

cont'd over/

recent charges would be the tip of the iceberg should Adamowski, who was personally protecting Morrison, win another four-year term. Among other looming problems was Adamowski's investigation of Daley's city commissioner of investigations, Irving "Sweep It Under the Rug" Cohen. According to Adamowski's chief investigator, Paul Newey, "It was Cohen's purpose to keep all the book joints going, but under wraps so that the media wouldn't make an issue of it during an election year. Daley knew it was wide-open."

"Gee, the mayor is fit to be tied, Curly," Pat Marcy informed Humphreys one day at Celano's. "He's letting the Polack, Adamowski, rib him, and he shouldn't do that," Humphreys replied. Humphreys then suggested that the "boys" should attempt to have a more friendly police commissioner installed to take the heat off of Daley. But all Humphreys' local politicking was soon to be dwarfed by a new assignment emanating from Hyannis Port, Massachusetts.

With the pundits predicting a virtual toss-up in the November election, the Kennedy patriarch had decided he needed the support of the Chicago Outfit, which was legendary for its ability to marshal foot soldiers to get out the vote locally and was known to be in control of many of the labor unions across the country. Papa Joe, knowing that Jimmy Hoffa would never endorse Bobby Kennedy's brother, concluded that the key players would also have to include the non-Teamster labor unions so often infiltrated by the likes of Curly Humphreys. Kennedy intimates make it clear that Joe intended to embark on his own to run the election show,

---

cont'd   When the dust settled, eight cops were imprisoned, and many more suspended. Also caught up in the fallout from the Summerdale Scandal were numerous Outfit-controlled police, who were being summarily reassigned. Concurrent FBI wiretaps disclosed that the thief, Richie Morrison, was the nephew of the mistress Curly Humphreys had taken on the lam with him to Mexico three decades earlier, Billie Jean Morrison. The Bureau also heard that after Morrison was arrested, Curly attempted to funnel money to Billie Jean to silence her talkative nephew. "This is gonna be the biggest thing that ever hit the mayor," Humphreys predicted. "This kid has got thirty coppers, he has them all set up . . . This will spread like wildfire." The Genius then pronounced his decree: "Well, boys, I don't see how the Democrats can win with this scandal. This will whip the hell out of this administration . . . I hate to do it but we got to watch out for this administration." As Humphreys told an associate at Celano's tailor shop, "We can tell [the aunt] to give him five thousand dollars and tell him to claim he was hypnotized."

dealing with these less savory elements, hopefully in ways that would not become public knowledge. Those who knew Joe could hardly be surprised at just how low the Old Man would go to fulfill his dream. Jack's aide-de-camp Kenny O'Donnell later acknowledged, "If Jack had known about some of the telephone calls his father made on his behalf to Tammany Hall-type bosses during the 1960 campaign, Jack's hair would have turned white." "You know, the old man is hurting you," a friend warned Jack. To which Kennedy responded, "My father is working for his son. Do you want me to tell my father to stop working for his son?" Former Speaker of the U.S. House of Representatives from Massachusetts, and longtime Kennedy family friend, Thomas P. "Tip" O'Neill recalled, "These things happened, although Jack didn't always know about them. But the Old Man made his own arrangements over and above the campaign staff. Jack certainly knew that his father was spending a lot of money." A stock joke of Kennedy's on the campaign trail had candidate Kennedy quipping, "I have just received a wire from my father. It says, 'Don't buy one more vote than is necessary – I'll be damned if I'll pay for a landslide.'"

Clearly, the candidate was not always aware of the details, but those very details, just now emerging, would later force the Kennedy family to play coy when the investigators into Jack's murder, three years hence, were desperate for a motive.

The decision reached, Joe began his secret liaisons with the Outfit, and many believe it was not a new occurrence. Joe Kennedy's alleged dealings with Capone notwithstanding, the patriarch had surely reached accommodations with Chicago's gangster element on other occasions. Chicago, after all, was the scene of one of Kennedy's greatest financial triumphs, the purchase of the enormously undervalued Merchandise Mart for $12.5 million, of which he was rumored to have put up none of his own money. (It was reputed to be worth five times that much, and by 1969 it was valued at $75 million.[10]) With the Mart located in the heart of Chicago's business district, it is virtually inconceivable that the Outfit-controlled unions did not have a vise grip on most if not all of the service and concession contracts that supported the behemoth. Joe Longmeyer, a

---

10. Years later, Kennedy's wife, Rose, observed, "Joe had a genius for seeing something and knowing it would be worth something more later on. And with the Mart, he was absolutely right . . . it skyrocketed in value and became the basis for a whole new Kennedy fortune."

veteran independent Chicago labor organizer, remembers one day when Curly Humphreys came into the furniture store where Longmeyer was working. "Humphreys arranged for the store owner to have entrée at the Mart," Longmeyer says. Such an opening allowed merchants to purchase wholesale goods in the Mart. "Since Humphreys had some kind of relationship with the management of the Mart, he got my boss in," Longmeyer added. Few old-time Chicagoans doubt that Kennedy, either by choice or necessity, formed some sort of alliance with the Outfit to guarantee the Mart's smooth running. As one of Giancana's drivers recently remarked, "Nobody does real business in Chicago without knowing Mooney. Joe [Kennedy] knew where the power was."

Joe Kennedy's first known election overture to Capone's heirs was the luncheon at Felix Young's, which Joe had had Johnny Rosselli arrange. However, when that summit produced no agreement, Joe Kennedy decided to approach the day-to-day boss, Mooney Giancana, separately. After all, they shared a mutual friendship with Frank Sinatra, whom Joe could use to press his case with Mooney.[11] One other commonality practically defied belief: Mooney Giancana, Johnny Rosselli, and Joe's candidate son all shared a girlfriend, Judy Campbell.

Joe and Mooney

In 1997, Meyer Lansky's best friend and close associate, Vincent "Jimmy Blue Eyes" Alo, consented to a first-ever interview in which he recalled his knowledge of Joe Kennedy's efforts to approach Mooney Giancana on behalf of his son:

> Joe came to me very early. Joe Kennedy and I had a mutual friend, Phil Regan, the actor and singer from Brooklyn. Joe sent Phil to see me.[12] We

---

11. Incredibly, there is evidence that even mob-hating Robert Kennedy may have acknowledged the need to court the crime bosses. Award-winning investigative journalist for *Newsday* Mike Dorman was told by New Orleans Mafia don Carlos Marcello that RFK traveled to the Crescent City, attempting to convince Marcello to deliver the Louisiana delegation to JFK in the Democratic convention. Marcello turned him down, politely informing him that he was backing Lyndon Johnson. Marcello was convinced that this was the genesis of Bobby's later obsessive crusade against both him and LBJ.

12. Phil Regan would go on to spend a year in jail for bribing a California zoning commissioner, eventually pardoned by California governor Jerry Brown.

met at the Sea View in Bal Harbour [Florida]. Phil told me that they had it [the electoral vote] figured out to the last detail. Even that early they knew that Chicago would make all the difference. I don't know how they knew it – this was before computers. The point is that they knew I knew Sam Giancana. Joe Kennedy wanted me talk to him about helping Jack in Chicago. I turned him down. I wasn't in the habit of interfering in elections. The next thing I hear is that they went to Sinatra.[13]

Although the Lansky faction, according to Jimmy Alo, had declined to serve as Joe's liaison to the Outfit, Joe had far from given up. As Alo later

13. Although Alo turned down acting as liaison with Giancana, some evidence suggests that Meyer did his bit to help in the election. In a letter written by a former employee of Las Vegas' Desert Inn Hotel to its owner, Moe Dalitz, the employee, Annie Patterson, had, in 1966, fallen upon hard times and wrote the former Cleveland-based gambler for financial assistance. In her letter, Patterson firmly links Joe Kennedy to Lansky. In the context of her letter, it is clear that Patterson had gotten to know Joe Kennedy at either the Desert Inn or the Flamingo. It is also clear that Kennedy had wronged Patterson in some way. She alludes to a letter she had written, in retribution, to J. Edgar Hoover that instigated wiretaps that somehow incriminated the Kennedys. She further states that the material was locked away because "apparently none wanted to cross with the Kennedys." The letter continued: "Meyer Lansky was not the one who I knew. Mr. Kennedy told me about him and all the money that he parlayed from Las Vegas for the presidential campaign . . . I did not feel welcome to write to the Flamingo because Mr. Kennedy went around me and at no time was I paid one penny for my work; nor would I have ever contacted Mr. Lansky because I know (or had been told by Mr. Joseph Kennedy) that they were very close friends; in fact, it was Mr. Lansky that caused wiretapping to start there in the first place. He continued to "needle" Mr. J. Kennedy that Mr. K. was not receiving his full share of the take and why – so the Kennedy clan got together. I sincerely don't believe that Mr. Lansky had any idea of the damage that he was causing anyone because he wanted to be socially accepted by the Kennedy clan . . . I feel sure that if I contacted the kind-hearted Lansky and requested help, I would receive it but that is against my principals. He is a friend of Mr. Kennedy – I have never met him personally but I saw him from a distance in Miami Beach. (They met me there for an appointment.)"

The Lansky election allegations appear to be supported by an FBI memo from a confidential friend of Lansky's noting that prominent Miami hoodlums "are financially supporting and actively endeavoring to secure the nomination for the Presidency as Democratic candidate, Senator John F. Kennedy."

heard through the mob grapevine, Joe Kennedy indeed called on Frank Sinatra, one of the best friends of Joe's son-in-law actor Peter Lawford.

When Lawford wed Jack Kennedy's sister Patricia in 1954, he introduced the rakish Kennedy to the world of his fellow Rat Packers, which included Frank Sinatra, Dean Martin, Sammy Davis, Jr., Joey Bishop, and Lawford. Throughout the fifties, young Senator Kennedy trysted with his new pals in Hollywood and Las Vegas. Not long after his announcement to run, Jack Kennedy celebrated at the Sands in Las Vegas with Sinatra and the Rat Pack, who were there filming *Ocean's Eleven*. An FBI airtel memo from local agents to Director Hoover noted, "Showgirls from all over town were running in and out of the Senator's suite."

Joe Kennedy knew that Sinatra had a special kinship with Mooney Giancana, an influence that might now be used to convince the Outfit to support the Kennedy master plan. Sinatra had been chummy with Mooney at least as far back as the early fifties, when Rosselli and the Outfit had given a push to the singer's stalled movie career. The two exchanged pinkie rings, and Sinatra often closed his shows by singing "My Kind of Town (Chicago Is)" as a tribute to Mooney. Fellow crooner and friend Eddie Fisher remarked, "Frank wanted to be a hood. He once said, 'I'd rather be a don of the Mafia than president of the United States.' I don't think he was fooling." However, in real mob circles, Sinatra was often derided as a "wanna-be."

In 1997, the author undertook new research for an ABC News film project that coincided with the release of the Seymour Hersh book *The Dark Side of Camelot*. One key task was to attempt to learn more about Joe Kennedy's election appeal to the Outfit. What was learned added much detail to the long-rumored Sinatra contact. Although Frank Sinatra had previously refused all interview requests concerning his contacts with members of the underworld, that silence would be broken in 1997. After speaking with her father, Tina Sinatra was authorized to relay the following account:

A meeting was called [between Joe and Frank]. Dad was more than willing to go. It was a private meeting. I remember it was over lunch. I believe it was at Hyannis. Dad said he was ushered in. He hadn't been to the house before. Over lunch Joe said, "I believe that you can help me in Virginia and Illinois with our friends. I can't approach them, but you can." Joe wanted Frank to approach the union leader with the most influence, which was Sam Giancana. Sam could rally his people – to make certain that neighborhoods were encouraged to get out and vote.

It gave Dad pause. I know that it did that because he said that it did that. But it still wasn't anything he felt he shouldn't do. So off to Sam Giancana he went. Dad calls Sam Giancana to make a golf game and told Sam of his belief and support of Jack Kennedy. And I believe that Sam felt the same way.

Apparently, Joe Kennedy decided that communicating with Mooney Giancana via Sinatra was unsatisfactory. Perhaps not trusting the crooner to make the case for Jack as strong as he could, Joe pressed to meet Mooney face-to-face. For years the talk of such a meeting has persisted in Chicago. Veteran *Chicago Tribune* Washington bureau chief Walter Trohan recently recalled what he had been hearing from ace police reporter (and two-time Pulitzer Prize winner) George Bliss: "He told me that in the course of seeking the presidency against Nixon, Joe Kennedy was dealing with Giancana. I couldn't believe it at the time." Former sports promoter and bookie Harry Hall, who knew Joe Kennedy, Mooney Giancana, and other luminaries, has a similar memory: "I spent a lot of time with the Kennedys in the Biltmore Hotel. Joe knew all the racketeers. I had heard he made a lot of promises to the Outfit for their support." Recent interviews seem to, at long last, put some teeth into the reports Bliss and Hall were receiving.

One of Joe Kennedy's oldest Chicago friends (and political allies) was the revered circuit court judge of Chicago William J. Tuohy, whom Kennedy had met in 1945. According to one well-placed source, when Joe needed to meet with Mooney Giancana, he asked Tuohy who might arrange it. Tuohy contacted the source, a close personal friend, who had served as an assistant state's attorney in his office in previous years and was now well-known to represent members of the Outfit.

Robert J. McDonnell was described by his legal peers as "the rising star" in the state's attorney's office in the 1950s. One newsman went so far as to say "McDonnell could've been governor one day." Born into a family (the Healys) that were the landed gentry of Chicago – McDonnell's father worked with Joe Kennedy on the purchase of the Merchandise Mart, and his uncle was the premier public-works construction contractor in Chicago – McDonnell's future seemed bright. However, along the way, McDonnell fell prey to the twin demons of booze and gambling. Soon he found himself working off his marker with the Outfit by defending them in court. This being the case in 1960, Tuohy knew McDonnell would know how to contact Giancana.

Although McDonnell knew many key mob players, at the time he had only a fleeting acquaintance with Mooney Giancana (in later years, he would marry the don's daughter Antoinette). McDonnell told Tuohy that the way to reach Mooney was through his First Ward spokesman, Pat Marcy, who in turn was secretary to First Ward alderman John D'Arco. Tuohy, who indeed knew Marcy, thought the entire business was distasteful and made it clear that he was doing this only at the insistence of Joe Kennedy.

"Pat Marcy came over and talked with Judge Tuohy," says McDonnell. "A few days later I was told that Mooney [Giancana] wanted to meet with me at the Armory Lounge." The day he got the call, McDonnell drove to Giancana's Forest Park headquarters. There Mooney informed him that he would attend the meeting, but only if it was kept secret. Two days later, Judge Tuohy called McDonnell. "The meeting is on for tonight at five o'clock in the judge's chambers," said the judge. "I want you there."

Tuohy and Kennedy were already on-site when McDonnell arrived. Soon, Pat Marcy walked through the courthouse doors escorting Mooney Giancana. After making the introductions, Bob McDonnell left the men to talk in private. "As I was leaving, Judge Tuohy said to me, 'Wait for me, Bob. I'm just going to tell them to shut the doors when they're finished.'" Tuohy and McDonnell exited, leaving the three men to their business. Exiting, Tuohy remarked to McDonnell, "I'm glad I'm not privy to this." "He was very dispirited," says McDonnell. "This was a man of the highest integrity."

McDonnell is quick to emphasize that he has no firsthand knowledge of what the three men discussed. "But I later heard that Joe Kennedy was asking Mooney and Marcy what help they could bring to the election of his son. He was obsessed with the election of John Kennedy – absolutely obsessed with it. And I don't know what deals were cut. I don't know what promises were made." Mooney's brother Chuck later wrote, "All Mooney said was that he was too busy meeting with Joe Kennedy, working out the details of their agreement for Jack's presidential campaign." McDonnell adds, "This was the biggest secret in Chicago. Everyone was sworn to secrecy. Bill Tuohy was a highly religious, very moral man. I think he felt himself debased by Kennedy's request. And I think he resented it. He did not discuss it again."

Although McDonnell had no firsthand knowledge of what deal was struck, Mooney was telling his associates that, as a quid pro quo, he expected a hot line to the White House.

Following form, Mooney Giancana had to seek approval for such an alliance from his puppet masters, Accardo, Humphreys, and Ricca. "Even at that time," Curly's widow recalls, "Mooney didn't make a move without the approval of the boys, you know." If that approval was granted, then it would be assumed that Curly Humphreys, the gang's political mastermind, would play a role in carrying out the directive. He did.

The episode is not only recalled by Jeanne Humphreys, but is recorded in her three-hundred-plus-page handwritten journal that details her extraordinary life with Curly. According to Jeanne, the "new business" was broached at one of the Outfit's Thursday-night business dinners at Accardo's Palace. She recalled her husband coming home the night the vote was taken to support the Giancana-Sinatra-Kennedy pact. "Mooney's talking about trying to get that Joe Kennedy's kid elected president," Curly informed his wife. "He's trying to impress Sinatra." Through her husband, Jeanne picked up bits and pieces of what had transpired at the Palace. "Apparently, Joe had promised that his boys would back off the Outfit, especially in their Las Vegas business," Jeanne said. "Mooney bragged about the assurances he got from Kennedy."

The initial vote was two for the deal (Accardo and Giancana), and one opposed (Humphreys). Just as he had at Felix Young's, Curly refused to fall in line. Jeanne said, "Murray was against it. He remembered Joe Kennedy from the bootlegging days – called him an untrustworthy 'four-flusher' and a 'potato eater.' Something to do with a booze delivery that Joe had stolen. He said Joe Kennedy could be trusted as far as he, Murray, could throw a piano." Of course hijacking hootch during Volstead was considered fair game, and Joe Kennedy may also have been such a victim. Doc Stacher, Meyer Lansky's boyhood friend and bootlegging partner, remembered an incident in 1927 in which a shipment of Joe's booze from Ireland was stolen in a Boston gunfight in which nearly all of Kennedy's men were killed by Bugsy Siegel's violent troops. When Siegel was upbraided by Lansky, Bugsy explained, "It really wasn't our fault. Those Irish idiots hire amateurs as guards."

Perhaps Humphreys had other reasons to be wary of the association: His old chum Lucky Luciano had been double-crossed when he'd made a deal with a previous presidential candidate, Franklin Roosevelt. And then there was Bobby Kennedy. As Humphreys' grandson George Brady recalled from his many trips to Chicago to visit Humphreys, "There was also trepidation about backing JFK because of Bobby. But, on the positive side, Frank [Sinatra] talked him up."

All that was needed was the vote of board member Paul Ricca, currently in "college" in Terre Haute. "Murray had to go to see Paul in prison," Jeanne remembers. "When he got back from seeing Paul, he said, 'They've all gone along with it now, that Jack Kennedy thing.'"

"Anyway, the vote was three to one in favor," Jeanne says. "Murray was stunned that the others voted with Mooney, but he later remarked about how the 'spaghetti-benders' all stick together." An entry in Jeanne's journal reads: "Murray said he thought Mooney was nuts and that he [Murray] was working on Paul's [Ricca] immigration problems, with no time for screwball ideas. He paced and mumbled." Regardless of his personal misgivings, Curly deferred to the majority vote. Jeanne asked her husband what this meant for his workload. "Nothing – if I can get away from it," Curly responded. "I've got enough on my hands." But in his gut, Humphreys knew there was no one else with his particular skills, and sooner or later, the election fix would become just one more piece of gang business on his plate.

The FBI, which had been attempting to follow Humphreys' every move, could attest to the gangster's hectic schedule. On May 23, the G followed Humphreys to Washington, where he lobbied the Outfit's agenda. The FBI followed the gang boss to O'Hare Airport, and one agent later described Humphreys' appearance, noting, "He was dressed in a very conservative black suit, wearing his glasses as always to conceal his blind eye. He had on a long-sleeved shirt, neatly showing an inch of linen. His shoes were bright polished, every inch of him looked like the CEO of Motorola or some other high profile Chicago company . . . he could have been anything he wanted in this world – an attorney, a congressman, a top legitimate businessman. I believe that."

On a later trip to Washington, Humphreys met with Congressman Libonati to confer on the Ricca parole. Also on the agenda was Curly's desire to have Libonati introduce legislation that would outlaw then–Attorney General Bobby Kennedy's surveillance techniques. Libonati had the temerity to tell a Chicago television reporter, "Yes, I know Giancana. [My] bill would cover him." When Bobby Kennedy heard of the Libonati bill, he ranted, "If Libonati shows up in Congress next year, I'll have him arrested!"

The Bureau watched as Curly left Washington's Woodner Hotel, carrying a small package, "believed to be a thick wad of cash," to Libonati's 224 C Street home, and leaving without it. From there, Curly proceeded to the Hamilton Hotel, where he met with Congressman Thomas J. O'Brien. Upon returning to the Woodner, the Bureau learned, Humphreys "went to the room of a well-known Washington call girl where he apparently spent the rest of the night."

Humphreys would return to the nation's capital two weeks later to meet with prominent mob lawyer H. Clifford Adler.

Back in Chicago, Giancana's soldiers coordinated the initial phase of the Joe Kennedy deal. The first order of business was to guarantee Jack Kennedy's victory in the upcoming West Virginia primary on May 10. Although Kennedy had won the recent Wisconsin contest, the margin was far too slim to convince the national power brokers he could win the nation. Tied to the misgivings was the rampant anti-Catholicism in many parts of the country. In Wisconsin, Kennedy had failed to win even one of the four Protestant districts. Thus, the Kennedy team deemed rabidly anti-Catholic West Virginia the make-or-break primary. But the very state that campaign chronicler Theodore White called one of "the most squalid, corrupt, and despicable" states was about to meet its equal, in the form of Joseph Kennedy.

West Virginia state senator John Chernenko recently stated that just prior to the all-important West Virginia primary, he received a call from Dick Wright, the Kennedy chairman of the West Virginia primary, and one of the most powerful Democrats in the state. Wright requested that Chernenko go to Mingo Junction, Ohio, just across the Ohio River from West Virginia, to meet with Frank Sinatra. "The purpose of the meeting was for Sinatra to review the campaign in West Virginia and to see how much financial assistance was needed," Chernenko said. No fan of Sinatra's, Chernenko declined the offer. But soon, mob-controlled jukeboxes across the state began featuring Jack Kennedy's campaign theme song, a reworded version of Sammy Cahn's current hit "High Hopes," sung by Frank. A Kennedy aide traversed the state paying tavern owners twenty dollars each to play the song repeatedly.

Nonetheless, as FBI wiretaps would later disclose, Sinatra's and Giancana's close friend Paul "Skinny" D'Amato, the manager of Atlantic City's 500 Club, spent two weeks in the state dispensing over $50,000 for the Kennedy effort. D'Amato clarified to writers Hellerman and Renner that it was not the money that mattered so much – the Kennedys already had plenty of that – but it was the gang's massaging of the poverty-stricken West Virginia pols. According to D'Amato, his boys' contribution was in the form of "desks and chairs and supplies for politicians around the state." The FBI taps also picked up a conversation wherein Giancana reminded Rosselli of "the donation that was made" to the Kennedy effort. What the FBI failed to learn was that, according to D'Amato, Joe Kennedy even paid him a personal visit and, in exchange for Skinny's aid, promised that, if elected, his son Jack would allow deported New Jersey mobster Joe Adonis to return to the United States. Once again, Joe Kennedy's zeal to see Jack elected would place his boy in a severely compromised position. (As president, Jack Kennedy refused to go along with the deal.) Corroboration for the direct Joe Kennedy-D'Amato contact was obtained in 1988 by historian Dan B. Fleming, who spoke with Skinny's next-door neighbor, Joseph DelRaso, now an attorney in Ft. Lauderdale, Florida. "Skinny told me Joe Kennedy called him directly to help in the West Virginia campaign," recalled DelRaso.

Kennedy eventually beat Senator Hubert Humphrey in West Virginia by a 60–40 margin. Humphrey complained, "I can't afford to run through the state with a little black bag and a checkbook." (Humphrey spent an estimated $25,000 compared to Joe Kennedy's $1–$2 million.)

Covert Conclaves at Crystal Bay

The contacts between Joe Kennedy and Mooney Giancana appear to have continued throughout 1960. Jeanne Humphreys remembered, "We went to Mooney's house in West Palm Beach in Florida, and there was a lot of conversation about it. Mooney was going out to California and meeting with Joe Kennedy, and it just kept evolving and evolving." When Curly began the laborious task of coordinating his unions behind Kennedy, Jeanne wondered why he had to do all the work; after all, the idea had been Giancana's. "I said, 'Where's Mooney?'" Jeanne recalls. "Murray said, 'He's taking care of his end, Blondie. He's with Joe Kennedy in California.' My husband didn't go into great detail." Although Jeanne was not privy to the "evolving" meetings in California, details have emerged about where they were likely held.

As one hoodlum friend of Joe's told writers Denton and Morris, "[Joe's] ties to the underworld intersected at a hundred points," and if the players in these intersections had a clubhouse where their furtive caucuses could be conducted, it was the Cal-Neva Lodge. Described in ads as "Heaven in the High Sierras," the Lodge consists of luxury bungalows, a swimming pool, and a casino. This idyllic venue is set on a parcel of land that literally straddles the California-Nevada state line on the north shore of Lake Tahoe, a region known as Crystal Bay. When gambling was illegal in both states, the owners of the Cal-Neva Lodge confounded raiding police by merely pushing the card tables across the room – and the state line – the direction dependant on which locale was conducting the raid. When Open Gambling was approved in Nevada, the gambling paraphernalia found a permanent home on the Nevada side of the casino room. The Lodge had been built in 1926 and purchased two years later by the "Duke of Nevada," real estate mogul Norman Biltz. In 1930, Biltz married Esther Auchincloss Nash, the aunt of Joe Kennedy's future daughter-in-law Jacqueline Bouvier. During the 1960 campaign, Biltz canvassed the Vegas Strip, collecting some $15 million for the Kennedy war chest. Jack Kennedy himself had made it clear that he coveted secret Sin City contributors, writing a note to pal Frank Sinatra, "Frank – How much can I count on from the boys in Vegas? JFK." The note hung in Sinatra's "Kennedy Room" for four decades.

At about the same time as Biltz's purchase, Joe Kennedy began frequenting the Lodge, a hunting and fishing escape that would be a lifelong getaway for him and his clan. Wayne Ogle, the longtime maintenance manager at the Lodge, has recalled how for years he would ship two ten-foot Tahoe pine Christmas trees from the Lodge's property to the Kennedy home in Hyannis.

Joe Kennedy was not the only former bootlegger escaping to the sanctuary of the Cal-Neva. In recent years, Mooney Giancana had been using the bucolic setting to escape the G's surveillance. According to both Mooney's people and the G, Giancana had viewed the Lodge as a personal haven from the Bureau. Although agents would tail him as he moved about the Las Vegas casinos, it was later learned that Mooney and his driver would go to a movie matinee, sneak out the back door, and drive to Crystal Bay, where the don could either relax or conduct business.

The Lodge changed hands numerous times, with many of the purchasers underworld dwellers. For a time, Bugsy Siegel's San Francisco partner, Elmer "Bones" Remer, took the helm; at another juncture, Bill Graham, who fronted for the Outfit at Reno's Bank Club, owned the Lodge. In 1955, Joe Kennedy's lifelong friend Bert "Wingy" Grober (so-named due to a shriveled left arm) took over the Cal-Neva. Grober, a sometime associate of Meyer Lansky's in Florida, had previously operated Miami Beach's Park Avenue Steak House, where his liquor and steak supplier was his pal Joe Kennedy. During Grober's five-year tenure, it was commonly believed that he was fronting for the real owner, Joseph Kennedy. As seen in the case of Morton Downey, Joe frequently hid his business interests behind other owners of record. Las Vegas chroniclers Roger Morris and Sally Denton recently located sources who claimed to know of the secret arrangement. "Wingy was old Joe's man there," one of the locals recalled, "and he looked after his stake in the joint." Another candidate for a Kennedy front was Charlie Bloch, Grober's partner in the Park Avenue Steak House. Bloch, it turns out, was Joe Kennedy's liquor distributor for the Southern region that included Miami and was believed by some to have been another of the Cal-Neva's many silent partners.

Two years after the fact, the FBI was told by a former New York-based federal prohibition agent named Byron Rix of a secret election-year liaison at the Lodge between Joe Kennedy and "many gangsters." Rix, who was personally acquainted with the Kennedy family and later worked in the Las Vegas gambling business, learned from numerous unnamed sources that Joe Kennedy had a nefarious meeting in 1960 at the Cal-Neva. In 1962, the FBI summed up Rix's information in a memo to then Attorney General Bobby Kennedy, noting that "this memorandum is marked 'Personal' for the Attorney General and copies are not being sent to any lower echelon officials in the Department in view of Rix's remarks concerning the Attorney General's father." The memo summarized Rix's story thus:

> Before the last presidential election, Joseph P. Kennedy (the father of President John F. Kennedy) had been visited by many gangsters with gambling interests and a deal was made which resulted in Peter Lawford, Frank Sinatra, Dean Martin and others obtaining a lucrative gambling establishment, the Cal-Neva Hotel, at Lake Tahoe. These gangsters reportedly met with Joseph Kennedy at the Cal-Neva, where Kennedy was staying at the time.

The Cal-Neva was uniquely equipped to cater to gangland gatherings, according to a Lodge hairdresser from the 1970s who set up her shop in Sinatra's old bungalow. When she took over the singer's gatehouse cabin, the hairdresser discovered that it concealed an extensive tunnel system that interconnected the various cabins and the main lodge, and which had allowed the stars and "underworld" bosses to come and go without being seen.

The Nevada Gaming Commission would later learn that one of the "others" in on the deal was Mooney Giancana. And, as will be seen, the group Rix mentioned would indeed buy the Cal-Neva from Wingy Grober (or the likely actual owner, Joe Kennedy) and install everyone's buddy, Skinny D'Amato, to run the casino.

By July, with the West Virginia primary behind them, the Outfit, at Mooney's request, escalated its electioneering efforts on behalf of Sinatra's friend young Jack Kennedy. Curly Humphreys, already fatigued from his regular duties, undertook the onerous chore of helping the son of the distrusted Joe Kennedy win the presidency. "[Murray] hated having to go along with the Outfit's vote to back Kennedy," Jeanne Humphreys recalls. "It was a constant source of aggravation for him." But, like it or not, Humphreys was a team player and thus once again settled into his role as the gang's political mastermind.

Luckily for history, Curly Humphreys decided to allow his wife, now the only living witness to the politicking, into the inner sanctums of the Kennedy effort. Jeanne remembers how one day in early July, Curly told her to pack her bags. "I thought perhaps Murray was lamming it again, and we'd be on our way to Key Biscayne, or God knows where." To Jeanne's dismay, she was informed that she had a choice: either hole up with Curly in Chicago or go alone to Key Biscayne or Vegas. When she was told that Curly would be in seclusion at the Hilton Hotel on Michigan Avenue for at least two weeks, Jeanne chose to stay with him, writing in her journal: "Realizing he would be alone practically across the street from the 606 Club and a few blocks from all those willing strippers, I opted to stay at the hotel. What I said was, 'I'll do my time at the hotel.'"

The couple abandoned their Marine Drive apartment and found two suites waiting at the Hilton, reserved for Humphreys in the name of "Mr. Fishman," a joke since Jeanne had developed an obsession for fishing in the Keys. Curly explained that what he was about to do had to be kept secret from the G-men, who were monitoring the gang's homes and regular meeting places. "They were looking for us everywhere," Jeanne recalls. "This was very secret." Once settled in, Jeanne wondered where the rest – Joe Accardo, Gussie Alex, etc. – were. "Murray said they were busy keeping Roemer and the G looking for them elsewhere, while we were getting things done." Getting what done? Jeanne wondered. As she quickly learned, her husband's big secret was the work of fixing Jack Kennedy's election.

Jeanne soon found herself a virtual prisoner at the swank hotel, which the locals still knew by its previous name, The Stevens, for two weeks, bored to tears while her husband worked himself to exhaustion. From Jeanne's journal: "I felt like the Prisoner of Zenda, Anne Boleyn in the Tower, Napoleon on Elbe, and Byron at Chillon. Murray said I was more like a bird in a gilded cage." One of Curly's gophers, Eddie Ryan, was the first to arrive, running errands for both his boss and Jeanne, who occasionally needed a change of clothes from home.

In 1996, Jeanne recalled for the first time what she witnessed at the Stevens/Hilton, scenes that were corroborated by her own contemporaneous writings. "Lists were everywhere," she wrote in her journal. "Murray was arranging lists in categories of politicians, unions, lawyers, and contacts . . . I could see that one list had at least thirty to forty names on it." Once the lists were developed, Humphreys began making contact with the power brokers whom he could order to back Jack. "Murray's phone rang off the hook – always politicians and Teamsters," Jeanne says. Soon the contacts began arriving at the Stevens from around the country to receive their marching orders from Humphreys. Among the regular visitors were Murray Olf, the powerful Washington lobbyist, Teamster official John O'Brien, and East St. Louis boss of the Steamfitters Union, Buster Wortman. "The people coming to the hotel were Teamsters from all over the country – Kansas, St. Louis, Cleveland, Vegas," Jeanne recently said. "They were coming in from everywhere, then fanning out again."

Although Jeanne knew no specifics about how the labor leaders were going to guarantee Kennedy's election, it is not difficult to deduce what was going on. At the time of the Kennedy-Nixon contest, the millions of unionized American workers tended to follow the dictates and endorsements of their leaderships. Although most Teamsters complied with Hoffa's endorsement of Nixon, tens of thousands of other non-Teamster unions across the nation were just waiting for the word from above. In a close election, these votes could make all the difference. Jim Strong, the *Chicago Tribune*'s labor reporter for twenty years, including 1960, recently spoke of the other weapons (besides the members' votes) that organized labor brought to the table. "With its nationwide links, the Outfit could reach out across the country," Strong says. "When the various locals endorsed a candidate, their modus operandi would be primarily to set up phone banks, get out the vote by driving voters to the polls, and write checks. That's how they did it." Factoring in the immense number of locals controlled by Humphreys, it becomes clear how he would be overworked at the Stevens.

Not allowed to go out due to the FBI's surveillance, Jeanne Humphreys tried to occupy herself by reading. Her best friend became Phil Itta, the hotel maître d', who kept her supplied with crossword puzzles, books, newspapers, and treats from room service. Itta, a trusted friend of Humphreys', swept the rooms for FBI bugs, handpicked the room-service waiters, and installed new tamper-proof locks on the suites' chests of drawers.

While Curly was holed up in the Stevens, his upperworld alter ego, Joe Kennedy, was likewise ensconced at Marion Davies' mansion in Los Angeles, his base of operations for maneuvering the delegates at the Democratic National Convention in the City of Angels. As one of his first moves, Kennedy brought in Chicago "backroom" pol Hy Raskin to deliver the convention delegates for Jack. Raskin was the number two man in the Democratic National Committee, legendary for his extensive Windy City contacts. By now, Joe Kennedy and other Washington insiders knew that Jack Kennedy's Democratic rival, Senator Lyndon Johnson, had already lined up the support of New Orleans boss Carlos Marcello, much as Nixon had done with Hoffa.[14] When the convention convened in L.A., Joe was conspicuously absent on the night of his son's nomination speech. His non-attendance didn't go unnoticed by the crowd, many of whom queried, "Where's Joe?" Randolph Churchill called it "a lovely party, but where's the host?" The perception was that

---

14. The key source of the information was Marcello's bagman Jack Halfen. Marcello had been paying Johnson, and many others to kill legislation that threatened slot-machine and wire-service gambling. For ten years, according to Halfen, Johnson was paid $100,000 per year. Johnson's voting record reflects that Marcello's money was well spent. Halfen initially gave many of the details (and proof) to award-winning journalist Mike Dorman in his book *Payoff*. More details were unearthed in my first book, *Live by the Sword*. Interestingly, when I obtained Halfen's list of bribe recipients, near the top of the list was Supreme Court justice Tom Clark, the same Tom Clark who, as attorney general, played such a key role in the early parole of the Outfit's Hollywood seven.

Joe did not want his personal history to mar this night with controversy. But that was only part of the rationale. As he watched the proceedings from the Los Angeles home of Marion Davies, eleven miles from downtown in Beverly Hills, Joe met with party bosses, and old friends who owed him favors. Besides Raskin, others, such as popular Southern author William Bradford Huie, were enlisted to distribute cash to various influential politicians on Jack's behalf.[15] Longtime family friend Judge Francis X. Morrissey wrote, "It was Ambassador Joseph Kennedy who made sure that the votes for the various delegations in the big key states, like New York, Pennsylvania, Illinois, and New Jersey, all went for Jack." It may never be known what promises were made by Joe on Jack's behalf, but it is a matter of record that Joe's promises to the underworld were among those that would severely handicap his son's administration.

When Jack successfully snared the nomination, Mort Sahl, the political satirist, attempted to put a humorous spin on the underhanded politicking, wiring the patriarch: "You haven't lost a son, you've gained a country."

With the nomination commandeered, the Humphreys repaired to their Key Biscayne home for some much needed R & R. To their dismay, however, they found that the G had been harassing Jeanne's brother's family, who also lived in the area. Not long after arriving, the Humphreys were attending a family get-together when Jeanne was approached by her seven-year-old niece, Diana. With tears in her eyes, the child said one of her schoolmates had asked her if her aunt and uncle were murderers. It turned out that the G, desperate to draw out Curly and Jeanne from their hiding place, had begun harassing members of Jeanne's family and friends, displaying Curly's 1934 mug shot. Diana's girlfriend's Cuban family was distraught over the prospect of being sent back to the island if they did not cooperate with the G. Curly had Jeanne's brother complain to the local FBI office, which claimed to know nothing of the encounter. The Family Pact, apparently, only applied to Roemer's jurisdiction.

---

15. Later, during JFK's presidency, Joe again called on Huie. This time the author was given a briefcase full of cash by the patriarch to deliver to Governor George Wallace, during his segregationist standoff against the Kennedy brothers. According to Huie's protégé, reporter Mike Dorman, Joe thought he could pay Wallace to "just go away."

Even as they attempted to unwind in Florida, the "Harts" saw their getaway home visited regularly by reminders of Curly's other life. In August, the Humphreys entertained Jimmy Hoffa at a time when their Key Biscayne neighborhood was enduring a fetid sewer backup. Still smarting from his treatment in Washington at the hands of Bobby Kennedy, Hoffa told Jeanne that he wondered if Bobby had fallen into Biscayne Bay, the stink was so awful. When the talk turned serious, Jeanne witnessed her husband explaining the Outfit's work in support of Joe Kennedy's son to the Teamster boss. "Of course I can't officially endorse it," Hoffa said. "But who knows? Maybe the Italians are right. If Jack feels he owes us one . . ."

Another visitor was Mooney Giancana, with whom the Humphreys dined at one of Giancana's favorite Ft. Lauderdale restaurants. The trio was chauffeured by Mooney's Florida driver, Dom, the parking valet at the Outfit's Miami Beach Kennel Club. Although Curly and Jeanne had hoped to escape the campaign, it was all that Mooney wanted to talk about. Jeanne Humphreys described the dinner conversation in her journal:

> Besides discussing what politicians had to be "turned around," what union heads had to be convinced, and how much good it would do in the end, I was amazed to hear that Jackie K. had to be told not to wear slacks anymore when campaigning. Since I wasn't included in the conversation I almost choked trying to suppress my laughter. There was a lot of "Frank said this" and "Frank said that" and "It'll all pay off" repetition. Mooney was exuberant. I could read M [Murray] like a book and saw his lack of enthusiasm. When there was a lull in the conversation I told Mooney I should be put on the campaign payroll. His exact words were: "We'll all get our payoff in the end." How prophetic!

As if Mooney Giancana had not injected enough drama into the year 1960, he embarked on yet another adventure while waiting for the November election. Apparently, the election fix was not a large enough marker to have over the Oval Office, especially if Joe Kennedy's kid lost the contest. Thus, Mooney, at Johnny Rosselli's instigation, concluded that the only sure guarantee of the Outfit's hold over the next president was its participation in a fanciful White House-CIA scheme to murder Cuban leader Fidel Castro.

17.

The Pinnacle of Power

Paul Ricca may have been incarcerated, but Humphreys and Rosselli likely felt an occasional twinge of envy, so exhausting was the year 1960. While Curly brainstormed Ricca's and Accardo's legal problems, cared for his mentally ill daughter and his grandson, entertained his new young wife, and worked the unions on behalf of Joe Kennedy's kid (all the while dodging the G), Rosselli was himself pulling overtime out West. This was the period when, according to his biographers, Rosselli "came to preside over every facet of business in the gambling capital."

For years, the original "Dapper Don" had been brokering complex Sin City financing partnerships – successes that left his associates in awe. "If Johnny Rosselli told [pension fund trustee] Allen Dorfman to go shit on the courthouse steps in Carson City," said legendary Washington influence peddler Fred Black, "he would shit on the courthouse steps." When not taking over the lucrative ice machine concessions for all Las Vegas, Rosselli was setting up power lunches in New York for Joe Kennedy. He also assumed hidden control of Monte Prosser Productions, which booked talent into the large local casinos and the worldwide Hilton Hotel chain. Billy Wilkerson, publisher and close friend of Rosselli, wrote in his *Hollywood Reporter* that the Hilton agreement was "the biggest deal in club entertainment history." At the same time, Rosselli was overseeing the hiring of the critical casino pit crews and backroom counters, many of whom were sending the skim back to Chicago. Johnny summed up his growing prosperity for a friend over a 1960 dinner conversation: "Everything's nice and cool. There's money pouring in like there's no tomorrow. I've never seen so much money." An FBI informant told the Bureau, "Rosselli was the 'power' in Las Vegas."

If Rosselli thought the binding on his day planner could not become more strained, he was wrong. The mob's ambassador was about to take a meeting with a man who wanted to enlist Rosselli's services in a secret White House–CIA operation so indelicate that its repercussions would be felt for decades and, in the opinion of many, would inadvertently result in the death of Joe Kennedy's boy Jack three years after its inception. For the next eight months, the planning of the operation would divert much of Rosselli's precious time from his Vegas work.

The dangerous enterprise commenced in August 1960, when Rosselli received a call from an upperworld friend living in Beverly Hills named Robert Maheu. A West Coast version of Mario Brod, private detective Maheu would later admit that he had a history of handling "delicate matters" for the Central Intelligence Agency. James O'Connell, deputy to the CIA's director of security, later testified that he had utilized Maheu "in several sensitive covert operations in which he didn't want to have an Agency or government person get caught." After a stint with the FBI in the forties, Maheu formed Robert A. Maheu and Associates (RAMA) and quickly negotiated a monthly retainer as a spy for hire with the CIA. Over the years, the Agency employed RAMA to produce and distribute propaganda aimed at destabilizing enemy states or potentates. Maheu himself admitted to running "impossible missions" for the CIA, many of which were brilliantly researched and reported in Jim Hougan's 1978 book, *Spooks*.

Although Maheu often told how he had met Rosselli a year earlier in Las Vegas, Rosselli was adamant in FBI debriefs and Senate testimony that their relationship went back to 1955, when the two were introduced by an L.A. insurance executive named Spitzle. Washington detective Joe Shimon corroborated Johnny's version, although Maheu's rendition is admittedly more colorful.[1]

Regardless of the details of their original introduction, by August 1960,

---

1. Maheu said that he had taken on a job to serve a subpoena on the owner of Vegas' El Rancho Hotel, Beldon Kettleman. The day before traveling to Sin City, Maheu found every hotel booked. In desperation he called old college buddy, and D.C. power attorney, Edward Bennett Williams, who then called Rosselli. Of all places, Rosselli, who had no idea of Maheu's mission, booked Maheu into El Rancho. "They rolled out the red carpet," Maheu later wrote. "[My wife] Yvette and I were given a beautiful bungalow, filled with flowers and fruit. And they told us everything was on the house. I was impressed. Johnny must be some kind of miracle worker." It goes without saying the booking by Rosselli effectively dashed Maheu's desire to serve Kettleman. When Johnny later found out about Maheu's awkward position, he "laughed his ass off," recalled Maheu.

Maheu and Rosselli were, by both men's admissions, good friends. "My children took to calling him 'Uncle Johnny,'" wrote Maheu. Sometime in August, Maheu was contacted by the CIA's office of security. "They asked me if I'd help 'dispose' of Castro," Maheu recently recalled. Maheu was informed by his CIA handlers that the assassination would not take place in a vacuum. "The men from the CIA kept me informed of the invasion plan," Maheu recently said. "The assassination plot was to take place just prior to the invasion, hopefully." It seems that some senior CIA officers had met Johnny Rosselli at a Maheu clambake the previous spring and were so taken with the Outfit's emissary that, when word came to the Agency that Castro was to be removed, the officers immediately thought of "Uncle Johnny." It is not known if Rosselli had spoken to the CIA boys at the clambake as he had to actor George Raft a year earlier in a Los Angeles bar. When Raft had mentioned that he had just returned from Cuba, where Castro was threatening to take over, Rosselli had bragged, "You give me a couple of guys with machine guns, we could go down there and take over the whole island." Whatever he had told the CIA officers in Maheu's backyard, Rosselli left a powerful impression.

There is no way of knowing if Maheu and his Agency contacts were aware that the men pushing the hardest for the CIA operation (to be coincident with an all-out invasion of the Cuban island) were Vice President Richard Nixon and his military aide, General Robert Cushman of the marines. However, other CIA luminaries such as Thomas McCoy, deputy to former CIA director William Colby, knew that Nixon was frantic to add a victory over Castro to his campaign rhetoric before the November election. "It was suggested by various people [in the State Department and the CIA]," McCoy said in 1996, "that there was substantial pressure coming from the White House to get the Cuban thing settled by October 1960 so that this would not be an issue that Nixon had to deal with in the '60 election." Another senior Agency man, Tracy Barnes, was confronted by an overworked project officer who asked, "What's the hurry? . . . Why are we working our asses off on this?" As CIA expert Peter Grose noted, "Barnes had the political savvy to understand that the person pressing the urgency was Vice President Nixon."

Regarding the planned invasion, Nixon himself wrote in *Reader's Digest* four years later, "I had been the strongest and most persistent for setting up and supporting such a program." The go-ahead for Operation Pluto, the code name for the invasion, was given at a National Security Council meeting on March 17, 1960, just prior to the Maheu

clambake. At Nixon's urging, Cushman met with exiled Cuban militar-
ists' for the express purpose of implementing the assassination of all
Cuban leaders when the invasion, later renamed the Bay of Pigs operation, commenced.[2]

Either the CIA or Nixon, or both, decided that their liaisons with the
unpredictable exiles might not produce the wished-for results. Hence, the
overture to Rosselli and the Outfit. As noted, the desired partnership with
Rosselli was merely a continuation of a long-secret relationship between
the feds and the underworld. However, Maheu was initially taken aback
by the unorthodox request for a murder, but after his Agency friends
likened Castro to Hitler and told Maheu the action was "necessary to
protect the country" and to save thousands of lives, the politically naïve
Maheu agreed to the assignment, even though it might place his own
family in jeopardy in the future.[3]

The CIA suggested Maheu contact the man they had met at the
clambake, hoping that his associates were still enraged at Castro for
taking over their casinos. The reluctant assassination accessory agreed to
play middleman with the Outfit's Johnny Rosselli, who agreed to meet for
lunch at L.A.'s Brown Derby Restaurant. Surrounded by film people
pitching scripts, the two discussed a real-life drama that dwarfed those
being advanced by the lunching movie moguls. Without telling Rosselli of
the larger invasion plan (he says he never told Rosselli of it), Maheu made
his pitch. If Maheu was surprised by the government's request, Rosselli
was positively stupefied.

"Me? You want me to get involved with Uncle Sam?" Rosselli asked.[4]

---

2. Regarding Nixon and the assassination of Castro, the reader is urged to read
Anthony and Robbyn Summers' *The Arrogance of Power: The Secret World of
Richard Nixon* (2000). In 1996, this writer conducted much of the research for the
Castro-Nixon portion of that book, which gives ample evidence that Nixon approved
the assassination plots.

3. "I had conducted a serious and dangerous assignment on behalf of my government
during World War II," Maheu recently recalled, "living with German agents for two
years. And I felt that if I could be responsible in saving lives and that the request was at
the behest of my government, I would take it on."

4. Maheu originally tried to convince Rosselli that the plots were backed by
businessmen, but Rosselli cut him off, saying, "I am not kidding. I know who you
work for."

"The feds are tailing me wherever I go. They go to my shirtmaker to see if I'm buying things with cash. They go to my tailor to see if I'm using cash there. They're always trying to get something on me. Bob, are you sure you're talking to the right guy?" Like Maheu, Rosselli was also initially disturbed by the essence of the request, political assassination. However, after Maheu played the Hitler card, the archpatriot Rosselli agreed to come to the aid of his beloved country – gratis. But as with all serious business, his Outfit bosses would first have to approve. Rosselli wanted verification that this was a government-approved murder plot, and Maheu promised to provide the proof. However, Maheu warned, under no circumstances would the G admit to the partnership, or even the operation. "If anyone connects you with the U.S. government, I will deny it," Maheu intoned. "I will swear you're off your rocker, you're lying, you're trying to save your hide. I'll swear by everything holy that I don't know what in the hell you're talking about."

According to Maheu, the appeal to Rosselli's nationalism clicked. "If this is for the government," Johnny finally answered, "It's the least I can do, because I owe it a lot." Although Maheu offered the Outfit representative a pot load of money, Rosselli declined the offer. Throughout Rosselli's long involvement with the G's assassination project, he not only never accepted a dime's payment, but refused to have his hefty hotel and travel expenses compensated. Among his friends, who learned of the plots decades later, this gesture was no surprise. "He was one of the most patriotic men I ever knew," remarked one longtime friend. Betsy Duncan Hammes, a Las Vegas singer and longtime Rosselli friend, remembers what Johnny told her after the plots were publicized years later: "He said it was his patriotic duty."

Despite the denial of support from the feds and the questionable chances for success, Rosselli agreed to take the notion back to his Chicago bosses, and the two friends agreed to meet in New York on September 14 and, hopefully, proceed from there. In Chicago, Mooney Giancana, more concerned with getting a marker on the G than patriotism, made a jest of Johnny's softheartedness. Detective Joe Shimon, a mutual friend of Mooney and Johnny's, recalled, "[Mooney] always used to say, 'Give Johnny a flag and he'll follow you around the yard.'" Of course, patriotism was not the only emotion that stirred in Rosselli; the partnership had practical business benefits. As Rosselli later told a gangster friend, "If somebody gets in trouble and they want a favor [from the G], we can get it for them. You understand. We'll have the fucking government by the ass." The idea of getting leverage on the G appealed to Mooney's innate gangster style, and he seconded Rosselli's proposal.

Although the Outfit's low-profile brain trust was skeptical about the Castro plotting, they apparently gave a tentative go-ahead. But Giancana's puppet masters were not unaware of the downside to Mooney's new high-profile friends, Sinatra, the Kennedys, his girlfriends Phyllis McGuire and Keely Smith – and now the CIA. On his forays back to Chicago, Mooney Giancana had been crowing about his blossoming relationship with the Kennedys. Columnist Taki Theodoracopulos, who wrote for *Esquire*, *Interview*, and other well-known magazines, became close with Giancana as a result of an introduction by Jack Kennedy's brother-in-law Peter Lawford. Taki recalled, "Sam Giancana was always talking about the Kennedys . . . It was clear that at some point he had met both brothers . . . [Lawford and Giancana] would talk fondly of their shenanigans with the first family . . . they used to talk about the girls Mooney used to produce for the Kennedys. Mooney was proud of it, very proud of his Kennedy connections."

According to Jeanne Humphreys, Curly and the rest were beginning to worry that both Mooney and Johnny might be putting their growing affinity for the high life ahead of their business sense. "They were starting to call Mooney and Johnny 'starstruck,'" Jeanne recalls. "The fear was that they were getting off on hanging out with Sinatra and CIA guys." Nonetheless, it appears that the decision was reached to play along if Maheu supplied proof of the government's authorization for the plot. That proof would be given at the upcoming New York rendezvous.

On September 13, while Johnny Rosselli was en route to his clandestine rendezvous with the G in New York, the G in Chicago was eavesdropping on an important conversation between Curly Humphreys, who had returned from his brief respite in Florida, and Gussie Alex. The agents listened in amazement as Curly spoke of his obtaining the jury pool list for the upcoming Accardo tax trial. The agents had a front-row seat as one of the nation's great criminal minds gave a seminar on how to succeed in the underworld. "Here's what we're gonna do," Curly said. "After we've decided which ones, then we'll decide how to make the approach." Alex offered that one potential juror lived in a town where a made guy, Joe Gagliano, had a cousin who owned a gas station. Humphreys then said, "You work on a plan. Do like an investigator would do. Find out if there's a connection there. Send Gags out there to talk to the gas station guy. Find out how well he knows this woman, then we'll decide." Regarding one potential juror, Curly hinted at the power he wielded through Hoffa's Teamsters: "Now I got a truck driver [juror]. We have an ace there."

The next day, Rosselli arrived at New York's Plaza Hotel for his meeting with Maheu. There, Johnny was introduced to Jim O'Connell, the CIA's chief of the Operational Support Division. O'Connell, using the alias Jim Olds, suggested to Rosselli that Castro be hit in a Capone-style "gangland rubout." Rosselli quickly disabused O'Connell of the dangerous notion, and the men agreed that poison made more sense. The inclusion of O'Connell was the imprimatur Rosselli needed, and he agreed that he would bring a man with extensive contacts in Havana named Sam Gold to Florida in about ten days, where the team would get down to business. Although he never told Maheu the reason for the timing, it was likely because Sam Gold, aka Mooney Giancana, had other pressing business to address: He was buying into Joe Kennedy's favorite resort, the Cal-Neva.

It was a perfect deal. Joe Kennedy wanted to demonstrate his seriousness, and Mooney needed a getaway retreat, especially one with the added lure of subterranean passages. On September 20, 1960, with Frank Sinatra fronting for him, Mooney purchased stock in the Cal-Neva for approximately $350,000 from Joe Kennedy's friend Wingy Grober. It has been widely misconstrued that Grober et al. sold the Lodge outright to Sinatra and Giancana. However, a close reading of the application put before the Nevada Gaming Commission reveals that the Sinatra purchasers (Sinatra; his manager, Hank Sanicola; and Dean Martin) only obtained a 49.5 percent interest in the operation, while Grober's group maintained a 50.5 percent controlling interest. Gaming board member Turner emphasized that "the operation would remain the same, that, in other words . . . the present controlling interest would remain as it is." Board chairman Milton Keefer added the Sinatra group's purchase "is not really a transfer, that it is a new acquisition of stock from the present 100 percent operation." However, if Grober was actually a front for Kennedy, and Sinatra was a front for Giancana, then, in essence, Bobby Kennedy's nemesis, Mooney Giancana, was now in partnership with Bobby's father. In an account that echoed the Rix allegation, Peter Lawford's biographer James Spada reported that Joe Kennedy's son-in-law Lawford was another of the resort's many silent partners, a disclosure that has led some to believe that Joe Kennedy staked Lawford in the deal, thus retaining even more interest in the business.

Connected people like Mooney's future son-in-law Bob McDonnell have known all along of Mooney's stake in the Cal-Neva. "Mooney Giancana backed Sinatra totally, put up all the money for the Cal-Neva," McDonnell says emphatically. The FBI also believed that Mooney Giancana was the "silent" owner of the hotel. Rosselli's friend Betsy Duncan Hammes says emphatically, "I know for a fact that Giancana put the money up for the purchase. Besides, Frank didn't have that kind of money back then." One of Mooney's drivers recently disclosed how he personally took the money from Chicago to Nevada for the transaction.

The allegations of Byron Rix add to the drama of the purchase. If Rix is accurate, then the transfer of Cal-Neva stock to Mooney was Joe's way of solidifying the deal with the Outfit to back Jack in the election. The secret meeting at the Lodge that year between Joe Kennedy and "many gangsters" may have indeed been, as Rix reported, another reason the hoods decided to support the Kennedy effort. Whereas some in Chicago believed that the reason Mooney brought the Kennedy request to them was a combination of his desire to get a marker on the G, and his groupie mentality toward Sinatra, it now appears that he had a third reason: Joe Kennedy had promised him a piece of the coveted Cal-Neva.

The transfer of Grober/Kennedy stock in the Lodge to Sinatra/Giancana may have been the show of sincerity Mooney and the Outfit needed to fulfill their end of the election bargain. But before that would occur, Giancana and Rosselli moved forward with their participation in Operation Pluto, a scheme that, even if unsuccessful, would ingratiate the Outfit with the Republican candidate, Richard Nixon. It was classic hedge-betting.

On September 24, Rosselli, Maheu, and the CIA's Jim O'Connell flew separately into Miami, which had been chosen as their logical base of operations. With O'Connell staying at another location, Maheu and Rosselli took adjoining suites at the Kenilworth Hotel. After a few days, "Sam Gold" arrived, and announced to Maheu that the Outfit was now an official partner with the government in its assassination endeavors against Fidel Castro. Gold, the actual Mooney Giancana, immediately moved the trio to the gang's home away from home, the Fontainebleau Hotel in Miami Beach. There they were ensconced in a five-room suite (with the requisite kitchen) on the penthouse floor. The experience was an eye-opener for Maheu, who had never before experienced firsthand the style and charisma of men such as those from the Outfit. Maheu watched as Giancana had beluga caviar, from a gourmet shop in New York, and champagne delivered daily. The Chicago boss cooked high-cuisine meals while the trio plotted murder. In his autobiography, Maheu described Mooney as dynamic, prideful, and charismatic. "When Sam Giancana walked through the lobby of the Fontainebleau Hotel," Maheu wrote, "it was like a king passing. People just made way."

Maheu also bore witness to the other side of Mooney, the side that had seen him succeed on the mean streets of the Patch. The private detective described one exemplary scene at the hotel: "One time, we were all sitting by the pool when a good-looking man walked up and immediately started talking tough. Without even looking at the punk, Giancana grabbed his necktie and yanked him close. Sam stared right into the kid's eyes and said, 'I eat little boys like you for breakfast. Get your ass out of here before I get hungry!'"

Mooney and Johnny soon engaged a third accomplice, who was introduced to Maheu merely as Joe the Courier. Joe was, in fact, Florida Commission member Santo Trafficante, as Maheu would soon learn when he casually perused a Miami newspaper *Parade* supplement, which prominently displayed a photo of the Cosa Nostra boss. Maheu was informed that Joe's cooperation was essential due to his extensive contacts in Havana.

Although an association with the G on official business had its practical benefits, there may have been an emotional component to the Outfit's acquiescence regarding the plots. Appearing on an ABC News documentary in 1997, Maheu reflected on a subtle expression he noticed in the hoods during his time with them:

> Rosselli and Giancana . . . had surveillances on them for years, they've known about it. They've suspected wiretaps by the federal government, they've known about it. And here, out of the clear blue sky, they are asked to help the government. Just think about that as a human being. This perhaps was the biggest compliment that had been paid them since they were in their teens. And I think to a degree that sparked maybe an innate loyalty that they wish had been there or that they had won a war someplace, or that they had been more cooperative with the government. That is the feeling they imbued in me.

Over the next few months, Mooney (Gold), Maheu, O'Connell (Olds), and Rosselli (Rawlston), made frequent return trips to Florida, where they linked up with Santo (Joe) to troll Miami's "Little Havana," seeking out exile accomplices. It had been decided to inform the exiles that a group of Wall Street businessmen with nickel interests in Cuba would pay $150,000 for Castro's head.

In a bizarre irony, the increased surveillance the gang endured in Chicago had followed them to Florida; the FBI was not privy to the Outfit's secret dealings with the CIA on Nixon's behalf. It is not known if the hoods noticed their FBI tails, but veteran detective Maheu, who already knew his room phone was tapped, could not help but discern them. "One night at dinner," Maheu wrote, "I noticed one agent following Rosselli into the bathroom. When Rosselli came back to the table, I went to the men's room and cornered the operative. I put him in the kitchen." Maheu was in the awkward position of not being able to disclose the operation to the FBI agents, but at the same time having to let them know they were found out, hoping that they would back off.

When Rosselli made return trips home, he also experienced the paradox. "I had to duck them [the FBI] in order to meet my contacts at the CIA," Rosselli would later testify. "One day, right in front of the [Los Angeles] Friars Club, I noticed a man. I walked over and opened the car door. He was on the floor of the car. I said, 'What the hell are you doing?' He said, 'Tying my shoelaces.' So I took his license number. Then I found out he was an FBI agent. He was there to follow me from the club . . . I told [Maheu] every time I would catch one of those fellows." And Rosselli showed great bureaucratic insight, later proven accurate, when he guessed at what it all meant. "I was beginning to feel," he testified, "that this was a pressure on the FBI's part . . . that they wanted to find out about the CIA."

Maheu recently commented on the atmosphere, saying, "Here we are, on the one hand, trying to get involved in a project that is presumably in the best interest of the United States government, and our efforts are being jeopardized by another branch of the government." Maheu decided to let the G in on the scheme. "I made sure that Hoover knew what I was doing," Maheu recently admitted, "because, from then on, I made all the calls out of the [tapped] suite at the hotel, collect to CIA numbers."

It is not known if Maheu's suspicion of tapped hotel phones was accurate, but the FBI was certainly beginning to pick up rumblings about the furtive anti-Castro plotting. Just days after his late-September meeting with Maheu, Giancana traveled to New York, where the notoriously indiscreet don bragged to an FBI informant that Castro would be "done away with" before the November election. FBI director Hoover quickly notified, of all people, Richard Bissell, the CIA's director of covert operations, and one of the small circle aware of the secret assassination efforts. At the same time, Hoover was picking up rumors that gangsters had been seen meeting with unnamed CIA officers in Florida. And on September 26, Hoover fired off a confidential memo to Allen Dulles, the director of the CIA, in which he informed Dulles that Miami-based Cuban exile (and future Watergate burglar) Frank Sturgis had been approached about mounting an operation against Castro. Hoover noted that the memo was classified "confidential" – "since [the] matter concerns a potential plot against the Castro government, the unauthorized disclosure of which could be detrimental to our national defense." In classic Hoover-esque, the director was letting the Agency know he was wise to the plotting. Any details that had thus far eluded Hoover were soon to be revealed, thanks to Mooney Giancana and his celebrity-chasing.

In late October, Giancana decided to take the measure of Maheu's loyalty. At the time, the boss feared that one of his best girls, singer Phyllis McGuire, was two-timing him with comedian Dan Rowan, who was appearing at the gang's Desert Inn in Las Vegas. Giancana told Maheu that either he bug Rowan's hotel room or he (Giancana) would have to abandon the Castro project and head to Vegas and straighten the matter out, Outfit style. Fearing not only Giancana's desertion, but the potential for him to tell McGuire what he had been up to in Florida, Maheu agreed to ask a CIA superior, Sheffield Edwards, for advice. "Shef told me that the Agency . . . would pay up to a thousand dollars if I wanted someone to do the job," Maheu later wrote. Maheu then enlisted a Miami private eye named Ed DuBois to install the bug in Rowan's room. However, when Dubois' technician was caught in the act, he told the police, and the FBI, that he had been hired by Maheu.

Eventually, Maheu had to admit to the Bureau the details of his secret plotting with the very hoods Hoover had been struggling to build a case against. Hoover supposedly hit the roof and quickly dashed off a series of memos to all key agencies in an effort to create a paper trail that would absolve the FBI in the event that the CIA's collusion with the Outfit affected the Bureau's ability to obtain convictions.

While the quartet worked the Miami streets, in Washington the CIA's Technical Services Division experimented, often futilely, with nefarious potions for the Miami plotters to somehow have delivered into Fidel's innards. Simultaneously, members of multiple branches of the U.S. military secretly toiled in Central America in a similarly futile attempt to coalesce a ragtag band of less than two thousand exiles into an effective invasion force. As is well-known now, neither the plotting in Miami Beach nor that in Central America would come to anything even remotely resembling success. But, in one way, that was beside the point, as the original purpose of the exercise was now moot: President Eisenhower refused to green-light the invasion in time for Richard Nixon to benefit in the November election. Now the operation would proceed under its own inertia, albeit with no raison d'être.

On October 21, while Mooney, Rosselli, and Trafficante plotted with Maheu in Miami Beach, the two presidential candidates were taking stage in New York for their fourth, and final, television debate. Although Jack Kennedy appeared to have bettered Richard Nixon in the previous three encounters, it would soon become apparent to Nixon just how much Kennedy craved a knockout blow in what was still predicted to be a toss-up vote just two weeks off. At this point, virtually all the principals had sullied their hands in the muck of political foul play: Joe Kennedy had sought out numerous gangsters; Lyndon Johnson had obtained the support of New Orleans crime boss Carlos Marcello; for a $1-million payoff, Richard Nixon had jumped into bed with Jimmy Hoffa and his Eastern mob buddies; and even Bobby Kennedy had made a futile approach to Marcello. Now it was Jack Kennedy's turn to deal from the bottom of the deck.

In the previous two months, candidate Kennedy had repeatedly been briefed on Operation Pluto, the Eisenhower-Nixon secret invasion plan for Cuba.[5] It is not clear if Kennedy was also advised of the accompanying assassination planning, currently under way in Miami. Two days before the last debate, Kennedy released a statement to the press that would not only jeopardize the invasion's chances, but force Nixon to deny the existence of the operation in order to salvage any hope of success. Of course, Nixon's denial would paint him as "soft on Communism," exactly what candidate Kennedy wanted – an irony given that Nixon had created his political persona by assuming an arch-anticommunist stance.

5. For details of the secret Kennedy briefings, see Russo, *Live by the Sword,* and Hersh, *The Dark Side of Camelot.*

"We must attempt to strengthen the non-Batista democratic anti-Castro forces in exile . . . *Thus far these fighters for freedom have had virtually no support from our government* [italics added]," Kennedy's statement read. When the debate commenced, Nixon was unable to admit that the "fighters for freedom" were in fact being supported to the hilt by the incumbent administration. Nixon later wrote in his autobiography, *RN*, "I had no choice but to take a completely opposite stand and attack Kennedy's advocacy of open intervention in Cuba. This was the most uncomfortable and ironic duty I have had to perform in any political campaign." In his memoir *Six Crises,* Nixon added, "For the first time I got mad at Kennedy personally. I thought that Kennedy, with full knowledge of the facts, was jeopardizing the security of a United States foreign policy operation. And my rage was greater because I could do nothing about it."

The ploy worked, with a Gallup poll showing that viewers, by a 43–23 percent margin, believed Kennedy had won the gabfests. Before one sheds any tears over Kennedy's treatment of Nixon, it should be remembered that Nixon's own history of political chicanery is virtually unmatched in American history. Not only did Nixon begin his career by smearing his congressional opponent, Helen Gahagan Douglas, as a Communist, but he conspired with the South Vietnamese to stall the 1968 Paris Peace Talks until after his election[6] and authorized virtual terrorism against political opponents in the 1972 contest.

Electing Jack

Back in Chicago, Curly Humphreys geared up for his role in the general-election push. Like his associates in Florida, Humphreys was placed in the contradictory position of carrying out a political function of international consequence while trying to evade the prying eyes and ears of Hoover's G-men. Once again, Curly gave his wife the choice of whether to accompany him back into the Stevens for two critical weeks in October, adding that this time the work would be even more intense than before. Once again, Jeanne Humphreys chose the luxury of the hotel prison.

Only after the fact did Hoover's eavesdroppers transcribe a gang

---

6. In 1996, as part of research this author conducted for Anthony Summers' *The Arrogance of Power,* the author convinced Anna Chennault to admit her liaison role with Nixon in the secret deal with the South Vietnamese delegation. The book goes into great detail regarding how President Johnson and Vice President Humphrey dealt with the electoral sabotage.

conversation that noted Humphreys' move to the Hilton Hotel. An October 28 report in Humphreys' FBI file notes the following secretly recorded recent conversation between Humphreys and underling Hy Godfrey in which Humphreys asked the aide to book him hotel rooms:

Humphreys: "How about this joint down the street?"

Godfrey: "Sheraton?"

Humphreys: "Yeah. See, sometimes it's easier to get a two-room suite than it is to get one room. Go downstairs and call them. Ask for a one- or two-room suite for a week . . . This time I won't check in under my own name. The hell with that."

Godfrey: "Curly, there's nothing available. Filled to capacity. Went to see [deleted] and [deleted] is there, and his contract is next to him. Also the Hilton [Stevens]."

Humphreys: "Get the Hilton. Get a two-room deal there."

FBI Summary: "At the conclusion of the above conversation, Godfrey left apparently to get a two-room suite at the Hilton Hotel under a different name."

The FBI mistakenly surmised that the purpose of the secret Hilton meetings was "to line up prospective witnesses in the defense of TONY ACCARDO."

The second sojourn at the Stevens became so arduous that Jeanne Humphreys was conscripted into action, helping her husband transcribe his lists. Jeanne quickly noticed that security was even tighter than before, with Phil the maître d' personally escorting all visitors to the Humphreys' suites. The couple's workday started at six-thirty in the morning and concluded late in the evening. "Votes weren't bought," Jeanne wrote about what she overheard. "They were commanded, demanded and in a few cases cajoled."

The transcribing and cajoling continued for two long weeks in late October. "After I made a legible list, Murray burned his copy," Jeanne wrote. Although she had no idea what purpose the rewriting served, Jeanne toiled away. "It would have been easier to compile a list of politicians he [Humphreys] didn't contact or meet with than otherwise," Jeanne noted in her journal. She sarcastically asked again if she would be placed on the Kennedy payroll. Once again, the familiar names of Wortman, O'Brien, and Olf popped up repeatedly, with a new name added, Jackie Presser. At the time, the Ohio-based Presser was a Cleveland jukebox racketeer, and one of Hoffa's key Teamster supporters. He would later succeed Hoffa as Teamster president. Curly had given up trying to convince Hoffa to back the Kennedy campaign. Considering all the characters working on bringing out the vote for Kennedy, the ever sarcastic Mrs. Humphreys noted, "It's ironic that most of the behind-the-scenes participants in the Kennedy campaign couldn't vote because they had criminal records."

Watching her husband's work ethic, Jeanne posed the obvious question: "How can you be so gung ho for something you think is a mistake?" Curly answered, "That's what I do." One night, however, Curly's frustration surfaced as he spoke of Joe Kennedy, whose visage had just appeared on the hotel television. "That old man's running things," he said. "It's his ball game. Mooney's making a big mistake. Nobody's going to control those punks as long as he's alive." Then, referring to Jimmy Hoffa's alignment with Nixon, Curly added, "Jimmy's right, I'm not going to push him [to switch]."

The self-imposed incarceration led to frayed nerves and occasional marital discord. On such occasions, Jeanne abandoned her list-making and stared at the TV. From her journal: "While millions of unsuspecting voters were debating which way to vote, the 'Fixer' was holed up with a harpie whose only interest was trying to spot Jackie Kennedy in slacks. God Bless America!"

About ten days into the stay at the Stevens, the Humphreys received word from Eddie Ryan that Jeanne's brother Bob had called on "our (safe) emergency number." Bob was distraught over recent IRS harassment of Jeanne's family, not only in Florida, but now also in St. Louis, where Jeanne's aunt was in tears. Curly told his wife to go and comfort her family, but that she would not be able to return to the Stevens. Curly enlisted Maurie Shanker, one of St. Louis' top criminal attorneys, to assist his wife's family. (According to its Humphreys file, the FBI verified five months later Humphreys' stay at the Stevens/Hilton: "During the fall of 1960, [DELETED] advised that MURRAY HUMPHREYS resided during the latter part of October, 1960, under the name FISHMAN in the Conrad Hilton Hotel in Chicago.")

In Norman, Oklahoma, Curly's first wife, Clemi, received a call from her former spouse, with whom she maintained a cordial relationship. After hanging up the phone she turned to their daughter, Luella, and nephew Ernie Brendle. "Father called," Clemi said. "He and the boys have agreed to support Kennedy. He said to tell the family." This came as a surprise, since up until this point, Curly had been pro-Nixon. Curly's niece Brenda Gage recently recalled, "Uncle Lew [her nickname for Curly] said he knew Kennedy would win. He was so sure about it long before the election. Later, I just thought he was so wise to know that." However, outside the family unit, the fix was to be tightly held.

As the election neared, knowledgeable insiders were tempted to parlay their awareness of the fix into a personal windfall at the Nevada bookie parlors. "I remember going to Vegas that year," recalls Jeanne. "I told Murray I was going to bet on Kennedy in the election. He became angry, saying I couldn't do it." Curly cautioned his young wife, "If we're seen betting on them, everyone will know what's going on." To which Jeanne now playfully adds, "I was only going to bet two dollars anyway." Joe Kennedy, however, was not so discreet. Legendary sports promoter/ bookie Harry Hall recently said, "I know for a fact that Joe [Kennedy] went to L.A. and put down twenty-two thousand, to win, on his boy," remembers Hall. "I knew Joe's bookie. Frank [Sinatra] and Dean [Martin] made big bets also." Las Vegas historians Morris and Denton located sources that recalled how Jack's brother Teddy Kennedy had a friend get down an election night $10,000 wager with the Outfit's Riviera Casino boss, Ross Miller. Hours later, as recalled by oddsmakers such as "Jimmy the Greek," Teddy apparently enhanced the wager when he had aide Stephen Smith phone up Wingy Grober at the Cal-Neva just before the polls closed and had him lay down an additional $25,000 on brother Jack. All this insider wagering seemed overly bold to the bookies, who rated the contest a virtual toss-up, "six to five, too close to call."

November 8, election day, brought continued behind-the-scenes manipulations. While Curly labored on the national front, Mooney Giancana worked hard to deliver his key city wards to the Democrats, an effort that not only aided Kennedy, but also worked against crusading state's attorney Bennie Adamowski. Scores of Giancana's "vote sluggers" or "vote floaters" hit the streets to "coerce" the voters. Giancana's biographer William Brashler wrote, "The 1960 Kennedy-Nixon election played into Giancana's hands . . . the master vote counters of the city's river wards worked feverishly to deliver their man." According to G-man Bill Roemer, there is no doubt that Giancana lent his considerable influence to the Kennedy effort. In 1995, Roemer recalled, "We had placed a microphone in Giancana's headquarters right after the election. There was no question but that Giancana had been approached by Frank Sinatra before the election to help the Kennedys."

The Outfit bosses were not the only ones working behind the scenes to fix the presidential contest. In Nevada, real estate mogul (and Kennedy insider by marriage to Jack's wife's aunt) Norman Biltz was rumored to have imported black voters from out of state, bribing them to cast illegal ballots for Kennedy. Biltz had employed the tactic years earlier when boosting the career of the seminal Nevada senator of the thirties and forties, Pat McCarran. In Texas, Kennedy running mate Lyndon Johnson's Democratic machine made its own contribution to the 1960 election fraud. Nixon biographer Earl Mazo wrote, "The election shenanigans [in Texas] ranged from ballot-box stuffing and jamming the Republican column on voting machines to misreading ballots cast for Republicans and double-counting those for Democrats." Mazo points out that in one county, the official tally had 148 for Kennedy-Johnson, and 24 for Nixon-Lodge, although only 86 people voted. The skullduggery proved critical to the Texas outcome, and likely the national tally. In a state where its favorite son should have led the ticket to a huge majority, Kennedy-Johnson managed only a 1 percent edge. It was not the first time Johnson's clique had been implicated in election fraud.[7] And there was more. In Alabama, Kennedy's popular vote was counted twice, as reported by Neal R. Peirce in his study of the electoral college, *The People's President*. If even just the Alabama totals had been accurate, Nixon would not only have won the state, but the nation as well.

*   *   *

---

7. Since 1948, Johnson had been pursued by nasty rumors about his ability to create close victories where none existed. In that year, Johnson's supporters helped erase a twenty-thousand-vote victory by Johnson's opponent, Governor Coke Stevenson, in the Democratic senatorial primary. For one solid week, new county-by-county totals appeared and turned the election into an eighty-seven-vote *Johnson* victory. In 1990, Luis Salas, the election judge in Jim Wells County (Precinct 13) admitted to *New York Times* reporter Martin Tolchin that under his supervision, and on orders of Johnson confidant and South Texas political boss George Parr, Salas stuffed the "Box 13" ballot with "votes of the dead, the infirm, the halt, the missing, and those who were unaware that an election was going on." When Stevenson attempted to have the election investigated, he was forestalled when Johnson's lawyer, Abe Fortas, appealed to the U.S. Supreme Court. Johnson later returned the favor when, as president, he appointed Fortas to the highest court. The Box 13 episode earned Johnson the hated nickname later utilized by Bobby Kennedy to get under his skin, "Landslide Lyndon."

From his Massachusetts home, Joe Kennedy continued to work the power-ful Daley front via Marty Underwood, a Chicago consultant working for the mayor. Underwood, who would be brought to work in Washington after the Kennedy victory, was originally brought into the fold early on by Kenny O'Donnell as an election adviser. "The old man [Joe Kennedy] wanted to maintain contact with Daley, but didn't want the phone calls traced," O'Donnell recalls. "I was dispatched to Minneapolis on election night to route the calls from Hyannis Port to Chicago." Underwood recently recalled an election night incident in which a Daley aide reported to the mayor that he wasn't able to retrieve all the "votes" from a Chicago cemetery, as some of the tombstones were overturned. Daley barked, "Well, lift them up, they have as much right to vote as the next person!" Underwood was thus a witness to a ploy that has been recounted by, among others, the longtime JFK friend from Palm Beach, Patrick Lannan. Lannan told author John Davis' literary agent, "Mayor Daley 'and friends' went to work stuffing ballots and resurrecting the voters from the dead." The 1960 election resurrected not just the dead, but an old Windy City proverb: "Death does not mean disenfranchisement."

It would later turn out that Hoover's FBI was spying not only on the Outfit, but its friend in the mayor's office, an undertaking that shed more light on the mayor's role in the 1960 vote-fraud wars. When Richard Daley's three-hundred-page FBI file was released in 1997 to the *Chicago Tribune,* the following passage was included: "on 11/18/60 [DELETED] advised that he had learned from [DELETED] . . . that a Chicago attor-ney . . . had told [DELETED] that Mayor Daley had paid for thousands of votes in the 11/8/60 election but had not received 25,000 of the votes for which he had paid."

Like his old friend Joe Kennedy, Los Angeles-based Frank Sinatra maintained an open phone line to Chicago via ward boss and Democratic national committeeman Jake Arvey, a known close friend of Mooney Giancana's. Arvey updated Frank every half hour on the Chicago tallies.

Back in Washington that night, *Washington Post* editor Ben Bradlee was at dinner with his friend John Kennedy. He remembered his conversation with the candidate: "Over dinner he told me how he [JFK] had called Chicago's Mayor Richard Daley while Illinois was hanging in the balance to ask how he was doing. 'Mr. President,' Kennedy quoted Daley as saying, 'with a little bit of luck and the help of a few close friends, you're going to carry Illinois.' Later, when Nixon was being urged to contest the 1960 election, I often wondered about that statement."

All night long, Illinois, and the nation for that matter, was a toss-up. At eight-thirty on Wednesday morning, Ann Gargan, Joe Kennedy's secretary, arrived to inform Jack that he had won Illinois. "Who says so?" inquired the exhausted candidate. "Your father says so," replied Gargan.

As it turned out, the election was so close that without Humphreys' union work, and the other noted machinations, Richard Nixon would certainly have prevailed. In Chicago, Mayor Daley held back his county's vote totals until the final tally was received from the Republican-stronghold farm belt in southern Illinois. It was common knowledge that the Republican pols in that region were counting thousands of uncast votes; Daley merely waited to see how many votes he would need to negate the downstate fraud. As the night wore on, Daley calculated that he needed to deliver a 450,000 vote advantage to Kennedy to carry the state; Kennedy took Cook County by 456,312 votes.

When the final count was tallied, out of almost seventy million votes cast nationwide, Jack Kennedy had won by a scant 113,554, less than one tenth of 1 percent of the total, and less even than his margin in just Cook County. Most pertinent, in the states where the Outfit had a strong union presence, Kennedy squeaked to gossamer-thin victories: in Illinois (+.2%), Michigan (+1%), Missouri (+.6%), and Nevada (+1.3%). These states accounted for a decisive 63 electoral votes, which, if given to Nixon, would have changed the outcome (269 were needed to elect; Kennedy obtained 303). With Curly Humphreys' charges ordered to get out the Democratic vote, which included the all-important ferrying of invalids to the polls, the Outfit's contention that it "elected Jack" is not without merit.

"I was an airhead," says Jeanne Humphreys. "I didn't know that a president could be elected on the whim of Chicago mobsters. In my ignorance, I thought majority ruled." In Illinois, the next morning's count showed that Nixon had prevailed in 93 of the state's 102 counties, yet lost Illinois by 8,858 votes, the result of the large Kennedy majority in Cook County, where Daley and the Outfit turned out a staggering 89.3 percent of the eligible voters, including the eligible deceased. Chicago veteran reporter Walter Trohan asked his old friend Richard Daley about his party's election shenanigans. "He never denied it," recalls Trohan. "He confessed that they stole to offset the Republican stealing downstate, which I didn't believe was on that grand a scale." Years later, nearing death, Daley told his friend Washington power attorney Edward Bennett Williams, "I have only one question: Will God forgive me for stealing the election from Richard Nixon?"

Of more pressing concern to Daley than even Jack Kennedy's victory was the simultaneous defeat of Daley's nemesis, Bennie Adamowski, the threatening state's attorney. Adamowski's chief investigator, Paul Newey, recently said, "We were creating bedlam in Cook County, so they knew they had to do something. That election was stolen from Ben – I have no doubt of it." Three weeks after his defeat, a bitter Adamowski told the *Chicago Tribune* that more than one hundred thousand votes had been stolen by Daley's machine.[8]

With typical sarcasm, Jeanne Humphreys made a notation in her journal that reflected on the decision of the bosses who had outvoted her husband: "Well, the election efforts were a success and the Senate Racket committee was to be disbanded; Bobby Kennedy would kiss and make up with Jimmy Hoffa and all Mooney's predictions of a respite from crime busters would materialize. What Dreamers!"

After the election, state Republicans conducted an unofficial recount and found that a switch of 4,500 votes in Cook County would have given the state to Nixon and reelected Adamowski. This unofficial recount, which established a gain of 4,539 for Nixon, was prevented from becoming an official tally by Mayor Daley. After Jack Kennedy's inauguration, a federal grand jury recommended a formal investigation of the vote fraud, but by that time the head of the Justice Department was Robert Kennedy, and the idea had predictably lost favor.

Richard Daley's help did not go unappreciated by the new president. The day after the inauguration, Daley became President Kennedy's second visitor to the Oval Office, just after Harry Truman. Daley biographer F. Richard Ciccone wrote, "Of all the Democratic leaders in the nation, only Richard J. Daley had been invited to spend part of Kennedy's first day in the White House with the new president. Camelot's

---

8. When Adamowski ran for county assessor ten years later, he ripped into the gross underevaluation of the Kennedy's Merchandise Mart. Although Kennedy friend Cook County assessor P. J. Cullerton set the behemoth's worth at $16 million, independent studies put the figure closer to $100 million. Deputy County Treasurer Peter Piotrowicz added that as a result of the undervaluing of the Mart and other Loop offices, the residents of Chicago faced a 17 per cent realty tax increase.

king had chosen the first knight for his Round Table." The Chicago mayor made frequent trips to the White House in the ensuing months, often returning home to find Chicago awash in federal moneys, which led to the great rebuilding of the Chicago highway system. As president, Jack Kennedy appointed numerous federal judges in Chicago and sent many defense dollars Daley's way. In three years, the city's main east-west artery, the Northwest Expressway, was renamed the John F. Kennedy Expressway. In stark contrast was the treatment accorded the Outfit for its powerful role in the election, part of a deal struck with Jack Kennedy's father, Joe.

Morris and Denton described a secret financial fallout from Kennedy's victory, the bookie payouts: "An unknowing Graham Hollister – a wealthy Sierra foothills Democrat and future official in the Kennedy administration – brought Teddy [Kennedy] his winnings in Los Angeles, guilelessly carrying the cash in a 'brown paper package,' as one witness remembered. Wingy Grober, it was said, sent the Kennedys their Cal-Neva winnings in similar wrapping."

In Chicago, Mooney Giancana was on the top of the world and said to be acting like "a preening peacock" by one associate. "He was really cocky," said another. On one occasion, Mooney told his and Jack Kennedy's mutual girlfriend, twenty-six-year-old Judy Campbell, "Your boyfriend wouldn't be president if it wasn't for me." Giancana bragged openly to the bosses that he had "elected" Kennedy, and that the gang would soon see a lessening of governmental harassment, both in Chicago and in Las Vegas. And as an added bonus, Mooney said, the hoods might even get Cuba back.

Giancana's swagger would have a life span of exactly one month, terminated when Jack Kennedy announced the unthinkable: He was appointing his mob-chasing brother Robert to be the nation's top law enforcement officer. It became dreadfully apparent to the wisest hoods, such as Curly Humphreys, that the decision to help Joe's kid get elected would prove to be nothing short of suicidal for the hard-won, forty-year reign of the Outfit. In her journal, Jeanne Humphreys opined about how history would have been different without the Outfit's participation in the 1960 election: "Nixon would have been elected. No assassinations, no Watergate, and most important to the Outfit, no Bobby Kennedy as Attorney General. The history of the United States from 1960 'til eternity was made by a mobster from Chicago's West Side who wanted to impress a crooner from New Jersey."

18.

The Kennedy Double Cross:
The Beginning of the End

Clark Clifford was speechless. Clifford, the legendary adviser to Democratic presidents for five decades, was assisting President-elect Kennedy with the transition when he was told of Bobby Kennedy's imminent appointment as attorney general. It was just days after the election when Jack Kennedy approached Clifford poolside at the Kennedys' Palm Beach retreat.

"I listened in amazement," Clifford later wrote about the impending announcement. Jack Kennedy explained, "My father said, 'I want Bobby to be attorney general. He's a lawyer, he's savvy, he knows all the political ins and outs and can protect you.'" Clifford had just finished warning Jack that an inexperienced attorney general could place him in great jeopardy, as had happened in numerous previous administrations. Jack agreed and asked Clifford to speak to "the Old Man." Clifford flew to New York and attempted to convince the patriarch of his ill-advised suggestion. "I made a carefully prepared presentation," Clifford wrote in his memoirs, "of why it was not in the interests of the new President, the Kennedy family, the entire administration, and Bobby himself to take the post." After what he thought was a persuasive argument, Clifford waited for Joe's response.

"Thank you very much, Clark," Joe said. "I am so glad to have heard your views." Then after a brief pause, Kennedy looked Clifford in the eyes and added, "I do want to leave you with one thought, however – one firm thought. *Bobby is going to be attorney general.*" Clifford noted that there was no rancor in Kennedy's voice, but that "he was simply telling me the facts. For a moment I had glimpsed the inner workings of that remarkable family, and, despite my admiration and affection for John F. Kennedy, I could not say I liked what I saw."

Jack Kennedy also enlisted a family friend, Senator George Smathers of

Florida, to try to talk to the father, again to no avail. In Smathers' presence, Joe Kennedy called young Jack over and upbraided him. "Jack! Come here!" Joe ordered. "By God, he deserves to be attorney general, and by God, that's what he's going to be. Do you understand that?" The president-elect responded like a scolded child, "Yes, sir."

Even Bobby, who had worked so tirelessly as his brother's campaign manager, resisted the idea. Although an arch-moralist, Bobby had tired of the grind from his tenure on the McClellan Committee. "I had been chasing bad men for three years," Bobby later said, "and I didn't want to spend the rest of my life doing that." And just as brother Jack had been warned by Clark Clifford, Bobby was likewise cautioned by columnist Drew Pearson: "You would handle so many controversial questions with such vigor that your brother in the White House would be in hot water all the time." (Those words would come to haunt Bobby three years later, when his intemperate handling of Cuban intrigues tragically backfired on his beloved brother.)

It is impossible to know how Joe Kennedy rationalized compromising his sons' well-being by making untold promises to the underworld to gain its support, only to do an about-face once Jack was elected. It has been suggested that Joe understood that the only way to avoid a Justice Department probe of the Kennedy election fix would be to place a Kennedy at the top of that agency. If that was the reasoning, in that, at least, he was proved correct. The numerous clamors for such a probe indeed fell on deaf ears once Bobby was sworn in.

By mid-November, newspapers such as the *New York Times* were reporting that Bobby Kennedy was being floated as the next attorney general. It is not known exactly when the Outfit bosses became aware that they had been double-crossed, but they certainly realized it by December 19, when the appointment was made official.

The announcement reverberated across the country, hitting the underworld enclaves hardest. In Los Angeles, mobster Mickey Cohen reacted by saying, "Nobody in my line of work had an idea that he [JFK] was going to name Bobby Kennedy attorney general. That was the last thing anyone thought." In Chicago, FBI mikes overheard Mooney Giancana complaining to ward boss John D'Arco about local state's attorney Roswell Spencer, comparing him to Bobby's double-crossing father. "He's like Kennedy. He'll get what he wants out of you, but then you won't get anything out of him." Giancana later told D'Arco, "Well, they got the whip and they're in office and that's it . . . They're going to knock us guys out of the box and make us defenseless." After the appointment of Bobby Kennedy, the FBI listened as Kansas City boss Nick Civella commiserated with Mooney in a phone conversation.

"If he [Kennedy] had lost this state here," Mooney said, "he would have lost the election, but I figured with this guy [Sinatra] maybe we'll be all right. I might have known this guy would fuck us."

Civella attempted to console Giancana, offering, "Well, at the time it seems like you done the right things, Sam. Nobody can say anything different after it's done."

"Well, when a cocksucker lies to you–" responded the distraught Giancana.

The Bureau similarly noted Curly Humphreys' rancor over the Bobby Kennedy development. In Curly's FBI file, agents summarized the gangster's conclusions: "Humphreys felt that if his organization had to endure eight years of the John Kennedy administration and eight years under the administration of Robert Kennedy, who he felt would succeed his brother John as President of the United States, that he and other top echelon members of organized crime in Chicago would be dead before a new administration might give more favored treatment to hoodlums."

The FBI report, however, fails to describe the depth of the gang's true feelings about the Kennedy double cross, and the repercussions for boss Mooney Giancana. Jeanne Humphreys remembered, "Everybody was sorry they got involved in it. And it all fell back on Mooney." Most important, she added, "Giancana lost face and that's when he started going downhill." Mooney's daughter Antoinette wrote in her autobiography about "the erosion of my father's stature as a crime boss" that began to occur. Mooney himself was not deaf to the whispering behind his back. Soon, his infamous temper was again rising to the surface.

According to his brother Chuck, Mooney had a heated phone conversation with Frank Sinatra immediately after Bobby Kennedy's appointment to make the crooner explain what was going on. Giancana ended the call by slamming down the phone and then throwing it across the room. "Eatin' out of the palm of his hand," Mooney yelled. "That's what Frank told me. Jack's eatin' out of his hand. Bullshit, that's what it is." The FBI also listened in as the squabble between Mooney and Frank played out. They overheard as Mooney, now fully cognizant of the effect of Bobby's appointment on his mob status, ranted about the Kennedy move. Giancana's FBI file describes one conversation caught by its surveillance: "Giancana claimed that he made a donation to the recent presidential campaign of Kennedy and was not getting his money's worth because if he got a speeding ticket 'none of those fuckers would know me.'" Concerning the 1964 presidential contest, Mooney said, "Kennedy better not think of taking this fucking state."

In time, Mooney and Frank would temporarily patch things up in their on-again, off-again friendship. The ubiquitous FBI overheard Johnny Rosselli report back to Giancana that Sinatra had recently insisted that Rosselli stay at his California home (the interior of which was designed by Sidney Korshak's wife, Bea, according to *Architectural Digest Magazine*). Rosselli said that while guesting at the Palm Springs estate, he was told by Sinatra that the singer had attempted to intervene with the Kennedys on Giancana's behalf. "I took Sam's name and wrote it down," Sinatra told Rosselli, "and told Bobby Kennedy, 'This is my buddy. This is what I want you to know, Bob.'" Rosselli added, "Frank saw Joe Kennedy three different times. Joe called him three times."

But Giancana wasn't buying: "One minute he [Sinatra] tells me this, and then he tells me that . . . he said, 'Don't worry about it. If I can't talk to the old man, I'm going to talk to the man [Jack Kennedy].' One minute he says he's talked to Robert and the next minute he says he hasn't talked to him. So he never did talk to him. It's a lot of shit. Why lie to me? I haven't got that coming."

Statements by Giancana and his associates suggest that the vengeful boss was not about to take the Kennedy affront lying down. It now appears that Mooney decided to subvert the Castro assassination plot, a decision that would doom the upcoming Cuban invasion to failure. And that failure ultimately led the Kennedy brothers to undertake an ill-advised anti-Castro sabotage operation that would come back to haunt the Kennedy family.

"Mooney's going to get even with the Kennedys," Curly Humphreys informed his wife soon after the Bobby Kennedy appointment. "My husband was very cynical about this latest 'brainstorm' by Giancana," says Jeanne Humphreys. "Before Kennedy was elected, from what I understand, it [the assassination plot] was legitimate in the beginning. But after the Kennedys started going after the Outfit, as they did after the election, Mooney decided to string them along and get even with them." Giancana also let on to friends such as Johnny Rosselli and D.C. detective Joe Shimon about the con. "I'm not in it," he said to one associate; or, "I just gave Maheu a couple names," to another. Giancana's son-in-law attorney Robert McDonnell has clear memories of the episode. "Sam thought it was hilarious that the government was paying him to kill Castro, very humorous," recalls McDonnell. "He never took it seriously."

Even Bobby Kennedy's Justice Department believed Giancana was selling the G a bill of goods. One of the earliest public hints of both the plots and Mooney's scam appeared in an August 8, 1963, article in the *Chicago Sun Times*. Quoting Justice Department sources, the article noted that Giancana had only pretended to go along with the CIA operation. He did this, the *Times* said, "in the hopes that the Justice Department's drive to put him behind bars might be slowed – *or at least affected by his ruse of cooperation with another government agency.*" (Italics added.) Chicago FBI agent Bill Roemer wrote, "Giancana's part in the scheme was a ruse." In his book *Roemer: Man Against the Mob,* Roemer added: "Here was the G coming to ask Sam a favor. They would put themselves in his hands and run up a 'marker.' What did Giancana have to lose by going along? . . . Giancana continued to give lip service to the CIA. He did so with a little smile on his face. But the whole time, I believe he was just playing along for his own reasons."

In Florida, the Outfit's plot confederate Santo Trafficante (Joe the Courier) also apparently received Mooney's memo. In a conversation years later with Jimmy Fratianno, Johnny Rosselli said, "Santo never did anything but bullshit everybody." The CIA's plans, Rosselli said, "never got further than Santo." Trafficante himself admitted as much. "Those crazy people [CIA]," he told his lawyer Frank Ragano, "they gave me some pills to kill Castro. I just flushed them down the toilet. Nothing ever came of it."

While Giancana continued to reel over the Kennedy swindle, the Humphreys were debating about how to respond to a missive that had just arrived by mail. Murray Olf, the powerful Washington lobbyist who had assisted Curly at the Stevens Hotel, had seen to it that Mr. and Mrs. Humphreys received an invitation to one of Jack Kennedy's five inaugural balls, where their mutual pal Frank Sinatra would be holding court. Although Curly thought the event might be fun, Jeanne was not so enthusiastic, and her journal records how Curly and Murray Olf tried to convince her to attend: "They argued and pleaded and even got me to Marshall Fields trying on ball gowns . . . A Trigere ballerina-length with a $1,200 price tag almost hooked me until the question of alterations, and shipment of same came up . . . Finally, I said to the saleswoman, 'Bullshit. I'd rather go fishing in Florida' . . . Anyway, I was mad at Jackie K. for not having the chutzpah to wear slacks on the campaign."

Bobby in Charge

Soon after Jack Kennedy's January inauguration, the Outfit began to feel the repercussions of the Kennedy double cross. In the attorney general's first magazine interview, Bobby Kennedy let it be known that organized crime was now the Justice Department's top priority, and in his first press conference he added that, in this effort, he had his brother's full support. In his book *Kennedy Justice,* Victor Navasky wrote that Bobby Kennedy possessed "a total commitment to the destruction of the crime syndicates," and according to former Justice official William Geoghehan, the new attorney general "got five anticrime bills moved through the Judiciary Committee so quickly that nobody had a chance to read them." Bobby Kennedy had soon drawn up a list of forty underworld "targets," ranked in order of priority.

Under Bobby Kennedy's watch, the number of attorneys in the Department's Organized Crime and Racketeering Section ballooned from seventeen to sixty-three; illegal bugs and wiretaps grew from only a handful to more than eight hundred nationwide; the IRS in another questionably legal Kennedy move, saw its man-days of investigative field work increase tenfold, from 8,836 to 96,182 in just two years; and within three months, New Orleans boss Carlos Marcello was grabbed off the street, under orders from Bobby Kennedy, and flown to Guatemala, a move Marcello's biographer John Davis called "arguably illegal," and Marcello's attorneys tersely labeled "kidnapping." Lastly, the list of "targets" expanded from an initial forty to a bloated twenty-three hundred, included among them Joe Accardo and Johnny Rosselli. If Accardo's intention in placing Giancana in the gang's forefront had been to make him the sacrificial lamb, it succeeded: Mooney was placed number one on Bobby's target list. And to guarantee success, Kennedy increased the number of G-men assigned to Chicago from ten to seventy.

Bobby Kennedy's obsession with destroying the underworld provoked him to trample the civil rights of his targets, the very laws he had sworn to defend. In 2000, attorney and syndicated columnist Sidney Zion wrote of his experience as a foot soldier in the Kennedy Justice Department:

I worked under Bobby Kennedy as an assistant U.S. attorney in New Jersey. I can tell you true that there never was and hopefully never will be an attorney general who more violated the Bill of Rights. It was Bobby who took this country into eavesdropping, into every violation of privacy ever feared by the Founders. He used his office as if he were the Godfather getting even with the enemies of the Family. Liberals cheered as he went after Jimmy Hoffa and Roy Cohn, but libertarians understood that what he did went far beyond these guys, that there was nothing more un-American than the decision that the ends justify the means.

Predictably, like the U.S. attorneys who had to carry out Kennedy's controversial orders, the underworld reacted strongly to the tactics of the new regime. FBI bugs soon began picking up the hoods' response to the goings-on at the Justice Department. In New York, they listened as mobster Michelino Clements told an associate, "Bob Kennedy won't stop until he puts us all in jail all over the country."

Pennsylvania boss Mario Maggio was heard saying, "[Bobby Kennedy] is too much; he is starting to hurt too many people, like unions. He is not only hurting the racket guys, but others." Maggio added that he feared "they are going to make this a family affair and [Bobby] wants to be president."

In Chicago, the FBI overheard Mooney remark to associate Potsie Poe, "I never thought it would be this fucking rough. When they put his brother in there, we were going to see some fireworks, but I never knew it was going to be like this. This is murder. The way that kid keeps running back and forth, I don't know how he keeps going."

As if to cast opprobrium at his own father, Bobby Kennedy took a personal interest in the persecution of Papa Joe's election-fraud accomplices in Chicago. Soon after taking his oath, Bobby traveled to the Windy City, where he met with the local G-men. From the Presidential Suite at the Hilton, the very hotel where his father's Outfit cohorts had worked so hard for Jack's election, he set up briefings with the FBI's special agent in charge (SAC), Marlin Johnson. On this first of his many trips to Chicago, Bobby Kennedy sat attentively in the local FBI office as agents set up a reel-to-reel tape recorder and played some highlights from their illegal bugs and taps. The first tape Kennedy heard was a recording from the First Ward bug nicknamed Shade. Although likely unknown to Kennedy, the first voice he heard belonged to the man who had brought Mooney Giancana to Joe Kennedy when the election deal was cut, ward boss Pat Marcy.

Demanding numerous replays of the tape, an enthralled Kennedy listened as Marcy and two bought-off cops discussed a plan to murder another uncorruptable cop. Agent Bill Roemer described Kennedy's reaction, writing, "This tape really got under Bob's skin. A Democratic politician plotting murder – of a police officer yet!" Kennedy, of course, never informed Roemer that Marcy's boss, Mooney Giancana, was at that very moment in Florida plotting the murder of the leader of a sovereign country – at the behest of another Democratic politician, Bobby's brother Jack.

During his tenure, Bobby Kennedy often returned to Chicago, where he brought his informal style to the briefings. In a 1996 article in *Real Crime Digest,* Roemer wrote, "Off would come his shoes and tie. With sleeves rolled up, he would go to the refrigerator, take out bottles of Heineken for all of us, and get down to business." Often, the business included the playing of more surveillance tapes. Four years later, when the courts finally put an end to the eavesdropping, Kennedy would allege, much as he would with the Castro assassination plots, that he had no knowledge that such a thing had occurred on his watch. (Bobby's moral stance was especially disingenuous given that he and his brother were simultaneously secretly recording many of the most secret Oval Office gatherings, unbeknownst to the other participants.) According to Roemer, Kennedy "said [the surveillance] was a violation of civil rights and that if he had known we were doing that, he would have put a stop to it." Although Roemer had grown to like Bobby, the fraudulent disclaimer destroyed their relationship. "Our friendship did not end smoothly," Roemer wrote. "When he came to Chicago [after 1965] . . . he never called anybody in the FBI again . . . I never heard from him again."

There can be no doubt as to the veracity of Roemer's side of the Hilton listening-party story. Immediately after the first tape-playing episode in Chicago, the cunning FBI director made certain the event was preserved for history. "Never a man to let an opportunity go by," wrote Hoover's intelligence chief, William Sullivan, "Hoover insisted on and got sworn affidavits from every agent present stating that Kennedy had listened to the tapes and had not questioned their legality."

For Curly Humphreys, 1961 saw a return to business as usual. High on his agenda was the brokering of a final intergang agreement on how to divide the shares of the skim from Las Vegas' Stardust Hotel. After negotiating with Moe Dalitz at his St. Hubert's Grill in the Loop in January, Humphreys returned to Celano's, where the FBI listened in as the exultant Humphreys crowed about this most recent triumph, which assured the Outfit a 35 percent cut of both the Stardust and the Desert Inn.

"We're right at the point where we can hit him [Dalitz] in the head," said Curly. He went on to brag that 35 percent was pretty good, given that Dalitz was "a Jew guy." Not coincidentally, the Outfit-controlled Teamster pension fund soon bequeathed $6 million to the Stardust Group for the construction of the Stardust Golf Course and Country Club. A similar Teamster loan had already financed the Desert Inn's golf course. These additions were viewed by the investors to be integral to selling lucrative housing lots that would ring the courses.

"Anyway, we got harmony now," Humphreys said. "It's all worked out . . . We didn't have to go through a showdown." As the Bureau tracked the activity of courier Ida Devine, they learned that the monthly split from Vegas now sent $80,000 to Miami, $65,000 to Chicago, $52,000 to Cleveland, and $50,000 to New Jersey. However, due to the illegal manner in which the Bureau was obtaining most of its current intelligence, it was unable to bring charges against the skimmers.

Joe Accardo used his share of the bounty to finance a very public show of familial affection. While the disastrous April 1961 Bay of Pigs invasion (sans Castro's murder) self-destructed, Accardo gave his daughter Linda Lee away at a lavish wedding, with the reception held at Mooney's Papa Bouché's Villa Venice Restaurant in Norridge, Illinois. Giancana had owned the facility since 1956, using as fronts owners-of-record such as Alfred Meo, and later, Leo Olsen. It was the same ploy he had used with the Cal-Neva and dozens of other properties he wished to hide from the IRS.

The reception was to be Accardo's last great shindig, and the boss made it his biggest. Among the more than one thousand attendees were the entire Chicago Outfit, with the exception of the imprisoned Paul Ricca. In addition to the Accardo family, Ricca's wife and children, Rosselli, the Humphreys, Giancana (with Jack Kennedy's mistress Judy Campbell), and virtually all the local underbosses, the heirs apparent, were present, among them Gussie Alex, Frank Ferraro, Jackie Cerone, Joey Glimco, James "Cowboy" Mirro, Phil Alderisio, Ralph Pierce, Hy Godfrey, Butch Blasi, Chuckie and Sam English, Joey Aiuppa, Pat Marcy, John D'Arco, Frank LaPorte, Joe Lombardo, Tony Spilotro, Dave Yaras, Ross Prio, Rocco and Joe Fischetti, Lou Lederer, Johnny Formosa, Frank Buccieri, and Marshall Caifano.

The attendance of the local bosses was no surprise, given their obsequiousness to boss Accardo. But what was most impressive was, as G-man Roemer wrote, "any mobster of stature anywhere in the country attended." With the press and undercover G-men outside taking names and photos, a virtual who's who of organized crime paid their respects to the most successful mob boss in the country.[1]

While the Outfit celebrated in Chicago, the Kennedy White House was in mourning. Only three months into the Kennedy brothers' regime, the disastrous failure of the Bay of Pigs invasion threatened to permanently cripple the new administration almost before it was up and running. Although Jack Kennedy surely knew that he shouldered the lion's share of the blame, since he had scuttled key components of the plan just days before its implementation, his knee-jerk reaction was to crack down on the CIA, the invasion's operational planners. In this effort, the president harkened back to something his father had said: "Bobby can protect you." Thus, at the request of brother Jack, Bobby agreed to place a name above Mooney Giancana's on his "list," Fidel Castro. The indefatigable thirty-six-year-old Bobby, with no experience in either the realm of intelligence or a criminal court, was now the boss of both the law enforcement and intelligence apparatus of the most powerful nation in the world. Few government careerists believed the nation would escape the period unscathed.

Although Bobby Kennedy's embroilment with Castro would sputter along fruitlessly, his war with Giancana was slowly driving the Chicago boss to self-destruction. Mooney's skirmishes now with the G demonstrated to all that the swarthy wheelman from the Patch possessed not a fraction of the prudence of his masters, Accardo and Humphreys. Jeanne Humphreys remembers that when she'd first met Mooney, Curly had warned his rapier-witted wife, "Don't be a wise guy with this fella. He's not the same as the rest of the fellas. He's different." It was now clear that Bobby knew how to push Giancana's buttons, using an illegal tactic that would have destroyed his own brother: He authorized the FBI to bug the bedrooms of Mooney and his lovers.

Since his ascension to boss, Mooney Giancana, ignoring the lessons of Capone, had escalated his high-profile lifestyle, to the continuing dis-

---

1. Among those ID'd were Gambino, Columbo, Profaci, Marcello, Alo, Buffalino, Bompensiero, Genovese, Patriarca, Lansky, Costello, Trafficante, Marcello, and Dalitz. As a final reminder that this was an effort to outdo the recent Bonanno-Profaci wedding in New York, the only mobster not invited was Bonanno, who was an outcast even in New York.

may of the Outfit brain trust. Of late, he had been squiring singing stars Keely Smith, after her divorce from bandleader Louis Prima, and Phyllis McGuire, of the popular McGuire Sisters singing trio. FBI bugs at Mooney's Armory Lounge headquarters often overheard Mooney demanding that the restaurant's jukebox be purged of all Smith records when Giancana was bringing over McGuire, and vice versa if Smith was in town. In the summer of 1961, Mooney was accompanying Phyllis as her group traveled the country on a concert tour. The unlikely lovers had met in 1960 at the gang's Desert Inn Casino in Las Vegas. Over the last year, Mooney had lavished on McGuire, whom he nicknamed Wonderful, such love tokens as a brand-new white Cadillac convertible. He also arranged for Phyllis' markers in the gang's casinos to be erased, or "eaten."

With Giancana busy partying in Las Vegas, the chore of running the gang's business there typically fell to the overwrought Curly Humphreys. The gang elder statesman watched in disbelief as Giancana's name, linked with the likes of Phyllis McGuire and Keely Smith, appeared over and over in local papers. On one occasion, when a local journalist requested an interview with Curly, the hood vented his feelings to an associate at Celano's: "I don't give a shit who the newspaper guy is. Why should I talk to him, I said, and don't you speak to any of our other guys." When Giancana actually showed up at Celano's, Humphreys seized the opportunity to set him straight. "Don't play around with the newspapers," Humphreys barked. "Just stand in the background. That's what I would do, Moe. You stay in the background." And on another occasion: "Giancana spends so much time away from Chicago when he has business here." Once when Mooney missed a meeting, Curly was unnerved. The FBI eavesdroppers summarized what happened: "Giancana got a hurry-up call and appeared to be unable to make the appointment that night. Humphreys sarcastically felt the call was from one of Giancana's girlfriends and appeared angered that Giancana let pleasure interfere with business."

The unsolicited extra responsibilities only accelerated Humphreys' desire to retire, but he knew that was impossible. In one monitored call to his ex-wife, Clemi, in Oklahoma, Humphreys waxed nostalgic about life before the Kennedy crackdown. "It's so bad now," Humphreys said, "that the coppers are even afraid to take money because they're afraid of the G . . . Honey, things were a lot different then, when you were here." His daughter, Luella, remembered a constant refrain whenever her father visited Oklahoma. "I'm so tired," he'd say. "I want out so bad, but I made my decision and I have to live with it." The FBI heard him say, "I got to sit around and control the underworld here."

The G-men summed up the growing tensions within the Outfit hierarchy: "Humphreys and the other leading Chicago Hoodlums have been unhappy with Sam Giancana . . . Humphreys and Frankie Ferraro apparently met with Giancana's predecessors, Tony Accardo and Paul Ricca, to discuss their feelings." In their powwow, the Outfit old-timers, who were old enough to remember Big Jim Colosimo's disastrous infatuation with a young singer named Dale Winter, worried about Mooney's infatuation with singers Phyllis McGuire and Keely Smith.

Mooney was not the only one shirking his responsibilities. Johnny Rosselli was increasingly absent from his Sin City post in favor of participating in CIA derring-do and bedding Vegas showgirls and Hollywood starlets. "Johnny became starstruck, like Mooney," remembers Jeanne Humphreys. "And he talked too much. The very first time I met him, he laughed about how he had whacked the wrong guy once by mistake. Murray was appalled that he would talk like that to me." In one Celano's conversation with Giancana, Curly spoke of how he had to repeatedly discipline Rosselli: "I've known Johnny, and I've always kind of liked him. But after all, you have to be honest when you talk to him." Curly recalled how he once scolded Johnny, saying, "Listen to me, you fucker. When I talk, this is it. Don't you give me this shit. I'm one of the old-timers. I'm not a young punk. You're talking to the wrong guy." Humphreys added, "So then he changed his mind."

Thus, like Mooney, Johnny Rosselli began to fall increasingly out of favor with his superiors. In his stead, the Outfit's other West Coast mouthpiece and labor relations consultant, Sidney Korshak, took up the slack. In 1997, *Vanity Fair* magazine devoted a sixteen-page article to the shadowy Korshak, calling him "one of the great hidden figures of twentieth-century organized crime . . . Las Vegas was one of his kingdoms." But what the article failed to note was that Korshak was totally controlled by Chicago, and specifically, by his handler, Curly Humphreys.

FBI wiretaps throughout the period detail Humphreys' command over Korshak, who was by now also negotiating contracts for top-flight Hollywood entertainers, many of whom desired to pad their wallets with lucrative weeklong engagements in Sin City. One bugged conversation showed Humphreys worrying that Korshak was "getting too big for his britches." Frequently, Curly would have to remind Korshak whom he worked for, as on the occasion when Sidney arranged a Las Vegas booking for singer Dinah Shore at a hotel not run by the Outfit. Since only Humphreys was allowed to contact Korshak, the idea being to insulate the valuable asset from gangster tarnish, it fell to him alone to straighten out Sidney. Humphreys, who continued to place calls to Korshak under the name Mr. Lincoln, was incensed and let Korshak know it.

After ordering Korshak to keep Shore "out of the wrong places," Humphreys added, "Anything you want to do for yourself, Sidney, is OK, but we made you and we want you to take care of us first . . . Now we built you up pretty good, and we stood by you, but anything else outside of the law business is us, and I don't want to hear you in anything else . . . Anytime we yell, you come running."

Korshak indeed came running to the Outfit's rescue whenever it perceived it was losing the public relations war. Such was the case with one of the underworld's most vocal opponents, composer and television pioneer Steve Allen. The Chicago native and creator of the talk show genre became an outspoken anticrime activist in 1954, when he chanced upon a photograph of a man who had been severely beaten after speaking out against the installation of pinball machines in a store near a neighborhood school. Allen, under the threat of advertiser desertion, produced a two-hour documentary on labor corruption for New York's WNBT, from where his *Tonight* show originated. After the documentary aired, one of the interviewees, labor columnist Victor Reisel, was blinded by an acid-thrower, and Allen endured slashed tires on his car and stink bombs set off in his theater. Then there came physical threats. One anonymous caller referred to the Reisel attack and told Allen, "Lay off, pal, or you're next."

But the hoods totally misread Allen, who was only emboldened by the threats. Over the years, Allen continued to take every opportunity to sound the clarion call, against not only the underworld, but also against its upperworld enablers. Allen made frequent trips to Chicago, where he spoke at benefits for the Chicago Crime Commission. His Van Nuys office contains more than forty binders labeled "Organized Crime," holding thousands of notes and newspaper clippings. But the entertainer's stance had a powerful impact on his career.

"I was blackballed in many lucrative establishments," Allen recalled shortly before his death in 2000. "I was only invited to play Vegas twice in my entire career." This alone deprived Allen of millions of dollars from a venue he would have owned if given the opportunity.

In 1963, Allen was hosting the syndicated late-night *Steve Allen Show* when he received a call from Sidney Korshak. "I was asked to take it easy on Sidney's friends," Allen recalled. Not long after politely refusing Korshak's request, Allen felt the power of the underworld-upperworld collusion once again. "We had a terrible time booking many A-list guests for the show," Allen explained. It was clear to Allen that Korshak, in connivance with Jules Stein's entertainment megalith, MCA, had chosen to deprive the *Steve Allen Show* of the MCA talent roster, which at the time represented most of Hollywood's top stars.

Despite the talent embargo, Allen concocted a wonderful program with his staple ensemble of brilliant ad-libbers such as Louie Nye, Don Knotts, Bill Dana, and Tom Poston, as well as quirky personalities like madman Gypsy Boots, and then unknown Frank Zappa, who appeared as a performance artist, bashing an old car with a sledgehammer. But Allen's 1963 run-in with Korshak would not be his last encounter with gangster intimidation.

While the fuming Accardo and Humphreys kept the organization afloat in Chicago, the man who was supposed to be the day-to-day boss remained on the nightclub circuit. In July 1961, the Bureau learned through its Las Vegas bugs that Mooney and Phyllis were going to transit Chicago on their way from Las Vegas to Atlantic City. Alerted, the Chicago Field Office dispatched five agents to Chicago's O'Hare Airport on July 12, with the intent of driving Giancana over the brink by serving a grand jury subpoena on Phyllis, whom Agent Roemer disparagingly referred to as Giancana's "mistress" (Giancana was a widower).[2] The plan was to separate the pair, with the former marine boxing champ Roemer assigned to sequester the volatile Giancana, while the others interviewed McGuire. According to both Roemer's and Giancana's versions, the confrontation was explosive, with Giancana launching into a profanity-laced tirade. Not only did Mooney repeatedly scream "motherfuckers" and "cocksuckers" at the agents, but he did the same to innocent travelers observing the altercation as they walked by.

At one point, Mooney chided the agents about their unrelenting

---

2. The agents were Harold Sell, Bill Roemer, Vince Inserra, Johnny Bassett, and Ralph Hill.

probing into his private affairs. He asked sarcastically if they knew that he owned 35 percent of Marshall Field's, 20 percent of Carson's, and 20 percent of Goldblatt's Department Store. He was then asked if he had any holdings in Las Vegas, to which he replied, "I own ninety-nine percent of Las Vegas. And in Florida I own the Fontainebleau, the Americana, and the Diplomat." Although these were obvious exaggerations, there was probably some truth in all the boasts, but given the Outfit's penchant for hidden ownerships, the truth will forever be elusive.[3]

"I know this is because of Bobby Kennedy," Giancana yelled at Roemer. Using hoodlum parlance, Mooney fumed, "You're going to report this to your boss, and he's gonna report it to the superboss . . . You know who I mean, the Kennedys . . . Well, I know all about the Kennedys, and Phyllis knows a lot more, and one of these days we are going to tell all . . . I'm going to light a fire under you guys and don't forget that." When Giancana was asked if he wanted the agents to call his aide Butch Blasi to give him a ride, Giancana said, "Yes, call Butch, and tell him to bring two shotguns with him." And to make absolutely certain Roemer got the point, the furious boss snarled, "Do you know how many people I've killed? I might have to be responsible for another one very shortly."

After being cursed at for an hour, Roemer also lost his cool and began his own shouting match with O'Hare patrons, yelling out to the unwary baggage-toting travelers, "Look at this piece of garbage, a piece of scum. You people are lucky to be passing through Chicago – we have to live with this slime. This is Sam Giancana, the boss of the underworld here. Take a good look at this prick."

Before being reunited with McGuire and catching their connecting flight, Giancana walked up to Roemer and pounded a finger into the agent's chest. "You lit a fire tonight, Roemer, that will never go out," Giancana threatened. "We'll get you if it's the last thing we do!"

At the Armory Lounge shortly after the confrontation (and with the G listening in), Giancana told an associate, "If a man would call me what I called them fellows [at O'Hare], I'd shoot them right there." The longer Giancana stayed on the topic, however, the hotter his temper grew. In a few moments, it had reached its extremely low kindling point, prompting the gangster to scream, "I've had enough of that guy [Roemer]. I'm

---

3. Regarding the Fontainebleau, Frank Sinatra's 1,275-page FBI file notes that Giancana associate Joe Fischetti "was deeply involved in this hotel" and arranged for Sinatra to perform there "without charge."

putting up a fund of one hundred thousand dollars to figure out how to get that cocksucker."

The absurd notion of whacking a G-man was brought before Giancana's bosses, who quickly disabused the fiery gangster of the idea. Mooney had requested such a sanction before, and the reply from Accardo was always the same: "That would be counterproductive. The whole FBI would come down on us from all over the country if we hit one of them. Call it off. Now." Giancana obeyed, although once out of earshot of his own "superbosses," he vented to his driver, "I'm the boss of this Outfit. Fuck anybody else!"

To be sure, Accardo and Humphreys had not turned their swords into plowshares, but their sanctioning of violence had greatly decreased in recent years, possibly due in no small part to their mellowing with age. Humphreys especially was deeply involved in charitable projects. In addition to his contributions to Native American children in Oklahoma, Curly was the sole executive in charge of the mob's "family pension fund," making certain that the gang widows of Capone, Nitti, Guzik, as well as Virginia Hill, were regularly compensated. Humphreys also found time to visit the terminally ill Frankie Ferraro daily at Wesley Memorial Hospital, and after Ferraro's passing, looked after both Ferraro's widow and his mistress.

When in Florida, one of the few forays Humphreys took away from his home was to visit Mae Capone and her boy Sonny on Palm Island. Humphreys alone sided with Sonny when he requested a $24,000 loan from the Outfit to shore up his foundering Miami Beach Restaurant; Curly was once again outvoted by "the spaghetti benders." Jeanne Humphreys remembers, "We had to sneak money to Mae. It was our own money." The FBI overheard discussions concerning Curly's anonymous contributions to the Red Cross, the Salvation Army, and "various Catholic and Jewish charitable organizations." With Libonati, Curly raised funds for Boys Town and helped to establish the American-Italian Welfare League in Chicago.

Like Humphreys, Joe Accardo was frequently linked to unadvertised philanthropy and displays of conscience. Once, when an FBI informer named Bernie Glickman had ratted on some crooked fight promoters, he was badly beaten by Phil Alderisio. Worried that the Outfit had put a murder contract out on Glickman, who had steadfastly refused to name Accardo, Agent Bill Roemer, using Ralph Pierce as intermediary, sought a sit-down with the man himself, Joe Accardo, a man whom he knew so much about, but had never met. After consulting with boss Accardo, Pierce called Roemer.

"In the Sears parking lot at North and Harlem at midnight," Pierce told the G-man. After his midnight arrival at the suburban intersection about forty-five minutes from the Loop, Roemer waited ten minutes before Pierce appeared from a Sears doorway.

"Walk west for a couple blocks," Pierce instructed, before walking away. Roemer did as instructed, and after about two blocks, the most powerful mob boss in the nation walked out from the cover of a tree. The two men shook hands, and Accardo allowed Roemer to search him for a wire (the meeting was not authorized by Roemer's superiors and he feared blackmail). "I'm the guy who should think *you'd* be wired," Accardo joked. However, as soon as the agent touched Accardo, six men exploded out of two cars parked nearby.

"Hold on," Accardo ordered his men. "I think it's OK."

Accardo suggested the two just take a walk and chat, and the two adversaries proceeded through the dark suburban streets "exchanging pleasantries," according to Roemer, all the while tailed by Accardo's cars.

"What is it you want from me?" Accardo eventually asked.

Roemer explained the situation with Glickman, assuring Accardo that the hood was not squealing on the boss.

"I want your word that he won't be harmed," Roemer said. "Call off the contract."

"You believe what you read in the papers, huh, Roemer?" Accardo chided. "Is there a contract?"

Roemer sidestepped that debate and told Accardo that Glickman had been left unprotected by the Bureau, which had resulted in the Alderisio attack, and that Glickman was in need of medical help and peace of mind.

"Roemer, I thought we were supposed to be the bad guys," Accardo said. "It seems to me here *you* are the fuckin' bad guys."

Roemer begged Accardo to show mercy to the infirm Glickman, who, the agent insisted, had shown undying loyalty to Accardo. After a few minutes of silence, the boss promised that Glickman would not be touched.

"You've got my word," Accardo said. Then the two men inquired about each other's families, as if they were old high-school classmates attending a reunion. The next day Roemer drove a stunned Glickman to Accardo's River Forest Palace, so he could hear could hear about his indemnity from the boss himself. In his book *Accardo: The Genuine*

Godfather, Roemer described what happened next: '[Accardo] took Bernie to his personal physician. The physician put Bernie in St. Luke-Presbyterian Hospital . . . and treated him while Bernie recuperated from his ordeal . . . Accardo had paid all the bills.'

The tensions with the G were temporarily ameliorated in the fall of 1961 as social gatherings held sway. On September 23, 1961, ten months after the election, Joe Kennedy threw a thank-you party for Frank Sinatra at the family's Hyannis compound. According to the Sinatra clan, Joe wanted to show his appreciation for Sinatra's enlisting the Giancana support in West Virginia, not to mention the Outfit's critical role in the general election. Two weeks later, Sinatra was in Chicago attending the coming-out party for Paul Ricca, who had just been released from prison.

The party atmosphere was not long-lasting, at least as far as the volatile Giancana-Sinatra relationship was concerned. Giancana had concluded by now that Sinatra had lied about intervening on his behalf with the Kennedys. Perhaps Mooney had expected some good word after Joe Kennedy's party for Sinatra in September. According to Sinatra biographer Randy Taraborrelli, the singer consistently lied to Mooney about pleading his case with Papa Joe. Taraborrelli spoke with Philadelphia mafioso Nicolas D'Amato, and Sinatra's fellow singer Dean Martin, both of whom were aware of the dangerous game Sinatra was playing.

"Sinatra was an idiot for playing both sides of the field like that," said D'Amato. "Playing Mooney for a sucker? What, are you kidding me? If he wasn't so fucking talented, he never woulda gotten away with being such a fink. With the boys, when you let 'em down, you got hit . . . And lie to Sam? Forget it. I can't think of anyone else who would've continued to breathe air after telling a story like the one Frank told to Sam." Dean Martin agreed, saying, "Only Frank could get away with the shit he got away with. Only Frank. Anyone else woulda been dead."

On December 6, 1961, the FBI eavesdroppers also caught wind of the escalating warfare between Sinatra and Giancana. On that night, Mooney was meeting in his Armory Lounge headquarters with Johnny Formosa, an underling used as a courier between Chicago and the West Coast, and who occasionally worked at Mooney's Cal-Neva Lodge.

"Let's hit Sinatra," Formosa advised Mooney. Formosa's rage was such that he relished taking out the entire Rat Pack. "Let's show those fuckin' Hollywood fruitcakes that they can't get away with it," Formosa said. "I could take the rest of them too – Lawford, that Martin prick, and I could take the nigger and put his other eye out." The suggestion echoed what the normally restrained Johnny Rosselli had also told boss Giancana. According to FBI wiretaps, Rosselli told Mooney that he should lash out at the those who had broken their word. "They only know one way," Johnny said. "Now let them see the other side of you."

But Mooney responded, "No. I have other ideas for them. You call those cocksuckers and tell them I want them for a month or else."

Giancana's "other ideas," which involved having the entire Rat Pack perform gratis at Mooney's Villa Venice, would take a year to reach fruition. In the meantime, a Chicago associate of Mooney's named Tommy DiBella learned just how close Sinatra had come to graduating from swing music to "trunk music." Mooney told DiBella he was considering putting a contract out on the double-crossing singer when he had an erotic epiphany. "[One night] I'm fucking Phyllis, playing Sinatra songs in the background, and the whole time I'm thinking to myself, Christ, how can I silence that voice? It's the most beautiful sound in the world. Frank's lucky he got it. It saved his life."

Sinatra's reprieve would be, like many of Mooney's other pronouncements, temporary. In the meantime, Mooney began making plans for Sinatra's payback for the Kennedy embarrassment.

Giancana's restraint was surprising, especially given the continued heat being placed on the Outfit by the administration they had helped elect. Bobby Kennedy, clearly not privy to whatever hollow deals his father had cut with the mob, now began to move on Vegas, the very city the Outfit thought it had protected when it had fallen in with Joe Kennedy. Before the Kennedy regime, the FBI had managed to tap only the Fremont Hotel. In Vegas, the FBI was now authorized to tap twenty-five telephone lines into Outfit-controlled, or Outfit-invested, casinos such as the Desert Inn, the Sands, the Stardust, and the Riviera. (The phone taps were discovered in 1963 by an engineer for the Fremont, the manager of which promptly enlisted the other casinos in a class action suit against the FBI. The suit was pending until 1967, when the Justice Department indicted them for the skim operation.[4]) The noose became so tight for the hoods that they had to put a prohibition on phone conversations altogether. One wiretapped conversation gave evidence of the agony the taps were inflicting on the underworld:

---

4. Even Nevada's lieutenant governor, Cliff Jones, found he was being watched when, in 1965, he found a microphone and phone-line-powered transmitter hidden in his office.

Hood One: "I need to get a hold of a guy in Las Vegas, and how the hell am I going to get ahold of him? They don't even want you to make a call there."
Hood Two: "You can't call the state of Nevada. That's the orders."

The tireless assault on the underworld did not appear to hamper the Kennedy administration's efforts regarding the rest of its agenda. Not unlike the overworked Curly Humphreys, Bobby Kennedy continued to burn the midnight oil in his zeal to bring down the number one man on his hit list, Fidel Castro. With the onslaught of millions of pages of recently released government documents, the evidence has become conclusive that Bobby Kennedy, like so many upperworld scions before him, attempted to walk the fine line between moral indignation and utilitarianism regarding associations with the underworld. For in his ardor to remove Castro from the scene, Bobby Kennedy almost certainly approved the ongoing CIA liaisons with Johnny Rosselli and others.[5] Years later, Rosselli was asked by a congressional committee if he had ever met the Kennedy brothers during the operation. He responded that the only Kennedy he knew was patriarch Joe Kennedy. Then he postulated that he might indeed have met Jack when he first met Joe. "The only recollection I have," Rosselli answered, "is I think when they were all kids out in California when his father was running the studio."

On December 11, 1961, Hoover began a campaign of slow torture against the Kennedy family by first alerting Bobby that Hoover's hidden mikes had heard all about Giancana's frustration regarding the double cross in the election deal he had cut with Joe Kennedy via Sinatra. It was just the sort of dirt that Hoover had historically coveted as his own guarantee of job security. He had gathered information on the private lives of powerful people for decades, occasionally letting the subjects discreetly know how vulnerable they were. The Bureau's head of intelligence at the time, William Sullivan, wrote, "[Hoover] kept this kind of explosive material in his personal files, which filled four rooms on the fifth floor of headquarters."

Hoover was especially concerned about his purchase with the Kennedy brothers and knew that this was the sort of intelligence that would

---

5. For more on Bobby and the use of the underworld in the Castro operations, see Russo, *Live by the Sword,* and Hersh, *The Dark Side of Camelot.*

forestall any attempt to remove him from the FBI. Even before the election, candidate Kennedy had let it be known that he was considering replacing Hoover. "Jack Kennedy disliked Hoover in return," wrote William Sullivan, "and wanted to replace him as Director." Now, it appeared, Joe's dealings had tied the brothers' hands.

Hoover biographer Curt Gentry powerfully described the charged atmosphere in his book *J. Edgar Hoover: The Man and the Secrets:* "What happened between the Kennedys during the next few days can only be surmised. Robert would obviously warn John that Hoover believed the story (that is, had yet another arrow to add to his quiver), whether it was true or not. Typically, the attorney general would have confronted Joe, certainly to ask about the tale and probably to rant and rave . . . And Robert Kennedy would surely be writhing furiously at this latest twist of Hoover's thumbscrew."

Gentry is quick to point out that seven days after Bobby learned of Joe's campaign shenanigans, and after a likely shouting match between the two, Joe suffered a massive stroke, from which he would never rebound. But Hoover was not yet finished with the education of Bobby Kennedy. In a few weeks, the director would apprise the self-righteous attorney general that he was fully cognizant of more examples of Kennedy family hypocrisy surrounding their dealings with the Outfit.

By the end of 1961, the Castro vendetta had transmogrified into a new joint White House–CIA venture code-named Operation Mongoose, which was typified by open sabotage against Cuba and more tightly held murder plots against its president. The man brought in to oversee this latest variation was a decorated CIA veteran and former FBI agent named Bill Harvey, who openly clashed with the impulsive and inexperienced attorney general over both style and strategy. By this time, Robert Maheu had long since extracted himself from the scheme, and Harvey had no desire to rerecruit him. When Rosselli was later asked about Maheu's departure from the scene, he explained, "[Harvey] never trusted [Maheu] since his FBI days . . . they were in the FBI together."

The perceptive Harvey also immediately cut Agency ties to Giancana and Trafficante, both of whom he rightly suspected were conning the White House. By the spring of 1962, Harvey had begun meeting Rosselli in Miami and elsewhere, and with Harvey as the conduit, the CIA passed four poison pills to Rosselli, which he in turn gave to a Cuban exile who promised to get them into Cuba with a team that would administer them to Fidel at the earliest opportunity.

Although he was shirking his Outfit responsibilities in Las Vegas, Rosselli enjoyed the CIA intrigue, and the strong bond he was making with new friend Bill Harvey. Like Rosselli, Harvey was an action man, who defied all bureaucratic refinements that slowed the pace. Both men were also strong patriots with a visceral hatred of all things Communist. Their bond would grow into a lifelong friendship, attested to by Harvey in congressional testimony, and more recently by Harvey's widow, Clara Grace, or "CG."

"Rosselli was a very good friend of ours," CG Harvey recently recalled. "He had dinner in our home." On those occasions when Rosselli showed up at the Harveys' Indianapolis home, he always brought gifts for their children, a recurring theme in the childless Rosselli's life. When the Harveys' son was in Hollywood, Johnny squired him around, introducing him to movie stars. "He would do anything for you he could possibly do," CG fondly recalled, "but Bobby Kennedy was hot on his neck." Although CG Harvey was not naïve about the ways of Rosselli's other life, she made no apologies for her affection for the charming gangster. "I know he had his bad side," she said, "but he was really doing things on our side that really counted. Bill defended Johnny, saying he was a loyal American. Bill said he would rather ride shotgun with him than anyone else."

Like Mrs. Harvey, Bill Harvey's coworkers also became aware of Harvey's fast-growing bond with Rosselli. An assistant CIA chief of station who worked directly under Harvey recently noted, "Bill was proud of his friendship with Rosselli. He bragged about it. These were guys that got things done, and that appealed to him."

As their friendship blossomed, Harvey granted Rosselli the privilege of an open door at the massive CIA base in Miami, from where Harvey's Mongoose raids were coordinated. Throughout the summer of 1962, "Colonel Rosselli," as he was known at the "JM/WAVE" CIA base, was a part of the Mongoose team, with all the excitement and bunkhouse camaraderie that such an undertaking entailed.

"[Rosselli] had virtual carte blanche into the highest levels of the [Miami] station," remembers Bradley Ayers, an army captain assigned to the CIA base. "It was clear that somebody had said, you know, give this guy whatever he needs." Ayers also saw in Rosselli what everyone else had seen regarding his devotion. "There was a quality to Rosselli that came off as the patriotic, true-blue, one hundred percent American. I could see the spark of patriotism there, and I guess that made it all palatable. We were all trying to get the same job done, although we were coming from entirely different places."

Over many months, Rosselli commandeered V-20 speedboats across the straits to Cuba in dangerous nighttime runs, infiltrating shooters onto the island. On one occasion, his boat was sunk by Cuban patrols, leaving the fifty-seven-year-old gangster to swim hundreds of yards in the cold ocean at night to reach a second boat. On another occasion, a sunk boat forced him into a dinghy, where he drifted for days before being rescued by colleagues who had given him up for dead. For all his devotion, however, Rosselli (and everyone connected to Mongoose for that matter) saw few successes. As time wore on, Bill Harvey began to see the assassination project as not only unwise, but immoral. And Johnny Rosselli had grown weary of the Cuban teams, which seemed far less capable than the hit men with whom he had been acquainted in his other life. According to Harvey's widow, also a CIA officer with whom her husband spoke freely, Bill Harvey began sandbagging the plots, hoping Bobby would just drop the idea.

At the end of 1962, Bobby Kennedy had drummed Harvey out of Mongoose for what he considered insubordination (Harvey had cursed out Bobby and his brother at a White House meeting). And Rosselli went back to his old life, only to find that the IRS was after him as well. Rosselli's biographers wrote that he "resented what he perceived as the government's double-standard – the pressure was increasing at the same time he was risking his life doing Uncle Sam's dirty work in the Florida Keys." Rosselli said as much to a Las Vegas associate, elaborating about the influence of Bobby Kennedy. "Here I am," Rosselli said, "helping the government, helping the country, and that little son of a bitch is breaking my balls."

The seriousness of the Mongoose enterprise was not without occasional comic relief. One such episode occurred during the summer of 1962, when Curly and Jeanne Humphreys arrived at their Biscayne Bay house after a recent Jamaican vacation. During the island jaunt, Jeanne had learned about how the Jamaicans had imported mongooses to solve their snake infestation problems. Coincidentally, the Humphreys were having a snake problem on their Florida property, and when the pair made a trip to Miami Beach to visit Rosselli at the Fontainebleau, the subject of mongooses was in the front of Jeanne's mind. Thus, while Curly was upstairs with some of "the boys," Jeanne remained poolside and made what she thought was innocent small talk with Johnny Rosselli.

In doing so, a simple intention to determine what the plural was for *mongoose* turned into a potential disaster for Rosselli. Jeanne remembers the following exchange:

> Jeanne: "What do you know about the word *mongoose*?"
> Johnny (nervously): "Is this a joke?"
> Jeanne: "Not to some people it isn't."
> Johnny: "Are you crazy? This Castro stuff is OK'd by the G. We're not supposed to talk about it. I can't believe Curly would talk about such a thing."
> Jeanne: "First, why on earth would Castro be concerned about the snakes in my front yard, and second, I'm the one who told Curly about them."
> Johnny (realizing): "Look, I just fucked up. Please don't tell Curly."[6]

The moral tightrope the Kennedys had been negotiating was about to become as fine as a human hair. Their use of the underworld, or castigation of it, depending on which was more politically advantageous at the time, was about to blow up in their faces, due ironically to Bobby Kennedy's pressure on Hoover to increase his surveillance on members of organized crime. If Bobby Kennedy had any doubts as to just how indistinguishable were the upperworld of his family, which he turned a blind eye toward, and the underworld of those he crusaded against, he had to look no further than his own brother's bedroom. The occurrence that crystallized the truism was put most succinctly by Hoover biographer Curt Gentry: "The bug in the Armory Lounge had gradually led [Hoover] to a discovery that even the old cynic must have found stunning. [Judy] Campbell, mistress of the president, was also romantically involved with Sinatra, Giancana, and Johnny Rosselli."

Although the Bureau had suspected the relationship since its inception two years earlier, it had now acquired hard evidence via phone records and other surveillance (all encouraged by Bobby Kennedy's mob crack-

---

6. Jeanne says that the confused byplay actually went on longer, although she cannot recall all the details four decades later. Once back at the Biscayne home, Jeanne could not restrain herself and brought up the hilarious non sequitur that had just occurred at the Fontainebleau. But just as with the election, Curly found nothing funny about the charade. "Forget about Mongoose," he told his wife. 'It's another crazy scheme of Johnny's.'

down) that Campbell had been in regular telephone contact with the president at the White House.

The information played right into Hoover's Chinese water torture of the Kennedys. On February 27, 1962, Hoover sent a memo to Bobby informing him that Hoover had become aware of the Campbell story; in March, Hoover similarly informed the president. And there was one more item. In May, Hoover sent a memo to Bobby letting him know that Hoover was fully aware of the CIA-Maheu-Giancana plotting against Castro. Although the Bureau had known the gist of the story for many months, they had recently been given the specifics by both the CIA and Maheu, both having been pressured to explain the Rowan wiretapping incident in Las Vegas.

The tug-of-war between the Outfit and the G was unrelenting. By this time, the Outfit knew of some of the FBI's bugs and wiretaps. Recall that Jeanne Humphreys has spoken of an FBI source cultivated by her husband. Even Agent Bill Roemer had become aware that Humphreys had obtained a highly confidential list of mobsters designated for targeting by Kennedy's Justice Department. According to Jeanne Humphreys, one celebrated Bureau infiltration represented nothing more than an elaborate Outfit charade.

On February 11, 1962, Miami agents listened to a bug they had illegally installed in Chicago boss Jackie Cerone's vacation home in Florida. The G listened in as Cerone conferred with fellow Chicago underbosses Fifi Buccieri and Dave Yaras. In great and violent detail the hoods discussed their past killings, and an attempted execution of rival numbers kingpin "Big Jim" Martin. Among other killings, they discussed the horrific torture murder of William "Action Jackson" Kelly, an Outfit juice collector. Agent Bill Roemer described the killing, which took place at a meat-rendering plant, in gruesome detail: 'They hoisted him a foot off the ground and impaled him on a meat hook through the rectum . . . They took a cattle prod . . . and attached it to his penis. They plugged it in . . . Then they poured water on the cattle prod, increasing the voltage . . . Then they smashed his kneecaps with a hammer . . . they stuck him with ice picks . . . They let him hang there for three days until he expired.'

As in the execution of Fred Evans, Roemer took credit for being the cause of the Kelly killing, claiming that the killers were trying to obtain a confession that Kelly had squealed to Roemer and his partners. In fact, the actual motive for the crime left many otherwise nonviolent insiders saying, "Kelly had it coming." According to recent interviews, what happened was that Kelly, a known sexual degenerate, had been trying to collect on a gambling debt from an Outfit-connected burglar named Casey Bonakowski. At the time Kelly came calling, Bonakowski was in prison on theft charges. Kelly therefore decided to collect the debt in the form of sexual favors from Mrs. Bonakowski, who put up a struggle before being raped. As if to put a signature on his depravity, Kelly bit off one of his victim's nipples and spat it on the floor. When word got back to Casey, he immediately took it up with the bosses, who made Kelly an example for future rapists of their women.

After the war stories concluded, the conspirators got around to the business at hand, planning the murders of Laborers International Union official Frankie Esposito and First Ward boss John D'Arco, both of whom were on route to the Sunshine State. The long session was highlighted by the following exchanges:

> Yaras: "I wish for Christ's sake we were hitting him now."
> Cerone: "Well, if we don't score by the end of the week . . . then we got to take a broad and invite him here."
> Yaras: "Leave it to us. As soon as he walks in the fucking door, boom! We'll hit him with a fucking ax or something . . ."
> Buccieri: "Now, if he comes in with D'Arco . . . we could do everybody a favor if this fucking D'Arco went with him."
> Cerone: "The only thing is, he [D'Arco] weighs three hundred fucking pounds."

The conversation continued for several minutes as the gangsters discussed in excruciating detail when and how to use their knives and axes, and whether to rent a boat, so as to deposit the bodies at sea.

Back in Chicago, the local G-men warned the alleged targets, who were disbelieving, to put it mildly. "That's all bullshit," Esposito told one agent who phoned him with the news of the threat. "Those guys wouldn't hit me, you guys are full of shit. I have no reason to talk to you." Esposito then hung up on the G. Even Bill Roemer, despite his later use of the tape to portray his prey in the worst possible light, admitted that he understood Esposito's response. "If I hadn't heard it myself on the tapes, maybe I would have thought it was all 'bullshit' too." According to Jeanne Humphreys, Roemer should have believed Esposito.

"The entire conversation was a farce, orchestrated by Murray," Mrs.

Humphreys recently recalled. "I was there at D'Arco's Hollywood Beach house when they rehearsed it. It was scripted. They knew the bug was illegal and they wanted to drive the G crazy." It is worth noting that neither Esposito nor D'Arco were ever even ambushed, let alone murdered. The Bureau's transcript of the incriminating conversation was leaked to *Life* magazine writer Sandy Smith and later used by Chicago agent Bill Roemer in his autobiography to illustrate not only the Outfit's violent ways, but the Bureau's great surveillance coup. No one was ever told about the rape of Casey Bonakowski's wife.

The occasional game-playing with the G notwithstanding, the situation became so intolerable that Jeanne Humphreys chose to spend the better part of 1962 in Zurich, Switzerland. Every March for years, she and Curly had been ferrying Outfit "pension" money to Virginia Hill, who had been living as an expatriate in the banking capital. According to Jeanne, Gussie Alex had been making the deliveries to Hill for a few years, until he was barred from going to Europe by the Outfit, who feared he was being followed. "I met Virginia in Gstaad," Jeanne recently said. "Her mouth was so foul, she made me look like Mother Teresa." Humphreys says that she smuggled $100,000 per year to Hill, the large-denomination bills hidden in Jeanne's nylon waistband when transiting customs. In 1962, after she and Curly had toured Africa, Egypt, and Europe and made their delivery to Ms. Hill, it was agreed that Jeanne should take an apartment in downtown Zurich. "My husband stayed for about three months, but had to return to Chicago to run the show," Jeanne recalls.

By the summer of 1962, the "Rosselli-Giancana-Sinatra Show" was becoming almost unbearable for the Outfit brain trust. According to the FBI's bug at Giancana's Armory Lounge, Giancana spoke with Rosselli about an assignation with still another celebrity, actress Marilyn Monroe. Over the years, numerous sources have stated that both Rosselli and Giancana had known Monroe, who like Judy Campbell had also been on Jack Kennedy's "nooky list." Also like Campbell, it appears that Monroe fell hard for the handsome president, who rarely let his emotions spoil a good romp. However, Monroe had recently been told the facts of life by numerous Kennedy aides, and very likely also by Bobby, and now fell into one of her recurrent self-destruct modes. Having no success in calming the actress, the Kennedys tried a different tack. During the last week of July, a distraught Monroe accepted an invitation from Jack Kennedy's sister Pat to join her and her husband, Peter Lawford, at Frank Sinatra's Cal-Neva

Lodge, where Monroe had previously visited when filming *The Misfits* in nearby Reno in 1960. Likely unbeknownst to the Kennedys, another occasional consort would be in attendance, whom Monroe had met through either Sinatra or Rosselli, the Lodge's true owner, Mooney Giancana.

A number of Giancana's closest associates assert that Mooney was intent on bedding Monroe, mostly as a swipe at President Kennedy, her other lover. According to Bill Roemer, who heard the Armory Lounge conversation between Giancana and Rosselli (who also knew Monroe), there was little doubt about what had transpired at Cal-Neva's Bungalow 52. As Roemer later wrote: "What I had gleaned was that Giancana had been at Cal-Neva, the Lake Tahoe resort, with Frank Sinatra and Marilyn the week before she died. There, from what I had been able to put together, she engaged in an orgy. From the conversation I overheard, it appeared she may have had sex with both Sinatra and Giancana on the same trip."

Meyer Lansky's partner and Las Vegas overseer, "Jimmy Blue Eyes" Alo, recently recalled, "I was there at the Cal-Neva in '62, when Peter and Frank were there with Monroe. They kept her drugged every night. It was disgusting." One of Frank Sinatra's photographers recently stated that a few weeks after the orgy, Sinatra showed him a proof sheet of photos Frank had taken in Monroe's chalet at the Lodge. The pictures showed a nauseated Monroe on all fours being straddled by Giancana, then kneeling over a toilet, then covered in vomit. At the photographer's insistence, Sinatra destroyed the proofs in his presence. Afterward, according to one Giancana confidant, Mooney derided both Monroe's body and her sexual inadequacy to anyone who would listen. But Mooney was satisfied just to have cuckolded the man who had double-crossed him and made him the laughingstock of the Outfit, Jack Kennedy. As the G listened in on the Armory bug, they heard Rosselli wisecrack to Giancana, "You sure get your rocks off fucking the same broad as the brothers, don't you."

Although the Lawfords struggled against the Sinatra-Giancana on-slaught at the Lodge, attempting to sober up Monroe, they had no success. A week later, the troubled Monroe was dead, a likely suicide by the lifelong manic-depressive. Worried that the death would somehow backfire on the Outfit, Humphreys and Accardo demanded more details on Monroe's controversial drug overdose. Mooney, however, hoped that the truth of Monroe's death would give him leverage over the dogged

Bobby Kennedy. According to Jeanne Humphreys, Rosselli showed up at the Humphreys' apartment a few months later, toting a thick manila envelope.

"Murray had no problem letting me read the first few pages – he rarely hid things from me," Jeanne remembers. "I only looked at three or four pages of the stash, which was about an inch thick. It started off with the medical report on Monroe's death. The way I understood it, Mooney and the other guys were very curious about her death. It was a topic of conversation." Jeanne Humphreys also heard whispers that "the boys thought maybe the Kennedys had hit her."

The practical effect of Rosselli's and Giancana's escalating high jinks was that the two fell even further out of favor with their Chicago bosses. And no matter how many times they were scolded by their superiors, the wayward playboys continued down their errant paths. In the fall of 1962, Mooney was ready to extract his pound of flesh from Frank Sinatra, the man who had sold him the bill of goods regarding the Kennedy "deal." Throughout 1962, Mooney had overseen a massive remodeling of his Villa Venice Restaurant, and according to some of his cronies, the entire undertaking was aimed at making a onetime killing, with Sinatra's Rat Pack as bait. According to Sinatra's daughter, Nancy, "The shows were Dad's way of paying back Giancana for the help he provided to the Kennedys."

Giancana's plan involved setting up a gambling operation on the grounds of the Villa, which, in order to attract Illinois' high rollers, had to first be rescued from its dilapidated state. Mooney's daughter Antoinette wrote of the result of Mooney's efforts: "[Guests] climbed into restaurant gondolas that were steered back and forth along a river by appropriately costumed gondola rowers, complete with music from the Old Country – all on the house, part of the ambiance. The seating capacity had been increased to eight hundred. The interior renovation was absolutely exquisite . . . the food was perfection and the table dinnerware was the finest that could be found in the Chicago area."[7]

But the most important addition to the compound was "The Quonset

---

7. Old-time Chicagoans are quick to point out that not many availed themselves of the gondola rides since the Des Plaines River, on which the boats traveled, was linked to an open sewer line, the effect of which removed much of the romance from the boating experience.

Hut," a gambling venue two blocks away, which could also be reached by shuttle bus for the more pampered guests. Starting on November 26, and for the better part of a month, Dean Martin, Frank Sinatra, Eddie Fisher, Sammy Davis, Jr., and Jimmy Durante appeared for free at the Villa Venice. During the sold-out run, there were lavish parties and receptions in Mooney's suite while the suckers were being ferried to the Quonset Hut to be relieved of their money at the craps, blackjack, and roulette tables.

Both the local press and the G, with its bugs, took a great interest in the proceedings at the Villa. The *Chicago Daily News* reported, "During the last twenty days . . . a heavy toll has been levied at the Hut on the Villa patrons. Individual losses of as much as $25,000 have been reported." The *Chicago Tribune* added, "The betting den began full-blast operations when Sinatra and his group opened at the Villa Venice . . . A host of gangsters were on hand for Sinatra's first night. Among them were Willie (Potatoes) Daddano, Marshall Caifano, Jimmy (the Monk) Allegretti, and Felix (Milwaukee Phil) Alderisio. Sinatra's gangland fans from other cities appeared too. The Florida contingent was led by Joe Fischetti, from Miami. A delegation of Wisconsin gangsters, including Jim DeGeorge, occupied a ringside table."

When the dust settled in December, Giancana (with the G listening) counted his profit, which exceeded $3 million. Hoping to learn more, the Bureau made discreet contact with some of the Villa's performers. With great candor, Sammy Davis, Jr. told them, "I can't talk about it. Baby, I got one eye, and that eye sees a lot of things that my brain says I shouldn't talk about. Because my brain says that if I do, my one eye might not be seeing anything after a while."

A few weeks after the monthlong party, Mooney abandoned the Villa, which curiously burned to the ground soon thereafter. Mooney Giancana would need every penny of his take from the Villa operation, as the new year would bring increasing pressures, both from the unyielding Bobby Kennedy and his own disgusted Chicago masters.

Part Six

The Party's Over

19.

The Outfit in Decline

Upheaval was the rule in 1963, with pressures both personal and professional mounting with each successive day. The intensified scrutiny even forced Joe Accardo into doing the unthinkable, selling his palatial mansion in favor of a more modest eighteen-room rancher he had built at 1407 North Ashland, also in River Forest. Although Accardo's ever-lowering public profile gave him an oasis of sorts, the others – Humphreys, Giancana, and Rosselli especially – began to whither under the strain. Most of the bosses sought refuge in constant travel, hoping to elude their government pursuers.

"It's a bad situation with the G on us," Humphreys said into the hidden mike at Celano's. "I stay around a week, and then go away for a week or so, that way they lose track of me. Then they get puzzled. I haven't been home for weeks." However, when the hoods moved about the Chicago environs, their lives were miserable. The local FBI's report on the game of cat and mouse is informative: "The hoodlums take the most elaborate precautions to prevent themselves from being placed under surveillance. These involve frequent changing of automobiles, the use of various types of public conveyances, including taxicabs, the devious and circuitous routes followed to reach a particular point and the confrontation of individuals whom they believe to be following them."

Humphreys' FBI file shows that J. Edgar Hoover himself ordered his agents to escalate their surveillance of Humphreys, who went to extraordinary lengths to elude them. In addition to keeping his loaded .38 in his jacket pocket, Humphreys gave his associates intricate codes for calling him, using a prearranged number of rings and hang-ups before answering, and a Morse code of sorts for knocking on his apartment door. At his Key Biscayne home, Humphreys had the height raised on the retaining wall that encircled his property (the G responded with helicopter flyovers).

On the streets of Chicago, Curly walked in zigzags, hoping to throw off the G. Given that one of Curly's many business triumphs was the local dry-cleaning concession, it was ironic that the G-men referred to Curly's evasive tactics as "dry cleaning." In one of their summary reports, the local feds wrote: "Humphreys located in vicinity of [King Arthur's] Pub. He dry cleaned and walked approximately fifteen blocks, entering and exiting buildings, drug stores, etc. [for twenty five minutes when] he entered restaurant." In another report, an agent described how Humphreys "left his Marine Drive residence and walked two blocks south . . . where he hailed a cab. It was again noted that during this two-block walk, Humphreys was constantly turning around and walking backwards and otherwise taking great pains to determine if he is being surveilled."

FBI agent John Bassett recently spoke of his personal travails in tailing Humphreys. Bassett remembered Curly's penchant for ducking into a large department store such as Marshall Field's, where he would immediately head for the first-floor cosmetics section, utilizing its myriad mirrors to observe his observers. The FBI also listened in as Humphreys proudly read aloud from a purloined Chicago Police Intelligence Unit report, which stated that the local cops, at least, "had no success whatsoever in surveilling him." Welsh historian Royston Webb aptly concluded, "No one knew the 'dry cleaning' business better than Hump."[1]

Even with the choke hold applied by his adversary, Humphreys was not without the occasional victory. In April 1963, Curly's never identified FBI spy came through with a document that Humphreys shared with his fellows at Celano's. As the eavesdroppers listened in shock, Curly read from a highly confidential Bureau memo that held the names on Bobby Kennedy's target list, which included not only the Celano's crowd, but their allies in Las Vegas. Humphreys discovered that the G had even ID'd the new courier the Outfit had brought in to replace the exiled Virginia Hill, Ida Devine.[2]

---

1. Located among the staff files of the Kefauver Committee is a report stating that Curly met his Intelligence Unit contact once a month at venues such as the Roosevelt Club coffee shop or the Bismarck Hotel. "The sole purpose of the meet," the committee's report stated, "is to chat and make a drop [payoff]."

2. The wife of one of Las Vegas' chief meat suppliers, Irving "Niggy" Devine, Ida brought the skim from Vegas by train to Chicago, where she was usually met at Union Station by perennial Outfit lawyers George Bieber and Mike Brodkin. After the money was cut, Devine trained on to mob strongholds such as New York, where she gave Frank Costello his share, or to Cleveland and John Scalish, or to Miami and Meyer Lansky.

Humphreys quickly forwarded a copy of the memo to Las Vegas, where the casino bosses were similarly shocked. The warning inspired the Las Vegas contingent to press their own sources, who also served up a plum. Later in the month of April, Las Vegas FBI agents listened in astonishment as Fremont Casino manager Ed Levinson read aloud from a just-written FBI summary of the skimming operation. "My God," Levinson lamented, "they even know about Ida [Devine]." The purloined memo sent the various casino executives scurrying throughout their physical plants in efforts to ferret out the illegal bugs. FBI mikes were soon ripped out of Levinson's office, the Dunes, and also the Horseshoe. Not all the mikes were found, however, but open talk of money was soon forbidden in the gambling venues.

Not content with the pace of his antimob crusade, Attorney General Robert Kennedy authorized the G to revert to its tried-and-true weapon, the IRS. Armed with the FBI's discovery of the Humphreys' luxurious Biscayne Bay home, the taxmen first sought to prove that it was impossible that the former $75-per-week dice girl Jeanne Humphreys, whose name appeared on the $55,000 mortgage, could have afforded either the home or the extensive improvements; likewise, the purchase was out of all proportion to Curly's income, as reported to the IRS.

When the IRS spoke with Curly, he informed them that Jeanne had indeed contributed $50,000 to the home. In seeking to determine if Jeanne was capable of such a purchase, the taxmen spoke with her former husband, Outfit bookie Irving Vine. Vine, who lived at a hotel owned by Humphreys aide Ralph Pierce, told the taxmen that his former wife maintained no such nest egg, and that he would agree to testify to that effect. Although Vine told the truth as he knew it, he was mistaken. During their marriage in the 1940s, Jeanne did indeed have a low income. But after they separated, Jeanne developed a high-class clientele in the better clubs. "I had one tip of fifteen hundred dollars," she says. "Another time I had a first-class vacation to Vegas paid for by one tip alone." By the midfifties, Jeanne had banked so much savings that she purchased her own home in Florida, thus to be near her brother who also lived in the Sunshine State. In Florida, Jeanne supplemented her savings by working at a dog track. Indeed, part of the money for the down payment on the Key Biscayne home came from the sale of her other Florida home. Thus, there was some truth in what Curly had told the IRS.

Some have postulated that Vine sought a possible payback on the man who he may have believed stole his wife, but Jeanne Humphreys emphatically denies it. "Our marriage broke up long before I began seeing Murray," she says. "In fact, our marriage broke up long before we separated. The last three years we only lived together out of convenience." Whatever his motivation, Vine unwisely agreed to testify against Humphreys.

According to the local press' ubiquitous unnamed "informed sources," the Outfit dispatched a number of soldiers who urged Vine to rethink his ill-considered persecution of underworld icon Curly. It is widely believed that when Vine ignored the warnings, the Outfit lashed out in a manner seen less and less frequently in recent years. After being called to Pierce's Del Prado Hotel on May 6 by a hysterical chambermaid, homicide detectives surveyed a scene that was explicitly described by writer Ovid Demaris: "Homicide detectives found Irving Vine lying on the floor, dressed only in blood-smeared shorts, his mouth and nose sealed with surgical tape, his legs also bound with tape, a shirt twisted loosely around his neck and a pillow covering his head. Three of his ribs were broken, his face was scratched and his knees bruised, but the real damage was to the lower part of his body where savage tortures had been inflicted with an ice pick during a period of several hours. Death was due to suffocation."

As first culled from Humphreys' massive FBI file by Welsh historian Royston Webb, the Bureau was told by informants that "Vine was murdered on behalf and under instructions of Humphreys, due to the fact that he was a prospective witness for the IRS . . . but also to serve the purpose of enabling Mrs. Humphreys to say that she received money . . . from Vine . . . She will now be in a position where she can throw the blame, not on Humphreys, but on Vine, now deceased." The G, however, was unable to track down the elusive Humphreys, who fled Chicago for Oklahoma and then Miami during the dustup.

"He flew to Florida the next day, worried that I had read the news of my ex-husband's murder," Jeanne recalls. "He told me, 'We didn't have anything to do with it. We don't do things like that.'" But Jeanne knew that when Outfit bosses believed they were betrayed, they *did* do things like that. She has always believed that her second husband authorized the murder of her first husband.

Returning to Chicago after the heat had died down, Humphreys maintained a furious workload, despite his own deteriorating heart condition, which periodically saw him hospitalized. In addition to his constant legal research on behalf of Accardo and Ricca, he also assisted

Ralph Pierce on a lawsuit he had filed against the police department; Buster Wortman, who was being prosecuted for intimidating a racetrack official; and Marshall Caifano, for whom Humphreys rigged a jury. On the business front, Humphreys' workload was equally daunting: He investigated gambling ventures for the Outfit in the Bahamas, Santo Domingo, and the Leeward Islands; brokered the sale of Pete Fish's restaurant; met with Kansas City boss Nick Civella; negotiated the heavyweight boxing match between Ernie Terrell and Eddie Machen; worked with Libonati in Washington and others in the state capital to defeat antimob bills; bought and sold properties and continued to seek avenues for expanding his dry cleaning empire; and spoke regularly with Hoffa, Korshak, and Rosselli to oversee the Outfit's national ventures.

Humphreys experienced some minor victories in his legislative partnership with Libonati, getting Mr. Malaprop to introduce legislation that would outlaw Bobby Kennedy's surveillance techniques. In one conversation (overheard by the G) with Pat Marcy at the First Ward headquarters, Libonati spoke of his warfare with the attorney general, bragging, "I killed six of his bills – that wiretapping, the intimidating informers bill . . ." The eavesdropping G-men summarized the balance of the conversation thus: "Libonati thinks that JFK is a sweetheart but RFK is cruel. Libonati describes how he opposed a RFK bill and got a call from Mayor Daley. Libonati told John Kennedy to stop Robert calling Mayor Daley on such matters. Bobby said on TV that his brother wants him to stay out of politics because he is the Attorney General. Libonati takes credit for this, saying, 'That was me.'"

With Humphreys working himself into an early grave, one can only imagine how he took the news that the so-called boss, Mooney Giancana, using the name J. J. Bracket, had spent two weeks in May with Frank Sinatra and Phyllis McGuire on the Hawaiian islands of Oahu (at the Surf Rider Hotel) and Maui (at the Royal Lahaina Lodge).

The constant surveillance became so bothersome that Humphreys decided to move from his Marine Drive apartment to new and hopefully more secure digs. Regretfully for Humphreys, the effort he put into the move had the opposite effect, although he never learned just how. Through their Celano's bug, Little Al, the G heard Curly speak of the move, but perhaps as a tease, he refused to disclose the new location. At the tailor shop, he told his associates that his new address would be so secret that "not even you guys are going to know."

After putting his furniture in storage with a friend, who adamantly refused to cooperate when the G came asking questions about where Curly was going to settle, the gangster decided on a shiny new twin-towered apartment complex, overlooking the Chicago River. Designed by famed architect Bertrand Goldberg, the two "corncob" towers consisted of pie-slice-shaped rooms radiating from a concrete core, with the first eighteen floors reserved for parking. The recently completed Marina Twin Towers sixty-story aerie was the tallest apartment building in the world, and much in demand with the city's high-rolling apartment dwellers. Part-time residents like Curly's upperworld alter ego Joe Kennedy were also quick to take apartments in the coveted habitat. FBI agent Bill Roemer claimed that, of all the apartments available in the Second City, he guessed that Curly was going to move into the Twin Towers and quickly moved to develop an informant, a secretary, inside the complex.

Although Roemer was allowed to see the building's register log, he failed to pick up on the name Eddie Ryan, Curly's longtime gofer, who had rented apartment 5131 in the East Tower. However, when Roemer's informant called to say that Ryan had just shown up with Humphreys, who was going to move in the next day, the G-man had to hustle. Illegally presenting their government IDs, a crew of agents gained admission to Humphreys' new dwelling later that same day, where they hid another microphone, which they nicknamed Plumb.[3]

After weeks of overseeing a meticulous painting and carpeting of the apartment, Humphreys moved in on Memorial Day, believing the FBI agents would be on holiday. Unaware of the G's bug, Curly followed form and G-proofed (he thought) the apartment. Ironically, while Humphreys secured the abode, the very adversary he was securing it against was listening in. Humphreys' very unofficial biographers in the FBI noted in Curly's file how he sought to protect himself: "[He spent] considerable time in his new apartment supervising the installation of additional locks.

---

3. Roemer writes that the name came from Humphreys' penchant for resolving problems by referring to what "Joe the Plumber," or Al Capone, would do. In their report, the agents described Curly's elegant, if not spacious, new fifty-first floor home: "Looking straight ahead, it commands an excellent view of Lake Michigan. Looking slightly to the left, it commands an excellent view of the Tribune Tower, and looking to the right, it commands a view of State Street, the most prominent street in Chicago . . . The apartment is one of the choicest at Marina City . . . it is furnished extravagantly with several expensive-looking paintings hanging on the walls, with a player piano, apparently new, and with very expensive-looking furniture."

He mentioned that although the G has expert lock-pickers, they will be unable to gain access to his apartment due to the expensive locks and bars he has installed on his doors and windows . . . Humphreys kicked a paper hanger out of his apartment because he was not convinced that the paper hanger was what he claimed to be."

The Bureau further stated that Curly and his aide Ralph Pierce were attempting to "locate someone who can manufacture equipment which will scramble or garble their conversations so that their conversations cannot be monitored by someone outside the room." And despite living on the fifty-first floor, Humphreys had bars and railings installed on his balcony, the perfect metaphor for the caged existence his was now forced to live when in Chicago. The FBI soon learned more about Curly's security precautions, as noted in his file: "The apartment now has a burglar alarm, three inside and outside locks, a tear gas device, bars and double-thickness glass on balcony window, pistol and shotgun." Curly also gave his maid a tear-gas gun that dispensed a dye that stained the offender for days. He also looked into the possibility of obtaining a "Tear Gas Watchdog," which would automatically fire on any intruder.

With Curly now thoroughly compromised by Plumb, the FBI refocused on Mooney Giancana, whom it rightfully believed could be pushed over the edge, thereby exacerbating internal gang strife. On June 8, 1963, the FBI watched as Mooney and Phyllis joined Sinatra at his parents' home in Hoboken, New Jersey. When he returned to Chicago, Mooney was met with a civil-liberties assault unparalleled in U.S. criminal history. In their effort to drive Giancana to self-destruction, the Chicago G-men, without the approval of their SAC (special agent in charge), Marlin Johnson, decided to complement their covert surveillance with blatant, round-the-clock, blanket coverage. The ploy had been used to a lesser degree thirty-three years earlier with Al Capone, when two uniformed cops tried unsuccessfully to unnerve Capone by following him everywhere after he left his voluntary incarceration in Philadelphia. Now, in 1963, the G called the technique lockstep, and the agents were certain that the attendant publicity would further ostracize the don from his associates.

For the next few weeks, the agents waited for Mooney to emerge from his Wenonah Park home in the morning, then followed him on all his sundry errands until he returned at night. When Mooney got out of his car, a team of agents likewise alighted from theirs, encircled the gangster at a radius of a few feet, and went everywhere he went: to the movies, restaurants, stores, golf courses, a walk, and even to church. Once again, the suburb was treated to the sight of the master wheelman coursing through its streets, his harassers in hot pursuit. When Giancana raced through his regular commercial car-wash tunnel, the employees cheered, "Go, Mo, go!" as he sped out the other end, spraying soap in all directions. On the golf course, the mediocre player Giancana and his playing partners were rushed by the FBI foursome behind them, with the agents often encircling the green and taunting Mooney as he putted. This was no small nuisance since Giancana took his game so seriously that he had had a putting surface landscaped into his backyard. Roemer described another aspect of the lockstep: "If he went to dinner, we went with him . . . [If] he got up from the table to go to the men's room, I'd get up and be at the next urinal. I found that really bugged him. He had shy kidneys. He couldn't do it when I was right there."

The tactic soon began achieving its desired effect, as Mooney started snarling at his unwanted companions, "Get away from me, you cock-suckers!" In his first serious effort to terminate the coverage, Giancana set a trap for the G-men by luring them to his lair, the Armory Lounge. Agents Roemer and Rutland followed Mooney into his headquarters and quickly realized that all of Mooney's most notorious musclemen were present. While some of the most dangerous men in America gave the G-men the Look, the agents wondered if perhaps they had gone too far and were now about to be ambushed. Surprisingly, the agents were allowed to leave the lounge unmolested. Minutes later, while the agents waited in their car for the Giancana party to exit, one of the gangster's aides, Chuckie English, came out of the restaurant and ran menacingly up to Roemer's car.

"Sam says to tell you that if Kennedy wants to sit down with him," English said, "he knows who to go through." He was of course referring to the same man Papa Joe Kennedy had gone through to get to Mooney for the election fix.

"Sinatra?" Roemer asked

"You said it," said English.

Mooney's flare-up with the G was immediately brought to the attention of Humphreys and Accardo. In a few days, the overweening agents listened to a conversation in Humphreys' apartment that proved their strategy was bearing fruit. The Bureau's transcript quoted one of Mooney's underbosses, Frank Ferraro, venting to Curly:

Frank: "So help me God, I'm about to jump out your fucking widow."

Curly: "What's wrong?"

Frank: "That fucking Giancana, wait until you hear what he's done now. He's not making good decisions."

Curly: "What happened?"

Frank: "Saturday night, Roemer and Rutland, they're on Giancana. He takes them to the Armory. They get in a fucking shouting match. Whole bunch of our guys and Roemer and Rutland. When it's all over, Giancana sends Charley McCarthy [English] out to see Roemer. What do you think he told Roemer?"

Curly: "What?"

Frank: "Charley McCarthy told Roemer that Mo told him to tell Kennedy to talk to him through Sinatra."

Curly: "For Christ sakes, that's a cardinal rule! You don't give up a legit guy! He tells Roemer that Sinatra is our guy to Kennedy?"

Frank: "More or less. I'm so fucking mad, I could jump out your window. We got to do something about this. The G is driving this man goofy. He's not right. He's making mistakes. He don't belong in that spot he can't take the pressure."

Curly: "I think this has to be brought to the attention of Joe [Accardo] and Paul [Ricca]. They've got to know the condition of this man's mind."

Within a few weeks, the Outfit conceded one battle to the G. On June 23, the gang abandoned Celano's forever. As a parting shot, Curly Humphreys, in full stage voice, announced for the last time, "Welcome to the eleven A.M. meeting of the Chicago crime syndicate. We hope everybody is tuned in."

That same month, Mooney Giancana virtually guaranteed the Outfit's presence on the front pages when he did the unthinkable: He decided to sue the FBI over their lockstep harassment. Outfit bosses were said to actually be secretly rooting for the FBI, since a government victory might result in a college stay for their starstruck boss, who had been in gross neglect of his responsibilities. But Mooney placed an ace up his sleeve when he enlisted famed civil-rights attorney George N. Leighton of Harvard Law School to come to his aid. Giancana turned on the charm, having Leighton over to his home, where the lawyer saw nothing but a loving extended family coming and going. Interviewed recently, Leighton said, "I found Giancana to be one of the finest persons I have ever known." Once aboard, Leighton devised a brilliant strategy, hiring a local production crew to film the G in action. Under the direction of private eye Don Ricker, the film crew accompanied Mooney on trips to the cemetery, church, golf course, and even the Armory Lounge. The FBI fully cooperated, not at all intimidated by the filmmakers. Occasionally, Mooney treated Ricker to the game of chase he played with the G, racing through the suburban streets, seemingly without disturbing the brake pedal. "I got my start this way," Mooney boasted to his white-knuckled passengers.

Much to his bosses' horror, Giancana's suit became a front-page staple and a lead television news story. When his suit was heard in court, a parade of Mooney's friends and relatives attested to the harassment. At one point, the courtroom lights were dimmed as Don Ricker projected the incriminating film. Comic relief was supplied on occasion, such as when attorney Leighton implored the judge regarding the filmed lockstepping on the golf course.

"Maybe you'll appreciate the position of a golfer," Leighton said, "who is about to take his eighteenth putt and looks up to see six FBI agents watching him."

"The most I ever had was four putts," Judge Richard B. Austin responded.

What happened next surely caused Humphreys, Ricca, and Accardo to turn pale: Giancana took the stand in his own defense, leaving himself open to cross-examination, and a possible rehash of the entire history of Chicago crime and all the Outfit leaders who controlled it. It was a rare opportunity for the prosecuting U.S. attorney's office, which made it all the more shocking, and infuriating, to the G-men when their lead attorney said to Judge Austin, "We have no questions, Your Honor."

It was later revealed that Robert Kennedy had personally instructed U.S. Attorney John Lalinsky to refrain from cross-examining the mob boss, ostensibly because the Justice Department did not wish to legitimize the judicial branch's authority over the executive. However, many have postulated that perhaps Robert Kennedy did not wish to risk giving Giancana a forum from which to hang out the Kennedy family's own dirty laundry: the Castro murder plots, the affairs with Campbell and Monroe, and the election fix. This possibility was buttressed many years later when Will Wilson, the assistant attorney general, Criminal Division, in the Nixon administration testified before Congress about a statement made to him by J. Edgar Hoover. Wilson told the committee that in 1971 Hoover recounted for Wilson how, during the Kennedy administration, the Bureau was about to arrest Giancana for racketeering when Bobby Kennedy burst into Hoover's office and prevented Hoover from going forward, saying, "He knows too much."

The degree to which the Bureau had been placed on the defensive was made abundantly clear when SAC Marlin Johnson took the witness stand, under subpoena from Leighton. While his subordinates languished in the audience, Johnson stole a page from Curly Humphreys' bible.

"Does William Roemer work for you?" Leighton asked.

"I respectfully decline to answer the question on instructions from the U.S. attorney general, order number 260–62," Johnson answered.

For a brief moment, it was as though the court had entered a parallel universe, where Bobby Kennedy's men were forced to plead their version of the Fifth Amendment for Giancana's probers. Johnson repeated the plea thirteen times, and the Bureau offered no defense, insistent that the court lacked jurisdiction. Judge Austin quickly ruled in favor of Mooney, who broke out a huge cigar in Austin's chambers, blowing smoke in Johnson's face as they signed the required paperwork. Per the ruling, the G was instructed to keep a reasonable distance when following their prey – and Marlin Johnson was fined $500 for contempt.

Although Mooney gloated over what was one of his few victories inside a court, his grin was quickly erased by a cold dose of reality. In a mere few weeks, the appellate court reversed the decision (and the contempt fine), and Cook County sheriff (and future governor of Illinois) Richard Ogilvie added his men to the FBI's lockstep carnival. Now, Mooney's home became a local attraction, as hundreds of curious mob-watchers showed up daily to watch Mooney curse at his tormentors. The circuslike goings-on did not go over well with the Humphreys-Accardo-Ricca triumvirate.

Giancana's biographer William Brashler neatly summarized the reaction in the Outfit's inner sanctum, writing, "Through it all the Outfit seethed . . . Accardo and Ricca were severely critical . . . Meetings were held without him [Giancana] in which strong underbosses railed about Giancana's lack of cool. Names like Sam Battaglia, Jack Cerone, even Giancana's own enforcer Willie Daddano were brought up as possible replacements."

The Clubhouse Closes

After spending all of six weeks in Chicago, Giancana headed West once again to continue his rolling party with Sinatra and McGuire, wasting no time in making front-page news in Nevada. According to his FBI file,

Mooney, with Phyllis in tow, guested at Sinatra's Palm Beach home, then went on to Las Vegas, where the mob boss cavorted with Eddie Fisher and Dean Martin, both of whom "made a big fuss over Giancana." From there, Mooney traveled to the Cal-Neva, where Phyllis and her sisters were scheduled to sing the week of July 27. According to McGuire's manager, Victor LaCroix Collins, the trio became involved in a drunken celebration at McGuire's Chalet 50. Collins got into a disagreement with McGuire, whom he attempted to force back to her chair. When she missed the chair and hit the floor, Mooney raced across the room and punched Collins above the eyebrow, cutting him with one of his osten-tatious diamond rings. The argument then escalated to an all-out brawl.

Hearing the ruckus, Frank Sinatra burst in and, in one telling, held Collins while Mooney punched him or, according to another, separated the two. Collins has said that Sinatra then warned Collins that the hoods would put a contract out on Collins for the affront to their boss.

"The only way they'll get me is from long distance with a high-powered rifle," Collins answered, "because none of them has the guts to hit me face-to-face. I'm not afraid of nothing, wop."

With that, the singer bellowed that because of the fight, he would now lose the Cal-Neva and his money.

"What do you mean, your money?" Collins shot back. "You don't have a dime in the place. It's all Mafia money and you know it."

As Sinatra predicted, the coverage of Mooney's presence at the Lodge, a violation of his Black Book listing, would indeed cause Sinatra to forfeit the Lodge, his 9 percent interest in the Sands, and his Nevada gambling license. The Gaming Board's decision was guaranteed after Sinatra launched into a tirade against a board investigator who called to hear Sinatra's version.

"Fuck you," Sinatra yelled. "I don't have to take this shit. Do you know who I am? I'm Frank Sinatra. *Frank Sinatra!*"

When the board immediately ordered Sinatra to divest himself of his Nevada interests, Mooney realized he would now never recoup his Cal-Neva investment. D.C. detective and Giancana confidant Joe Shimon remembered running into Mooney soon after the board's decision. "He told me that Frank cost him over $465,000 on Cal-Neva," Shimon told Sinatra biographer Kitty Kelley. "He said, 'That bastard and his big mouth. All he had to do was keep quiet, let the attorneys handle it . . . but no, Frank has to get him on the phone with that damn big mouth of his and now we're going to lose the whole damn place.'"

Then governor of Nevada Grant Sawyer recalled how President Kennedy was making a stop in Las Vegas to speak at the Convention Center during the Cal-Neva flare-up. In the limousine from McCarran Airport, Kennedy asked Sawyer, "What are you doing to my friend Frank Sinatra?"

"Well, Mr. President," Sawyer answered, "I'll take care of things here in Nevada and I wish you luck on the national level."

As early as 1961, the FBI had heard Sam express concern about his Cal-Neva investment. Speaking with Johnny Rosselli at the Armory Lounge, Mooney had said, "I'm gonna get my money out of there [Cal-Neva] . . . [or] I'm gonna wind up with half of the joint and no money." Now, according to a source close to Mooney Giancana, the hot-blooded boss did not take the loss of his getaway retreat lying down. According to the source, who wishes to remain anonymous, the idea of killing Sinatra was again revived, this time by Mooney himself. "From what I was told," the source says, "Mooney was furious that Sinatra refused to give back his investment, so he put out a contract. Frank begged the New York boys to intercede for him again, and Mooney called it off." Shortly after the Lodge's closing on Labor Day,[4] Giancana was at the Armory Lounge with aides Charles Nicolletti, James "Cowboy" Mirro, and the source when who should arrive, drunk to the gills, but Frank Sinatra and Dean Martin.

"What the hell is he doing here?" Mooney snarled. "That motherfuck-er is lucky to be alive – and he comes here?" In short time, the inebriated duo were escorted to their waiting limousine and whisked to O'Hare Airport, where a commercial plane had been kept waiting.

While Mooney continued to self-destruct, so too did Curly's marital bliss. With Jeanne having spent much of the last year on her own in Switzerland and Key Biscayne, Curly once again began skirt-chasing. According to government informants, Curly was becoming a frequent habitué of a "twist" club called The Scene, and the Playboy Club, where he began dating club "bunnies." His FBI file notes that "he was observed . . . on three occasions early this year in company of young women apparently not his wife." Humphreys' dalliances may have been warranted, given the treatment he was receiving from his young wife on her infrequent visits.

The Bureau's illegal Plumb mike planted in Curly's new apartment now

---

4. The Cal-Neva was reopened in January 1964 under new ownership.

became more a fount for FBI voyeurism and less for insight into Outfit business, its ostensible raison d'être. "[Jeanne] appears extremely unhappy in her new apartment at Marina City because of its lack of room and its location," noted one Bureau report. "I was used to large homes, with animals," Jeanne says. "There was no way I was going to be happy in an apartment, no matter what the address was." Another file notes how Jeanne demolished one of the expensive balcony windows: "She had pounded the window twenty times before she even got it to crack . . . Humphreys advised his wife that she was a maniac." From another report: "Source advised that over the weekend, Humphreys' wife became extremely intoxicated and apparently attempted to throw Humphreys off their fifty-first storey balcony."

"I don't remember trying to throw Murray off," Jeanne now says, "but there was one time when I was trying to bash him with a frying pan and he locked himself in the bedroom. I climbed out on the balcony in my nightgown and tried to break the bedroom window to get to him."

On August 28, 1963, the Humphreys' *amour fou* marriage was dissolved in Chicago divorce court. Curly agreed to pay Jeanne a staggering $18,000 per month alimony, on top of the $6,000 he was sending to Clemi in Oklahoma. However, Curly maintained a cordial relationship with Jeanne, much as he had with Clemi. His FBI file illustrates many instances in which he continued to visit Jeanne in Florida, and to tend to her legal problems, including "fixing" a case for her.

On the occasions where the pair attempted to rekindle their marriage, the Peeping Tom agents memorialized the goings-on for J. Edgar Hoover. A report filed six months after the divorce noted that on one recent visit "Humphreys cabareted her until the early morning and then brought her to his apartment where he became enamored of his former wife."

"I was impossible to live with, there's no denying it," Jeanne Humphreys says about the breakup today. "I found out years later, when I began having seizures, that I had been been in the early stages of a form of epilepsy that made me uncontrollable. After I was finally diagnosed, I was put on medication that stopped the outbursts, but as a side effect I acquired diabetes." Jeanne adds that her husband shared some of the blame for the failure of their marriage. "Murray was extremely jealous," she says. "When we were in Italy for Lucky's [Luciano] funeral, he wanted to kill an Italian that he thought was flirting with me."

Bobby's Reign Cut Short

It was just after 10:30 A.M., Pacific time, on November 22, 1963, when Johnny Rosselli was awakened at the Desert Inn by a call from Hollywood. The caller was an old friend, a producer at Columbia Studios named Jonie Tapps. When told that Jack Kennedy had been shot, Rosselli thought he was dreaming. "I didn't believe it at first," Rosselli later testified, "because I was in a deep sleep." Rosselli soon accepted the news after Tapps persuaded him to turn on his radio.

"I got shocked," Rosselli told Congress thirteen years later, careful to censor his language. "I said, 'Gosh Almighty, those damned Communists' . . . You know, that was the first thing that came to my mind because a few months before that, Castro had made a speech, and I read it in the newspapers, and it sounded just like him, that he was threatening the establishment here."[5]

Johnny had expounded on his theory three weeks after the assassination with fellow hood Jimmy Fratianno. During their chat, Fratianno lamented that the press was openly speculating that organized crime was responsible for the hit. "You know, Johnny," Fratianno said, "the more of this bullshit I read, the more I'm convinced that we've become fucking scapegoats for every unsolved crime committed in this country. What's this mob the papers are always talking about, for Christ's sake? It's against the fucking rules to kill a cop, so now we're going to kill a president."

"No question in my mind," answered Rosselli. "I think [Castro] hit Kennedy because of the Bay of Pigs operation . . . But it's got nothing to do with us." Of course, Johnny Rosselli, unlike virtually everyone else monitoring the tragedy that day, also had firsthand knowledge of the secret White House assassination plots that could have motivated "those damned Communists." Rosselli's opinions were shared by many in the American intelligence establishment, especially those who had worked with the Outfit on the Castro assassination plots, which were hidden from

---

5. On September 6, 1963, in a public speech in Havana, Castro indeed said: "We are taking into account . . . the Caribbean situation, which has been deteriorating in the last few days due to piratical attacks by the United States against the Cuban people . . . Kennedy is a cretin . . . the Batista of our times . . . If U.S. leaders are aiding terrorist plans to eliminate Cuban leaders, they themselves will not be safe. Let Kennedy and his brother Robert take care of themselves since they too can be the victims of an attempt which will cause their deaths."

the official investigators into Kennedy's murder – the repercussions were just too awful to contemplate.

Throughout the country, the FBI huddled around their illegal surveillance apparatuses, trying to learn if organized crime had finally gotten even with the hated Robert Kennedy. What they consistently heard convinced them that the country's underworld would never even contemplate such an action. In Buffalo, local boss Stefanno Magaddino lamented, "It's a shame we've been embarrassed before the whole world by allowing the president to be killed in our own territory." He added that Kennedy was one of the nation's greatest presidents and, as noted by the eavesdroppers, "blames the assassination on his brother, Robert Kennedy." In Miami, a bug in the home of Charles Costello heard that boss voice a different lament: "It's too bad his brother Bobby was not in that car too." In northern Pennsylvania, the G heard Russell Buffalino agree, saying, "They killed the good one [Jack]. They should have killed the other little guy [Bobby]."

In Key Biscayne, Jeanne Humphreys had just been coming home from a boating party when the phone rang. It was Curly in Chicago.

"Did you hear what happened?" Curly asked. After Jeanne responded that she had, Curly said, "That's no concern of ours." Then after a pause, "We're not connected with it, but they got the wrong one."

In Chicago, Mooney had spent the morning with aide Chuckie English and singer Keely Smith. The FBI heard the don say, "Attorney General Robert Kennedy will not have the power he previously did." That weekend, the Giancana family was glued to their television set like most of the world. While watching the assassination coverage, Mooney's daughter Antoinette remembered what her father had said after the 1960 double cross: "Someday Jack will get his, but I will have nothing to do with it." When the eventual actually happened, Antoinette recalls her father being saddened, but saying little. Three days later, after the pro-Castro Lee Oswald was charged in the murder, Mooney was again with English and the two engaged in a bit of twisted wordplay worthy of *The Sopranos:*

English: "This twenty-four-year-old kid was an anarchist. He was a Marxist Communist."

Giancana: "He was a marksman who knew how to shoot."

Hearing the Outfit discuss Kennedy's killing, Agent Roemer concluded the same as his fellows around the country, later writing his summation of the atmosphere in the Outfit's inner sanctums: "The mobsters discussed the Kennedys constantly . . . But never in any way did they indicate they were interested in assassination . . . After the assassination, they talked about it frequently. They weren't at all unhappy about it, but they gave absolutely no indication that they knew about it in advance or that they had anything at all to do with it."

After Jack Kennedy's murder, his brother Bobby retreated not only from his work at Justice, but from life itself. Convinced that the vendettas against the people on his 'list' (either Castro or the mob) had backfired on his brother, Bobby fell into a deep depression. His withdrawal, and the subsequent appointment of a do-nothing attorney general by the new president, Lyndon Johnson, briefly encouraged the underworld, but J. Edgar Hoover, with congressional legislative support, let it be known that the pursuit of the nation's underworld would continue.

In the spring of 1965, a federal grand jury investigating organized crime in Chicago deposed Mooney Giancana. The FBI listened as Curly Humphreys counseled Mooney and the other hoods about pleading the Fifth. With the belief widespread that the illegal bugs would sink the government's case, few in Chicago feared this umpteenth grand jury probe. However, no one suspected that the G would grant Giancana immunity, thus forcing him into a no-win situation: If he still refused to talk, he would be cited for contempt; but if he talked honestly about organized crime in the Windy City, the Outfit would hit him faster than he could say stool pigeon.

Mooney's first instinct was to put the word out on the streets that he would pay $100,000 to the man who could extricate him from his dreadful situation. When help was not forthcoming, Giancana believed it was time to tell his lawyer, D.C. power attorney Edward Bennett Williams, about the many governmental secrets (and those of the Kennedy family) to which he had been privy. Williams shrewdly contacted Bobby Kennedy's close friend and chief of Organized Crime at Justice, William Hundley, to give him the bad news. The Justice Department, still populated by many of Bobby Kennedy's disciples, agreed to cut a deal, promising to ask Mooney only a handful of benign questions about petty crime. It looked as if Mooney had obtained a sweetheart deal, but as it turned out, the don had second thoughts once on the witness stand. Leaving the courtroom to meet his attorneys (lawyers are barred from the grand jury), Mooney gave them the bad news.

"I couldn't make myself answer the questions," Mooney told his stunned attorneys. It became clear to his team that the code of *omerta* (silence) was all-encompassing, preventing Mooney from even admitting that he had ever even bootlegged a bottle of beer.

Mooney chose to keep quiet and accept imprisonment. It is unclear whether the government or the Outfit was happier to have Mooney out of commission. When Giancana was released a year later, the Justice Department prevented the state's attorneys from going after him again. When the original judge in the case, William E. Campbell, later learned of the CIA plots with Giancana, he became convinced that the spy agency had prevailed with Justice to let sleeping dogs lie.

If the loss of the gang's front man induced no grief among the bosses, such was not the case when one of the Outfit's guiding lights breathed his last later that year. The loss of Curly Humphreys, combined with the semiretirement of Accardo and Ricca (and the death years earlier of Jake Guzik), dictated that Al Capone's heirs turn their focus away from the grandiose expansions for which they were famous, in favor of merely struggling to maintain the status quo.

20.

Endgames

As Mooney Giancana settled into his new digs at the Cook County jail, the Outfit breathed a sigh of relief. And it was more than Mooney's removal that caused the bosses to relax. With the guilt-ridden Bobby Kennedy traumatized to the point of catatonia, and the new president more concerned with healing the nation's wounds and trying to wrap his backroom-specialized brain around the knotty problem of Jack Kennedy's Southeast Asian undertakings, Bobby Kennedy's "list" became less of a priority.

On July 11, 1965, under increasing pressure from court decisions that upheld the Fourth Amendment's right-to-privacy provision, President Johnson ordered the FBI to remove its illegal bugs from the underworld lairs.

In Chicago, as elsewhere, the removal order placed the G-men in great peril, as they once again had to surreptitiously enter the mob hangouts and pull out the sources of their hard-won intelligence. "It was a heinous slaughter," wrote Bill Roemer, "devastating to our coverage of the mob." While the G risked life and limb, they seethed as they learned of former attorney general Robert Kennedy's disavowal of his knowledge of the illegal microphones. But they saved their public vitriol for President Johnson. Roemer wrote: "I can only surmise that [Johnson] was afraid that sooner or later the bug[s] would reveal something of his activities . . . [regarding] the days when he was amassing his wealth as a senator from Texas . . . It was enough to raise suspicions that he had some things to hide somewhere along the line. There were those who even thought he might have been on the take, that the mob had gotten to him."

As if to rub salt into the wounds of the agents, President Johnson's vaunted 1965 Commission on Law Enforcement produced little of value, even relegating a sixty-three-page report on Chicago corruption by Notre

Dame professor G. Robert Blakey to four footnotes. It is conceivable that Blakey's report was so treated due to the Pandora's box it threatened to open, for the professor's censored thesis stated frankly: "The success of the Chicago group [mob] has been primarily attributable to its ability to corrupt the law enforcement processes, including police officials and members of the judiciary . . ." Two years later, the deputy director of President Johnson's Crime Commission, Henry S. Ruth, cut off Henry Peterson, the head of the Justice Department's Organized Crime Division, in midsentence when he launched into his findings regarding corruption in the Teamsters. "We're going to move on to another subject," Ruth said.

The relief felt by the Outfit was to be short-lived, however, as the stresses of a life in organized crime were about to catch up with its irreplaceable mastermind, Llewelyn Morris "Curly" Humphreys.

The last year and a half had been a whirlwind for the ailing sixty-five-year-old gangster. Although twice divorced, Curly continued to see both ex-wives frequently. In 1964, Humphreys took his first wife, Clemi, and daughter, Luella, on a two-month tour of Europe, with stopovers in Switzerland, France, Greece, and England. In what may have been Curly's way of bringing his life full circle, the last stop on the itinerary was his father's homeland, Wales, Curly's first-ever visit. Daughter Luella described her father's reaction: "He went around and visited with cousins over there and he truly enjoyed himself. He stayed and settled the estate and sold the land because he knew he was on borrowed time . . . and he made sure everyone got a deed to property . . . He was just thrilled he made it home."

In January 1965, Humphreys took one of his many return trips to Oklahoma, this time to bail his daughter out of her financial woes, largely the result of a recent divorce. After returning home to Chicago, Humphreys was seen by the FBI dating numerous women, including his second ex-wife, Jeanne. On her thirty-seventh birthday, Jeanne received a $37,000 gift from Humphreys in a futile gesture aimed at winning her back.

Even as he attempted to keep a low profile, only Humphreys could finish the mob's work that he had initiated. Humphreys continued to lobby the state capital on behalf of antigambling legislation and against wiretapping proposals. Before pulling its bugs, the Bureau heard Curly's glee when the wiretapping bill was defeated. "The fight is not over," Curly instructed his associates, "and that fight versus other anticrime bills, especially the immunity bill, must continue." When he failed to defeat one set of antimob legislative proposals, Curly was heard to complain, "I had thirty-five labor organizations attacking these bills, but they couldn't do a thing."

The final act in Curly Humphreys' dramatic life commenced when he appeared before a grand jury on May 19, 1965, and refused to answer questions. So confident was he that he also declined to invoke the Fifth Amendment, saying instead that he refused to answer because he had no idea what the prosecutors were talking about. But in doing so, Curly was too clever for his own good, committing a rare legal miscalculation. When he failed to reappear for a another round of questioning on June 25, a warrant was issued for his arrest.

Humphreys was located the next day in Oklahoma, where he was placed in lockup for the weekend. His bank-robber cellmate wrote his son about the legendary gangster: "We played quite a few hands of Chicago style gin rummy . . . He is a very interesting character, friendly, soft-spoken, considerate, smart, and above all loaded with long green. He wound up a good friend of mine."

On his return to Chicago, Humphreys posted bail and worried to his brother Ernest that the gross miscalculation might ruin his reputation. The FBI noted that the brother assured him differently, comparing "the lifelong success of his brother in organized crime to the perennial domination of baseball by the New York Yankees."

After a few months of fruitless testimony by Curly's peers, it was decided out of desperation to charge him with contempt and perjury (Humphreys had testified that he was unaware of the scheduled June 25 court appearance). Agent Roemer was charged with serving the arrest warrant on Curly, but he refused. "I did not want to execute it," Roemer wrote. "I was fond of the guy and did not want to be the one who snapped the handcuffs on him." At one-thirty in the afternoon, Thanksgiving Day, 1965, three FBI agents went to Curly's apartment and knocked for several minutes. Finally, a distraught Humphreys opened the door, his trusty .38 pointed straight at the agents. After disarming the sixty-five-year-old hood, the agents began to search the premises, albeit with no search warrant.

At that point, the agents became interested in Humphreys' safe and asked him for the key. When Curly refused, the agents attempted to pry his hand from his pocket. Curly became hysterical and fell onto his bed tussling with FBI agent Danny Shanahan. After tearing Curly's pocket, the key was retrieved, giving the G access to Curly's safe. Once opened, the safe revealed $25,000 in cash and a letter that related to the Willie Bioff Hollywood scandal. After the money was counted twice in Curly's presence, the gangster was taken downtown, where his pal Morrie Norman posted his $45,000 bail about 6 P.M. While signing his release papers, a disgusted Humphreys sniped at reporters, "Here we go again." However, when an attractive TV reporter named Jorie Luloff asked Curly if he had a comment, the aging lothario quipped, "None, except, my, you are a pretty girl."

Returning to his apartment, the fastidious Humphreys set about cleaning up the residue of his struggle with the G. While pushing his vacuum cleaner, his heart also sucked in detritus, a blood clot. Curly fell dead, his head hitting a table in the fall. At eight-fifty, Curly's brother Ernest discovered the body.

The phone rang at Bill Roemer's home that night. It was *Chicago Tribune* reporter and FBI confidant Sandy Smith, calling with the news of Curly's death.

"I felt like I had taken a punch in the stomach," Roemer later wrote. "Honestly, it was as if a part of me died that night. No more Hump? What would my life be like? He was a major reason I enjoyed what I was doing." Roemer also felt responsible for having helped piece together the "two-bit" perjury case, without which "Hump would still be alive."

An autopsy was performed out of fear that Humphreys may have been poisoned by an enemy. However, it was determined that he died of a blood clot in the heart. His Oklahoma family flew in for the private funeral at the Donnellan Funeral Home. Only ten mourners, names unknown, attended the wake. After the ceremony, Curly's remains were cremated, although he had wished for his body to be donated for medical research.

After the funeral, the Oklahoma contingent repaired to Morrie Norman's restaurant, where they were met by a grieving Bill Roemer. "I told them all how much I respected their husband, father, and grandfather, and that I deeply regretted what had happened," the agent later wrote. Turning to Curly's grandson, George, Roemer said, "He was a fine man." Summing up his feelings for Humphreys, Roemer wrote in his autobiography, "There was a *style* about the way he conducted himself. His word was his bond. I surely was to miss him. My work would lose some of its glitter."

Humphreys' ashes were taken to Oklahoma, interred under a huge stone on his property that said only "Humphreys."

The news coverage befitted Curly's stature. HIS EPITAPH – NO GANG-STER WAS MORE BOLD announced Sandy Smith's headline in the *Chicago Tribune*. "Humphreys died of unnatural causes – a heart attack," quipped Mike Royko, who also noted that "Humphreys turned Sam Giancana from an unknown semiliterate into a well-known semiliterate." On a more serious note, Royko stated, "[Humphreys] devised legal strategies and political fixes that have yet to be equaled. He engendered appreciation for his immense intellect, his finesse, and again within the perspective of his vocation, his civility." The *Daily News* opined, "His brains spoke louder than his muscle . . . At the time of his death, Humphreys was still the crime syndicate's master fixer, the man who could 'reach out for' a judge, a policeman, or even a congressman."

Among the personal effects seized at Curly's apartment by the FBI was a seventeen-page sheaf of notes containing the notation "No. 46-400 at 20." Since Humphreys owned pieces of Las Vegas casinos, in addition to every other Outfit gambling enterprise, investigators hoped the cryptic code would lead them to a stash of millions in a Swiss bank account, but Swiss law prevented the banks from responding to inquiries about Curly's alleged nest egg. However, almost immediately after her father's passing, Luella Humphreys Brady began what would be a yearly trip to Zurich, Switzerland, where she would raid the Swiss bank account of her deceased father, the fruits of his four-decade career with the Outfit. In 1984, Huw Davies, the comptroller of a prestigious Welsh public television station, encountered Luella in transit on one of her yearly forays to Zurich. In his Cardiff office, Davies was shown one stash of over a million dollars, which Luella was transporting back to Oklahoma.

In Key Biscayne, Jeanne sold the house, bequeathed to her in Curly's will, for $205,000.

The corpses continued to pile up: Not long after Humphreys' death, Joe Bulger, the Unione Siciliana consigliere, and the Outfit's mysterious "secret boss," died when the small plane he was piloting to Miami crashed; on March 24, 1966, forty-nine-year-old Virginia Hill finally succeeded in poisoning herself to death in Kopple, Austria. Jeanne Humphreys believes Hill was despondent because March was "payday," and it had been Curly alone who made certain her yearly "pension" was delivered. As noted, Hill was just one of many who had benefited from Humphreys' generosity. In Florida, Mae and Sonny Capone had used Outfit disbursements to finance a Miami Beach restaurant, The Grotto. Shortly after Curly's arrest, they lost the business and Sonny was charged with shoplifing $3 worth of sundries from a supermarket, his only run-in with the law.

In California, Johnny Rosselli was also experiencing the passing of the torch of organized crime. On May 11, 1966, Los Angeles FBI agents informed Rosselli that they knew his real name was Filippo Sacco, and that he was an unregistered alien. Although Rosselli did not know it at the time, the Bureau had obtained the intelligence from a man who had functioned as Rosselli's courier, delivering yearly $10,000 gifts to Rosselli's mother in Boston. "We got nothing against you, John," said one of the agents. "It's a matter of national security."

"Talk to my lawyer," was Rosselli's response to the agent who brandished nothing more than a pesky misdemeanor violation, albeit with a hint that he was after bigger fish. The next day, Johnny flew to Washington to meet with his CIA contacts, Shef Edwards, still with the Agency, and Bill Harvey, by then an attorney in private practice. Rosselli assured his partners in the assassination plots that he was not going to jeopardize national security by singing to the FBI. However, upon his return to the West Coast, Rosselli was told by the FBI that what they actually wanted was the goods on the Outfit's skimming operation in Las Vegas. Rosselli politely refused. (After one year, however, the INS case had refused to go away, and the CIA had as yet not come to Johnny's rescue. Rosselli began leaking part of the assassination story to syndicated columnist Jack Anderson, with the proviso that Anderson not use any gangsters' names. Anderson's column thus became the first public disclosure of the CIA-Mafia plots sanctioned by the Kennedys. Frightened that Rosselli would soon give up more, the CIA, according to its own records, finally intervened with the INS, and the immigration threat was dropped.)

Although the Outfit's Mr. Smooth was supremely confidant that he could deal with the immigration bother, he was unaware that one of his side ventures was set to blow up in his face. Since the early sixties, Rosselli had taken a cut from a card-cheating scheme run at the Beverly Hills Friars Club. The cheating had been devised by Maury Friedman, a businessman for whom Rosselli had brokered a complex partnership in the purchase of Las Vegas' Frontier Hotel. With illegal high-stakes gin games holding sway on the third floor of the Friars, Friedman had holes drilled in the roof, from where lookouts would tip their playing partners via a radio hookup. In this manner, regular patrons such as entertainers

Zeppo Marx, Tony Martin, Phil Silvers, and others were relieved of
approximately $40,000 nightly. As a matter of courtesy, Rosselli was sent
a percentage of the take. After years of successful celebrity fleecing, the
scam was about to become unraveled.

Back in Chicago on Memorial Day, 1966, Mooney left prison and was
immediately summoned by the two remaining bosses, Joe Accardo and
Paul Ricca, who had not forgiven him for both bringing the suicidal
Kennedy fix to them and for his front-page-grabbing style. Informants
told the FBI that the meeting between the bosses was a hot-tempered
screaming match, with Mooney on the losing side. Accardo and Ricca not
only removed Giancana from his leadership role, but ordered him out of
the country until further notice. A recalcitrant Giancana left family
behind and fled to Mexico, while Accardo and Ricca tried to salvage
their empire.

The original Outfit was now crumbling, the combined effect of processes natural and man-made: Curly Humphreys and Jake Guzik had
passed on; Rosselli had been placed under increased official scrutiny;
Mooney Giancana had been banished; and Jimmy Hoffa was exhausting
his appeals on two thirteen-year terms for his misuse of the pension fund.
Only Accardo and Ricca were left, and they longed for retirement. There
would follow a succession of temporary front men to take Giancana's
place, trusted bosses like Sam Battaglia, Phil Alderisio, Jackie Cerone,
Joey Aiuppa, Joe Ferriola, Sam Carlisi, and John DeFronzo. But invariably, the key decisions were made by the gangsters' last links to Big Al
Capone, "Joe Batters" Accardo and Paul "the Waiter" Ricca. And
although the Outfit's final years saw the members more often on the
defensive than not, a handful of lucrative conquests were still to be had
before they too abandoned the mortal coil.

In 1966, one year before Hoffa went away, he and Allen Dorfman
approved a $20-million pension-fund loan to hotel magnate Jay Sarno,
for the building of Las Vegas' most garish paean to gambling yet, Caesars
Palace Hotel and Casino, a seven-hundred-room retreat (later expanded
to twenty-five hundred) that features Romanesque fountains; the eight-
hundred-seat Circus Maximus Theatre, patterned after the Roman Col-
osseum; numerous marble and concrete-over-chicken-wire replicas of
classic Roman sculpture, frescoes, and murals; and an Olympic-size pool
formed out of eight thousand pieces of Italian marble.

Although Sarno appeared to have a clean reputation, the FBI had learned two years earlier, just before its bugs were pulled, that the Caesars grand strategy had long been in the planning and that its putative owner would be just another in a long series of front men used by the Outfit and its partners. Before the casino opened in August 1966, the Bureau leaked a nine-hundred-page bug and wiretap report to Chicago reporter Sandy Smith, who in July of that year wrote a two-part exposé in the *Chicago Tribune,* followed by another in *Life* magazine. Since the Bureau was embargoed from using the illegal tap evidence, they decided to leak the material in hopes of arousing public disapprobation. Smith's articles stated emphatically that the soon-to-open Caesars, like many other Las Vegas casinos, was actually owned by a gangster consortium that ultimately answered to the Outfit. In his *Life* series, Smith also named "The Lady in Mink," Ida Devine, as the Outfit's new courier and even displayed an FBI surveillance photo of her at the train station (the only way she would travel).

The FBI was later told by an informant that the deal to cut up the Caesars skim was arrived at in October 1965 at a Palm Springs house rented by two Las Vegas showgirls. In what came to be known as the Palm Springs Apalachin, mob bosses from around the country, including Joe Accardo, Longy Zwillman, and Jimmy Alo, arrived to work out the details.

The disclosures in the Smith articles reverberated throughout gangland. "Jimmy Blue Eyes" Alo advised his Las Vegas partner Meyer Lansky to sell out. "Let's take the money and have a quiet life," Alo said to his lifelong friend. Chicago entrepreneurs took a similar tack, but with a critical distinction. With Jimmy Hoffa packing for college (and Allen Dorfman not far behind), Joe Accardo devised a temporary solution to the G's Vegas onslaught. He would instruct Johnny Rosselli to keep an eye out for squeaky-clean suckers with deep pockets, then start unloading the gang's holdings, with one key proviso: The Outfit would manage the casinos. "Timing is everything" goes the aphorism, and Accardo's timing could not have been more fortuitous. On Thanksgiving Eve, 1966, Howard Hughes, the "billionaire kook" as he was known to the mob, moved into the penthouse suite of the gang's Desert Inn Hotel. Hughes, a total recluse, liked the habitat so much that he refused to leave on checkout day, much to the rancorous objection of the hotel's other pampered high rollers.

"Tell them to go to hell," Hughes ordered his aides after the hotel managers attempted to evict him.

As fate would have it, Hughes, the sole owner of Hughes Tool Company, had just sold his stock in Trans World Airlines for $546 million, and it was burning a hole in his pajama pocket. Thus, the famous agoraphobe felt it less troublesome to buy the Desert Inn than to move out and instructed his key staff to work out the details. And Joe Accardo's good fortune did not end there, for Hughes' right-hand man was none other than Robert Maheu, friend of Johnny Rosselli, Las Vegas' greatest partnership broker, most recently tasked to find a purchaser for his casinos – and who better than a man who would never surface to testify in court.

Bob Maheu instinctively turned to his old assassination chum Rosselli to get the ball rolling. "I told Mr. Hughes that I thought I had found a person fitting the background that he had requested me to seek," Maheu later testified in court, "a person who had connections with certain people of perhaps unsavory background. . ." In his autobiography, Maheu admitted, "Johnny smoothed the way." Although the Outfit had decided on a new front man, its mob partners in other cities had to be convinced. Using the skills that later earned him the sobriquet The Mafia's Kissinger, Johnny Rosselli spent three months convincing the partners to agree to the Hughes buyout. For his diplomatic legerdemain, Rosselli was paid a $50,000 "finder's fee."

It is not known if Maheu or his boss were aware that they had become merely the newest pawns in the Outfit's front-man motif, but years later Maheu told Chicago investigator Jack Clarke, "Johnny told me who to hire to run the casinos and pit crews." Las Vegas *Review-Journal* reporter Sergio Lalli divined what had happened when he wrote, "The mob went about its business as usual." Historians Roger Morris and Sally Denton called the sale nothing more than "a classic Las Vegas shell game." And Johnny Rosselli himself told Jimmy Fratianno, "The whole thing was a Syndicate scam . . . We roped Hughes into buying the Desert Inn." Fittingly, Hughes took over on April Fools' Day, 1967. Shortly thereafter, the hoods sold their newest sucker the Frontier, the Sands, the Castaways, and the Silver Slipper, for a total of $45 million. Before he pulled up stakes four years later, on another Thanksgiving Eve, Hughes was relieved of another $50 million via the skim.

It would take Howard Hughes four years to realize that he was being robbed blind in his casinos' count rooms. In 1970, he put his Las Vegas holdings up for sale, as his Mormon Mafia aides secreted him out the back door to the Bahamas. In a parting shot, Hughes called Bob Maheu "a no-good, dishonest son of a bitch" who "stole me blind." Thanks to the 1969 passage of the Corporate Gaming Act, corporations were finally permitted to own casinos in Nevada, and they seized the baton lustily, moving quickly, as one local historian put it, "to purifying the wages of sin." Overnight, upperworld bastions such as Hilton Hotels, MGM, Holiday Inn, the Ramada Inn Corporation, and impresarios Kirk Kerkorian and Steve Wynn began their irreversible push to give Sin City a superficial veneer not unlike that of Disneyland – but at the heart of it all would remain gambling activities shamelessly rigged in the casino owners' favor.

Before they were completely finished with Las Vegas, however, the Outfit would find one more sucker to front for them in Sin City.

The Hughes purchases were not the only occurrences causing celebration in underworld enclaves in 1967. Although they were not the architects of Jack Kennedy's murder, the nation's organized-crime bosses, not unlike Fidel Castro, became the chief beneficiaries of Lee Harvey Oswald's marksmanship. President Lyndon Baines Johnson, the Democratic successor to Jack Kennedy, appointed one do-nothing attorney general after another. After a stint by Nick Katzenbach in which little was done to continue Bobby Kennedy's war on crime, things only got better for the bosses.

President Johnson brought still more smiles to the faces of Accardo and Ricca when he appointed Ramsey Clark, the son of Supreme Court justice Tom Clark, to be the new attorney general, replacing Nicholas Katzenbach. (Tom Clark resigned his Supreme Court chair to avoid conflict-of-interest charges.) The reader may recall that it was Tom Clark who had facilitated the early paroles of Ricca and his cohorts in the Hollywood extortion case two decades earlier; Clark had also restricted the FBI's probe into vote fraud in the Truman-Pendergast stronghold of Kansas City in 1947. The Outfit's enthusiasm for the appointment of Ramsey Clark would prove well-founded, as the new AG made it clear from the beginning that he was not going to authorize bugs or wiretaps, both of which he felt were infringements of privacy rights, in addition to being "wasteful and unproductive." Incredibly, Clark also abandoned the G's one ace in the hole when it came to bagging the most wanted hoods, the Internal Revenue Service. The new AG surely warmed the heart of Joe Accardo, who had been fighting the taxman for years, when Clark testified that it is "not OK to select organized crime cases" for scrutiny by the IRS. When Congress passed the Omnibus Crime Bill of 1968,

Clark made it clear that he would not utilize the wiretapping provisions of the bill.

In place of the surveillance, which had actually proved of immense use to the FBI's understanding of organized crime activities, Clark expanded the regional Strike Force operations, which by 1967 had only one outpost, in Buffalo, New York. Under Clark, the Strike Force set up shops in Detroit, Brooklyn, Philadelphia, Chicago, Newark (N.J.), and Miami. However, having been stripped of their most effective tools, and receiving little encouragement from their standard-bearer, the Strike Forces under Clark saw few successes. Clark Mollenhoff, the reporter who had persuaded Bobby Kennedy to join the McClellan Committee, wrote in his book *Strike Force,* "The Organized Crime Division wea-kened under Acting Attorney General Nicholas de B. Katzenbach, and all but expired as Ramsey Clark became the Attorney General . . . His bleeding for the poor criminals was so extensive that some joked that he must be in quest of the Mafia vote." Ramsey Clark indeed harbored short-lived presidential ambitions and faced the prospect of challenging the leftist, antiwar positions of candidate Robert Kennedy. Mollenhoff surmised that Clark's views on privacy rights "appeared to be the only way for a young man with obvious presidential aspirations, who at that time was backed by everyone from the *New York Times* to President Johnson, to move to the left of Senator Kennedy."

When Richard Nixon again ran for president in 1968, the "law and order" candidate aimed much of his campaign rhetoric at Ramsey Clark, whom he charged with "leading an official retreat" in the battle against organized crime. "If we are to restore order and respect for law in this country," Nixon fulminated upon accepting the Republican nomination, "there's one place where we're going to begin: We're going to have a new attorney general of the United States of America."

After Nixon won the 1968 contest, thanks to his own election high jinks, he indeed appointed as attorney general a bug-happy John Mitchell, who charged up both the FBI and the regional Strike Forces in their antimob prosecutions. Of course, President Nixon's motives may not have been entirely grounded in morality: He obviously remembered how organized crime had helped steal the 1960 election from him, and he was now in a position to prevent a reoccurrence in 1972. And Mitchell's prosecutions turned out to be straw targets, especially after Mitchell's sloppiness resulted in the dismissal of nearly seven hundred federal indictments that were based on improperly authorized wiretaps.

More troublesome for the underworld was the passage of the Organized Crime Control Act of 1970, the most important aspect of which
was a section entitled "Racketeer Influenced and Corrupt Organizations," or RICO, crafted largely by one of Bobby Kennedy's Justice
Department subordinates, G. Robert Blakey. Now the G would be able to
indict not only entire crime organizations by showing a pattern of
criminal activity over a ten-year period, but also anyone who could be
shown to be involved in said organization. Such associations would not
be easy to prove, but at least it was now possible to make war on the
"organized" part of organized crime.

Combined with the Omnibus Crime Control and Safe Streets Act of
1968, Title III of which sanctioned court-approved wiretaps, RICO
would eventually decimate criminal organizations in every major city.
(During the next decade, more than twenty Mafia bosses were indicted,
and most were convicted.) The FBI heard one New York mob boss
complain, "Under RICO, no matter who the fuck we are, if we're
together, they'll get every fuckin' one of us." Interestingly, the first
prosecutor to successfully navigate the intricacies of RICO was an Italian
U.S. attorney in New York City named Rudolph Giuliani, who worked
tirelessly for years to create the templates for the first RICO convictions.

The Outfit and Hoffa's Presidential Clemency

In 1971, Nixon was under pressure from many directions to offer executive
clemency to Jimmy Hoffa, imprisoned since 1967 on jury-tampering and
pension-fund kickback convictions. Without presidential intervention,
Hoffa was likely to serve out his two concurrent thirteen-year terms. Both
the rank and file, and the interim Teamster boss Frank Fitzsimmons, who
counted Nixon as a close friend, had been lobbying for Hoffa's release.[1]
Nixon may have been leaning toward such a move, since he felt he owed
Hoffa for the million-dollar contribution he had made to Nixon's candidacy
in 1960. However, it now appears that Nixon was finally convinced by the
promise of another fat check, this one from none other than Joe Accardo.

According to White House tapes released in 2001, Nixon informed
Henry Kissinger on December 8, 1971, "What we're talking about, in the
greatest of confidence, is we're going to give Hoffa an amnesty, *but we're*

1. Other influential constituents such as Ronald Reagan, World War II hero Audie
Murphy, and California senator George Murphy all lobbied Nixon on Hoffa's behalf,
hoping to obtain either Teamster business or pension-fund financing for pet projects.

going to do it for a reason." (Italics added.) Nixon then whispered about "some private things" Fitzsimmons had done for Nixon's cause "that were very helpful." In February 1973, fourteen months after Hoffa's release by Nixon, and just as Nixon was frantic to raise "hush money" for the 1972 Watergate burglars, Accardo, Dorfman, and Fitzsimmons met at "the mob's country club," LaCosta, to make good on a promise to Nixon. It was fortuitous timing for the president, who would five weeks later be informed by aide John Dean that the Watergate burglars would require one million dollars to bite their collective tongues.

"You could get a million dollars," Nixon replied. "You could get it in cash. I know where it could be gotten." Many journalists, such as Hoffa chronicler Dan Moldea, author of *The Hoffa Wars,* believe Nixon was referring to the money that he had just been promised by the Teamster-Mob alliance.

In the period of Hoffa's incarceration, the Outfit seems to have grown to like Frank Fitzsimmons (and partner Dorfman) more than Jimmy Hoffa, who only used the mob loans to help strengthen the Teamsters; he was never considered "one of ours" by the hoods. Hoffa was also known to have become a government informant against Fitzsimmons.

Before going away in 1967, Hoffa had said to his board about Dorfman, "When this man speaks, he speaks for me." He made similar statements about Frank Fitzsimmons. Now the duo surpassed their iconic colleague in his appeasement of the underworld. Under Fitzsimmons and Dorfman, Moe Dalitz was loaned $27 million to expand LaCosta; Frank Ragano, Santo Trafficante's lawyer, received $11 million in a Florida real estate deal; Irving Davidson, Carlos Marcello's D.C. lobbyist, received $7 million for a California land purchase; and in addition to Caesars, the fund was tapped to construct the skim-friendly Landmark, Four Queens, Aladdin, Lodestar, Plaza Towers, and Circus Circus. All told, the pension fund, controlled by Curly Humphreys' Chicago protégé Allen Dorfman, had loaned over $500 million in Nevada, 63 percent of the Fund's total assets, and most of it went to the hoods' favored casinos. But, perhaps most important, Fitzsimmons had decentralized Teamster power, which benefited local mob bosses, who could now easily outmuscle small union fiefdoms without having to bargain with an all-powerful president.

Now at LaCosta, the conspirators, who included an FBI informant, devised a new scheme wherein California Teamsters would be mandated to funnel dues into a prepaid billion-dollar health plan, 3 percent of which would be kicked back to something called People's Industrial Consultants, which was nothing more than Joe Accardo and what remained of the Outfit. For the scheme to work, Fitzsimmons had to remain at the top of the Teamsters. According to high-placed FBI sources, the purpose of the LaCosta meeting was to coordinate a delivery of one million dollars in Las Vegas skim to the besieged Nixon, who had released Hoffa with the stipulation that he not run for the Teamster presidency. It was also reported that the money would guarantee that Nixon-Mitchell would take it easy on investigations of pension-fund loans. According to a secret FBI report, one mobster who attended the LaCosta meetings stated that half of the payback, $500,000 in cash, "had been requested by White House aide Charles Colson, who handled the administration's relations with the Teamsters." When Colson was later asked about this by the Senate Watergate Committee, he pled the Fifth Amendment.

While the schemers met at LaCosta, Nixon was at his nearby San Clemente home, with aides John Dean and John Haldeman, both of whom drove to LaCosta where Accardo et al. were in the midst of their four-day meetings. Although no one can prove that the two camps met, it is known that Fitzsimmons flew back to Washington aboard Air Force One with Nixon. According to mob sources located by author William Balsamo, Fitzsimmons told Nixon on the flight, "We're prepared to pay for the request I put on the table . . . You'll never have to worry about where the next dollar will come from. We're going to give you one million dollars up front, Mr. President . . . and there'll be more that'll follow to make sure you are never wanting."

Soon after, John Mitchell indeed scuttled investigations into the Teamster loans and rescinded the taps on Accardo and friends.

Hoffa's conditional release was not the Outfit's only behind-the-scenes power play in 1971. One of its unheralded successes simultaneously displayed how thorough had been the gang's commandeering of the nation's labor unions and also treated the world's movie fans to what has been called "the best three hours one could spend in a movie theater."

At the time, Las Vegas real estate millionaire Kerkor "Kirk" Kerkorian had just seized control of MGM Studios in Hollywood and thought to use the association with the MGM film *Grand Hotel* to construct another Las Vegas theme hotel, $106-million megalith to be called the MGM Grand Hotel, the largest hotel in the world. A millionaire many times over, having recently sold his Trans International Airlines for $100 million and having built the hugely successful International Hotel, Kerkorian could build anything he wanted. However, all of the money in the world could not overcome the stranglehold Accardo and Humphreys had placed on the nation's labor force, and the Outfit wanted something in return for its cooperation: They wanted one of MGM's contract actors for a production by another studio.

At the time, Paramount producer Robert Evans was attempting to package a film project based on Mario Puzo's wildly successful novel *The Godfather,* for which Evans owned the movie rights. A problem arose when the director, the as yet unsuccessful wunderkind Francis Ford Coppolla, insisted on an unknown, diminutive actor named Al Pacino for the lead role of Mafia boss Michael Corleone. The fly in the ointment was Pacino's unbreakable contract with Kerkorian's MGM. Evans first called MGM's president, Jim Aubrey. "With the emotion of an IRS investigator," Evans wrote, "he turned me down."

The way Bob Evans saw it, he had no choice but to call the Outfit's Hollywood dealmaker, Sidney Roy Korshak. The producer had been a great friend of Korshak's since the early fifties and claimed that the pair met every day until 1980, when they had a falling out. Like most upperworld achievers, Evans was well aware of the Outfit's knack for getting things done – they were, after all, action men. Years later, Evans wrote of the power Sidney Korshak, and by proxy the Outfit, now wielded: "A nod from Korshak, and Santa Anita closes. A nod from Korshak, and Madison Square Garden stays open. A nod from Korshak, and Vegas shuts down. A nod from Korshak, and the Dodgers suddenly can play night baseball. Am I exaggerating? Quite the contrary. In the spirit of confidentiality, it's an underplay."

Among Korshak's Tinseltown triumphs was the critical assistance he had given Screen Actors Guild president Ronald Reagan in settling the 1966 actors' strike. In 1971, the same year Evans faced his *Godfather* predicament, Korshak served as uncredited legal adviser for the Las Vegas-based James Bond film *Diamonds Are Forever.* Korshak had recommended his friend Jill St. John for the costarring role of "Plenty O'Toole."

As recounted in his memoir, *The Kid Stays in the Picture,* Evans, who was in New York at the time, placed a call to Korshak at his New York office in the Carlyle Hotel:

"Sidney Korshak, please."

"Yeah?"

"Sidney, it's Bobby."

"Yeah?"

"I need your help."

"Yeah?"

"There's an actor I want for the lead in *The Godfather*."

"Yeah?"

"I can't get him."

"Yeah?"

"If I lose him, Coppola's gonna have my ass."

"Yeah?"

Evans advised Korshak of his turndown by MGM's Aubrey, a revelation that elicited a nonstop recitation of *yeah*s from Korshak.

"Is there anything you can do about it?"

"Yeah."

"Really?"

"The actor, what's his name?"

"Pacino . . . Al Pacino."

"Who?"

"Al Pacino."

"Hold it, will ya. Let me get a pencil. Spell it."

"Capital *A*, little *l* – that's his first name. Capital *P*, little *a, c-i-n-o*."

"Who the fuck is he?"

"Don't rub it in, will ya, Sidney. That's who the motherfucker wants."

As Evans tells it, twenty minutes after the friends hung up, an enraged Jim Aubrey called Evans.

"You no-good motherfucker, cocksucker. I'll get you for this," Aubrey screamed.

"What are you talking about?"

"You know fuckin' well what I'm talking about."

"Honestly, I don't."

"The midget's yours; you got him."

That was Aubrey's final statement before slamming the phone down on a befuddled Evans, who immediately called Sidney. The master fixer advised the producer that he had merely placed a call to Aubrey's boss, Kirk Kerkorian, and made the request. When Kerkorian had balked, Korshak had introduced his Outfit connections into the negotiations.

"Oh, I asked him if he wanted to finish building his hotel," Korshak told Evans. "He didn't answer . . . He never heard of the schmuck either. He got a pencil, asked me to spell it – 'Capital *A*, punk *l*, capital *P*, punk *a, c-i-n-o*.' Then he says, 'Who the fuck is he?' 'How the fuck do I know? All I know, Bobby wants him.' "

The rest, as they say, is history. Not only did *The Godfather* redefine the cinema, but Al Pacino became a star, and Kirk Kerkorian completed his MGM Grand, earning him the moniker Father of the Mega-Resort.

When the film was screened for a party of Hollywood insiders at a Malibu estate, antimob crusader Steve Allen somehow made the guest list. "There was the usual crowd there," Allen said in 1997, "but there were also a few swarthy Vegas boys who had 'organized crime' written all over them. After the movie, my wife, Jayne, made a remark about gangsters that caused one producer, who was friendly with the mob, to get in her face. 'You have no idea what you're talking about, lady,' this character told her."

Allen says he intervened before the face-off got ugly, and soon thereafter, he and Jayne made their exit.

"The next morning, while I'm just waking up," Allen said, "our housekeeper came banging on our bedroom door."

"Mr. Allen! Mr. Allen!" called the frantic woman. The entertainer rushed out and followed his housekeeper to the front porch, where, in a scene reminiscent of the movie he had just seen, he found an enormous severed leg and shoulder of a horse. Allen knew the name of the producer who had had the set-to with Jayne and, in a show of defiance, had the carcass delivered to his home. (The producer, whom Allen identified for the author, was a close friend of Johnny Rosselli's, whom Allen believed also attended the screening.)

Sidney Korshak's behind-the-scenes role in the making of *The Godfather* was merely one illustration of many such maneuverings. Korshak also facilitated the production of another Paramount box-office success, the 1976 remake of *King Kong*. In 1975, according to the film's chronicler Bruce Bahrenburg, "Paramount was looking for another 'big' picture in the same league as their recent blockbusters, *The Godfather* and *The Great Gatsby*." When the project was announced in the trades that year, Universal Pictures sued the new film's producer, Dino De Laurentiis for $25 million, claiming it alone held the rights to the remake of the original 1933 RKO production. Universal simultaneously filed suit against RKO, which had sold the rights to De Laurentiis, after it had supposedly already done the same to Universal.

De Laurentiis countersued for $90 million, as the legal morass became more entangled with each successive day. "The legal issues surrounding the copyright to Kong," Bahrenburg wrote, "are as puzzling as a maze in a formal British garden." With the lawsuits casting a shadow on the film, Paramount nonetheless went ahead in early January 1976 with principal photography, and it now became imperative that the legal issues be resolved. Although the courts had failed to bring about a deal, there was, of course, one man who was famous for just that, and he already had a track record with Paramount and Universal, whose parent company, MCA, was run by his close friends Lew Wasserman and Sid Sheinberg. The master negotiator was, again, Sid Korshak.

According to a source close to the film, a luncheon was arranged at Korshak's Beverly Hills home between executives of Paramount and Universal (MCA). "Sidney was the court," says the source. "In a couple hours, a deal was arrived at that made everybody happy. Sidney had done more over his lunch hour than dozens of high-priced attorneys had done in eight months." The source, a producer at Universal, adds that Korshak was paid a $30,000 fee for his 120-minute business lunch.

Variety later reported that Universal agreed to allow Paramount to make the film with Universal maintaining the rights to a future sequel. "I am very pleased," De Laurentiis told the press, "and would like to thank MCA's Lew Wasserman and Sid Sheinberg for their understanding and generosity in making such accommodations possible." Per custom, Sid Korshak's name never surfaced in connection with the resolution.

Back on their home turf, Accardo and Ricca periodically surfaced to pass judgments on various individuals who threatened the Outfit's common good. They were particularly hard on soldiers who broke the cardinal rule that forbade trafficking in narcotics. It is believed that ten drug dealers were slain in one week on Accardo's orders; others who received the ultimate sanction included "street tax" scofflaws, who refused to pay the mandated tithe to the men who made it all possible.

Among the more unsettling news the duo was receiving was that from Mexico, where Mooney Giancana, ever the survivor, was making a fortune. Since his settling in a walled estate called San Cristobal in Cuernavaca, Mooney had been constantly in transit, using contacts he had made over the years to set up gambling cruise ships and casinos throughout the Caribbean and Central and South America. The former boss' passport was stamped by the customs agents of Lebanon, Iran, Spain, Peru, Jamaica, the Bahamas, Greece, and every major European destination.

Mooney's gambling ventures were not only legal, but wildly successful, netting him untold millions in profit, according to the FBI's best information. Giancana's biographer William Brashler wrote, "Five gambling boats in particular were gold mines for Giancana." When word of Giancana's prosperity reached Accardo, the boss suddenly decided that Mooney was, in fact, still in the Outfit and was thus required to send a cut of his profits back to Chicago. Accardo instructed an aide, Richard Cain, who was also an FBI informant, "I want you to go to Mexico and explain the facts of life to him. I mean the facts of *life*, do you understand what I'm saying?"

When G-man Roemer heard that Accardo might be gearing up to hit Mooney, he worried that the murder would bring the G down on Accardo. Roemer was clearly conflicted: He had been chasing Accardo for decades, but now when the whacking of Giancana threatened to backfire on Accardo, Roemer realized that Chicago could live with an original Outfit member, but not with another boss who might have no rules of conduct. Roemer thus arranged another neighborhood stroll with his ostensible adversary.

"I think you know you're the right guy for the job you've got," Roemer said. "And we think so too. You keep the Outfit out of narcotics, you only do what you have to do with the heavy stuff . . . Watch out on the hit on Mo. It'll backfire on you."

"Roemer, I appreciate your thoughts," answered the boss. "There are worse guys than you around. But I don't think there's any good in you coming around. You do your job and I'll do mine. Whatever is gonna happen will happen."

With that, the two men shook hands and went their separate ways, with Roemer not knowing that his plea had absolutely no effect on Joe Accardo's ultimate decision.

And Then There Was One

On October 11, 1972, after years of successfully stalling IRS and Immigration probes, seventy-five-year-old Paul "the Waiter" Ricca was felled by a fatal heart attack, in what was becoming a cardiac epidemic among Outfit bosses. In addition to his legal entanglements and occasional rulings with Accardo, Ricca had spent his declining years in relative quiet, often lolling about the Al Italia arrivals gate at O'Hare Airport, where he would chat with deplaning Italian tourists in the language of their shared inheritance. The day after Ricca died in his own bed, his lifelong friend Joe Accardo stood by his casket and greeted well-wishers as though it were his own brother who had passed. When the wake concluded, Ricca was buried with the full rites of the Catholic Church.

After his role in the Hughes takeover negotiations, Johnny Rosselli was imprisoned in the Friars Club scam in 1971. At sixty-five years of age, the man who had grown accustomed to tailored silk shirts was going back to prison blues, sentenced to a five-year term. He ultimately served two years and nine months, but by the time he left McNeil Island Federal Penitentiary, his relationship with Chicago was completely severed. In three years, he would have one last appearance in the headlines, although not by his own choosing.

Although the Outfit had de facto expired with the loss of Curly Humphreys, it was now officially over. The original gang that had seized the baton from Big Al Capone had a reign of forty-one years, a duration that far eclipsed that of any other underworld enterprise in U.S. history. What followed would have Joe Accardo, the ultimate survivor, attempting to pass on the vast network of national upperworld business partners, co-opted labor unions, legitimate businesses, and corrupt politicians to another generation.

The Chicago Underworld Today

At its peak, the Chicago Outfit employed hundreds of full-time "associates," and thousands of soldiers, in its quest to expand its influence from coast to coast. The outposts established by Accardo et al. in locales such as Miami, Hollywood, and Las Vegas are now run instead by the local underworlds and have become so enmeshed with the legitimate sphere as to be virtually indistinguishable from their white-collar counterparts. It is unknown if these local power brokers still pay a tithe to Chicago, but it is a matter of courtesy that when an associate of the gang that founded Sin City arrives there for a spree, mountains are moved to make his stay enjoyable.

Since the Strawman setback (see Epilogue), and the deaths of the original Outfit bosses, the Windy City underworld has greatly contracted, content to run rackets in the Cook County vicinity. Chicago crime historian Howard Abadinsky, a professor of criminal justice at Chicago's St. Xavier University, has opined, "The Outfit is a business and they've learned that having a smaller core is good business."

Today there are believed to be as few as fifty Chicago organized-crime members in what *Chicago Magazine* recently called "Mob Lite." Whereas local crews traditionally numbered seven, that figure has dwindled to a mere three, on the North, South, and West Sides. From these strongholds, the new, lean Chicago underworld continues to mine the traditional sources of treasure: gambling and labor unions (for both pension kickbacks and extortion of businesses who require their services). One such labor union believed to be controlled by Chicago's Mob Lite is the nineteen-thousand-member Laborers' International Union of North America, which sits on a $1.5-billion treasury. Controlling the unions allows the Mob Lite to have implicit, and usually legal, influence on work contracts. Abadinsky calls the new regime's approach "remarkably sophisticated."

The new Chicago mob has gone so low-profile that experts cannot even agree on who heads it. Some well-informed mob historians believe that John "No Nose" DiFronzo, seventy-one, an Accardo-style CEO, is the current chieftain.[2] Others assert that Joe "the Clown" Lombardo, another seventy-one-year-old, and a survivor of the Strawman purges, is in charge. Local G-men believe that sixty-eight-year-old Joe "the Builder" Andriacchi, a construction mogul, is running the show. Lastly, there is the strong possibility that all three run the local rackets by committee. This is the view of Professor Abadinsky. "It's fantastic. It's unbelievable," Abadinsky recently said. The crime chronicler explained that mobs have often designated straw front men as boss to confuse the G. "But the Outfit has gone even further; they've purposely made no effort to designate anyone as boss, so no one really knows. They realized that there's an inevitable conclusion to being a dapper don. Just look at [New York boss John] Gotti . . . He's in jail now for the rest of his life."

When he was paroled in 1992, Joe Lombardo went so far as to make a public pronouncement about his lifestyle, attempting to convince the locals that they had nothing to fear from him. That year, his classified ad appeared in the *Chicago Tribune*: "I am Joe Lombardo, I have been released on parole from federal prison. I never took a secret oath with guns and daggers, pricked my finger, drew blood, or burned paper to join a criminal organization. If anyone hears my name used in connection with any criminal activity, please notify the FBI, and my parole officer, Ron Kumke."

The increased low-profile extends to the adoption of a modus operandi

---

2. DiFronzo obtained his moniker in 1949 when a part of his nose was shot off by a bullet that was standard issue for the Chicago police department.

at greater odds than ever with the use of violence and the trafficking in narcotics. "That they've managed to stay out of street-level drug deals is an amazing success story for the Outfit," Abadinsky told *Chicago Magazine*. "The temptation, the money, is so incredible. This is true discipline." A friend of Joe Lombardo's recently claimed that Lombardo decreed in the early nineties that murder and mayhem were now forbidden, except in the most extreme cases, and then only when given the green light from above. It has been asserted that there were only six Outfit-sphere murders between 1990 and 1994, and even that number might be exaggerated. Abadinsky told *Chicago Magazine*: "When you have fantastically lucrative businesses like gambling, in which victims willingly participate and no one's getting beaten up or killed, it draws much less attention from law enforcement – no one's complaining. And when you're not shaking down every bookie or restaurant owner on every street corner, when you're not peddling drugs at the street level, you don't require as many employees." Wayne Johnson, the current chief investigator for the Chicago Crime Commission, says of the Outfit descendants, "They won't take bets from just anyone, and when someone can't pay, the penalty will often be as simple as blacklisting the guy and letting everyone in the business know that he's a stiff."

Regretfully, the abhorrence of street violence by the heirs to Accardo and Humphreys is not shared by the Young Turks that comprise the inner-city cocaine-dealing gangs with ties to Russian, South American, Chinese, and Mexican drug cartels. Turf wars and drive-by shootings in sectors such as Cabrini Green are regular occurrences, with Glock Nine-toting terrorists putting Capone's "Chicago typewriter" gunmen to shame.

As the Chicago underworld continues to profit from its traditional sources of revenue, sectors of the city's officialdom likewise continue to form partnerships with their alleged prey. Not only are the requisite pliant pols kept happy, but the city's designated law enforcement officers are continually hit with a barrage of corruption allegations. In 1997, Chicago police superintendent Matt Rodriguez was forced to resign when his close friendship with convicted felon Frank Milito came to light. In 2000, retired deputy police superintendent William Hanhardt was charged with leading a nationwide band of jewel thieves who stole over $5 million in precious gems between 1984 and 1996. It has been charged that Hanhardt utilized his contacts at police headquarters to identify his jewelry salesmen targets. And when vice cops recently raided adult bookstores and peep shows owned by alleged mob associate Robert "Bobby" Dominic, they were met by the men hired by Dominic as security, the Chicago Police Tactical Unit's Detective Joseph Laskero and Officer Anthony Bertuca, both coincidentally assigned to the raiding vice unit.

Chicago area politicians also made news recently when nine officials of Al Capone's Cicero were charged in 2001 with stealing and laundering $10 million from the town's health insurance fund. Among those indicted was the town's president, Betty Loren-Maltese. One month earlier, a federal jury awarded former Cicero police chief David Niebur $1.7 million, after he had been fired by Loren-Maltese for working with the FBI on investigating corruption in Cicero.

Many of the survivors of the original regime have realized the immigrant gangster dream by making the transition into legitimate business. When recently asked what has become of the old-guard hoods, Jeanette Callaway, the director of the Chicago Crime Commission, laughed. "They're everywhere," Callaway says. "They've become involved in every possible Chicago business." It is a truism in Chicago that when strolling down Michigan Avenue's "Magnificent Mile," one is surrounded on both sides by enterprises successfully entered into by former Outfit members.

Ironically, the Outfit's own progeny appear to have no interest in the underworld, but have instead fulfilled their parents' desires to embark on careers that gained them upperworld acceptance. It is a sacrosanct Italian dictate that holds that one's offspring become better educated and more successful than one's self; the next generation must improve upon the previous one. A child of one of the original top bosses, who asked not to be named, recently said, "My father would not discuss those kinds of things with the family. He was very closemouthed, but it was clear he did not want us to follow in his footsteps." Mooney's daughter Antoinette Giancana received a similar message from her father: "I don't think any of these guys wanted their kids to get involved in crime."

Consequently, the Outfit's heirs took whatever trusts were allotted to them and either went into business or pursued higher education; a number of them are Realtors, stockbrokers, restaurant owners, etc. Some, like Jackie Cerone's son, became prominent attorneys. Joe Accardo set up numerous family members with careers, such as his brothers John (who became a movie projectionist) and Martin (a tavern owner). Joe's granddaughter Alicia became a highly regarded Hollywood script supervisor.

There were occasional obstacles such as when Joe's son, Anthony Accardo, Jr., attempted to set up a travel agency in the early sixties. According to one of Tony's closest friends, "Bobby Kennedy got wind of this and sent out his goons to talk to potential clients – telling them they'd have IRS problems. The agency never materialized. That's a story you can take to the bank."

Epilogue

The passing of Paul Ricca carried with it an ominous undertone, one appreciated by few outside the Outfit's world. It had been Ricca who had first brought Mooney Giancana to the Outfit as his driver, then later remained his chief booster as he rose through the ranks; Ricca was one of the few who had stood by Mooney during his constant breeches of gang protocol. Now, with Ricca gone, Giancana was without his sponsor. In Accardo's eyes, if Giancana refused to capitulate soon, the upstart exile's fate was all but sealed. It was one of many circumstances Accardo would have to confront in the years ahead as the last survivor of the original Outfit.

The final acts in Accardo's career are here briefly summarized due to the constraints of space.

1974

Increasing his distance from the front lines, Joe Accardo purchased a $110,000 condo that bordered the fairway of Palm Springs Country Club Golf Course. The home, in a gated community on Roadrunner Drive in Indian Wells, California, kept Accardo far removed from the wiretap fray and gave his wife, Clarice, the retired life she had so long coveted. When in Chicago, Accardo stayed at his home on Ashland Avenue, which he retained after his Indian Wells purchase.

Throughout this period, the Outfit's day-to-day boss was Joey "Doves" Aiuppa, so nicknamed for his 1962 prosecution on charges of illegally shooting, along with his shotgun-toting soldiers, more than fourteen hundred mourning doves in Kansas. (Bobby Kennedy had been so excited by the conviction, he flew to Kansas for the sentencing.[1]) Along with

---

1. In response to his conviction, Aiuppa established the Yorkshire Quail Club south of Chicago in Kankakee County. Joey's club catered to underworld   *cont'd over/*

powerful underboss Jackie "the Lackey" Cerone, Aiuppa oversaw a regime infamous for its strict enforcement of the Outfit's code. Aiuppa's tenure was bloody, typified by more executions for drug dealers, as well as for bookies and juice men who neglected their "street tax."

Before totally abandoning the Vegas casinos, a crime consortium that included Kansas City, Milwaukee, Cleveland, and Chicago (represented by Aiuppa for Joe Accardo) sang its swan song in Sin City, its new lead singer named Allen Glick. A sucker with far shallower pockets than Howard Hughes, local entrepreneur Glick naïvely thought (or so he later claimed) that he could obtain a $62-million loan from the Teamsters pension fund with no stings attached. His subsequent 1974 purchase of the Stardust, Fremont, Hacienda, and Marina casinos gave the underworld one last chance at hitting the gambling capital's jackpot. However, this time, the hoods would finally learn what it felt like to lose in Las Vegas. All except Joe Accardo, that is.

At this time, the first RICO successes were yet to be secured, thus the gangs believed they could raid the golden goose one more time. With the endorsement of Milwaukee "theater owner" Frank Bal (who was in fact Milwaukee mob boss Frank Balistrieri, and who was ultimately subservient to Chicago), Glick obtained his Teamster loan. However, before the first set of dice were polished, Glick was told by Bal, under orders from Accardo and the consortium, to hire Chicago's Frank "Lefty" Rosenthal to be in charge of operations. "If you interfere with any of the casino operations," Rosenthal warned Glick, "or try to undermine anything I do here . . . you will never leave this corporation alive."

Over the next three years, the cartel skimmed $7 million per year from the slots alone (investigators believe, but cannot confirm, that a similar amount was taken from the tables). In four years, Glick would be ordered to sell his Argent Corporation to an even more pliant owner or his children would be killed. He did as told and disappeared into southern California obscurity with a tidy profit.

The same year Glick was being booted from Nevada, Mooney Giancana was receiving the same sentence in Mexico, rendering all his hard work in

---

cont'd   members around the country, who traveled to Yorkshire when their blood-lust needed sating. Aiuppa had come far since his days manufacturing the gang's slot machines in his Cicero plant, the Taylor Furniture Company.

the gambling-junket business for naught. On the night of July 18, 1974, the Mexican government seized Mooney in his pajamas and slippers, after eight years in exile. In a surprise abduction by Mexican immigration authorities, Mooney was deported on a charge of being an unwanted visitor. After being driven to Mexico City, where authorities alerted the FBI, he was sent to San Antonio, Texas, and met there by Chicago agents who bought the penniless Giancana a one-way plane ticket to Chicago. And due to local law, Mooney was never able to retrieve the millions he had deposited in Mexican banks. It was a frail, unshaven Giancana, outfitted in a blue work shirt and a pair of pants four sizes too large (given him by authorities in Mexico City), who unceremoniously boarded the flight back to the Second City.

Tipped to Mooney's arrival, longtime adversary and macho man Bill Roemer raced to O'Hare Airport to get in his face, for old times' sake. However, when Roemer confronted the aged former boss and heard his greeting, Roemer backed off. The G-man later wrote that Giancana "was undoubtedly the wealthiest person on that plane, but he looked like some Italian immigrant landing at Ellis Island, destitute and frail."

"I'm not gonna be involved in anything anymore," Mooney whispered. "You'll soon find out that I have nothin' goin' for me here. I'm out of it. So, please, just leave me alone. Nothin' personal like it was between us before. If it takes an apology, then this is it. Let's just forget what has been before."

Although he had been intent on goading Mooney into another fight, Roemer became disarmed by the gangster's feeble visage. However, the agent quickly found a way to relieve his frustration. "I think at that moment," he later wrote, "I realized that I had won."

1975

On June 18, 1975, Mooney Giancana was shot to death in his basement. For months, the ailing Mooney had been telling friends that he would do anything to avoid "rotting in jail." The don was currently the subject of another grand jury proceeding and had agreed to meet with investigators for the Senate's Church Committee, which had been investigating, among other things, the Kennedy administration plots to murder Fidel Castro. The same committee had also called Johnny Rosselli, who voluntarily agreed to testify. Now, Mooney's prospective testimony, under subpoena, would virtually guarantee more unwanted front-page coverage for organized crime in Chicago, a prospect that, in addition to Mooney's refusal to pay tribute to Accardo, likely sealed his fate.

On his last night alive, Giancana had been cooking his favorite meal of sausage, escarole, and *ceci* beans in his basement kitchen sometime after 10 P.M. His daughter Francine had visited that evening, and as she drove away around ten, she saw Mooney's longtime aide Butch Blasi pull into the driveway. Blasi's car was also observed there by Chicago detectives who were patrolling the suburban homes of a number of bosses that evening. About two hours later, family friend and Giancana tenant Joe DiPersio went downstairs to check on Mooney and discovered the body. Giancana had been shot seven times with a silencer-equipped .22, once in the back of the head, once in the mouth, and five times under the chin in an upward direction.

Although it has been reported that the killer took no loot, that may not be the case. "Mooney had a velvet bag full of diamonds and other precious jewels," remembers his son-in-law Bob McDonnell. "He always used to call it his 'escape insurance,' something he could use if he ever had to leave the country in a hurry." Mooney's daughter also remembers the valuable cache, which has never been located. Until it was recently brought to her attention that Accardo was feuding with Mooney over money, Antoinette never considered that the missing jewels may have been taken by the killer. All told, Giancana's assets at the time of his death (in cash, property, trusts, and investments) totaled about $1 million, although he was reportedly worth $25 million at his peak. It has never been determined whether any of his resources are gathering dust in a Swiss account or a buried stash.

In 2001, a source who was close to Butch Blasi at the time stated that Blasi admitted to having been the perpetrator. A few months after Giancana's slaying, a village worker found the murder weapon on a patch of grass located halfway along a route to Blasi's home. After a long bout with dementia, Blasi passed away, an occurrence that effectively ended authorities' interest in the case.

On June 24, only six days after Mooney's murder, the don's assassination-plot partner Johnny Rosselli gave his first testimony in Washington before a rapt Church Committee, once again placing the underworld in the media spotlight. The exquisitely tailored Rosselli was in great form and, totally disavowing Curly Humphreys' dictum to say nothing, spared no details. "It has always puzzled me," committee member Senator Richard Schweiker later said, "why he came in, and why he was so forthcoming."

"John gave a fully detailed description," his lawyer Leslie Scherr later recalled. "Everything that had gone on in '61 and '62, everything from that era, and every one of those guys were mesmerized by John. He was hypnotic. The guy would have made a wonderful lawyer." At one point, Rosselli brought the room to convulsive laughter when answering Senator Barry Goldwater's query as to whether he had taken any notes during the plotting.

"Senator, in my business, we don't take notes," Rosselli deadpanned in response. After being excused, Rosselli agreed to return for a second round on September 22. With Rosselli's testimony to be sealed for the next twenty years, underworld leaders across the nation surely feared that the garrulous gangster, now totally chastened by his late-life prison stay, must have divulged secrets that would cause Curly and Paul to spin in their graves. Like so many other underworld players of his era, Johnny Rosselli was now living on borrowed time.

On July 30, just five weeks after Mooney's murder, Jimmy Hoffa disappeared. He had placed himself in jeopardy in April 1973 when he had declared his intention to take back the Teamsters. However, most experts believe that the underworld was already happy with Fitzsimmons and decreed otherwise, for reasons stated. "Hoffa was also a government informant," says Dan Moldea. "All the Teamster presidents occasionally talked against their associates to the government, that's how they survived." Moldea believes the contract to kill Hoffa, meant also as a warning to Fitzsimmons, was put out by Carlos Marcello of New Orleans and Santo Trafficante of Tampa, and from there it was given to East Coast bosses Tony Provenzano of New York and Russell Bufalino of Pennsylvania. Both the FBI and Moldea agree that the actual killer was Sal Briguglio, an enforcer for Provenzano. What the hoods never knew was that Fitzsimmons, in fear of both the mob and the IRS, quietly followed Hoffa's lead and began informing for the G as well. "Fitzsimmons was a stoolie for [IRS investigator] John Daley," a partner of Daley's recently confirmed. "That's how he stayed out of prison. It's also one of the reasons the government was able to start building its case against the mob's pension-fund loans in Nevada."

1976

After a third meeting in Washington with members of the Church Committee, a semiretired Johnny Rosselli traveled to Plantation, Florida, to visit his sister, Edith. Anxious to make another score, Rosselli called Hollywood producer-friend Brynie Foy and pitched him a new film idea, a thinly veiled roman à clef in which a patriotic gangster helps the White House kill Fidel Castro, but the operation backfires when Castro gets his own people to plan the American president"s death. Perhaps Rosselli was trying to cash in on his recent Church Committee testimony, the salient points of which had leaked to the press. According to some, Foy believed the story was too implausible to get interest from the studios.

On a May 1976 trip to Los Angeles, Johnny had a relaxed dinner with old chum Jimmy Fratianno, of the L.A. underworld. The California hood was clearly worried about Johnny, and given Rosselli's recent testimony and attempts to sell his Mafia-CIA story to the studios, it was small wonder.

"Johnny, be careful, will you," Fratianno implored. "This thing of ours is treacherous. You never know when you're going to make the hit list. Don't let Trafficante or [Jackie] Cerone set you up."

"Will you stop worrying?" Rosselli nonchalantly responded. "I'm all right. Everything's under control."

On July 28, during another visit to Plantation, Florida, Rosselli borrowed his sister's car and drove off just after noon with his golf clubs. It was the last time he was seen alive. That night, the family began their frantic search, with Rosselli's brother-in-law recalling that Johnny had once said, "If I'm ever missing, check the airports, because that's where they usually leave the car." It was an eerie prognostication: His car was found two days later at Miami International Airport, and seven days after that, on August 7, Johnny's grisly remains were found. He had been strangled to death, then dismembered, stuffed into a rusted oil drum, and dumped at sea. Rosselli's metal coffin washed ashore not far from the former Biscayne Bay home of Curly Humphreys.

Fred Black, a Washington influence peddler and close Rosselli friend, was among those certain that Santo Trafficante had ordered the hit. That it had taken place in Trafficante's domain was telling. For years, the Florida boss was believed by many to have been playing a dangerous game, operating a numbers racket (bolita) out of Havana in partnership with Castro, while living among the Castro-hating exiles. The theory goes that Trafficante feared reprisal from Castro if his role in the CIA plots surfaced, or from the exiles if his game with Castro was revealed. Beyond the speculation, there was never a suspect officially named in the murder.

"I was saddened," CG Harvey recently said, "like I would be with any friend." Just two months earlier, on June 8, CG had lost her husband, Johnny Rosselli's great CIA chum, Bill Harvey, due to heart failure.

1977–78

In January 1977, while the Accardos were in Indian Wells, their Chicago home was burglarized by the most foolhardy band of thieves imaginable. Joe's houseman, Michael Volpe, informed Accardo, who then instructed Aiuppa to "bring in Spilatro." Tony Spilotro, one of Aiuppa's most savage and uncontrollable enforcers, had been posted in Las Vegas, where he and his soldiers made short work of cheats and rival gangs.

When word got out that Accardo had ordered the stalking and executions of the guilty, there was a reported mass exodus from Illinois of thieves and cat burglars, who worried that they might mistakenly be linked to the crime. It took some time before Accardo's men could crack the case, all the worse for the guilty parties, since Accardo's anger only escalated with each passing day. Finally, in January 1978, the guilty parties were identified and the bodies quickly began piling up, as the sound of "trunk music" once again reverberated throughout Cook County.

On January 20, the first burglar was discovered, having been shot to death. Over the next eight weeks, the remaining six were found in various states of morbidity: Some had been tortured with castration, one had his face burned off with an acetylene torch, and most had either been shot to death or had their throats slashed.[2] One year later, the two executioners likewise turned up murdered. Suffice it to say, no one ever again laid so much as a glove on Joe Accardo's properties.

In 1977, according to the FBI, Joey Aiuppa journeyed to Atlantic City for an important Commission meeting, the subject of which concerned future expansion in Las Vegas. At the time, New Jersey's Gambino crime family was making rumblings about buying into Sin City, much to the dislike of Accardo-Aiuppa. Fortunately, the state of New Jersey had just legalized casino gambling, an eventuality that gave the two parties a way out of their disagreement. It was decided that the Eastern families could keep

---

2. The burglar victims were identified as Bernard Ryan, Steven Garcia, Vincent Moretti, Donald Swanson, John Mandell, John McDonald, and Bobby Hartogs. Their executioners were believed to be John Borsellino and Gerry Carusiello.

what holdings they had in Vegas, but that was all. As a trade-off, they were given complete lordship over Atlantic City, a shrewd move by Accardo, since Atlantic City had an aggressive antimob Casino Control Commission in place before the first craps tables were set up.[3] As a result, the New Jersey mob was never able to strangle Atlantic City the way Chicago and New York had Las Vegas.

On October 5, 1978, Michael Volpe, Accardo's longtime housekeeper, vanished, an event believed by some to have been connected to his grand jury testimony five days previous. In response, the FBI executed a search warrant on Accardo's eighteen-room Ashland Avenue home. With Joe's daughters Linda Lee and Marie escorting them, the G spent over seven hours in a sacrosanct abode they had seen only from the outside since its construction in 1963. On the rancher's first floor, the agents found little besides the indications of upscale urban domesticity. The basement, however, was another story.

The lower region of the home consisted of a long hallway, its walls covered with Joe's photos and glass cases housing his gun collection. The hallway divided a large do-it-yourselfer's workshop on one side, and Accardo's conference room on the other. The large, carpeted conference room was commanded by a huge round table encircled by thirty chairs. "How many strategies had been plotted there?" mused FBI agent Bill Roemer.

Adjoining this room was the requisite kitchen; however, in this case it was an industrial-sized affair with walk-in pantries, coolers, and a wine cellar. One of the pantries contained a locked door that none of the house keys opened. The agents broke down the door and found that it concealed a bank-size vault. Accardo was called in Palm Springs and he reluctantly gave the G the combination to the vault. Inside Accardo's ten-by-fifteen-foot vault, the agents found two .38-caliber Smith & Wesson revolvers, a pile of bullets, and fifty-five stacks of $50 and $100 bills totaling $250,000. The G confiscated not only the weapons, but the loot, forcing Accardo to spend weeks in courts to have it returned.

---

3. According to a July 15, 1985, article in the *Reno Gazette-Journal*, New Jersey was spending $3.4 million annually on casino regulation, fully ten times what was allocated in Nevada; also, New Jersey appointed 92.3 policing officials per casino, as compared to 1.1 in Nevada.

1981

On June 4, 1981, Accardo was arrested in Chicago, taken downtown in handcuffs, and charged along with sixteen others in a Miami-based scheme to receive $2 million in kickbacks from the medical plan of the 550,000-member Laborers International Union. Using crack Chicago attorney Carl Walsh, Accardo was able to show that the indictment was, for once, specious, there being only hearsay innuendo connecting him to the fraud. When the case was adjudicated, only six of the defendants were convicted. The case was a good example of overzealous prosecutors attempting to utilize RICO, but not taking the time to prove the necessary linkages.

1982–84

In late 1982, as a result of a massive FBI surveillance operation called PENDORF (Penetration of Dorfman), Allen Dorfman was convicted of defrauding the Teamsters pension fund, a display of the proper uses of RICO and Title III. On January 20, 1983, while awaiting sentencing, Dorfman was murdered in the Hyatt Hotel parking lot in Lincolnwood, Illinois. Some believe he was hit to prevent him from cutting a deal with the G; apparently he had been hinting at such a strategy. Gang insiders also claim that boss Joey Lombardo, also convicted in the case, expected Dorfman to bail him out; when he failed to deliver, the murder was ordered. Those same insiders assert that "the big hit" was so important that no Italians were used as executioners, and that mob bail bondsman Irwin Weiner, who had accompanied Dorfman to the Hyatt, had set him up.

But the biggest blow was still to come. Since the late seventies, when the Carter administration had got serious about corruption and ordered hundreds of taps, the FBI, in a two-phase operation code-named Straw-man, had learned of the mob consortium that was skimming the Tropicana (Phase One), and the Stardust, Hacienda, and Marina casinos (Phase Two). At the trial, Teamsters president Roy Williams (who had succeeded Frank Fitzsimmons, who died in 1981) admitted being paid by the mob. Combined with Glick's incriminating testimony, the damning tapes from the conspirators' phone conversations, and a retrieved ledger that described how the skim was divided, the case was so airtight that some of the defendants pled guilty before the jury returned verdicts. Amazingly, Glick claimed to have no idea that Frank Bal was mobster Frank Balistrieri. Bill Ouseley, the lead FBI investigator on the case, said recently that Glick's contention was absurd. "Glick was a brilliant guy," said Ouseley. "Vegas was a cesspool at that time, and everyone knew how the game was played. However, after a long period of working to obtain Glick's testimony, we reached agreement wherein he would be a neutral witness, and we were happy with that."

As a result, many of the mob bosses received stiff sentences, ranging from thirteen to thirty years. In all, there were more than thirty defendants, only one of whom was acquitted. Fronting for Accardo, bosses Joey Aiuppa, then seventy-seven years old, and Jackie Cerone each received a twenty-eight-year term. Once again, Accardo was unscathed. Lead government prosecutor David Helfrey recently opined, "Accardo was definitely involved, but we can't convict without the evidence." Helfrey explained that since Accardo was ostensibly retired in Palm Springs, he was not under electronic surveillance and thus had no incriminating links to convicted boss Joey Aiuppa. And since the defendants did not take the stand, there was no opportunity to draw them out on Accardo. It was a classic use of the Outfit's strategy of the front man/flak-catcher.[4]

On February 23, 1984, a frail, seventy-seven-year-old Joe Accardo appeared under subpoena before the U.S. Permanent Subcommittee on Investigations, which at the time was conducting a scaled-down organized-crime inquiry along the lines of McClellan. Under advice from counsel Carl Walsh, Accardo refused to answer the probers' questions, not citing the Fifth Amendment, but his belief that the foundation for the questions was arrived at through the use of illegal wiretaps. After being cited for contempt of Congress, Accardo's appeals wound their way through the courts until he was ultimately ordered to answer the questions.

On June 21, Accardo appeared before the federal tribunal again, and this time he answered the questions, but in a manner that would have been laughable had they not been coming from a man who appeared as everyone's kindly grandfather.

"I have no knowledge of a crime family in Chicago," Accardo meekly answered Senator William Ross (R-Del.). "I've never been boss." To another query, Accardo said, "I only know about [organized crime] from the newspapers." Incredibly, Accardo claimed that he had no idea what

---

4. For details of the Strawman operation, the reader is urged to read the brilliantly researched *Casino* by Nicholas Pileggi.

Joey Aiuppa did for a living. His sole admission was that he had broken the law many years ago when he had gambled.

Accardo's appearance, altered by the ravages of bouts with cancer and heart disease, apparently affected his inquisitors. Although a perjury citation would obviously have prevailed on appeal, the lawmakers allowed Accardo's testimony, and Accardo himself, to stand unmolested. It now appeared a certainty that Joe Accardo's parroted boast that he had never spent a night in jail would be a permanent memorial.

1992

The year began ominously, with the passing of Joe Accardo's longtime First Ward mouthpiece, Pat Marcy. On May 27, 1992, eighty-six-year-old Joe Accardo, the last surviving Outfit boss, died of heart failure at Chicago's St. Mary of Nazareth Hospital. With all of his best friends having preceded him into the Great Beyond, Joe's wake consisted mostly of family. Buried in the Queen of Heaven cemetery in suburban Hillside, Accardo (as usual) is flanked by allies: the remains of Paul "Ricca" De Lucia on his right and Sam Battaglia on his left. While over at Mt. Carmel Cemetery, Frank Nitti, Dion O'Banion, the Gennas, and Roger Touhy keep Big Al Capone company.

On July 27, 1992, Curly Humphreys' only child, Luella Brady, died, like her father and most of his pals, of heart failure in Norman, Oklahoma, at age fifty-seven. Since Curly's death in 1965, Luella had made yearly pilgrimages to Switzerland to avail herself of her father's nest egg, secreted in a numbered bank account in Zurich. However, due to a combination of mental instability, drug addiction, and, in an ironic twist, given her father's acumen, a naïve business sense, Luella had managed to squander every penny of her father's accumulated treasure. Two years earlier, the Oklahoma State Supreme Court disbarred attorney Coy McKenzie for preying on Luella's instability when he'd convinced her in the early 1980s to invest the last of her inheritance, over $400,000, in a racetrack-purchase scam. The *Daily Oklahoman* summarized the tawdry affair: "A Norman attorney's effort to save a failed racetrack in Stroud led to financial ruin and disbarment for him and left a millionairess destitute and without food."

Adding insult to injury, McKenzie had convinced Luella to put up the 320 acres near Norman that she had also inherited as collateral for a loan when her money ran out. The bank foreclosed on the property, which was eventually sold to a Realtor who parceled out ninety-nine lots that sold for a combined $2.25 million.

1996

On June 20, 1996, the last member of the early Outfit brain trust, Sidney Roy Korshak, died at his home at 808 North Hillcrest Road in Beverly Hills, his brother and confidant, Marshall, having died just the day before in Chicago. Sidney's *New York Times* obituary headline read: SIDNEY KORSHAK, 88, DIES; FABLED FIXER FOR THE CHICAGO MOB. Among those in attendance at Korshak's wake were Barbara Sinatra, Robert Evans, Tony Martin and Cyd Charisse, Angie Dickinson, and Suzanne Pleshette.

And in a last great Outfit money mystery, Sidney Korshak left his wife nothing but their homes. The money had vanished.

Afterword: The Outfit, and Organized Crime, in Perspective

The heirs to Al Capone had an unquestionable impact on twentieth-century America, from their establishment of lotteries and interstate offtrack betting to envisioning Las Vegas, to promoting the ascendancies of Jimmy Hoffa and John Kennedy, to their establishment of key components of the entertainment industry. Of course, the question must be asked, but at what cost? Through its use of murder and mayhem (usually against equally hooligan competitors), the Outfit oversaw a virtual nonstop assault on the Internal Revenue Service, its perennial target, fleecing it out of every cent possible.

What overwhelms the researcher, however, is the degree to which the number of actual Outfit "innocent" victims is out of all proportion to the response of Congress and the Department of Justice. It is a sad fact that underworld crimes pale in comparison to the institutionalized abuses of the upperworld, many of which were committed in partnership with the more vulnerable immigrant hoods. Yet the history of U.S. law enforcement paints a consistent picture of a country that chooses to live in denial of its own national ethos, a choice that condemns it to fostering crime at every level of society. Since its inception, the United States has routinely attacked crime from the bottom up, when, in fact, it is the free ride given the upper class that has inspired generation after generation of new arrivals.

The History of True Organized Crime

The demonization of the lower-class criminal had its roots in the conceptual foundations of Anglo law, formulated in Middle Ages England, and appropriated by the architects of the New World. In attempting to equalize the legal rights of the landed aristocracy and the emerging industrial rich, these two entities reached an understanding wherein they became equal under the law. The lower classes were exempt from the negotiations. By combining an adversarial system of justice with a representative-democracy form of government, the upperworld all but guaranteed that Aristotle's prediction would come to fruition: These dicta would result in the swift evolution to a plutocracy, or government by the rich. (In one year, it was estimated that of thirty successful Senate candidates, twenty-eight of them spent more than their defeated opponents.) In Aristotle's construct, the upper class would always be free to gamble, plunder, and buy alcohol and sex. Because it could afford to hire the best attorneys and to elect puppet officials to create the needed loopholes, the new gentry were allowed to flagrantly break the law in ways cartels such as the Outfit never imagined. Laws were passed to prohibit usury, or loan-sharking, thus to eliminate competition with the upperworld banks. The problem became exacerbated when the banks often refused to make loans to risky, newly arrived citizens, who needed money to survive just as much as those with good credit. Juice men quickly rushed in to fill the void.

Just as the loan sharks filled a vital need for the immigrant wave, so too did the numbers kings, racketeers, and bootleggers, who employed countless unskilled, illiterate workers who would otherwise have been placed on the public dole or, worse, resorted to violent crime.

It has never really been a secret that the American upperworld economy, to say nothing of its legal institutions, is powered by the triple engines of greed, hypocrisy, and, for lack of a better term, linguistic prestidigitation. The nineteenth- and twentieth-century immigrant arrivals deduced this soon after arrival, and some (the underworld) decided to exploit the apparent invitation to villainy, knowing they would likely not be punished if they could quickly make the transition to the thoroughly indemnified upperworld.

Historian Curt Johnson wrote: "An impartial observer might conclude that a history of the United States could be written around instances of the triumph of greed over principle and compassion." Johnson added that the only difference between the upperworld gangsters and the underworld variety was that the lower-class criminals "had guts to spare." He might have added that, at every turn, crime organized by the underworld was dwarfed by that constituted by the upperworld. Sociologist Stanley D. Eitzen determined that the monetary impact of white-collar crime surpassed all forms of street crime by a factor of ten. More important, the American system of justice consistently gives the flagrant white-collar offenders virtual carte blanche, while plastering the nation's front pages with tales of arrests of bank robbers, gambling bosses, bookies, and labor racketeers. This feat of prestidigitation served the purpose of engaging the reader with tales of Capone and Accardo, while distracting them from the far bigger story of massive, routinely sanctioned white-collar crime.

Sociologist Edwin Sutherland, who coined the term *white-collar crime*, pointed out that "white-collar criminals are by far the most dangerous to society of any type of criminals from the point of view of effects on private property and social institutions." (White-collar crime has been defined to include bribery, kickbacks, payoffs, computer crime, consumer and banking fraud, unsafe working conditions, illegal competition, deceptive practices, embezzlement, pilferage, and securities theft.) Sutherland concluded that these "established entrepreneurs" "make Mafias and Crime Syndicates look like pushcart operations." Sutherland described the chief difference between underworld and upperworld crime thus: "[The underworld gangsters] have indeed the requisite qualities of ruthlessness and unscrupulousness but lack finesse." Professor David Bell, a former chairman of Columbia University's department of sociology, also challenged Congress' and the Department of Justice's tunnel vision. Bell concluded that underworld crime represented merely a stepping-stone, if a vulgar one, used by some immigrants to overcome extreme prejudice on their way to legitimate lifestyles. There was no mysterious international "Mafia" committed to crime for crime's sake. In Bell's view, Estes Kefauver, for example, failed to understand "the process of ethnic succession."

The protocols that gave white-collar criminals a wide berth in the United States were established when the first English settlers arrived in the New World in the seventeenth century. According to Randall M. Miller, author of *The Dictionary of African American Slavery,* approximately six hundred thousand Africans were abducted from their homeland over a 350-year period. Eventually, their descendants, also slaves, numbered some four million (by 1860). The abhorrent practice was legitimized by Thomas Jefferson and the Founding Fathers, who together crafted what should have been called "The Declaration of Independence for White Anglo-Saxon Protestants." It has long been painfully obvious that the Founding Fathers' high-minded talk of liberty and virtue was mere rhetoric designed to disguise the new country's true mandate to sanctify greed, or, in their euphemism, "manifest destiny."

Benjamin Franklin and George Washington broke with Great Britain not merely over a quest for personal liberty, but also a desire to be free to take "Indian" property west of the Appalachians, a policy that the Brits had prohibited. John Hancock signed on because, as one of the biggest New World smugglers, he stood to lose a fortune if forced to pay British import taxes.

Under the Founders' watch, the systematic destruction of the Native American culture was undertaken. Before the Revolution, Jefferson had written in *A Summary View of the Rights of British America* that the land and the riches in the New World were "undoubtedly of the allodial nature." Untwisting this tortured language, what the racist Jefferson was saying was "To the victor go the spoils." Jefferson showed his more compassionate side when he suggested that the WASP invaders should initially attempt to steal the natives' possessions nonviolently. He wrote that the Chickasaw tribe should be encouraged to run up unpayable debts at the government stores. "They will always cede lands," Jefferson wrote, "to rid themselves of debt." When that gambit proved not speedy enough, the erudite framers looked the other way as the West was taken through outright slaughter. Colin G. Calloway, author of *American Revolution in Indian Country*, wrote, "Thomas Jefferson wanted to see the Ohio Shawnees exterminated or driven from their lands." At the time, the native population was estimated to have exceeded eight million. By 1900, that figure had plummeted to 120,000. When the Nazi's acted similarly in the twentieth century it was rightly called genocide.

Jefferson simultaneously established a brothel near his University of Virginia so that the white-collar intelligentsia would have a respite from the stresses of academic life.

The Blue Bloods Set the Standard for America's Underworld

Law? What do I care for the law? Hain't I got the power?
                                                    –Commodore Vanderbilt

I owe the public nothing.

                                                    –J. P. Morgan

If you steal $25 you're a thief. If you steal $250,000, you're an embezzler. If you steal $2,500,000, you're a financier.
                                                    –An unknown Roaring Twenties journalist

Simultaneous with the Western land grabs was the consolidation of the American infrastructure by the "robber barons." These upperworld gangsters (Rockefeller, Morgan, Whitney, Vanderbilt, etc.) systematically bribed and/or blackmailed state and federal officials to allow them to loot the country's natural resources such as oil and iron ore. During the upperworld's formative years in the New World, they manipulated enough congressional votes to have the government turn over all the land they needed to construct railroads, an area equaling that of the state of Texas. Instead of taking over the unions, à la Curly Humphreys, the white-collar criminals destroyed them, allowing the entrepreneurs to mine the new country's natural resources by utilizing the sweat of slaves, indentured or otherwise. After destroying labor unions such as the National Labor Union and the Knights of Labor, the industrialists forced Irish, Italian, Chinese, and other non-WASP immigrants to build their railroads and dig their mines.

Worker safety was rarely addressed, and then only if it increased the profit margin. Nineteenth-century mine fatalities alone are estimated at two thousand per year. Working fourteen-hour days, six days per week, men, women, and children took home a scant $15 per week, while one of the wealthiest men in the country, Secretary of the Treasury Andrew Mellon, slashed the taxes of the upper class from 50 to 25 percent (while the poor saw a minuscule drop from 4 to 3 percent.) In the 1930s, billionaire Andrew Mellon told a Senate committee that he indeed used thugs to break workers' unions in building his empire. "You couldn't run without them," he callously testified. In his 1976 study, *Gamblers and Gambling,* sociologist Robert D. Herman concluded, "Many of America's great family fortunes were not so much built as taken."

In creating his oil monopoly, John D. Rockefeller in essence formed what Capone biographer Laurence Bergreen called "the most lucrative racket in the country." The notorious monopolist used bribery, collusion, and predatory pricing to establish Standard Oil. As America's biggest racketeer, Rockefeller also burned down the oil derricks of competitors such as Pennsylvania's Sun Oil. When one feisty competitor, Tidewater Pipeline Company, refused to cave in, Rockefeller's boys plugged up its pipelines and bribed judges to enjoin its bonds. His great-grandson Senator John D. "Jay" Rockefeller admitted, "The business practices then were completely different from those of the modern era." Capone's descendants must wish they could use the same excuse.

In the Outfit's home base of Chicago, financier Samuel "Emperor" Insull, the founder of General Electric, invested in rigged stocks and, like Capone, contributed heavily to the campaigns of the corrupt Mayor Bill Thompson, the better to guarantee that his power monopoly remain unscathed by officialdom. When Insull required protection from his many enemies, he hired none other than Capone and the Syndicate, who obliged until they learned that the stingy Insull refused to pay the bodyguards' salaries. Likewise, publishing magnate Moe Annenberg built his fortune on the backs of Capone's and O'Banion's gangsters.

The institutionalized crime of the upperworld became so flagrant that poet-songwriter Woody Guthrie memorialized it in his song "Pretty Boy Floyd":

> Now as through this world I ramble,
> I see lots of funny men,
> Some will rob you with a six gun,
> And some with a fountain pen.
>
> But as through this life you travel
> And as through your life you roam,
> You won't ever see an outlaw
> Drive a family from their home.[1]

In the very year that Al Capone was sent to Alcatraz for cheating the IRS out of $215,000 in income tax, the richest man in the world, J. Pierpont Morgan, paid not one cent to the taxman. Supreme Court justice Louis Brandeis wrote that J. P. Morgan symbolized 'monopolistic and predatory control over the financial resources of the country.' (Morgan's father had made a fortune during the Civil War, in which he dodged service, by buying defective carbine rifles from the government and then selling them back to the unsuspecting feds at an enormous profit. Morgan was not the only upperworld Civil War profiteer. The Du Pont family formed a cartel of gunpowder manufacturers by bombing their competitors' plants into oblivion.)

As if to construct a physical metaphor for the double standard of justice that allowed them to thrive, the white-collar criminals used their plunder to appropriate all the prime Long Island beachfronts, then walled out the great unwashed. Robert A. Caro, in his profile of builder Robert Moses, *The Power Broker,* brilliantly depicted how the upperworld gangster elite used their collective clout to prevent city dwellers from availing themselves of the beautiful North and South Shore waterfronts. Not only did they

---

1. *Pretty Boy Floyd* by Woody Guthrie Copyright © 1958 (renewed) by SANGA MUSIC, INC. All rights reserved. Used by permission.

purchase immense tracts of land, much of it used only to prevent public access, they also prevented the roadways from being repaired or expanded beyond two lanes. During the steamy New York summers, the upperworld scions sat outside at their walled estates, laughing at the bumper-to-bumper traffic that searched in vain for a public beach. "If they swam on Long Island," Caro wrote, "they swam in their cars in their sweat."

"They feared that [New York's] 'foreigners,' hordes of long-haired Slavs, hook-nosed Jews, and unwashed Irishmen, would descend on and befoul their beautiful beaches at the first slackening in their vigilance," wrote Caro. When the Mosquito Control Commission solicited contributions for spraying, blue bloods such as Mrs. Robert Hollins declined, fearing that without the pests, more "foreigners" might attempt to move in. "I'd rather have the mosquitoes," said Hollins.

By 1934, both AT&T and Western Union, which had made millions leasing their wires to the mob, had smooth-talked their way out of congressional censure and Justice Department indictments. When Truman's underworld sponsor, Tom Pendergast, was convicted in 1939, little attention was given to his upperworld partners, executives of four insurance companies who had paid Pendergast $750,000 in bribes, then skated free. Likewise, when the American Tobacco Company was caught bribing federal judge Martin Manton to the tune of $250,000, Manton was convicted; the tobacco executive who had made the bribe arrangements was promoted to vice president of the company.

The upperworld gangsters extended their reach throughout the hemisphere, where they routinely paid for the overthrows of unfriendly heads of state. In Europe, the Du Ponts and Fords joined International Telephone and Telegraph building factories that profited through selling planes, tanks, and fuel to the regime of Adolf Hitler. And when World War II ended, these same entities collected $27 million from the U.S. government as reparations for damage the Allies had inflicted on their German factories.

In the early fifties, Meyer Ditlove, Joe Siciliano, and others were jailed for their roles in Chicago's "horseburger" episode. The spiking of ground beef with horsemeat was not known to have sickened, let alone killed, anyone. At the same time, according to the U.S. Department of Agriculture, upperworld-owned food-processing plants knowingly sold food contaminated with cockroaches, flies, rodents, mouse droppings, fecal and urine waste, pesticides, mercury, and salmonella, resulting in four thousand food-poisoning deaths per year and millions of cases of nonfatal food poisoning. The deaths were expedited by the routine bribing of U.S.

Department of Agriculture inspectors by the food industry. It is believed that, unlike the horsemeat scammers, no food industry executive has ever been imprisoned for the processing crimes.

In 1954, Westinghouse and General Electric held secret meetings in a conspiracy to acquire lucrative government contracts, the result of which cheated government out of $1 billion. After a seven-year investigation, forty-five executives were indicted, but only five went to prison, for twenty-five days each.

Also during the midfifties, Brown & Williamson Tobacco executives discussed in secret memos "burying unfavorable test results" on their product, which they confidentially referred to as "nicotine delivery systems." One such memo noted that the product contained the powerful carcinogen benzopyrene. Since the midfifties, it is estimated that cigarette smoke has killed more than fifteen million people. No tobacco executive has served a day in prison.

In 1958, Hooker Chemical Company learned that the twenty million pounds of chemical waste it had dumped in an abandoned waterway near Niagara Falls, New York, contained not only dioxin, but benzene, which was considered, according to Hooker's own documents, "the most powerful carcinogen known." In efforts to avoid a $50-million cleanup, Hooker failed to tell the Love Canal school board, to whom they had sold the property to erect a school. The chickens came home to roost years later, when many of those who had attended the elementary school grew up and tried to have their own children. A survey by the New York health commissioner noted: "In a neighborhood not far from Love Canal, only one of the sixteen pregnancies in 1979 ended in the birth of a healthy baby, while four ended in miscarriages, two babies were stillborn, and nine were born deformed." After sixteen years of court wrangling, Hooker's parent company, Occidental Petroleum, agreed to pay for the cost of the clean up. No one went to prison.

Similarly, the Environmental Protection Agency (EPA) found that Dow Chemical, best known for producing napalm, Agent Orange, and feel-good television commercials, was releasing six times the accepted limit of dioxin into the air around its Midland, Michigan, plant, the cause, or so suspected by the EPA, of a local infant mortality rate 67 percent above normal. No one has ever been charged.

Even before they sold their first Pinto model in the 1970s, the Ford Motor Company discovered that the car had a gas tank design flaw that would cause the car to explode on rear impact. Although the company's actuarial studies predicted more than 180 deaths would occur, they calculated that settling the resultant lawsuits would be far cheaper ($49.5 million) than retooling the production line ($137 million) and thus decided to sell the deadly fireball compact car. In doing so, the callous executives were merely following the dictates of their founder, Henry Ford, who once said, "There is something sacred about big business. Anything which is economically right is morally right."

Ford spokesmen later said that only twenty-six people had died from the Pinto explosions, but independent studies by others such as Ralph Nader put the figure closer to five hundred. No Ford executive was ever imprisoned for what the families of those victimized accurately termed serial murder. In 1979, writer Mark Dowie observed: "One wonders how long Ford would continue to market lethal cars were Chairman Henry Ford II and [President] Lee Iacocca serving twenty-year terms in Leavenworth for consumer homicide." One can only imagine the outcry had Joe Accardo or Mooney Giancana murdered five hundred total strangers in order to fill the Outfit's coffers.

In the 1980s major cocaine smuggler Bert Gordon flew Columbian coke from the Bahamas into the United States, using Florida's Homestead Air Force Base as a landing point. Gordon did this with the assistance of U.S. customs agents. "We'd come into Homestead," Gordon told senior NBC investigator Ira Silverman, "and they'd use a customs van, back up to the plane, and we'd load it up – about one thousand kilos at a time." Although Gordon was eventually sent to prison, the customs officers went unscathed; one now operates a lucrative commercial fishing venture in the Bahamas.

On July 17, 1981, a concrete skybridge on the Kansas City Hyatt Hotel collapsed, killing 111 and injuring another 200. Although the National Bureau of Standards found that engineers had knowingly violated Kansas City building codes, no one was even indicted.

Meanwhile in Washington, the Reagan-Bush administrations guaranteed that corporate greed would be encouraged and rewarded. During the 1980s, thanks to federal decrees, the income of the country's wealthiest 5 percent increased by 60 percent, while the poorest 20 percent saw only a 3 percent rise; the wealthy also realized a 10 percent tax decrease, while those in the lowest 20 percent bracket experienced a tax *increase* of 16 percent. As the widening financial gulf between the rich and the poor exacerbated the polarization of the social classes, the crackdown on underworld crime escalated, with the Department of Justice trumpeting its RICO successes.

In the mid-1980s, after Operation Strawman, the upperworld took over Las Vegas and pronounced that everything was now sanitized enough to bring the kiddies along. Much of "the New Vegas" was financed by fraudulent "junk bonds," floated by Michael Milken and others. The new veneer in fact only eliminated the underworld gangs' skim operations; the essential immorality of the rigged games remains in place. B. J. Jahoda was an Outfit soldier in charge of running the games in the Vegas casinos from 1975 until the Strawman trial, in which he was a key witness. In 1992, Jahoda wrote to Robert Fuesel, the director of the Chicago Crime Commission, and gave his educated opinion of "the New Vegas":

> All organized gambling, legal and illegal, is a zero-sum game intentionally designed so that, over time, the player ends up with the zero and the house ends up with the sum. It has always been so and so it will always remain.
>
> Organized gambling creates and manufactures nothing except smoke, false promises, and hard dollars at the expense of the unwary.
>
> And while all forms of organized gambling are parasitic by their very nature, none, not even the Outfit's, can match or exceed the predatory and rat-hearted level at which many of the major casinos routinely operate.

It was just as Commission partner Meyer Lansky had predicted in his diary, which was released by his granddaughter Cynthia Duncan in 2001. "The whole thing will be taken over by the Puritan establishment," Lansky had written years earlier. Lansky added, "My crime is now accepted and made legal in most of our states. And gambling taken over by the hypocritical mob of stock swindlers with the protection of all law enforcement who until now would call casino gambling immoral."

In the 1990s, the new "clean" Vegas owners contributed over $16 million to both political parties in a successful attempt to stall legislation aimed at outlawing betting on college sports (a $2-billion-per-year business), which remains legal only in Nevada. The college betting boom started in 1974, when Vegas bookies "persuaded" Congress to drop the 10 percent tax surcharge on sports betting to a negligible 2 percent. The game-rigging, bribes, and point-shaving that have since gone hand in hand with "the Vegas line" have resulted in the expulsion and imprisonment of numerous college athletes, many of whom shaved points to get out from under massive gambling debts. National politicians such as

Trent Lott, Richard Gephardt, Orrin Hatch, and Charles Rangel have received the royal treatment, including junkets on corporate jets, from Vegas moguls such as Steve Wynn, founder of the Mirage. Senator Hatch initially promised to cosponsor the remedial legislation, only to do a last-minute about-face. A Senate staffer told *Time* magazine, "[Hatch] told them it would impact his ability to raise money for [the GOP's Senate fund-raising committee] from the gambling industry." Although the NCAA favors a legislative ban, they are not allowed to make congressional contributions due to their tax-exempt status and have minimal lobbying funds available to counteract the corporate deluge.

The cost of paying off Phoenix real estate developer Charles Keating's debts for his fraudulent S&L, Lincoln Savings and Loan, came to $3.4 billion, far more than the total loss in all the bank robberies committed by the underworld *for the last hundred years.* Yet 91 percent of hoods who are convicted of bank robbery go to jail, while only 17 percent of those convicted of major bank embezzlement are sent away – and an even smaller percentage of embezzlers are ever convicted in the first place. During the period of the Lincoln S&L scam, the Keating family was paid $34 million, at a cost to twenty thousand bank customers who were knowingly sold worthless junk bonds to finance the scheme. One Lincoln sales memo noted: "The weak, meek, and ignorant are always good targets." Keating was eventually convicted on seventy-three counts, which could have called for a 525-year prison term. Keating served a mere three years before his federal conviction was overturned in 1996 on a technicality.

In 1988, the Ford Motor Company was once again shown to have sacrificed lives in its zeal to save money on gas tank repairs. In its desire to avoid making $76 million in improvements to the gas tanks of its bus fleet, Ford allowed unsafe vehicles to be sold to the unsuspecting public. On May 14, 1988, the gas tank of a Ford-built Kentucky school bus exploded, killing twenty-four children and three adults. In the lawsuit that followed, the court said, "The conduct of Ford's management was reprehensible in the extreme. It exhibited a conscious and callous disregard of public safety in order to maximize corporate profits." Ford was fined $10 million in the 1988 episode, the same year it turned nearly a $500-million profit.

In 1989, a Department of Energy nuclear weapons plant in Rocky Flats, Colorado, was found to be so contaminated that it will remain dangerous for twenty-four thousand years. The cleanup is estimated to cost $2 billion. Worse still was the finding that Rockwell International, which ran the plant, had been dumping radioactive waste into local rivers. In 1989, the Justice Department refused to sign criminal grand jury indictments, opting instead to accept a plea-bargained $18.5-million fine. However, the Department of Energy simultaneously gave Rockwell a $22.6-million "performance bonus," which resulted in a $4.1-million profit for the year. No one went to jail.

Recently, it has been learned that numerous U.S. financial institutions have quietly been fostering the drug cartels that currently enslave those who thought they were emancipated by Lincoln or the Civil Rights Act. In 1996, Los Angeles customs agents began an elaborate sting operation, named Operation Casablanca, aimed at penetrating money laundering of the Colombian drug cartel's profits in the Southwest. At the time, it was estimated that an astounding $600 million was being laundered *per day*, worldwide. The customs agents set up their own money-laundering setup just outside L.A. and, over two years, washed $180 million in their scheme to penetrate the intricacies of the international money-laundering enterprise.

When the operation reached fruition in 1998, three Mexican banks, dozens of their executives, and high-ranking members of the Mexican government were shown to be involved in the drug cartel's money-laundering scheme. Although this part of Operation Casablanca was widely reported in the U.S. press, what was not covered was the complicity of U.S. financial institutions in the massive lawbreaking. One of the customs officers involved told investigators Denton and Morris, "Not a dollar was laundered by a Mexican bank that wasn't in a U.S. account under American scrutiny at one time or another." Based on their research, Denton and Morris concluded: "Operation Casablanca would document over a hundred money-laundering accounts in the case tracing to more than seventy U.S. banks, including many of the nation's most powerful and respected – among them, Chase Manhattan, Banker's Trust, Bank of New York, Chemical Bank, Citibank, Great Western, Nationsbank, Norwest, American Express Bank, and scores of others."

Denton and Morris found that in just the Florida banks implicated, the fraudulent trade transactions conducted by the banks to cover the laundering cost the American public $50 billion per year in lost tax revenue.

Despite the discoveries of Operation Casablanca, no U.S. banking executive has even been charged, nor will they likely be.

Another way the upperworld facilitates the money-laundering desires of the cocaine traffickers is by allowing them to purchase hundreds of millions of dollars in U.S. goods, which are then shipped to South America to be resold legally. The companies involved include many on the country's most high-profile corporations. In 2000, IRS investigator Michael McDonald told PBS's *Frontline* producer Lowell Bergman for his "Drug Wars" program, "Most of these companies know that they're getting paid with money that comes from the black market. And the black market is fueled by the drug trade." Greg Passic of the DEA told Bergman, "We've got the Fortune 500 involved in our drug-money laundering process." The legal concept is known as 'willful blindness,' and although hundreds of major U.S. firms are known to be committing it daily, no executive has even been charged. But interestingly, cigarette giants Philip Morris and British American Tobacco have been accused in a *Colombian* civil action of laundering drug money through sales of their tobacco products.

All told, according to the U.S. Chamber of Commerce, white-collar crime accounts for a minimum $40 billion annual loss to the U.S. economy, above and beyond the tax issue. And yet John Gotti's life in prison still gets the lion's share of press attention.

Government Crime

The abduction of half a million Africans and the holocaust perpetrated against the Native American culture were but the first chapters in the history of government-sponsored organized crime. Although every stratum of officialdom has been implicated, the example has often been set at the very top: The administrations of Presidents Ulysses Grant, Martin Van Buren, Warren Harding, and Harry Truman were all tainted by scandals involving influence peddling and insider profiteering. Lyndon Johnson rose to prominence via fixed senatorial elections in Texas; Dwight Eisenhower installed a dictatorial shah in oil-rich Iran, against the desires of the populace, resulting in the murders of hundreds of thousands of dissidents; John F. Kennedy's father enlisted the underworld in his son's cause; Richard Nixon conspired to prevent the incumbent president, Lyndon Johnson, from succeeding in arranging Vietnamese peace talks in 1968 and then, as President, presided over the deaths of two million Asians and authorized the wholesale trampling of the U.S. Constitution to save his political skin; Ronald Reagan's aides blocked the release of the Iranian hostages to prevent President Jimmy Carter from winning the 1980 contest; George Bush presided over the slaughter of hundreds of thousands of Iraqis to keep U.S. oil interests assuaged; and George, Jr.'s administration backed the Olympic bid of repressive China (which executed seventeen hundred political prisoners in 2000 alone), largely to appease the expansionist interests of U.S. upperworld businesses.

In 1932, the U.S. Public Health Service began a forty-year project to withhold curative treatments from four hundred black male syphilis sufferers in Tuskegee, Alabama. The men, who were regarded as guinea pigs not unlike the Jews in Hitler's World War II death camps, were not even told of their illness. When the abomination came to light in 1972, an Alabama court awarded the survivors, many of whom were now blind or insane, the grand total of $2.50 for each day they had been in the experiment. Unlike at Nuremberg, no one was ever imprisoned.

Toward a New Definition of "Organized Crime"

For those Americans not in denial of their history, the term *organized crime* has always meant something other than Al Capone, Mooney Giancana, or Meyer Lansky. Without doubt, the best organized crime in the United States is a coalition of upperworld businessmen, pliant politicians, and corrupted law enforcement officers. "Corruption is as American as cherry pie," wrote author and former Senate staff member Nathan Miller. "Graft and corruption played a vital role in the development of modern American society and the creation of the complex, interlocking machinery of government and business that determines the course of our affairs."

The crimes of this shadowy partnership surpass in spades the criminal escapades of underworld cliques like Chicago's Outfit. However, this very upperworld paradigm gives both rationale and inspiration to the underworld gangsters we choose to vilify in their stead. As a society we no longer have to purchase our vices from gangsters: We can merely sit at home and, thanks to the General Motors-owned DirecTV, have pornography delivered straight to our television sets (or to our Hilton Hotel room in Vegas); through state-sponsored commercials, we are enticed to play the G's lottery, a game so tilted in the state's favor as to make the hoods' numbers racket seem like charity.

A modest proposal: Both the press and the Justice Department should suspend their infatuation with gangsters and instead direct their resources toward the criminals who, in proportion, deserve the long overdue attention. There is little belief here that this will or can actually happen unless the citizenry demands it. It is my earnest hope that this book will in some small way help awaken the sleeping giant.

Appendix:
The Outfit and Gambling

It has been called the "meat and potatoes" of organized crime, providing an uninterrupted flow of income for the nation's generations of hoods. Gambling was also a close runner-up to booze and sex as the most desired vice secretly coveted by the repressed Puritans of early America. Boston mob boss Vinnie Teresa opined, "Gambling is the standby and the foundation. From it comes the corrupt politicians and policemen, the bribes and the payoffs, and sometimes murder. If you could crush gambling, you would put the mob out of business."

Gambling, like alcohol consumption, was recognized by the nineteenth-century Euro immigrants as a fundamental human drive that would probably someday be legalized. Luckily for them, it wasn't yet, allowing the new arrivals to have the playing field to themselves if they so desired. The early gangs knew what it took officialdom many years to admit. In 1985, law professor Jerome Skolnick told the President's Commission on Organized Crime something it probably already knew: "Clearly, gambling is not perceived as a deplorable evil by an overwhelming majority of Americans." Dr. Gustav Carlson, a sociologist and gambling expert, pointed out that gambling is a universal human activity.

Although gambling is most obviously tied to the genetic mandate for self-preservation (i.e., money = security), Skolnick pointed out that there was much more to the subject. He noted that the compulsion to gamble is an extremely complex drive, but is clearly linked to a person's desire to exponentially increase his interest in any event he or she is observing. "Gambling seems, above all, then, to offer self-interested recreational involvement," Skolnick said. And it does not take a large wager to greatly affect the gambler's interest in an observed event. "A ten-dollar bet is what keeps a Chicago fan from turning off a televised football game

Miami and Chicago," Skolnick testified. The eminent University ...fornia scholar went on to point out the many paradoxes in the long ...ry of illegal gambling, especially noting the otherwise antigambling ...holic Church's flourishing bingo enterprises. Social scientist Robert ...erman, writing in *Gamblers and Gambling,* asserts that the tug of gambling is also linked to the need for personal autonomy. Herman wrote, "[Gamblers] seek an activity that allows them to set themselves individually apart, to establish their distinctiveness, and their autonomy."

Skolnick also addressed the more serious gambling associated with horse racing and casinos, noting that "deep play" was a mark of social status dating back to sixteenth-century English noblemen. Anthropologist Geoffrey Gorer, in *The American People: A Study in National Character,* called the gambler's winnings "the adult equivalent of the marks and grades which signified the schoolchild's relative position in regard to his fellows." Legendary Las Vegas oddsmaker Nick the Greek perhaps summed up all the theorizing most succinctly: "Money is just a way of keeping score."

It is doubtful that Joe Accardo and his crew spent any time debating the allure of gambling. But they certainly were experts in the ways of satiating the gamblers' cravings. Like alcohol, gambling (especially lotteries, off-track betting, and slots) would eventually be legitimized by the upperworld. But until that day, gangs like the Outfit were more than happy to fill the supplier void.

Chicago enjoyed a long history with gamblers and their culture. And since the days of nineteenth-century gambling czar Mike McDonald, Chicago officialdom happily looked the other way – at least as long as the graft kept flowing. After McDonald, Jacob "Mont" Tennes took up the baton, using the newly devised telegraph wires to transmit instant horse-racing odds and results to "handbook" operators (authorized bet-takers operating in poolrooms and bars). In 1911, Tennes spent a rumored $20,000 to insure the election of Mayor Carter H. Harrison. Former director of the Chicago Crime Commission (CCC) Virgil Peterson wrote: "With the election of Harrison it was commonly understood that gambling would be permitted to flourish without interference from the police." The CCC learned that the number of gambling establishments in the Loop was doubling every two months. Harrison's City Hall and police department were even found to have sided with Tennes in his war with the wire service competitor, the Payne New Agency. A Civil Service Commission inquiry concluded that the pols had conspired with Tennes' General

News Bureau to drive out "nonsyndicate" gamblers, essentially guaranteeing an uninterrupted flow of payoffs to the corrupt officials. It also guaranteed the constant reelection of Harrison, who served for five terms.

After the Tennes-Harrison association came the Capone-Thompson arrangement, which permitted the Capone Syndicate to propagate in the twenties. Now, with Capone's heirs running the games, the latest pushover to occupy the mayor's office was the notorious Ed Kelly. When Outfit adversary Mayor Anton Cermak was assassinated in 1933, it fell to Cook County Democratic Party chairman Pat Nash to appoint a successor. Nash, a tax cheat to the tune of $175,000, chose the even more corrupt chief sanitation engineer, Ed Kelly, to assume the mayoralty. Kelly had already been indicted three times for fraud involving civil workers who had grown rich off patronage without having worked a single day. Kelly later admitted that, while with Sanitation, he had an annual salary of just over $13,000, but a total income of $66,000.

In the years after Kelly's mayoral ascension, the Internal Revenue Service found that he had grossly underreported his income. It seemed Kelly had earned at least $750,000 per year above his salary from "incidental income" – in other words, graft. That estimate may have been conservative. The Chicago Crime Commission estimated that the Kelly-Nash machine received $20 million per year from the Outfit alone to allow its gambling empire to proceed undeterred. "The fix is in at the top," said one local observer. The CCC's Virgil Peterson called the Kelly-Nash machine "one of the most ruthless political organizations in American political history." The machine operated smoothly for fourteen years, thanks in large part to the self-perpetuating nature of the patronage system and the flagrant vote fraud that accompanied Kelly's reelections. Adding in the muscle of the Outfit for good measure, Chicago had the greatest vote-producing machine in American history.

Much like Volstead's nonimpact on America's thirst, the outlawing of gambling parlors in the nineteenth century only forced the players to go underground, and not very deep at that. Thus, before legalized casino gambling in the twentieth century, the only place a blackjack, craps (dice), or poker aficionado could obtain any real action was at illegal gambling parlors run by the local crime syndicate. Often, the big-stakes players were forced to locate a movable feast, otherwise known as a floating game. In this version, only gamblers who were known to the organizers were directed by intermediaries to the one-night-only site for the big game, usually in a well-guarded rural locale.

The Chicago underworld not only profited from indoor table games, but from outdoor sporting events such as horse racing. It is generally believed that Al Capone became involved in the races in 1927. At the time, the sport of kings was in transition. When horse racing debuted in nineteenth-century Europe, it was the domain of the leisure class. However, the lower classes soon co-opted the sport for themselves, not by competing for ownership of the expensive equines, but by wagering on the races they ran. This led to rampant race fixing by anyone with access to the stables: jockeys, trainers, stable boys, etc. In America, the Whitneys and Vanderbilts were shocked to learn that their "pets" were being routinely doped, jabbed with electric prods, or raced under false names. In 1894, industrialist J. P. Morgan joined banker August Belmont in providing low-interest loans to a failing U.S. Treasury. Their resultant influence in Washington virtually guaranteed that the government would take a laissez-faire attitude when Morgan, Belmont, and others set up their own racing monopoly in New York, The American Jockey Club. This trust gave the upperworld total control of licensing for jockeys, trainers, and owners. In 1905, Morgan and Belmont built Belmont Park racetrack in New York.

But the abuses continued unabated, and pressure mounted from prohibition-type reformers to enact the thoroughbred version of Volstead. Much as they would with the sale of alcohol, most states outlawed horse racing altogether during a reform wave in 1908. Some entrepreneurs, such as Kansas City boss Tom Pendergast, ran "underground" horse-racing tracks despite the bans. By the 1920s, operators like Al Capone embraced dog racing, as yet not rendered illegal, as their entry-level sport. Fronting for Capone, before the ascent of Accardo, were Johnny Patton and "Artful" Eddie O'Hare, nicknamed for his sartorial splendor. Patton was known as the Boy Mayor, being the twenty-five-year-old mayor of the Chicago suburb of Burnham. He was known to associate with the Syndicate since at least 1925, when he convinced Johnny Torrio to purchase the Arrowhead Inn and convert it into a brothel/saloon (see Prologue). Torrio made Patton the club's manager, and Mayor Patton hired his chief of police to tend bar while many Burnham town officials moonlighted as waiters. That same year, 1925, the Boy Mayor was briefly arrested with Frank Nitti. After Torrio returned to New York, Patton was absorbed first into the Capone gang, for whom he also dabbled in political fixes, and eventually the Outfit.

A natural athlete who excelled at golf, horseback riding, and swimming, Edward O'Hare was a cultivated and skilled attorney, who gave the impression that his only criminal activity involved his racing businesses with Capone and Patton. "You can make money through business associations with gangsters," O'Hare said, "and you will run no risk if you don't associate personally with them. Keep it on a business level and there's nothing to fear." It was a fine line that O'Hare futilely attempted to walk. In actuality, during prohibition, O'Hare had been arrested for using his office to store $200,000 worth of whiskey for national bootlegging king George Remus. He was released only after cutting a deal with Remus, with each refusing to testify against the other. In addition, it is commonly understood in Chicago that O'Hare took a hefty agent's fee for managing the gang's Wall Street investments. As with innumerable other upperworld businessmen, O'Hare was happy to use the gangs to get rich, but would sell them out at the drop of a hat. When he tried to scam the Outfit, his luck ran out. Years after the Big Guy's conviction, Nitti and Accardo learned that O'Hare had tipped off the court that Capone possessed the jury list and was prepared to fix his 1931 tax trial. (Recall that it was the last-minute jury switch that sealed Capone's conviction.) O'Hare had also pointed the feds to Capone's bookkeeper, a turn that became a critical component of the prosecution's case. Worse still, "the boys" were told that O'Hare had continuously informed for the government in the years after Capone's trial. Thus on November 8, 1939, while the stoolie O'Hare was driving down Ogden Avenue, another car pulled alongside and its two occupants drew their shotguns, blasting him into oblivion. Eight days later, Al Capone was released from prison. Those on the streets of Cicero understood that O'Hare's murder was intended as a coming-out gift for the Big Guy. So much for there being "nothing to fear."[1]

The Capone-Patton-O'Hare triumvirate chose Capone's town, Cicero, as the site for their first dog track, the Laramie Kennel Club, later renamed the Hawthorne Kennel Club. (In a few years, the track would be switched over to harness horse racing, once Capone's councilman, "Mr. Malaprop" Libonati, introduced legislation authorizing the change. In this incarnation, the track would be called Sportsman's Park.)

The Syndicate's racing gig was so successful that it began expanding across the country. From Florida to California, Patton-O'Hare-Capone

---

1. After World War II, Chicago renamed its airport after Eddie's son, Butch, who died a war hero.

opened new tracks. The expansion also helped reinforce bonds with other crime cartels. In Coral Gables, Florida, for instance, the Syndicate partnered with its slot-machine colleague New York boss Meyer Lansky in running the Tropical Park track. With regional gangs working in concert, racing seasons were scheduled so as not to conflict. In Florida, Johnny Patton, already skilled at the art of the fix, greased the palms of the local pols, assuring that the mob tracks in Coral Gables, Miami, and Tampa were given wide berth. Patton eventually contributed $100,000 to the successful 1948 gubernatorial campaign of Warren Fuller.

With the gangs now running both legal and underground tracks, abuses quickly appeared. Horse-doping with drugs such as cocaine, bribed jockeys, and the use of ringers occurred regularly. After Volstead was repealed, it was wrongly believed that legalizing the tracks would drive the gangs out. Thus, after prohibition ended, the horse-racing ban was also lifted. But the gangs remained in control. In fact, descendants of the Capone family continue to run Sportsman's Park to this day.

Vegas

When the Chicago underworld expanded its gambling empire into Nevada, it chose a locale uniquely positioned to accept legalized gambling.

At about the same time that Thomas Jefferson was putting the finishing touches on the Declaration of Independence, a band of Spanish conquistadores led by Padre Escalante ventured northward from Mexico into a territory later annexed by Jefferson's new world and subsequently named Nevada. When the explorers discovered an artesian spring in the southern part of the region, they christened the area Las Vegas, or the Meadows. After the conclusion of the Mexican-American War in 1848, the Spaniards ceded the harsh terrain to the new nation, and the settlement became little more than a comfort station between major cities. In 1855, Mormon leader Brigham Young dispatched missionaries to Las Vegas from Utah in a vain attempt to convert the Paiute Indians. After three years, the mission foundered, but the Mormons retained a strong presence in northern Nevada, especially in the area that would become Reno and the state capital, Carson City. The Mormons became the dominating force in the Nevada state legislature, where they inserted their belief system into the state's legal code and licensing procedures. One of the religion's core tenets is the superiority of fair-skinned people, with the Mormons holding that they are descended from a sixth-century explorer to the New World named Nephi, who was "white and delightsome," as opposed to his brother, the evil Laman, who was "dark and loathsome." The Mormons' dogmatic resentment of darker-skinned peoples would become important a century later when olive-skinned Sicilians appeared before them requesting gambling licenses. And although the Mormons were strictly forbidden to gamble, their leadership encouraged them to provide not only the workforce but the financing for the profitable casino industry. A century after the failed missionary settlement, the Mormon-owned Bank of Las Vegas would provide critical capitalization for some of the city's most lucrative casinos.

Around the turn of the century, southern Nevada experienced a temporary gold and silver rush in the arid Eldorado and McCullough mountain ranges that encircle Las Vegas. With grizzled prospectors in need of R&R, Vegas became a low-class vice district that featured gambling, which was sporadically legal throughout this period. After the mines had been stripped bare in a mere ten years, many southern Nevada towns, including Las Vegas, began the slide toward their previous status as ghost towns. It now appears that when state officials considered ways to rejuvenate the state's stalled economy, they were aided in their discussion by Curly Humphreys and the Outfit, who were conveniently expanding their dog-racing ventures in the state. The relaxing of Nevada's gambling laws, which proved beneficial to both the Outfit and the Mormon gentry, was likely the result of graft dispensed by Johnny Rosselli and Curly Humphreys in 1931. And although the Outfit appears to have played a critical role in "opening up" Nevada in 1931, they became distracted from its potential for over two decades. Meanwhile, hordes of less organized hoods from all over the country flocked to Nevada, where they believed they could seize their last chance at the American Dream.

The remarkable history of this desert city is rich with irony. One would have been hard-pressed to find a Spanish explorer who would have believed that this parcel of uncultivatable desert would become the fastest-growing city in the world by the end of the twentieth century. Early Mormon missionaries would be appalled to know that their descendants would one day provide the indispensable workforce for America's paean to hedonism and divorce, aka Sin City. Gold prospectors would likely have laughed off the suggestion that in time gullible tourists might journey here from points remote to voluntarily part annually with $20 billion of their hard-earned wages. As with the other Outfit rackets, the Las Vegas one would be superficially sanitized in advance of its complete takeover by the upperworld.

Sources

1. Interviews

Howard Abadinsky, Allan Ackerman, Steve Allen, Vincent "Jimmy Blue Eyes" Alo, Jack Anderson, Senator Frank Annunzio, Senator Howard Baker, Ed Becker, August Bequai, Sam Betar, John Binder, Charles Bluth, William Brashler, Ernest (Humphreys) Brendle, David Bushong, Michael Cain, Anna Chennault, Jim Ciatloa, Jack Clarke, Miles Cooperman, James Deakin, John DeCarlo, Cartha DeLoach, C. Douglas Dillon, James Dowd, Morton Downey, Jr., Julius Lucius Echeles, Lou Farina, Clark Fettridge, Brenda Gage, Antoinette Giancana, Jerry Gladden, Joey Glimco, Jr., Andrew Goodpasture, Harry Hall, Betsy Duncan Hammes, Senator Gary Hart, Clara Grace Harvey, David Helfrey, Maury Hughes, Jr., Robert Hughes, Jeanne Humphreys, William Hundley, Wayne Johnson, "Ruth Jones," Constantine "Gus" Kangles, Tom King, Irwin Klass, Herb Klein, Boris Kostelanetz, Ed Kovacic, Joe Langford, Teddy (Mrs. Meyer) Lansky, Michael Lavelle, Jack Lavin, Honorable George N. Leighton, Howard Liebengood, Richard Lindberg, Joe Longmeyer, Mike Madigan, Sherman Magidson, Robert Maheu, Richard Mahoney, Honorable Abraham Lincoln Marovitz, Jake McCarthy, Robert McDonnell, Walter Metzer, Dan Moldea, Roger Morris, George Murray II, Bernard Neistein, Dave Nissen, Ben Novak, John O'Brien, Madeline Foy O'Donnell, Wayne Ogle, Patrick O'Malley, Jimmy O'Neill, Bill Ouseley, Irwin Owens, Sharon Patrick, Art Petaque, Marty Philpott, Nick Pileggi, Andy Postal, Frank Ragano, Oliver "Buck" Revell, William Roemer, Douglas Roller, Frank "Lefty" Rosenthal, Joseph P. Santoiana, David Schippers, Joe Shimon, Toni Shimon, Sandy Smith, Thomas Sobek, Brownie (Mrs. Billy Wilkerson) Stewart, Governor William Stratton, Jim Strong, J. Randy Taraborrelli, Jay Tischendorf, John W. Touhy, Red Tracton, Walter Trohan, Bethel Van Tassel, Santo Volpe, Carl Walsh, Royston Webb, Vern E. Whaley, Will Wilson.

My sincere thanks to all the above, as well as to those who preferred to remain on background or go unnamed – and profound apologies to anyone I've overlooked.

2. FBI Files

A number of FBI files were obtained, some by new Freedom of Information Act (FOIA) requests, others from the FBI reading room in Washington, the FBI Electronic Reading Room on the Web, and the National Archives II in College Park, Maryland. Those file subjects include Anthony Accardo, Al Capone, Moe Dalitz, Paul De Lucia, Sam Giancana, the Bobby Greenlease kidnapping, Murray Humphreys, Estes Kefauver, John F. Kennedy, Joseph P. Kennedy, Sidney Korshak, the assassination attempt on Franklin Roosevelt, Johnny Rosselli, Benjamin Siegel, and Frank Sinatra. In addition, the FBI's report on the parole scandal was located by the Department of Justice and made available.

3. Government Reports

Federal Communications Commission Report on the Telegraph Industry; December 1939.

Committee on Expenditures in Executive Departments (House); 80th Congress, 2nd session; 1948; report and hearings ("Parole Investigation").

Subcommittee of the Committee on Interstate and Foreign Commerce (Senate); 81st Congress, 2nd session; May 1950; "Transmission of Gambling Information" (race wire) ("McFarland").

Hearings Before the Committee on Interstate and Foreign Commerce (House), regarding proposed legislation to prohibit interstate sale of gambling machines (slots, etc.); 81st Congress, 2nd Session; June 1950.

Special Committee to Investigate Organized Crime in Interstate Commerce (Senate); 81st and 82nd Congress; 1951; reports, hearings, and working papers ("Kefauver").

The Report and Hearings of the Select Committee on Improper Activities in the Labor and Management Field (Senate); 86th Congress, 2nd Session; June 1960; reports, hearings, and working papers ("McClellan").

Report of the Inspector General of the Central Intelligence Agency; May 23, 1967; "The Plots to Assassinate Fidel Castro."

Interim Report of the Select Committee to Study Governmental Operations with Respect to Intelligence Agencies (Senate); 94th Congress, 1st Session; November 20, 1975; reports, hearings, and working papers ("Church").

Report of the Select Committee on Assassinations (House); 1979; also twelve volumes of hearings, and working papers.

The President's Commission on Organized Crime; June 24–26, 1985; "Organized Crime and Gambling."

Parole Board and Bureau of Prisons records at the National Archives at College Park, Maryland.

The Papers of Representative Fred E. Busbey in the Special Collections holdings of the Robert Manning Strozier Library at Florida State University at Tallahassee.

4. Court Filings and Transcripts

U.S. v. Schenck & Moscowitz (Federal Court, Southern District, New York).

U.S. v. Campagna et al. (Federal Court, Southern District, New York). – Both supplied by Boris Kostelanetz.

Hoffman v. United States (4/25/51) (U.S. Supreme Court).

U.S. v. Aiuppa (2/7/52) (Northern District Court).

Aiuppa v. United States (12/11/52) (Sixth Circuit Court of Appeals).

Papers of the Brooklyn, New York, District Attorney's Office, especially the "Murder, Inc." files stored at the New York Archives.

State of Illinois v. Sam Jantelezio, Michael Campobasso, and Michael Gibellina (March 1962); re voting fraud in the 1960 election.

U.S. v. William A. Hanhardt et al. (October 2000) (Northern District of Illinois); re jewelry theft ring.

5. Books

Abadinsky, Howard. *Organized Crime*. Boston: Allyn and Bacon, 1981.

Albanese, Jay. *Organizational Offenders: Understanding Corporate Crime*. 2nd ed. Niagara Falls: Apocalypse Publishing Co., 1988.

——. *Organized Crime in America*. 2nd ed. Cincinnati: Anderson Publishing Co., 1989.

Albini, Joseph L. *The American Mafia: Genesis of a Legend*. New York: Appleton-Century-Crofts Educational Division, Meredith Corporation, 1971.

Allen, Steve. *Hi-Ho, Steverino! My Adventures in the Wonderful Wacky World of TV*. Fort Lee: Barricade Books, 1992.

——. *Mark It and Strike It*. New York: Bartholomew House, 1960.

——. *Ripoff: The Corruption That Plagues America*. Secaucus: Lyle Stuart, 1979.

Anderson, Jack, and Fred Blumenthal. *The Kefauver Story*. New York: Dial Press, 1956.

Andrews, Robert Hardy. *A Corner of Chicago*. Boston: Little, Brown and Company, 1963.

Arnaz, Desi. *A Book*. New York: Buccaneer Books, 1976.

Asbury, Herbert. *Gem of the Prairie: An Informal History of the Chicago Underground*. New York and London: Alfred A. Knopf, 1940.

Bahrenburg, Bruce. *The Creation of Dino De Laurentiis' King Kong*. New York: Pocket Books, 1976.

Baker, Bobby. *Wheeling and Dealing*. New York: W. W. Norton and Company, 1978.

Balboni, Alan. *Beyond the Mafia: Italian Americans and the Development of Las Vegas*. Reno: University of Nevada Press, 1996.

Balsamo, William, and George Carpozi, Jr. *Crime Incorporated: The Inside Story of the Mafia's First 100 Years*. Far Hills: New Horizon Press, 1991.

Barkley, Alben. *That Reminds Me*. Garden City: Doubleday, 1954.

Barth, Alan. *Government by Investigation*. New York: Viking Press, 1955.

Behr, Edward. *Prohibition: Thirteen Years That Changed America*. New York: Arcade Publishing, 1996.

Bequai, August. *Organized Crime: The Fifth Estate*. Lexington: Lexington Books, 1979.

Bergreen, Laurence. *Capone: The Man and the Era*. New York: Simon and Schuster, 1994.

Berman, Susan. *Easy Street*. New York: Dial Press, 1981.

Blakey, G. Robert, and Richard N. Billings. *The Plot to Kill the President: Organized Crime Assassinated J.F.K.: The Definite Story*. New York: Times Books, 1981.

Bonanno, Bill. *Bound by Honor: A Mafioso's Story*. New York: St. Martin's Press, 1999.

Bonanno, Joseph, with Sergio Lalli. *A Man of Honor: The Autobiography of Joseph Bonanno*. New York: Simon and Schuster, 1983.

Bonanno, Rosalie, with Beverly Donofrio. *Mafia Marriage: My Story*. New York: William Morrow and Company, 1990.

Brandeis, Louis. *Other People's Money and How the Bankers Use It*. Fairfield, N.J.: A. M. Kelley, 1986.

Brashler, William. *The Don: The Life and Death of Sam Giancana*. New York: Ballantine Books, 1977.

Brill, Steven. *The Teamsters*. New York: Simon and Schuster, 1978.

Brownstein, Ronald. *The Power and the Glitter: The Hollywood-Washington Connection*. New York: Pantheon Books, 1990.

Bunch, William. *Jukebox America: Down Back Streets and Blue Highways in Search of the Country's Greatest Jukebox*. New York: St. Martin's Press, 1994.

Campbell, Rodney. *The Luciano Project: The Secret Wartime Collaboration of the Mafia and the U.S. Navy*. New York: McGraw-Hill Book Company, 1977.

Caro, Robert A. *The Power Broker: Robert Moses and the Fall of New York*. New York: Knopf, 1974.

Carse, Robert. *Rum Row*. New York and Toronto: Rhinehart and Co., 1959.

Chambliss, William, J. *On the Take: From Petty Crooks to Presidents*. Bloomington and London: Indiana University Press, 1978.

Ciccone, F. Richard. *Daley: Power and Presidential Politics*. Chicago: Contemporary Books, 1996.

Clarke, Thurston, and John J. Tigue, Jr. *Dirty Money: Swiss Banks, the Mafia, Money Laundering and White Collar Crime*. New York: Simon and Schuster, 1975.

Clifford, Clark, with Richard Holbrooke. *Counsel to the President*. New York: Random House, 1991.

Cohen, Adam, and Elizabeth Taylor. *American Pharaoh: Mayor Richard J. Daley: His Battle for Chicago and the Nation*. Boston: Little, Brown and Company, 2000.

Cohen, Rich. *Tough Jews*. New York: Vintage Books, 1999.

Collier, Peter, and David Horowitz. *The Kennedys: An American Drama*. New York: Warner Books, 1984.

Collins, Gail. *Scorpion Tongues: Gossip, Celebrity, and American Politics*. New York: William Morrow and Company, 1998.

Conklin, John E., ed. *The Crime Establishment: Organized Crime and American Society*. Englewood Cliffs: Prentice-Hall, 1973.

Conrad, Harold. *Dear Muffo: 35 Years in the Fast Lane*. New York: Stein and Day Publishing, 1982.

Cowan, Geoffrey. *The People Versus Clarence Darrow: The Bribery Trial of America's Greatest Lawyer*. New York: Times Books, 1993.

Davis, John H. *The Kennedys*. New York: McGraw-Hill, 1984.

——. *Mafia Kingfish Carlos Marcello and the Assassination of John F. Kennedy*. New York: Signet, 1989.

Davis, Kenneth S. *FDR: The New Deal Years, 1933–1937: A History*. New York: Random House, 1986.

Deakin, James. *A Grave for Bobby: The Greenlease Slaying*. New York: William Morrow and Company, 1990.

——. *Straight Stuff: The Reporters, the White House, and the Truth*. New York: William Morrow and Company, 1984.

Demaris, Ovid. *The Boardwalk Jungle*. New York: Bantam Books, 1986.

——. *Captive City: Chicago in Chains*. New York: Lyle Stuart, 1969.

——. *Judith Exner: My Story*. New York: Grove Press, 1977.

——. *The Last Mafioso: "Jimmy the Weasel" Fratianno*. New York: Bantam Books, 1981.

Denton, Sally, and Roger Morris. *The Money and the Power: The Making of Las Vegas and Its Hold on America, 1947–2000*. New York: Knopf, 2001.

Doleschal, Eugene, Anne Newton, and William Hickey. *A Guide to the Literature on Organized Crime: An Annotated Bibliography Covering the Years 1967–81*. Hackensack: National Council on Crime and Delinquency, 1981.

Dorman, Michael. *Payoff*. New York: Berkley Medallion Books, 1972.

Dorsett, Lyle W. *The Pendergast Machine*. Lincoln and London: University of Nebraska Press, 1968.

Drosin, Michael. *Citizen Hughes*. New York: Holt, Rinehart and Winston, 1985.

Dunar, Andrew J. *The Truman Scandals and the Politics of Morality*. Columbia: University of Missouri Press, 1984.

Edmonds, Andy. *Bugsy's Baby: The Secret Life of Mob Queen Virginia Hill*. New York: Carol Publishing Group, 1993.

——. *Hot Toddy: The True Story of Hollywood's Most Sensational Murder*. New York: William Morrow and Company, 1989.

Eitzen, D. Stanley, and Maxine Baca-Zinn. *Social Problems*. Boston: Allyn and Bacon, 1986.

Evanier, David. *Making the Wise Guys Weep: The Jimmy Roselli Story*. New York: Farrar, Straus and Giroux, 1998.

Evans, Robert. *The Kid Stays in the Picture*. New York: Hyperion, 1994.

Farrell, Ronald A., and Carol Case. *The Black Book and the Mob: The Untold Story of the Control of Nevada's Casinos*. Madison: University of Wisconsin Press, 1995.

Ferrell, Robert H. *Truman and Pendergast*. Columbia and London: University of Missouri Press, 1999.

Fetridge, William Harrison. *With Warm Regards: A Reminiscence*. Chicago: Dartnell, 1976.

Fido, Martin. *The Chronicle of Crime: The Infamous Felons of Modern History and Their Hideous Crimes*. New York: Carroll & Graf Publishers, 1993.

Fleming, Dan B., Jr. *Kennedy vs. Humphrey, West Virginia, 1960: The Pivotal Battle for the Democratic Presidential Nomination*. Jefferson: McFarland, 1992.

Fletcher, Connie. *What Cops Know: Cops Talk About What They Do, How They Do It, and What It Does to Them*. New York: Villiard Books, 1991.

Fontenay, Charles L. *Estes Kefauver: A Biography*. Knoxville: University of Tennessee Press, 1980.

Fox, Stephen. *Blood and Power: Organized Crime in Twentieth-Century America*. New York: Penguin Books, 1989.

Franco, Joseph (Joe), with Richard Hammer. *Hoffa's Man: The Rise and Fall of Jimmy Hoffa As Witnessed by His Strongest Arm*. New York: Prentice Hall Press, 1987.

Fraser, Steven. *Labor Will Rule: Sidney Hillman and the Rise of American Labor*. New York: Free Press, 1993.

Freidel, Frank. *Franklin D. Roosevelt: A Rendezvous with Destiny*. Boston: Little, Brown and Company, 1990.

Fremon, David K. *Chicago Politics Ward by Ward*. Bloomington and Indianapolis: Indiana University Press, 1988.

Fried, Albert. *The Rise and Fall of the Jewish Gangster in America*. New York: Holt, Rinehart and Winston, 1980.

Friedman, Allen, and Ted Schwarz. *Power and Greed: Inside the Teamsters Empire of Corruption*. New York: Franklin Watts, 1989.

Gabler, Edwin. *The American Telegrapher: A Social History, 1860–1900*. New Brunswick and London: Rutgers University Press, 1988.

Gage, Nicholas. *Mafia, USA*. Chicago: Playboy Press, 1972.

Gambino, Richard. *Vendetta: A True Story of the Worst Lynching in America, the Mass Murder of Italian-Americans in New Orleans in 1891, the Vicious Motivations Behind It, and the Tragic Repercussions That Linger to This Day*. Garden City: Doubleday & Company, 1977.

Geis, Gilbert, and Robert F. Meier. *White-Collar Crime: Offenses in Business, Politics, and the Professions*. New York: Free Press, 1977.

Gentry, Curt. *J. Edgar Hoover: The Man and the Secrets*. New York: Penguin Books, 1991.

Giancana, Antoinette, and Thomas C. Renner. *Mafia Princess: Growing Up in Sam Giancana's Family*. New York: Avon Books, 1984.

Giancana, Sam, and Chuck Giancana. *Double Cross: The Explosive, Inside Story of the Mobster Who Controlled America*. New York: Warner Books, 1992.

Goodwin, Doris Kearns. *The Fitzgeralds and the Kennedys*. New York: St. Martin's Press, 1987.

Gorer, Geoffrey. *The American People: A Study in National Character*. New York: W. W. Norton and Company, 1948.

Gosch, Martin A., and Richard Hammer. *The Last Testament of Lucky Luciano*. Boston: Little, Brown and Company, 1974.

Gottfried, Alex. *Boss Cermak of Chicago: A Study of Political Leadership*. Seattle: University of Washington Press, 1962.

Gould, Jean. *Sidney Hillman: Great American*. Boston: Houghton Mifflin Company, 1952.

Granger, Bill, and Lori Granger. *Lords of the Last Machine: The Story of Politics in Chicago*. New York: Random House, 1987.

Grant, Robert, and Joseph Katz. *The Great Trials of the Twenties: The Watershed Decade in America's Courtrooms.* Rockville Centre: Sarpedon, 1998.

Green, Paul M., ed. *The Mayors: The Chicago Political Tradition.* Carbondale and Edwardsville: Southern Illinois University Press, 1987.

Grose, Peter. *Gentleman Spy: The Life of Allen Dulles.* New York: Houghton Mifflin, 1994.

Halper, Albert, ed. *The Chicago Crime Book.* Cleveland and New York: World Publishing Company, 1967.

Hamby, Alonzo L. *Man of the People: A Life of Harry S. Truman.* New York and Oxford: Oxford University Press, 1995.

Harris, Patricia. *Adlai: The Springfield Years.* Nashville and London: Aurora Publishers, 1975.

Hellerman, Michael, with Thomas C. Renner. *Wall Street Swindler.* Garden City: Doubleday & Company, 1977.

Herman, Robert D. *Gamblers and Gambling: Motives, Institutions, and Controls.* Lexington: Lexington Books, 1976.

Hersh, Seymour M. *The Dark Side of Camelot.* Boston: Little, Brown and Company, 1997.

Hinckle, Warren, and William Turner. *Deadly Secrets: The CIA-Mafia War Against Castro and the Assassination of J.F.K.* New York: Thunder's Mouth Press, 1992.

Hoffa, James R., as told by Oscar Fraley. *Hoffa: The Real Story.* New York: Stein and Day Publishers, 1975.

Hoffman, Dennis E. *Scarface Al and the Crime Crusaders: Chicago's Private War Against Capone.* Carbondale and Edwardsville: Southern Illinois University Press, 1993.

Holmes, Burnham. *The American Heritage History of the Bill of Rights.* Englewood Cliffs: Silver Burdett Press, 1991.

Hougan, Jim. *Secret Agenda.* New York: Ballantine Books, 1984.

——. *Spooks: The Haunting of America: The Private Use of Secret Agents.* New York: William Morrow and Company, 1978.

Ianni, Francis A. J., and Elizabeth Reuss-Ianni. *The Crime Society: Organized Crime and Corruption in America.* New York: New American Library, 1976.

James, Ralph C., and Estelle Dinerstein James. *Hoffa and the Teamsters: A Study of Union Power.* Princeton: D. Van Nostrand Company, 1965.

Jennings, Dean. *We Only Kill Each Other: The Life and Bad Times of Bugsy Siegel.* Englewood Cliffs: Prentice-Hall, 1967.

Jennings, Francis. *The Creation of America Through Revolution to Empire.* Cambridge: Cambridge University Press, 2000.

Johnson, Curt, with R. Craig Sautter. *Wicked City Chicago: From Kenna to Capone.* Highland Park: December Press, 1994.

Josephson, Matthew. *Sidney Hillman: Statesman of American Labor.* Garden City: Doubleday & Company, 1952.

Kallina, Edmund F., Jr. *Courthouse over White House: Chicago and the Presidential Election of 1960.* Orlando: University of Central Florida Press, 1988.

Katz, Leonard. *Uncle Frank: The Biography of Frank Costello.* New York: Drake Publishers, 1973.

Kelley, Kitty. *His Way: The Unauthorized Biography of Frank Sinatra.* New York: Bantam Books, 1986.

Kelly, Robert J., ed. *Organized Crime: A Global Perspective.* Rowman & Littlefield Publishers, 1986.

Kennedy, Robert F. *The Enemy Within.* New York: Popular Library, 1960.

Kessler, Ronald. *The Sins of the Father: Joseph P. Kennedy and the Dynasty He Founded.* New York: Warner Books, 1996.

Killian, Michael, Connie Fletcher, and F. Richard Ciccone. *Who Runs Chicago?* New York: St. Martin's Press, 1979.

King, Rufus. *Gambling and Organized Crime.* Washington, D.C.: Public Affairs Press, 1969.

Kleinknecht, William. *The New Ethnic Mobs: The Changing Face of Organized Crime in America.* New York: Free Press, 1996.

Knoedelseder, William. *Stiffed: A True Story of MCA, the Music Business and the Mafia.* New York: HarperCollins Publishers, 1993.

Kobler, John. *Capone: The Life and World of Al Capone.* New York: G. P. Putnam's Sons, 1971.

Kostelanetz, Andre. *Echoes: Memoirs of Andre Kostelanetz.* New York: Harcourt, Brace, Jovanovich, 1981.

Kunen, James S. *Reckless Disregard: Corporate Greed, Government Indifference, and the Kentucky School Bus Crash.* New York: Simon and Schuster, 1994.

Kyvig, David E. *Prohibition: The 18th Amendment, the Volstead Act, the 21st Amendment.* Washington: National Archives (GPO), 1986.

Lacey, Robert. *Little Man: Meyer Lansky and the Gangster Life*. Boston: Little, Brown and Company, 1991.

Landesco, John. *Organized Crime in Chicago*. Chicago: University of Chicago Press, 1929.

Larsen, Lawrence H., and Nancy J. Hulston. *Pendergast!* Columbia and London: University of Missouri Press, 1997.

Lasky, Victor. *J.F.K.: The Man and the Myth*. New York: Macmillan Company, 1963.

Lawford, Patricia Seaton, with Ted Schwarz. *The Peter Lawford Story: Life with the Kennedys, Monroe, and the Rat Pack*. New York: Carroll & Graf Publishers, 1988.

Lawrence, Carol. *Carol Lawrence: The Backstage Story*. New York: McGraw-Hill Publishing Company, 1990.

Lindberg, Kirsten, Joseph Petrenko, Jerry Gladden, and Wayne A. Johnson. *The New Faces of Organized Crime*. Chicago: Chicago Crime Commission, 1997.

Lindberg, Richard. *To Serve and Collect: Chicago Politics and Police Corruption from the Lager Beer Riot to the Summerdale Scandal*. New York: Praeger, 1991.

Longstreet, Stephen. *Chicago: An Intimate Portrait of People, Pleasures, and Power: 1860–1919*. New York: David McKay Company, 1973.

Lundberg, Ferdinand. *The Rich and the Super-Rich*. New York: Bantam Books, 1968.

Maheu, Robert, and Richard Hack. *Next to Hughes: Behind the Power and Tragic Downfall of Howard Hughes by His Closest Advisor*. HarperCollins Publishers, 1992.

Mahoney, Richard D. *Sons & Brothers: The Days of Jack and Bobby Kennedy*. New York: Arcade Publishing, 1999.

Mast, Gerald. *Howard Hawks, Storyteller*. New York and Oxford: Oxford University Press, 1982.

Mazo, Earl. *Richard Nixon*. New York: Avon, 1960.

—— and Stephen Hess, *President Nixon: A Political Portrait*. London: McDonald, 1968.

McCarthy, Todd. *Howard Hawks: The Grey Fox of Hollywood*. New York: Grove Press, 1997.

McClellan, John L. *Crime Without Punishment*. New York: Duell, Sloan and Pearce, 1962.

McCullough, David. *Truman*. New York: Simon and Schuster, 1992.

McDougal, Dennis. *The Last Mogul: Lew Wasserman, MCA, and the Hidden History of Hollywood*. New York: Crown Publishers, 1998.

McPhaul, Jack. *Johnny Torrio: First of the Gang Lords*. New Rochelle: Arlington House, 1970.

Messick, Hank. *Secret File*. New York: G. P. Putnam's Sons, 1969.

Miller, Nathan. *Stealing from America: A History of Corruption from Jamestown to Reagan*. New York: Paragon House, 1992.

Miller, Richard Lawrence. *Truman: The Rise to Power*. New York: McGraw-Hill Book Company, 1986.

Miller, William "Fishbait." *Fishbait: The Memoirs of the Congressional Doorkeeper*. Englewood Cliffs: Prentice-Hall, 1977.

Milligan, Maurice M. *The Inside Story of the Pendergast Machine by the Man Who Smashed It*. New York: Charles Scribner's Sons, 1948.

Mills, James. *The Underground Empire: Where Crime and Governments Embrace*. Garden City: Doubleday & Company, 1986.

Mintz, Morton, and Jerry S. Cohen. *America, Inc.: Who Owns and Operates the United States*. New York: Dell Publishing Co., 1971.

Moehring, Eugene P. *Resort City in the Sunbelt*. Reno and Las Vegas: University of Nevada Press, 1989.

Mokhiber, Russell. *Corporate Crime and Violence: Big Business Power and the Abuse of the Public Trust*. San Francisco: Sierra Club Books, 1998.

Moldea, Dan E. *Dark Victory: Ronald Reagan, MCA, and the Mob*. New York: Viking, 1986.

——. *The Hoffa Wars: Teamsters, Rebels, Politicians and the Mob*. New York: Paddington Press Ltd., 1978.

——. *Interference: How Organized Crime Influences Professional Football*. New York: William Morrow and Company, 1989.

Mollenhoff, Clark R. *Strike Force: Organized Crime and the Government*. Englewood Cliffs: Prentice-Hall, 1972.

Moore, William Howard. *The Kefauver Committee and the Politics of Crime, 1950–1952*. Columbia: University of Missouri Press, 1974.

Morgan, John. *Prince of Crime*. New York: Stein and Day Publishers, 1985.

Munn, Michael. *The Hollywood Connection: The True Story of Organized Crime in Hollywood*. London: Robson Books, 1993.

Murray, George. *The Legacy of Al Capone: Portraits and Annals of Chicago's Public Enemies*. New York: G. P. Putnam's Sons, 1975.

Nash, Jay Robert. *People to See: An Anecdotal History of Chicago's Makers & Breakers*. New Century Publishers, 1981.

Neff, James. *Mobbed Up: Jackie Presser's High-Wire Life in the Teamsters, the Mafia, and the F.B.I.* New York: Atlantic Monthly Press, 1989.

Nelli, Humbert S. *The Business of Crime: Italians and Syndicate Crime in the United States*. Chicago and London: University of Chicago Press, 1976.

Nielsen, Mike, and Gene Mailes. *Hollywood's Other Blacklist: Union Struggles in the Studio System*. London: BFI Publishing, 1995.

Nixon, Richard. *RN: The Memoirs of Richard Nixon*. New York: Grosset & Dunlap, 1978.

North, Mark. *Act of Treason: The Role of J. Edgar Hoover in the Assassination of President Kennedy*. New York: Carroll & Graf Publishers, 1991.

O'Connor, Kenneth P. *Johnny We Hardly Knew Ye: Memories of John Fitzgerald Kennedy*. Boston: Little, Brown and Company, 1972.

O'Connor, Len. *Clout: Mayor Daley and His City*. Chicago: Henry Regnery Company, 1975.

Ogden, Christopher. *Legacy: A Biography of Moses and Walter Annenberg*. Boston: Little, Brown and Company, 1999.

Peirce, Neal R. *The People's President: The Electoral College in American History and the Direct Vote Alternative*. New Haven: Yale University Press, 1981.

Pepitone, Lena. *Marilyn Monroe Confidential: An Intimate Personal Account*. New York: Simon and Schuster, 1979.

Peterson, Virgil W. *Barbarians in Our Midst: A History of Chicago Crime and Politics*. Boston: Little, Brown and Company, 1952.

——. *The Juke Box Racket*. Chicago: Chicago Crime Commission, September 1954.

Petro, Sylvester. *Power Unlimited: The Corruption of Union Leadership*. New York: Ronald Press Company, 1979.

Pileggi, Nicholas. *Casino*. New York: Pocket Star Books, 1995.

Poague, Leland A. *Howard Hawks*. Boston: Twayne Publishers, 1982.

Ragano, Frank, and Selwyn Raab. *Mob Lawyer*. New York: Charles Scribner's Sons, 1994.

Rappleye, Charles, and Ed Becker. *All American Mafioso: The Johnny Rosselli Story*. New York: Doubleday, 1991.

Rattray, Everett T. *The South Fork: The Land and the People of Eastern Long Island*. New York: Random House, 1979.

Rattray, Jeannette Edwards. *Rum-Running Tales from the East End*. Privately published, 1963.

Reid, Ed, and Ovid Demaris. *The Green Felt Jungle*. New York: Trident Press, 1963.

——. *The Grim Reapers: The Anatomy of Organized Crime in America, City by City*. New York: Bantam Books, 1969.

Reiman, Jeffrey H. *The Rich Get Richer and the Poor Get Prison: Ideology, Class, and Criminal Justice*. New York: Wiley, 1979.

Robb, Peter. *Midnight in Sicily: On Art, Food, History, Travel, and La Cosa Nostra*. Boston: Faber and Faber, 1998.

Roemer, William F., Jr. *Accardo: The Genuine Godfather*. New York: Ivy Books, 1995.

——. *The Enforcer – Spilotro: The Chicago Mob's Man over Las Vegas*. New York: Ivy Books, 1994.

——. *Roemer: Man Against the Mob*. New York: Ivy Books, 1989.

——. *War of the Godfathers*. New York: Ivy Books, 1990.

Rosoff, Stephen M., Henry N. Pontell, and Robert Tillman. *Profit Without Honor: White-Collar Crime and the Looting of America*. Upper Saddle River: Prentice-Hall, 1998.

Rothman, Hal K. *Devil's Bargain: Tourism in the Twentieth-Century American West*. Lawrence: University Press of Kansas, 1998.

Rothmiller, Mike, and Ivan G. Goldman. *L.A. Secret Police: Inside the LAPD Elite Spy Network*. New York: Pocket Books, 1992.

Royko, Mike. *Boss: Richard J. Daley of Chicago*. New York: Signet, 1971.

Russo, Gus. *Live by the Sword: The Secret War Against Castro and the Death of JFK*. Baltimore: Bancroft Press, 1998.

Salerno, Ralph, and John S. Tompkins. *The Crime Confederation: Cosa Nostra and Allied Operations in Organized Crime*. Garden City: Doubleday & Company, 1969.

Sanders, Coyne Steven, and Tom Gilbert. *Desilu: The Story of Lucille Ball and Desi Arnaz*. New York: Quill William Morrow, 1993.

Sasuly, Richard. *Bookies and Bettors: Two Hundred Years of Gambling*. New York: Holt, Rinehart and Winston, 1982.

Sawislak, Karen. *Smoldering City: Chicagoans and the Great Fire, 1871–1874*. Chicago and London: University of Chicago Press, 1995.

Schem, David E. *Contract on America: The Mafia Murders of John and Robert Kennedy.* Silver Spring: Argyle Press, 1983.

Schlesinger, Arthur M., Jr. *Robert Kennedy and His Times.* New York: Ballantine Books, 1978.

Schoenberg, Robert J. *Mr. Capone.* New York: William Morrow and Company, 1992.

Sebilleau, Pierre. *Sicily.* New York: Oxford University Press, 1968.

Sheridan, Walter. *The Fall and Rise of Jimmy Hoffa.* New York: Saturday Review Press, 1972.

Sinatra, Nancy. *Frank Sinatra: An American Legend.* Santa Monica: General Publishing Group, 1995.

——. *Frank Sinatra, My Father.* New York: Pocket Books, 1985.

Smith, Alson J. *Syndicate City: The Chicago Crime Cartel and What to Do About It.* Chicago: Henry Regnery Company, 1954.

Smith, Hedrick. *The Power Game: How Washington Works.* New York: Ballantine Books, 1988.

Smith, Sally Bedell. *In All His Glory: The Life of William S. Paley: The Legendary Tycoon and His Brilliant Circle.* New York: Simon and Schuster, 1990.

Soule, George. *Sidney Hillman: Labor Statesman.* Amalgamated Clothing Workers of America, 1939.

Spada, James. *Peter Lawford: The Man Who Kept the Secrets.* New York: Bantam Books, 1991.

Stone, Irving. *Clarence Darrow for the Defense.* New York: Doubleday, 1989.

Sullivan, Edward D. *Rattling the Cup on Chicago Crime.* New York: Vanguard, 1929.

Sullivan, William, with Bill Brown. *The Bureau: My Thirty Years in Hoover's FBI.* New York: Pinnacle Books, 1979.

Summers, Anthony. *The Arrogance of Power: The Secret World of Richard Nixon.* New York: Viking, 2000.

——. *Goddess: The Secret Lives of Marilyn Monroe.* New York: Macmillan Publishing Company, 1985.

——. *Official and Confidential: The Secret Life of J. Edgar Hoover.* New York: G. P. Putnam's Sons, 1993.

Swados, Harvey. *Standing Up for the People: The Life and Work of Estes Kefauver.* New York: E. P. Dutton & Co., 1972.

Taraborrelli, J. Randy. *Sinatra: Behind the Legend.* Secaucus: Carol Publishing Group, 1997.

Teresa, Vincent, with Thomas C. Renner. *My Life in the Mafia.* Garden City: Doubleday & Company, 1973.

Terkel, Studs. *Coming of Age.* New York: New Press, 1995.

Theoharis, Athan, ed. *From the Secret Files of J. Edgar Hoover.* Chicago: Ivan R. Dee, 1991.

Thomas, Evan. *Robert Kennedy: His Life.* New York: Simon and Schuster, 2000.

Thornton, Russell. *American Indian Holocaust and Survival: A Population History Since 1492.* Norman and London: University of Oklahoma Press, 1987.

Touhy, Roger, with Ray Brennan. *The Stolen Years.* Pennington Press, 1959.

Trohan, Walter. *Political Animals: Memoirs of a Sentimental Cynic.* Garden City: Doubleday & Company, 1975.

Truman, Margaret. *Harry S. Truman.* New York: Quill, 1972.

Tuohy, John W. *When Capone's Mob Murdered Roger Touhy.* Ft. Lee: Barricade, 2001.

Turkus, Burton B. *Murder, Inc.: The Story of the Syndicate.* New York: Da Capo Press, 1992.

Turner, Wallace. *Gambler's Money: The New Force in American Life.* Boston: Houghton Mifflin Company, 1965.

Van Tassel, Bethel Holmes. *Wood Chips to Game Chips: Casinos and People at North Lake Tahoe.* Reno: privately published, undated.

Walsh, George. *Public Enemies: The Mayor, the Mob, and the Crime That Was.* New York: W. W. Norton & Company, 1980.

Washington Post. *The Presidential Transcripts.* New York: Dell Publishing Co., 1974.

Watkins, T. H. *Righteous Pilgrim: The Life and Times of Harold L. Ickes, 1874–1952.* New York: Henry Holt and Company, 1990.

Webb, Royston. "The Life and Times of Llewelyn Morris Humphreys." Doctoral dissertation, 2000.

White, Theodore H. *The Making of the President 1960.* New York: Atheneum Publishers, 1961.

Willoughby, Malcolm F., Commander USCG (Rt.). *Rum War at Sea.* Washington, D.C.: U.S. Government Printing Office, 1964.

Wilson, Earl. *Sinatra: An Unauthorized Biography.* New York: Macmillan Publishing Co., 1976.

Zeller, F. C. Duke. *Devil's Pact: Inside the World of the Teamsters Union.* Secaucus: Carol Publishing Group, 1996.

6. Articles

Allen, Robert S. "How Congress Scuttled Kefauver." *U.S. Crime,* December 7, 1951.

Bartlett, Donald L., and James B. Steele. "Throwing the Game." *Time,* September 25, 2000.

Bilek, Arthur J. "Hit Team for the St. Valentine's Day Massacre." *Real Crime Book Digest,* spring 1995.

——. "St. Valentine's Day Massacre Chicago Rat-tat-a-tat." *Real Crime Book Digest,* spring 1995.

"Bioff Show." *Newsweek,* November 10, 1941.

Brashler, William. "How the FBI Put the Heat on Giancana." *Chicago,* February 1977.

Candeloro, Dominic. "A Personal Essay on Italian Americans in Chicago and Illinois Politics in the Twentieth Century." (Internet).

Chandler, J. D. "Frank Sinatra and the Mob." *Crime Magazine,* June 13, 2001.

"Chicago Rebels Against Filly de Mignon." *Life,* February 11, 1952.

Clemens, Bob. "The Las Vegas Strip." *Variety,* December 7, 1954.

Earl, Phillip I. "The Legalization of Gambling in Nevada, 1931." *Nevada Historical Society Quarterly, Notes and Documents,* spring 1981.

"Estes Kefauver, RIP." *The National Review,* August 27, 1963.

Gilfoyle, Timothy J. "Making History Writing Law and History in Chicago: Interviews with John Hope Franklin and Abraham Lincoln Marovitz." *Chicago History* 25, no. 3 (all 1996).

Greenberg, David. "Was Nixon Robbed? The Legend of the Stolen 1960 Presidential Election." *Slate Archives,* October 16, 2000 (Internet).

Gribben, Mark. "Bugsy Siegel." (Internet).

Hopkins, A. D. "Capone Connection." *Las Vegas Review-Journal,* March 21, 1999.

——. "The Developer's Developer." (Internet).

IIT Technical Institute and the Chicago Crime Commission. "A Study of Organized Crime in Illinois." 1972.

Jackson, David. "Sordid Ties Tarnished City Police." *Chicago Tribune,* October 22, 2000.

Kelly, Jack. "How America Met the Mob." *Forbes American Heritage,* August 2000.

Kennedy, William. "Under My Skin." *The New York Times Magazine,* October 7, 1990.

Kurson, Robert. "Mob Lite." *Chicago Magazine,* December 2000.

"The Mafia of Domenico Airoma." Institute for the Doctrine and the Social Information, undated (Internet).

Lindberg, Richard. "The Death of the Don: The Legacy of Tony Accardo." *Illinois Police and Sheriff's News,* September 1992 (Internet).

——. "The Memoirs of a Street Agent." (Internet, undated).

Lombardo, Robert M. "The Genesis of Organized Crime." (Internet, undated).

Long, Russ. "White-Collar Crime." (Internet).

Longmeyer, Joseph. "Blood, Sweat and Picket Lines: An Ex-Organizer's Very Personal Account of How Unions Kill Themselves." Undated.

——. "Gus & Lenny: Mob Marauders from the Security Set." Privately published.

Machi, Mario. "Chicago." American Mafia.com. undated (Internet).

Maloney, J. J. "The Greenlease Kidnapping." *Crime Magazine,* 2000 (Internet).

Marinacci, Michael. "Joseph Weil: The Yellow Kid." (Internet 1997).

Martin, John Bartlow. "Who Killed Estelle Carey? The Murder That Lifted the Veil on the Syndicate." *Harper's,* June 1944.

——. "Al Capone's Successors." *American Mercury,* June 1949.

May, Allan. "The First Shooting of Frank Nitti." (Internet, February 22, 1999).

——. "Havana Conference." Internet, December 22, 1996.

——. "The History of the Race Wire Services." *Crime Magazine,* undated (Internet).

——. "The Last Days of Lepke Buchalter." *Crime Magazine,* 2000 (Internet).

——. "A Sicilian Bedtime Story." *PLR International,* 1999 (Internet).

McWilliams, Carey. "Chicago's Machine-Gun Politics." *The Nation,* March 15, 1952.

"Mobsters Zeroing In on White Collar Crime as Lucrative Path to Riches. *Organized Crime Digest* 18, no. 4. (February 19, 1997).

'Moodys: Public Utilities, 1945," (Western Union, AT&T).

Moore, William Howard. "Was Estes Kefauver 'Blackmailed' During the Chicago Crime Hearings?: A Historian's Perspective." *The Public Historian* 4, no. 1 (winter 1982).

Mosca, Alexandra Katherine. "Funerals of the Infamous." *American Funeral Director,* July 2000.

"The Mystery of Joe Kennedy." *Newsweek,* September 12, 1960.

Nellis, Joseph L. "Legal Aspects of the Kefauver Investigation." *Journal of Criminal Law, Criminology and Police Science,* July-August 1951.

Nichols, Ron. "Lucky Luciano." *The Crime Library,* undated (Internet).

"Outcry of IBEW's Jurisdictional Fight vs. IA May See New Officers." *Variety,* August 22, 1933.

Piccolo, Steve. "Chip Venues & Their History." *Chequers Magazine,* August 2000 (Internet).

Posner, Gerald. "The Fallacy of Nixon's Graceful Exit." *Salon.com Politics,* undated (Internet).

"Rat Pack's Hot Harem Nights." *Globe,* April 21, 1998.

Roemer, Bill. "A Place in the Sun: Las Vegas . . . from Capo to Corporate." *Illinois Police & Sheriff's News,* 1995 (Internet).

Roth, Andrew. "Bevan's Bid for Power." *The Nation,* March 15, 1952.

Rowan, Roy. "The 50 Biggest Mafia Bosses." *Fortune,* November 10, 1986.

Smith, John L. "The Double Life of Moe Dalitz." *Las Vegas Review-Journal,* undated (Internet).

Smith, Sandy. "The Mob." *Life,* May 30, 1969.

Stevenson, Jack. "The Jukebox That Ate the Cocktail Lounge – the Story of Scopitone." (Internet, 1999).

Stewart, W. M. Scott. "Kefauverism: A Protest." Papers of Robert P. Patterson, Library of Congress.

Thomis, Wayne. "Abraham Lincoln Marovitz: A Moving Profile and His City." *Chicago Tribune,* May 21–26, 1967.

Tosches, Nick. "Hipsters and Hoodlums." *Vanity Fair,* December 2000.

——. "The Man Who Kept the Secrets." *Vanity Fair,* April 1997.

Tuohy, John William. "Accardo." *Gambling Magazine,* undated (Internet).

——. "Extortion 101." *Gambling Magazine,* undated (Internet).

——. "Gone Hollywood." *Gambling Magazine,* (undated (Internet).

——. "Guns and Glamor." *Gambling Magazine,* undated (Internet).

——. "The Guns of Zangara." *Gambling Magazine,* 2000 (Internet).

——. "The Last Days of Al Capone." *Gambling Magazine,* undated (Internet).

——. "The Last Gangster: The Life and Times of Roger Touhy, John Factor and the Mob." *Gambling Magazine,* undated (Internet).

——. "Power Play: The Nitti Shooting." *Gambling Magazine,* undated (Internet).

——. "Roger Touhy, Gangster." *Gambling Magazine,* undated (Internet).

——. "The Sands." *Gambling Magazine,* undated (Internet).

——. "Ten Percent Tony: The Story of Chicago's Most Corrupt Mayor." *Gambling Magazine,* undated (Internet).

——. "Do the Mobs Dictate Your Crime Laws?" *Reader's Digest,* March 1953.

——. "Secret 'Mr. Big' of Florida." *Collier's,* May 5, 1951.

Velie, Lester. "The Capone Gang Muscle." *Collier's,* September 30, 1950.

——. "'The Man to See' in New Jersey." *Collier's,* August 25, 1951.

——. "Rudolph Halley – How He Nailed America's Racketeers." *Collier's,* May 19, 1951.

Warren, James. "Nixon's Hoffa Pardon Has an Odor." *Chicago Tribune,* April 15, 2001.

Wolcott, James. "When They Were Kings." *Vanity Fair,* May 1997.

Weberman, A. J. "The Godfather Part III: Why the Mob Rubbed Out Rosselli." Assassination Archives and Research Center, undated.

Zill, Oriana, and Lowell Bergman. "U.S. Business & Money Laundering." Transcript of *Frontline,* October 10, 2000.

7. Assorted Private Holdings

Cal-Neva Resort Report, Lake Tahoe 2, no. 3 (fall-winter).

Chicago Crime Commission (CCC). "Action Alert." Fall 1995.

——. "Action Alert." Winter 1996.

——. "Annual Report." 1993.

——. "Annual Report." 1995.

——. "Public Enemy Number One: Gangs, 75 Years of Fighting Crime in Chicagoland." 1995.

Cuban Information Archives. Document 0126: "Santo Trafficante, Jr." 1961.

Hoffman, Dennis E. "Business vs. Organized Crime: Chicago's Private War on Al Capone, 1929–1932." CCC. 1989.

Peterson, Virgil W. "Criminal Statistics: A Report on Chicago Crime for 1967. CCC.

——. 'A Report on Chicago Crime for 1961." CCC.

——. "A Report on Chicago Crime for 1962." CCC.

——. "A Report on Chicago Crime for 1964." CCC.

——. "A Report on Chicago Crime for 1965." CCC.

——. "A Report on Chicago Crime for 1968." CCC.

"State by State Popular Vote and Electoral College Breakdown of the Presidential Election of 1960."

Acknowledgments

In some respects, the Outfit's story has been told before. Although there is much in this book that is new, the foundation was laid years ago by writers such as George Murray, Virgil Peterson, Sandy Smith, Art Petaque, Ovid DeMaris and many others. The history of Chicago crime has also been compiled by dozens of FBI agents, whose reports are scattered in various files at the Bureau's headquarters and archival repositories. *The Outfit* owes a great debt to all of these trailblazers who have long deserved a wider audience for the intricate story they helped compile. I viewed my role as twofold: to coalesce all this reportage into a single narrative, and to add new material in the form of recently released documents and original interviews. However, this book could not exist without the contributions of my predecessors, and I thank them first for making *The Outfit* possible.

That this dizzying trove of raw data is readable at all is due in large part to the initial line and copy editing of talented New York documentary producer Sally Rosenthal, who cheerily donated her time to the cause and consistently extricated me from the writing doldrums with her witty missives (she also got Boris Kostelanetz to pose for her). Sally's work was further refined by Panio Gianopoulos at Bloomsbury. Any gaffs that remain are most certainly due to my occasional stubbornness in ignoring some of Sally's and Panio's suggestions.

I also benefitted from the expert eye of Jack Clarke, possibly the most knowledgeable person regarding organized crime in Chicago. Jack took the time to read the manuscript and offer suggestions, leads, and critiques.

I am further indebted to Jeanne Humphreys, who in 1996 decided to break her long silence and tell me her story, sharing her photos and handwritten journal in the process. Sadly, within days of my delivery of *The Outfit* manuscript, Jeanne passed away. Jeanne was that rare treasure who not only had a bird's eye view of some of the most important conclaves in the history of twentieth century underworld America, but possessed a sharp memory, unaffected cynicism, and a total indifference to profiteering from her priceless stories. It was a privilege to be her friend and confidante.

Chicago native and entertainment legend Steve Allen opened up his crime files to me at his Meadowlane office in Van Nuys, California. My work there was facilitated by Steve's assistant, Gioia Heiser, and the Meadowlane staff. When I visited California, Steve, as Abbott of the Beverly Hills Friars Club, treated me (and likely all of his friends) like visiting royalty at Club events. In addition to the great void in comedy and music, America lost a passionate voice for civility and ethics with Steve's tragic passing in 2000.

Tony Romano of Magellan Filmed Entertainment started as a business partner, and has since grown into a great friend, who both encouraged and supported me when I needed it most. Tony has a passionate interest in storytelling, and an astonishing insouciance regarding the Hollywood glitter and self-absorbtion that surrounds him. I doubt there is anyone quite like Tony working in Hollywood today, except perhaps Larry Berman – but that's another story.

Graphic artist and friend Steve Parke of What? Design in Baltimore unselfishly provided his expertise in executing the photo spread and other visual elements of the book, and I am forever indebted. Steve was assisted in the photo spread typesetting by colleague Susan Mangan, who answered the call on short notice. Royston Webb shared his doctoral dissertation on Murray Humphreys with me, and I am most grateful for his brilliant untangling of the FBI's massive file on the Outfit's grand strategist. Royston also introduced me to Welsh television producer Don Llewellyn, who graciously provided his photographic collection. In Oklahoma, Humphreys' nephew Ernie Brendle not only provided photos and documents from Curly's personal papers, but opened doors to other Humphreys relatives, including Curly's only surviving descendant, grandson George Brady.

A number of federal employees were tireless in their efforts to help me gain access to government documents, many previously unreleased. Among those who assisted me were Linda Kloss in the FBI's FOIA Office; Fred Romanski at the National Archives Civil Records Branch; Thomas McIntyre, chief of the Department of Justice FOIA office, Criminal Division; Katherine Day and Natasha Taylor at the Bureau of Prisons FOIA Office; and, as always, Steve Tilley at the National Archives in College Park, Maryland, who quickly responded to my many requests for documents from the organized crime files in the JFK Collection.

I was fortunate to become the first journalist to gain access to the eighty-seven cubic feet of records compiled by the staff of the Kefauver Committee. The process was expedited initially by Senator John McCain, chairman of the Senate Committee on Commerce, Science, and Transportation, which oversees the records. Committee general counsel Joanie Wales coordinated the release with Michael L. Gillette, director of the Center for Legislative Archives at the National Archives. From there, archivist Kristen Wilhelm quickly processed the files I requested. In the National Archives research room, Bill Davis helped with Kefauver Finding Aids. Nancy Velez, head of Photographic Unit of the Library of Congress, toiled diligently to deliver photos on a tight schedule.

Thanks go to Jim Agnew in Chicago who early on loaned me his copy of Virgil Peterson's *Barbarians in Our Midst,* and also alerted me to the writings of John Bartlow Martin and others. Jim's periodical *The Real Crime Book Digest* was an important journal of crime and corruption, and it's termination was a great loss. In addition to being interview subjects, Bob McDonnell and Antoinette Giancana have become friends who always happily responded to my late-night phone queries (and sent jars of delicious spaghetti sauce). Also in Chicago, chief investigator Wayne Johnson, director Jeanette Callaway, and assistant Lee Lyons of the Chicago Crime Commission, all provided material from their voluminous files. Detective Charles Schauer (ret.), of Accardo's River Forest precinct, kindly provided photographs from his personal files. The staff of the Harold Washington Library in Chicago assisted me with their fragile microfilm, thus allowing me to copy hundreds of ancient newspaper articles from the collection. John Binder gave me access to his massive FBI file on Murray Humphreys, and Leith Rohr and Keshia Whitehead at the Chicago Historical Society helped with photo searches. Carolyn Berry retrieved court filings at the Cook County Criminal Court in the Daley Center. Local crime historian Bill Helmer put me in touch with other Outfit photo collectors.

In Nevada, the following individuals provided insight and documentation: Chris Driggs at the Nevada State Archives in Carson City; Eric Moody of the Nevada Historical Society in Reno; Joanie Jacka at the Nevada Gaming Commission; and David Millman at the Nevada State Museum and Historical Society in Las Vegas. Additionally, authors Roger Morris and Sally Denton pointed me in research directions regarding Las Vegas, while T. R. Fogli, Nancy Greene, and Bethel Van Tassel helped with the Cal-Neva specifically.

In New York, Mark Obenhaus and the gang at Lancer (especially Ed Gray, Richard Robbins, Linda Patterson, Kristina Wallison, Trina Quagliaroli, and Eric Davies) were great working partners in the initial ABC News project that amplified my interest in the ways of the Outfit. Also in New York, Lois Swaney shared her prohibition research with me.

In Washington, D.C., colleagues Mark Allen, Ray Farkas, Dan Moldea, Laurence Leamer, W. Scott Malone, Sy Hersh, and Ira Silverman all shared their work and advice. As with my first book, Julie Ziegler's work as researcher extraordinaire was invaluable.

In California, my work was supported wholeheartedly by pals such as Steve Molton and Pamela Galvin-Molton, Bill Gable, Jon Karas and Irene Webb at Infinity Management, Lynn Hendee at Chartoff Prods, and Hil Anderson of UPI. Former U.S. State attorney David Nissen graciously provided photos from his prosecution of Johnny Rosselli, and Los Angeles investigative reporter Dave Robb contributed his papparazzi style picture of the notoriously camera-shy Sidney Korshak.

At Baltimore's treasured Enoch Pratt Central Library, Joe Arcieri, Nancy Yoh, Harriet Jenkins, and Doug Adolphsen all retrieved hard-to-locate books and Congressional reports from the distant past. Assistance and support in varied forms came from other friends and relatives such as Jay Greer, Kevin Perkins, Al Miller, Tony Russo, Bob Russo, Steve and Janet Nugent, Carol Banks, Dutch Snedeker, Cinda Elser, Toni and Phil Sommo, Anotol Polillo, and Irish colleagues Anthony and Robbyn Swan Summers. Trusty companions Scout and Mrs. Teasdale were extremely tolerant of my absences.

A special thanks to friend and colleague Kristina Rebelo Anderson, who recommended me to her (and now my) literary agent, Noah Lukeman. Noah, now affiliated with AMG/Renaissance, proved a strong advocate in placing the book quickly and negotiating my contract with Bloomsbury USA. At Bloomsbury, Chief Editor Karen Rinaldi and her associates Susan Burns, Andrea Lynch, and Panio Gianopoulos all gave me the perfect mix of encouragement, expertise, and critique. Bloomsbury's support is best exemplified by their willingness to accept a manuscript that was one-third larger than contracted for, a rarity in today's publishing marketplace. There is no substitute for the enthusiastic support of one's publisher, and I was fortunate to receive it.

The assistance provided by all these friends and associates in no way implies their agreement with any of my conclusions. However, any errors herein are most certainly theirs (NOT!).

Index

A NOTE ON THE AUTHOR

Gus Russo is the author of *Live by the Sword: The Secret War Against Castro and the Death of JFK*, which was nominated for a Pulitzer Prize in 1998. He is an investigative reporter who has worked for various major television networks, including PBS' Frontline series.